IVO VAN HOVE ONSTAGE

Since his emergence from the Flemish avant-garde movement of the 1980s, Ivo van Hove's directorial career has crossed international boundaries, challenging established notions of theatre-making. He has brought radical interpretations of the classics to America and organic acting technique to Europe.

Ivo van Hove Onstage is the first full English language study of one of theatre's most prominent iconoclasts. It presents a comprehensive, multifaceted account of van Hove's extraordinary work, including key productions, design innovations, his revolutionary approach to text and ambience, and his relationships with specific theatres and companies.

David Willinger is Professor of Theatre at the City College of New York and the Graduate Center (CUNY), USA.

Ivo van Hove

© Leo Van Velzen

IVO VAN HOVE ONSTAGE

Edited by David Willinger

Routledge
Taylor & Francis Group

LONDON AND NEW YORK

First published 2018
by Routledge
2 Park Square, Milton Park, Abingdon, Oxon, OX14 4RN

and by Routledge
711 Third Avenue, New York, NY 10017

Routledge is an imprint of the Taylor & Francis Group, an informa business

British Library Cataloguing-in-Publication Data
A catalogue record for this book is available from the British Library

Library of Congress Cataloging-in-Publication Data
Names: Willinger, David, author.
Title: Ivo van Hove onstage/ed. David Willinger.
Description: Milton Park, Abingdon, Oxon; New York, NY: Routledge,
2017. | Includes bibliographical references.
Identifiers: LCCN 2017036616 | ISBN 9780815366072 (hardback) |
ISBN 9780815366089 (pbk.) | ISBN 9781351260084 (ebook)
Subjects: LCSH: Hove, Ivo van, 1958—Criticism and interpretation.
Classification: LCC PN2708.H68 W55 2017 | DDC 792.02/33092–dc23
LC record available at https://lccn.loc.gov/2017036616

ISBN: 978-0-815-36607-2 (hbk)
ISBN: 978-0-815-36608-9 (pbk)
ISBN: 978-1-351-26008-4 (ebk)

Typeset in Bembo
by Sunrise Setting Ltd., Brixham, UK

Visit the eResources: www.routledge.com/9780815366089

This book is dedicated to Clara Haesaert.

CONTENTS

FIGURES

CONTRIBUTORS

Johan Callens is affiliated with the V.U.B. (Free University of Brussels [Flemish]) where he is a Professor of English. His books include: *Dis/Figuring Sam Shepard* (2007), *Crossings: David Mamet's Work in Different Genres and Media* (2009), and *Dramaturgies in the New Millenium: Relationality, Performativity, and Potentiality* (2014). His essays have appeared in American Studies/Amerikastudien, The Journal for Dramatic Theory and Criticism, Modern Drama, Theatre Research International, Text and Performance Quarterly, The Drama Review, Theatre Journal, PAJ: A Journal of Performance & Art, and the Yearbook of Research in English and American Literature, European Journal of American Culture, Miscelánea: Journal of English and American Studies, the Journal of American Drama and Theatre, the Journal of Contemporary Drama in English, and the theatre studies journal Documenta.

Serge Goriely works in the faculty of l'Université Catholique de Louvain. He has authored the books *Le théâtre de René Kalisky: Tragique et ludique dans la représentation de l'histoire and L'imaginaire de l'Apocalypse au cinema*. Often writing about the intersection between theatre and film, he has written articles in books and journals on such subjects as: Michael Haneke, Fassbinder, cinema and religion, images of the Shoah on stage, the grotesque, and Jewish humor.

Charlotte Gruber is on the research staff of the Theatre Department at the University of Ghent. Her Masters thesis from the University of Amsterdam is entitled *Interactions – Actual and Virtual Spaces as Stages of Interest*. Since, she has focused her research specifically on Antigone, with a doctoral dissertation *The Other Antigone[s]: Spotting the difference in Contemporary Tragedy*. Her articles have appeared in Gender & Performance and Performance Research.

Francis Maes works in the Music Faculty of the University of Ghent where he teaches musicology and music history. His books include: *A History of Russian Music, Het stempel van Roland Mortier, Opera: achter de schermen van de emotie, The Empire Resounds*, and *De klanken van de Keizer*. His articles have appeared in European History Quarterly, Music Theory and Analysis, DSCH Journal, Russian Review, Martinu-Studien, Canadian Journal of History, among many others.

Johan Reyniers was chief editor and a frequent contributor to the Flemish theatre journal Etcetera. He was also the long-time artistic director of Kaaitheater in Brussels, and is currently the chief dramaturg for Toneelgroep Amsterdam.

Johan Thielemans is author of Het paard begeerte: aspecten van het toneel van Hugo Claus. Influential journalist, theoretician, and television personality, he has published widely on the Flemish theatre in Etcetera, Contemporary Theatre Review, Documenta, and elsewhere. He was host of a popular show on Flemish television about theatre and culture.

PREFACE

This book offers a rounded and detailed, if not absolutely exhaustive, portrait of Ivo van Hove's work, from its inception to the present. It endeavors to explain his specialness and significance as well as to fill in blanks for the better understanding of the renowned director's artistic evolution. The chief area for inquiry will be the productions themselves. Our underlying premise is that theatre directors produce works of art that are worthy of study for their formal qualities, for consideration of the social context out of which they grow—that can somehow be reflected within them—and for what they may say about the theatre scene at large. We emphasize first and foremost the shows as theatrical experiences. It is the staging, design, the acting, soundscape, and the relationship with the audience that is the stuff of the director's domain. But next, van Hove's productions, apart from a handful of early works, are grounded in dramatic texts; while having been influenced importantly by performance art, he is not primarily a post-dramatic creator or champion of devised theatre for whom the playscript is an incidental.

Van Hove's unfolding career stretches over thirty-six years, so that much of this work has acquired an historical amplitude. The theatre has changed along with his evolution, with independent trajectories undergone by each of his audiences in Belgium, Holland, England, France, Germany, and the United States, each a part of a related history. Along with the productions, we will be recalling numerous reviews, essays, and interviews that have accompanied these developments. Some of the critics whose voices we include have had an outsized impact on his choices along the way, but were known only in a small echo chamber until now; this is particularly true for the Flemish and Dutch critics who've offered some of the most detailed and sharpest analysis in print, writing for a small community of readers and impenetrable for most English speakers. Their voices will be heard here. Since van Hove only really emerged as a major figure once he started directing at New York Theatre Workshop and assumed control of Toneelgroep Amsterdam, this book will be making accessible both the works and their history from his early career in Belgium and provincial Holland before that recognition came. Most of the latter are forgotten or dimly remembered by the few who were privileged to see them. A director's achievements are condemned to oblivion or at best a fragmentary, if legendary, recall once a show is over. It will be my aim, in however small a degree, to bring these productions back to life in the imagination of the reader, and to illustrate some milestones along van Hove's highly variegated career thus far. This work then, will be one of salvage, reconstruction, and appreciation in the fullest sense of the word.

The interest in van Hove, along with that in Jan Versweyveld, lies in his daring approach to theatrical design and startling theatre imagery in general; to his fresh readings of classics; to his introduction of film scripts into the theatre canon; for recovering and discovering new life in discarded works; to his often surprising casting; to his propensity for flipping subtext to the level of strong inter-character confrontations; for his ability to concatenate theatrical surprises; for discovering theatrical means to express and present worlds of feelings that reveal the world of today to the audience of today; and for his superb timing in giving international audiences a "new" for which they longed unknowingly. These achievements are what make him remarkable, and so are the areas we have explored in some depth.

No major artist does everything. Van Hove has not pioneered a novel system of acting, revolutionized the directing process, or forged exceptional models for the way theatre companies function, as Ariane Mnouchkine, Augosto Boal, or Ann Bogart have done; nor yet has he formulated major theories of performance in the fashion of Peter Brook, Jerzy Grotowski, or Richard Schechner. In the hyper-intellectualized environment of continental culture, all major experimental directors are expected to engage with the theories of the day, to "talk the talk," as it were.[1] As opposed to the United States, where a theatre artist has only to throw around the word "deconstruction" (in a sense that would horrify Derrida) to be seen as hip beyond belief, in Europe, the discourse of academic and artistic praxis have merged. But van Hove stands apart, a pragmatic journeyman who adapts to his real-life situation and figures out how to get to the results he envisions without a heavy sidecar of verbiage. While much may be said regarding van Hove's intuitive, malleable way of working, it is not that nor the originality of his performance theories that have galvanized the world's attention, and it is not where we have put ours.

There are a number of things this book does not foreground. It is not a biography; elements from van Hove's life will be referenced insofar as inferences may reliably be drawn as to their impact on his work, but it is not our intention here to give a full accounting of his life or character as a private individual. Nor have we showcased his work process. There are plentiful mentions of his collaborators, especially Jan Versweyveld, whose work justifiably gets equal time. But we have not interviewed the many actors, dramaturgs, designers, composers, or technicians with whom he worked or delved into his production books. In no sense do we mean to diminish the contributions of those many individuals who have unquestionably had major impacts on those shows. It is just that we are primarily interested here in what can be wrought by the art of directing, as practiced by an inspired individual, one who makes no bones about his place at the top of the creative hierarchy. Studies into biography, collaboration, and process will be left for other authors to undertake, as we have reason to believe they are indeed underway at this writing. Those and other books and articles will serve as complements to this one. We have tuned our writing so that it is comprehensible not only to practiced scholars and theoreticians, but to undergraduates, theatre artists, and to the general reading public with a curiosity to know more about the director whose work is having such an impact. Thus, while we engage in an "academic conversation," we endeavor to make it a transparent and expansive one. Again, our work does not preclude others from subjecting the van Hove oeuvre to special theoretical methods for more select audiences; indeed, we wish it to be seen as an open invitation to do so. Van Hove is a big enough subject to merit a variety of approaches in separate treatments.

My own long monograph covers van Hove's career globally: in the first section it moves vertically, identifying salient qualities that recur regarding subjects such as play choice and interpretation, design and space, acting, the political aspect, and so on. The second section horizontally pinpoints and describes selected paradigmatic productions in detail; it is an unabashedly personal selection. Other commentators may, and should, elaborate on different shows entirely.

The other five essays cover in depth important lacunae in my own. Eugene O'Neill is van Hove's favorite playwright, and that is evidenced by the relatively large number of O'Neill productions he has done. Although I do discuss *Desire Under the Elms*, Johan Callens' discussion embraces the entire set of O'Neill as a discrete opus. Along the way, he provides a most interesting chronicle of the shifting leadership configuration amongst various Flemish and Dutch theatre organizations throughout the period, detailing the game of "musical chairs" of artistic directorships through the 1980s and 90s.

It is one of van Hove's undisputed breakthroughs to reverse the usual procedure and to draw on film as a basis for theatre adaptation. Sometimes he has even brought to the theatre film scripts that had earlier been playscripts. Serge Goriely goes into these works, again as an independent set, but his emphasis is on how this special adaptive process, distinct from all others, operates.

Charlotte Gruber singles out the important production *Antigone* as a paradigm of what can go awry between van Hove and his critics. Her aim is to explain the gap between certain negative criticisms this highly anticipated work received and to square them with misapprehensions of the show's ambitions.

Apart from his theatre work, van Hove has had extensive experience directing opera, notably the world premiere of *Brokeback Mountain*. His greatest achievement, however, was to stage Wagner's entire *Ring Cycle*, the first time it had ever been attempted in Flanders. Francis Maes explains why this rendition failed to gain the notoriety it deserved, and goes on to analyze the groundbreaking interpretation.

Johan Thielemans explicates the recent production *Kings of War*, the second celebrated Shakespeare history trilogy, after *The Roman Tragedies*, that van Hove undertook. In it, he seeks to draw general conclusions as to van Hove's approach to classics, history, and the social context.

We round out the picture with a translation of an important Dutch-language interview with van Hove conducted by Johan Reyniers, along with a new section conducted expressly for this book, which will allow the director's own voice to be heard at some length.

Also appended is a chapter devoted to *The Roman Tragedies*. Since this production, more than any other, received serious analysis in a number of periodicals, we include two of the most perceptive of them and avoid reinventing the wheel.

Available as **online supplements** to this book are dossiers on van Hove's first two productions: *Rumors* (1981) and *Disease Germs* (1982). Included are:

1) my articles from the time, reprinted from *The Drama Review*;
2) samples of press coverage (mostly for *Disease Germs*, as *Rumors* received virtually no press in Belgium);
3) the playtexts written by van Hove himself, translated to English;
4) and the introductions to the plays I wrote at the time, when they were incorporated into my anthology of Belgian drama.

NB: *All critical passages and excerpts from reviews, interviews, and essays originally in Dutch and French have been translated by myself.*

Note

1   David Whitton is quoted, speaking of an emerging trend of "uncompromising intellectualism" in French theatre, with Mesguich as a prime example. [Jim Carmody, "Daniel Mesguich: 'Unsummarisable mises en scène,'" Maria M. Delgado and Dan Rebellado, eds., *Contemporary European Theatre Directors* (London and New York: Routledge, 2010), 125.]

ACKNOWLEDGMENTS

Christel Staelpaert has acted as godmother and midwife to the book, and it would not have appeared in its present form without her. Effusive thanks to Hugo Haesaert for going over all my translations of Dutch-language quotations from interviews and secondary sources for accuracy; his ideas for alternate renditions were most inspired. Bart Magnus, formerly of the Flemish Theatre Institute (now merged into Kunstenpunt in Brussels), not only was extremely helpful in expediting my research at VTI, but was also kind enough to read the entire text for accuracy, as was Gitta Kruisbrink, my able guide through the Toneelgroep Amsterdam labyrinth during my research visit. Thereafter she kindly consented to read the text and steered me away from misstatements of several facts. Klaas Tindemans and Peter Boenisch provided a number of highly useful suggestions, and I am grateful to them. I am also particularly grateful to the anonymous peer reviewers whose enthusiasm and helpful suggestions energized me in the rewriting process.

At Toneelgroep Amsterdam, van Hove's staff has been more than helpful: Ingrid Deddes lavished mountains of hard-copy documentation on me, an astonishing amount of which has proven germane; Andre Tabak generously sent me away with a number of duplicate DVDs of productions; both Renée Roetman and Marlene Kenens have made links to recordings of productions available; Henri Verhoef worked hard to provide us with the illustrations for the book. The person who has been most dogged in seeing that I was provided with recordings of productions from TGA and other venues was Ramon Huijbrechts. I thank him from the bottom of my heart for his patience with my endless requests and persistence in hunting down recordings.

Serge Goriely and Régine Van Belle have proven to be loyal and sensitive *companions de route* in this project, always willing to discuss aspects of van Hove's work, share their shrewd insights, suggest secondary sources, or entertain any ideas I needed to try out. They have also perused sections as I churned them out. Thanks go out to both of them for their willingness to read and comment on the text, as also to my colleague at City College, Kathleen Potts, a generous and staunch confidante. Thanks to Pieter Vermeulen for his contribution to the translation work with me on the Johan Reyniers interview. Jaak Van Schoor, who chaired AKT/Vertikaal's board of directors in the 1980s, offered valuable insights on the theatre scene in Flanders during Ivo's formative years as well as sharing certain key documents. I thank him as well as his wife Magda and son Jarel for all Magda's delicious meals we've enjoyed, many spent musing over Ivo van Hove's remarkable destiny. Pol Arias shared recollections regarding his long and sympathetic spectating and commenting on van Hove's career from his influential platform on Flemish radio, and gave free access to his considerable personal archive of documentation. Deep gratitude goes to Pinucchia Contino, who together with Sélène, Reuben, and Noémi Goriely offered splendid Belgo-Sicilian hospitality on so many occasions, and to Manu Tiebos for so many offers of "Antwerps" hospitality.

To all those whose energies converged to bring about my initial discovery of van Hove and Versweyveld in 1981: Clara Haesaert, the late Niki Bovendaerde, Karel DeSloovere, Bob Van Aalderen, Ingrid DeKetelaere, the late lamented Luc Deneulin, and, as ever, my late deeply missed teacher and advisor, Daniel Gerould, who prevailed on me to go to Belgium. The amazing Marvin Carlson proferred advice that was as kind as it was erudite, and I offer him profound thanks for directing me to the work of several relevant thinkers, but more for the breadth of his wisdom and experience. Thanks also to Mechthild Kalisky, Suzanne Burgoyne, Ivo Moyersoen, Jean Churchill, and Brandon Judell for engaging with me on various aspects of the study. Jill Stevenson instigated me to explore van Hove and Versweyveld's types of space usage in a systematic way and perceptively guided my thinking in that area. Ben Piggott of Routledge has been the most sensitive and encouraging editor an author could wish for. His assistant Kate Edwards cheerfully and graciously steered me through the publication process. Colin Read and his staff assiduously addressed a vast number of small textual errors and thus managed to gigantically improve the book. And thanks, as ever, to Peggy Dean, for her careful reading of the manuscript and for all sorts of selfless support she offered at every stage of the research and writing process.

I am very grateful to Ivo van Hove for making himself available on numerous occasions to offer clarifications on puzzling issues, and for putting the TGA staff at my disposition. Effusive thanks especially to Jan Versweyveld for the numerous photo images he provided and for extraordinary production assistance.

The following have graciously granted permissions: M.I.T. Press for reprint of "Staging the Twitter War," originally in *The Drama Review*, as well as reprints of my articles on *Geruchten* (*Rumors*) and *Disease Germs*; Toronto Press for reprint of "The Politics of Distraction," originally in the *Canadian Theatre Review*; to Johan Reyniers for permission to translate and include his interview with van Hove that originally appeared in *Etcetera*; to the following photographers for permission to use photos as follows: Leo Van Velzen the portrait of Ivo van Hove; Luc Peeters (Keoon) for Figures: 1.2, 1.13, 1.15, 1.22, 1.23, 2.1; Deen Van Meer for Figures: 1.4, 1.5, 1.24, 1.25, 2.2; Herman Sorgeloos for Figures: 1.3, 1.26; Chris Van der Burght for Figures: 1.1, 1.29, 1.30; Jan Versweyveld for Figures: 1.6, 1.7, 1.8, 1.9, 1.10, 1.11, 1.12, 1.14, 1.16, 1.17, 1.18, 1.19, 1.20, 1.21, 1.27, 1.28, 1.31, 1.32, 1.33, 1.34, 1.35, 1.36, 1.37, 3.1, 3.2, 4.1, 5.1, 5.2, 5.3, 5.4, 6.1.

The research for this book was supported in part by a grant from PSC-CUNY.

SELECTED CHRONOLOGY

(Toneelgroep Amsterdam Productions which later toured to the United States, the United Kingdom, France and Germany are indicated by: US, UK, F, and G respectively.)

1958	Ivo van Hove born in the small town of Heist op den Berg (Belgium)
	Raised in Kwaadmechelen
1970s	Studies in Antwerp (Law School) and Brussels (Het RITCS, Flemish directing academy)
1981	Founds, with Jan Versweyveld, AKT (Antwerps Kollektief voor Teaterprojekten)
	Rumors (*Geruchten*) self-authored
1982	*Disease Germs* (*Ziektekiemen*) self-authored
1983	*Like in the War* (*Als in de oorlog*) authored with Gie Laenen, adapted from Sophocles' *Oedipus at Colonnus*
	The Servant (*De Lijfknecht*) by Harold Pinter
1984	AKT merges with Ghent theatre company Vertikaal to form AKT/Vertikaal
	Agatha by Marguerite Duras
	Wild Lords (*Wilde heren*) adapted from *The Wild Boys*, by William Burroughs
1985	*Wonders of Humanity* (*Wonderen der mensheid*) adapted from *The Constant Prince* by Calderón
1986	*ImitationS* (*ImitatieS*), collective work
	Russian Overture by Heiner Müller
	Troilus and Cressida by Shakespeare (a student production at the Antwerps Conservatorium)
1987	AKT/Vertikaal merges with Antwerp theatre company, De Witte Kraai ("The White Raven") and gives birth to the company De Tijd ("The Time")
	The Bacchae by Euripides (DT)
	Macbeth by William Shakespeare, DT
1988	*In the Loneliness of Cotton Fields* by Bernard-Marie Koltès, DT
	Don Carlos by Friedrich von Schiller, DT
1989	*Mourning Becomes Electra* by Eugene O'Neill, DT
	Lulu by Frank Wedekind, DT

1990   Ivo van Hove is appointed artistic director of Zuidelijk Toneel in Eindhoven,
        Netherlands (ZT)
        Richard II by William Shakespeare, ZT
        Jakov Bogomolov by Maxim Gorky, ZT
        South by Julien Green, ZT
1991   *Ajax/Antigone* adapted from Sophocles, ZT
        'Tis Pity She's a Whore by John Ford, ZT
1992   *Desire Under the Elms* by Eugene O'Neill, ZT
        Tabataba by Bernard-Marie Koltès, ZT
        Saved by Edward Bond, ZT
1993   *The Bacchae* by Euripides (Hamburg, in German), ZT
        Hamlet by William Shakespeare, ZT
1994   *More Stately Mansions* by Eugene O'Neill, ZT
        Splendid's by Jean Genet, ZT
1995   *Desire Under the Elms* by Eugene O'Neill (Stuttgart, in German), ZT
        A Streetcar Named Desire by Tennessee Williams, ZT
1996   *Caligula* by Albert Camus, ZT
1997   *The Unloved* (*Les Mal-aimés*) by François Mauriac, ZT
        Faces (*Koppen*) adapted from John Cassavetes, ZT
        More Stately Mansions by Eugene O'Neill (first residency at the New York Theatre Workshop
        [NYTW], in English), ZT
1998   Ivo van Hove is appointed director of the Holland Festival
        Romeo and Juliette by Peter Verhelst, adapted from Shakespeare, ZT
1999   *Lulu* by Alban Berg (Vlaamse Opera, Antwerp and Ghent), ZT
        India Song by Marguerite Duras (also performed in English at the Edinburgh Festival), ZT
        A Streetcar Named Desire by Tennessee Williams (NYTW, in English)
2000   *The Lady of the Camellias* adapted from Alexandre Dumas's play, ZT
        Rent by Billy Anderson and Jonathan Larson (commercial production in Amsterdam)
        Alice in Bed by Susan Sontag (Amsterdam [Holland Festival] and NYTW)
2001   Ivo van Hove is appointed artistic director of Toneelgroep Amsterdam (TGA)
        The Massacre at Paris by Christopher Marlowe, adapted by Hafid Bouazza, TGA
2002   *True Love* by Charles Mee, TGA
        Con Amore by Jef Aerts adapted from *L'incoronazione di Poppea* by Monteverdi, TGA
        Carmen by Oscar van Woensel adapted from Prosper Mérimée's novella and Georges Bizet's
        opera, TGA
        The Makropoulos Case by Leoš Janáček (Het Muziektheater, Amsterdam)
2003   *Othello* by William Shakespeare, TGA
        The Three Sisters by Anton Chekhov, TGA
        Mourning Becomes Electra by Eugene O'Neill, TGA (Second Version)
2004   *Iolanta* by Tchaikovsky (Het Muziektheater, Amsterdam)
        The Norman Conquests (*Kruistochten*) by Alan Ayckbourn, TGA
        Hedda Gabler by Henrik Ibsen, NYTW (in English)
        Resigns from directorship of the Holland Festival
2005   *Scenes from a Marriage* adapted from Ingmar Bergman, TGA (UK, F)
        The Taming of the Shrew by William Shakespeare, TGA
        Faces adapted from John Cassavetes's film script (Stuttgart [Theater der Welt], in German)
        A Perfect Wedding by Charles Mee, TGA
2006   *Opening Night* adapted from John Cassavetes's film script, TGA (F, G)
        Das Rheingold by Richard Wagner (Vlaamse Opera, Ghent)
        Hedda Gabler by Henrik Ibsen, TGA (in Dutch) (F, G)
        The Miser by Molière (Germany)

2007	*Die Walküre* by Richard Wagner (Vlaamse Opera, Ghent)
	Roman Tragedies (*Coriolanus, Julius Caesar, Anthony and Cleopatra* by William Shakespeare), TGA (US, UK, F)
	The Misanthrope by Molière (NYTW, in English)
	Siegfried by Richard Wagner (Vlaamse Opera, Ghent)
2008	*The Lady of the Camellias* adapted from Alexandre Dumas (Hamburg, in German)
	Angels in America by Tony Kushner, TGA (US, UK)
	Götterdämmerung by Richard Wagner (Vlaamse Opera, Antwerp and Ghent)
	Rocco and His Brothers adapted from Luchino Visconti's film script (Bochum [Ruhrtriennale], in German, then TGA, in Dutch)
2009	*The Human Voice* by Jean Cocteau, TGA
	Cries and Whispers adapted from Ingmar Bergman's film script, TGA (US, F)
	The Antonioni Project adapted from from Michelangelo Antonioni's film scripts for *L'Avventura, La Notte, L'Eclisse*, TGA (UK)
	Teorama adapted from Pier Paolo Pasolini's film script (Bochum [Ruhrtriennale], in German; then Amsterdam, in Dutch, TGA, followed by the Lincoln Center Festival on Governor's Island, New York)
	Amsterdam (original film)
2010	*Summer Trilogy (ZomerTrilogie (The Villeggiatura Trilogy))* by Carlo Goldoni, TGA
	Idomeneo by Wolfgang Amadeus Mozart (De Munt, Brussels)
	The Misanthrope by Molière (Berlin, in German) (F)
	The Little Foxes by Lillian Hellman (NYTW, in English)
	Children of the Sun by Maxim Gorky, TGA
2011	*And We'll Never Be Parted* by Jon Fosse, TGA
	Ludwig adapted from Luchino Visconti's film script (Munich, in German)
	The Russians! by Tom Lanoye adapted from *Platonov* and *Ivanov* by Anton Chekhov, TGA
	The Miser by Molière, TGA
	Edward II by Christopher Marlowe (Berlin, in German)
2012	*Husbands* adapted from John Cassavetes's film script, TGA (F, G)
	Der Schatzgräber by Franz Schreker (Het Muziektheater, Amsterdam)
	Macbeth by Giuseppe Verdi (Opéra de Lyon)
	After the Rehearsal/Persona adapted from Ingmar Bergman's film scripts, TGA (US, UK, F, G)
2013	*Mazeppa* by Pyotr Ilyich Tchaikovsky (Komische Oper, Berlin)
	Strange Interlude by Eugene O'Neill (Munich Schauspielhaus, in German)
	Long Day's Journey Into Night by Eugene O'Neill, TGA
	A View From the Bridge by Arthur Miller (Young Vic, London) (US, F)
2014	*Scenes from a Marriage* adapted from Ingmar Bergman's film for television, NYTW (in English)
	Maria Stuart by Friedrich Schiller, TGA (F)
	Brokeback Mountain opera by Annie Proulx and Charles Wuorinen (Teatro Real, Madrid)
2015	*A View From the Bridge* by Arthur Miller, Lyceum Theatre, Broadway, New York
	The Secret Power (*De Stille Kracht*) by Louis Couperus, TGA (G)
	Antigone by Sophocles (Paris, London, New York at BAM)
	The Fountainhead by Ayn Rand, TGA (USA, F)
	Kings of War (*Henry V, Henry VI, Richard III* by William Shakespeare), TGA (US, UK, F)

2016	*Song From Far Away* by Simon Stephens (London, then TGA)
	Lazarus by Enda Walsh and David Bowie, NYTW (UK)
	The Crucible by Arthur Miller (Walter Kerr Theatre, Broadway, New York)
	The Damned (*Les damnés*) adapted from Luchino Visconti's film script (Comédie-Française at the Festival of Avignon, then brought to Paris)
	The Things That Pass (*De dingen dat doorbijgaan*) by Louis Couperus, TGA
2017	*Obsession* adapted from Luchino Visconti's film script (Barbican in London)
	The Diary of One Who Disappeared (*De dagboek van ene verdwenne*) opera by Leoš Janáček (Co-production with Muziektheater Transparant, Amsterdam)
	Network, by Lee Hall, based on Paddy Chayefsky's film, London

Van Hove shows have also toured to Buenos Aires, Moscow, Wroclaw, Hong Kong, Taipei, Zurich, Luxemburg, São Paolo, Milan, Vienna, Barcelona, Zagreb, Saint Petersburg, Santiago, Sydney, Adelaide, Belgrade, Seoul, Dublin, Lisbon, Modena, Quebec, Stockholm, Montreal, Melbourne, Athens, and elsewhere.

ABBREVIATIONS

BAM   Brooklyn Academy of Music
DT   De Tijd
IVH   Ivo van Hove
TGA   Toneelgroep Amsterdam
ZT   Zuidelijk Toneel
NYTW   New York Theatre Workshop

1

VAN HOVE, VIRTUOSO

David Willinger

Theatre is a sponge.

Ivo van Hove

The stage floor is a metaphor for all existence.

Jan Versweyveld

If the text doesn't serve to make the spectator jump out of his seat, what good is it?

Bernard Crémieux

Introduction

It may be wondered why we choose this moment in particular to undertake a book-length study of this director, who, now in his fifties, still has much of his career ahead of him. Over the course of thirty-six years, Ivo van Hove has made a profound impact on the theatre life of several countries. Now, at the height of his powers, he is churning out productions at breakneck speed, including plays, operas, and hybrid musical works. He has become a major point of reference for theatre-makers, scholars, and aficionado audiences alike, much in the same way that Peter Brook made an impact in the 1960s, modeling a creative framework for an entire generation.

It is no exaggeration to assert that van Hove has come to a critical juncture. Precisely because his youth is decisively behind him, he can no longer lay claim to be a *wunderkind* and *enfant terrible*, labels which both haunted and catapulted his earlier career. And it appears that he has now decisively "gone to the next level" of acceptance and "arrival," to have "crossed over," if you will, in the major metropolises where he practices his craft on both sides of the Atlantic. Critics have conferred on him such august titles as: "the most important director in the theatre right now," "one of the very few masters of European theatre," "the most provocatively illuminating theatre director," a "visionary director," and a "revered director." One blog breathlessly proclaims: "Ivo van Hove is God!"[1] Formerly a star of the margins, an iconoclast who drew attention through controversial bold theatrical strokes that flew in the face of convention often at the risk of being shunned, he is now approaching a new equilibrium, a sort of enshrinement, where his ambiances, choices, and approaches would become a new institutional norm. "The strange, fascinating thing about van Hove," says one critic, "why we keep lapping his work up for more effrontery—is that he styles himself as [both] a rebel and an establishment figure" (Gener 2009: 83).

In a real sense, he appears to have fulfilled a plan he had laid out for himself: "that's my mission as a theatre director," he once told an interviewer. "I want to make the most extreme work possible, without compromise, shown to as many people as possible." This places him in a tradition together with van Hove's heroes, Patrice Chéreau and Peter Stein, but most eloquently summed up in Antoine Vitez' formula: "Elite theatre for all."[2] Van Hove has been featured in the Festival of Avignon and lauded in Paris. He has had long-running hits in London's West End and has more in the works. His collaborations with mediatized stars, like Juliette Binoche, Phillip Glass, Jude Law, and David Bowie, have added further luster to the Flemish director's "brand." The list of honors bestowed on him is getting too long to include them all.[3] One might say that a decisive leap from elitist highbrow for a select few *cognoscenti* to middlebrow for the general public, a move he has made no secret of desiring, is accomplished and ensured.

At this point, a critical one because it is so obviously littered with perils, possibilities, and temptations, it behooves us to look backwards to his obscure beginnings, take stock of his earliest aspirations and reception, and chart our way back to the crux at which van Hove now finds himself. Before he had emerged from the second-tier cultural capitals of Belgium and Holland and onto the world scene, he had already put a great deal of interesting work behind him. The present recognition of his talents will almost certainly elicit curiosity about these early shows. The ephemeral nature of theatrical art means that the chance to glean reasonably detailed impressions from that not so distant past is rapidly slipping away, and it is one of this book's main purposes to fill in some of these critically important blanks. Having digested the large majority of his mise-en-scènes, we are faced with the difficult challenge of defining what inner and outer qualities epitomize the entire substance of this major director's artistry—one so multifarious as to nearly traverse all boundaries.

Do we need to justify the notion that a theatre director is an artist in the same sense as and of equal interest to a playwright? It is true that far fewer books have been written about stage directors' productions than about dramatists' scripts. But a sea change has been taking place in the art of theatre since the advent of the modern theatrical director in the 1870s, when the Duke of Saxe-Meiningen and his hired hand, Chronegk, laid down a marker for this new profession with the innovation of process-oriented rehearsals and a steeply higher artistic standard for production values (Koller 1984: passim). It seems to me indisputable that pioneering theatre directors, no less than pioneering film directors, about whom there is perhaps less controversy, merit serious consideration as a discrete artistic category of creator and should not be written off as negligible interpreters. Notable film directors collaborate with camera people, editors, and other important creative contributors, yet are lionized as *auteurs*. Why would it be different for a theatre director whose special vision is recognized as determinant in what the audience gets to see?[4]

In a revitalized theatre in which scripts are mined for their visual and auditory life in unconventional ways, the thrall of the narrative is reduced. As images suggestive of states of being come to the fore instead, the directorial function assumes outsized proportions. Elinor Fuchs describes the current new prestige and parity that theatre workers beyond the playwright have attained, overturning the famous prescription that dramatic action is the most important of component elements:

> In the theatre of difference, each signifying element—lights, visual design, music, etc., as well as plot and character elements—stands to some degree as an independent actor. It is as if all the Aristotelian elements of theater had survived, but had slipped the organizing structure of their former hierarchy.
>
> *(Fuchs 1996: 10)*

With such a reconfigured hierarchy of Artistotelean elements, the director/designer, who after all is master of the formerly denigrated "spectacle," gains a concomitant new prestige over Aristotle's previously privileged element of dramatic "action," which is historically the play-wright's domain.[5] "The stage director," as Rancière says, "is no longer the regent of the interregnum. He is the second creator who gives the work this full truth that manifests itself in becoming visible" (Rancière 2011: 125). I trust that the discussion which follows will be a self-justifying one, speaking to "respect for directing" when it comes to an innovator such as Ivo van Hove.

For want of a common, rigorous vocabulary for describing theatre directing as an art, I will be borrowing from others and, in certain cases, introducing terms of my own as they become necessary, trusting that this approach will be comprehensible to all. In framing the discussion of van Hove, I will have recourse to certain influential, already canonical, modern performance theoreticians—Elinor Fuchs, David Savran, Hans-Thies Lehmann, and others—whose works all appear to me germane to the discussion and were written roughly over the time period through which van Hove's efflorescence has taken place. Underpinning all I write are also the ideas and vocabulary of older, today seldom referenced theoreticians—Susanne Langer and Bernard Beckerman. That does not imply, however, that van Hove himself has absorbed or has been responding to any of these particular writers' commentaries in his productions. It is certain that he hasn't; it will be shown that his reading interests lead him elsewhere. The truth regarding van Hove, if not for many of his European brethren, is as Fuchs suggests that "postmodern theater practice . . . takes little interest in theoretical debate, just as the theoreticians are less aware of actual theater than of any other art" (Fuchs 1996: 95; Pavis 2003: 26). And yet, certain of his artistic statements—and especially his practice—coincide marvelously with elements of their theories.

Progression and patterns

Van Hove's first two shows were plays he wrote himself. *Rumors* (1981) was his first production and it showcased four performances in the setting of a disused laundromat (see Figure 1.1). He wrote and directed it, with Jan Versweyveld designing all elements of the show:

> Through a theatrical structure that is not narrative but imagistic and poetic we are presented with subjective fragments of the life experience of a young man become schizophrenic. The ensemble of decimated architecture; mobile, multi-colored fluor-escent lights (designed by Jan Versweyveld); abrasive sound-track of words and music; ambivalent text and acting all suggest the inner world of the schizophrenic's mind spatially and sonorously.
>
> *(Willinger 1981: 116–118)*

FIGURE 1.1 *Rumors*

© Chris Van der Burght

So many elements contained the seeds for things that returned in more polished forms in later shows: the precarious theatricality of the set, the semiotics of the lighting, the use of an "elect performer" whose silent gaze leads the audience's interpretations (like the maid characters in *Hedda Gabler* and *Things That Pass*), the uncanny framing of the lower halves of the bodies (which we see again much later in *Ludwig* and *Edward II* in mediatized versions), the film-stage ambiance, which pops up again in *The Antonioni Project* and *Opening Night*, the figure of the inarticulate outsider hero trying to find himself, and so on.

I would also say that the text stands up despite its fragmentary nature. It is still one of the best pieces of dramatic writing to come out of modern-day Flanders. Van Hove emerged from the *Rumors* experience confident of his directorial abilities. Not so for writing. He later said that he resolved to leave writing to others as he didn't have the knack, but that playwriting, along with singing in a rock band, remains one of his unrequited ambitions (Willinger 2014). I've never heard him sing, so I can't weigh in on his assessment on that front, but I do regret the plays he never wrote, owing to lack of confidence.

Van Hove's second play, *Disease Germs*, is like some camp grand opera, in which the uniformly female cast of characters is played by men (see Figure 1.2). In sensibility, *Disease Germs* is not so very different from the Genet of *The Maids* or Werner Fassbinder's hysterical operatic film *The Bitter Tears of Petra Von Kant*.

And by operatic, I intend a very particular connotation. There is no explicit singing (in fact all the musical selections are borrowed paradigms of recorded kitsch: James Bond soundtracks, *Citizen Kane*, *The Merry Widow*, etc.), but the characters bemoan their fate through operatic postures, by way of spoken arias and duets. There is something Wagnerian about the feverish

FIGURE 1.2 *Disease Germs*

© Leo Peeters (Keoon)

emotional tone of these set pieces, so that all genuine feeling gets expanded in the crucibles of operatic convention and cliché.

Looking back from this point in time, it is clear that in *Disease Germs* van Hove and Versweyveld were laying down certain markers that have recurred in new iterations throughout their extensive oeuvre: the insertion of kitsch pop songs and tunes, the masterful use of spatial planes and shuttering off of parts of the space, from the Typist's office at the furthest remove down to the intimate closing scenes with Jeanne and Joanne, the emphasis on physical and visual action, the addition of stunning visual treats—in this case, a real, working automobile—and the tropes of gender exploration. In these earliest shows, there is a blatant, cruel humor, which is hard to detect in most of the later work, but which is great fun.

After some time, it became apparent that van Hove was not going to be a theatre director in the mold of Richard Foreman or Tadeusz Kantor; one who would mine a single signature vein of style and process throughout a long career. Neither did he go through one stylistic or thematic period, then leave it behind forever to start a new one, forging coherent, neatly defined periods. A look at his chronology confounds all efforts to compartmentalize his career into phases of literary interest, theme, or style. Rather, his trajectory resembles that of Patrice Chéreau, the notable French director he admired, who juggled a varied, but definite set of interests and tendencies.

In his first decade of directorial activity, van Hove established many of the threads he would follow in the future, leapfrogging over one to another. In his earliest two productions, *Rumors* and *Disease Germs*, he shook up the audience by inviting them to derelict and gutted industrial spaces. Having introduced this use of site specificity, he dropped it and went on to other challenges. Thus, he eludes any easy labeling—in this case, being branded as a director of the site specific. But lo and behold, thirty years later, he exploits a disused cavernous warehouse on Governor's Island in New York harbor for his American production of *Teorema*. He is both faithful and unfaithful to his experiments.

For van Hove is an oscillator: one who oscillates between fulfilling the role of standard director of European repertory theatre introducing moderately unusual choices (*The Russians, South, Lulu*) and unleashing his *auteur* instinct (*Faces, Cries and Whispers, Roman Tragedies*) to stage break-ins on our comfort zone; he also oscillates between scandal and respectability, between competence and transcendence, between gay and straight tropes, between being a pioneer of sound, silence, and image theatre and explicator of text theatre. His stages may be empty or cluttered. He is both an avatar of high art and an unabashed purveyor of pop kitsch; works with tech-centered theatre and organic theatre of the human body. He is both mercurial and faithful, bull-headed and equivocal. He wants to borrow and adapt, embark on the unknown and nestle down into the safe modes of expression too. In the beginning, his work burst out with youthful impetuosity and, frequently, rage. Now, the two energy batteries of impetuosity and mastery pump in alternation and often intertwine.

With the succinct self-observation: "I'm a bungee jumper of the theatre" (Szalwinska 2011). Van Hove acknowledges ownership of this far-ranging, if erratic, pattern. Elaborating on the multiple modalities of theatre, that have never ceased to interest him, he pushes back against those who would pigeonhole him:

> In contrast to more analytical kinds of plays, I also did many productions, such as the recent *Con Amore*, based on Monteverdi or *India Song* by Duras in which I strive to get an intuitive, direct audience reaction. My first plays were even entirely constructed based on a journey in search of a new image language. This show [*Carmen*] belongs in that line. It also tracks with a new sensibility in the world of performance: the boundary between theatre and other media is growing ever thinner. A new theatre language is everywhere developing, with a strong influx of video artists, new technology, musicians. . . . All those folks are clamoring to take a crack at theatre. [. . .] With Jan Versweyveld too [Ivo van Hove's steady set designer] I sense an interest in the impure, the performance art aspect of theatrical production.
>
> *(T'Jonck 2002)*

Van Hove is, then, ever in flux. But despite the polyvalence of his works, which allows for wild, if erratic, variation in scale, texture, scenic strategies, dramatic sources, and approaches to acting, I would argue, for all that, that the stamp of a van Hove production is unmistakable. His shows couldn't have been produced by any other of his contemporaries, even though at times they seem to be "quoting" each other.[6]

Van Hove's success is undeniable, and yet he has flaws and weaknesses. One can look back and understand how certain earlier works formed part of a longer experimental process: how one can discern his direction in these works and why he hit walls or went down blind alleys. But—we will assert—certain "alleys" he considered blind or negligible, and which commentators considered failures, are worthy of reconsideration. A director is allowed his failures. He tries things out in the public eye, then returns to work on what interests him. Temperamentally and contextually, van Hove is an exemplar of the great European director who brings something idiosyncratic, yet who reserves the right to reinvent himself.

When we say van Hove we don't mean it

To illuminate this artistic voyage, to know its many adventures and the ways they interconnect, one would have to have seen, if not all, then many, many shows in several countries over the course of thirty-six years. No one, to the best of my knowledge, has been privileged to do so, except for his closest associates. Even among those accompanying actors, designers, dramaturgs, critics, and assistants, who of them has been everywhere van Hove has created? Flemish critics such as Pol Arias, Geert Sels, and Fred Six will have seen his Flemish plays and many of his Dutch productions. But would they have seen those in New York or Germany? Dutch critics like Hein Janssen and Hana Bobkova know his work in Amsterdam and much of what he did in Eindhoven, but prior to that? I would venture to say: only Jan Versweyveld, who provides the set and lighting design, has been in a position to have seen them all. Whenever one invokes van Hove, Versweyveld is also implied. Their creative process has been so intertwined and mutually dependent that separate ownership cannot be defined. The director has most eloquently expressed the nature of their symbiotic and productive partnership in this way: "We are really both responsible for the design together. It is our common child. We also ought to write that it's actually a show by Ivo van Hove and Jan Versweyveld. That's the way I feel it" (Bots 2005).

One should properly say, when alluding to their works, that they are van Hove/Versweyveld shows, in the same way Merchant/Ivory films seems a natural description. But somehow, it doesn't sing in the same way. So for easy reference we call them van Hove shows, knowing full well we are unwarrantedly but wittingly reducing, even falsifying. For the truth, as van Hove also says is: "Jan and I make *Gesamtkunstwerke**: it's almost impossible to say where design leaves off and the directing begins" (Wensink 2015a).

I was most fortunate to be present at the dawn of both their careers, the 1981 production *Rumors*, and am pleased to have been able to play a role in their early renown.[7] I have seen a number of live productions since, but have filled in the lacunae with video recordings, photos, and reviews. Those I have not seen in some form are the very few of which no recording was made.

The Flemish and Dutch historical context

The Belgium of van Hove's youth was rather a backwater. The Belgian inferiority complex is a cliché with more than a bit of truth to it. The francophone section of Belgium in large part looks to Paris for its trends, whereas the Flemish half looks north to the Netherlands, where they speak the same language, only with a different accent. Since the seventeenth century "brain drain," when the intellectuals of the Southern Lowlands fled north to escape the Catholic occupation by Spain, Flanders has been looked down upon as a cloddish, backward cousin. Within Belgium, the Flemish section has had to struggle to achieve parity with the francophone half; this long, slow process being known as the Flemish Movement. In the 1970s, when van Hove came of age, Flanders was on its way to surpassing Wallonia economically, but there remained a strong vestigial sense of unfairness. Flare-ups were fresh in memory, and many were still being played out in schools and suburbs. At the same time, Flanders has a rich past of writers and artists who have gained recognition: Hugo Claus, Maurice Maeterlinck and Michel De Ghelderode (the latter two who wrote in French), James Ensor, Marcel Broodthaers, Rik Wouters; the list is really quite long. But that doesn't mitigate the sense of always playing catch-up with the surrounding dominant-culture nations with the irresistible cultures: of the United Kingdom, the Netherlands, France, and Germany, all of whom cast long shadows. Despite their central position geographically and a defiant pride in their heritage, Flemish artists sensed that they were always two steps behind the others.

Ivo van Hove has, in Belgium, Netherlands, and America, arrived on each scene during a moment of—perhaps vacuum is too strong a word—slump. His contribution always seemed to make up for an extant creative deficit. The theatre scene in Flanders had reached an impasse by 1981. The three major state theatres in Brussels, Antwerp, and Ghent housed longstanding fixed repertory companies, each of which had resolved into complacency and staleness (Den Butter 2005). The play selections lacked inspiration; the actors' work tended to be perfunctory; and the directing was derivative and mechanical. A culture of bureaucratic inertia prevailed. Audiences were aging and dwindling. Formerly, the theatres of Flanders had served a major cultural function. They were a hub where the Flemish language, denigrated and delegitimized by the dominant francophone establishment, could be spoken, communally shared, and celebrated. By 1981, despite and perhaps because of the success of the Flemish Movement, the sense of communal imperative had ebbed away.

What wasn't clear was that this stasis had practically reached a point of no return where something would have to give. When it did give, it was initiated from above in a bureaucratic shift. Officials at the Flemish Ministry of Culture, such as a visionary Minister Bert Anciaux, exasperated at how artistically stagnant their theatres were and how poorly attended, reversed the basis of the entire funding structure by rewarding and penalizing theatres according to their degree of creativity; funding was targeted using a different formula—based on exciting innovation. At the same time, a large number of young directors were drawing intrigued audiences and positive critical comment for their iconoclastic works in marginal venues. These included Luk Perceval, Guy Joosten, Jan Fabre, Guy Cassiers, Arne Sierens, and Ivo van Hove. Established theatre critics such as Pol Arias, Wim Van Gansbeke, and Jef De Roeck agitated for a fundamental change. The government officials heeded them and went to see for themselves. Modern Flemish dance, due to the rise of Anna Theresa De Keersmaeker and Wim Van De Keybus, was having its own renascence, and was being recognized internationally. In parallel, the rising Flemish theatre directors were being appointed as artistic directors of the big theatres (Perceval and Cassiers), evolving as world class opera directors (Joosten), or as general performance stars (Fabre), these developments constituting "The Flemish Wave."[8] The old artistic directors and their stables of actors were summarily put out to pasture, and the best of them reintegrated into a new, looser arrangement as freelancers. Prior to this, Dutch theatremakers had been in constant demand in Flanders; now it was the young Flemings who were being invited to direct and assume control over theatres in the Netherlands (Willinger 2016b). Flemish theatre became a point of reference and sought-after commodity in the dominant-culture countries, and its directors were invited to work in England, France, Germany, and beyond, often setting trends rather than following them.

The creations van Hove and Versweyveld made while still students at Het RITCS, *Rumors* and *Disease Germs*, were done under the aegis of their own little production company, AKT (Antwerps Kollektief voor Theaterproducties). Shortly thereafter they fused with another extant company in Ghent to become AKT/Vertikaal. In 1987, AKT/Vertikaal then formed a loose cooperative with yet another theatre company, De Witte Kraai, and became known as De Tijd. This conglomerate, which lasted three years under the joint leadership of van Hove, Sam Bogaerts and Lucas Vandervorst, retained its experimental character while at times aspiring to the ambitious scale of a repertory institution.[9] By 1990, van Hove accomplished the remarkable feat of securing the artistic directorship of a Dutch state-supported regional theatre, the Zuidelijk Toneel in Eindhoven. Leaving his home country, he claimed, finally relieved him of chronic anxieties regarding finances,[10] although his was one chapter in a larger movement. Van Hove's rise, curiously, tracks with the consolidation of Brussels' role at the heart of the European Union. The Berlin Wall fell. Shortly after that major event, Europe unified its currency and Brussels was established as the seat of government. Just as van Hove was leaving Belgium for the Netherlands, his homeland was gaining unprecedented prestige and importance.

By the time he'd finished his service as artistic director of the provincial theatre, Zuidelijk Toneel, the Netherlands, too had hit its own sort of creative wall. The Dutch theatre community graduated from their traditional notion of theatre in the 1970s, with the advent of the historical movement called the Tomato Action (*Aktie Tomaat*). Tomato Action grew from the spirit of May '68, when young radicals took to the streets with the utopian idea that they could change the world; their activist strategy extended to the theatre. Young experimentalists of the time and their sympathizers stormed the auditoriums of the institutionalized state theatres of Holland and literally threw tomatoes at the stages until the artistic directors simply abdicated in favor of the young tyros (Drukman 1997; Van Engen 1996; McConachie 1990). The audience seemingly adapted their tastes to the fresh, new kind of theatre identified with those artists who came to the fore.

The renovators of the Dutch theatre, now ensconced in seats of power, including Gerardjan Rijnders, brought their productions across the border to Belgium when on tour, and van Hove recounts being inspired as a young man by the innovative Dutch shows, so alive and open in contrast to the ossified local Flemish official theatre (Hillaert 2009). By the 1990s, when van Hove replaced Rijnders as artistic director at Toneelgroep Amsterdam (TGA), protest movements had run their course and with them the styles of theatre they engendered. The Tomato Action generation had seen its time, in turn, come and go. While Rijnders had long expressed the wish to step down and devote himself to writing and directing, when the reality that a replacement candidate would arrive dawned, both he and the TGA company were ambivalent.

Van Hove, meanwhile, had achieved the double coup of being named artistic director of Toneelgroep Amsterdam, the largest institutional theatre in the Netherlands,[11] at the same time as heading up the prestigious Holland Festival, for which his assigned mission was to add more theatre, rebalancing the predominance of music and dance (Editorial Board NRC 2002). Two such assignments would be stunning for anyone; they were all the more remarkable for a Fleming to become so recognized in Holland. His parallel careers in America, Germany, and England took shape over time. Van Hove took over the TGA in 2000. Shortly thereafter, the 2001 US terrorist attacks took place; as the world began to alter, so did van Hove's vision of his own artistry. Beginning in the 2006–7 season, he greatly expanded the number of productions and performances that TGA offered in their home building, the Amsterdam Schouwburg, and also vastly increased the amount of touring they did—first to the Dutch provinces and Flanders, but as time went on—to far-flung places including the Far East, the Americas, and Australia. TGA, under van Hove's leadership, has a much larger footprint than it had when he started. Van Hove's international career has not only enhanced his prestige at home, of course, but also that of the TGA.

Delgado and Rebellato have discussed the ways in which the evolution of the European artistic director can be at odds with that of the innovative stage director who has the luxury of assuming a "subversive" stance of "cultural opposition." When entrusted with the running of an institutional theatre [like TGA], a revolutionary stage director comes to embody, "particular bourgeois ideals of individual attainment, entrepreneurialism and capitalist enterprise. . . ." Thus, "directors across the festival circuit—[that are seen to be] suppressing 'the local in favor of the transportable, privileging the symbolic over the realistic, the metaphorical over the referential,'" (Delgado and Rebellato 2010) have become the norm. That norm in every particular describes van Hove. He is happy to discuss his strategies for making up shortfalls in government funding through sponsoring, strategic cuts, and new touring schemes. The subversive stance as a stage director, which he wears as a badge of honor, cohabits in seeming harmony with that of an unabashed entrepreneur, effective at circumventing the convulsions of neo-liberal "democracy"; although market pressures for rendering works accessible to heterogeneous audiences on the touring circuit only in part account for van Hove's globalist tendencies. They may have something to do with the "suppression of the local" and "the privileging of the metaphorical" that is so prevalent in his work. It remains to be seen whether he has stayed entirely true to his avant-garde roots, moved on to institutional respectability, or achieved something that straddles the two.

The director seen from multiple angles

A theatre of experimentation and excess

Transcending traditions and challenging norms

In our quest to identify the quintessence of Ivo van Hove's artistry, the elusive elements that set him apart from his contemporaries, one must drill down into the nature of his artistic vision and production. This encompasses what he has introduced to the global theatre that is truly new, and where he piggybacks on previous pioneers' innovations. And of course, it should be remembered that what appears to be brand new and startling for an American audience might not carry the same shock for a European one. In some measure, when it comes to his productions at NYTW and Brooklyn Academy of Music (BAM), these were virgin voyages for the current generation of New York audiences into territory that is *vin ordinaire* for European ones. Thus, the American critic Randy Gener may write, "The irony is that while he is blessed by controversy here, in Europe van Hove's unabashed *auteurism* is very much a mainstream staple. Some observers consider him conservative, even," and in the same article add in seeming contradiction:

> Van Hove's classical revivals in New York entice, challenge and astonish for the opposite
> reason—because his go-for-broke technique creates uncommon stage realities that allow
> far greater room for the physical, the incongruous, the animalistic and the poetic than
> U.S. audiences are accustomed to seeing. . . . Through his idea of naturalism in extremis,
> van Hove rattles our arthritic conventions.
>
> *(Gener 2009)*

The notion of reducing the set of *A Streetcar Named Desire* to a single bathtub center stage, as he did in his notorious New York Theatre Workshop (NYTW) production, would not have had the same charge in Belgium, France, or Germany as it did in New York. Continental audiences would be rather more surprised to see a normal, completely detailed naturalistic rendition of the sort American audiences are inured to when it comes to the mainstream theatre-going experience. But European critics would deem that too literal. They disparagingly call such an approach "theatre of the first degree" or "illustration of text."[12] More typically, Europeans would expect scenic life that takes the text to a "secondary degree"; something American audiences and critics reflexively think of as "avant-garde," "way out," or just plain weird. That heightening, abstraction, and disjunction between text and spectacle is exactly the kind of standard theatre now seen all the time in the large, established institutional theatres of Belgium and Holland. Yet, van Hove often digs in his heels in such a way as to give the impression that his theatre is most conventionally grounded:

> I am not the kind of director who puts the text aside and starts fantasizing images. I am really a text director. The only reference is the text. I do drive everyone crazy, because I question every line and, in an opera, every note. Why is that line there? Why this crescendo there? I want to know the why behind the text. Every text needs an interpretation. It needs to be taken care of. To be looked at. There is not one truth about the text—not one truth. You have to find your own truth.
>
> *(Gener 2009)*

In fact, his insistence on text-centeredness conforms to the more general trend for what Richard Schechner calls "today's" avant-garde, which he re-dubs a "niche-garde":

> Alongside the emergence of the avant-garde tradition is a strong return to the written text. And here, ironically, may be the only really new thing about today's niche-garde. Rejection of the written text and what it stood for, authors and authority, was a hallmark of the historical avant-garde. Avant-garde manifestos called for burning libraries and wrecking museums.
>
> *(Schechner 2015)*

Even if we take van Hove at his word, there is a lingering sense that he is not a text director in the same sense as most first degree American naturalistic directors are; otherwise his contribution to the American scene would lose all importance. Rather he conforms to Patrice Pavis's nuanced corrective portrait of the modern director who, "half semiologist and half 'sorcerer's apprentice,' makes up his own performance text" (Pavis 2003). For although van Hove does see himself as a "text director," which implies fidelity to some orthodox reading, in fact, he uses his close analysis of the traditional text to refashion a performance text that often borders on subverting the original, or at the very least, the spectators' preconception of it.

Belgian critic, Fred Six, writing in 1993, clarified where Ivo fits in the European creative space in this way, asserting that van Hove and Versweyveld:

> profile themselves as inspired designers in what is finally a traditional pattern of the major repertory undertakings. Their productions are in line with the De Tijd's [van Hove's theatre company before going to Zuidelijk Toneel] stated intentions not to alter a centuries-old theatre tradition, but to 'enrich' it with a modern vision based on previous experiences in an experimental and idiosyncratic dramaturgical past. . . . He never pushes things so far that he goes at the play to use it either as ally or antagonist in relation to his own ideas. Therefore: no rewriting, no parodying, cutting or adding [all things for which he had come in for criticism previously in his AKT production, *Like in the War*, an adaptation of *Oedipus at Colonus*]. He doesn't pad the dialogue with extra text, but rather assimilates it in a personal manner. In that sense, he is more servant/priest than rebel or prophet.[13]

In the same vein, van Hove himself has said in a European interview: "In New York I'm an avant-gardist. Here, I'm official theater" (Phillips 2003). The purportedly radical approach, for example, to *A Streetcar Named Desire* or *More Stately Mansions* that took critics aback in New York, when viewed at Toneelgroep Amsterdam, the largest institutional theatre in the Dutch nation, is simply considered normal theatre.[14]

Van Hove favors classics, but that does not mean he is interested in presenting them "classically." Rather, he gives the text an empirical analysis, which leads to unnervingly original stagings of scenes it was assumed could only be done one way. As one New York critic noted, as though he were alerting us to a deficiency in van Hove's directing abilities: "Almost all the elements in [his] interpretative approach appear opposite to our preconceived ideas" (Goldberg 2004). Van Hove once recounted with an unashamed giggle how actors stand open-mouthed during rehearsals whenever he lays out his vision of what he sees them eventually doing onstage. "'How in the world did you come up with that?! What a sick mind!'" he gleans them thinking to themselves or saying out loud.[15] Van Hove violates many assumed theatrical traditions with the force of fantasies issuing from his imagination.

His reinterpretations of *Othello* are a good example. The usual interpretation of the title character has the general maintaining his cool through the first half of the play at least. For example, in the extremely early action of van Hove's *Othello*, where ingrained tradition has trained us to expect a besmitten, contained, and consummately diplomatic tragic hero, the audience instead witnesses the general striding downstage towards Desdemona in order to slap her violently, hurl insults, and furiously track her back upstage. As the downstage area is defined as a civic space, this uncontrolled violence is a public embarrassment and reveals a chink in the armor of the political chief—in full view of society.

Many characters play out their submerged desires and urges in all tactile frankness. Iago, when he comforts Desdemona, touches her sensually, intimately even, caressing her hair and face. When he buries his face in her belly, she caresses his hair. Violating conventional wisdom, which assumes Desdemona's absolute purity and fidelity, she accepts all these overtures from her husband's lieutenant as though they were natural. Emilia, who is standing by observing it all seems to think nothing of it either. Othello literally glimpses Desdemona's supposed adultery with Cassio, thus blurring the line between paranoia and objectivity. As we witness these flagrant inversions of Shakespearean interpretive tradition, we are forced to ask whether these carnal liaisons and violent gestures, that contrast so greatly to customary productions, are meant to be taken as imaginary wish fulfillments, as actual violations of the marriage contract, or as phantasms? Challenging assumptions regarding where to draw the boundaries of reality is one of the enjoyable and unsettling aspects of van Hove's theatre.

For the past thirty-six years Belgium and the Netherlands have welcomed van Hove's adventurousness and encouraged it, so long as it provided lively, even controversial fodder for conversation, and so long as his overall trajectory was fruitful.[16] While it appears that van Hove has now won over the American public and theatrical establishment, which is notorious for chewing up and spitting out its most celebrated artists, van Hove can seemingly do no wrong despite the fact that indulgence over the long haul is not a customary hallmark of the American scene. The French have elevated him to a status higher than their own, as has Great Britain. Yet, in the latter context, cracks have started to open, as the London critics proved quite divided, and even disgruntled with his recent productions, *Lazarus* and *Obsession*.

Van Hove can take credit for much of what he represents, but does not hesitate to acknowledge figures from the past who have influenced him and served as models in a variety of ways.

Antecedents

Antonin Artaud

During an interview, van Hove described his time at the Brussels directors' academy, De RITCS. His principal teacher, Alex Van Royen, told his students that "there were basically three theories in the twentieth century worth referring to: Artaud, Brecht, and Stanislavsky," and that having studied them all, the prospective director took Artaud as his inspiration.[17] When I asked van Hove which of Artaud's ideas had particularly impacted him, he rushed to a bookshelf and pulled out the dog-eared copy of *The Theatre and Its Double* he'd bought in 1980. Thumbing through it, he said that during his student years he'd underlined the points which particularly struck him. "'Actors should be like hieroglyphs,'" he quoted aloud from randomly thumbed, underlined passages. "'Theatre should wake us up—should wake up our heart and our nerves,'" he read, and then added his own comments:

> Artaud considered theatre to be a visceral thing, a physical thing. And this is still what I'm trying to do. Theatre was meant to be a living, important urgent thing. Everything that exists in crime, in love, in war, in madness, that's what should give it its urgency. . . . Artaud spoke of theatre as a plague.
>
> *(Willinger 2017a)*

He noted further that the visionary character of Artaud's statements, their very lack of precision in contrast to Stanislavsky's methodicalness, opened a door "so you could fantasize about acting. . . . It inspired me to be experimental. Theatre is a world of imagination. You can create. You can create things that are not really there" (Willinger 2017a).

Looking back, one can see how some of those exalted flashes of insight from the French prophet gave van Hove a key for unlocking his own artistic freedom. They represented approval to conduct his trial and error approach for working with actors, which he took as both a license and a directive to be wild and push boundaries—his own, the actors' and the audience's. Still, Artaud didn't hand down specific tools in the form of exercises or chronicles of his rehearsal work method as we have from Stanislavsky and Grotowski. Artaud's own practice at directing was painfully circumscribed, notably to one abbreviated season of three shows he managed to mount with Roger Vitrac in 1927, under the banner of their shortlived Théâtre Alfred Jarry. A contemporary critic, Bernard Crémieux, when describing Artaud's production of Strindberg's *A Dream Play*, attempted to capture the essence of what he saw there, observing "certain parts are so violently real" that:

> they make a poetical use of daily life, and that, as far as the actors go, it's all a question of nerves; they are questing after a theatre of nerves. . . . For better or worse, they sprinkle the text with shouts, groans, contortions and moans. For if the text doesn't serve to make the spectator jump out of his seat, what good is it?
>
> *(Dort 1979: 257)*

While, from these laconic comments it would be impossible to reconstruct what actually took place on that stage, when combined with Artaud's manifestos and letters, later directors form a composite *impression*, which serves as a template for their own work. Van Hove was left in a situation where he'd have to make up a concrete work process as he went along using trial and error. But it gave him guideposts. For example, there is no question that it has been a central aim for van Hove over the years to come up with images, actions, and stage effects that will cause the audience to "jump out of their seats." These shocks to habitual perceiving, as we shall see, manifest in reconfigurations of the audience/actor relationship, casting choices, revisioning of clichéd interpretations of character, blatant sexual business, anachronistic use of music, and a variety of pyrotechnical stage effects. He invariably qualifies his affinity for shock value with the caveat that he means for all shocks to awaken the audience into greater awareness and availability for inner transformation; there he is in lockstep with Artaud's program.[18]

Artaud took stands on most issues that became central to van Hove's set of interests. Having flirted with a democratic work process, following the pattern laid down by the Living Theatre and taken up by such contemporary Flemish theatre groups as De Trojaanse Paard,[19] van Hove quickly returned to a paternalistic approach to working with actors. Indeed, in the essay, "Mise en scène and Metaphysics," Artaud advocates the necessity for a director to take undisputed charge of all the stage elements. These passages in Artaud remind us of Gordon Craig's call for an all-powerful über-director. Artaud (and Craig) assert that "the language of theatre" must supercede the authority of the dramatic text, and that it is the director, not the playwright, who is the wrangler of those elements (Artaud 1958: 57).

Artaud concerned himself with scenic design as well, although as usual, his discourse is more suggestive than pragmatic:

> Present-day theatre . . . cultivates illusion—and then it's worst of all. Nothing is less capable of deluding us than the illusion of the fake prop, of cardboard and painted cloths which the modern stage offers us (Artaud 1989: 42). These trappings, this visual display are what we want to cut down to the bare minimum and immerse in a solemnity and a spirit of disturbing action (Ibid., 42) Our aim is to materialize the most secret movements of the soul by the simplest and most naked means. (Ibid., 37) To show an unexpected side of the most hackneyed, most banal situations. . . . (Ibid., 38) Everything which cannot be depicted as it is, or needs the illusion of artificial colouring, all this will be kept off the boards.
>
> *(Ibid.: 42)*

Over and over, van Hove and Versweyveld have followed through on these instructions, broadly traced out though they are by Artaud, in the scenic life of their productions. Artaud insists on a stripped down theatrical space as a precondition for gleaning the "secret movements of the soul." One is contingent on the other. Versweyveld's sets evince that refusal toward detailed representation. The starkness of the space clears the way for "a spirit of disturbing action" to "materialize the most secret movements of the soul." While it is difficult to parse this exalted, romantic language van Hove and Versweyveld have managed to translate it into specific praxis.

The kind of communication that interested Artaud bypasses the intellect and, incoherent as it might seem, makes itself understood loud and clear by the soul. Lights, for Artaud, speak a language the soul can comprehend. Versweyveld has taken him at his word. They are to have a new and special function within the entire production scheme:

> The lighting will not be restricted to illuminations but will have a life of its own, it will be considered as a state of mind. (Artaud 1989: 78) . . . The lighting effects, like gesture, will also stand for a language, and in this attempt to achieve a single, integrated theatrical language light will constantly be associated with sound in order to produce a total effect.
>
> *(Ibid.: 78)*

It is not particularly clear here what the visionary Artaud was getting at when it comes to actual design and execution; theatre's technology of his day was very restricted. But indeed, Versweyveld's lights—through the use of unconventional instruments as well as their deployment—are frequently used like a parallel language, a gestural language whose meaning is often just beyond the grasp of intellect, but which succeeds in unnerving us. Versweyveld makes no attempt to make his lighting imitate that in the natural world.

The tricky question of *"the real,"* that elusive quality, which van Hove and Versweyveld claim they are questing after, in contrast to *realism*, is a binary that finds its roots in Artaud's discourse. Bernard Dort attempts to parse the crucial distinction:

> The theatre that [Artaud] refuses is that of *illusion*, that which is nothing but a 'game' and a lure. And the theatre he's calling out for is a theatre which is 'a veritable reality.' 'That,' writes Artaud, 'is the most serious part of all: The formation of a reality, the unprecedented eruption of a world. The theatre must present this ephemeral world to us, a world that is tangential to the real world. It will have to be that very world or else we'll just have to get by without the theatre entirely. . . . The false in the midst of the true, that is the ideal definition of this mise-en-scène.
>
> *(Dort 1979: 261)*

Artaud's envisioned theatre would, paradoxically, create "an absolute theatrical reality which is self-contained," although employing "the most hackneyed, the most banal situations," and use "simple objects from life." As Dort asserts, "We think of Artaud as organic, but it's also a theatre of monstrosity, of grandiosity—as we see so clearly with the uncanny imagery in *A Jet of Blood*" (Ibid.: 262). Again, a binary of organic reality (see above the critic Crémieux's description of Artaud's directing as "violently real") as well as monstrous and grandiose—all the same seeming incompatibles that regularly coexist on van Hove's stages.

Artaud sometimes advocated ridding the theatre of text entirely (Artaud 1958). At other times, he embraced the necessity of using extant text, providing it was made subservient to a magnanimous directorial will. While van Hove, after his beginnings in self-authorship and collaborative creation, became closely identified with "text;" lurking behind was a sense that the texts were pre-texts for a prolonged project of staging certain secret places in the human soul, in consonance with Artaud's own skeptical attitude towards text. The season at the Alfred Jarry included extant plays by Strindberg and new ones by Roger Vitrac. Accounting for the seeming inconsistency, Artaud downplayed text, insisting that:

> we are not creating a theatre so as to present plays, but to succeed in uncovering the mind's obscure, hidden and unrevealed aspects, by a sort of real, physical projection. We are not aiming to create an illusion of things which do not exist, as was done heretofore, as has been done up to now in the theatre (Artaud 1989: 35) . . . Servility to the author, submission to the text, what a load of rubbish! But each text has an infinite number of possibilities. The spirit of the text, not the letter! But a text demands more than just analysis and insight. There is a kind of magnetic intercommunication to be established between the mind of the author and the mind of the director.
>
> *(Ibid.: 35)*

And on the thorny questions of aestheticism, of images for their own sake, answers are provided by Artaud in his sweeping expostulations:

> a theatre which aims at demolishing everything in order to get down to the essence, to seek by specifically theatrical means to achieve the essence, cannot be an arts theatre, and cannot be so *by definition*. To produce art, to produce aestheticism, is to aim at amusement, at furtive effect, external, transitory effect, but to seek to exteriorize serious feelings to identify the fundamental attitudes of the mind, to wish to give the audience the impression that they are *running the risk* of something by coming to our plays, and to make them responsive to a new concept of *Danger*, I believe that that is not to produce art.
>
> *(Artaud 1958: 71)*

Van Hove repeatedly, rejecting the notion of art-for-art's-sake, also identifies his imagery with a dangerous drilling down into the human heart and soul.

But even as he rejects "aestheticism," along with Artaud, he is equally leery of using the theatre for unmitigated political advocacy. After Artaud witnessed the Surrealist Group's flirtations with the political left, he became disenchanted:

> Should you wish to create a theatre to put across political or other ideas, I will not be a party to it. In the theatre only what is essentially theatrical is of interest to me, making use of the theatre to promote any revolutionary idea (except in the domain of the mind) seems to me to be of the basest and most repugnant opportunism.
>
> *(Artaud 1958: 47–48)*

Artaud's targets for denigration, as we shall see, tally surprisingly closely with van Hove's regarding the role of psychology as well. Psychology in the theatre is thrown into the same obsolete buckets as conventional scenery:

> dragging all the literary and artistic ideas down with it in this destruction, along with the psychological conventions, all the plastic artificiality, etc., on which this theatre was built, by reconciling the idea of theatre, at least provisionally, with whatever is most feverish in life today.
>
> *(Artaud 1958: 47–48)*

Indeed, van Hove often seems resolved to sweep the audience up in that which is most feverish in *stage* life today. In those shows where van Hove has leaned furthest into realizing an Artaudian vision—such as *Rumors, Splendid's, A Massacre at Paris*, and *True Love*—it has chiefly meant taking a wild throw into vocal exploration, which is perforce connected to mining actors' untapped emotional zones. The audience enters an atmosphere in each case that is dense and palpable. An invitation is conveyed to the audience to participate in a radical separation from daily life, an immersion into a tangential reality. These shows are unique of their kind. But they have certainly not been van Hove's most popular. Implicit in Artaud's program is dragging the audience out of their comfort zones and through unpleasant states of being. It is a select audience indeed that will willingly give in to such an intrusion. Other shows in which there is a whiff of Artaudianism without it engulfing the experience—*Cries and Whispers, Opening Night, Persona, Lazarus*, to name a few—have been among the most compelling. From van Hove's earliest beginnings as a director, no theatre theoretician has ever displaced Artaud for his primacy, although we can see this influence far more strongly in certain productions than in others.

Patrice Chéreau

Van Hove has on many occasions asserted that his model, the director he admired most when a young beginner just starting out, was the Frenchman Patrice Chéreau. To this day, he claims to buy every book that comes out on the subject (Willinger 2017a). As with Artaud, his discovery of Chéreau was thanks to Alex Van Royen. He recounts his teacher coming into class one day in transports. Avowing that he'd always hated the opera, Van Royen had just seen a production—by Chéreau—which was so extraordinary that it caused him to reconsider the entire art form (Ibid.) Based on his teacher's recommendation, he went to see for himself.

Though van Hove was too young to see Chéreau's early work, he did attend live productions of his *Hamlet, Henry VI, Richard III*, and *Platonov*:

> I saw all three versions of his *Loneliness of the Cotton Fields* (by Koltès), all of them different. The last version was the most stunning thing I ever saw. I was the second person in the world to direct it. The third version I saw five, six times. [The 1987 version toured to the Halles of Schaerbeek in Brussels making access easy for him.] I told my actors at Zuidelijk Toneel: 'we're going to see that show, and sent them all to see it.' I saw his *The Dispute* by Marivaux and *I Am the Wind* and *Autumn Dream*, both by Jon Fosse. I saw *Lulu* by Alban Berg on video. *Lulu* was his real breakthrough.
>
> *(Willinger 2017a)*

He saw many of Chéreau's other opera productions as well, most significantly his *Ring Cycle*. There is much in Chéreau's approach and choices that shed light on van Hove, whose career in many ways refracts the elder director's, in some cases consciously and in others serendipitously. Van Hove expresses reservations about certain aspects of Chéreau as a person: "He was on drugs a lot, which I'm not. . ." and avows that while establishing a theatre school attached to a theatre was a fundamental component of Chéreau's artistic identity, which he greatly admires, it is not something he's managed to do with Toneelgroep Amsterdam (Ibid.). What is most significant is that what drew him to Chéreau's theatre were the directorial craftsmanship, notably his mastery in deploying actors onstage and the Frenchman's iconoclastic approach to staging:

> I've never seen anyone use the chorus so well. When he brought the chorus on, it was magic. Staging, moving people around the stage. Sound. He used sound off-stage, far off-stage, creating a sound of anticipation. The other thing is that he could find the most wonderful theatrical solutions for real issues. For example the ghost of Hamlet. He had Hamlet's father ride across the stage on a horse with his sword raised high, like a Kurosawa image. He translated psychology into physical behavior.
>
> *(Ibid.)*

Like van Hove, Chéreau had a long-term, inseparable partnership with a designer, Richard Peduzzi, but unlike van Hove, it wasn't also a love relationship. For a director like Chéreau who declared that the theatrical representation is first and foremost a question of "place," [*lieu*] the director-designer bond was crucial to his creative identity (Benhamou 2015: 241). In the early part of their collaboration, they sought out, like van Hove and Versweyveld later, crude but stunning site-specific locations. Also, not content with conventional scenographic construction, they experimented with all sorts of unusual and elemental materials, whose textures freed and constrained the actors by turns: "stage floors full of sand, water, mud, rough cement, walls of brick or cement" (Ibid.: 15). In *The Dispute*, the stage floor was covered in a material like a pebbly beach (anticipating van Hove's *Long Days' Journey* and *View From the Bridge*), just one instance of Chéreau/Peduzzi's proclivity for including natural elements underfoot and for forming plastic shapes out of the very air. For example, in their 1994 *Don Giovanni*, they used stage fog sculpturally, analogous but not identical to the way Versweyveld later used it in *The Quiet Force*. Photos of the sets for the 1991 Botho Strauss' *Le Temps et la Chambre* reveals a vast and vacuous set bounded by three walls and ceiling, with high windows stage right that admit rectangular shafts of light, a very close replica of van Hove/Versweyveld's 2016 *The Crucible*.

We see van Hove's Macbeth riding a real horse as well; that was followed up by a Noah's Ark of other animals in so many productions that it has become one of his signatures. Johan Thielemans cites a number of examples in Jan Versweyveld's early designs where he endeavored to achieve an equivalent monumentality to Chéreau and Richard Peduzzi, his set designer's concepts—*Macbeth*, *Don Carlos*, and *Hamlet*—with far less financial means than Peduzzi enjoyed, using a series of wind machines in the first, giant banners in the second, and moving towers in the third (Thielemans 2007/2008). Versweyveld has certainly acknowledged his influence.[20] In one case, van Hove anticipated Chéreau, with his real automobiles that actually drive onstage in the 1982 *Disease Germs*, a pyrotechnic production element Chéreau used one year later for Koltes' *Combat de nègre et de chiens*.[21]

Van Hove's repertoire, too, corresponded in many cases to Chéreau's. Most of the early pieces van Hove was too young to have seen, but heard about and later staged himself: *Richard III*, *Lulu*, and *Massacre at Paris* (1972).[22] The elder director put on plays by Jon Fosse. Along with Chéreau's house playwright, Koltès, Fosse was one of the very few contemporary playwrights van Hove has staged. Most importantly, Chéreau crowned his career with a groundbreaking *Ring Cycle* by Wagner, and was indeed the first to have put on the entire cycle in France, as van Hove later did in Flanders.

Much we can read about his path locates van Hove swimming in his wake. It has been said that "there were many Chéreaus" (Fancy 2010: 51). His trajectory was "a tissue of contradictions and about-faces" (Dort 2001: 324), his career lurching forward in a pattern of high-flying "parabolas" akin to van Hove's "bungie-jumping," and, according to the distinguished French critic Bernard Dort, "the duality of theatre remained his central preoccupation" (Dort 1988: 5–13). He had a reputation for being a "smasher" (*briseur*) of classics and was frequently called an "enfant terrible." There is no question either that van Hove's method of analyzing classic texts in such a way that they are not reset in some definite period, but wrenched from history altogether to resonate for present times, is modeled after Chéreau's example (Dort 1979: 191). The elder director endured many of the same controversies, prevaricating between popular and elitist tendencies, navigating the fault lines running between political involvement and aesthetic practice, and was instrumental also in striving to redefine the notion of theatrical realism. He was known for pushing his actors to "go further" toward more extroverted and emotionally extreme performances, and he led them to explore and expose the salacious and otherwise unsuspected undersides of their characters. For many, Chéreau precisely incarnated the figure of the "sovereign" stage director in the France of his time. And ultimately, all he accomplished he did while deliberately avoiding enshrining his diverse experiments as a personal system (Dort 2001: 329).

Marivaux's *The Dispute* was a show van Hove declares he found stupefying on viewing a video version (Willinger 2017a). It contained nudity and tropes of lesbian love. Chéreau dedicated himself to a theatre at once sophisticated, often provocative and shocking, yet popular. At the same time, he wished to be universally loved and adulated. Dort attempts to capture the essence of Chéreau's directing:

> He goes all out with what might be considered artificial, sham, the illusionistic. And he shows the underside of it too: the impoverished and stripped away. He transmutes the real in theatre, but in doing so, he brings into existence to all that is most concrete, most immediate. He confronts opposites: the theatre's toolbox of pyrotechnics along with its material constraints, the splendor of the machine for acting along with its prosaic reality.
>
> *(Dort 2001: 326)*

His stages were replete with:

> clinches, punching matches, falls, hand-to-hand combats of desire or hatred, characters pressed up against each other or thrust apart in the space like two wild animals, smarting in turns from a combat or a coupling-off, such is the nature of the specifically dramatic part of Chéreau's universe.
>
> *(Benhamou 2015: 47)*

These might equally be free-form descriptions of the physicality the Artaudian "extremity" of van Hove shows a decade later. Chéreau's theatre, which was often on a monumental scale, just as often brimmed with sexuality and eroticism. For Dimitri Dimitriadis' *Le Prix de la révolte au marché noir* (*The Cost of the Revolt on the Black Market*, 1968) and Neruda's *Splendor and Death of Joachin Murieta* (1970), among his earliest projects, Chéreau featured characters defiantly transvestite carrying on with brazen delight in a kind of campy music-hall atmosphere. When Chéreau appeared in his own production of *Richard II* in the title role, he played it in full cross-dressing make-up and surrounded by young male lovers, a manifestly gay King Richard. But while he made no bones about incorporating gay tropes in his work, we can almost hear van Hove's voice when he asserted:

> I never wanted to specialize in gay stories, and gay newspapers have criticized me for that. Everywhere love stories are exactly the same. The game of desire, and how you live with desire, are the same.
>
> *(Kirkup 2013)*

Chéreau's designer, Peduzzi, had a bent for the monumental on stage; after several attempts at emulating it, van Hove's designer, Versweyveld, went his own separate way. Throughout the 1980s at his theatre in Nanterre, Chéreau's work tended more and more to strip away inessentials from the scenic space, including a strict reduction in the number of props. The progressive "denudation" of the environment was coupled with an increasing emphasis on the body of the actor, an extreme of which was disproportionality reached in *Solitude in the Cotton Fields*, the production van Hove reports admiring above all others. This along with Chéreau's quest to depict a reality "tangential to the real," perhaps provide keys to the source of van Hove's penchants.[23] In short, while the two directors are each creatures of his own time, an examination of the elder one's struggles and choices goes a long way to illuminate his disciple's.

Rainer Werner Fassbinder

The third key figure to impact on the young Ivo van Hove, whose example continues to mark him thirty-six years later, is the German cult filmmaker, Rainer Werner Fassbinder. When one interviewer asked if he had "a spiritual father, a shining example," van Hove responded, "If I had to name one it would be Fassbinder. His combination of coolness and melodrama I find especially interesting" (Vaes 1988). The renegade cultural icon died prematurely, at the age of thirty-seven, from an overdose of barbiturates only one year after van Hove started directing. Before becoming a filmmaker, Fassbinder had been a prolific playwright, director, and actor.

Fassbinder crammed the production of his entire oeuvre of some forty movies into a mere fourteen years, in the late 1960s and 70s, years that corresponded to van Hove's impressionable phase of early adulthood. The heyday of Fassbinder's live theatre work in Germany had petered out by 1974, and it was primarily through his cinema work that he became known to the budding artists of Antwerp. Hungry for models to emulate, they discovered his work at the local art film theatre. Beyond the films, it was the German director's selfhood or the self-created image of the "possessed," "disturbed," "exhibitionist" *auteur* who refuses to live up to his social responsibilities that most impressed itself on the young Flemish artist (Shattuc 1993: 50). Fassbinder stood out in high relief on the cultural landscape. "A conspicuous member of his generation, he 'represented' the counter-culture of the 1970s, being both a figurehead and a scapegoat" (Elsaesser 1996: 17). "I was influenced by Fassbinder, who said 'I use film like other people might throw a bomb,'" van Hove paraphrases (Willinger 2017a). It was the Fassbinder stance—grungy and scornful of propriety—as well as the German director's propensity for shock and provocation, which van Hove and his crowd embraced. "We were in a way the Fassbinder generation: with leather jackets, and we could give a shit about everything, but thought we were hot stuff" (Hillaert 2009). What van Hove appears to have coopted from Fassbinder first and foremost was his particular pose as an artist—an image.

Fassbinder scholar Thomas Elsaesser's observations hold true for van Hove:

> the work as a whole has become invisible, consumed by Fassbinder's life. What drew the gaze of audiences, but also distracted it, was the enigma of the man who had made these perplexing, provocative but absorbing films: the scandal of openly flaunted homosexuality, the purported self-abuse and the abuse of others seemed to fuel an awe-inspiring productivity, as if a Faustian pact had been sealed with sulphurous thunder. Especially since his death, his lifestyle and the posthumous revelations about it have invariably upstaged the films, it seemed if one wanted to understand the films, one had to look at his life.
>
> *(Elsaesser 1996: 7)*

Fassbinder was typified both by a refusal to conform to any standard whatever as well as a penchant for lashing out at both the German establishment and the counter-culture alike. We can hear van Hove's voice blending with his in the statement, "All my films have something very personal to do with my life" (Shattuc 1993: 54), although in the filmmaker's case, the autobiographical connection was more palpably direct. His highly public personal relationships were full of a sordid sadomasochistic perversity that formed the basis of his decadent film idiom (Ibid.: 50).

While he came out of left-wing politics, flaunting connections with the terrorist Baader Meinhof Gang (Ibid.: 55), he heaped scorn at the feebleness and futility of the German left, as he perceived it. And he pushed back against any obligation to serve as tribune for any political stance: "I don't throw bombs. I make films" (Elsaesser 1996: 36). Like Patrice Chéreau, having incubated in a profoundly political milieu, "Fassbinder's vision became 'political' in the (then commonplace phrase) 'the personal as political,'" rather than polemical, in that "he gave priority to the depiction of emotional microcosms. The psycho-dynamics of the characters tend to usurp issues of political economy" (Ibid.: 4, 42). The same, as we shall see, is true for van Hove.

Having been turned down by the Berlin Film Academy, Fassbinder struck out on his own and made films exactly as he wanted, working on a shoestring. Yet, he maneuvered the system of subsidies and film festivals to gain optimal advantage. While heaping scorn on those institutions, he benefited from them more than others of his generation. But he always gave the impression of being autonomous from a system he could walk away from at a time of his own choosing. His career, however, reveals someone getting ever more bound up in it. His early films had a rough, homemade, experimental quality. But when the chances were offered, he didn't see himself as cheapened or selling out by directing more polished films and television series with much higher budgets and wider distribution, such as *Despair* (with film stars Andrea Ferriol and Dirk Bogarde), *Berlin Alexanderplatz*, or *The Marriage of Maria Braun* (launching Hanna Schygulla as a mainstream film star). Having made a name for himself with self-authored films from all kinds of provenance (Johnston 1981/1982: 69), he was equally comfortable adapting modern narrative classics by Döblin, Fontane, or Nabokov.

Though gay, he refused to be cubbyholed; he had a brief marriage with a woman and was intimate with many others right up until his death. When he depicted homosexual relationships, as with *Fox and His Friends*, they were notable for making such relationships into a new normal, warts and all. His refusal to idealize them gained him accusations of homophobia. His sometimes negative portraits of women gained him charges of misogyny. While openly defiant toward the dominant heteronormative, bourgeois culture, he equally flew in the face of what later became known as political correctness.

For all the film scripts van Hove has brought to the stage, he has yet to adapt a Fassbinder. One might note, however, that the overt decadent mood of certain van Hove shows, down to the recent *The Damned*, and the unapologetic immersion in "the popular veneer of melodramatic" are shared by both (Shattuc 1993: 51–52). Each in their own divergent way have pioneered a style that rejects realism, but quests after an internal authenticity. As Elsaesser says, "Fassbinder's worlds are of resolute and uncompromising artificiality" (Elsaesser 1996: 21–23). That, plus van Hove's proclivity for aggressively pushing what is disgusting and offensive in much physical stage business, is related to Fassbinder. His kitschy use of extant pop musical pieces also finds a precedent in the German film director.

In his public persona, Fassbinder's flamboyance was in sharp contrast to van Hove's restrained personal style. Still, van Hove did appreciate Fassbinder's "coolness." Fassbinder, even when cheerful, declined to smile (Schlumberger 1992: 16). But he was in his element when wreaking emotional havoc both among his intimates and out in the world. Van Hove professes to prefer stability and a conflict-free environment. Apart from a few upheavals, not many open conflicts have come to light about his relations with artistic peers. It is more in terms of artistic freedom, the ability to navigate exactly where he wishes, and devil take the hindmost, that we see van Hove referring back to Fassbinder's example.

The common thread that binds these three forebears is an example of freedom, the freedom to liberate oneself from society's prescriptions, from hidebound textual parsings, from reason and logic, and even from consideration for others; to allow individuality to shine out, whatever the cost. This, according to Ionesco, is the artist's first prerogative:

> Freedom of imagination is not flight into the unreal, it is not escape, it is daring and invention. And invention is not evasive or abdication. The paths of imagination are without number and the inventive powers are boundless. On the contrary, the way is barred only when we find ourselves within the narrow confines of what we call some dreary 'thesis' or realism, whether it be socialist or not. The latter has already withered, its revelations have faded, it is academic and conventional, it is a prison.
>
> *(Ionesco 1964: 82)*

They all went against the grain, rebelling against both "establishment" and socially acceptable forms of progressivism, rubbing many the wrong way. They refused to be cubbyholed. They were highly imaginative and achieved a measure of notoriety. Their stock in trade was images. Indeed, a particular image in van Hove's 2017 show, *Obsession* is emblematic. The hero goes on the road to escape from all the constraints of his life, his past, and encumbering relationships. He comes to a stop. His back to the audience in silhouette, he faces a vast screen filled with footage of a crashing sea. It is a quote of German Romanticist, Caspar David Friedrich's famous painting, "Wanderer Above a Sea of Fog." The Romanticist artist is confronted with the mystery of the universe—quite alone.

Such subjectivity in an artist that flirts with downright derangement can be a difficult equation to square with all the responsibilities of an artistic director who leads a major institutional repertory company, a role that requires a keen objective sense of how the establishment works and good survival skills. Artaud failed miserably to embody both; Chéreau was much better at it; and Fassbinder did as well, but at a terrible cost. Van Hove in that respect, most emulates Chéreau.

A repertory from left-field

Van Hove was to be the first to direct an impressive number of plays in the Benelux, including the Jacobean classic that is frequently performed in the anglophone world, *'Tis Pity She's a Whore*. Furthermore, when in America, he revived several virtually discarded modern American classics, getting Americans to see them through new lenses. His success spurred a revived wave of interest in forgotten American drama. And beyond that, he has become closely identified with introducing film scripts to live theatrical production with his Bergman, Cassavetes, and Visconti shows. *The Little Foxes*, *South*, *Massacre at Paris*, *Strange Interlude*, *More Stately Mansions*, and *Children of the Sun* form a list that bespeaks an unlikely, even far-fetched, repertory: cosmopolitan, gawky, and varied. One journalist pinpointed this "preference for unknown plays with classical allure, to which he means to add strong theatrical effects." He quotes van Hove, who says much the same thing:

> Taking a detour into the past enables me to tell my own story. . . . I love plays that practically nobody's ever seen, that one can take in with a fresh glance, that can be viewed with naiveté. That's the keyword for me: naiveté.
>
> *(Geerlings 1993)*

It is a rare mind that can find excitement both in proven classics such as *Othello*, *Macbeth*, and *The Misanthrope*, and who can also repeatedly perform acts of artistic archaeology to rescue what many would consider old chestnuts and lemons from obscurity: the forgotten and unlikely, retrieved from reject bins. Wildly different as they are, van Hove's choices are all plays about the tendency of human beings to slip down into an animal condition, as some few strive to move upwards against the current and break free.

One salient example of a successfully produced forgotten work is a dreary post-war family drama by François Mauriac, *The Unloved* (*Les Mal-aimés*; in Dutch, *De Onbeminden*). The life Ivo discerned in its leaden dramaturgy brought him and the actors to a quirky, upbeat though grotesque style, which both mocked and remained respectful to the play, and totally justifies choosing it. Hein Janssen's glowing review gives some idea of this show for which no complete video exists:

> Ivo van Hove has fashioned an overwhelming show out of this heavy-handed family drama. The majestic space is adorned with carpets that cover the floor and walls, and dark antique pieces of furniture are everywhere. The De Virelade house is a mausoleum into which daylight never penetrates. . . . *The Unloved* is an ever-intensifying accumulation of theatrically stunning scenes. . . . the proud knight Alain rides in on his Citroën to elope with Elisabeth, the right action at just the right time. Chris Nietvelt, practically sinking to her knees with unfulfilled longing, is so aroused she rubs up against the car. Doing it against the guy would be more than she would dare.
>
> *(Janssen 1997)*

It is often some relational configuration between the characters that draws [van Hove] to a work, and allows him to see past the thick layer of dust that conceals its potential interest. Gerben Hellinga feels van Hove directs better when he finds a text without the ghosts of past productions accreted to it:

> Ivo van Hove is clearly a director who's at his best with theatre texts that have no production tradition associated with them. I found his weakest production in recent years to be *Hamlet*, a well-chewed-over text indeed, about which whole libraries stuffed with writing are packed full.
>
> *(Hellinga 1994)*

There is something to this point, while it doesn't always apply. Ivo's productions of *Romeo and Juliet* and *The Three Sisters*, among the most famous plays from the canon, were also generally considered among his weakest shows.

Van Hove is attracted to certain *patterns* in dramatic works that most have rejected as too leaden, clunky, and often too melodramatic to revive. In both *Mourning Becomes Electra* and *The Little Foxes*, the mother of the family finds a way to free herself from her husband by murdering him. Coincidentally, both Christina and Regina precipitate a heart attack in their respective husbands, Ezra Mannon and Horace Giddings. Christina, though, helps it along with poison in place of medicine, whereas Regina merely withholds the medicine. In both cases, the victim's husband has a strong, passionate link with his daughter. We discover this same father/daughter link again in Mauriac's *The Unloved*. In *More Stately Mansions*, the mother has disposed of her husband before the action begins and is vying for mastery of her son's soul with her daughter-in-law; in *Mourning Becomes Electra* that mother is in competition for her son's soul against his sister.

And then there are all the boys who share a "sacred little world" with their mothers—Simon with Deborah (*More Stately*), Orin with Christine (*Mourning*), Edmund with Mary (*Long Day's Journey*), Edward and Polly (*True Love*), Martin in *The Damned* with Sophie—an unabashedly "out" Oedipal relationship repeated over and over. Perhaps these recurrent interpersonal dyads and triads that form the essential web of these mid-twentieth century plays' dramatic life, written in the wake of the then novel Freudian craze, are just incidental to van Hove's love of them. The paradox is that he has claimed on more than one occasion not to be interested in psychology, and yet favors O'Neill, that most psychologically oriented of playwrights, whose fascination with Freud led him to repeatedly dramatize Oedipal and Electra Complexes, which were such an intellectual novelty for the American bourgeoisie in the 1920s and 30s.[24]

The word "psychology" is troubled in the van Hove discourse. To get to the bottom of what he means by it, I asked him whether all the above examples of relationships he so enjoys working on correlate with the disdain for Freud he maintains. In that interview, he rejoined that certain of his shows, notably his TGA version of *Mourning Becomes Electra*, were much more heavily affected by his affinity with Jung, with character fragments that collide within an individual's psyche (Willinger 2017b). But finally, it seems that what he has no patience for is actors who use the notion of the "psychological" to justify playing it safe, and not necessarily Freud's own concepts. He refuses, for example, to participate in the common rehearsal practice of an actor building a personal history for their character, as in his experience, it leads to a kind of literal and confining straitjacket construct. "This character would or wouldn't do such and such," is the common kind of claim from an actor which he finds counter-productive. He wants the freedom in rehearsal to elicit seemingly inconsistent behavior if it could be of theatrical interest, and the actor's mantra of psychology often precludes such unboundaried explorations (Willinger 2017b). My own hypothesis is that real Freudian psychology is not at all incompatible with van Hove's interests, but that he has only had access to those ideas in distorted, received forms.

He also favors the cultural critic, Camille Paglia, who makes an earnest case for restoring Freudian tropes of sexuality, notably that of the Oedipus Complex, to feminist discourse, and as we have seen, van Hove has no trepidation about bringing dynamics of mother/son sexual attraction to the fore.[25] For his rendition of Shakespeare's *Henry VI*, which constitutes the second section of *Kings of War*, he strips the historical elements away and boils the sprawling historical trilogy down into a mere hour-long heady essence of unapologetic Oedipal family drama.

The Unloved is a van Hove paradigm for characters who are struggling to free themselves from social and psychological constraints, a pattern that forms the basis of so many other play choices. *Othello* kicks off with a father attempting and failing to keep his daughter from marrying a suitor not of his choosing. *The Taming of the Shrew* (2005) and *The Miser* (2006), by contrast, feature fathers trying to marry their daughters off to suitors not of their choosing as the precipitating context for the action. In all three cases, the mother is non-existent without explanation, and the daughter's fate is in varying degrees dependent on her father's good will or will, plain and simple. In *Othello*, Emilia is an ineffectual stand-in for a mother, and in *The Miser*, the marriage broker, Frosine, is an older female whose only project is to make more money for herself, not to protect the young lady. But in all three cases, an incipient and obnoxious marriage is at stake, wished for or resisted by the eligible young lady in question.

Several of van Hove's obscure play choices are initially baffling. Then one looks further and finds several recurring narrative leitmotifs at their basis—that they contain characters, for example, who are eating themselves up with unrequited love. In Maxim Gorky's play, *Children of the Sun* (*Kinderen van de zon* in Dutch), this trope of unreciprocated love is like a chain reaction that runs through the whole cast. A pattern of frustrated attraction holds for Lieutenant Wicziewsky and Regina of Julian Green's *South*, many of the antagonists in Chekhov's *Platonov* and *Ivanov*, and for the monodrama, *La Voix Humaine*, where another suicide results from love deprived of a willing partner. We see it yet again in Marguerite Duras's *India Song*, in which the Vice Consul follows the frigid, withholding, but fascinating Anne-Marie Stretter all over South-East Asia. He even stalks her to the remote island where she drowns herself. *The Things That Pass* problematizes an extra-marital relationship where forbidden lovers are driven to kill the woman's husband. Their crime of passion paralyzes them for the next fifty years of their lives; they have exchanged one type of psychic prison for another. None of these plays, stylistically, is an obvious choice for van Hove to have undertaken, nor do they otherwise resemble each other. But they do all repeat this consistent pattern of characters desperately, vainly in love, battering their heads against a wall of desire for a partner who coolly or frantically turns them down.

Overkill

One hallmark of van Hove is that he wants there to be *a lot* of theatre in his shows. Sometimes he achieves this by simply doing a very long show with very little cutting, piling on stage-time. Of course, he's not the first to demand that audiences sit for long stretches in the theatre. This addresses a key aesthetic issue of tempo. He refuses to rush through a show via what is known universally and traditionally in the profession as "pacing."[26] He won't force a scene to move faster simply to get the audience out onto the street earlier if dramatic value could be gained through the addition of lengthy pauses or languorous line readings. Peter Stein, one of his role models, favored epic theatrical ventures, which exacted an absolute thoroughness and exhaustive treatment of subjects, as for example a 22-hour long Goethe's *Faust* and a 10-hour long version of Schiller's *Wallenstein*. Robert Wilson, Peter Brook, and other *auteurs* from an earlier generation, too, opted for "the long form," as did Patrice Chéreau, who van Hove claims as "his idol."[27] He does the whole *Angels in America* trilogy in one evening. *More* is one way of being outrageous, and it isn't asking too much of an audience to hunker down for the long haul of a generous theatre experience. Van Hove calls this grouping system his "mega-productions," and is proud his theatre company has the means to produce them.

It isn't enough to do one Shakespeare history play; he must concatenate three in one monumental evening in *Roman Tragedies*, and yet another three into *The Kings of War*. Often, he will include two or more related but separate texts in one evening, piggybacking one on the other. The experiment succeeded best with *Roman Tragedies*. The most successful case of blending several works into one is *The Antonioni Project*, where three film scenarios are seamlessly interwoven with each other under one ineffable atmosphere. The three seemingly interminable, actionless film scripts on which this show was based were intercut with each other to create a new theatre text, actually making it all seem much more eventful than the films felt when apart. The pattern of switching back and forth between distinct narrative threads, obliging us to continually refocus and remember where we left off, is thus an antidote to ennui.

In some of the other cases, the bulking up is just counterproductive. One long Chekhov play isn't long enough on its own; Van Hove intertwines both *Platonov* and *Ivanov* into an evening he entitled *The Russians (De Russen)*. Nor will one Greek tragedy suffice: it must be both *Antigone and Ajax* (1991). He piggybacked Ingmar Bergman's *Persona* onto his *After the Rehearsal*, although either on its own would have been a full evening of theatre. It must be asked if more is always more—in the sense of deeper, harboring more surprises and delights, greater insight—or simply if exhaustive won't simply lead to exhaustion, both of the audience's energy and of the dramatic excitement. While the audience can have no complaints about being given their money's worth, this overkill can get stultifying by the fourth or fifth hour as diminishing returns set in. Still, in an age of quick sound bites and terse YouTube fragments, an extended, continuous camping out in the theatre for a deep confrontation is refreshing, and is essentially a return to theatre's native, classic roots of the Greek trilogy format—a submersion in artistic experience that palliates the superficiality of brief shocks and bumps in the night.

Scenes From a Marriage, which first came out as a television mini-series, was not initially intended to be watched in one sitting. But van Hove stuffs it into one evening. In a binge of forced feeding, the series of false endings of the married couple's relationship ultimately starts to make unreasonable demands on the audience's patience. *The New York Times* reviewer didn't seem to have this criticism (Brantley 2014a), but the audience I was sitting with that seemed so engaged and galvanized until halfway through Act II, started to visibly sag and lose interest from that point on. The piling on of inconclusive conclusions wound up dissipating the considerable dramatic impact of the show.

Macbeth *as prototype*

The first major classic van Hove took on was *Macbeth*, a 1988 production under the AKT/ Vertikaal rubric. It became what he calls a "prototype" production, one not absolutely successful in and of itself, but full of fodder for future ones (Willinger 2016b). Up to that point, he had established himself as an interesting, distinctive experimentalist, often using intimate plays from the contemporary canon, including those by Duras, Koltès, Pinter, and Müller. But negotiating a large cast with Shakespeare's well-known intricacies of language and options for period style was a challenge he needed to assume. In retrospect, it served as a trampoline to become artistic director for a major regional theatre, and he has made no bones about saying that at the time it was his dream to do large-scale productions in a theatre with sufficient means.[28]

Macbeth was a prescient and densely packed, transitional work, where van Hove tried out many ideas he would return to later. It was overstuffed with innovations, as though, unconvinced that he had a long, fruitful career as a director ahead of him, there would only be this one chance to say and do it all.[29] While his production gets off to a rocky start in the interpretation of the Witches, and throughout remains a kind of bric-a-brac of contradictory radical interpretations, the production does finally accrete into a show with power and substance. It is worth examining, if only as a germinating tray for many of the ideas he later reverted to and developed. Others tried out in this production were never to be used again.

Upstage there is a wall of enormous vertical Stonehenge-like stones encircling the space, a powerful statement. These great slabs ultimately are seen to revolve, and reveal themselves painted scarlet on the backside. At first, only one of them is reversed, forming a red alcove that is used for bloody scenes and deeds, but finally all the slabs present their red sides to the audience, as the play gets more and more incarnadine. Down center there is a large transparent bowl that remains present throughout the spectacle. This set piece has multiple purposes: as a kind of wishing well—as a window to the supernatural beyond, where the noble thane's successful future is rendered visible—as a mirror reflecting the tragic hero back at himself, as a simple pond, and so on. When the Witches present Macbeth with a series of apparitions, it is in the pool that he sees them. And it is in this prominently placed pool that Macbeth ultimately meets his end.

The Witches are represented as large emerald blue lozenges that waver and quaver. While there is no corporeal presence, the lines are hollered out from their vicinity in a harsh, grating way. It is a good idea, perhaps, but falls flat in the event. Even so, van Hove revives the use of endowing abstract ovular forms with life in his later production of Marlowe's *Massacre at Paris* to much better effect. All the Scottish characters wear salmon-colored shirts, white pants stained with burgundy splotches, dangling belts, and tatters of plaid kilts hanging down, which create an impression of their being dabbed with former bloody murders. This costuming hovers between a jagged post-modernist statement about refusing pure period style, and coming across as simply dirty and ragged.

When Duncan greets the victorious soldiers he stays stolidly behind his desk, repeating another pattern in the van Hove oeuvre that began with King Phillip in his 1988 production of Schiller's *Don Carlos*—turning royalty into executives of some modern-day capitalist enterprise. Lady Macbeth wears a severe gray suit. Depictions of powerful period-appropriate aristocrats and burghers transformed to high-ranking members of the contemporary plutocracy become legion. From Julius Caesar and all his Roman cohorts to Caligula's (by Camus) associates and Richard II, from Harpagon in Molière's *The Miser* to Alceste in *The Misanthrope*, the equation of classic royalty with modern corporate leader or European Commission bureaucrat, the two of which are interchangeable, is van Hove's fallback position. This shorthand image of an authoritarian corporate ruler from the "one-percent" instantly strips Duncan of the sympathy he usually gains in most productions.

Duncan and his retinue stand there imitating sound effects of nature—bird calls, crickets and frogs too, which recur at the very end of the play as the lights dim—a distancing or alienating effect. It surely alienates us from any catharsis, as we chuckle against our own better judgment. It is an irreverent brand of theatricalism redolent of stand-up comedy, one reminiscent of certain of Jan Fabre's trademarks and of the post-dramatic antics the Flemish group, TG STAN specializes in (Willinger and Van Belle 2014). An easy and even juvenile attempt at humor, it is the kind of thing that, once tried, van Hove never repeated.

A different pattern is established when Macbeth offers his "what will come hereafter" soliloquy, rationalizing the murder to come. He does so with an oral delivery that is unadorned, accompanied by fluttering his hands, nervous and pensive. Van Hove has stripped him of all that is pretentious, going for a quiet approach that contrasts with the many gimmicks that litter this production. He is presented as a haunted, modest, unactorly Macbeth, who occasionally accrues a comic tone. Indeed, the tone tilts wildly throughout the production. Matters almost descend into Punch and Judy (or into King and Queen Ubu) as Lady Macbeth boxes Macbeth's ears to get him moving and answer the hammering at the door.

The Porter who enters next is bent over double, concealed in a voluminous cape with hundreds of keys at his waist and hanging from his neck. As the "knocking without" multiplies and magnifies ever more insistently, he counts and goes through each key systematically, seemingly endlessly, in real stage time. He mutters his famous soliloquy to himself in totally incomprehensible gibberish, a choice of delivery that a director in an Anglophone production would be hard put to opt for, as it obliterates the sacred text. On his return stage cross, where van Hove has him fleeing into exile, The Porter, still bent double, creeps across the stage, stabilizing himself with two giant valises, slow as molasses. This Porter has been turned into a Beckett character.

Artaud is in the air when a distracted Macbeth's clasping of his hands finally escalates until it is uncontrollable. The fluttering of Macbeth's hands returns at moments of guilt like a musical leitmotif. Macduff too, when he discovers Duncan's death, places himself in the red enclave

FIGURE 1.3   *Macbeth*

© Herman Sorgeloos

with his hands wavering emblematically above and to the sides of his head like frightened birds. He bows forward and back cataclysmically and howls over the murder of the king. When it is Lady Macbeth's turn to be overcome with guilt, at the entrance of Banquo's ghost, she goes into a kind of quiet delirium, replete with facial and physical tics. Van Hove also pursued his interest in live animals by seating Macbeth on a monolithic farm horse for his "Tomorrow and tomorrow and tomorrow" speech (see Figure 1.3). This conceit, which may have been a further attempt at ironic distantiation, drew negative attention from critics who complained that the novelty of the horse's dominating presence detracted from the introspective power of the moment:

> van Hove demystifies this play. This works great when a farm horse is brought onstage and the audience is more fascinated by how the nag got there than with Macbeth's reaction to the news that his wife had hung herself.[30]

(Schouter 1987)

So, the show is an odd mix of styles and ill-fitting business.[31] But it was useful as a way station for later occasions when more coherent uses of these many disparate ideas recurred.

Unlikely casting

In his casting choices, van Hove has often broken the mold. At one point, emphasizing how crucial casting can be in changing the tenor of a narrative, he told an interviewer he preferred "anti-casting" to typecasting (Geerlings 1993). When he has undertaken texts that are familiar to us, and in many cases sacrosanct, he has departed from the traditional image of a given character, and offered to the audience an alternative icon for their consideration. This has been one of his principal strategies for shaking up the play's meaning and breaking into some new interpretation. Consider *Hedda Gabler*, beginning with the title character's husband, George Tesman. Normally cast as an unappealing and ungainly dork, a pedant who is wandering about the bibliographical archives to tease minutiae out regarding his specialized field, the handicrafts of Brabant in the Middle Ages,[32] he is characterized both in Ibsen's text and legion productions as remarkably thick-headed and unsympathetic—a mild-mannered, unwittingly dangerous bumbler. But van Hove cast him in two iconoclastic ways, first in the American production, and then differently again in the Dutch production.

Regardless of who directs this modern classic, a nagging question must, in some way, be addressed: Why did the beautiful, stylish, caustic termagant Hedda marry Tesman? The explanation in the text is supposedly covered when she confides in Judge Brack that she had simply "danced herself out;" in other words, she'd tilted precariously close to the end of the marriageable age at the same time accruing a nasty reputation, a combination that left her an unacceptable candidate for marriage to most respectable men. At the New York Theatre Workshop Tesman was a glib, petulant Bunthorne figure—a young dandy. If he wasn't gay, then he was certainly ambivalent. Physically he was lithe, feline, and in both clothing and verbal drawl, fashionably trendy. Casting Tesman as a sexually ambivalent metrosexual fills the bill. It certainly doesn't look like this Tesman will give Hedda a child or molest her very much at all, which leaves her, in that sense, free within her marriage. If she can't have Eilert Lovborg, at least she won't be subject to any undesired overtures.

Then in the Dutch production he was cast as a charming, amiable puppy of a man, an unremarkable heterosexual "guy," truly affectionate, aiming to please, and impossible not to like. Again, we can see that he would be an "acceptable" choice for a husband who could have been talked around by his brothel buddies into hooking up with Hedda, oblivious to the scandalous social response it would engender.

Van Hove transformed the miniscule character of the Maid in *Hedda Gabler* into a lead. By giving the extravagant Polish transplant Elzbieta Czyzewska the role in New York, and setting loose all her diva tendencies, he wittingly put the maid on a par theatrically with her new mistress, the title character. She, in effect, competed with Hedda for dominance of the household. Czyzewska had been a star back in Poland, but as an émigrée performer with a heavy accent, was long struggling to establish herself in a prominent position in New York theatre. Here, despite the few lines at her disposal, she was given scope to steal the show.

Tesman's Aunt Julie is another re-visioning of a traditional prototype. American directors invariably follow the obvious clues that Ibsen has embedded, portraying her as a self-effacing, loquacious busybody, socially clumsy, but well intentioned, usually played by a small, bird-like actress. Van Hove changes gears entirely, making her into the epitome of the social-climbing bourgeois Antwerp matron—cold, imperious, and unforgiving. The new image doesn't arise out of whole cloth, but is based on a clue in the text that the character is highly ambitious for her nephew, having invested every penny she owns into his advancement. He is the only progeny her family has spawned, so she is prepared to take any road, even the low road, to assist his rise to the top of his profession and society. The van Hove rendition of Aunt Julie clearly spurs her nephew Tesman on in his ruthless vendetta against his rival Eilert Lovborg, and manages to help him to squelch the evident fondness with which Tesman also holds for Lovborg. Van Hove shows how social Darwinism runs in the family through this bit of unexpected casting and interpretation that overturns the going preconception.

A wiry, supple central male figure with small, regular facial features and close-cropped hair, sometimes ramified by a slew of similarly slender, agile male supporting actors with modest good looks, is the prototypical van Hove default casting disposition, regardless of national or stylistic tradition. Even when the role is that of a mature man, such as Harpagon in Molière's *The Miser*, where the commedia convention would dictate using a very squat or very lanky, angular figure with a pointy nose, in his place we find a fit, neutrally clothed man of early middle age, with the bland even features that one imagines abound in the contemporary European boardroom or European sub-commission. The only exception that proves the rule in the Toneelgroep Amsterdam company is the burly Fred Goossens. Naturally, once Ivo assumed command of Toneelgroep Amsterdam, which is structured along traditional European repertory company lines, van Hove has had to resort to the actors available from the company instead of jobbing them in according to each given role's unique requirements. But it is van Hove himself who, over time, has determined the composition of this company, and the men in it have come to share the rather homogenous physique described above.

When he directs for NYTW, he can put his ensemble together *ex nihilo*, and then it generally seems like he is going for exactly the same look. A case in point is his production of *The Little Foxes*. In the character description that Lillian Hellman provided of Ben, the malign uncle and head of the family, he is specifically pictured as having the light movements that heavy men so often have. The hulking George C. Scott for example, true to type, played the role in the 1967 Lincoln Center production. But van Hove is having none of that, and we were confronted with Marton Czokas, a feline, square-jawed, actor seemingly without love handles, slithering about the stage. Van Hove has kept the light-footed part of Hellman's requirements, but dispensed with the paunch. Long sinews, but no concomitant bulk, are the male hallmarks. Yet another case in point occurs in his recent reimagining of John Proctor in the Broadway production of Miller's *The Crucible*. Ben Whishaw has a markedly slighter build than the sturdy character described by the original text and than Proctor is generally cast to look. When he is described in the play as appearing like a "great bird" sitting offstage in his solitary confinement cell, one is hard-put to make the verbal image correspond with the unimposing actor we've been watching.[33] As a general rule of casting, van Hove stays in the center of the human spectrum, applying consciously or unconsciously an unmistakable litmus test that excludes extremities of height, weight (especially obesity), or very unusual features in any particular direction.

As for what Ivo's male actors wear that offer expressive content, he has come a long way from the post-modern experiments he tried out for *Macbeth*. The costumes are now usually a standard generic version of clothing. That usually includes straight-legged pants. Shirts may be t-shirts or button down shirts, but almost none are showy or detailed. If suit jackets are sometimes added for an official or slightly formal touch, they are plain and generally unaccoutered with ties. As the bodies must be covered, it will be done with as minimal ambition as possible for expressing any particular thing beyond what dry necessity requires. In fact, the overall impression from the point of view of style is not just that the costumes are unobtrusive, but that they are denatured. The same may be said for most of the actresses, with notable exceptions. In period shows they may evoke a reference to historical particularity, but the costumes are never accurate period renditions. In *The Crucible*, for example, the well-known Pilgrim garb is absent. There are no big buckles, high-brimmed hats, or voluminous capes and frock coats. But the costumes with modern lines retain a black sobriety and modesty, keeping much of the body well covered. Still, the women wear pantsuits in preference to dresses. Sophie Okonedo who played Mrs. Proctor in *The Crucible* confided that, "he wants the men and women to wear the same kind of stuff, so they're rather androgynous" (Okonedo 2016).

Acting and emotions: not the Method or a method

Emotions are difficult for everyone to grapple with, whether regarded as a skill set or technical challenge, and this is no less true for European theatre directors and acting pedagogues. And they are difficult for critics such as myself to talk about with any precision. Still, many go to the theatre precisely because the emotional charge can be so immediate and stimulating. This issue of emotions, whatever the difficulties in articulating it, is an essential bedrock of the live theatre genre. It's a subject that clearly has long preoccupied van Hove and for which he has definite ambitions. What is clear is that he loves the extreme ends of emotional expression, the noisy explosions and the numbed out passages. Both have the power to shock and disarm. The question of how to achieve the former, though, has proved tricky.

Stanislavsky, for whom helping actors to reliably access emotions was a central tenet, never made the same pivotal and long-lasting inroads on French, German, and Belgian theatre as he did on the American. Indeed, for France and Belgium, The Actor's Studio and the entire school of 1950s American "Method Acting" has the kind of legendary, exotic, and unattainable status as— say—French wines might in Podunk. John Strasberg, the famous Lee's son, set up a shop as an acting guru in Paris, and French actors trooped to study with him. Certain of Strasberg's acolytes gave workshops in Flanders in the 1980s as well. But that does not mean that the Stanislavsky system, in a broader sense, has been integrated into European acting pedagogy as the Lecoq system and the rhetorical Comédie Française tradition have.

In post-war Flanders, acting was taught at the Studio Herman Teirlinck and the Brussels Conservatorium using theories and techniques originating with Jacques Copeau, Lecoq, Laban, and Tairov, as culled and expounded by the great post-war cultural innovator Teirlinck and his acolytes. Stanislavsky was not disregarded, but little practiced or understood. And certainly the offshoot teachings of the American epigones of the Stanislavsky system, so lionized across the Atlantic—Strasberg, Adler, Hagen, Meisner—were not part of the mix at all.

Van Hove himself didn't have an acting-based training. At Het RITCS, where he studied directing, there were no student actors on-site for the student director to direct, nor was any organized, hands-on method taught. So he started by essentially following his instincts and inventing his own way of approaching the great mysteries surrounding what stage emotions are and how to elicit them. He gleaned what he could about it as a sensitive viewer from his extensive film, performance art, and theatre-going, and worked out a not very systematic trial and error approach, sometimes stumbling on felicitous results. For better or worse, his praxis has never evolved into a system. Rather, he adjusts his contours to the context.

Having now worked in many nations, each with its own theatre traditions, he acknowledges certain broad differences between Flemish, German, and American actors respectively, claiming that emotions are the special forte of the Americans:

> As a director who works in several countries, does he think there is any longer such a thing as a national style of theatre? 'For me, not,' he says instantly. 'Well, yes,' he revises, equally instantly. 'American actors are much more emotional. And German actors tend to observe their own characters from the side, almost commenting on them while they are playing them. Belgian actors play from the belly. They are very earthy. . . . Yes, there are these little differences,' he finally decides. 'What is important is that you create a sense of ensemble. And once you manage that, you have done 50 per cent of the work.'
>
> *(Hemming 2015)*

In a separate interview, when asked what distinguishes the Belgian spirit, he answered:

> Now I often notice—and here I'm surely exaggerating—that Dutch actors are most concerned with how I should move and how should I walk, and then they think, once they've figured that out, they've come up with a character. A Flemish actor dares to paddle around in the puddle of uncertainty a whole lot more.
>
> *(Geerlings 1993)*

And in yet another:

> we have our feet on the ground. That's our Flemish side. I like it when actors perform as much with their emotional intelligence as with their bodies. Which isn't the Dutch way. They're more rational.
>
> *(Perrier 2012)*

Yet, Amsterdam has been Ivo's artistic home base for many years now, and it may be that Dutch actors' rationality has been cramping the director's style in the work at TGA.

From the beginning, van Hove was questing to find an idiosyncratic formula. In his early works, it seems that he simply hurled himself from one approach and style to the next with an impetuosity that, like some whirlpool, sucked his young, inexperienced collaborators into its vortex without too much analysis of how they got to the intended end. The compelling acting in his first play, *Rumors*, emerged in large part from the shared sense of mission among all who participated in it. That first ensemble he pulled together consisted largely of totally untrained actors, mostly students from the academy for visual arts with few preconceptions about acting, who were drawn by the young charismatic leader's implacable and lofty vision that galvanized their simmering and heretofore untapped longings. And they threw themselves into a creative endeavor they found compelling. The play's subject and the unconventional circumstances of its genesis seem to have been enough to forge a unified, and unusual, convincing performance style. He then tilted to extreme Mannerism and artificiality in *Disease Germs*.

Wild Lords (*Wilde Heren*, 1984) whose playtext grew out of improvisations, was both in subject matter and the process by which the collaborators plumbed it, a quest for authenticity. It represents a coming to terms with gayness and concomitant emotional responses to male identity.[34] The actors were led—more through Grotowskian than Stanislavskian practices—to break through the accretions of defense and denial to a place of addressing their contempt for themselves and others—their mortification and shame inextricably linked to their deepest attractions and longings—and to ultimately arrive at a measure of acceptance. As the actors were periodically called upon to present a version of their own lives, at times without the intermediacy of playing characters, and without any particular training in psychology, van Hove was trawling on the borders between creative work and drama therapy.

Following these early gropings involving a period of employing non-literary texts he evolved with the actors, van Hove undertook a wide variety of extant dramatic texts by established authors. His quest for emotional truthfulness in acting was carried forward. But the evidence in production reveals that *truthfulness* is only one criterion he is looking for regarding emotions. For van Hove, *suddenness* is equally valued. And *volubility*. And for preference, *sudden and voluble* at the same time.

From legion evidence, in contrast to the extreme indulgence he exercised in *Wild Lords*, he started demanding that actors' emotions explode out of seeming nowhere and hit an instant crescendo, an exigence that puts emotional truthfulness at risk. Actors caught in between both imperatives may sacrifice truth for volume, volume for truth, or achieve the rare blend of both. Though not absolutely reliable as objective records of a rehearsal process, a few examples of actors' accounts from a recent production serendipitously contain some hints about how he works now. To all appearances, with Visconti's *The Damned*, he succeeded in forging a unified style in record time, having a mere three weeks to rehearse, with the Comédie Française, a company he'd never worked with before. Denis Podalydès, Elsa Lepoivre, and Guillaume Gallienne, who play Konstantin Essenbeck, Sophie Essenbeck, and Friedrich Bruckmann, each spoke glowingly of van Hove's work process:

> Like all the great masters, Ivo van Hove surrounds himself with an impressive staff and works in the most total calm. Which put us the actors into a state of natural availability, as if our inner program had been totally updated, and all the preceding layers cleared away. You arrive onstage with an awareness that a gigantic phase of preparation has been affected back upstream in the process, and the work ahead suddenly appears quite simple, allowing one in a very short time to rise to a high level of intensity of acting and expression. For the scene with the Night of the Long Knives [the mass assassination of the SA by Hitler and the SS, during the night of 29 June 1934], all Ivo van Hove had to do was pronounce this phrase: 'It's a bacchanalia.' That said it all. All that remained for us to do was to push things to their ultimate formal and theatrical consequences.
>
> *(Darge 2016)*

And another:

> For the majority of us this work with the onstage camera is totally new. And yet, its presence never stifles the acting: in the dialogue which he sets in motion with it, Ivo van Hove seems, on the contrary, to encourage our theatricality. I can act forcibly with all of this terrible woman's [the role of Sophie Von Essenbeck the actress was playing] colors of impotence and frustration: her perversion has to come from somewhere, even if that's no excuse for her acts and her thirst for power, which for me, remain an enigma. But in the film, Ingrid Thulin plays her in a very perfumed, cat-like way in her little silk negligees. I wanted to aim for something cruder, more monstrous, and Ivo encouraged me to do so.

> He wants to show the interplay of paroxystic forces onstage carried along by the kind of acting that burgeons to the absolute limit. I adore it.
>
> *(Darge 2016)*

And finally:

> Ivo van Hove doesn't drag a huge amount of theoretical baggage along with him, but a structure for directing the show that's already shaped in its entirety. The blocking, the relationship to the video and the music, it's all worked out in advance to the max, the way it would be with opera. And the characters are never approached in a psychological manner: Ivo rather exhorts us to follow what's in the score and pushes us to engage with the character's thought process. The other day I was kidding around with him, saying that he'd got me to stop being a psychological actor! I often ask for explanations about things when the theatre itself amply suffices, but he gives me that confidence to permit me to get past it. It feels good, at 44 years old, to finally be able to leave all that behind!
>
> *(Darge 2016)*

This may not be the same way he works with his company in Holland or with American actors at the NYTW. Suffice it to say that van Hove's strongest work has come about whenever a given ensemble of actors under his direction has happened on a quicksilver adventitious partnership of believable and profound interaction, paired with an inspired vision for the mise-en-scène of staging, set, lighting, costuming, music, and, at times, electronic imagery. However much one would like to discern replicable and systematic causes at work, the force of kismet cannot be underestimated.

The American alchemy

Between 1997 and 2016, Ivo van Hove has had sixteen productions produced in New York City: a series of seven in English he has mounted with American actors at the New York Theatre Workshop in the East Village, six Toneelgroep Amsterdam productions in Dutch using English super-titles, which have played mostly at BAM in Downtown Brooklyn, as well as one (*Teorema*) sponsored by Lincoln Center, that performed on Governor's Island in the East River. And now he's occupied Broadway twice, once in 2015 and once in 2016. He's returned to BAM in the fall of 2016 with *Kings of War*, and *The Fountainhead* is planned at BAM for November 2017.

In the fall 2015 season, three van Hove shows were on the bill in New York—*Antigone* with Juliette Binoche at BAM following its European tour, *Lazarus* (in collaboration with David Bowie, who died in the middle of the run) with an American cast at NYTW, and the hit London production of *View From the Bridge* transported to the Lyceum Theatre on Broadway. Then, in the spring of 2016, he followed up this impressive array with Miller's *The Crucible* at the Walter Kerr Theatre. To be *the* director with four major productions in the American theatre capital in this one season, despite or because of being a foreigner, is unprecedented. No previous European theatre director who doesn't live in the United States, except perhaps for Zeffirelli and certain other opera directors whose many productions premiered at the Metropolitan Opera, have done the like. The only comparable cases in memory in the theatre are those of Peter Brook, Liviu Ciulei for a short time, and Andre Serban; but then he actually settled in New York, only periodically returning to Romania.

With the Tony Award for *View From the Bridge*, there is no longer a question of a small confidential following, but rather of van Hove's absorption into the general New York theatre scene. Initial hostility from the critics, which gradually gave way to grudging praise, now most often soars with superlatives. One might devote an entire study to the foremost tastemaker of the middlebrow, principal *Times* critic Ben Brantley's conversion over time as a paradigm for this mounting acceptance.[35] Along the way there were inevitably malicious pot-shots lobbed from a battalion of detractors who balked at anything but an orthodox approach to classics. Lately, such critiques have been muted or absent. The real influence van Hove has had on the American theatre scene would be impossible to calculate at this moment of great flux. What is tantalizing to consider here is the way his experiences of working with American actors and of undergoing the initial trial by fire from New York theatre critics may have left an imprint on his European work.

By and large, for his NYTW and Broadway productions, van Hove forged ahead with the audacious project of staging American realistic classics in America with his foreigner's touch (O'Neill's *More Stately Mansions*; Williams's *A Streetcar Named Desire*; Hellman's *The Little Foxes*; Miller's *View From the Bridge* and *The Crucible*) (Willinger 2010). It was very much a conscious, calculated project, as is clear in his answer to a Dutch interviewer just before he first set off to America to stage his first American classic drama with American actors at New York Theatre Workshop (NYTW):

> And of course it's thrilling to direct right in O'Neill's own lion's den in a manner that will hopefully be unusual for the Americans. We'll just have to put up a fight against a substantial O'Neill tradition. The plays by the great American writers such as Tennessee Williams and Eugene O'Neill are still always put on with all the bells and whistles in their native productions. It is that realism that we mean to break through.
>
> *(Janssen 1996)*

FIGURE 1.4 *A Streetcar Named Desire*

© Deen Van Meer

His famous production of *A Streetcar Named Desire* at NYTW used the reduction principle to outrage the audience and shock them out of their complacent expectations as to how such an American classic has, must, and will be approached (see Figure 1.4). The attention the visiting Flemish director grabbed, much of it negative at the time,[36] precipitated a heated debate on the New York fringe theatre scene and ensured van Hove perennially full houses for all his return engagements to the Big Apple. The gamble he took in mounting a revered American classic with all its accretions of habitually associated production values in peoples' minds, but with all those "bogus materials" in fact taken away, proved a publicity coup.

Whether he underestimated the depth of possessive chauvinism that attaches to the classics in the American context is unclear. With a certain amount of defiance and contempt for the entrenched production tradition, van Hove saw himself as a "missionary" out to prozelytize and reform (Bots 2005). This rather condescending view for traditional theatre practice went hand in hand with respect and even reverence for the quintessentially American plays themselves, as he often asserts in interviews.

Additional works he has produced in New York include European classics already considered part of the Western "canon," Molière's *Misanthrope* and Ibsen's *Hedda Gabler*, which he repeated in Amsterdam with Dutch actors (and for a third time in London in 2017), and the world premiere of Susan Sontag's monodrama recounting life with cancer, *Alice in Bed*. He further remounted a Dutch production of Bergman's *Scenes from a Marriage* in English, but with a New York cast.

The New York scene van Hove arrived to find was ripe for a new voice it could deem "avant-garde." The city, through the 1960s and 70s, had gained a justly deserved reputation as a hotbed of theatrical risk-taking and innovation. Groundbreaking companies such as Beck and Malina's Living Theatre, Joe Chaikin's Open Theatre, and Richard Schechner's Performance Group (which later morphed into Elizabeth Lecomte's Wooster Group) were the tip of the iceberg. In such venues as Ellen Stewart's La Mama, Theatre Genesis, Judson Poets Theatre, and Café Cino, which ultimately numbered in the hundreds, rough-hewn theatre of all varieties was essayed. Over time, Richard Foreman and Robert Wilson started their theatre work, as did the collective Mabou Mines under Lee Breuer, Joanne Akalaitis, and Ruth Malaczech. Ensemble groups now forgotten, but nonetheless remarkable for their attempts to create new forms, such as Creation Company, the Manhattan Project, the Shaliko Company, Theatre of the Open Eye, the Chicago Project, John Jesurun, and so on, were extraordinarily prolific. All of this occurred under the umbrella of "Off-Off Broadway." The boundary between professional and amateur was blurred, as everyone did the work they found compelling for its own sake. Part and parcel of the creative explosion was the existence of numerous outlets for journalistic response. *The Village Voice* alone had some fifteen critics reporting on theatre on a weekly basis; they were themselves playwrights and directors, and had a personal stake in the health and positive direction of the burgeoning movement. *The Soho Weekly News*, a major organ, had several theatre critics; there were others such as *Theatre Week*, *The Chelsea-Clinton News*, and *The Villager* with in-house critics. Cheap rents, the availability of storefronts, churches, and community centers made ventures possible that operated on a very narrow financial margin. Through the 1970s, New York slid into financial insolvency as crime rose, garbage piled up, and tourism plummeted. All these negative factors were a boon that made cheap and free space for artists feasible.

As the Hippie Generation gave way to the "Me Generation," communal and cooperative ventures began to fall into disrepute, and with them the notion of the experimental director. Materialism was on the rise, and theatre artists wished to be remunerated for their work.

As New York once more became a tourist destination with the return of safe streets and a general cleanup and modernization, real estate values rose. The churches and community centers sought more lucrative ways to cover overheads. A new slate of *Village Voice* critics showed themselves merciless and intolerant of risk. Sympathy and encouragement gave way to a tendency to demolish and attack minor flaws. Theatres started to boast computers; computers metastasized into a giant machinery of arts administration that wagged the creative dog. Over time, performance art, most often one-person affairs, and staged readings, both of which could be produced with far less money and less rehearsal time, started to edge out the elaborate, uneconomical spectacles wrought by directorial innovation.[37] Text theatre was back in fashion, much of it stylistically conservative, which in America means naturalistic. What innovation there was was also relegated to playwriting. Suzan-Lori Parks, Tony Kushner, Paula Vogel, Mac Wellman became a sort of dramaturgical avant-garde, and directors were relegated to a back seat (Aronson, 203); playwrights camped out in the rehearsals to protect their texts from directorial experimentation. Boldness consisted in writing on topics of social justice with less emphasis on stylistic innovation. In the avant-garde of the 1960s, there was a commitment to "process," whereby theatre artists endeavored to sincerely set aside the compulsion to "get somewhere," to know exactly where they were going in their work and be sure that it reflected a goal they had pre-determined. They followed Joseph Chaikin's zen koan, that to go from one known place to another known place is not to move (Chaikin 1991). However, starting in the late 1980s, New York artists and audiences alike wanted consumer-like guarantees from the theatre they would partake of:

> Spectators, scholars, funders, and festival-bookers know what to expect when they dial the Wooster Group and other 'classic' avant-garde masters. Along with identity politics, political correctness, and academic orthodoxy, today's avant-garde depends on its being known before it is experienced.
>
> *(Schechner 2015: 21)*

By 1984, Bonnie Marranca could look back and say:

> A dozen years ago I was one of only a handful of spectators seeing . . . work in a grungy loft or little theatre in a part of the city few people wandered into. Now I sit among people for whom this theatre has no urgency. Avant-garde theatre has moved into the culture machine but it still has no real impact in American cultural life and letters the way other arts do. All important theatre is dying from lack of attention in the discourse of American life, it has no input in the way we view our experience as a people. In fact, the whole feeling of going to the theatre and being part of the theatreworld has changed in [this] brief span of time. (Marranca 1984: 18) . . . The avant-garde, begun in opposition to the museum concept of the arts, has now been absorbed into the museum. (Ibid., 17) . . . Avant-garde theatre has got to reinvent itself at this juncture of art/history: it can be the loud, thoughtful voice of a radical critique (political and aesthetic) of culture, it can go underground, or it can cry itself to sleep.
>
> *(Marranca 1984: 133)*

Arnold Aronson put it even more succinctly: "The American avant-garde that began in the late 1940s faded away in the 1990s" (Aronson 2000: 203). By 1997, the negative sea-change had become so thorough that the Off–Off Broadway scene had become a ghost ship. Theatre experimentation or innovation by directors was an ever rarer phenomenon. The remnants of the former avant-garde were represented by an "institutional," "established," or "traditional" avant-garde ("oxymoronic domains"): the Wooster Group and Richard Foreman's Ontological-Hysterical Theatre at Saint Marks; BAM welcomed a dribble of certifiably official avant-garde pieces from overseas (Halstead 1992). *The Village Voice*, which had been partially responsible for killing off experimental theatre, no longer had a theatre to comment on and had long since become a free publication with barely any readership. *The Soho Weekly News* was on its last legs, as were the surviving more ephemeral newspapers. The theatre was in a state of intense stagnation, but didn't know it was.

The New York theatre scene van Hove came intending to revolutionize was a desert, thirsty for new energy. The collaborators he was confronted with at New York Theatre Workshop, like most American actors coming out of almost any training academy, shared a faith in, and a vocabulary from, some iteration of the Stanislavsky System. Such actors would have seemed dubious before a director who demanded that they shout without having summoned up a precipitating inner prompting to do so. There is some basis in the cliché of the Actor's Studio acolyte refusing to follow a direction before the question, "What's my motivation?" gets thoroughly hashed out.

For his part, van Hove has expressed frustration on occasion, saying "it's hard for American actors to move from one emotional moment to another without demonstrating the psycho-logical process!" (Horwitz 2001). This statement suggests what his productions confirm: that he prefers actors to jump into emotions on the dime and spin the dial to their highest intensity, which is in contradiction with the American practice of making space and trusting to emotions to steal upon an actor unawares. Actors of the Strasberg school advocate accessing them through a step-by-step associative process of emotional recall, which may be that technique of "demonstrating the psychological process" van Hove finds so alien.

Sometimes, as in the NYTW production of *Hedda Gabler*, American actors have attempted to comply with the van Hoveism of empty yelling, detached from impulse, and the result is every bit as awful as it is when Dutch actors do it. In a sense, the *Hedda Gabler* cast was *too* pliable and eager to please. But, overall, the collision of European director and American actors has ulti-mately enriched both. As critic Linda Winer remarked: "Say this for van Hove: He certainly inspires good actors to go to the brink for him" (Winer 1999).

Van Hove has had to coax American actors into his way of working and to swallow, what is for them, a radical vision for the theatre. And he has certainly had to modify his own methods to get the best work out of them. Tom Sellar insinuated himself into the NYTW rehearsal hall for *The Misanthrope* in 2007 to investigate how the Flemish director's work process would interface with American theatre culture. He assumed he'd be using some exotic approach to arrive at an outlandish result, but was pleased to report that Ivo van Hove "is a naturalist at heart. What looks like avant-garde revelry turns out to be his extensions of, well, scene work and Molière's text." Using the naturalist-based parlance of American acting studios, Sellar notes that van Hove:

> invents circumstances but leaves it to each actor to thread them together. Conflict? Observed behavior? Building roles? This is practically Stanislavsky talk—and here in his American studio, van Hove appears wholly comfortable with it.
>
> *(Sellar 2007)*

He asks the actors to explore subtext, with the difference that he expects the subtext to turn into explicit, extreme stage business, prompting his cast to let those hidden drives and impulses play out on the level of observable behavior. What a contrast with the French actors in *The Damned* who exulted that Ivo entirely relieved them of bothering about subtext and a "psychological" approach.

In contradiction to Sellar, who seems to find the European director's rehearsal technique pleasantly in keeping with American ways, Sophie Okonedo, who played Elizabeth Proctor from *The Crucible* sounded rueful that "he doesn't really talk about character. He sets a world" (Okonedo 2016). Van Hove himself puts it this way: "What fascinates me during the performance is 'the event': how the audience gets pulled into it, needs to get inundated, needs to get emotionally impacted. The actors in effect embody an atmosphere. They are emotions in the flesh" (Jans 1987).

An American method-oriented director who doesn't talk about a character's psychology and history first and foremost would be hard to find. But the truth of how exactly van Hove works with American actors only grows murkier the more you hear from them. Thomas Jay Ryan who acted in van Hove's production of *The Misanthrope* at NYTW praised him, saying, "Ivo is a true actors' director. It's not the angle I expected. Nothing comes that isn't from a logical organic impulse." Bill Camp, another actor in the same production, reports that, "Ivo has an amazing ability to find given circumstances I can't ignore, using all the elements" (Sellar 2007).

Having found himself faced with so many clashing cultural contexts and actor training philosophies over time, van Hove has apparently evolved a malleable way of dealing with the disparate types of actors he encounters:

> Never with me will we have the first 'table reading' where the director dissects the lines before they're rehearsed. Talking about scenes is too intellectual. In life does anyone know why they act in such and such a way? Why would actors know any better? First and foremost situations must be brought to life, the play has to be discovered through acting it. And in its own order. Chronologically. Only the most banal way, you see. . . . I have no method, since each actor is different. Some need to understand the psychology of the character, and others not. I'm not a guru. On the contrary, I try to adapt to the needs of each one. If I like to provoke confrontations in rehearsal, I'm also allergic to conflicts. I need harmony when I work.
>
> *(Pascaud 2016a)*

This remark suggests that he's come to bend to the contours of those he's working with, wherever that may be, rather than insisting on a given method, which formerly put him in opposition to his performing partners.

Van Hove has formed close, highly creative and productive partnerships with such American actors as Elizabeth Marvel, Bill Camp, Jenny Bacon, and Joan MacIntosh. In the cases of the former two, they will have had a training at Juillard, NYU, or some other reputable MFA acting program, but at any rate, a Stanislavsky-based one with heavy emphasis on voice and diction production. In the case of MacIntosh, this prominent veteran of Richard Schechner's Performance Group productions, whose acting in the 1970 *Commune*, which garnered her an Obie, and whose 1975 *Mother Courage* brought her brief cult renown, found a natural artistic ally in van Hove.[38] Like those so many actors who incubated in the experimental theatre movement of the 1960s and 70s, she was imbued with Grotowski methods and standards, the tumultuous ambiance of alternative theatre. And it was specifically alternatives to the Method that were being sought. Today many of that generation go sadly neglected in the naturalistically oriented American establishment, which doesn't know what to do with them. But van Hove rediscovered and was happy to cast Joan MacIntosh in *Alice in Bed*, *More Stately Mansions*, and *The Misanthrope*. His experimental approaches were in total harmony with those she brings from years of Off-Off Broadway avant-garde experiences. In a sense, she is his ideal actor.

Over time, the director gained in adeptness at working organically, and the American actors managed better to fuse their own organic training with conceptual directing. In turn, it is highly likely that van Hove's interaction with most American actors he's dealt with taught him something about new ways to work with his Flemish, Dutch, and German interpretive partners. It may very well be that his American adventure was *determinant* for his maturation and synthesis of European strengths with American strengths. He imported something important and then exported something back; the alchemy of that interchange was instrumental in bringing him to maturity.

A poetics of precarious theatrical space

As Hans-Thies Lehmann notes, the traditional verbally centered aspect we are used to privileging in theatre often takes a back seat to what he calls a "visual dramaturgy" on the contemporary scene. Image and stage picture may now demand primacy over *logos*. The first thing that greets an audience on entering any theatre is the set and the specific performer-audience configuration. Those elements subliminally proclaim and initially embody the style that is elaborated for the duration of the evening. Arnold Aronson ventures to suggest that for most spectators, "it is the apprehension of space that may be the most profound and powerful experience of live theater although, admittedly, it is one that is most often felt subconsciously" (Lehmann 2006: 93; Aronson 2000: 1). Van Hove and Versweyveld productions are perhaps best known for their innovations in set, light, and media design. Beyond narrative and acting, the visual aspects of their plays take on agency and harbor elements of dramatic suspense and surprise to an unusual degree. This, the longest chapter of this essay, will be concerned with giving detailed consideration to some recurring scenic ideas they have developed over the years. Florence March's kaleidoscopic recapitulation evokes the plenitude of their spatial experiments:

> Labyrinthine, maximalist or minimalist, juxtaposed or embedded, veiled to play with transparence or opacity, multiplied by the effects of mirrors and the presence of cameras and screens, conjugating on-screen and off-screen, far and close shots, Ivo van Hove's spaces call forth different and complementary modes of seeing, as well as a certain dexterity of vision. Alternating between the empty and the full, centrifugal or centripetal, reversible, polyvalent, and unstable by turns, they break the linearity of the dramatic plot, braid several narrative threads simultaneously, encourage the development of parallel or interpenetrated actions.
>
> *(March 2016: 55)*

Certain identifiable and traceable templates for defining space concocted by van Hove and Jan Versweyveld, his longtime partner and designer, have been in conversation with each other from production to production, a lengthy back and forth debate or dialectic that spans more than three decades.

Versweyveld describes the stylistic mission that governed their discoveries as follows: "The challenge has really been to avoid degenerating into some ersatz realism, and instead to develop a new sort of theatrical reality" (Hillaert 2006). Note: he is calling for a "new sort of theatrical real*ity*," and not a new form of "theatrical real*ism*."[39] As Meyerhold, following Lügne-Poe and the Symbolists, the first director to break with the Naturalistic style, proclaimed: "A dramatic performance depends on laws peculiar to the theatre" (Aronson 2000:17; Braun 1969: 253), which may be opposed to those which govern life.[40] Van Hove and Versweyveld work with unabashedly theatrical space that declines to conceal its performative role, while selectively adding back elements which recall "the real" to it.

An announcement for a 1988 exhibit on Versweyveld's design techniques for the theatre, put the accent on "real" materials, in other words tangible stuff, none of which was manufactured expressly for the theatre:

> The design for *The Bacchae* (1987) was founded on the basis of natural materials: zinc, linen, leather, paper. Starting with the concept—working with pure, unsullied materials and natural colors—the form of the show started to take shape. The set for *Macbeth* consisted of existing objects recycled from the industrial world (steel pylons, wind and smoke machines). The costumes too, and the jewelry which are assemblages from extant costumes and jewels. Objects are dragged out of their actual context and, through the addition of the directing and how the actors deal with them, gain a new meaning. The setting is real, untreated, but in the world of the theatre begins to lead its own life.
>
> *(Thielemans 1988)*

Aiming for authenticity, but eager to steer clear of "ersatz realism" (their derogatory term for the naturalism of Zola/Antoine), van Hove/Versweyveld have often contrived something palpably different, which both they and critics have struggled to label variously as: "naturalism in extremis" (Bobkova 2007/2008), "supra-realism" (Thielemans 2007/2008), "spectacular realism," "essential realism," and "hyper-realism."[41]

But do we really need the word realism at all to describe their theatre, simply because it strikes us as being automatically associated with reality? Despite or because of its allure, the word Realism has been used to mean anything and everything, thus finally meaning nothing. In the visual arts, Realism was commonly ascribed to the paintings of Corot and Millet, and so, to define a certain sort of recognizable aesthetic surface. In the theatre, however loosely the term has been used, it is the aesthetic surface to Naturalistic theatre of the Hauptmann, John Osborne, David Storey, and Clifford Odets variety where it finds its most stable and generally recognized definition. It is noteworthy that in his quest for "the real," Versweyveld looks for visual inspiration to the least realistic of visual artists—Beuys, Rothko, and Francis Bacon are some he's cited, but never such as Andrew Wyeth (Thielemans 2007/2008).

Realism is the thing itself in its most functional, non-auraed manifestation. But is that what appears in a van Hove/Versweyveld approach to theatrical design? "The stage floor is a metaphor for all existence," is how Versweyveld sums up his very different, if immodest project (Hillaert 2006). The metaphorical theatricalization Artaud and Versweyveld both refer to is the fruit of the inner eye that recognizes the *inner* life of the characters and draws it to the surface, to project outward a construct which can contain *that* life, what Susanne Langer called "virtual life." By virtual what is meant, quite distinct from the current parlance which invokes the internet or the web, is the life set apart by an assumed frame regardless of art-form or style.

Van Hove was unwittingly speaking about Langer's virtuality and coincidentally paraphrased his theatricalist forebear Meyerhold when he stated, "I don't create theatre . . . as a mirror of reality, but try to create a theatrical universe in and of itself" (Six 1993: 322–335). Johan Thielemans cites a number of specific features from Meyerhold's theatricalist stagecraft that van Hove and Versweyveld engage, such as breaking open the boundary between audience and stage; moving placards in *Roman Tragedies* announcing news of the world; projecting a live feed of the street in front of the theatre, as in *The Misanthrope*. Van Hove never mentions any filiation with Meyerhold, but he is clearly working within the theatricalist tradition of radical interpretation initiated by the turn-of-the-century Russian innovator (Thielemans 2007/2008). "'Theatre stands separate from life.' The stage is the realm of the imagination. It uses its imagining to give shape to motives and problems it finds interesting" (Lampo 1990).

David Cole has conceptualized a lucid template for how such transmutations of fantasy into spatial constructs occur:

> Theatrical production is, in its essence, a process of making mental constructs (scripts, improve premises, stories, etc.) happen as events in space; and each of the resources it employs to this end—gesture, blocking, setting, light, etc.—functions by translating imaginative relationships into spatial relations. Theatre work makes it possible for us to enter physically mental structures which otherwise would exist for us only on the level of thought and fantasy. In other words, theatre accomplishes by its very nature the transformation of abstract structure into spatial experience which—as the spatial vocabulary of one abstract discipline after another reveals—those fields are longing to accomplish.
>
> *(Cole 1978: 45)*

He goes on to distinguish between two generic kinds of structures: "Shakespeare's or Ibsen's places, whatever their symbolic overtones, are still places," but in such works as Strindberg's *Dream Play*, Evreinov's *Theatre of the Soul*, Richard Foreman or Mabou Mines productions, "it is an abstract 'field' within which images can be laid out and juxtaposed" (Cole 1978: 45).

Making a different distinction, Bonnie Marranca parses conventional sets and the type of performative space she has seen in any number of non-linear events:

> Setting entraps a play in historical time; it is merely scenery, information, the dressing that frames a play in a set of gestures, speech styles, and moral values. That static view of space encourages closure, pre-occupation with causality, motivation; it is possessive of dramatic characters, reducing all their gestures to a specific time and environment, as if there were no world beyond the fourth wall. It separates the human being from the world, forcing the two into opposition. The concept of space, on the other hand, is dynamic, open to the world, it allows more light in a play; it is cosmopolitan, engaged, performance-oriented. In its three-dimensionality it assumes the attitude that human behavior has global significance and reverberates beyond the single gesture, as ongoing narrative. All gesture, thought, language and action travel beyond the performance space, overwhelming the idea of linear time. Space institutes a far-ranging context for human life by reinventing the experience of time in the drama which is transformed into a dramatic field, and this freedom brings high definition to the nature of presence in theatrical experience.
>
> *(Marranca 1984: 197)*

That "far-ranging context," which invites creative freedom, is also meant to liberate the spectator's mind-set, and keep matters from being too narrowly construed. It is tempting to detect in the type of approach Jan Versweyveld uses the application of David Cole's concept of "field" and Bonnie Marranca's notion of "space," even when there is *also* a fictional "place" established.

Dutch essayist, Hana Bobkova, analyzes Versweyveld's special treatment of place throughout the decade of the 1980s; his overall approach hasn't changed since:

> In their performances from this period, there is talk of the existence of a visual dramaturgy. . . . Versweyveld often creates a microcosm and a universe at the same time; a space that is compact or empty, an associative space in which no realistic illusion of objective reality is pursued. It is striking that, especially for those plays written in a realistic/naturalistic style, no location or place indicator is given, as the author's stage directions mandates.
>
> *(Bobkova 2007/2008)*

In the 2000s, critic Geert Sels has seen Versweyveld's designs trend toward, "less materiality, less illustration, and more openness," in a direction of purification, which he identifies with the influence of Adolphe Appia. It may be that Versweyveld's frequent work on creating wide open "meaning spaces" for choreographer Anna Teresa De Keersmaeker has filtered into his conception of theatre space as well (Sels 2007). For after all, what van Hove and Versweyveld wish to clear room for within any dramatic narrative is the insinuation of forces whose provenance cannot be determined or defined. Depending on the parameters of a given show, are they emanations from the unconscious mind, imagination, numinous spheres, or culturally and historically determined doom that drifts in to disorganize, wreak havoc, or delight? Any, all, or others should be enabled within these theatrical contexts. Finally, it is the interplay of "virtual powers," in Susanne Langer's terms, which take over seeming concrete human interactions.[42] At a minimum, the overlay of both realms—place and space—doubles the layers of stage reality being presented. Despite going for a *stylistic* unity, Versweyveld explicitly tries to avoid a *perceptual* finality that pins down or confines the spectator's experience:

> There's probably a terror that I might over-decorate so that [essential] sense of opening closes down, which is why we make sure that everything continues to breathe, in order that the entire space may accrue a number of ways of being interpreted.
>
> *(Thielemans 2007/2008)*

Beyond the doubling of space and place, Hana Bobkova detects even more layers, as she describes the set for *More Stately Mansions*:

> The universal space and time of the story were placed in a mystical sphere of ur-history, in the concrete space of physical desire and torment, and in imaginary space, in its simultaneous attraction to and alienation from reality.
>
> *(Bobkova 2007/2008)*

Her last comment about an imaginary space that both attracts and alienates reality seems to come closest to Versweyveld's long-term method.

The majority of flats, platforms, and other set pieces, as well as furniture, that generally turn up in van Hove productions share a tendency to be unobtrusive, and are characterized as "industrial." While clearly modern, having no molding or finicky decorative touches, neither are they especially flashy in the manner of hi-tech. They convey no personal touch. They are blandly devoid of style. Not just the style of the period in which the text is ostensibly set, but any style.[43] These blank shells, whether opaque or transparent, in Bonnie Marranca's words, criticize "the box set and the ideology of traditional domestic realism that it alludes to."[44] Van Hove and Versweyveld were stunned by *Point Judith*, from the *Places in Rhode Island* trilogy, which they saw with their own eyes during the determinative trip they took to New York in 1981, immediately prior to embarking on their first show *Rumors*. The Wooster Group's scenography at the time clearly served as one point of departure for Versweyveld.

But for all the prevailing steel-grayness and flatness, there is no question but that these environmental shells harbor the potential for extreme spectacularity. The key word is potential. As such, they are akin to the technique Bernard Dort calls the *lieu-piège* (booby-trapped space) employed by Chéreau and his scenographer, Richard Peduzzi—sets that harbored two worlds at a minimum (Dort 1979: 154), which in their atemporality form "a potent mix of the concrete and the abstract" (Fancy 2010: 57). For what is *not* self-abnegating about their visual life is the arrangement and startling dramatic evolution of the scenic components in relation to the human bodies that inhabit them over the course of a given show. The space delocalizes and dehistoricizes the narrative through the industrial non-style of furniture and lack of decoration on the surrounding walls. The actors' bodies and voices, are identical with those we know from life, but are deliberately stripped of particularity through innocuous costuming. They are part of an imagined image, and initial appearances notwithstanding, not one of actuality. Thus, the space can refuse its utilitarian function, or ramify into a symbolic, emblematic, nostalgic overlaid existence.

Artaud: "We must accept things as they are, and not seek to compete with life" (Artaud 1989: 42). *Things as they are.* So, in *The Crucible*, the theatre's own *jolie-laid* brick wall is visible, along with a mundane slops sink. In *Obsession*, an unadorned standing pipe provides real water. Set off, as they are, from a generalized illusionistic realism in a stripped down, abstracted environment, the objects acquire an unaccountable aura, "a sense, an application, of a new spiritual order given to the ordinary objects and things in life," as Artaud envisioned (Dort 1979: 261):

> In the simple exhibition of the objects of reality, in their associations, in their sequence, in the relationships, between the human voice and lighting, there is a whole reality which is self-sufficient and doesn't need any other to come alive.
>
> *(Artaud 1958: 54)*

Geert Sels calls such singular objects in Versweyveld's designs, "icon-objects," things from the real world that accrue more auric glow and potential for interpretation, but no specific one (Sels 2007). Also, the shell that had seemed impermeable and unaccoutered, contains surprises of all sorts, often quite pyrotechnical; therein lies the trap. Clear see-through glass transforms to mirrors. Subversive scenic elements are lurking in innocent walls, bringing into the theatrical realm what Zygmunt Bauman has called in the global sociological realm a "space of flows" (Bauman 2007: 48).

The flows are predominantly realized through lighting. Versweyveld has insisted that as a consequence, surpassing even his quest for the most "purified" scenic elements, and a space stripped of illustrative or fussy decoration, "lighting forms the motor of the production" (Hillaert 2006). A separate study could be devoted entirely to Versweyveld's idiosyncratic approach to lighting. Starting with *Rumors*, his preference for unusual lighting instruments, many lifted from industrial contexts, instead of, or in addition to, the normal array of stage lighting was one of the most striking elements of the show. This combined with the instruments' often unsettling placement and cues which lead to abrupt shifts, like a change in the conversation, produce a sophisticated semiotics of light itself. In his own words:

> I've always been fascinated by light. Maybe that's why I have an aversion to traditional theatre lighting. The truth is that in the 80s theatre lighting was mostly quite dreary and was used to evoke 'moods.' I was trying to find chunks of reality such as the yellowish light you can see in cities at night, the chilly light of a *frites* stand or the luminosity of a department store. And so I chose all sorts of alternative industrial light sources.[45]
>
> *(Bobkova 2007/2008)*

We see another means of creating "chunks" with the unusually sculptural, but shifting use of fog in *The Hidden Force*. But, in general, the more he has sought to remove the ponderousness of "things" from his stages, the more he has become reliant on lighting to perform the dramatic tasks (Ibid.). Then, mediatic elements of video and projection often transform the environment, adding unforeseen dimensions, including time travel and emanations from the supernatural. The audience, depending on the particular show, is likely to be startled by sudden incursions of such non-sequitur substances as scores of balloons or ping pong balls descending, portending hilarity and hollowness; solitary wolfhounds prowling through, or pools of liquid white scum that might unobtrusively seep in and fill the stage surface; insidious nightmare horrors. I would, for want of a more apt term, call these items theatrical objective correlatives—concrete images that not only astonish, delight, and punctuate theatrically, but encapsulate a mood, emotional resonance, or even an idea. The ultimate recourse of the given scenic structures is simple, sudden collapse.

While the sets include highly selective elements that suggest the stuff of daily life, in order to invoke an indeterminate world that is both universal and contemporary, utilitarian and metaphorical at the same time, if there is a thrust toward representation at all, it is first and foremost a visual emanation of how life *feels*, and not necessarily how it literally *looks*.

The initially innocuous set will, in Bonnie Marranca's phrase, "gather its own thematics," over the course of the performance (Marranca 1984: 41). It follows that we should ask what aspects of "felt life," including "thematics," van Hove is interested in examining, and by what theatrical means he renders them virtual. If one common *dramatic* element can be discerned that runs through the multifarious texts that van Hove has chosen, it involves a character or characters who are trying to break *out* of a reality which is confining them. Some succeed, but in just as many cases, the semblance of reality *breaks down*, as forces either from inside or from outside erupt and wreak havoc. That collapse of an entire world of complacent assumptions, beliefs, and social arrangements is embodied through the spatial action: the human residents lose their agency and can only fight a losing battle to keep pace with these cataclysms. As contemporary life has its latent dangers and possibilities, Versweyveld's sets are machines for the revelation of that precarious, but ineluctable condition.

Through all the diverse literary and cinematic styles that van Hove has subsumed into his theatre, there lurks the possibility for total upset, for chaos to set in and overturn any assumed perceptual order—"chaos" being a concept he invariably reverts to when talking about his art. This reflects the draw, in terms laid down by some of the theoreticians to whom van Hove subscribes, Judith Butler, Zygmunt Bauman, and Richard Sennett, of *precariousness*. All that one knows and assumes about life's parameters that lends stability and reassurance may at any moment explode, implode, or slip away to give way to some sort of hallucination or half-life existence. The sets remove much that is familiar were they to be merely representational, but leave a few resonant artifacts in each case—simulacra of walls, plates to eat off, water spouts and sinks, showers, and so on—that retain just enough recognizability and practicality to reassure, which makes them a perceptual booby-trap. In many cases, their practicality goes beyond customary theatrical norms (as with the running water, presence of animals, and actors' nudity).

They seem (illusorily) to comprise frozen and durable space, whereas they are a front for an entirely malleable space. The sets seem solid, but turn out to be permeable. They seem stable, but turn out to be fragile. They seem safe, but they are only one step away from dissolution. They appear to be utterly benign, but they are loaded with pyrotechnical display, akin to the energy of a geyser, earthquake, or sinkhole collapse. Throughout their productions, Judith Butler and Zygmunt Bauman's notion of precarity is most eloquently expressed in van Hove and Versweyveld's theatrical spaces. If there is realism to be found in Versweyveld and van Hove productions, it can be termed *precarious realism* or *devastating realism*, although I would prefer to call it *precarious theatricality*, which in any case converts to fictive image what some important thinkers consider to be the dominating issue of contemporary existence.

As long ago as 1988, there were critics who began to tag certain rudimentary principles and patterns in Versweyveld's sets. "No matter what the set pieces may be, you may discern in them diverse, overlapping artistic strategies, in all their ambiguity, for creating a meaningful context for a theatrical event" (T'Jonck 1988). Since that time, those strategies have come into clearer focus and been applied and reconfigured in multifarious ingenious ways that they may be laid out as a coherent taxonomy. Self-imitation is rife; a good idea can be recycled and recombined with others many times without reducing impact. As Versweyveld said, "You can take and redesignate the same thing a thousand times" (Hillaert 2006).[46] You might say that he uses a modular approach, inserting successful ideas as needed. Van Hove, too, when it comes to the larger production scheme, does so as well.

The broad categories of principles governing van Hove/Versweyveld's scenic configurations may be expressed as: **Reduction**, as with *A Streetcar Named Desire*, in which the entire Kowalski household was embodied in a single bathtub set center-stage; **Proliferation**, as with *Desire Under the Elms*, in which O'Neill's farm-home was rendered in a crush of detritus, or Christopher Marlowe's *The Massacre at Paris*; **Isolation**, as with Gorky's *Children of the Sun*, Pasolini's *Teorema*, Bergman's *Persona*, and Ibsen's *Hedda Gabler*, in which a home is encased in a hermetically sealed rectangle; or **Dispersion**, as with John Cassavetes' *Faces*, in which the audience is distributed throughout the various fictional homes and cafés that are each suggested with the most minimal of objects, or Genet's *Splendid's* where each character does most of his acting on an isolated platform around which the audience circulates; or else a synthesis of several of the above, as in Ingmar Bergman's *Scenes from a Marriage*, Visconti's *Rocco and His Brothers*, or Charles Mee's *True Love*.[47]

Tasteless containment chambers

We'll start with van Hove's most distilled rendition of domestic environments. It comes in the context of traditional proscenium framing and Italianate stage/auditorium combinations.[48] The configuration in question is a morphing from what Henry James called "the tasteless parlors" of Ibsen plays and a plethora of late nineteenth and twentieth century naturalists, replete with all the stuff of human existence, into what appear to bear resemblance to sterile freezer cabinets, based on a spatial strategy we'll call **Isolation**. Here, van Hove resorts to an atomization of life within a single part of a larger house, whose other spaces remain unseen and unknown to the audience. A great many van Hove productions (*South, Hedda Gabler, Children of the Sun, Teorema, After the Rehearsal/Persona, Ludwig, The Little Foxes, Husbands,* etc.) are designed as rectangular spaces delimited by encasing walls, forming a simple box with the audience on the fourth open side. They are usually white, although some are black, others with insulation material exposed. They are, in essence, a re-visioning, and critique of, the late nineteenth century box set—the aforementioned tasteless parlor.

But with each successive production that uses this strategy, the seemingly simple box eventually gains more individualized metaphorical life. It could be either a jack-in-the-box that pops open or even explodes, or a Pandora's box that contains all manner of surprises cached in odd nooks and crannies. It could even be a skull, as Jan Versweyveld has discerned in his set for *Lazarus*. Initially unsuspected elements lurk concealed in the walls, the way they are cunningly hidden away in airplane or spaceship cabins to economize on space and render them maximally utilitarian: scenery, props, doors, windows, and staircases, and especially television monitors, initially out of sight or unremarked, manifest gradually throughout the action.

FIGURE 1.5 *South*

© Deen Van Meer

The earliest example I have found of this Isolation principle in van Hove's oeuvre is in his production of Julian Green's play *South*, set in the southern Confederacy before the American Civil War, which is done in a simple spare space (see Figure 1.5). It represents the home of a venerable patrician family whose present generation are the progeny of a stately heritage, yet whose younger members are seething with unsatisfied transgressive desires. There is a door unit far extreme upstage left, with a unified wall of wooden slats across the upstage that goes very, very high—five times' human scale—an adaptation of the box set, though extended into the upper reaches. The outsize scale and impermeability of the wall connote how it protects the inhabitants and shuts out other ways of living. It is also suggestive of the cumulative weight of history and hide-bound tradition against which the intimate domestic drama will be set in relief. A large majestic table with monumental organically formed animal legs and feet and tablecloth, an imagistic encapsulation of southern dignity, dominates the entire centerstage area.

Just downstage of the door unit, there is a plain bench. Stage right there is an equally simple, truncated step unit, for making entrances and exits. A hidden cabinet is set into the upstage plank wall. And a gratuitous element making the stripped-down space strange is a big fishbowl on a tall, narrow table and inside it a single tropical fish. To top it all off, extending far out high up from the sidewall is the prow of a ship with a female figurehead attached to its underside, looming incongruously over the stage floor. In many ways, there has been a reduction to an absolute minimum. It is not exactly a replica of a gallant southern plantation mansion as Zola might wish it to be; it's an intentional distortion of one, an ideation rather, with a very few peculiar additions, notably the fishbowl and ship's prow that call the whole into question. The table is used much the way tables are often used by van Hove, right down to his more recent *Scenes From a Marriage*: to have sex on. Its majesty, solidity, and dominance of the space are established only to be deconsecrated by the sexually repressed, steamily libidinous characters.

The walls in the Isolation-based type of set represent the boundaries that contain modern life—or all life, whether they primarily be social constraints or the psychic restraints bolstering a frail sanity a character is liable, at some point in the action, to lose. Ultimately eerie lights seep through the cracks between the planks in the high walls, splaying over the audience and, contrary to the unassailable way they'd seemed, revealing how porous and vulnerable the barriers' true nature had always been. In other Versweyveld's shows, the seemingly stable box may be compromised in other ways. Walls' destiny is—before the end of the show—to collapse or in some other way to disintegrate partially or totally. Sometimes, toward the end of the play, all the walls of the three-way enclosed chamber become video screens, which transformation is another kind of disintegration of that which was formerly solid. In van Hove's production of Cassavetes's *Opening Night*, the walls literally fall away at the climax, opening up the formerly contained spatial and mental horizon to a vastness.[49]

Another example can be seen in the 2009 TGA theatricalization of Pier Paolo Pasolini's film classic, *Teorema*, which was restaged in a warehouse on Governor's Island in New York in the summer of 2010, a paradigm for this mode of stage imagery (see Figure 1.6). The original film by Pasolini is a largely non-verbal exercise in style. Not bound by stage constraints, the cinematic medium permits a large number of locations. It masquerades as a bourgeois family drama. The father owns a factory. He ultimately surrenders control of it to his workers, as a result of having been transfigured upon contact with the intruder, Emilio. In the film, we see the actual factory. There is the family home, a grand manor house with a vast garden that fronts a dilapidated city street amidst an industrial landscape. We are also taken to the rustic farm the faithful family servant was born in and to which she returns, there to become a saint who eats only nettles. Glued to a bench

FIGURE 1.6 *Teorama*

© Jan Versweyveld

from which she conducts true healings on the crowds who flock to see her, this formerly unexemplary person finally levitates high in the air. We follow the lady of the house as she picks Emilio up in her car and takes him to a hotel room, and so on. Like so much post-war Italian cinema, the film has a deceptive neo-realistic style, but the earthy details of the recognizable, true-to-life physical settings give way before an uncanny string of events, which rather belong to magic realism and spiritual allegory. While serial sex is implied, as Emilio makes conquests over each successive member of the household, no sexual act is explicitly portrayed. For even though the film is redolent of erotic promise, it remains fastidiously chaste in what it shows, particularly in comparison to other Pasolini films such as *Salò*.

In the van Hove production, the Versweyveld design substantially restricts and concentrates the entire action into a singular environment. A black-walled box and black floor is a container for a barren status quo the play's nuclear family has become stuck in even before the action starts. The condition that the space expresses is sterile, stripped, and perfectly rectilinear. There are a few stray pieces of black furniture here and there—table, benches, with clean aluminum features. The space is enclosed and spare as the family lives in an equally involuted mental and moral system that affords no sustenance. Actors announce the stage directions cribbed from the screenplay aloud. However, they do not then enact or illustrate what the stage directions say, for example riding a motorcycle, but may simply sit or stand. The stage directions, as they're written by Pasolini, are lyrical and in themselves worth hearing, but they don't transport the audience beyond the black shell.

The mother sits on a streamlined chaise longue watching a television monitor set into the wall, which plays a stream of irrelevant images, notably shots of endearing exotic animals that nuzzle up against each other. There are in fact many hidden compartments set into the wall, mysteriously waiting to be used. There is also a turntable with a headset that one of the characters operates, from which apparently issues the incidental free-flow music, the first number being the American pop classic "Suddenly It Just Happened."

Once each of the family members is established, the intruder Emilio appears over the rear wall, in a very concrete sense dropping into their lives out of the clear blue sky, and brandishing a white piece of paper. Up to that point, the purported box set had seemed impenetrable, representing not just a protective house, but the mental defenses built up by the family over time. But Emilio chisels out his own unlikely avenue of access, jumping down inside the enclosure. Once in, he runs around brandishing the page in their faces. They seem unmoved, uninterested, not acknowledging his presence. He finally puts the missive into the aged maid's hand. She brings it over to the father, who opens the envelope and reads it aloud: "I'm coming tomorrow," an anachronism that puts paid to any further sense of realism because he is very much already present. In the film, the maid responded to a knock on the door and simply picked up the note left anonymously on the doorstep. The duration of the play is comprised of Emilio incrementally laying claim to the family members, and according to the theatrical language of the production, to the physical space.

When he has accomplished his ultimate project and, so to speak, gained possession of their souls, rather than exploiting the dominant position he has gained over the household, he suddenly and inexplicably departs. Indeed, the father sends him away, whereupon bright light shoots out from openings under the flats and streams through the open door by which he vanished. A sound of machinery and factory clangs out, destroying the preceding quiet (the silence of death) that had reigned in their lives. Stagehands come into view and change the entire environment amid the half-light and dissonant racket. The cacophony comes to a sudden stop as lights come back up on total disorder. Even the formerly invisible orchestra has been repositioned front and center. So empty barrenness is succeeded by a no less unsatisfactory chaotic mess.

Jason Fitzgerald, in his review of the Governor's Island version, observes that, "the massive set . . . is filled with overturned chairs, tables, desks, and floor panels, like an office after an earthquake" (Fitzgerald 2010). The alteration is depicted as so disturbing that the large garage/warehouse space surrounding the hermetically sealed and contained walls of the home space appears to dwarf and jeopardize that space.[50] The characters in the family all lose their grounding and bearings. The acting until this point had been cool and understated, but now they all act as though they'd been afflicted by rabies. So it's not just a matter of domestic orderliness, but of all internal psychological organization being profoundly devastated by Emilio's visitation.

Chaos in the walls and under the floorboards

Emilio had upset the family's homeostasis by injecting himself into their midst. But his exit leaves a sense of loss and disharmony in its wake, represented by the chaos of the spatial arrangement. Pieces of the flooring have come undone, exposing the wood beneath. Many parts of the walls are gone. Nothing is in its right place any longer. All coherence has drained away, as the characters each narrate and enact the subsequent way they go about annihilating their past selves. The last to go, the old servant lady walks along dragging a suitcase on a wheeled carrier, then leaves the house she'd been an integral part of since time immemorial. The great open and empty warehouse that encases the theatre space becomes gradually visible as light unprecedentedly filters in—high and empty and barren—as the play ends. It is as though all space, the entire cosmos beyond the home, is revealed to be a desert. It will be remembered that in his film Pasolini had realistically suggested this modern desert in his own way by surrounding the factory owner's luxurious mansion with dead industrial terrains and seedy vacant lots that the audience got to see throughout the film whenever characters entered or left the house.

For the 2010 production of Maxim Gorky's forgotten play *Children of the Sun* that van Hove unearthed, about the moral ambiguity of scientific advances, Versweyveld uses Isolation as a scenic strategy, but adds several interesting twists over the course of the play's action. For this *echt* early twentieth century naturalistic play, written by one of Stanislavsky's house playwrights, the onstage room at first resembles even more closely a naturalistic set to match the playwriting. Later on in the show, the barren home environment reveals itself as the mere false seeming of one. The upstage area is arrayed with a white wall divided into cabinets, and a sink unit stage left. There is a table with a TV on it upstage center. An old-fashioned oven is located up right alongside a door. There are doors everywhere recessed into the wall and a black and gray checked floor. A little staircase set into the wall leads to an unseen upper story for one more exit option. So, in this case, van Hove opted for a middle approach that shuttles between pure naturalism where objects look the way they're supposed to and his usual more radical stripping away of utilitarian objects. It is the home of a scientist whose experiments are the central subject of the action. The blinding whiteness, where verisimilar walls would naturally have peeling wallpaper or distempered patches, instead suggests the sterility of a laboratory even though it's an ordinary communal apartment. Critics have also suggested that it evokes an image of an ivory tower.[51]

Still, contrasted with *Teorema*, it is a pretty filled-up stage, and for once, everyone has props that they use as people in life use small useful objects. Yet, the samovar we would expect to see has been changed out for an anachronistic glass teakettle, and there is the anomaly that all the furniture additions are stuck up against the rear wall.

The play starts with a girl, Liza, doing repetitive aerobic exercises clumsily. She is taking her moves from an exercise show on the TV, placed on top of the refrigerator. The TV, also highly anachronistic for 1905, instantly takes us out of any sense of bygone "period," and plays unobtrusively throughout the whole show, establishing the dull drone of the outer political context in the usual relationship it has with the modern home: omnipresent, but easy to tune out. Following the epileptic Liza's explosive monologue at the end of Act I, there is an explosion of visual scenic technology to match, seemingly erupting from Liza's cerebral short-circuit.

Over the hyper-sentimental pop tune "What a Wonderful World," which blasts out exuberantly, various projected figures, ape-like and human-like, creep all over the white walls, which have accrued a new function as a screen surface. Van Hove sees an opportunity in Liza's losing her mind to open up the enclosed space by splashing the screens with all kinds of footage of various twentieth-century disasters, as though they were spouting out of an unbalanced, but prescient sensibility. A seer or prophet, Liza's visions transform the walls from static barriers into unsuspected and unpredictable spaces brimming with ever-changing dimensions. The ape-like creatures are eventually replaced by Liza's own face that takes over the entire space. As the act ends with the actress writhing in a dance, her actual body too is engulfed by the image of her own face.

In the resolution to Gorky's play, the ignorant townspeople gather to menace the scientist whose discoveries have disturbed the balance of their community. Gorky's stage directions invoke the sound of the clamoring masses outside the door howling for the scientist's head. Van Hove ignores Gorky and replaces that sound tapestry, suggestive of a lynching in the making, in this way: the small TV image rapidly metastasizes into various Russian faces superimposed over the upstage wall, filling the set, as the sound of sirens and marching take over. Huge masses of seething humanity are projected over the stage—a montage of scenes from various classic Russian films, perhaps Eisenstein's. Then, as *The Internationale* plays and gets deformed, loud popping is heard. Great gashes are punched in the walls. A series of dictators from all lands, not just Russia, and quick clips depicting many wars and various atrocities from barely discernible current events pass over in rapid succession. The wider world, which had formerly been contained in the unobtrusively droning TV box, has invaded the intellectuals' ivory tower and taken over. As the video imagery recedes, many characters are discovered lying bloodied on the stage. Are we to understand that science-based technology unleashed a violence that led to the scientist's demise along with those of his friends and family? Or is this an allusive way to suggest that the world following the fall of Communism has become even more fraught and unmanageable? It is a Frankenstein's monster trope, whereby the modern-day scientist whose inventions bring evil along with progress ultimately falls victim to his creation.

As can be seen, van Hove frequently problematizes the disorganized immensity lurking within or outside the domestic spaces, masquerading as the homes he and Versweyveld erect onstage. In *Children of the Sun*, as at a crucial point in several other shows, outsized video images depicting global horrors bursts out within a local and specific home environment, swamping it with a vaguely defined but universal social catastrophe that is already with us or on the way to engulfing us. Sometimes working with great power, this theatrical technique aligns with the notion of precarity, as "great historical trajectories that suppose a culture moving from stability— whether rooted in reality or in illusion universally accepted as actuality—toward and into a new instability of which theater becomes both model and agent,"[52] an apt description of the highly disconcerting juggernaut van Hove repeatedly allows to invade his sets. As never before, today's theatre has the means to bring macrocosmic upheavals into the middle-class living room, and van Hove exploits those means to expand the scope of the dramatizable. Van Hove's characters live with precarity as a precondition, concretized in the image of presumably stable walls that eventually crumble or dissolve. Insofar as the flimsy walls are bulwarks of civilization, van Hove over and over demonstrates how they are prey to the chthonian, the dark forces that well up from below which can undo the whole social arrangement in a flash.[53]

Writing itself becomes dramatic activity and commanding image at one and the same time. A technique of chalked meanderings of a disordered mind scrawled on the walls and floor that van Hove used in his 2011 German production *Ludwig II* (2011) makes a comeback in the very recent production of Arthur Miller's *The Crucible* that played on Broadway in spring of 2016. In that show, a blackboard is placed prominently up center. There is a poem inscribed on it, as well as the image of a tree and a house. The blackboard is employed in fits and starts by characters, notably Mercy Warren, who, in Act II, under pressure to name names of those who accompanied her to see the devil in the woods, repeats incontinently, "I cannot," and then proceeds to write the same phrase all over the board in bold letters. At a still later point, a flock of tiny projected white birds, recognizable at first only as chalk marks that start to move around, flutter all over the blackboard, and then spread to the surrounding walls. The startling device of characterization through graphic means, first introduced in the 1970s in performance art events as Elinor Fuchs chronicles, has become such a standard of the contemporary theatre by now that it has surely lost any of its initial avant-garde charge, a fact that does not diminish its efficacy in these particular productions (Fuchs 1996: 74).

These multiple examples allow us a glimpse into all the ways seemingly normal domestic walls are turned into subjectively determined and societally swarming ones by van Hove. Through video, writing, and—as an oft-repeated last resort—demolition, van Hove challenges a series of assumptions regarding the safety and equanimity with which we all invest a home's walls. The mind of the individual and the unruly social forces swirling about the microcosmic home enclosure lead to its abrogation and elimination.

People in glass houses

Next we'll consider a scenic principle of Ramification, as applied to several scattered productions. The word ramification has two divergent dictionary meanings: subdivision and upshot. Ramification as it works in these shows means that the audience's gaze into the ensemble of characters' issues and sub-plots is subdivided, made multiple. Where it's a matter of a family, as it often is, the audience can absorb within one theatrical frame the misery, frolics, and doom of more than one isolated family member at a time, observing how they behave when they think themselves to be private and are separated from the others. Through cunning interaction of the scenic materials with the play of light, we watch the characters too ramifying, split into two or more and refracting each other. The second dictionary meaning of ramification is also pertinent, as the characters' behavior and their conflicts are the upshot of the way they have been living, internally and with each other, and due to the impact society has had on them.

Quite often, the lights of a van Hove/Versweyveld production will come up on a scenic interior consisting of an arrangement of soldered and bolted rectilinear metal scaffolding demarcating receding planes of space separated by plexiglas sheets. The configuration taken in its entirety embodies a domicile on a grid that is divided into separate chambers, some downstage, some upstage, some in the center, and some on the periphery of the action (Bobkova 2007/ 2008). It is no accident that van Hove and Versweyveld have most often reserved this metal and glass aesthetic (the same materials we associate with skyscrapers) for plays with life centered about the domestic sphere, notably in four of their more successful productions: Shakespeare's *Othello* (2003) and *The Taming of the Shrew* (2005), Molière's *The Miser* (2006), and *Cries and Whispers* (2009, based on the film by Ingmar Bergman).

How is the metal and plexiglas aesthetic of these home spaces distinct from Zola's turn-of-the-century idea of slice-of-life drama? In some sense, there is no difference. Zola wanted to peek inside at denizens of his own time and study the details of their behavior—how they dress, the furniture and other objects that occupy their attention, the actual colloquial manner of their speaking, and their insignificant habits and tics. To that end, architectural minutiae, a plethora of typical hand props, verisimilitude in costuming according to profession, class, and character temperament, were all hallmarks of the characters' lives and social quagmire:

> The essential point is to increase illusion by reproducing environments more for their dramatic usefulness than for their picturesqueness. The environment should determine the character. Once a setting is studied from this point of view, so that it gives the impression of a description by the Balzac come to life, once, at the curtain's rise, we get our first idea about the people in the play, about their character traits and their habits, merely by looking at the place where they live, we will perhaps understand how important an accurate setting can be.
>
> *(Zola 2003: 365)*

The 1880s innovation of looking through the keyhole of a three-sided stage-set from which the front, fourth wall had been ripped off provided an opportunity to regard human relations as a

Petri dish under laboratory conditions. The principal operative identified with this concept was the director André Antoine at his Théâtre Libre, whose little stage was able to manifest one single, detailed, and delimited locale at a time, each of which was assembled and struck in linear fashion whenever a play depicted various locales. An act curtain would generally come down to conceal scene changes from the audience in the interest of maintaining an illusion of reality, but impinging on fluidity of action.

Later naturalists such as Lee Simonson and other American set designers of the 1930s, 40s, and 50s evoked multi-roomed houses designed as unit sets for the scripts of Eugene O'Neill, Paul Green, and others. Sets consisting of such exposed warrens of habitation graced productions like *Porgy*, *Street Scene*, and *Desire Under the Elms*. They emphasized the regional, the organic, and the recognizably topical. The non-naturalistic avant-garde evolved these experiments in Ramification, for example, the early Wooster Group under Liz Lecompte's direction, notably with *Three Places in Rhode Island* (*Sakonnet Point* [1975], *Rumstick Road* [1977], and *Point Judith* [1979]), the latter which Versweyveld and van Hove saw. Sets made with raw wooden armatures with sawed out apertures enabled us to look through them and in on peoples' lives. Here too, the subject was the family—Spalding Gray and his actual family specifically—that was the subject of this voluntary voyeurism and exhibitionism, but in a markedly more abstract environment. We see the same principle at work with a Belgian director contemporary with van Hove, Arne Sierens who, parenthetically, worked for him on several shows for a time as his translator/adaptor. In 1997, together with Alain Platel, Sierens recreated a cluttered multi-chambered multi-storied dwelling on stage in their *auteur* creation *Indians All (Allemaal Indianen)*.

In their own representation of a home that van Hove and Versweyveld have erected on so many occasions, individual family members' simulacra of rooms can be discerned. But depending on the lighting and orientation of the actors, the function and ownership of a given part of the stage may change throughout the show. The key factor about this scenic aesthetic is that it allows for simultaneous, juxtaposed actions in several parts of the house/stage at once; that things may happen in one part of the house/stage of which other members of the family, *who are also in view*, are unaware; that some areas may be brought into sharp focus as the recessive life goes on for the others who either remain in view or temporarily vanish from our consciousness; and that an impression emerges of exposed confidentiality.

Generally plumbing the classic repertoire for his texts, van Hove resets them in a depersonalized and generalized "today" with an iconic array of electronic media—TV and computer monitors and a spate of cell phones littering and accoutering all the clean lines, the aggregate of stuff meant to improve the inhabitants' lives. What happens to the people residing within the clean lines and behind the brittle plexiglas surfaces, however, is anything but neat and clean. Despite their advanced design, these domiciles continue to be the same pain-factories as families' houses depicted in the drama have ever been. A metal and glass sectioned slice of a skyscraper is no less a crucible for seething, roiling passions—animosities and attractions, yearnings, and stiflings—to burble up and spill over than old fashioned slums or manor houses constructed of brick and stone and filled with knick-knacks. It is a holding pen and a wrestling ring. It is contemporary society's channeling apparatus for intra-familial hostilities and battles over dominance and subjugation. The architects of the modern steel and glass abode intended to create a streamlined, perfectly functional structure, presumably to house ever self-perfecting family units. But no parallel interpersonal evolution has occurred to match the architectural one. Indeed, the vapidity and aridity of the house or apartment together with the isolation generated by the prevalence of personal electronic devices exacerbates the alienation within the family construct. As Camille Paglia observed, "The middle-class nuclear family, where the parents are white-collar professionals who do brainwork, is seething with frustrations and tensions" (Paglia 1991a: 27). There is a sense that society—or at least bourgeois society—is attempting to elim-inate all organic life from its precincts and managing to flourish better than ever, on the same principle as hydroponic plants, without benefit of the psychological equivalents of oxygen, water, and soil. Benjamin R. Barber elaborates:

> It is what Neil Postman calls 'technopoly', the submission of all forms of cultural life to the sovereignty of technique and technology. McWorld can be criticized for its 'pervasive materialsim.' Zbigniew Brzezinski 'who has blamed the temptations of tribalism on the West's 'pervasive cornucopia,' that breeds materialist self-gratification and a 'dominant cultural reality' defined by the 'dynamic escalation of desire for sensual and material pleasure.' . . . The complaint against McWorld represents impatience not just with its consumption-driven markets and its technocratic imperatives, but with its hollowness as a foundation for a meaningful moral existence.
>
> *(Barber 1995: 274–275)*

Zola and Antoine's keyhole theatre was paired with a social/political agenda: to scrutinize the poor and deprived, to better understand the root social causes for human suffering. Van Hove's, though, is not a theatre of social-political-economic protest against the plight of the under-classes, in the spirit of the early naturalists.[54] For such family dramas as *The Miser*, *Othello*, and *The Taming of the Shrew*, the contemporary bourgeois world van Hove wants to depict is stripped of national identity and specific local flavor, although it finds its analogue in the aristocratic and bourgeois purlieus of the French and English Renaissances from which the texts are drawn.

Versweyveld dates the origins of this quest to depict the world of "the post-industrial bourgeoisie" back to the earlier 1989 Zuidelijk Toneel production of Wedekind's *Lulu* (Bobkova 2007/2008). In fact, this design concept entered the van Hove/Versweyveld visual vocabulary even earlier, in their third production, *Like in the War* (*Als in de oorlog*) in 1983. That show was an initial foray in many respects: it was their first attempt to adapt an extant text rather than self-authoring one (van Hove and his former literature teacher from boarding school Gie Laenen did the writing), it was based on a classic (Sophocles' *Oedipus at Colonus* in the context of the annual Europalia Festival in Brussels, that year dedicated to Greek works), and they retooled the outsized tragedy as an intimate "family drama," thus laying down several significant markers for future work. The actors never left the stage, but were all visible in their exposed sectors, whether they had dialogue or not (Van Rompay 1983).

In 2003, Versweyveld brought that basic schema back once more. On an open thrust stage he erected a multi-layered fretwork of architectural pillars, beams, openings, and corridors for the great jealousy tragedy, *Othello* at Toneelgroep Amsterdam. *Othello* is a good illustration of the way deceptively simple materials such as a metal armature with plexiglas dividers and curtains, when combined with all the innovative lighting instrumentation with which Jan Versweyveld is continuously experimenting, are the technical basis for astonishing visual transformations and consequent new dramatic spins throughout the show. In the playtext, the opening scene is merely identified as, "Venice. A Street." The van Hove show begins neither outside nor in the domestic world, but in a contiguous one over which Shakespeare's Act I, Scene 1 dialogue gets superimposed: a boxing gym that serves as a prologue site to all that follows. Here, the males bond through violently acting out with each other, but from which the females are excluded by the palpable boundary consisting of imposing blue drapes hanging upstage. The lounge of a health club is replete with comfortable low-slung chairs distributed at random over the space. Stage right are benches and a clothes rack, with hooks and so on, where the actors' clothing is hanging. A punching bag is suspended from the flies. The scenic arrangement promotes unabashed physical exposure and an exclusively male communion through pugilistic physical release. Opening the play in this auxiliary public/private environment dominated by males who choose each other's company establishes the social ground of masculine domination and aggression for the co-ed family drama that ensues.

Once this scene is over, the blue overhanging drapes, in a majestic scenic gesture, are released and float impressively to the ground, revealing the main set that remains for the duration of the show. It consists of an armature, painted battleship gray, composed of a platform with a roof over it (see Figure 1.7). This open shelter contains a bed and very narrow horizontal windows. It is an aluminum and glass rendition of a lady's chamber, but looks more like the vestibule in a modern apartment building replete with the clean cold lines suggestive of a ship's cabin or a bank vault. A bank vault is an apt scenic image for Desdemona's chastity. The bed in the vestibule is a low industrial, solid white rectangular altar, whose visual purity suggests both the sanctity of the Othello couple's marriage and the coffin it will eventually become to contain Desdemona's unsullied remains. There is also a golden palm tree, an object that is both natural and ceremonial, but above all strangely kitsch. The garish tree is cousin to the fishbowl on the set in *South*, another disconcerting simulacrum of life plunked down in an inorganic ensemble. The vestibule is enclosed in glass at both upstage and downstage ends, thereby leaving the marriage bed on view to the "public" from all angles. Standing guard on the roof, an alert military figure stares into the middle distance.

Othello is played by the imposing Hans Kesting, who in his uniform bears a strong and surely not accidental resemblance to Colin Powell. Despite or because of the indisputable fact that he is

FIGURE 1.7 *Othello*

© Jan Versweyveld

a white actor playing a person of color, his otherness is stressed by a string of pejorative, racist pronouns applied to him by other characters in Hafid Bouazza's adaptation.[55] Given Othello's role as modern man of state, his entire life must be on display; no corner of his undertakings—even his carnal relations with his wife—may be kept out of sight from his constituents in this modern day. The military figures that silently prowl in view beyond the upstage glass, casting brazen glances into Othello and Desdemona's domain as they pass, are on sentry duty. They are akin to the secret service, which haunts modern-day heads of state, denying them any true privacy. However, in a larger sense, they are males purporting to guarantee the safety of the bridal bower, but, in the end, abetting its destruction. Ann Shanahan, who writes about modes of women's theatrical space, alludes to:

> a plot-based connection between the house and the woman's creativity (sexual, artistic, and/or intellectual); a pivotally-plotted transition for the woman in relation to the house (sale, abandonment, or removal); significance of borders to the house and inner rooms or remote spaces; the threat or actualization of violence; a climactic, unexpected death or departure of the central female character (from a significant location in the house); and finally, communal reaction to this death or departure dramatized in denouement.
>
> *(Shannahan 2017)*

She is referring to plot in a dramatic text, but plot in a production interacts with spatial choices in a seamless manner; they are indivisible. Dramatic moments are actualized *some*where on stage, that somewhere perhaps critically altering its meaning. Like so many public figures, Othello and his wife live perpetually surrounded, and threatened even, by the men charged with protecting them.

The aggressively irrational, dream-logic in van Hove's *Othello* becomes downright vertiginous as we approach the play's climactic homicide; indeed, it is a visual tour de force. The grueling climax of Desdemona's murder is occasion for the glass and curtains of the set to provide a crescendo of imagistic complexity. Here we see the full panoply of Ramification possibilities unleashed. The gender-determined landscape becomes a well-oiled machine of devastation as the destructive male energies penetrate and destroy the vulnerable female principle. The glass box allows for several lives to be witnessed at once, although only one character or pair of characters engages in actual utterance. While Desdemona joins Emilia behind the glass partition to prepare for bed, spreading sheets and arranging pillows, Roderigo enters downstage simultaneously and rails at the treatment he's received at Othello's hands through Iago's manipulation. Then, the bed made, as Desdemona confides to Emilia her foreboding anecdote about the servant Barbary, Othello adds to the tension by prowling in silence far upstage of the glass bedroom. Having completed her tasks, Emilia exits and leaves Desdemona alone. Othello closes the glass door. A relentless hard rock beat starts, which in the event, summons up the characters' animistic sides, and primal urges are unleashed. Lights go up more intensely in the glass bedroom and dim down everywhere else. Othello is in silhouette, a still figure.

An extended silent hysterical and savage free-for-all that isn't in Shakespeare ensues between Iago, Bianca, Emilia, Cassio, Roderigo—violent fighting, assaulting, leaping on each other to hard rock accompaniment. This Dionysian unraveling, which is entirely van Hove's invention, suggestive of a total suspension of social forms and a surrender to elemental impulses, prepares the way for the bloody resolution. Once the violent melée subsides, lights come up in the bedroom, which is now surrounded by darkness. Othello, who had been outside the house in two-dimensional silhouette the last time he was visible, is now suddenly discovered standing over the bed totally and three-dimensionally naked, declaiming calmly. Desdemona invites him into bed. He pulls the sheet off of her, and the audience sees she too is lying there totally naked. As Othello prepares for the murder, he isolates the entire room from the audience by closing the white voile drapes on tracks. Once the chamber is eclipsed, Othello's shadow, superimposed on the drapes as the actual Othello moves about, follows him. The noble Othello is being tracked and doubled by his own lower, paranoid self. As he pursues Desdemona, she attempts an escape by opening the sliding glass door, but gets caught by him in the drapes (which were identified with the male world in the prologue at the gym). Then he gets her back on the bed, and smothers her using pillows as her naked legs thrash about grotesquely in silence for an extended time.

Emilia, also seen only as a black shadow, runs by, and then from offstage informs Othello of Cassio's injury. Reentering with his back to the glass in silhouette, grasping the curtain, the still naked Othello is suddenly hit by a bright spotlight just in time for him to relate and justify his murder of Desdemona. As Iago enters and Emilia berates them both, she flings the curtains open to reveal the body, evidence of both Othello and Iago's guilt. The actress playing Emilia improvises freely, shrieking uncontrollably, and repeating, "I will speak. I will speak!" Iago, with frightening decisiveness, but in total silence, forces her down onto the floor, strangling her methodically, just as Othello had strangled Desdemona. Othello then faces downstage, in full frontal nudity, while Iago sits downstage of him, but facing upstage. Both are reflected uncannily in the upstage glass wall, Othello from the back, Iago from the front, so that spectators see both their faces coming from either direction (see Figure 1.8).

Not only does this image pair Othello and Iago as though they were flip sides of the same entity, but it pictorializes both characters' dual personalities.[56] Throughout the segment, the Ramification principle, whereby shadow and mirror effects give an impression of a manipulator and his dupe doubling up on each other's crimes, is at play. The nemeses are no longer

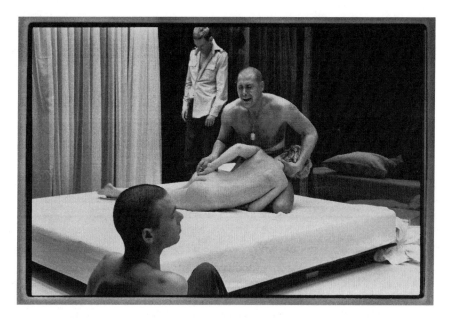

FIGURE 1.8 *Othello*

© Jan Versweyveld

separate, but multiple and interpenetrating. When characters appear on different planes separated by glass partitions that can be seen through, or even on the same plane that is walled off, those partitions reinforce their separateness and aloneness. But the partitions also act as mirrors. In those cases, the separateness is multiplied and reinforced, but they also inexorably link discrete characters to each other. This ulterior mirroring effect also links the audience back to the earlier mystifying moments in the show, as when Iago had caressed Desdemona back in Act I, and brings them full circle dramatically. French scholar Florence March, signals the mythic overtones captured in this spatial treatment that is reconfigured for the 2005 Toneelgroep Amsterdam production of *The Taming of the Shrew*:

> In *Othello* the final tragic scenes take place in a transparent box posed at the center of a black box, a chamber in which Eros and Thanatos vie with each other, where the little death and death itself get played out. The same procedure is found once more in *Taming of the Shrew* where the sonorized glass cage delimits a polyvalent room whose purpose gets periodically redefined, now bedroom, now living room, intimate space or recreational space. Both embedded and embedding spaces entertain a complex relationship, and are sealed off or accessible by turns depending on whether the glass doors are open or closed.
>
> *(March 2016: 55)*

In the 2005 show, van Hove again went for a variation of the metal and plexiglas motif. Upstage center, in an inner chamber totally open to view, was a grand piano, iconic of a creative spirit with which the two sisters on the marriage market, Katherine and Bianca, are identified. The forestage is immediately established as a macho male domain, one where brute force dominates. Two characters, Lucentio's servants, throw heavy metal boxes down on the forestage with a slam, that harsh gesture setting the keytone for the show.

On the furthest downstage plane are two male characters in modern-day jackets and cardigans. Like the clean, modern lines of the set, the costumes are also innocuous, flavorless. Tranio and Lucentio plunk themselves down on their box downstage right watching the whole scene of thwarted courtship within the totally open home-space. There, inside, Katherine makes a show of mopping the floor and tidying up as Bianca plays the piano. Although van Hove has cut Shakespeare's extensive prologue, which frames the entire play meta-theatrically, he creates a new one by putting Katherine, her family, and the suitors on display for Tranio and Lucentio, who are situated to act as their audience. Of course, the crucial voyeuristic party who is being visually invited into the various chambers of the domestic refuge that is democratically exposed to their gaze is the audience.

Kate and Bianca's existence within the house seems free and easy and antic as Bianca sets a mattress on top of the piano and stretches out on it. Then Kate enters and spins around in a swivel chair and Bianca does a pole dance. Kate and Bianca have been tapped for arranged marriages, and until that point, are confined to a hot house, as the glass enclosure suggests, or perhaps an icebox, where their range of action is curtailed. While they need not toil, they are left to spin in futile aimlessness. For example, though Katherine, the subversive sister, gives an impression that she is cleaning in her house, over time she actually creates greater disorder, throwing stuff around at random.

These are images of fun, but also of futility, which ultimately pave the way for Kate to act with unwarranted cruelty to her more desired sister. They portend two carefree damsels whose childhoods are coming to an end, kept on ice as it were until now, who must now venture forth (i.e., downstage) into the alienating male-dominated world of the marriage market. It is worth quoting Hanna Scolnicov extensively, as she lays out a theory of feminine theatrical space, which has application to van Hove's scenic organizing principle at work here and in several other shows:

> The structural division of space into the interior and the exterior of the house carries with it social and cultural implications. Gender roles are spatially defined in relation to the inside and the outside of the house. Traditionally, it is the woman who makes the house into a home, her home, while the world of commerce, war, travel, the world outside, is a man's world. As Simone de Beauvoir noted, 'man is but mildly interested in his immediate surroundings because he can find self-expression in projects;' whereas for woman, the house is the centre of the world, 'reality is concentrated inside the house, while outer space seems to collapse.' From the spatial point of view, the world of man and the world of woman meet on the threshold. Thus, the very shape a play gives its theatrical space is indicative of its views on the nature of the relationship between the sexes and on the position of woman in society. 'Women,' wrote Virginia Woolf, 'have sat indoors all these millions of years, so that by this time the very walls are permeated by their creative force.' . . . Traditionally, the house has been associated with woman's social place, but it can also be seen to stand for her body and her sexuality.
>
> *(Scolnicov 1994: 16–17)*

Scolnicov is referring to spaces evoked in written scripts, but these spatial definitions are even more graphic when realized scenically in a production such as this, renders architectonic the configuration she maps out.

When the aggregate of male characters are all together in their downstage sphere "outside," they horse around, shouting macho fashion, piling up on each other, lugging each other around, and talking about available women with a lot of noise and forced camaraderie. As they go on simulating a football game, mooning each other and the like, Kate dances a frenetic solo in her house, the transparencies in the set design allowing spectators to see these actions happening concurrently. The frolicking men claim their space downstage of the house and pass by upstage of it, but the actual conquest only occurs once Petruchio and his cohorts manage to penetrate into the middle ground between the two: Kate's home, which, as we have implied, is the outer shell of her sentient self. "[T]he male space, lends itself naturally to a plot the goal of which is man's conquest of the house" (Ibid.: 8). Kate is wild—a termagant—but are the men any more civilized? They are like a marauding party out of a 1940s Western movie, who reappear through the transparent walls and have the stagecoach surrounded. But what kind of sympathy can there be between two such incompatible species as they are presented here? How can they ever pair off in harmony? What an alienated portrait of young, available men and women in contemporary society!

While there is not much hilarity either aimed at or achieved in this rendition of Shakespeare's supposed comedy, some does arise through the use of a small white cabinet. Before his famous scene of verbal jousting with Katherine, Petruchio sits on a bench downstage right, and thus outside the house, to deliver his soliloquy. Simultaneously, Katherine, in preparation for the unavoidable marriage proposal, wheels out a small white cabinet or freezer, opens it, slips inside it, and shuts the door on herself. Petruchio refuses to acknowledge that she is evading him, and treats the cabinet as though it were Katherine herself: he lays the cabinet on its side, kisses it, lies on it, keeps wooing her through its walls. After all, she has called him "a moveable," that is,

FIGURE 1.9 *The Taming of the Shrew*

© Jan Versweyveld

a piece of furniture, so his riposte is to treat the furniture in which she takes refuge as though it were she herself, turning her into an object. Katherine intends for the opaque white box to be a means of gaining some privacy within the exposed plexiglas home, where nothing may be concealed. But even there, Petruchio pursues and possesses her (see Figure 1.9).

Van Hove uses a variation on this "bit" again when Valère, the spoiled brother in his German production of *The Miser*, has a tantrum and goes to sit in the refrigerator. It's a good sort of place to pout and one in which a vulnerable party—in both cases children of imposing fathers—may finally get some provisional respite from a situation in which they, the offspring, are suffering diminishing control over their own destinies. The ubiquity of this technique in van Hove's productions, as for example when Hedda and Judge Brack duck down behind a sofa for a moment of who knows what—even as their vagaries must be totally exposed to view from behind to anyone chancing to pass by—is yet another variant on the same trope. In contemporary homes, the denizens require privacy, and, though the need for such a hiding place is seemingly universal, it is only to be had through the most awkward of ad hoc arrangements.

Jan Versweyveld calls the wide array of small private spaces he provides characters "*huisjes*," (little houses), and he does it quite consciously on this regular basis: "What I really like doing is giving actors a spot that truly belongs to them, a spot which helps them regain their energy. If I were an actor I too would like to have a spot in the middle of the stage that is intimate nonetheless" (Bobkova 2007/2008). Geert Sels notes that the first example of "*huisjes*" on a Versweyveld set could be found "in rudimentary fashion," in the early production of *Ajax/Antigone* (Sels 2007).

In *The Taming of the Shrew*, as in *Othello*, van Hove takes advantage of the set's transparencies that are virtual windows, to achieve a plethora of Ramification effects, such as when Petruchio and Kate, who are standing stock still, are turned into silhouettes. A bright fluorescent light bathes the rest of the stage while the outlines of their bodies are seen, pressed together. Instead of having them pantomime the debacle of their wedding literally, van Hove uses this still image to ramify Biondello's narration of how Petruchio has misbehaved outrageously in the church—where he acted out as the veritable male shrew.

In 2006, van Hove and Versweyveld undertook Molière's *The Miser* (*Der Geizige*) in Germany, a Dutch version of which followed five years later in 2011. It is another classical comedy, made essentially unfunny by the Flemish director, bent on exposing the essential vapidity and brutality of contemporary middle-class family life.[57] The set for *The Miser* features a wrought iron super-structure filled out with plexiglas, divided into modules that can be curtained off, and so concealed or revealed as needed. Midway upstage is found an unobtrusive, low black metal railing running parallel to the proscenium line, which comes in handy throughout the show in various cunning ways despite its deceptive simplicity, as well as a bed one plane further back that half conceals actors who are on it or behind it. The only sign of organic life is a tropical plant with big leaves, suggesting perhaps the Mediterranean—one of those strange-making touches we have seen van Hove use elsewhere. Otherwise, everything is clean-lined, with unadorned, modern furnishings. The actors are costumed accordingly: ordinary t-shirts, hoodies, panties. The older men wear simple white button-down shirts and black pants, and Frosine, the matchmaker, a frowsy moo-moo.

As *The Miser* opens, muted rap music plays and an actress, who we later learn plays Elise, daughter of the family, sits up in bed naked and starts getting dressed. Her brother Cléante is revealed in a separate rectangular space adjacent to Elise's trying on black pants, a flashy silver-black blouse, and various mod jackets. His room, adjacent to hers, is simply comprised of racks full of hanging clothes. There is much emphasis on clothes in the text—Cléante later complains to his father that he has nothing to wear—but right here in his room, in plain sight, there is a wide clothing rack with scads of suits to choose from and, of course, another TV monitor. The kids, in contrast to the circumstances indicated by Molière's text, are actually spoiled and super-endowed with "stuff." Van Hove has always maintained that the theme of the play is avarice, but this detail in what's hanging in Cléante's closet throws the play thematically off-kilter. It is Harpagon's self-centeredness that is the source of suffering in his family, and all family members suffer from the same malady. The director's professions notwithstanding, he has, in effect, belied the title and visually rewritten the play, and in so doing significantly broadened its import. While they've been lavished with a surfeit of clothes and video equipment—both the latest, no doubt—neither their father nor the world they inhabit nourish their hearts and souls. Apart from making liars of them, it is that inner sterility, not their father's parsimony, which the set makes manifest.

Harpagon, the miser of the title and father of the house, and La Flèche, Cléante's manservant, both in black pants and white shirts, are then discovered, poised amidst this re-visioned construct of domesticity, surrounded by chairs, computer terminals, and so on, downstage. So what in the text are a succession of two-character "French scenes," all of which traditionally are played in a single self-contained and concentrated all-purpose locale typical of the neo-classical stage, are executed here by picking up on one area of the stage after another. It is, effectively, a complicated unit set representing the network of the subdivided modern-day apartment. Thus, the linear temporal and spatial organization envisioned by Molière, dictated by the neo-classical unities, has become one of cinematic fluidity and simultaneity. As with *The Taming of the Shrew*, wherever the principal focus is then developing, the plexiglas and metal structure with its inherent transparencies between sub-units, allows for evolving simultaneous action elsewhere. It is a realization of Baudrillard's visionary promise for a future domestic environment: "a poly-functional nucleus, an ensemble of 'black boxes' with multiple input-outputs, the locus of con-vection and of destructuration" (Baudrillard 1983: 78). Whenever a bloody argument has run its course, the contestants, like boxers at the end of a round, go back to their respective computers and TV monitors in their own private nooks (*huisjes*).

Harpagon natters on downstage on his cell phone, the living image of a businessman in a tough negotiation, or reads off a computer screen the list of moneys he has squirreled away, and—eureka!—we have post-modernized renditions of the classic soliloquy. At the very same time, his daughter Elise undresses upstage, and wearing only underwear, climbs into yet another of Jan Versweyveld's *huisjes*, a hiding place in the form of a giant plastic bag. There, Valère discovers her and climbs in, for a session of physical intimacy. On the same plane stage left, Cléante, again simultaneously, shuffles through his outfits and is *further* ramified in yet one more upstage plane, reflected back in a mirror. At other times, the stage action physically expands so that these atomized existences within narrowly established boundaries are abrogated (see Figure 1.10). So the entire stage is taken over by one single unifying action. For example, Harpagon, upon learning that Cléante is pursuing the same woman he is, tears up a document and goes into a fit, chasing and kicking his crawling son. This physical fight ranges over the entire stage, until his young antagonist can only slink out of the apartment entirely.

At a certain point Harpagon says: "Your job is to clean up all around, and do be careful not to rub the furniture too hard." In the playscript he delivers these orders to his servants, but here he gives them directly to his family members. As the song "Stayin' Alive" from *Saturday Night Fever* is pumped out, the ensemble of wrangling family members and hangers-on form themselves into a merry procession and circulate single-file over the multi-chambered space, tossing all the garbage that's laying around up in the air or kicking it along. Whatever order one character manages to create is undone and exacerbated by the one bringing up the rear, so we can't tell if they're cleaning up or creating more chaos. Throughout this segment the pater familias, Harpagon, expatiates without pause over the Bee Gees' voices.

Following the ritualistic anti-clean-up in this motherless home, the ensemble of actors go and grab items from the refrigerator, munch snacks, and reassemble down left in what could be "the family room." Van Hove depresses that comic potential in the "actual" scenes Molière and Shakespeare provided, but then gratuitously adds in these upbeat physical segments that the authors hadn't provided for. The friendly, bouncy atmosphere of this post-dramatic insert ends

FIGURE 1.10 *The Miser*

© Jan Versweyveld

abruptly as Harpagon screams for the music to be turned off. There is a sharp, hard and immediate shift to sober business matters concerning marriage.

The low metal railing mentioned earlier that separates the single apartment into two, with upstage and downstage divides, gives us the hint that we've crossed over to a different character's space, as needed. Most of the time, the bar is unobtrusive and unobserved, but periodically it comes into sharp focus as it serves some critical dramatic purpose. For instance, Monsieur Anselme, Harpagon's handpicked suitor for Elise, takes his place immediately upstage of the fence as though it were the bar of the law that supports his otherwise weak case for matrimony. In another instance, all Harpagon has to do is lean on it with his face tilted down and the audience knows that he's out on the balcony to his apartment, looking obsessively at his cell phone.

As we approach the climax, Harpagon's preparations for his own wedding to the very same girl his son covets draw close to their sinister fulfillment. Things slow down markedly. It is almost as though the reality of the resolution—that both children will be deprived of their desired partners by their unloving father—is so terrible to contemplate that the characters go into an opium state of detachment and muzziness to avoid it. Electric metal music plays. It is a descent into chaos. Then, with the sound of motorcars drifting up from below, Harpagon violently sweeps the contents of the coffee table onto the ground and stands on the black railing facing upstage as though he was going to jump and commit suicide. It is implicit that he does indeed plunge to his death, in a blatant violation of Molière's original dénouement and the standard upbeat classical comedy resolution. It's a definitive way out of a family quagmire that he himself architected. He, a self-styled master of the universe and would-be destroyer of his children's happiness, is the ultimate victim of the social establishment from which he was spawned.

Each family member believes themself to be misunderstood and bereft. Those are qualities of alienation that *could* elicit empathy, but when replicated in cordoned-off spaces by many at once they accrete to form an impression of a generalized culture of self-involvement and self-indulgence. When family members do meet in a common space, to plead their cause, to open their hearts, to give vent to their discontent, it leads to instantaneous conflagration, as the other characters take this insistence as further proof of how they themselves are misunderstood and alone with their suffering. Each asserts the privileged nature of their own case. So rather than communing in empathic response, they bounce off each other and recoil to nurse their wounds in separation. As Zygmunt Bauman, whose ideas regarding how negative globalization has affected the family unit had direct impact on this production, wishes us to realize:

> In such a world there are not many rocks left on which struggling individuals can build their hopes of rescue and on which they can rely in case of personal failure. Human bonds are comfortably loose, but for that same reason frightfully unreliable, and solidarity is as difficult to practice as its benefits, and even more its moral virtues, are difficult to comprehend. The new individualism, the fading of human bonds and the wilting of solidarity are engraved on one side of a coin whose other side shows the misty contours of 'negative globalization.' In its present, purely negative form, globalization is a parasitic and predatory process, feeding on the potency sucked out of the bodies of nation-states and their subjects.
>
> *(Bauman 2007: 24)*

The loosening of traditional familial bonds is palpable in this microcosmic setting. All this drama of aggravated disappointment is witnessed by an audience allowed into all private chambers at once, to form in their minds an overarching image or dream of a society-at-large that is lost.[58]

Hoarders on-stage

As lights slowly gather through the early part of the Zuidelijk Toneel production of O'Neill's *Desire Under the Elms*, we ultimately see that the scenic space works from a principle of **Proliferation**. The stage is literally packed with stuff—furniture and disparate junk over the various areas. The rustic furniture, exceptional for Versweyveld, is fitting enough, but the absence of walls betokens a distorted image of a farm, rather than "the real thing," however real each item within it appears. The proliferation of furniture, tools, milk cans, people, and cows over a small surface democratizes the space, rendering milk can, cow, and human equal—all on the lowest level possible—and robs all of privacy. Everything, organic and inanimate, is subject to a generalized gaze and rendered incestuous. The audience is party to all manner of private goings-on, even though the characters are supposedly shut out from them, though no physical impediment blocks their view. Not even the most confidential act of sex or evacuation is concealed, but offered indiscriminately to the audience's gaze.

There are three areas on a gigantic stage. In this spatial formulation there are no flats or walls to delimit the functions or proprietorship of the stage areas. Only the way the characters utilize them over time furnish those informational keys. As there are no physical impediments to set one apart from any other on this otherwise highly detailed stage farm, the characters strip and bathe in full view of each other. The father gradually grows suspicious that his young wife is carrying on with his son, although it appears from the audience that the actor who plays him has visual carte blanche to the entire affair and could know at the first sign of it. In *Othello*, the abused husband has full access as he stares through transparent plexiglas barriers, thus seeing through supposed walls and plumbing the infidelity lurking in his wife's heart. Here, in contrast, a total absence of barriers creates a different paradox: characters are unable to see what is happening literally right under their noses. The total absence of walls together with all the physical signs of the farm environment speak to why Johan Thielemans was tempted to call it "spectacular realism." Not even the real-as-real cows, with which the farm-folk cohabit, are separated from each other by stalls that *mere* realism, or as Jan Versweyveld pejoratively calls it, "ersatz realism," would dictate.

In addition to Marlowe's *Massacre at Paris* (see pp.170–174), where the congestion is caused by an aggregate of abstract forms, he uses this principle of filling up the stage yet again in Chekhov's *Three Sisters*. The floor is white. The upstage area groans under the brooding presence of big, heavy, brown cabinets and wardrobes. Far upstage is a grandfather clock in characterless formica modern. Just downstage of the grandfather clock is a metal ladder, the side of which functions as a simple boundary, and just upstage of which is a little alcove nook for intimate tête-à-têtes. All of the metallic cabinets have clean, modern lines and slick varnish. A samovar, emblematic of Russian country life, gets placed on a short white step unit, a post-modern iteration of a shrine. And furthest upstage, beyond the cabinets and wardrobes, are metal platform units whose armatures are exposed. The stage we see has all the allure of a rehearsal space—with neutral substitute units in place of the lovely period pieces we have come to expect of Chekhov productions. Regardless, the primary tone of this set is a crowding and accumulation, which allows very little room for movement. The actors are forever squeezing in between things to get anywhere onstage.

Where the audience becomes the clutter

In Genet's *Splendid's* and Cassavetes's film *Faces* (*Koppen*), van Hove resorted to a Grotowskian kind of "empty space" typified by the scant definition of the Reduction principle, but joined with a scenic configuration of **Dispersal**. By that I mean an environmental arrangement of the audience forced into the middle of the action for more direct immediacy and confrontation with the performers, even as the performers are scattered throughout the audience and in diffuse relationship to each other.

Grotowski had earlier explored this kind of confrontational actor/audience relationship in such works as *Akropolis*, *Kordian*, and *The Constant Prince*,[59] as had Richard Schechner's Performance Group in experimental works like *Dionysus in 69*, *Mother Courage*, and *The Balcony*. Schechner's extensive experimentation with environmental seating arrangements led him to theoretical conclusions as to how the spatial innovations push both actor and audience member into paradoxical stances. For the actor:

> This is not Stanislavski's famous 'as if.' This is the actual situation of the action, not its imaginary projection. This is the 'what is.' Environmental theater performing is both naturalistic (= 'show himself as he is') and theatricalistic (= 'in the extreme situation of the action').
>
> *(Schechner 1973: 126)*

So the performer is encouraged by the non-traditional space into a more immediate sense of self-presentation. It also produces a binary rubber band of audience response:

> This less sharply delineated division of roles, actions, and spaces leads not to deeper involvement, not to a feeling of being swept away by the action—the bottomless empathy, enhanced by darkness, distance, solitude-in-a-crowd, and regressive, cushioned comfort of a proscenium theater—but to a kind of in-and-out experience: a sometimes dizzyingly rapid alternation of empathy and distance.
>
> *(Ibid.: 18)*

The revolution in theatrical space was part and parcel of Grotowski's theory of "Poor Theatre" that called for a removal of all material trappings endemic to traditional performance spaces and going beyond even such former innovations as theatre-in-the-round. Echoes of *The Connection* by The Living Theatre may also be felt, although van Hove would never have actually seen any of these iconic works. Van Hove had first tried out this Dispersal principle six years earlier, scattering the audience throughout the dramatic action, in a deeply flawed 1986 student-acted production of Büchner's *Danton's Death* at the Antwerps Conservatorium Toneel. The lobby of the theatre with its glass walls, sterile pillars, and neutral lighting of overall whitewash resisted any evocation of the decadent atmosphere he was going for. A gelatinous formlessness prevailed in that experimental foray, but one can see within it the germs of ideas that recur in *Splendid's* and *Faces* with far greater consummation. By the time van Hove worked with this technique in *Faces* (*Koppen*), the echoes of 1960s avant-gardism had long passed from the scene, but an analogous 1990s trend toward "living room theatre" had come into practice in Europe. Indeed, with all the sofas and beds littered among the café tables, *Faces* has a vibe of bringing the audience right into the intimacy of private homes.[60] The audience is forced into complicity with the disconcerting, invasive action and made to be extremely involved with the actors in the most literal sense.

The environmental audience arrangement that we are calling Dispersal gained in piquancy and paradoxicality when van Hove employed this 1960s anti-materialist-derived aesthetic to depict a set of characters as deeply entrenched in the parallel suburban middle class, profoundly materialistic world of the 1960s as those in Cassavetes's *Faces* are. The set and audience space, which are one and the same, littered with café tables and chairs, sofas, and recliner beds, declares that it isn't a standard theatre space at all, but rather evokes a jazz club or living room ambiance.

Versweyveld latched onto "The Loser's Club," one of many locales depicted in the source film, and established it as a master or meta-setting—a place of unabashed, presentational performance—to contain the smaller "private spaces" in which the actors take refuge with each other. These supposed hideouts are manifestly on view, not to say blatantly invaded, by the audience. The actors squeeze themselves through the tight passages allowed between spectator seating groupings, and enter small areas just large enough for scenes to be played. Highly intimate encounters occur in very circumscribed islands, largely taken up by double beds, restricting movement—in the audience's laps as it were—although a great deal of highly physicalized performance occurs even on the outer fringes of the space behind the audience, forcing them to twist around to see it. Parts of the thus fragmented audience are forced to keep their legs raised and their heads resting against the headboards of the king-size beds throughout the performance. The band is embedded throughout the space as well. In these licit and illicit renditions of bedrooms, the suburban characters "perform" their circumscribed social roles, bursting at the seams to find escape from inner and outer inhibitions.

In van Hove's production of Charles Mee's *True Love*, modular blocks are rearranged throughout the show and used in various ways like an erector set. When they are reorganized, the audience is forced to stand up and move. Van Hove also sporadically resorts to an analogous environmental approach to scenography in later productions with great effectiveness, notably the *Roman Tragedies*.[61]

Coming full circle to a magic circle

To a greater and greater degree, we see Ivo van Hove, in his most recent work, setting aside the strategies enumerated above and falling back on a visual clean sweep. This tendency had great currency in the 1960s, in the wake of Grotowski's "Poor Theatre." A number of European directors, notably Patrice Chéreau, worked this concept into their productions and Peter Brook theorized it in his highly influential book *The Empty Space*.[62]

As we have seen, van Hove has been as apt to have a cluttered stage as an empty one. Or a transparent one; or a transformative one. He's not identified with only one spatial concept. But in much of his earliest work, a principle of **Reduction** was already in play. In the cavernous warehouse in which *Disease Germs* performed, the actors and limited scenic pieces, consisting only of a real automobile and a windowed booth-like office in the far distance, were dwarfed by the ambient, yawning containment shell. And while played on normal proscenium stages, other early works—*Wild Lords*, *Imitations*, and *Wonders of Humanity*—all began with an assumption of a bare stage to which only the barest minimum of set pieces and furniture were added. They remained boldly theatricalist environments more redolent of possibility than definition. For van

Hove and Versweyveld, clearing away the traditional bric-a-brac of theatre was an exciting revolution in and of itself. As van Hove has said:

> It was a revelation when we figured out that the rear side of a set ought to be as much on display as the front side. On the rear side loiter the actors for hours on end, so why should that be less on view? That was a whole other approach to theatre. Also the use of materials: bogus materials were eliminated, flat painting and the stuff of illusion-manufacture swept away. What was left on stage was real. Same for minimalism: you have only to place a table on stage and you already in fact have a set. A table too, as Jan always says, is rising onto higher ground.
>
> *(Hillaert 2009)*

Once a relative void is created, it remains to determine what little ought to be added back. In general, those set pieces would be selected according to the play's "commanding image," a concrete or abstract artifact that contains the overarching life of the play. For a classic farce like *Summer Trilogy*, doors are the chief mechanism through which the apparatus of the farce gains its (il)logic. For the poetic realism of *A Streetcar Named Desire*, the bathtub encapsulates Blanche Dubois's vanity, obsession with self-preservation, and the need to self-tranquilize. It concretizes her invasion and occupation of the Kowalski household. It is the physical locus of her essential conflict with Stanley, one both sensual and proprietary. In some realistic productions, once that commanding image is discerned, the conventional set designer might find a way to give it emphasis in the context of a functioning, pictorial set. As for when Versweyveld applies the Reduction principle, all other context becomes superfluous, and that image is all there is onstage in all its bald, resonating simplicity.

The Reduction principle, in and of itself, is neutral in more ways than one, and its impact depends heavily on context. When used abroad in the present-day Dutch theatre, for example, staging a not very well-known Italian classic on an Empty Space basis actually reinforces conventional norms and reassurance for the middlebrow European theatre-goer. Van Hove's *Summer Trilogy* by Goldoni (2010) for a Dutch audience, in which the only scenic elements were some self-supporting doors, stands out as a conservative production. A lot of comic mileage came from running through the doors and slamming them behind. But when van Hove and Versweyveld, European interlopers, stripped one of the most revered American classics of its familiar appurtenances, the scenery in and of itself was sufficient to be perceived as a gesture in the vein of burning the American flag; at least a portion of the audience and critics took it that way. There was a level of personal affront in their responses that signaled that some foundational ethical line had been crossed. The empty space as applied to *Streetcar* in America proved subversive, however much the approach was meant to reinforce or get closer to the essential dramatic qualities of the text.

More recently, we have seen a spate of this reductive modality deployed by van Hove: in his German production of *Strange Interlude*; his English production of *A View From the Bridge*; his Dutch *Mary Stuart*, *The Fountainhead*, *Long Day's Journey Into Night*, and *The Things That Pass*; his American *The Crucible*; his French *The Damned*. In both *Strange Interlude* and *View From the Bridge*, a quadrilateral open pen contains all the action; the floor is filled with sawdust or sand, which is the only spectacular element in the frame for most of the show. The substance on the floor is physically malleable enough to be manipulated and sifted for its metaphorical possibilities. *Mary Stuart*, in a proscenium arrangement, works with a wide open space, with an enclosing wall upstage, having in addition a mere two benches pressed up against it. This show's visual life consists almost exclusively of moving actors around in different harmonious stage groupings like chess pieces, hardly an innovative approach.

Along with the stripping of the stage space, in this particular set of productions, comes a paring down of language and physical movement. The language is efficient, crisply enunciated and well projected, although van Hove's actors have invariably worn body mikes for several decades now. The actors' bodies, whether standing, sitting, or walking, tend to be relaxed, and gestures are saved for special moments. Stage crosses and business also remain at a minimum. The spoken text is king, and all other elements are relegated to support it, as in much traditional theatre.

Mix and match

In their theatrical rendering of Ingmar Bergman's film scenario, *Scenes From a Marriage*, van Hove/Versweyveld combine three of their established spatial strategies, to lay before us the multifarious inner workings of a single, paradigmatic heterosexual connubial unit. For Ingmar Bergman's made-for-television mini-series, the ramification of space using transparent surfaces and industrial materials as it worked in *Othello*, *Taming of the Shrew*, and *The Miser* is merged with the isolation chambers we've seen used in *Hedda Gabler* and *Children of the Sun*. Van Hove/ Versweyveld completely gutted, then reconfigured, the space of New York Theatre Work-shop into three drab, beige claustrophobic, partitioned off spaces. They divided the audience into three sub-groups as well, and then poked just enough holes in the dividing walls so that the sub-groups led into the the triangular chambers could glean whiffs of action simultaneously being performed in the other two compartments, periodically sensing as well the presence of the other two audience coteries. And who is onstage in each of the three reduced stage areas? The audience gradually pieces together that it is the same husband and wife, Marianne and Johan, repeated three times at different ages by three sets of actors. They get to see into Marianne and Johan's married life at its inception, its middle period, and its debacle, but not necessarily in that order. Each pair of actors, assisted by other characters added as needed, will play the same scenes over thrice-running for each successive third of the audience who are led from space to space. Those three scenes, in varying order according to audience rotation, constitute Act I.

So while van Hove achieves the kind of compartmentalization and compression of relationships as he does in *Hedda Gabler*, he simultaneously, by enabling slight glimpses through the windows and doors, manages also to effectuate the voyeuristic audience/ performer relationship he had introduced to *Othello*, *The Miser*, and *The Taming of the Shrew*. But here it is not other characters that are glimpsed, but uncannily the *same* characters played by different actors, only earlier or later in their marriage. Occasional shouted lines from other periods of the marriage manage to seep through the opaque but insubstantial dry-wall, so that all phases of the marriage, early, middle, and late, are consequently contained within each other. The causes and effects of the marriage's demise are alive in the meta-space all the time. The beginning contains its own destruction, and that destruction was a certain consequence of the relationship's earliest days, given who the characters are. Johan and Marianne are surprised by what they do and what happens to them throughout their marriage, but the play's structure, both temporally and physically, suggests that all that happens was innate, and meant to follow this course through its eventual mellowing and ultimate hollowing out. The dispersed, confused treatment of the narrative allows the audience to vicariously experience the fragmented, irrational, almost accidental process by which the couple has stumbled into major decisions throughout their married life.

In each space, there is either a single table or bed, indeed with no room to spare for much more. The table may ultimately be used as a bed in one of the stages, and the bed used like a table. Standing in for the Ikea-infused spare but authentic Scandinavian homes in Bergman's movie, are bland and unadorned reductions of domestic environments, hyper-compressed (viz. *Streetcar*) into one iconic piece of unlovely, unadorned furniture. Above each furniture piece is a single rectangular fluorescent light, only slightly amplified by a few supporting ungelled lighting instruments. The homes are thus converted into surgical operating theatres with the offstage common space behind each and in the center of all, serving as fulcrum for the three, reminiscent of one of those administrative work stations found on every floor of modern hospitals. We are placed in the position of witnesses to the surgical post-mortem of this marriage, horrified at the knife wounds the partners inflict on each other's spiritual flesh, but dispassionate before them as well. We are back in the psychically distanced, but physically intimate, Brechtian spaces of the Wooster Group's *Point Judith* and *Rumstick Road* replete with their contemporaneous claustrophobia, inevitability, and see-through voyeurism.

For Act II, when the audience is called back from a half-hour intermission, a major and perceptually transgressive alteration to the space has been accomplished. All the separating walls have been removed, leaving one single wide open space with the three audience segments now in an in-the-round formation and reunited for the ultimate playing out of the remaining phases of Johan and Marianne's marriage. They include the signing of the divorce papers and Johan's departure for Australia, his return as a man remarried to a different woman, his reuniting with Marianne, re-married to a different man, the resumption of their now illicit relationship with each other, and, at last, the termination of this adulterous phase. So, a plethora of after-lives subsequent to their legal marriage play out.

In one of the most original and refreshing moments of the entire show, all three couples representing Johan and Marianne mix and match in the open space, sometimes speaking and acting simultaneously. Different Mariannes arbitrarily pair up with any of the three Johans for tender or hostile moments on parade. This makes for some piquant stage business. When one Marianne goes to fetch her diary to read it aloud, she grabs two extra versions of the diary from a cabinet and passes them out to her fellow Mariannes. They then read segments from the diaries one after the other. When Johan wants to kiss Marianne goodbye, all six congregate in one concentrated spot, and smooch, passing back and forth between all the female and male partners and giving the impression of an orgy, although it's really just one couple, subdivided. Here the space itself isn't ramified through window and mirror effects, nor do objects proliferate and crowd. Rather, all ramification is achieved through a joining of the various selves, and it is the characters within the space who proliferate. When one Marianne phones for a taxi, the other Mariannes add "two," then "three" taxis to the phone order. They are all after-images of each other, like a Muybridge serial photo, sometimes joining, sometimes breaking up into autonomous existence throughout the protracted scene, one couple paradoxically divided *and* multiplied to be deployed within itself.

There have been other mixes and matches of two or more spatial strategies in a single production. Van Hove's theatrical version of Visconti's film *Rocco and His Brothers* is played in a large cavernous space with the audience in the round. In the center is a gigantic open platform that functions as the central metaphorical and situational image of a boxing ring. Rocco and at least two of his brothers are seeking their fame and fortune as boxers. The master environment proclaims itself as an "empty space," undefined and redolent of possibilities. But the initial impression of vacuity is contradicted over time as the areas abutting the platform on all sides grow cluttered with a dense accretion of stuff, leading once more to a principle of Proliferation.[63] These areas, which resemble storage spaces where someone has indiscriminately shoved unwanted objects, will come to represent the various tight, claustrophobic rooms the straitened economics of Rocco's family force them into. The film on which the show is based is a prime example of Italian post-war Neo-Realism in the direct tradition of Zola's Naturalism, with all its typifying detritus. Van Hove's clutter—the usual set of black, generic, clean-lined forms—isn't at all detailed or verisimilar in the same way as Visconti's convincing evocation of post-war Italy.

To reinforce the already complex and self-contradictory environment, Versweyveld has added rectangular towers at the four points of the rectangular space alongside and slightly behind the audience bleachers. These monumental structures house several scaffolded stories, parts of which are curtained off, still others exposed to view through clear or translucent windows. They represent the family kitchen, offices of boxing ring impresarios, and other locales. The interior chambers in the tower, in effect, lead once more to a Ramification where the audience gets to peep through transparencies. With the audience split in four risers quadrilaterally arranged around the boxing ring, its attention is forever shifting throughout the show onto the central empty space, away to the cluttered peripheral spaces, or to the adjacent tower spaces, in unpredictable patterns. So the set taken as a whole promotes yet a third spatial principle, that of Dispersal. The variety of visual experience, that also produces a dynamically changing audience-actor relationship, keeps the energy alive and prone to unexpected disruptions. It reproduces, without any electronic means, the rhythm of a movie, with its blend of flow and sudden jumps. The audience is treated to an ever-changing tempo of alternation between public and private, intimate and societal, micro and macrocosmic. Thus have van Hove and Versweyveld translated the verisimilar world of cinematic expression into a work that conforms to the abstract visual languages and possibilities of live theatre.

The brave new world

Richard Shechner describes the way today's live avant-garde theatre has become intertwined and indistinguishable from commercial theatre and other media:

> What we have today is a triangular, surprisingly stable, trilectical tension among the avant-garde, the mainstream, and the social media. Works of a particular kind can and do show up under any of these categories, sometimes sliding easily from one to the other.
>
> *(Schechner 2015: 18)*

In the later phase of van Hove's work, he is very liable to eschew technology altogether, reverting to a more traditional "linear-successive" mode of perceptual arrangements (Lehmann 2006: 16). *Perfect Wedding*, with its blank stage and minimal stagecraft, exemplifies this tendency. Other recent shows with little or no mediatization are *Streetcar*, *The Little Foxes*, *Mary Stuart*, *Persona*, *Scenes From a Marriage*, and *Antigone*. But as much as Ivo can be an acolyte of Peter Brook's Empty Space, on a parallel track, he has also evinced a bent for accoutering live theatre events with post-modernist landscapes, including *The Antonioni Project*, *The*

Massacre at Paris, and *Mourning Becomes Electra*. He has used this toolbox to advance the art of dramatic narrative into the twenty-first century, but no less importantly to give the audience spectacular treats to amaze them:

> 'The Mephisto of theatre technology,' he's recently been called. 'The theatre of today,' he says, 'brings all sorts of artists, including writers, together. I think that's an extremely positive development. People have started to return to the theatre to get their perceptual kicks. There are continual inventions being introduced in the theatre for new ways of telling old stories.'
>
> *(Van Vierken 2000)*

Quite often the post-modernist landscape bristles with a plethora of monitors and video screens littering and hanging over the stage and brings about a "simultaneous and multi-perspectival approach" to audience reception; *Roman Tragedies*, *Cries and Whispers*, *The Damned*, and *The Miser* being prime examples. This particular aspect van Hove's scenography leads him also into the realm of what Elinor Fuchs calls the *meta-dramatic* (Fuchs 1996: 102). The intrusion of electronic media on his stages alongside newly minted renditions of well-known characters meta-dramatizes them in startling ways.

Ivo's use of monitors was first tried out in the early production, *Antigone* (1991), and it was six years later when he made another more important foray with *Caligula*. In his own words:

> Video and microphones are the tools of today. Why not use them? In the times of the Greek tragedies, they used masks—which were like huge close-ups of an emotion. But I never use cinematic methods in a purely aesthetic way. I try to make it dramaturgically necessary.
>
> *(Szalwinska 2011)*

In the modernized ambiance he grafted onto the Ancient Greek world, the actors playing social leaders held their press conferences with their faces projected on a series of monitors along the horizontal line of the forestage, a shorthand medium for expressing that the same sorts of power struggles and political tropes are being repeated in our own times.

Indeed, his most successful, sophisticated uses of technology where all the experimentation later converged with appropriate dramatic necessity were with the politically inflected *Roman Tragedies* and the socially inflected *The Antonioni Project*. His early experiments in this area contained, due to the more rudimentary technology available, a far reduced number of witty perspectives than the multiplicity he ultimately came to command in the later shows. Here we have the realization of Baudrillard's giddy vision: "We live under the ecstatic sign of the technico-luminous cinematic space of total spatio-dynamic theatre" (Baudrillard 1983: 39).

It began as a kind of imitation or homage. The Wooster Group has been feted and lionized internationally, but no place more than in Flanders where imitators have abounded, especially Jan Lauwers's Needcompany (LeCompte; Shewey; Erika Rundle). Guy Cassiers and many small young companies as well have rendered them homage.[64] While Needcompany became identified with these and other Wooster Group scenic strategies over the years, including the extensive use of desk microphones, van Hove, you might say, merely flirted with them. That flirtation can especially be seen first in his *Antigone* (1991), the set for which was comprised of a spiraling configuration of rectilinear tables—conference tables in effect—with a rectangular overhanging canopy that had lines of neon lights recessed in it. The tyrant Creon's place is at the far end of the conference table in an authoritarian position, with all the others arrayed as though they were members of a board of directors. This network of long tables is also reminiscent of Grotowski's set for *Faustus*, irrefutably one of the earliest influences on the Wooster Group aesthetic under its earlier rubric as the Performance Group.

Ivo further refined the idea, and came even closer to duplicating the Wooster Group's 1980s and 90s signature arrangement six years later in *Caligula* (1996). There, the monitors were hung over the stage in a line and the live actors frequently placed beneath them in a parallel horizontal line behind a long set of tables, thus highly reminiscent of The Wooster Group's approach from such Liz Lecompte productions as *L.S.D.: Just the High Points*, their pastiche of Arthur Miller's *The Crucible* and *Routes 1 & 9*, a radical spin on Thornton Wilder's *Our Town*. The Wooster Group was an important point of reference for van Hove from the time he and Versweyveld saw *Point Judith* in New York in 1981. He later brought their *Hairy Ape* to the Holland Festival when he was its artistic director (Arian 1998). In *Caligula*, there is a wide-open rectangular space with a series of tables way upstage arranged in a horizontal line. One can lie back on them, as Caligula's mother Drusilla does in a particularly lascivious moment, similar to the way we have seen a table used in *South*, for sitting on, standing on, for copulating on. Far upstage reposes the upright figure of Caligula, visually distinguished by his great height, in contrast to the prevailing horizontality of the tables. Van Hove here also introduced an onstage cameraman, giant camera slung over his shoulder in plain sight, filming a live feed, and apt to go right up into the face of the live actor playing Caligula. The far distant live figure of the emperor that normal perspective renders insignificant in size instantly replicates as a giant on screen, addressing us seductively and intimately. The other characters are picked up on other small screens simultaneously, where we observed them stuffing their faces. In that show he also, for the first time, cribbed the Wooster Group's use of electronically amplified sound, a technique he has since incorporated for all shows.

Van Hove's *Mourning Becomes Electra*, especially, operated in a flattened out, metonymic, and hyper-technologized space. The constricted, non-representational jigsaw edifice of raw wood in front of which the live actors operate, sitting at desk surfaces variously oriented so as to alienate the actor/operators from each other, are laden with laptops. This ambiance in no way suggests the bygone days in New England, but rather makes for an abstracted physical and social context, and an extreme of aesthetic frigidity. As Zygmunt Bauman has written:

> Society is increasingly viewed and treated as a 'network' rather than a 'structure' (let alone a solid 'totality'): it is perceived and treated as a matrix of random connections and disconnections and of an essentially infinite volume of possible permutations.
>
> *(Bauman 2007: 2)*

The image of society as network shows up increasingly. The mediation of cameras, cords, and monitors disrupts all direct connections the performers have with each other.[65] The Wooster Group coupled their networks with sardonic distance, always holding direct passionate outbursts at bay. Van Hove and Versweyveld's admiration notwithstanding, they uncoupled the environmental designs they found so compelling from emotional coldness typifying the Wooster Group, which was alien to them, and went full steam ahead with mediatization.

Ben Brantley describes the ubiquitous use of video in van Hove's rendition of John Cassavetes' *Opening Night*:

> Our disorientation is compounded by the plethora of simultaneous versions of the same scene: those that occur in the flesh on the stage; those reflected in the glass doors at the back of Jan Versweyveld's soundstage-like set; and those that are projected in video onto an assortment of screens large and small. . . . This use of technology suits well the portrayal of people whose sense of self is forever in flux. . . .. For Mr. van Hove the camera is much more than a gimmick here. The tool may magnify and clarify performance, yes, but also distort. It seems telling that a show about a woman reclaiming her soul should end, as this one does, with two performers, Ms. [Elsie] de Brauw and Mr. [Jacob] Derwig, by themselves onstage, without their video doubles. At that moment they seem larger and more solid than ever before.
>
> *(Brantley 2008)*

By the time he did *Opening Night*, in 2008, van Hove had moved far beyond his initial Wooster Group emulations, but his evolution didn't end there.

The radical blowing up of the normative audience/actor relationship in *Roman Tragedies*, in which *Antony and Cleopatra*, *Coriolanus*, and *Julius Caesar* were performed in succession on one bill, was only possible through its use of video. While set in a classic proscenium-style theatre, the entire stage space was organized to accommodate parts of the audience throughout it (see Figure 1.11). On a rectilinear grid, easy chairs, sofas with their side tables and coffee tables, all

FIGURE 1.11 *The Roman Tragedies*

© Jan Versweyveld

facing in different directions including toward the back wall of the theatre, could be occupied by audience members and actors alike without differentiation, creating a democratized leveling between the viewer/performer hierarchy. All through the stage space were distributed small monitors on the tables in addition to the extremely large screens available to those members of the public remaining in their traditional seats. In between acts and plays, the audience was invited to come up onstage or return to their former seats so they could experience portions of the show from radically different perspectives.

There were several cameramen circulating throughout the action, who approached dangerously close to the audience members to get the desired angle and distance for their shots, even as the actors themselves were disseminated in extremely close proximity to the loungers, often performing beats of high emotional intensity and getting into perilous physical altercations inches away from audience members' noses. At the same time, projecting out from the edge of the stage were podiums for the more rhetorical moments of public address all these plays contain, as well as a horizontal line of conference tables with table mikes planted on them, for the sorts of press conference scenes that recall the earlier work *Caligula*.

The drama of the political and personal narratives is thus rendered multi-layered and multi-perspectival, as each audience member in a sense creates their own show simply through the choice of where they sit. Focus can wander from large screen to live actor or from large screen to smaller screen(s). And just as the near proximity of an actual actor lounging in the neighboring sofa can bring the action into a disconcertingly familiar intimacy, beckoning the show into a personal living room kind of space, so in a different way can the monumental images of close-ups revealing the actors' very nose pores, be intimate in their way, albeit preserving a formal actual distance. And reciprocally, audience members' faces are just as apt to be singled out by the live cameras and splayed out on the larger screens, transforming them into plebian characters who get fifteen seconds of fame. Taken altogether, this show problematizes the public and private lives of political figures in a world that feels like today. They are always on view, their lives invaded and exposed for consumption through television and social media, and in effect are living out multiple simultaneous existences, immediate and vicarious. They become members of our own family, just as alive and familiar to us as the actual ones are, having penetrated to our very own living rooms, epitomized by the sofas and easy chairs that litter the stage, so near and yet so far.

The Antonioni Project breaks new media ground in other ways still. This show, comprised of three movies by the great Italian experimentalist, *La Notte*, *L'Avventura*, and *L'Eclisse*, rather weaves the three disparate casts and narratives together into one intricate whole. Contrasted with *Roman Tragedies*, it retains its psychological distance, keeping the actors separate from the audience on a proscenium stage, and features only one large screen above that principal aperture and another somewhat smaller one upstage behind a raised platform. The two screens don't necessarily display the same images as each other, which makes for two perspectives at any given time at a minimum. In this production, beyond the content of the three scripts, van Hove wittily plays with the notion of filmmaking itself, and with the art of making narratives in general.

The stage is quite open and sparsely defined, but through the use of live video feeds, with cameramen roaming freely, by introducing high booms, a circular track, and cart for dollying, a movie stage is suggested. Depending on the angle of the boom, the relative tightness of the frame image, and the position of the camera, various nooks and crannies over the stage space, even those hidden behind tall flats, may fill the screen, dwarfing the broad view of the live-action stage by magnifying minutiae with which it is juxtaposed. There is a mix of pre-recorded footage along with the live feed. Live actors may act against that footage, which becomes background to them, or video images of the actors in live feed may be melded into the pre-recorded footage, yielding three layers of reality available for consumption. The use of video here is particularly appropriate: the specific intertwining narratives from the film scripts losing importance alongside the meta-narrative of actors being filmed and living actors acting. As the separate strands of the three filmscripts start to lose their integrity and blend together, interest gets further displaced onto how the stories are being transmitted more than on their specific content.

In his recent works *Lazarus*, *Kings of War*, and *The Damned*, Ivo has found further ways to amplify, stun, and stimulate the spectator's perceptual aperture. In the former, the central character self-multiplies by his image separating out from his living figure and taking over the entire upstage space. In the latter, not only does a character's figure replicate behind him in multiple versions, limberly expanding and contracting like parts of a spring, but we are privy to life offstage even as we remain onstage. Then we are even brought into the world of the recently deceased to learn what life is like within coffins. Those poor souls, unremarked by surviving characters, remain with the oblivious living, howling for attention in vain. In the *Henry V* section of *Kings of War*, the life on the video screens, together with daring lighting shifts, make manifest liminal states on the evening before the Battle of Agincourt. First, large panels alternate sea-green and dull blue, as various small monitors flicker with short-circuiting imagery—more rhythm than content—to evoke a state between sleep and wake. Then the camera penetrates into a virtual corridor of drowsing soldiers, bathed in blood red. This soporific mood gradually gives way to a bacchanalia of swaying, drunken bodies whose faces are frequently masked. In both *The Damned* and *Henry V*, van Hove permits himself a dive into an ambiance of surrealistic decadence on the mediatic plane that gets away from the sterile ambiances of corporate contexts that prevail in the stage dimension. The recurring van Hove trope of chaos, internal and external, invades the stage through the video inserts. As the on-screen orgy subsides, so the live king on his knees before his army cot with dawn gathering comes to the fore in simple supplication. Through these technical essays, the very notion of reality opens further into unsuspected realms. Paradox and contradiction are more than ever the stuff of theatre. And, as van Hove says: "The boundary between theatre and other media is growing thinner all the time" (T'Jonck 2002).

Persistent leitmotifs of gender identity

Sex acts/acting sex

One Dutch critic who has followed van Hove closely said of him: "He hops from lap to lap, because violence and sex always go hand in hand for van Hove" (Janssen 2001a). Nine years later, on the same theme: "Love becomes lust, celebration becomes chaos, theatre becomes a carnival of vanity" (Janssen 2010). Throughout the early phases of his career, van Hove laid down numerous markers identifying him with both sex and violence onstage. It was enjoyed or deplored, but it was news. Here is a small selection: "with Ivo van Hove we're often placed in the domain of eroticism and passion" (Van Heer 1988). And: "The high point of their [the two male actors in *In the Loneliness of the Cotton Fields*] unfortunate 'exchange initiatives' is a long tongue kiss, one of the longest that's ever been seen in a theatre" (Ibid.). "There's a lot of physical violence going on in his plays. And nudity is practically a must with van Hove, someone's always taking off their clothes—or getting dragged out of them." This critic goes on to marvel that women piss real urine on his stage (Zijlmans 1994). "He lets his shows play with a lot of fondness for erotic images, as we are accustomed to getting from him" (Oranje 1991). "After *Lulu* and

FIGURE 1.12 *The Miser*

© Jan Versweyveld

South, Ivo van Hove once more [in *More Stately Mansions*] introduces an interesting theatre play in which sexuality is the motor for human behavior" (Hellinga 1994). At times, Hove appears to cultivate this salacious image in his public pronouncements, such as: "'I have lots of fantasies about violence that I need to get out of my system'" (Zijlmans 1994), and, "I make fierce theatre, but theatre is all about fantasies, and those are often violent or sexual" (Van der Van 2005).

An American critic, having seen a number of his shows, was amazed to finally attend one where no one undressed or made love, as they are that prevalent (Phillips 2003). The reputation for sexual obsession and explicitness has followed the director throughout his career both in Europe and America, although it is dissipating recently with his most recent ventures, which sublimate or entirely avoid sexual tropes, at least on Broadway (see Figure 1.12). Van Hove is not only interested in the feelings arising between a couple in love, but is also fascinated by the creative challenge of putting carnality itself before his public. Carnality is a very appropriate word to express the quality his actors invest in such performance passages. The movements and gestures representing love-making themselves are used as a provocation that bypass the media's steady barrage of sexual arousal that has left everyone blasé. His ability to succeed in getting under the skin can feel especially destabilizing in live performance.

To mis-paraphrase Tolstoy, all renditions of theatrical sexuality are not the same. Van Hove's are highly idiosyncratic. For one thing, no actual or even simulated penetration happens on his stages. The sex acts, such as they are, tend toward the gymnastic, the fetishistic, and sex is often used as a window into psychological power relations. The best way to grasp the flavor of it would be to cite a fair number of specific examples from some prototype productions, first of all going back to *Macbeth*. Lady Macbeth's first speech, reading the letter from her absent husband, is straightforward and intense, but ends with bestial lasciviousness as she anticipates her absent husband's return, upon which he is suddenly there with her. On his arrival, she leaps into his arms and plays the whole scene right up against him, belly to belly, as he feverishly tries to undress her. The exact duplicate of this sex-charged stage business resurfaced in van Hove's recent show, *The Things That Pass*, when Ottilie jumps into both her sons' laps in succession.

The frank sexuality of the Macbeths' relationship, while not especially original,[66] heralds a tendency we can see throughout the van Hove canon: to bring subtextual sexuality between intimate partners explicitly to the fore. Later in the play, when Macbeth complains to his wife of the miserable, guilty nights he undergoes for the several murders he has committed, her response is exclusively to sensually massage his shoulders and back, and bring him back to her through tactile wiles.

Lord and Lady Macbeth are not the only loving couple in *Macbeth* as depicted by van Hove. The brothers, Duncan's sons, hold each other round like lovers. Macbeth and Banquo embrace like lovers as well, united in grief (feigned grief in the former's case) at the death of the king. Macbeth hastens to respond to Macduff with an embrace that is tight and almost sexual. In sum, the actor Lucas Vandervorst plays him as a highly eroticized Macbeth throughout, one who uses proximity and sexual energy to elicit loyalty from his subalterns. Even Macbeth's death has an erotic kick to it. After losing the battle at Dunsinane, he sinks voluptuously down onto the bench, vital energy palpably leaking out from all sides. Following his own triumph on the field of battle, Macduff arrives and taps his nemesis from behind. Then gently, tenderly, he leads him by the neck around to the back of the picnic bench and sticks his head into a receptacle filled with water in a shocking gesture that is both sadistically cruel and intimate. The murder on the field of battle is presented like snuff sex.

In the early 1986 student production of a particularly verbose play, Büchner's *Danton's Death*, van Hove embedded the rhetoric of the revolution within a series of explicit sexual acts performed by the political activists. As in so many other cases, he uses sex on stage to cut and dilute the potential tedium of excessive wordiness. However, the unremitting sexuality becomes numbing in its own right as excess is piled on excess. The political upheaval of the French Revolution bristles with an unleashing of orgiastic energies. A female character starts to sing "The Marseillaise," standing across from Danton. What starts off pleasantly, gradually changes into something raucous and obnoxious, as the hero of the revolution joins in. They both vie to make the paean to liberty as discordant and bestial as they can, blurting it into each other's face, like verbal vomiting, after which she starts masturbating and undulating as she speaks. Her speechifying continues unabated as Danton makes rhythmic love to her from behind. She then leads him around on his knees with her fingers jabbed into his mouth, fol-lowed by a kiss. She drops down invitingly, seeming to offer fellatio, lies back as though she is ready for it, and then reverts to a fetal position, talking, talking all the while. Next, she stands over him while he lies splayed out on his back. She sits on Danton's stomach making love to him as he delivers one of his longer political tirades.

In *Desire Under the Elms*, sex is a vital barometer for who in the father–son–stepmother triangle has power over whom. The stepmother is the stake that both men gamble for, but she refuses to be a pawn in their game, preferring to play her own game of sexual dominance over both of them. It is a question of whom she will choose, and in the event, she chooses both in turn, leaving the other to skulk. When the sex act does finally occur it is a no–holds–barred affair, with emotions fully engaged and voices unleashed to spill out deeply repressed angst, as would certainly not have been the way in a traditional American production. O'Neill doesn't indicate anything of the kind in the stage directions. In this revival, the sex act becomes a rite of passage as well as an abrogation of all restrictions.

In a play like O'Neill's *More Stately Mansions* (*Rijkemanshuis*, 1993), explicit sex, which again is certainly not indicated onstage in the original text, serves to cut the great author's extreme prolixity. But when we see these characters act out their most intense sexual desires without apparent hesitation or reserve, it spirals so far beyond the socially permissible conventions of the period, that we must wonder if what they are doing is occurring on the objective plane or else is a fantasy wish that is not actually being realized at all. When Joe starts to make love to Sarah, prompted by her innocuous line from the script, "It's so long ago that you've kissed me that way," he devours her, kisses her all over her body, and flips her upside down, exposing her backside, underwear, and so on—which is a highly typical rendition of van Hove lovemaking— before going right back into one of those endless O'Neill monologues. The tour de force physicality of these interchanges is reminiscent of Wim Vandekeybus muscular choreography— a signature of the Flemish Wave.

Talking and lovemaking, which often occur simultaneously and incontinently can both be over the top in van Hove productions. Again in *More Stately Mansions*, Joe proposes that he and Sarah live together as unmarried lovers. Her response: "I'd like nothing more." He interprets her willingness as a green light to indulge in an orgy of fetishism, first removing her bra and panties. Next he sits on a stool across from her and repeatedly gets her to open her legs so he can see her vagina, leaning back to get a better look.[67] All the while he rattles on about their relationship and future, then repeats the compulsive voyeuristic ritual once more. Joe takes a cool, distanced, clinical approach during this compulsively repeated action. Again, it could be the stuff of the unconscious mind or an extremely unspontaneous wish fulfillment of a remembered secret obsession from childhood.

Without any warning, the tables are turned between the couple as Sarah's sexual hunger is aroused, and she starts pulling *his* clothes off, suddenly and swiftly. He sits back on the stool wearing only socks, as she runs over and sits on his lap, grabbing him in a bear hug. She falls back on the floor and pulls him down on top of her. But he, detaching himself, walks robotically off, talking about his plans for the future, while she lies there on the floor, writhing with dissat- isfaction. They keep talking, he cool, she in a frenzy of sexual need. She crawls around on the ground on all fours, approaches him, and pushes his protectively joined hands off his lap. She gets him to slide down off the stool and onto the floor once more as they proceed to "make love" athletically in all kinds of twisted Kama Sutra positions—to the accompaniment of somewhat satirical piano music. They then both get themselves organized and dressed.

While all this activity is decidedly uninhibited, it is less sensual than animalistic and athletic— with a lot of carrying and dragging of bodies, inverted postures, and so on, ultimately forming one of the extended non-verbal segments, which are emblematic of van Hove, that he inserts between dialogue-dominated segments. Pushing the body to extremes is, historically, a gro- towskian tendency and is also derivative of later performance artists of the 1970s, "who sought the transgression of socially repressive norms through the experience of pain and danger."[68]

Zygmunt Bauman claims that the prohibition against incest was humanity's "first act of culture." How natural then that such a taboo gets taken up so regularly by van Hove; it is an infallible subject for unnerving an audience. Incest, at the heart of '*Tis Pity She's a Whore*, where a brother and sister fall in love with each other, is a trope van Hove explored earlier, first in *Like in the War*, his adaptation of Sophocles' *Oedipus at Colonnus*, in Marguerite Duras's *Agatha*, where the sister was played in drag, and it gets taken up yet again in *Desire Under the Elms* and Charles Mee's *True Love*, these times between boys and their stepmothers. In the latter, where the age differential between son and stepmother is much greater than in the former, sex acts are prominent, and sex itself the theme of the play. However, sexual expression is treated with a certain ambivalence: in-your-face for the chorus representing society-at-large, but verging on prudery for the mother/son couple. Following the pattern for sexual display laid down in *Danton's Death*, in the midst of one of the many extremely long monologues about sex that pepper this show, the stepmother in love with her young step-son commences to masturbate and achieve orgasm, yet never stops talking. Moving from self-stimulation to putting her fantasy into action, she initiates a tickling match with her son, which evolves instead into a large group orgy-like scene involving the entire cast. Van Hove saves the display of sex for the super-numeraries, as the transgressive couple is concealed behind the mass. To spare us seeing the mother and son actually making love, van Hove diverts the show into ever widening circles of distancing, covering it over with in-unison foot-stomping by the ensemble.

In one of van Hove's more recent productions to be staged in America—Bergman's *Scenes From a Marriage*—lovemaking is once more front and center. Here, though, sexual longing and deprivation within a legally sanctioned heterosexual marriage provide the fodder. When the central character Marianne wants to prevent her husband Johan from fulfilling his announced project of leaving her and the children, she takes off his shirt and presses the flesh of his back, her fingers desperately recalling to him what her words fail to.

If one sees this scene a-chronologically as I did, one is left with the assumption that it was she whose demand for more sex than he was willing to supply and it was that that was causing him to flee from an over-exigent partner, only to find out later in the theatre-going experience in another anachronistic segment that the opposite was the case. It was she who had emotionally abandoned her highly sexed spouse, leaving him randy and unsatisfied, thus propelling him into the arms of another woman. Then in Act II, when all three of the couples who represent one single couple at different points in their marriage find themselves onstage at the same time, get pissed off, and try to get out the door en masse, their lingering attraction keeps them in the room. Instead of walking out on the offending partner, the six of them wander from one to the other in a virtual clump, kissing and caressing at random, unable to let go. Is all this tactility erotic for the audience? That doesn't seem to be the point. It is more to do with the "social choreography," of the relationship, as van Hove puts it. The grasping and clinching that precedes the leaving develops into yet another sustained non-verbal van Hove composition segment, a choreo-graphed set piece whose antecedents are in performance art or the dance-theatre of De Keersmaeker and Pina Bausch.

The exception to van Hove's proclivity for staging sexual exploits, one which proves the rule for its exceptional delicacy, is seen in *Angels in America*. In a famous scene depicting gay male seduction in a public setting, van Hove had the obvious cue to explore it in his usual carnal way. He instead sets the action of that scene at the extreme upstage point of a deep stage space at BAM, with the participants' bodies entirely covered and concealed in hoodies. Rather than exposing anything and drawing the spectators in, he effectively exiles us to a far removed perspective of interfering passers-by. With low voices and whispered monosyllables, the men furtively hook up and slip behind large dark flats, suggesting the concealed chambers under a boardwalk on Coney Island or some far-flung nook in the subway system, where their activities go on well out of the audience's sight. Thus, van Hove, rather than exulting in the sexual liberation that gripped the gay world in the 1970s, quarantines it in a periphery of shame.

Despite Amsterdam's reputation as a sex capital, van Hove appears to be fighting an uphill battle against a certain prudery concerning displays of gay sex, which may account for his own uncharacteristic modesty in this production. When interviewed by a gay magazine about his *Angels in America* production in Holland, his disappointment in the younger generation of Dutch peoples' attitudes was palpable:

> What's really taken me aback has been the reactions to an educational project that we've been conducting around this play. It appears that it's difficult to bring up a theme such as homosexuality, so instead we use skits on topics like separation and mourning. Toneelgroep Amsterdam often develops programs for getting middle school pupils to respond to themes from its productions, and they run with it. Even acting out scenes, for example. But this time we've encountered a lot of resistance; kids have no desire to play gay people, or even deny that they exist. I thought that we'd come further on the road to acceptance than that.
>
> *(Van der Elst 2008)*

As far as nudity goes, van Hove has taken the measure of his disparate publics' tolerance levels for scabrousness. In his 2015 staging of Simon Stephens's monodrama *Song From Far Away* first in London, then in Amsterdam, the solo actor Eelco Smits spends the lion's share of the evening naked. But in this case, the unclothed body is more of a signifier for vulnerability before cosmic indifference, "unaccommodated man," than an occasion for prurience (Lauwaert 2015). For his French productions a great deal of nudity is on display, for example in his 2016 production of *The Damned*. The S.A. Commandant Konstantin Essenbeck and his young lieutenant strip down and disport themselves, belly-flopping unclothed through a self-created pool of beer. Their carry-ings-on are echoed on a large video screen behind them by a virtual squadron of young S.A. officers who remove their clothes and engage in a drunken orgy before passing out and getting butchered by the S.S. The border-pushing androgynous Martin plays all manner of forbidden games. During a round of hide-and-seek with his young female cousins he almost does *some*thing illicit while playing possum with one of them in a dark closet that causes her to scream for the help of her nanny. He later prompts her to touch his body all over. Just before her hand ventures to a really objectionable area the game is interrupted. The sibylline Martin undresses as well, as does his regal mother, Sophie. Still later, after thoroughly showering his mother with the pent-up invective of years' wrongs done him, she and he crawl toward each other on the floor and get dangerously close to sharing a highly sexualized kiss.

For his recent Broadway shows, on the other hand, there has been virtually no disrobing; only Ben Whishaw who took off his shirt in *The Crucible*. Van Hove has been very insistent that he only agreed to work on Broadway provided there was no interference in his artistic choices from his producer, Scott Rudin. And I'm sure it was accurate when he claimed that Rudin assured van Hove he would not make any artistic stipulations whatsoever (Willinger 2014). But the environment itself has its own, perhaps irresistible, bewitching grip. For the Puritan-dominated *Crucible* in the self-censoring Walter Kerr Theatre context, the apostate Proctor tackles his erstwhile mistress Abby for only a few quickly stifled and chaste clinches. Thus, the Broadway audience is sub-jected to only a severely curtailed rendition of normal van Hoveist gymnastic sex. Not non-existent, but nothing much to offend an out-of-town tourist couple either. When van Hove had included rawer sexuality and more scantily clad bodies in his earliest NYTW productions, he got a lot of pushback. Now, having won over the cutting edge crowd, but crossed over to the land of *Wicked* and *Mary Poppins*, the equation may have changed. The subversive advantage of administering shocks to the moral sensibility are weighed against the possibilities of a drastic loss in popularity or being forever banned. In each locality, what it means to push the envelope is different.[69]

The difficult woman

The van Hove brand (to use an all too common word that puts great artists and laundry detergent on the same level) is not limited to spatial experimentation. Some tropes of character definition keep returning very strongly throughout the Flemish director's career, notably the prototype of the "Difficult Woman." In the 2004–5 season alone, he picked plays from the standard repertoire that contain two of the most iconic troublesome women in dramatic history—Hedda Gabler from the play of the same name and Kate from *The Taming of the Shrew*. Add in the unstable, charismatic women from the Cassavetes shows that same year, and it comes into high relief that there is something definite van Hove is trying to explore or work out. Both Hedda and Kate are idle women who at the same time are highly cantankerous. They both have pianos that they don't know how to play. Their random diddling on the keys epitomizes the aimlessness of their lives and tips us off to the ominously unchanneled but aggressive energies roiling beneath the surface of their personalities. Once having kick-started into intentionality, those energies could be either constructive or destructive—toward others or themselves. Kate is a termagant who is being thrust into a marriage contract, presumably against her will. It is made abundantly clear that Petruchio wants her for the material benefits that are to be his, a very good reason for Kate to mistrust the match and resist it.

But subdue her he does. Throughout Acts III and IV, Petruchio puts Katherine through the "taming" treatment of the title, a spirit-chastening process portrayed in this production as a version of shock therapy, with very dynamic use of both set and lighting design to compound the horror to which she is subjected. Sudden blinding flashes pick her out of the darkness, abject and half naked on her hands and knees, reduced to a pitiful, sobbing, howling state, and begging for affection. The show is essentially a grim breaking down of an ill-conditioned, badly behaved woman through a "tough love" treatment reminiscent of lobotomizing, and that by a man more rudely behaved than she.

Hedda Gabler, by contrast, has voluntarily entered into her own undesired match and is attempting to have her cake and eat it too. Unsuccessfully playing the supportive, second-string housewife role, she simultaneously attempts to salvage her late tempestuous life by wresting Eilert Lovborg away from Thea Elvsted and dragging him back into his former alcoholism and debauchery. Running through these plays we recognize the prevalence in great Western drama of the trope of the marriageable girl/woman, that mainstay of drama from the Renaissance right through the early twentieth century. It is the same trope in *The Miser*, wherein Harpagon is attempting to impress his daughter Elvire into an undesirable but profitable marriage, even as he himself is pursuing a young woman out of lust. His tyrannical reign corners his daughter into a hated destiny, and she responds by acting out as a petulant, whining, intractable harpy—yet another "Difficult Woman."

It becomes obvious that van Hove is drawn to twisted, domineering, manipulative female characters. He avows this, what he calls, "fascination," with euphemistically designated, "strong women" (Vander Veken 1982; T'Jonck 2002). As Camillie Paglia says, "Those who revere and live with great art recognize Clytemnestra, Medea, Lady Macbeth, and Hedda

Gabler—conspirators and death-dealers of implacable will—as equally the forebears of modern woman"[70] (Paglia 1991a: 25). Assembling all of van Hove's women characters in one paragraph parts the curtain on a veritable pantheon. Not only Hedda, Blanche Dubois, and Shakespeare's shrewish Kate, but Wedekind's demonic Lulu, toxic Regina from Lillian Hellman's *Little Foxes*, and fallen women, Carmen and Camille, have all trod his stages. Even Desdemona, normally depicted as bland, blameless victim, in the van Hove version boldly flirts with Cassio and allows Iago to maul her, giving Othello's jealousy palpable fodder to feed on itself. Variously borderline, alcoholic and bi-polar, these ladies draw van Hove and us in only to abuse everyone around them. Sometimes, like Hedda, they lure their male adversaries to their demise. Like Ottilie from *The Things That Pass*, they have been literal murderers, or like her daughter Ottilie (Lietje), eat men up and spit them out. Or else they self-destruct, sometimes getting the tables turned on them, as happens in *The Taming of the Shrew* and *A Streetcar Named Desire*. Another of the same ilk is the solo role in Cocteau's *The Human Voice*, a nameless woman who parades up and down in her isolated apartment, pleading into the telephone receiver for her lover to come back to her, and ultimately jumping out the window in despair.

Charismatic and perverse women appear as early as in van Hove's second production, the self-authored *Disease Germs*. The hieratic, grotesque tone from the campy Fassbinder cult classic, *The Bitter Tears of Petra Von Kant*, crept into this remarkable *oeuvre de jeunesse*. The larger than life women of *Disease Germs* are thrust into a converted warehouse, pumping up the scale and stridency of their performances to match, and throw their passions around in unembarrassed self-indulgence. The curious point about this production is that all the women were played by men in drag. Was the fascination for women concealed by this gender-bending theatrical strategy, or is his subsequent direct portrayal of women characters played by women really subterfuge gay dress-up? Resorting to over-the-top camp was a way for van Hove to get at taboo zones of human emotional pain while keeping it at arm's length. In later shows, he addressed such pain more directly. Indeed, the show managed to wring a good deal of poignancy and melodrama out of the event despite the prevailing camp mood.

Agnes, the heroine of Bergman's *Cries and Whispers*, is a difficult woman whose fatal illness has pushed her over the brink, making her an utterly impossible one. Her condition from the start of the show is known to be terminal and unbearable, with no painkiller adequate to assuage its torments. Her symptoms are humiliating and swamp the lives of all who are close to her, notably her sisters and the family servant. We don't know that much about her character before her illness, but at this point, she is demanding, emotionally overwrought, and irremediable. In contrast to Hedda or Kate, who have pianos they can't play too well, earlier in life, Agnes is reported to have channeled her constructive energies into painting. Van Hove has taken that allusion and brought it into the foreground, expanding and exploring the image of Agnes's painting into one of the most central and memorable of the production. Her former creativity has degenerated into abandoned splashing of paint onto every surface in her immediate vicinity.

In the 2006 stage adaptation of John Cassavetes's film script *Opening Night*, the main character in the play-within-a-play, the veteran actress, Myrtle, is another extremely irascible woman whose psychological meltdown commands both attention and affection. A celebrity in decline, she is uncomfortable in the role ("Virginia") that is assigned her in the play within the play that we see being rehearsed, which she's accepted in an attempt at making a comeback. The rehearsals start to go off the rails during what is supposed to be a run-through without stops. A certain dramatic moment's been planned for her to receive a stage slap, but instead of going with the intense flow of the scene, she breaks out laughing. Indeed, she falls on the ground, so uncontrollable is her hilarity.

Then, departing from the script, she commences a tirade attacking "Virginia," the lady she's supposed to perform. She laces into the fictional character's want of logic, her lack of humor, the unrealistic way she is drawn as a character, the insults precipitating a crying fit by the insulted playwright who is sitting right there in the first row. Her hurt feelings don't prevent Myrtle from launching into further repeated and loudly proclaimed denunciations. Dismay at getting older—which playing this character role makes her confront—is behind all her disruptive diva shenanigans. For if she turns out to be plausible in such an older role as Virginia, it would mean her aging process must be visible to the whole world. Apart from throwing tantrums, Myrtle crosses the line of professionalism and starts having an affair with the—married—director even though her former husband is also in the cast. Her jealousy of the latter's young second wife is yet another irritant spurring her to drag these personal dramas into the "fictional" one.

A further complication derives from the repeated intrusions of a perky young fan of hers—Nancy. At the beginning of the play, Nancy pops up from nowhere, confesses her undying admiration for the veteran actress, and runs out once more. Without further ado, she gets her brains spattered on the glass front door, supposedly having been hit by a car right outside the theatre. Although Nancy had at first seemed totally plausible as an impulsive fan who bursts in to see her idol, it gradually dawns that she had been a figment of Myrtle's disordered imagination all along. Despite her sudden, gory demise, Nancy insists on reappearing at Myrtle's elbow, and keeps her on her toes, now bowing down before the elder woman's great talent, now taunting her cruelly, none of which the other characters can see or hear. But while we think of her presence as a consequence of Myrtle's excessive drinking, there is also room for a more spiritualist interpretation. Myrtle later takes her to be a manifestation of her younger self that she is wrestling with, and ultimately stamping out, in her rite of passage toward greater self-acceptance. So the phantom Nancy dovetails with and reinforces the central inner action of the drama.

More than Hedda, Blanche Dubois, Kate, or any of the other leading ladies in prior productions or some in later ones such as Mary Stuart, Abigail Williams, or Sophie Essenbeck, Myrtle in Elsie de Brauw's interpretation comes through as a multi-dimensional figure—not just difficult or charismatic in some emblematic way, but a person with a whole series of contradictory psychological pulls and preoccupations. It's not only that she evokes sympathy and irritation, but is ultimately one we wouldn't mind knowing and struggling along with. She and her alter ego, Nancy, for all their difficulty, are highly compelling even as they make a mess. All the more so since the men who surround her—fellow actors, paramours, and director—are such ciphers by comparison.

Today's man

And then there is manhood. "It so happens that men in my shows are often rather passive. And the women strong-willed" (Den Breejen 2002). Van Hove's statement tends to be borne out. In van Hove's 1986 *Macbeth*, the male characters wore clothes that, while unconventionally so, were Elizabethan in cut—with tights and jerkins, and coats-of-mail. In his 1988 production of Schiller's *Don Carlos*, the critic reports for the first time that "the players run around in rather timeless but extremely contemporary fashionable costumes" (Vaes 1988). There was once again a strong suggestion of period outfits in *'Tis Pity She's a Whore* for many characters—yet he had the central male character of the latter, Giovanni, wear a simple suit and even a wristwatch in that post-modernized Jacobean universe. This approach signposted where he was headed.

By the time van Hove is appointed artistic director of Zuidelijk Toneel in 1990 and undertakes *Richard II*, a critic may remark that "the performers run around in somewhat timeless but unmistakably contemporary-style costumes," a one-size-fits-all look (Ibid.). Picture, if you will, a slender, clean-limbed young man with close-cropped hair and a square jaw and an almost delicate but sharply defined bone structure. He wears straight-legged, perfectly fitting pants and a t-shirt or simple button-down shirt, sometimes with a sports jacket, with a narrow belt and—crucial detail—loafers. This is a description of the iconic van Hove hero. Spare and sleek, a subduedly stylish image of contemporary manhood, exemplified by van Hove's earliest leading man of choice, Bart Slegers, then a young juvenile,[71] who defines the look of the van Hove hero, and most of the supporting male characters as well. Analogous to Magritte's ubiquitous fetish-Man in a Bowler Hat, the young Slegers image is a prototype that persists in slightly modified forms down to van Hove's most recent shows. He is reborn in such current members of the TGA actor stable as Eelco Smits, Robert De Hoog, Harm Duco Schut, Jip van den Dool, and Alwin Pullinckx. The addition, however, of the slightly more fleshy Aus Greidanus is a sign, perhaps, of a concession to more visual diversity.

Older characters invariably are distinguished by wearing jackets and button-down white shirts, but still most often no ties. Loafers on the feet constrain the wearer to a certain kind of walking—efficient, neither macho nor effeminate—but definitely anti-dramatic in enforced flat-footedness, of which Richard II was the early exemplar. The usual brooding, mousy, hesitant portrayal of the ineffectual king was jettisoned for a matter-of-fact, young executive type, whose costume and bearing failed to set him apart from all the other similarly costumed and loafer-shod young executives on the scaffolded unit set. This default image of manhood recurred over and over through the Zuidelijk Toneel years well into his time at Toneelgroep Amsterdam, even into *The Russians*, where the Platonovs and Ivanovs all projected a similar image.

The prototype for this gender image might have origins in American film stars of the late 1950s and early 60s such as Paul Newman in films like *Hud*,[72] the descendant of the character Hal, in William Inge's *Come Back Little Sheba*, who was described by John Clum as "just another 1950s rough trade fantasy, all body but not much in the way of brains, the male equivalent of the dumb blonde . . ., the drifter stud [who] has not been domesticated" (Clum 2012: 167). Van Hove's iteration, while retaining much of the outer semblance of this image, is far from dumb; he is even glib. Transferring easily to Cassavetes or Pasolini pieces from the 1960s, this prototype is also assimilable in late nineteenth century characters such as George Tesman and Eilert Lovborg in *Hedda Gabler*. We are then reintroduced and made to see afresh formerly togaed figures such as Coriolanus, Brutus, Marc Antony, or even Alceste from Molière's *The Misanthrope*, now in suits. Royal status in *Henry V* and *Henry VI* is indicated by the addition of sports jackets and ties. As the catalog expands to include figures from all parts of theatre and film history, it becomes clear that fidelity to period will be no obstacle to infiltration by this ubiquitous statement and trademark. Concessions to the awkwardness of Henry VI and contortedness of Richard III are granted by having their jackets cut short and riding high on their haunches, and a bit too tight so they must be fastened with one button mid-stomach.

By 1995, this image had become so deeply imbued within the van Hove sensibility that it carried over into his casting choice for Stanley Kowalski in his NYTW production of *A Streetcar Named Desire*. The American actor he settled on, the late Bruce McKenzie, was a spitting image of the young Bart Slegers—an image of a millennial Antwerper transplanted to the American heartland of the 1950s, thus a jarring violation of the Stanley Kowalski stereotype American audiences have grown to expect and which Williams describes in the stage directions. This is a streamlined, cool, even androgynous Stanley, a choice that accentuates his insinuating side over the affable, rutting bull in a china-shop stereotype. When Kowalski was then packaged in t-shirt, khaki pants, and loafers it seemed as though the director was simply trying to replicate his Dutch fetish actor with one who had all the same endowments, only English-speaking.

Although unaware of the provenance of the iconography that typified van Hove back in Flanders and Holland, Ben Brantley still called attention to the disparity between conventional expectations (including his own) and the actual incarnation at NYTW, summarily dismissing the McKenzie revisioning as "a scrawny, charisma-free Stanley" (Brantley 1999). The costume and bearing of this prototype could apply equally well to a straight, gay, or bisexual, and in the van Hove canon, it does. This man neither swaggers, nor minces; he is certainly no gaudy butterfly; nor is he crudely macho. He is simply modern man, who does not wear his sexual preference on his sleeve, but leaves it to be discovered according to the stage partners he chooses through the dramatic action, at hazard. It is almost as if van Hove is refusing to cubbyhole his male characters in a given sexual identity.

However, when a male character is blatantly effeminate, van Hove will accessorize slightly to tip the audience off. The aging homosexual, Julian, in Charles Mee's *Perfect Wedding* (2006), as played by Joop Admiraal, is permitted a red scarf flung about his neck to stand out from his otherwise standard van Hove uniform. This accessory, coupled with a sinuous, sibilant physicality, announces his gayness and paves the way for his sizzlingly subdued, unrequited love scene with the priest, Father Thane, played by Fedja van Hûet, also wearing the trademark costume, with the slight concession of a clerical collar. Several of the women characters in the production are also gay or bisexual, their orientations emblemized by their straight-lined tailored suits. The male actor, Kay Barthalomaus Schulze, who plays the Queen in the German production of Marlowe's *Edward II*, is distinguished from the other prison denizens by the bright red lipstick he sports. Another effeminate character, from Mee's *True Love*, a middle-aged archly leering, old-fashioned "queen," played by Fred Goossens, is unmistakably attired in bright and pastel colors, including a loud Hawaiian blouse. He throws his gayness around with merry outness as though he were silently singing "I Am Who I Am" to himself all the while. That is a major exception to the norm.

A new queer aesthetic

In *Disease Germs*, van Hove introduced a camp, kitschy aesthetic to Flemish theatre, with all the female parts played in the grand style by men. Similar approaches, which had been rampant for years in America with Robert Ludlum's Theatre of the Ridiculous, the San Francisco Angels of Light, and others, were virtually untried in Belgium. Queer Theatre as such arrived very late in a country known for its Catholic piety, in contrast with the more liberated Netherlands to the north that had roiled since the 1960s with alternative cultural experiments in hippie culture, feminism, and various outgrowths of the protest movements.[73] Van Hove dove into theatrical transvestism and gender-bending in such productions as *Disease Germs*, Bernard-Marie Koltès's *In the Loneliness of the Cotton Fields*, and Marguerite Duras's *Agatha*. In the latter, two male actors, playing brother and sister, are costumed in identical "dainty ready-made suits and stylish striped slips" (Caris 1984). There is no question that such choices were bold and innovative considering the context. Still, gender dressing up, while it offers a kind of liberation, may also be a kind of cover—a literal disguise, hiding behind camp and poses.

He repeated and enlarged on gay issues, imagery, and gay feelings in an unmasked way—a thoroughly vulnerable way—in certain scenes of *Wild Lords*.

For a Belgian avant-garde production to specifically explore gay intra and interpersonal feelings, using the performance vocabulary of the Living Theatre and Grotowski's Poor Theatre to do so, was unprecedented. The core notion both Grotowski and Living Theatre founders, Julian Beck and Judith Malina, introduced was one of stripping down to the authentic and the essential, getting rid of what they considered bourgeois society's and bourgeois theatre's illusory trappings. While Frédéric Flamand's collective PlanK displayed two near-naked men onstage in Grotowski-influenced devised theatre pieces such as *Real Reel* in the 1970s, they were operating in the French-language side of Belgium. It is a sign of how divided the tiny Belgium was that van Hove never saw or knew of this work. Still, from a wider historical point of view, it constitutes a stepping-stone toward *Wild Lords*.

The physicalized camaraderie between the clumps of male friends that have recurred in van Hove shows over the years is an outgrowth of van Hove's fascination with boys in early ado-lescence sitting around a campfire in the final scene of *Wild Lords*, an *oeuvre de jeunesse* in more ways than one (see Figure 1.13). The experimental structure of the play allowed for the emergence and free play of concealed yearnings. Van Hove's iterations of gay identity in his early works were performed in a headlongedly primal way. It was courageous of both him and the performers to so personally commit themselves, for the real risk that a cross-section of the press would respond homophobically was borne out in the event.[74] These early plays (i.e., *Disease Germs*, *Wild Lords*, and *Imitations*) were self or group-authored under van Hove's aegis. In a separate phase, when he crossed over to text theatre, resorting to the repertory of Koltès, Duras (in his gender-bender rendition of *Agatha*, which was about brother/sister incest, but where van Hove had men play both roles), and Genet, again we find a tropism to the gay.

FIGURE 1.13 *Wild Lords*

© Luc Peeters (Keoon)

For someone who was a bold pioneer in his early years, he had a resistance to owning it. In interviews, van Hove never makes any bones about his identity and his extraordinarily durable liaison with Jan Versweyveld. But he had been quick to assert that straight tropes interest him just as much if not more and firmly refused a label of "gay artist" or the notion that he was bound to direct "gay theatre," insisting that he was simply interested in love in all its forms.[75] In 1992, a Dutch gay paper prefaced an interview with an indictment of him for not being more forthright:

> It's striking that in his work and also outside it he's so slightly explicitly homosexual. What's more, he initially refused to be interviewed by *De Gay Krant*. Van Hove didn't want Zuidelijk Toneel to be labeled as a gay group. And that while he was almost exclusively surrounded by homosexuals in his post.
>
> *(Kraijeveld 1992)*

But in the interview proper he stuck to his guns:

> I don't relish talking about [being gay] because I don't consider it important for my work. People who need or want to know, figure it out for themselves, but I don't think it's my subject. Someone like Derek Jarman, who that issue aside, I admire greatly, has taken homosexuality as his main subject. More power to him, but I don't think it's the principal theme of my work. . . . But I'm Ivo and I do it in my way. And regarding my preference for homosexual plays; only *South* in part deals with it. And as for most of my actors being gay, I consider that a matter of chance. With De Tijd and Toneelgroep Amsterdam it was entirely different, and that's all there is to it. It has nothing to do with why I work with certain actors. . . . I don't think there's any blanket way that gays experience theatre. Yes, in fact I find it an annoying subject for discussion. Do you categorize other peoples' work as heterosexual? I like using an expression of Fassbinder's who often said: 'I'm fifty percent homosexual and as for the rest I do other things.' It depends on whether homosexuality brings added value to your work or not. In my work I find it's not the case. I make things I think are beautiful, not because there happens to be some homosexual aspect present in it.
>
> *(Ibid.)*

In 2002, he pithily responded to a journalist who was pushing him to identify his art as gay theatre:

> I don't try to hide my sexual preference under chairs or benches, but it isn't true that my productions are all about that. In the words of Fassbinder: I'm not a fulltime homosexual. There are plenty of other themes from life which grab me. I've been making theatre for twenty years now. In only two productions was homosexuality actually a theme: in Julien Green's *The South*, and in Jean Genet's *Splendid's*. The rest of my shows have absolutely nothing to do with it. In point of fact heterosexual love is always central to my productions.
>
> *(Stuivenberg 2002)*

On the one hand, he is being disingenuous or literal, for *Disease Germs*, *Wild Lords*, *Agatha*, and *In the Loneliness of the Cotton Fields* play with gender-bending as well as the two he references. In defining artistic identity this way, he is comparable to the American playwright Edward Albee who, though gay, was a dramatic bard of heterosexual marriages in *Who's Afraid of Virginia Woolf* and a plethora of plays. As such, he has been variously assailed for being unqualified to dramatize the lives of straight couples, or of cloaking portrayals of gays in the personae of straights.[76]

Lately, van Hove's discourse on gayness is changing. By his own admission, life for gays in Holland is getting tougher, as they find themselves the target of opprobrium, and he feels the imperative to offer himself as a role model for vulnerable young people and to seek out occasions to broadcast his gay identity without disclaimers (Sels 2016a). Once he had switched over and settled into being a "text director" for good, plays with gay subjects, sub-plots, or treatments haven't predominated, but neither were they so uncommon. To the earlier list are now added: *Ludwig II*, *Edward II*, *Angels in America*, *Perfect Wedding*, *Song From Far Away*, *The Damned*, and *The Things That Pass*.

It is true though, that over time, particularly once he assumed directorship of Zuidelijk Toneel, he wound up doing far more works that explore straight families and heterosexual relationships—albeit dysfunctional ones. It is not that he went back into the closet, but that he may have felt impelled to address the interests and orientation of his primary, generally conventional, local audience in the provincial Dutch city of Eindhoven. It is also true that heterosexual subjects, characters, and interactions undeniably intrigue him, as he claims, and that he brings his own subversive gaze to bear on them. Queerness, as David Savran has it,

> is less a fixed attribute of a given text or performance than a transient disturbance produced between and among text, actor, director, and spectator. It might be said to be an effect of knowledge or lack of it, in relation to dissident sexual desires and identities.
>
> *(Savran 2003: 59)*

Viewed from this extremely inclusive vantage point, we can detect queerness in works set in the most ostentatiously straight milieux where such "transient disturbances" erupt to their fictive members' consternation.

Van Hove frequently finds dramatic justification for staging clusters of heterosexual men. In all later works where the guys disport with each other, such as *The Taming of the Shrew*, *Faces*, *Husbands*, *Rocco and His Brothers*, and *Othello*, same-sex attraction may be deduced or assumed, but the closest it gets to being expressed is in the fun-aggressive group pile-ups these productions all have in common (see Figure 1.14). The gay has gone underground, but it may be a motive force in the heterosexual milieu, in the form of what Eve Kosofsky Sedgwick calls "male homosexual panic," which she confidently states, "became the normal condition of the male heterosexual entitlement" (Sedgwick 2002: 159). By its endemically furtive nature, it must lead to aggression, self-destruction, and destruction of others, both male and female; Van Hove dramatizes this dynamic over and over. According to Savran,

> heterosexuality (like the bipolar system of gender it requires) is itself a performance that imitates 'a phantasmatic ideal of heterosexual identity.' . . . Thus heterosexuality is always predicated on lost—and unmourned—homosexual catheses. . . . the male bond is always the site of intense anxiety, and the homoeroticism that perpetually threatens it is being constantly dislocated, abstracted, or (more ominously) translated into violence between men.[77]
>
> *(Savran 2003: 74, 146)*

FIGURE 1.14 *The Taming of the Shrew*

© Jan Versweyveld

Othello, which illustrates this point, opens with male aggression space—the lounge area in a modern-day gym or health club—foregrounding the corporality of the male body at sport. In the darkness, the sound of someone striking a punching-bag primes us for the swaggering world that is about to greet us. The stage is invaded by an abrupt flood of toned male flesh and virile voices. Roderigo is at the punching-bag—and all the guys are almost naked. Thus the keynote and atmosphere is established for this play about heterosexual love. The men are dressed only in exercise shorts (somewhat adapted to culottes, hanging down to the knees and ever so slightly feminizing them, as van Hove did previously for the men's kilt-like costumes from his early approach to *Macbeth*) and boxing gloves—sans shirts, shoes or socks. Before the scene is over, all the men will have stripped entirely to buff and dressed again, covering up in the usual signature business uniforms.[78]

In *Faces*, the men spontaneously break out into a game of Cowboys and Indians, and in *The Taming of the Shrew*, the suitors descend into macho, rough but affectionate tactile horseplay at the drop of a hat, with butt-patting, and "nuggies" of knuckles pressed into skulls, as though they were members of a basketball team.[79] In all these cases, men are shown jockeying for the affections of a circumscribed group of available women, but that proprietary combat does not preclude genuinely affectionate physicality between the men; in fact, it's just the flip side of the same gender coin. It is as though van Hove wants to show that Hedda and Kate, just to cite a few, are ultimately run over not by one empirical man, but by a male steamroller of tight networks and sub rosa understandings. That chummy male network, so redolent of misogyny, confirms Kosofsky Sedgwick's assumption that behind it all is homosexual panic, a terror that she suggests is not based:

> on an essential differentiation between 'basically homosexual' and 'basically heterosexual' men, aside from the historically small group of consciously and self-accepting homosexual men, who are no longer susceptible to homosexual panic. . . . If such compulsory

relationships as male friendship, mentorship, admiring identification, bureaucratic sub-ordination, and heterosexual rivalry all involve forms of investment that force men into the arbitrarily mapped, self-contradictory, and anathema-riddled quicksands of the middle distance of male homosexual desire, then it appears that men enter into adult masculine entitlement only through acceding to the permanent threat that the small space they have cleared for themselves on this terrain may always, just as arbitrarily and with just as much justification, be punitively and retroactively foreclosed.

(Sedgwick 2002: 157)

The black-suited trio of friends in *Husbands* operates in that same "small space," as do all the others. The entire first act of the play is a spate of male bonding following the funeral of a mutual friend. They retire to one of their finished basements, where they go through the same routines of horsing around and playing competitive games we see in other van Hove shows. Every so often they pop out with sexual come-ons toward each other, outbursts of homosexual feelings that just as quickly get reinterred. In *Faces*, two pairs of supposedly straight men, all of whom display a gratuitous homophobia, go to visit the call-girl Jeannie, yet seem to be especially eager to watch the other man having sex with her, not merely to have it with her themselves. While clutching at a frail deniability in the context of a rugged straight ritual—going to a prostitute—they are trying to commandeer a little gay fun in the process. One could argue that such urges are behind all the straight posturing Cassavetes's men specialize in. Van Hove senses it and has an affectionate chuckle at their expense.

Van Hove has the three women in *Husbands*—the widow of the friend whose death they are mourning, a prostitute, and a stray party woman—all played by one actress. The trio of men treat each woman in the same way: as an opportunity for a come-on. And come on they do, with clumsy brutality; but they absolutely fail to make any connection with them, not even getting the minimal amount of casual sex they say they're after. They can connect with each other, however unsatisfactorily, but can't find any way at all to do so with the woman.

Sometimes the subtextual gayness may be unearthed as it was in *Rocco and His Brothers*. Here is a show about an aggressively male and macho environment, the world of boxing that van Hove had superimposed on *Othello*, but which is integral to this world as scribed by its author, the cineast Visconti. Van Hove's version presumes a gayness woven into the woof of this circum-scribed social milieu. He unearths same-sex impulses and even sex acts that Visconti, if he imagined them, left firmly in the subtext. In van Hove's show, the five brothers all sleep together on one bed packed in like sardines. When Simone goes to the impresario, Morini, the latter, even as he berates the former champion Simone for losing matches, kneels down in front of him and tempts him sexually, an unmistakable overture that the drunken Simone finally repulses. It's just a brief moment of stage time, but a very life-like one.

Apart from the tenderness and vulnerability displayed between the brothers, exceptional in the van Hove gallery of male buddy groupings, we are also presented with the character of the brothers' friend Guido. Here is an explicitly gay character who is both accepted and casually abused by the brothers, especially the dissolute Simone, for whom he performs many services. This hanger-on and go-between is depicted in the live version as a gay admirer of the entire family, something more out of *Last Exit to Brooklyn* than from Visconti's source film. The massages and salubrious rubdowns he administers are motivated more by sexual appreciation of the flesh than for their mere thera-peutic value. Simone affects not to notice the sexual intent of Guido's touch even as he benefits from the contact, and so manages to have it both ways. All this suggests that Simone's insecurities around women, and even his misogyny, may mask or go hand in hand with homosexual yearnings.

The men in this play go after women aggressively. A territorial battle over one woman in particular is unquestionably at the heart of the drama. Even so, they are heterosexual characters with more fluidity of preference and identity than the source text suggests.

Between 2008 and now, van Hove has returned at times to stage texts with explicitly gay subjects—*Edward II, Ludwig II, Angels in America*, the world premiere of the opera version of *Brokeback Mountain* he did in Spain, and so on. Most recently, he has brought his stage adaptation of Visconti's perverse and homoerotic historical epic film *The Damned* to the Avignon Festival and Paris. *Edward II, Ludwig,* and *The Damned* are among his most fulfilled and original works. But as David Savran says, "Why must a queer theater remain fixated on the imaginary stability of that most unstable of identities? And why not acknowledge the fact that a writer's [or a director's] work will always exceed, and often belie, his or her avowed identity?" (Savran 2003: 81).

Van Hove has brought to shows a harsh analytical vision of heterosexual male identity as a construct and mask. To this end, he has often deliberately chosen especially aggressively hetero-sexual pieces—Cassavetes filmscripts, for example—or brought to the surface the macho under-pinnings of unlikely scripts, such as *Othello, Hedda Gabler,* and *The Taming of the Shrew*. It is as though, having grown fascinated with the topic of male aggression within the framework of camaraderie, the choice of any given text is incidental and arbitrary. He can use *Rocco and His Brothers*, a text *about* boxing, or equally well make *Othello into* a play about boxing, and with it explore the trope of choice: why, in order to be close to each other, do men have to be so rough?[80] And how is it that affection can flip into homicidal hostility? So, in *Faces*, for example, the suburban husbands' affectionate horseplay invariably morphs into wrestling, with bruised limbs and rueful feelings throbbing painfully in the wake. It is the absence of free homosexual expression between these straight characters, Eve Kosovsky Sedgwick might aver, the refusal of the campfire erotic closeness at the end of *Wild Lords* depicted as a universal yearning among boys for each other, which deprives men of harmony with their peers, and renders their relations with women so distorted. Taken into the realm of the political in *Coriolanus* or *Julius Caesar* (both constituent parts of the *Roman Tragedies*), this mutual male roughness, which goes hand in glove with a refusal of open mutually exchanged male eroticism, can lead to war and the rise or fall of whole dynasties.

The continuum between agit-prop and aesthete

How are the politics in the sites where van Hove's shows are created and all the places they are shown interwoven into the shows themselves? How are they involved in his role as artistic director of the most significant theatre in the Netherlands? As a private person? These are complicated questions with complicated and incomplete answers. Inasmuch as van Hove has achieved such popularity and esteem, including a reputation for being a political artist, it warrants in-depth examination. In the first place, an evolution has taken place over the course of his career, just as the world itself has changed. It should also be observed that in his case, as in that of so many artists, it is surely a mistake to take public and private pronouncements regarding political stances to mean that those stances are reflected directly or even indirectly in the artwork; they may or may not be. The artist may sincerely believe they are when nobody else sees them there. And conversely, audiences and critics may see much there in the artwork that the artist never intended to insert. It is especially worth examining as the case of Ivo van Hove, given his current charmed position vis-à-vis world culture, is so curiously paradigmatic.

When I asked what drew him to theatre work, he described being an avid reader of the German avant-garde monthly theatre magazine *Theater Heute* (Willinger 2017b).

This large-format periodical was always bristling with images of the latest shows in Germany. He says he learned German expressly so he could read it.[81] In other words, van Hove in the first instance was fascinated by theatre as a visual medium and specifically by the striking (still) images that imaginative directors could produce. It should also be remembered that what stood out to him about Patrice Chéreau's work was the craft of skillfully and artistically deploying groups of actors on a stage—in other words: his stage pictures. I don't believe these responses should be underestimated; on the contrary, they should guide our understanding of the kind of theatre artist van Hove is and which way his natural inclinations most strongly tend.

It should also be determined what is meant by political theatre. One point of view has it that politics in art are inescapable, even if an artist is bent on creating purely escapist art. An artist can't *not* be political. Thus, it has been asserted that theatre, like all arts, must either be explicitly political or else is implicitly political by default, because all theatre occurs in a political context and is impacted by it.[82] One may grant that yet there is theatre which has no perceptible political content, which may be about human relations, may be a machine for making people laugh, or simply be an aesthetic experiment.[83] Some recent theoreticians of the political in theatre, for example Dominic Johnson, will detect "covert" politics in such a play as Tennessee Williams' *Cat on a Hot Tin Roof*, simply on account of its evocation of a character who is probably in "the space of the closet" (Johnson 2012: 10).

Van Hove states that the events of the 2001 US terrorist attacks represent a cut-off point, after which his work changed. There is no reason to question the sincerity of his transformation, although he may not have had much choice in the matter, as the 2001 US terrorist attacks gave the theatre, along with all the arts a seismic jolt.[84] Van Hove, among others, drifted into a much more socially minded stance, and it is reflected in his shows.[85] Prior to that point, the authors he looked to for inspiration were chiefly theatre authors—"Artaud, Grotowski, books about American performance art"—although elsewhere he also attributes influence to the American cultural commentator Camille Paglia, who wrote extensively about gender and feminism, often going against the grain of political correctness.

Since the turning point of the 2001 US terrorist attacks, van Hove has become a voracious reader of a certain type of social commentator. They come variously from sociology, philosophy, political science, and so on, but share an overarching worldview. In interviews he has referred to the influence of Zygmunt Bauman and Jacques Rancière. Upon close questioning, the list expands to include: Judith Butler, Benjamin R. Barber, Richard Sennett, Giorgio Agamben, Amin Maalouf, Peter Sloterdijk, and Martha Nussbaum (Willinger 2017a and b). Many of these writers quote each other. There are several intellectual threads that unite them. Much of their thinking about the contemporary scene was precipitated by the American government's responses to the 2001 US terrorist attacks—the sharp increase in surveillance; the introduction of torture; the tightening of restrictions of all sorts; the increasing polarization between the West and Middle-Eastern peoples; and the unwarranted wars that traumatized masses, displaced unprecedented numbers, and destabilized the region as had been predicted. They are also profoundly concerned with the tectonic shifts in civilization since the fall of the Soviet Union, after which the old political equations are up for grabs. This includes such effects of "negative globalization" (Bauman 2007: 24), as xenophobia, the masses of the displaced who loiter in a liminal realm out of Westerners' consciousness or sense of responsibility, the reliance on the internet and technology, runaway consumerism, the disjunction between the world's haves and have-nots, "the *disposability* of humans," and so on (Bauman 2003: 81). Barber formulates it as a new world order in which the forces of, "Jihad," which "pursues a bloody politics of identity," governs alongside "McWorld, a bloodless economics of profit" (Barber 1995: 8). Barber further comments:

> If the political totalism of the fascist and communist world once tried, at horrendous human costs, to subordinate all economic, social, and cultural activity to the demands of an overarching state, the economic totalism of unleashed market economics seems now to be trying (at costs yet to be fully reckoned) to subordinate politics, society, and culture to the demands of an overarching market.
>
> *(Barber 1995: 295)*

In other words, these writers chart a macro-sociology of present times, going into the sweeping trends that affect everyone's relationships, including the relationship to oneself. They are solicitous of protecting democracies, although several assert that present governments have slipped their democratic moorings, and that a parallel force—one that is market-driven—is the actual body governing humanity. But it is democratic principles in their ideal form for which they are advocating, and for the potential for humanism to survive in an age when so many powerful forces are afoot to defeat and undermine democratic and humanistic values. The primary emotion identified with these seismic shifts in which a terrorist attack, closing of a factory, or the arrival next door of uprooted peoples could cause a slip into non-existence or complete disarray, is deep-rooted anxiety, the doom of living with "the spectre of inadequacy" (Bauman 2007: 58). It is a universally experienced existential state that Bauman has called "precarity."

> With skills falling out of demand in less time than it takes to acquire and master them, with educational credentials losing value against their cost of purchase by the year or even turning into 'negative equity' long before their allegedly lifelong 'sell-by' date, with places of work disappearing with little or no warning, and with the course of life sliced into a series of ever shorter one-off projects, life prospects look increasingly like the haphazard convolutions of smart rockets in search of ephemeral and restless targets.
>
> *(Bauman 2003: 93)*

They have explained how this differs in essence from existential terrors previous generations have had to contend with. It is the confluence of all these conflicts that have threatened (and thus far failed) to bring extreme right wing elements to power, exemplified most recently in the 2017 Dutch elections with the narrow defeat of Geert Wilders and the French elections that brought Emanuel Macron to power and greatly diminished Marine LePen. In this context, practically any other candidate of any political stripe who can manage to forge a coalition toward the center of the spectrum is deemed to be a savior of the status quo. In the new politics, where the evaporation of Communism has made the old left and right obsolete, "Social Justice" causes have come to dominate the discourse: an umbrella value to defend rights of all segments of disenfranchised peoples, from LGBTQ to the exponentially growing number of "stateless persons;" from unwed teenage mothers to ethnic minorities. The vocabulary of political correctness has concomitantly risen, whose presumed excesses, to the surprise of many, became one of the prime grievances that helped to elect Donald Trump. The point of view that safeguards and stands up for democratic prerogatives has gained in urgency, even as the far right has achieved ever greater currency in Dutch society, as it has throughout Europe. Anti-totalitarian bulwarks that were installed following World War II have never been so threatened as they are today. In a nutshell, the far-seeing and sympathetic Zygmunt Bauman concludes: "You cannot make this world kind and considerate to the human beings who inhabit it, and as accommodating to their dreams of dignity as you would ideally wish it to be. *But you must try*" (Bauman 2003: 84).

The logical question is to what degree are these authors' ideas or the developments described represented in van Hove's shows, and my answer is: only marginally insofar as content goes. This brings up the split in his functions—director on the one hand and artistic director on the other (in Dutch: *regisseur* and *directeur*). While van Hove is talented in both roles, and both are kinds of leadership roles, they are very different; what the director produces is very different from what the artistic director produces. The artistic director of such a prestigious and established institution as TGA—the most established theatre of the nation—plays the role, in a very real sense, of a prominent moral and ethical authority. He is one of the chief spokespeople for the interests of culture within Dutch society, but also regarding the general political life of the nation. And inasmuch as he has achieved extraordinary international recognition, so have his opinions and initiatives gained greater prestige. Neo-liberal forces, which have also risen in recent years in Holland just as in the United Kingdom and America, and a point of view that questions the value of government underwriting the arts along with all the other protections established in a socialist environment such as the Netherlands, create a situation in which cultural establishment figures are regularly called upon to take appropriate action to resist cuts.

So from that standpoint, van Hove must safeguard his theatre, which is a seat of free expression, from a political scene that undervalues that type of culture. But is he also obligated to do explicitly political theatre? And does he? It seems that there are forces—critics, audiences, and market forces—which militate toward that expectation. But what would such theatre look like, and is Toneelgroep Amsterdam producing it? Based on the many public interviews with the director and what critics say, you might think they do. But, I would say the truth lies elsewhere. On the strength of his aforementioned socio-political readings, van Hove refers to the pressing issues of the day—oppressed and marginalized minorities, endangered liberties, immigrants and xenophobia. Yet we see precious little of any of this reflected in his productions. I believe it is because, despite a sincere wish on van Hove's part to do his share on the political scene, that is simply not the kind of artist he ever was or now is. And yet, there is an unmistakable sense in the image the world has of him, that he is a political, even engaged artist. There appears to be a gap between the image and the reality, one he may not even be entirely aware of.

To explain the conundrum in which van Hove has found himself, it's worth a digression into an earlier historical episode known at the time as "The War of Images," in which the man van Hove cites as his primary artistic model, Patrice Chéreau, played a crucial role. In the post-war period in France, intellectual politics were dominated by the political left that led to heated debates between Stalinist, Trotskyite, and Social Democratic factions. The theatres drew strongly on Brechtian models for "critical" and epic approaches. Throughout the 1950s, the influence of the Berliner Ensemble was heavily felt in France, and many theatre critics came at their task from a Marxist point of view as well. This political engagement sharpened dramatically with the Algerian War and later with the uprising in the streets in May 1968. A leftist wing following the Maoist Chinese model came to dominate the discourse. It was in this highly politicized context that Chéreau had his debut and beginning years as a director. His earliest projects took a highly Brechtian tilt, both in play choice and scenic expression. He was "driven by faith in social and historical progress, confident in his own capacity to do his part in the transformation of the world" (Benhamou 2015: 75).

The theatre establishment became one of the sites where intense cultural debates got played out, and they centered on the role of the director. (S)he was seen to have a key social responsibility; the artist's subjectivity needed to be subsumed by "an ideologization" of the theatrical image being produced. The theatre was meant to become a peoples' theatre. A large number of theatre leaders, among them artistic directors and directors, in May 1968, in solidarity with the revolutionary tide, united to sign a "Declaration of Villeurbanne." This document called on the theatre public to reconsider its ties with "bourgeois culture," and to render the theatres sites for political interchange. There should also be an effort made to bring "the non-audience"—that is a non-traditional audience of the proletariat—into the theatres, so that the theatres might, once and for all become "popular," in fact and not just name. The work done would be designed to artistically and politically educate these new audience members drawn from the masses (Ibid.: 78).

It seems that two influences from outside the French context, in the event from the United States, galvanized the French theatrical landscape at the time, and split it into two opposing camps—the Living Theatre and Robert Wilson's *Deafman Glance*—which had both been doing European tours (Dort 1979: 191). Their examples put at loggerheads those on the one hand who were struggling to establish a communitarian theatre structure in which the whole creative team— director, actors, designers, technicians, and stagehands would have an equal say in a show's development, and for whom the role of theatre was essentially as a cultural/political tool of revolutionary utopianism. At the other end were those who, captivated by Wilson's grandiose, non-narrative approach, were moved to create their own abstract shows in which text was subordinated to beautifully realized images. Chéreau, as a willing signatory to the "Declaration of Villeurbanne," initially committed to the former camp, but then—spectacularly—was the first to defect to the latter. He lost the conviction that theatre professionals could succeed at creating a viable workers' theatre for an audience of workers. After a year of efforts spent producing a proletarian, polemical type of theatre he officially divorced himself from that initiative, in favor of developing "the craft [*l'artisanat*] of theatre in and of itself," a different sort of commitment which had been germinating in him since working under Giorgio Strehler in Italy (Benhamou 2015: 75). He proclaimed that "the only theatre which had a right to the epithet 'political,'" the only one,

> that can claim the right to be called truly politically active is that born in the streets in a time of revolution, and can only be a theatre of and for the proletariat, one that comes into being historically, and not as the fruits of an aesthetic choice made by theatre professionals.
>
> *(Dort 2001: 324)*

Asserting, "I'm a theatre director, not a tribune" (Ibid.), he publicly renounced his part in the "Declaration," and asserted that his primary interest would henceforth be pursuing the craft of directing, rather than preaching, teaching, converting—or even delivering particularly clear messages. . . . that from then on "his own artistry would be the sole subject of his militantism" (Peduzzi 2016: 380). Political and experimental theatre were two incompatibles, he asserted (Benhamou 2015:78). Directors all over Europe underwent comparable disillusionment: In the 1970s, Peter Stein, for example, resigned himself to abandoning the utopian ideal: "the company came to the conclusion that agit-prop work was better left to the workers themselves and, moreover, that it was not what the company could do best" (Bradby and Williams 1988: 200).

This turn around did not go unpunished, as more and more French theatre leaders, following suit, renounced the terms of the "Declaration of Villeurbanne," producing a snowballing movement in the reverse direction, to the consternation of the left-wing press. Chéreau's next plays were Moliére's *Don Juan* and Shakespeare's *Richard II* in which he cast himself in the title role. The virulent attacks against his new emphasis on stage imagery began to multiply. The verbal dimension, the development of a dialectic, that had been so central to the Brechtian school, was now relegated to a back bench in favor of visual spectacularity. Complaints centered around actors being inaudible and inarticulate. The shows were accused of decadence. Actors' prerogatives were said to have been ignored under a tyrannical director. But it was his 1972 production of Marlowe's *Massacre at Paris* that served as "a particularly provoking theatrical manifesto," representing the kind of theatre Chéreau intended to pursue that raised especial ire (Benhamou 2015: 28).

Thus Jean-Pierre Léonardini in *Travail Théâtral*:

> *The Massacre at Paris* is exactly that, a feast of beautiful images without any true center of gravity. One stretches one's ear in vain to finally hear an explosion with any measure of sense, which gets sacrificed to the visual machinery. . . . The script itself is guilty of . . . political irresponsibility, a decadent fascination for death, the aestheticist gesture, and finally, a total absence of subject matter.
>
> *(Benhamou 2015: 29)*

Bertrand Poirot-Delpech in *Le Monde* ramped up his attacks on this aestheticist direction:

> Even if all the scenic picturesqueness of his Marlowe could be justified, even if he has attained great beauties of decadent jubilation in the fashion of Visconti, it is clear that he is totally unconcerned with the play's contents, which when it comes down to it is reactionary—history is presented as nothing more than a cesspool . . . he is graced with the luxury of cheapening his very privileges as an artist through beauty itself. Chéreau's contempt for social commitment has caused him to neglect his research and service to the public . . . and to lose himself in aesthetic refinements.
>
> *(Benhamou 2015: 30)*

As late as 1977, the distinguished left-wing critic Gilles Sandier would attack Chéreau and the entire image-oriented tendency in the following description which degenerates into personal insults: ". . . A purely formal show. . . a gratuitous succession of tableaux vivants of an absolute, formal beauty. . . Nothing but sophisticated scholasticism, a theatre of imposters" (Benhamou 2015: 28). Over time, such opposition was worn down and the very qualities for which Chéreau was attacked in the early 1970s came to be seen as virtues. He was proclaimed "the best of our painters in the theatre" (Ibid.). The critical establishment was won over:

> He was a director for whom the direction of the actor counts less than the feel of the composition, whose 'passion for creating tableaus' has all the same, never ceased, since his earliest days, aiming to make a dramatic impact, properly speaking, that is to say, the evocation of an emotion which will put the audience and the stage in strong relationship where they may both participate in the direction it takes.
>
> *(Benhamou 2015: 21)*

While the theatre scene in Belgium in 1981 had not been subject to the same convulsions as that in France, the dialectic represented by the War of Images was in the air there as well. The Flemish scene, when van Hove entered it, was rather more fragmented, as an unwholesome relationship between the multiplicity of political parties across the spectrum existed, with specific theatres linked to a given party's program, dependent on that party for its subsidies—extending even beyond partisan politics to patronage by the Freemasons, which even today has a strong influence on the Belgian cultural scene. Still, what passed for the Flemish avant-garde at the time had a strong left-wing political tilt, as represented by such groups as the Internationale Nieuwe Scene (again influenced by Brecht and the Living Theatre), aspiring to make the same sort of proletarian alliances as advocated in "The Declaration of Villeurbanne," and De Trojaanse Paard, which had a heavy didactic flavor.

During the 1980s, there were three critics who in the main exercised influence in the Flemish theatre scene—Pol Arias, Jef De Roeck, and Wim van Gansbeke. All three had good will for the theatre and did their best to nudge it in a positive direction, one of renewal. Of the three, van Gansbeke, although popular and charismatic, could be the most severe. As one observer remarked, his words were as sharp as his voice and facial profile, for indeed, his voice was squeaky and his features sharp (Vander Veken 2016):

> the experimental new aesthetic had limits for Van Gansbeke, and they're not so far off from what today's audience members sometimes dare to complain about with subsidized theatre: a compelling formalism at the expense of coherent content, a refusal to communicate clearly, the self-aggrandizement of certain creators, the lax application of rules for declaiming text, or heavy-handed aesthetic conceptualism. This latter for example explains why Van Gansbeke never became a big fan of Ivo van Hove. He did in fact recognize his qualities, but found his stagings too studied, and that they betrayed too little emotional depth. [He said:]: experimentation must remain a means to arrive at something, and when it becomes a goal in and of itself becomes as loathsome as whatever it's trying to oppose.
>
> *(Hillaert 2010: 66)*

He reacted particularly acerbically to van Hove's third play, *Like in the War*, and laced into him for over-aestheticizing at the expense of other facets:

> Ivo van Hove's direction is based on a carefully thought out concept and there's marvelous looking scenery—and lighting design—but his text remains hermetic and often stripped of meaning—which doesn't mean that there's nothing to mean about here—and the directing of the actors comes up scandalously too short. Not in respect to form, because the physical aspect of the performance brings the set artfully to life, but the content of the acting, the transmission to the spectator, the organic dynamics of the production. There's a curious vacuum that gets you through an hour and a half without being really bored, that keeps your attention going, but for that same hour and a half it keeps you from getting involved, since in all that time you haven't found a way to get past the form to the shocking kernel of the show's content. The tight formalism of van Hove's previous productions here reaches a high point, while accessibility simultaneously reaches a low point. But van Hove is still young and perhaps will just have to get through this learning curve. For it can't be denied that this fellow does think carefully about what he's doing, looking for a solution in visual aspects. If these qualities ever dovetail with greater depth and verbal power we can expect to see a masterpiece.
>
> *(Hillaert 2010: 182)*

While van Gansbeke's remarks probably weren't politically motivated in the way Chéreau's French reviewers' were, he was wedded to traditional values of clarity, text, and emotional catharsis, and felt the show sacrificed depth of feeling for a brittle, recherché visual surface. He gave a familiar lambasting to the inaudibility, inadequate coaching work with the actors, and obliviousness to textual concerns, just as Chéreau's early critics had done. He wasn't the only critic who took van Hove to task for that production. The critic from the influential avant-garde Flemish theatre periodical, *Etcetera*, accused him of treating the actors as purely compositional elements on a par with set pieces and lighting. That article was the most detailed and serious analysis of van Hove's work to that point. It was also the harshest, certainly sterner than van Gansbeke's. It belabored an insufficiency in directing of the actors, whose work the critic found superficial and caricatured. In fact, the critic had many problems with the show, starting with the language: "A clear, clean, pure use of language—justifiable in the vernacular context—here gets tangled up with content-less and superficial babble." He also criticizes such additions as an inserted flashback concerning the young Oedipus' loss of his virginity with his mother on the eve of his twelfth birthday. And yet, he finds occasion to praise Versweyveld's David Hockney-infused design concept, the lighting, to which he attributes the presence of any multi-faceted connotations that seep in, and certain powerful moments, such as when Oedipus takes a shower; then, "electricity is in the air" (see Figure 1.15). He finds that the production portrays the mythic king as, "a split personality, an aggressive and ultimately cold-blooded Oedipus in relation to his four incestuous children" (Van Rompay 1983).

And a feature article meant to show the fledgling director in a positive light in the most read magazine in Flanders, *Knack*, was scathing regarding the opacity and fragmentation

FIGURE 1.15 *Like in the War*

© Luc Peeters (Keoon)

of the narrative, the abstraction of which went hand in hand with emphasis on visual images:

> AKT as van Hove's group is called, never shows simple stories. The plot doesn't develop according to a series of chronological events. AKT tells them associatively, enveloping itself in a depth-psychological or mystical language-adornment style. The plot, in any case, is never transparent. And great efforts are necessary to plumb the atmosphere ever so slightly, with very slight concomitant rewards.
>
> *(De Bruyne 1982)*

We can deduce that van Hove was for the first time introducing and playing with certain of his signature ideas. *Like in the War* was one of his "prototype" productions. In an interview he gave at this early point in his career, he delineated three formal phases he'd already been through. There was a certain pomposity to doing so, as he'd only been directing for four years at that point! (Penning 1985). By 1992, he had a more modest assessment to make of his early career: "'I suppose you've got to consider the early part of my career as a great learning process. In retrospect, I'm glad that I didn't start right in on classics'" (Kraiijeveld 1992). He seems to have forgotten that he *did* start with a classic—*Oedipus at Colonnus*, adapted as *Like in the War*. While it wasn't well received, it offered promise for the future. His apparent amnesia suggests that the bad press he got made a profound impact. Elsewhere, Jan Versweyveld confessed that his growing enthusiasm for theatre was greatly "dampened" by that show, and that he'd much rather forget it ever happened. This despite the fact that he as designer received only praise, in fact, stealing the thunder from van Hove (Thielemans 1988).

I believe van Gansbeke's review, well-meaning as it obviously was, coming from an authority figure the young director could not help but be in awe of, together with the other pans, left a lasting scar. One even more immediate impact was that, taking van Gansbeke's harsh commentary on the text to heart, van Hove permanently stopped writing his own plays. And while he rushes to minimize its significance today and quickly points to the fact that van Gansbeke later relented,[86] he became permanently defensive about being associated with any hint of "aestheticism." Indeed, van Hove's theatre is neither purely aesthetic nor markedly political, although at times it has gravitated in the direction of both. The director's various statements on the subject over the years are worth revisiting and juxtaposing.

In his 2013 interview with Johan Reyniers that can here be found as an appendix, the director elucidates his and Jan Versweyveld's initial stance toward the politics of the early 1980s:

> We weren't that political. We weren't interested in Reagan and Thatcher. We didn't make any political statements, unless perhaps indirectly. Nuclear weapons, now that was something. I lay awake for three nights running after our teacher explained to us how the atom bomb worked and the damage it could do. The awareness of evil. The 1982 anti-nuclear demonstration is the only one I ever participated in. Indeed there was a lot of unemployment, but we didn't give a damn about money. We were deliberately *outside* of the social context. Not opposed, but outside.
>
> *(Reyniers 2013)*

It is not surprising, then, that he saw his theatre work, more or less up until the year 2001, as apolitical. Aversion to political theatre, by which he here seems to mean theatre that comments directly on current events—that pushes a given opinion on a hot-button issue—began to surface in some of the earliest interviews:

> 'I once saw a show by the Internationale Nieuwe Scene [Communist/Anarchist Flemish theatre group]. *Putsch* it was called. And then I thought: those people should go into politics instead. There are a lot more direct ways of saying the same thing than through theatre.' Is Ivo van Hove somebody who runs off to join the crowd in a large Brussels peace demonstration? Ivo: 'No. Ivo van Hove is someone who would rather stay home. And work on theatre.'
>
> *(De Bruyne 1982)*

This despite open avowals that as a teenager he had a rebellious and even left-leaning streak. "I rebelled against my parents, against the school, against the priests, against Capitalism, against everything." He reported that he left law school in his third year to study directing because he found the Belgian legal establishment, "a reactionary world" (Van der Speeten 1988). Yet, his point of view about how politics should figure in his and others' theatrical work hadn't changed markedly nineteen years later:

> Theatre for me is not the stuff of dogma, but of imagination. Imagining—that for me is the essence of theatre. As when I dream and fantasize at night. It gets my juices flowing. Theatre as an art form may also bring changes in its wake to society, but not in a direct way. If that's what you really want to pursue, then you'd do better to go into politics.
>
> *(Smith 2002)*

And even as recently as five years ago, his exasperation at explicitly political theatre is still palpable:

> 'That's . . . my problem with the German theatre: they always want theatre productions to be political, whereas I find that the theatre ought to be subversive and not political.' Subversiveness [the interviewer then paraphrases] is that which injects disturbance into one's thoughts, which triggers upsets and rejects horizons that are parachuted in ahead of time.
>
> *(Perrier 2012)*

After all these frank professions, it would behoove us to take seriously that political theatre is clearly a long-standing aversion. In the years following 2001 however, due to cataclysmic events in the world, the pressure built to seek out nuance in his anti-political bias, and a new kind of rhetoric crept in:

> I think that my work with Toneelgroep Amsterdam has become much more 'socially minded.' It's in relation to the important themes of the day, such as migration: *Rocco and His Brothers* for example is about that. In *The Antonioni Project*, sure there's a lot about love stories, but they also have a very hard time holding their own against a forward-moving, changing, urban world. At this point in time I'm going to find that side of things a lot more compelling. Thus, as you take a look backwards you can easily see that there've been a vast array of themes. You don't live isolated from the world. When two airplanes fly into a tower then you can't just stay off in your own world, unless you withdraw way deep down

inside your own world. I think that's totally fine too, but for me personally, I felt the need to develop an exact opposite way of relating to it.

(Hillaert 2009)

In the reference to the 2001 US terrorist attacks, he shows that his readings in contemporary philosophy and sociology have brought him to feel a responsibility to respond in some way to the pressing issue of the day within his theatre work. He is echoing the ideas of Judith Butler, Zygmunt Bauman, Amin Maalouf, and other social commentators close to his heart. The very fact that he reads them and brings them up figures into that sense of responsibility. He claims in interviews that he hasn't read any theatre theory since the long-past days when he drank in Artaud and Grotowski; now it's only these social authors.

In the press release for his recent production of *The Damned* in France, for which he is probably not directly responsible, the blaring squib designed to attract an audience thundered it's no more nor less than "political theatre!" (Pascaud 2016b). On the TGA website, the synopsis of *The Things That Pass*, which premiered last year, is quick, in the first paragraph, to assert that at base the show isn't a family chronicle (which it most manifestly is), but a visionary take on how the West has lapsed into decrepitude vis-à-vis its former Asian colonies (which would be a major interpretative stretch). The new social orientation dominates. Even when van Hove elected to stage a certain series of domestic dramas and comedies that he designated under an umbrella term of a "marriage cycle" in the 2004 to 2006 period,[87] he hastened to lay stress on the seriousness of their content, apparently defensive that someone might consider them frivolous choices:

> This marriage cycle has a political character. And in that I am referring to politics in the Greek sense of the word, namely all that deals with society. We live in a time of great changes, there are great stresses, the world is almost ablaze. In such a period it behooves me to take a good hard look at people. Marriage is a special bond: it's the smallest unit in which treaties are signed, in which eternal faithfulness is sworn, and in which tiny wars are waged.
>
> *(Gompes 2005)*

What Zygmunt Bauman calls "life politics" (Bauman 2003: 23), expressed in Fassbinder's context of the 1970s in the catch-phrase, "the personal as political" (Elsaesser 1996: 40–41), the interactions in a home setting between family and lovers are rhetorically reframed within a context of actual wars. This reasoning seeks to dignify the material and to justify a potentially derisory artistic decision, given the global backdrop against which momentous events are playing out. Indeed, van Hove divides all dramatic literature as stacking up between "family drama" or "history plays" [*koningsdrama*]:

> There aren't many other many other conceivable structures; because those are the two great structures by which the world is organized. That's just the way it's developed till now. *Oedipus* is a family drama. *Ajax* too. The fact that I often direct classical texts is that by taking a detour into the past is the best way to tell my own story.
>
> *(Janssen 1994: 7)*

Indeed, he reduces many classical plays to their family armature, subtracting or minimizing the historical pattern. His latest idea, that history plays will problematize leadership itself, again brings potentially expansive political tropes to a microcosmic dimension of the personal.

His social turn has proven convincing to the world-at-large. Ivo van Hove had the distinction of being included in the magazine *Foreign Policy*'s highly select pantheon of "Leading Global Thinkers of 2016," specifically for, "unmasking fear from the stage." The editors' encomium captures and perpetuates an image of van Hove as a tribune for social justice issues and model of ethical rectitude:

> This year, a Belgian director revived classic American theater and sharpened its edges, cutting to the very heart of the neo-McCarthyism currently poisoning swaths of U.S. politics. In critically praised productions of *A View From the Bridge* and *The Crucible*, Ivo van Hove pared down Arthur Miller's signature overt moralism, as well as indications of the plays' historic periods, with minimalist sets, bland costumes, and tense pacing. This avant-garde approach exposed the scripts' darkest themes—xenophobia, homophobia, suspicion, social hysteria—as universal, timeless, and unnervingly familiar. Van Hove's vision of theater as a means of holding up a mirror to audiences' lived reality won him two Tonys, for Best Revival and Best Director of a Play.
>
> *(Rothkopf 2016)*

Van Hove's dramaturg, Bart Van den Eynde, speciously I believe, explains the grounds for the honor, burnishing the director's political/ethical credentials:

> His approach is topical. We see how societies get driven by terror and seek to cling to their belief systems. What Ivo does is an important political activity. After Brexit and the American election people have become spooked out by the choices they made. Ivo doesn't judge people, but takes them seriously and brings out their motives.
>
> *(Sels 2016b)*

While it is true that Arthur Miller wrote *The Crucible* with specific politics in mind, at the height of the McCarthy fever in America, van Hove revisioned the play in many definite ways, largely by stripping it of those associations. He left it not at all clear which belief system in the play—that which saw witches and believed in them or that which knew there were none—had right on their side. Miller saw no such ambiguity.

Van Hove's immersion in Shakespeare's history plays, first with the three-play cycle *Roman Tragedies* and next with a second three-play cycle, *Kings of War*, is his most blatant foray into material that could be perceived as explicitly political. But there is a far cry from presenting images of political struggles, personalities, and patterns, which is what we see these shows doing, and advocating for one side or another (or even clearly delineating which side is which and how those sides have parallels on the contemporary political scene), that they decidedly do not. Rendering the politics murky, however, does not diminish the plays' power. As Randy Gener describes the electrifying experience of spectating *Roman Tragedies*,

> The Dutch actors pulled no punches in their raucous portrayals of anchormen, senators, generals, cameramen, businessmen and so forth. The razor-sharp exchanges, petty jealousies, backroom politics and blatant hypocrisies seemed not just incredibly real but were also hugely magnified by the cameras and TV screens scattered around me. In this simulacrum, there were no intermissions, but there was an explicit body count. Every so often I was slapped back to my senses when footage of American soldiers in Iraq was shown

or a soldier was killed in the play; his body was laid on a slab and projected onto a large screen for all of us to contemplate. I wondered: can a show such as this be produced or presented on American stages?

(Gener 2009)

Indeed, it later was presented at BAM, and while the large, typically progressive audiences were electrified, they certainly manifested no sense of being offended by the presumably critical references to the war in Iraq. Firstly, it was not clear that they *were* critical. Then few in America's intelligentsia would still defend the wisdom of launching into that conflagration. Unaccountably *The New York Times* sent no critic. We thus have no particular journalistic record or response to Gener's question. But I would venture to say, having seen it at BAM, that had it gotten some press or gone on tour through the country, many would have found it galvanizing for its theatrical values, few controversial for its political content. And it is not certain that a significant part of the audience associates the Shakespearean politics of Rome with the War in Iraq as Gener did. So much is going on onstage that it's easy to miss or identify that footage.

> Compellingly, *The Roman Tragedies* used 17 actors (48 participants in all, counting the crew) to stage declarations of war and public debates as global media events that unfolded in our living rooms. The dramatic-installation concept made so much sense that I, as a powerless spectator-citizen both in the world of theatre and in the world of the play, felt deeply implicated in the media's illusion of closeness and truthfulness, especially in relationship to the centers of so-called democratic government and corporate strength.
>
> *(Gener 2009)*

Gener describes a theatrical event that makes world events feel immediate in such a way that he felt his citizenship of the world more keenly and his habitual sense of powerlessness challenged. Still, it is not clear that this confrontation could imply any equivalency with specific events of the day. Similarly, a Dutch critic reports that, as he watched the same spectacle, "I now and then get a shock to be reminded of politicians such as Fortuyn, Melkert, Bos, Balkenende and Wilders," all controversial figures in the Dutch political landscape (Arian 2007). But for international audiences who wouldn't recognize Fortuyn, Wilders, et al. in the guise of Antony, Coriolanus, or Brutus, it is the universal meta-pattern that gets showcased. And again, I raise the question as to whether many Dutch audience members would take the Roman characters to represent Fortuyn and Wilders. As van Hove himself has said, "The need to make explicit connections to social issues is by definition inartistic" (Reyniers 2013).

Agnes Heller, whose book guided his thinking in this production, writes: "The worst historiography would be for Shakespeare to believe in one single interpretation of a fact as in something final" (Heller 2002: 30). Van Hove's a-historicism is of a kind that allows the audience members, in their individuality, to allow their imaginations to fly in multiple directions . . . or simply take the show on its own terms without associations. His statement, "I'm more interested in question marks than in exclamation points," essentially expresses what he wishes to communicate and his aim for audience reception (Reyniers 2013).

Considering how theoreticians have played fast and loose regarding what constitutes the "political,"[88] I felt it was crucial to understand what van Hove specifically means by it. His answer, "I use it in the way of the Greeks—it deals with society, what is important for the 'Polis'" (Willinger 2017a), remains problematic. Given van Hove's adherence to the many social writers who defend democracy and are so solicitous of the interests of the masses, it is curious that he has regularly eliminated all the proletarian characters and scenes from his history plays. There is literally no "polis" present in his performed image of history. The spotlight is on those at the top. It may be true that, as Randy Gener says above, the audience is cast in the role of the citizen, but the citizen's plight goes unexamined.

Van Hove insists with increasing frequency that *leadership* is the key political issue in today's world. The reasons for that emphasis may have a personal, inductive provenance. In line with his oft-repeated assertion that his shows are autobiographical documents, even a seemingly political production like *Roman Tragedies*, in a sense, gets boiled down to a meditation on what makes an effective leader. But is it, even more than that, a divided portrait of the leader of an arts organization?

> It's about people who grant that society is malleable, but who are compelled to arrive at a consensus with each other. Coriolanus is therefore far too surly. He's totally inflexible. And that's why he founders. At the opposite extreme is Octavius (who later becomes Emperor Augustus), here acted by a woman, Hadewych Minis. She heads the empire as though it was a big company. She focuses on business plans and has no friends. She has only coworkers who carry out her decisions. The buck stops with her, but that's not because I particularly favor her character over the others, although I do have a great deal of empathy for her. I head a company myself. I'm a manager myself. I know how decisions get brought to a successful conclusion.
>
> *(Arian 2007)*

Van Hove started using classics, whose characters are invariably royals, as a mechanism for exploring the position of the modern administrator at the top of the bureaucratic food chain as early as his 1988 production of Schiller's *Don Carlos*:

> In a breathtaking set (by Jan Versweyveld) full of hidden references to his empire, King Philip governs over his imperium like a lonely bureaucrat. In his empire over which the sun never sets, his only contact with reality is a little bell that sits on his desk, used to constantly set his trusted men to their tasks throughout his rebellious provinces.
>
> *(Vaes 1988)*

It is interesting that the bureaucratic head in this powerful image is depicted as isolated and detached from the realities of his realm.

Although van Hove is undeniably a highly effective artistic director, that assumption didn't always go unchallenged, particularly in his early years at Toneelgroep Amsterdam. Although Gerardjan Rijnders, former artistic director of Toneelgroep Amsterdam, had long let it be known he wanted to step down from his position, once he was replaced by van Hove, ambivalence reigned throughout the company, keeping a low-grade feeling of instability simmering. The new leader had a dual role as Artistic Director of the Holland Festival,[89] took other international directing assignments, and had been immersed in directing the Wagner *Ring Cycle* in Antwerp, which only exacerbated the situation, as did an accusation that his management style was cold, remote, and uncaring (Kagie 2003). The fact that not all his shows got good press didn't help either. In 2003, three years after assuming his administrative role in Toneelgroep Amsterdam, there was a revolt by a coterie of actors; accusations flew; a series of meetings, official and clandestine, proliferated. Three mainstays of the company, Pierre Bokma, Lineke Rijxman, and Hans Kesting, walked out.[90] The extended brouhaha became a major media event. The subtitle to one article averred that, "Clearly providing leadership is not his strongest suit" (Takken 2003b). The event took on truly Shakespearean proportions. This was the moment of van Hove's greatest emergency, although there have been other lesser ones. While he projects confidence in his leadership abilities and enjoys the role, he has inevitably been forced to take stock of his style and choices.

The artist's personal identification is much more persuasive as a motive force for the turbulent stage dynamics depicted in the history plays than any particular political stance relating to current events. The trials and tribulations of leaders is a highly compelling theme for van Hove. In one breath, he avows his fascination and identification with Steve Jobs and equally with the character of Caligula in Camus's play—because the two of them, wildly different as they are, yet both like him, must grapple with how to be good leaders (Sels 2016a). Elites are elites, whether they be government officials, heads of artistic institutions or private enterprises. When under siege during the 2003 uprising at TGA, van Hove defended his policies using a commercial analogy, "If Coca-Cola is in crisis, that's no reason to change the taste of the drink either" (Kagie 2003).

His production grouping *Julius Caesar* with two other "Roman" Shakespeare plays is a different animal than, for example, Oskar Eustis' highly controversial *Julius Caesar* in New York's Central Park in the summer of 2017, where Caesar was unmistakably portrayed as Donald Trump. The interpretation of the public assassination of Caesar/Trump was to show how political violence only leads to escalating chaos. Eustis claims that this idea is borne out by the plot, but, if so, was generally misinterpreted by the wider public as a call to assassinate the president. The fall-out was intense, leading to sponsors withdrawing support, stealth protesters stopping performances cold, and death threats going out to producers of Shakespeare theatres across the nation. The way this production became an instant media event and elicited such violent responses reveals its political bona fides. It's not necessarily a *better* approach; indeed, it is a highly literal one, meant to be unambiguous; also one presumably legible to a mass audience. Strategically it could prove disastrous. It may even have precipitated an unintended backlash that harms progressivism, not to mention funding for theatre. But it is a more *engaged* approach and one that makes theatre relevant to the wider society. It's an approach that van Hove would be loath to take. As Johan Thielemans says in his article in this volume, "With [van Hove] a tyrant like Richard III won't be found sporting a Hitler moustache" (p.299).

And that goes for other subjects drawn from history. For his stage rendition of *Ludwig II*, mad king of Bavaria, van Hove pushes verisimilitude away, warning the audience not to expect a period recreation: "We're not making historical theatre with the perfect glasses in the perfect décor and all the historically correct costumes. Our *Ludwig II* is an existential drama, not an historical drama" (Janssen 2011). There is candor in that statement, and it was a highly successful, if apolitical production.

As regards how he sees another history play he directed, his production of Marlowe's *Edward II*:

> For the production of *Edward II* at the Schaubühne we were influenced by Giorgio Agamben and his reflections on "the state of exception." I thought of the camp at Guantànamo where extreme torture was considered normal by the American government, a form of barbarism that they'd never have accepted from any other nation in the world. So boom, our *Edward II* takes place in a prison. . . . Yes [the author of the article

goes on to say], the omnipresence of finance in our lives and on our minds, cupidity vaunted as a universal value, led him to take on *The Miser*.

(Perrier 2012: 76–79)

There is a chance that a prescient audience member might link van Hove's production to the contemporary public figures and events he says served as jumping off points for him—Donald Rumsfeld, his colleagues, and the Guantànamo Bay detention camp. But, apart from the prison setting van Hove has added to the Elizabethan history play, there is nothing explicitly in the production that evokes them. The prisoners aren't portrayed as Muslims or prisoners of war. Their costumes do not evoke those in Guantànamo. Nor are any in solitary confinement. If Obama or Guantànamo weren't referenced in production notes or interviews there is little likelihood that an audience member would associate that extrinsic narrative as the lens through which to view this production. *Othello* however, is an exception: in it, van Hove clearly depicts the political leader as a Colin Powell figure, and emphasizes the racist attacks to which he could be subjected, thus giving a famous love tragedy the resonance of present-day issues.

In his production of *The Miser*, which van Hove refers to above as a commentary on cupidity—implying that the audience will be invited to consider the world of high finance—the central character's purported stinginess is subverted by showing the way his children have been spoiled materially. The lack in the house is a want of love and connection, not cash. This certainly illustrates Bauman and Barber's points about the pitfalls of rampant materialism, which are critical issues to dramatize, but that hasn't yet made it about the egregiously disproportionate distribution of wealth in twenty-first century capitalism that is so central to public discourse. So a subject leads van Hove to direct a script, which by the end of the process, may no longer be a central theme or any part of the ultimate production; this is just such a case.

Van Hove recounts being criticized for putting on his "Marriage Cycle" at time when Pim Fortuyn had just been assassinated:

> They found it scandalous that I was doing that while two people in the Netherlands were lying dead on the streets, so to speak. 'In Berlin they're organizing an evening around Theo van Gogh, and what are you doing?' I told them: At this particular moment I think Amsterdam needs something different, more warmth. I find those events incredibly important, but I don't know what to do with the subject on stage *right now*.

(Reyniers 2013)

When van Hove himself, in spite of that, asserts some connection between real life figures in his show and events, it should be taken with a grain of salt.[91] For example, van Hove considers his most recent billing of Shakespeare history plays, *Kings of War*, and explains that it:

> will be about leadership. These are themes we still have to deal with. You see it with Obama. He started so promisingly, but now even the most Democratic figures say they are disappointed. What happened? What kind of leaders do we want? Shakespeare wrote about all these things.

(Sels 2016a)

The fact that Obama is nowhere to be found in *Kings of War* does not make it a lesser show, only that a dubious expectation of topicality is being raised.

Another frequent van Hove technique for referencing the political sphere is the insertion of video montages of various historical cataclysms into live productions such as *Teorema* and *Children of the Sun*. The sudden shift from one medium to another and the vividness of the imagery showing social turmoil, in and of themselves, have visceral impact. But the subject matter is painted with the broadest of brushstrokes and often bewilderingly so, so that what we are meant to construe from these segments is open to conjecture. As scholar Simon Hageman observes:

> Whether these images are susceptible to interpretation as commentaries on the action, as in [Erwin] Piscator's approach, or whether they correspond more closely to the characters' interior world, the spectator is invited to an associative montage between what is said and seen onstage and what passes by on the screen. That is unless his attention isn't distracted from the play's dramatic action where, in the cases of the broadcasting of video clips and animated films, certain images seem to resist interpretation and rather advance their own signification.
>
> *(Hageman 2016: 87)*

Images of totalitarianism and disaster are presented without attempting to discriminate between various types of tyranny or even between natural and political cataclysms. They are essentially conglomerate images of a world that is exploding, precarity tipping over into chaos: people on the move in patterns of irrational emergency, and hordes at the mercy of leaders and events out of their own control—enduring what Butler and Bauman call "bare life," and "life in suspended zones" (Butler 2004: 67). Judith Butler has plaintively reminded us that we turn away from marginalized masses of people at the expense of our own humanity: "The question that preoccupies me in the light of recent global violence is, Who counts as human? Whose lives count as lives? And finally, *What makes for a grievable life?*" (Ibid.: 20) While van Hove's video images of mass tumult impress, tapping into the anxieties of precariousness, they do not bring us closer to valorizing the lives of those depicted. The persons within the moving images of "superfluous masses of people forced to move and live in 'permanently temporary' facilities," existing in "the unfathomable space of flows," remain unidentified, unindividuated, remote, and alien (Bauman 2007: 45, 48). From a dramatic point of view, they aren't grievable. Rather, they are a simulacrum of the seething wave of horror engulfing remote parts of the globe, a veritable tsunami that the West would much prefer to be indemnified against; it could be argued that they are the nightmare image of the world out there that exists or which could invade, as within the subjectivity of the characters in *Teorema* and *Children of the Sun*. As they are mediatized in these productions, one perception might be that the masses are diminished and distanced precisely since they come into the lives of Westerners first as video images. As Bauman says, "distant misery and distant cruelty" go hand in hand (2003: 96).

Luk Van den Dries tries to define van Hove's way of integrating social issues into the domestic sphere while simultaneously skirting the "political," in his comparison of two of van Hove's middle-period productions, Edward Bond's *Saved* and O'Neill's *Desire Under the Elms*:

> It is also and above all in their theatrical approach that the two plays share common ground. In both cases the dramaturgy is not based on any historical-sociological foundation for the dramatic action (strict Protestantism in *Desire*, social decline in *Saved*). There is therefore no portrait of an historical period, but in the theatricalizing process, a search is pursued for emotional constants through which the conflicts retain relevance for our own epoch. This is expressed as much in the use of language and costuming as the scenic design.
>
> *(Van den Dries 1993: 44–46)*

The "theatricalizing process" Van den Dries alludes to is text that partially strips away historical particularity, but also the foregrounding of "emotional constants" that universalize the production, and presumably open the way for a contemporary connection to be made. When asked to identify political themes in his recent production of *The Damned*, based on the Visconti film of the historical chronicle of the Krupp family (prominent armament manufacturers for the Third Reich), van Hove responded: "For me, Visconti hasn't made a film about Nazism, but the potential overturning of values in all society. He shows how the world can become barbarous in the name of basic economic and financial interests." He goes on to recount the trajectory of the play's anti-hero, the CEO of the firm, summarizing:

> He will have learned nothing from existence, one in which, capable of every excess under the sun, he winds up with only his violence for all the world to see. A jihadist? A militant of the extreme right? *The Damned*, which is set in the years 1933–1934, for me contains a troubling topicality here in Europe where everything might be overturned from one day to the next.
>
> *(Pascaud 2016b)*

In this telling analysis of his own work, van Hove masks the particular time and place explicitly depicted in his show (Nazi Germany), as well as the particular political movement (Nazism), to refocus the source text on universal values that are lost whenever material interests come to dominate (see Figure 1.16). This essentially places all emphasis on the meta-historical pattern of societies in dislocation. Such universal social issues and patterns provide the audience with the

FIGURE 1.16 *The Damned*

© Jan Versweyveld

threads to connect to their own time and context. But is an unprejudiced audience likely to tease out the interpretations van Hove extrapolates from a show that has brownshirts and SS men overrunning the stage and a narrative in which Jews are exterminated? It seems to me to be another case where his assertions in interviews clash with implanted elements of the show. But it is noteworthy that he wishes it to be possible that audience members might connect the character of the CEO with that of a contemporary jihadist or right-winger. Still, the choice remains with the spectator.

One British critic at Avignon took the bait, proclaiming van Hove to have been "uncannily prescient" in choosing this play, because it "resonates now" with the Trump election, with "ideologically driven terror," and Brexit (Todd 2016). In my view, this has connected a dubious latency in the production to an associative and arbitrary subjectivity. The historical and socio-political indeterminacy of the theatrical text leaves the field free for the viewer to see any connections with issues past or present—or none at all. This viewer earnestly *wants* the show to be that topical, but there is nothing in the production itself to ineluctably lead to that conclusion.

Patrice Chéreau had his "War of Images." The young van Hove had to wage his own little "War of Images" with critics such as Wim van Gansbeke. Being branded an "aesthete" or "formalist" for experimenting according to his interests put him on the defensive. "For me it was totally untrue. I just didn't want them to put me into a box" (Willinger 2017a). He admitted that van Gansbeke was "tough on them"—that is, the members of AKT, van Hove and Versweyveld—and preferred his contemporary Luk Perceval to whom van Hove was forever being compared and, yet, was opposed to new trends in stage lighting and video that he and Versweyveld were introducing (Laveyne 2010). But van Hove also dismissed the controversy as a dead letter issue whose importance passed with the end of the 1980s. Yet, it is a source of consternation he can still be heard grappling with in 2010, following his extremely formalist experiment *The Antonioni Project*, which puts it two years after the death of Wim van Gansbeke: "Now I don't think I'm an aesthete at all. To me it's beside the point how beautiful something looks. An image only starts to be beautiful on account of the emotional charge underlying it."[92]

An emotional charge, it need hardly be pointed out, isn't a political statement. But let us recall, it was exactly the emotional charge that van Gansbeke found missing, sacrificed to visual imagery in the 1983 show *Like in the War*. Right up until 1992, when van Hove found a new approach with *Desire Under the Elms*, his and Versweyveld's search for a visual style was their primary concern, the image explorations linked with such abstract, opaque texts as Marguerite Duras' *Agatha* and the theatre collage *Wonders of Humanity*. Certain critics in the 1980s felt called upon to ardently defend van Hove's eschewal of narrative clarity, as for example:

> Although the average theatregoer still swears by 'a story,' text theatre, according to van Hove, is definitively a thing of the past. His Concept is an associative sort of theatre through which the audience creates their own 'stories.' It isn't easy, but it can't leave you unaffected.
>
> *(De Win 1985)*

Van Hove was later completely converted to the very text theatre he had denigrated as "a thing of the past." But when periodically drawn back like a moth (or bungee jumper) to a highly visual, anti-narrative kind of theatre with *Massacre at Paris* in 2000, *Con Amore* in 2002, and *The Antonioni Project*, critics tended to make the same complaints of narrative incoherence, opacity, and emotional detachment. Even in 2012, regarding his emotionally satisfying—but highly imagistic and narratively iconoclastic—adaptation of Bergman's *Persona*, we hear him at pains to differentiate his artistic brand from more formalistic peers:

> We're not trying to impose a style, like Bob Wilson, Peter Sellars, or Christoph Marthaler, who put on purely visual or purely conceptual shows, but rather to go to the extreme limit with a text, with all the means at our disposal, and without ever illustrating the text or situating it in a realistic world.
>
> *(Perrier January 2012)*

The above statement is one that most nearly approaches an accurate manifesto of van Hove and Versweyveld's essential aesthetic vision. It invokes the triad between visuality, primacy of text, and a refusal of Zolaesque realism.

A show for which he was lambasted for over-aestheticizing, Marlowe's *Massacre at Paris*, may actually have been a serious commentary on power politics. But the reviewers missed it at the time, blinded by the elaborate aesthetic surface. One critic six years after the show's premiere retrospectively retracted his own dismissal of the production. He admits to having overlooked or underestimated the play's theme of butchery in the Counter-Reformation in the name of religion:

> By his own admission van Hove 'isn't a director who's going to storm the barricades with a clenched fist.' He is furthermore someone who, as in *The Roman Tragedies*, addresses political matters coolly. Still, with the first production as artistic director of Toneelgroep Amsterdam six years ago he issued a stern warning against religious struggles and civil wars. It perhaps came in too pretty a package which caused attention to be diverted, but Marlowe's *The Massacre at Paris* in Hafid Bouazza's adaptation didn't get the appreciation it deserved. Maybe it arrived too early. For in 2001 [one year later] a whole slew of civil wars, terrorist attacks, and political assassinations with religious pretexts began that before were still a glimmer on the horizon.
>
> *(Arian 2007)*

It may be that much of the hype the play received about its intricate design made it impossible for critics at the time to separate out the action of the play with its endless, protracted butchery in the name of opposing religious sects. This critic, again, sees topicality in a far-off historical chapter, rendered highly imagistically in a style that tends to universalize and distance. Images and politics can merge, seems to be the critic's point.

As noted earlier, and at his most candid, van Hove has articulated a key predilection he feels for the *subversive* over the *political*, in the precise way in which he defines both. One might translate subversive as rebellious or determinedly perverse, a tendency that he confessed to without reserve in his earliest interviews. It governed his attitudes and choices then and may never have entirely dissipated. As an adolescent, rebelliousness had a political tint, but when he started directing, that compulsion for the subversive and provocative found its target in the audience. By depriving them of the easily accessible narrative forms they were used to and unleashing the sex and violence of his "sick mind," he sought to awaken the audience. But in recent years, notably after the 2001 US terrorist attacks, he has drifted toward interest in—what he terms—"the sociological," or even more broadly—the ethical. As one journalist would have it, van Hove has set out on "an embarkation into current events, a diffuse sociology of the everyday" (Perrier January 2012). Benjamin Barber's thoughts on subversion and the implicitly political are apropos:

> In fact, opposition has been art's familiar posture throughout the modern era. Molière took on orthodox clericalism in his clerically enshrouded France and although his plays were paradigms of classical comedy, they were sufficiently subversive of the established church to be banned by the monarchy. Brecht mocked capitalist ideology, Ibsen undermined Victorianism, and George Bernard Shaw took on bourgeois democracy and its complacent imperialism with a wily wit. Such opposition could be explicitly political and didactic—think Tony Kushner—but more often the political dimension has been implicit.
>
> *(Barber Spring/Summer 2011)*

How do opposition and subversion function in van Hove's shows? To take a few examples he has cited, when the Parondi family in *Rocco and His Brothers* migrates from the heartland of Italy to the big city, van Hove may claim, as he does, that his theatre is concerned with the issue of immigration. Similarly, the self-involved sybarites in *The Antonioni Project* complain of feeling dislocated. And again, van Hove asserts that this illustrates how they are victims of modern precarity. In either case, one hears the voice of the artistic director with moral and ethical responsibilities speak of social ills which justifies, and I think distorts, the work of the director, who happens to be himself; the latter attracted to those texts because . . . well, just because. The often transgressive relationships between the characters fascinate him. The artistic challenges, including the opportunities for vibrant image life, draw him too. *Rocco and His Brothers* is much more to do with male image and bonding than migration. And *The Antonioni Project*, much like the original films upon which it is based, is saturated by existential anomy, rather than being about how the technological revolution is leaving human values behind. The centrifugal pressures of van Hove's dual roles open a gap between his discourse and practice.

In 2008, van Hove was invited to give the Machiavelli Lecture, an annual event in which a public figure speaks about some subject of general social interest. He uncharacteristically came out with a detailed written public polemic on the role of the artist in society, and the place of politics in theatrical art, and it's as good a window into his thinking on the subject as any other. A summary of the main points of this lengthy address reads as follows:

1) Just as Artaud made the analogy between the theatre and the plague, here van Hove analogizes theatre as a wild beast that may seem tame and domesticated, but which unpredictably attacks and devours:

    > There is 'a persistent tendency' in the Netherlands to imagine that political art will lead to a better society. . . . Politics has to concern itself with order, and artists have to concern themselves with chaos. Politicians nibble away at the dividing line between chaos and order. . . . Art gets put into a cage, like a wild animal that needs to be tamed. But art follows its own nature and its own laws, like a wild beast that can't be tamed. Art that matters is wild like a tiger. When I go to a theatre I want to become immersed in chaos. The artist needs to break free from reality.
    >
    > *(De Volkskrant 2008)*

Society likes to keep art around, but is shocked when it acts like the wild beast it is. Theatre ought to be immune to attack from politicians but it, the theatre, reserves the right to criticize both politicians and the citizenry, so long as it stays within certain bounds. Otherwise society runs the risk of acting as a censor.

2) The government (The Dutch government at any rate), on the one hand prefers to stay outside of the affairs of the arts, but funds them, even guaranteeing their survival. The government recognizes the value of the arts so long as they can be associated with other more "useful" agencies such as education. Why don't the arts naturally have an autonomous right to the government's support? Government claims to wish to enter into social discussions with the arts, but actually has no intention of doing so—seeing it on the one hand as a matter of box office income, and on the other, an appendage to education. The discussion never materializes.

3) Art is autonomous, and neither digests nor discusses the political world in the same way or as effectively as the media, journalism, and so on. The proper grist for art's mill is the human soul, not political issues.

4) Art is both analogous to dreams and to wild animals; it plumbs the depths of the human soul and wallows in its darkness. Art is society's most acute spectator/interpreter, but does not reflect the image in the mirror. It peeks, rather, at the dark recesses lurking behind the mirror, and reserves the right to utterly smash it.

5) Artists have an obligation to engage with the social issues of their time, and absorb them as themes into the artwork.

In the first, third, and fourth points, I hear Artaud speaking through van Hove using wild, intuitive images. The fifth sounds like Brecht. The first and third points seem to be contradicting the fifth—the first two refusing politics as a subject for the arts where as they most definitely are natural grist for journalism—and next asserting art's solemn responsibility to make social issues its subject. The paradox, as stated, mirrors that which haunts van Hove's art and his related rhetoric. I would say that the first and third points are enunciated by van Hove, the artist, who identifies with the wild animal, ready to bite and bent on unleashing "chaos," but the fifth point is uttered by the artistic director, immured in responsibility and his own social role. The two roles are in perpetual dialogue and debate.

In his Machiavelli Lecture, where he came close to condemning the far right (but stopped short of doing so), he referenced Harold Pinter, who in his last years spoke out on social issues such as opposition to the war in Iraq and other Bush and Blair Administration policies. It will be remembered, however, that his most remarkable and durable plays—*The Homecoming*, *The Birthday Party*, *No Man's Land*, *Old Times*, and so on—weren't essentially political, but could easily be thought of as subversive. The British avant-garde playwright became the exemplar of the artist who finally takes a stand and devil take the hindmost. Like van Hove, Pinter's political life continued on outside his artistic work. Another aspect is that an artistic director could risk jeopardizing his theatre's stability with rash, offensive remarks; recall also that van Hove the artist eschews the viewpoint that it is theatre's place to take incontrovertible stands. However, ever-intensifying circumstances may not allow him to stay on the sidelines. The middle ground is disappearing. The spotlight is on him, and Richard Schechner speaks for many when expressing dissatisfaction with a generation of theatre-makers who eschew politically radical theatre: "Many of these [contemporary] artists are on the left personally, but in their artistic practice, in terms of venues, audiences, and effects on the political world, this left is apolitical, a style left rather than a worker's left" (Schechner 2015: 27).

But is an artist such as van Hove really obligated to bend his theatre to political ends? Flemish theatre critic Fred Six writing, in 1993, what was up to that point the most thorough, thoughtful, and sympathetic early history of van Hove's work, introduced a fresh element to the discussion:

> I find that we must open ourselves entirely to the mystery of the text. No cynicism, therefore, as regards the text, but collision with its inscrutable enigmas; the business mustn't be reduced to things we know or are capable of grasping.
>
> *(Six 1993)*

And van Hove has said virtually the same thing, articulating a position I believe to be totally defensible, if only he would stick to it: "I don't believe in a theatre where what is there is all there is. Theatre is precisely the context in which you attempt to express what cannot be expressed. . . . That's why it is so very hermetic" (Penning 1985). He situates himself in a line with his fellow countryman, Maurice Maeterlinck, in wishing to express the deepest mysteries of life onstage.[93] From *Rumors* in 1981 to *The Things That Pass* in 2016, much of his strongest work has invited the numinous into its precincts.

I would conclude that van Hove uses politics the way he uses love, as a subject for theatrical image-making after all. He turns subject matter to dream images with all the distortion and underlying reality that that implies. He reserves the right to problematize mystery, and cannot be forced into analytical clarity. This doesn't make him what he would term an aesthete, as these are not pictures devoid of content or relations of pure form, as certain shows by Robert Wilson or Richard Foreman have tended to be. In my opinion, there would be nothing wrong with it if they were, but certain forces, which he is sensitive to, condemn pure form.

Among the images he creates, van Hove arrays before us all the roles in the political process— the leaders, the toadies, media personnel, the masses, the leaders' spouses—including their explosive interactions, and how society is swept along by broad, roiling waves of historical events. His shows give instance to discussions and debates, but he himself, the *auteur* who has released all this energy, is neither presenting a Brechtian dialectic, nor is he taking sides, whether through the elements that comprise the show or when commenting on his work. Despite his understandable aim to clearly state his positions in the press and to show himself to be an articulate spokesman for culture, for his theatre, and explicator of his own productions, he also reserves the right and necessity for the shows themselves to defy reason and discursive explanations altogether. But whenever he says something to that effect, he is seen to be on shaky ground in an age where "social justice" is prime currency in intellectual and cultural circles. So he then retreats from that position.

I think he is intuitively at pains to expound a notion that is the foundation of Susanne Langer and Bernard Beckerman's rigorously worked out theories: that the arts, including theatre, don't work the same way journalism, sociological or philosophical texts work, that what they present to their audience is a different order of phenomenon. In contrast, they are profoundly non-discursive and produce expressive content that cannot, must not, be reduced to logocentric statements that are perforce squeezed out of the show on a false premise. As the playwright Ionesco said:

> Drama is not the idiom for ideas. When it tries to become a vehicle for ideologies, all it can do is vulgarize them. It dangerously oversimplifies. It makes them too elementary and depreciates them. It is 'naïve,' but in the bad sense. All ideological drama runs the risk of

being parochial. . . . A work of art cannot have the same function as an ideology, for if it did it would *be* an ideology, it would no longer be a work of art, that is to say an autonomous creation, an independent universe with its own life and its own laws.

(Ionesco 1964: 24–25, 80)

Or as Patrice Pavis expresses it:

> no audience wants to be lectured at. Brechtian epic theatre, with its sharp edge, is supposed to touch the audience at the heart of its interests, to highlight contradictions and nail down the gestus of the characters. But for fear of being too direct or too painful, the neo-director softens the dramaturgical analysis, staying in the realm of the general or the ambiguous. There are hardly any 'Brechtian' directors left, nor much overtly political theatre. . . . As we understand it today, mise en scène need not be clear, readable or self-explanatory. Its role is not to mediate transmitter and receiver, author and audience, to 'smooth things out.' Instead of simplifying and explicating, it remains deliberately opaque. After the clarity of Brechtianism, it instead favours ambiguity and vagueness. This has been apparent in very unorthodox and rather 'aestheticising' (as one would say during the militant post-'68 years) productions.

(Pavis 2010: 397–398)

This, despite the fact that van Hove, public figure that he is, participates in the interviews that help to propagate the misunderstanding. Like many artists, he seeks inspiration from non-theatrical works and seems to feel that those non-fictional ideas give his productions greater substance and body; it seems they also give him a motive force with which to get started on a given work. But the work of art, despite the fact that it may be nourished by philosophy, psychology, sociology, or history, is itself none of those things, and despite the artist and his commentators' earnest intentions to make it susceptible to thorough explanation, remains—in director Daniel Mesguich's term—stubbornly "unsummarizable," he sees it as a series of experiences that the spectator negotiates (Delgado and Rebellato 2010: 18).

What inheres within the work, in Langer's term, is "significant form," emotional and sensory life captured symbolically, which resists decoding in the same fashion.[94] In the theatre, an irreducible image or set of images may yet lead to a profound experience. At times, lurking among van Hove's many public statements, we may glean a heart-felt plea for his shows to be allowed downright incoherence. Then, through a passage of chaos, can his actual role plainly emerge: a prophet signaling wildly at us through the flames. The shows seem to be making an impression on critics and audiences alike as socially subversive; as Artaud himself was profoundly subversive in rejecting any specific political role for the theatremaker whatsoever. Van Hove's chief means remains the striking theatrical images, as they always have. He practices, in Maaike Bleeker's term, a certain "ethics of vision" (Bleeker 2008: 44). This process by which even implicitly political art may be instrumental against social ills is eloquently captured by Benjamin Barber:

> Our first impulse when we think about art is to think about something oppositional, something subversive to power, to the established order, to conventional paradigms. Something that can exhilarate and discomfit us, something other than a perfect mirror of the society in which art finds itself. Radical or conservative, art confronts society, even

(particularly when) society is democratic. If we understand art as a way of seeing and hearing through the imagination that allows us to see and hear anew, then we know that whatever its relationship to the state and society in which it finds itself, it is going to rest less than comfortably under their control.

(Barber 2011)

Language and its double

The diction in the shows van Hove directs in Dutch makes only subliminal impact on English speakers. They are relieved to have the super-title translations at their disposal and wouldn't consider themselves competent judges of the nuances of the verbal utterances they were hearing. All they require is to be able to understand the meaning of the words being said. And yet, the variants of speech sounds make a huge difference to the texture and emotional life of the theatre-going experience of his Dutch-language productions. Van Hove was born in Flanders, where Dutch is an official language, but in many homes and small communities, multiple local Flemish dialects dating back to the Middle Ages and beyond are the lingua franca. These dialects, while being part of the same general language, contain variants of grammar, vocabulary, syntax, and especially radically different pronunciations. For general usage, a sanitized and standardized form of Dutch called "*Algemeen Nederlands*" (A.N.) is resorted to but, even so, Flemish-sounding official Dutch is different, especially in certain speech sounds like "the hard [g]," compared to the Dutch-sounding dialects to the north. These differences are accidents of history.

In a show like *Desire Under the Elms*, van Hove and his Flemish adaptor Arne Sierens played with the peasant characters speaking Flemish-sounding variants, which added to the pleasure of the experience for some, myself included. Some Belgian critics claimed to be perplexed by, or scornful of, these attempts, particularly as some of the Dutch actors in the show apparently weren't especially skilled at reproducing convincing Flemish dialect. *Splendid's*, like *Desire Under the Elms*, is an adaptation done by Arne Sierens, and it is hard to resist the impression—from the point of view of diction, accents, and language—that they were among the most interesting work in van Hove's career. It may be that "proper" diction occasionally suffers, but the earthy Flemish flavor contributes to liberating a primal voice issuing from an elemental core. The depiction of small-time criminals as one example and Flemish farmers as the other was all the more plausible. And the performers drew startlingly close to the Artaudian ideal of a performer who becomes spiritually immolated during the performance, with which that earthy Flemish dialect sound is integrally involved.

However, since assuming control over Toneelgroep Amsterdam in Holland's cultural capital, even though the occasional Flemish actor is employed there, van Hove has perforce hewed to extremely Dutch-sounding official Dutch—the rough equivalent of the King's English that was formerly spoken at the RSC.[95] The dialogue at TGA is generally clearly spoken, but can lack much character or spice in itself. Clarity triumphs over grit, except in a heavily Artaud-influenced show like *Massacre at Paris* (van Hove's very first with TGA) where the actors ventured more vocal experimentation. In most recent productions, as van Hove has targeted an ever more general audience, the spoken language has become more homogenized.

From his early declaration that "text" was passé to arriving at the point of conversion when he trumpeted that he was a "text director," with the statement, "the theatre world needs to be purified using great texts" (Vaes 1988), van Hove showed himself to be part of a mounting trend in Europe toward a "new faithfulness to the authorial text" (Bradby and Williams 1988: 214),

But with this transformation, van Hove not only meant that he interprets other writers' texts, but that he loves language for its own sake and is interested in mining it for its intrinsic value. Thus he gravitates toward playwrights who indulge in extremely long monologues, notably O'Neill, Charles Mee, Schiller, Büchner (at least the Büchner of *Danton's Death*), Genet, Camus, Ayn Rand, and Molière. While one might think that modern audiences have less tolerance for both long rhetorical passages and long evenings in the theatre, van Hove, again going against the grain, gravitates toward both. And the audiences seem not to mind.

But there is also a non-verbal aspect that surfaces with regularity. Sounding like Artaud himself, van Hove declares "The theatre has a vital twin function: it's a feast of the irrational and a place to pose questions without trepidation or reservation" (Bots 2005). He also connects his affinity with the irrational to performance art, especially Marina Abramowic's work. Whether we see this strong tropism as Artaudian or post-dramatic, van Hove "production texts" typically include lengthy inserts of non-verbal action, which often have a ritualistic facet. Despite many statements of fidelity to text, normal speech and dialogue can be put on a far-back burner. Hans-Thies Lehmann expounds on non-Aristotelian forms of the type that van Hove, in many cases, foregrounds:

> The aesthetic function in any kind of *ceremony*, the aesthetically 'isolating' moment inherent to all *festivity*. It is evident that there is always a dimension of the ceremonial in the practice of theatre. It is inherent to theatre as a social event—derived from its religious and cultic roots that mostly disappeared from consciousness. Postdramatic theatre, however, liberates the formal, ostentatious moment of ceremony from its sole function of enhancing attention and valorized it *for its own sake*, as an aesthetic quality detached from all religious and cultic reference. Post-dramatic theatre is the replacement of dramatic action with ceremony, with which dramatic-cultic action was once, in its beginnings inseparably united.
>
> *(Lehmann 2006: 69)*

Dutch critic Hana Bobkova describes this aspect of van Hove's best work as: "a language that holds its tongue more than it speaks. And more than that: a language of the two glued together, crawling to each other and finally—after a silence, no talking and inexpressiveness—an impotent scream" (Bobkova 1992).

We see examples of entire shows that function ceremonially to the detriment of normal dramatic narrative, such as *Splendid's*. But in his preponderantly linear-sequential text-based shows too, such as *The Miser* or *The Taming of the Shrew*, the ceremonial element may dominate the course of extended segments. These could include choreographed or very aleatory dance; it could be long passages of sexual interaction without words; it could be a segment of extended physical violence; or it could simply be a charged silence, as in *The Damned*, where four characters sit at a table in silence for many moments, eating with a tension so thick it could be cut with a knife. These segments are very seldom indicated by the authors in stage directions and so represent taking a major directorial liberty, one generally away from naturalism but toward some inner truth and the quest for immediate-feeling theatrical presence. In this sense, van Hove is an exponent of live theatre's *many* available languages and codes.

Signatures and tics

If one had attended enough Peter Brook productions over the course of decades, one would have become inured to seeing gigantic Persian carpets hanging upstage by way of cycloramas.

They were colorful, tasteful, and minimal. They exuded a suggestion of the East, and of the Gurdjieffian brand of spirituality that was secreted throughout all of Brook's productions. In Richard Foreman's productions, from the mid-1970s onward, there were the famous series of horizontal wires strung across the proscenium, along with many other artifacts such as the blinding lights shone in the audience's eyes, and the mellow voice of the omniscient narrator insinuating itself through the loudspeakers. These are just some examples of directorial signatures. In the above two cases, they are so ubiquitous and compulsive they might even be called tics. And they are not necessarily a bad thing. Camille Paglia insists that they are a sign that art is before us: "Fixation is at the heart of art, fixation as stasis and fixation as obsession" (Paglia 1991a: 29).

Despite the multiplicity of styles that have diverted van Hove's interests, some curious scenic items recur repeatedly including three fetish objects: pianos, TV monitors, and showers. Pianos pop up in *Carmen*, *The Three Sisters*, *Hedda Gabler*, *The Taming of the Shrew*, *Ludwig*, and the very recent Louis Couperus adaptation of the novel *The Hidden Force* (*De Stille Kracht*), where a grand piano emblemizes all Western culture in a colonial context. Grand pianos, uprights, and spinets all make appearances. In a few cases, they are indicated in the stage directions of the original script. Other times, they are added by van Hove and make integral sense to the play's action. In still others, they are dumped onstage . . . just because. But they seem to embody the creative impulse, regardless of the dramatic situation.

In countless productions, including *Teorema*, *Kings of War*, *Cries and Whispers*, and *Mourning Becomes Electra*, apart from the video monitors that are used as mixed media, there are additional functional monitors and laptops woven into the characters' stage lives conjuring what Romain Piana has called, "a virtualization of the space" (Piana 2016: 166). They tend to stay turned on as background noise and image beneath the stage action, ignored or watched as the case may be. No one thinks to turn them off. They are as casually and universally accepted in the image of today's world van Hove is projecting as a heartbeat. Indeed, their emissions are often used to mark the changing tempo for the entire production. In the theatres of antiquity, a holy shrine would be placed front and center. The ubiquity of monitors and laptops on van Hove's stages suggests that in the modern world, the role of sanctified repository for contemporary civilization's pulse has been transferred to the electrified screen.

Stark bare-boned, open showers with real running water, too, may be seen in a large number of van Hove productions: *Like in the War*, *Othello*, *Con Amore*, *Rocco and His Brothers*, and *Edward II*. If one were to add in related tropes of water, including baths, water falls, pools, monsoons, real and imaginary, and so on, the list would be expanded to include *A Streetcar Named Desire*, *Ludwig*, *Persona*, *The Antonioni Project*, *The Hidden Force*, and *Obsession*. Of course, just having water or any other natural element, such as fire and sand onstage (which he also has had at times) is sensational in and of itself. The naturalistic convention teaches us that water onstage should generally be imaginary. It is an aleatory, seemingly uncontrollable element that is also a technical challenge to introduce. It is therefore a treat when it's real, as in all these van Hove shows where naturalism is paradoxically eschewed.

In a van Hove show, a shower or bath has an erotic dimension as well. In every case where it's used, there is a fantasy suggestion of possible illicit relations, more often the queer trope of sweaty gym-exercised bodies reveling in the sensual rush of water on the upturned face. But occasionally, women find themselves under the spigots as well—or splashing in tubs (cf. *Streetcar* and *Obsession*). Water also has an oneiric power, as used in *Ludwig* and *Persona*, where its presence is the keynote for magic realist and surreal ambiences. Water unleashes the imagination and the unconscious mind as it does with the paint that gets splattered in *Cries and Whispers*, the blood that comes showering down (a different kind of shower) in *View From the Bridge*, and the white ooze that engulfs the stage floor in *Lazarus*; each incarnates a different kind of invasion from deep within the psychic lives of the plays' characters.

In certain aspects of performing too, vocal and physical tendencies can morph into personal tics. There is no question that van Hove has always wanted his shows to work with extremities, including extremities of emotional expression. And without the rehearsal language and methods of Stanislavsky-based acting in his tool-kit, he initially prompted the actors in his charge to push and push further again, which has often led to a *cul de sac* of unremitting yelling. As remarked above, yelling, at times effective and at others arbitrary, has often become a tic of his productions.

Another sign for extreme emotions is the van Hove version of stage combat, generally taking the form of a shower of open-handed stage slaps incontinently raining down on a character's head as he shields himself from actual pain. This overused technique is another default stand-in for extreme passion to be used at a moment of crisis in conflictual scenes. The slap-fest too sometimes falls flat when it is unwarranted emotionally.[96] In any case, it has become the theatre critic's mantra that van Hove indulges every opportunity for sex and violence. There is a kernel of truth in this supposition. A fascination with random cruelty and violence led him to direct David Storey's one-act play *Saved* about a bunch of hoods who kill an infant in a baby carriage. In its time when it first opened in England and then America in 1965, it was initially censored and gained notoriety for crossing an unprecedented line into a brand of gratuitous violence. The shock it gave was undiluted when van Hove revived it in Holland in 2002, as very few directors have done since its inception.

A third piece of theatre business that is ultimately a tic or fallback is for one character to summon up a gob of saliva and let it drop onto another's face. As an expression or extrusion of consummate contempt it does not fail to get a rise out of the audience—a squirm of disgust and discomfort—that might qualify as Artaudian. Eilert Lovborg opens a can of beer, drinks some, and pours the rest over Hedda's head. Forcing her to the ground, he spits the remainder of it in her face. It is thus made unmistakably clear that the sex he invites her to share is debasing sado-masochism, with him in the sadist's role. Next, he dribbles sputum onto her face from above. This particular form of vileness has been seen in other van Hove shows. In *Desire Under the Elms*, in what passes for a courtship maneuver down on the farm, the father spews food halfway across the stage towards the woman he covets. At the climax of a fight with his new wife for dominance, the triumphant husband forms a giant clod of spit before gravity draws it humiliatingly onto her face below him. For a spectator who only witnesses this business in one van Hove show, it might be startling. But when it has been seen in "x" number of productions, and is both predictable *and* disgusting, the novelty gives way to a certain malaise.

Each component of a van Hove/Versweyveld production glows with an aura of originality and idiosyncrasy. As early as 2010, a Dutch critic was able to compile a short list of components that are virtual van Hove "identifiers":

> The set takes up the entire width of the stage and is quite spare in appearance: an off-white wall with a video screen, a shiny floor, glass walls everywhere, 25 half-lit fluorescent lighting instruments, and a ubiquitous cameraman—those are his tried and true ingredients in the theatre of van Hove and his permanent designer Jan Versweyveld.
>
> *(Janssen 2010)*

Once that set of "identifiers" starts to lose its aura, however, it has almost the fizzle and pique of falling out of love, as seems to have occurred in the spring 2017 Barbican production of Visconti's *Obsession*. The very same elements, such as arbitrary bursts of pop music and bland, understated sets, which so recently fascinated London audiences, now begin to pall when reiterated once too often or applied clumsily. Then the system behind them starts to show through the cracks, which appears fatal. "Followers of van Hove's career will note many similarities to his recent take on *Hedda Gabler* at the National Theatre—there's a sense here of ideas and gestures being recycled," writes one critic, who is part of a general chorus of one-time advocates, now turned detractors:

> What follows should feel raw and dangerous. Yet there's nothing sultry here, no blistering chemistry or sweltering cabin fever. At times Eric Schleichim's sound design is ravishing, even if the bursts of opera and Woody Guthrie are heavy-handed. But visually the production is either bland or ugly, except when adorned with exaggeratedly romantic projections of seascapes. The vast, empty set is punctuated by a handful of curious props—a treadmill on which Gino runs wildly as he attempts to flee, a dangling engine that spurts oil on the cast at key moments, and a tank in which Gino and Hanna wash the oil off their nearly naked bodies. . . . we're left with something cooly stylish and portentous.
>
> *(Hitchings 2017)*

Naked bodies, the mix of classical and pop music, the neutrality of the set relieved by surprise mechanisms, real water, garbage that proliferates are all recognizable van Hove elements. They formerly amazed, but now apparently stultify. Dean of London critic Michael Billington, a real van Hove supporter, pays tribute to the acting, but takes van Hove to task for, "swath[ing] the action in artistic refinement" (Billington 2017). Billington recounts that van Hove has—as was true of the shows Billington so recently praised, and praises once more in this article (*Hedda Gabler* and *View From the Bridge*, "which showed that there are alternatives to reality")—dislocated the action: "There is no specific locale and the stage is largely bare except for a motor engine, a water tank and Perspex-windowed doors" (Ibid.). It's the old charge resurrected once more: van Hove is an aesthete who saps his show of genuine passion.

By subtracting the "sordidness and poverty," in other words, the naturalistic social milieu from the Visconti film, van Hove has "softened" the "harsh, murderous story" (Billington 2017). What is perplexing is that van Hove had merely applied the very same treatment to all three shows, the two Billington praised and this that he disparages! Other critics grant the talents of Jude Law and his co-star from Toneelgroep Amsterdam, Halina Reijn. They are rhapsodic about the Hollywood star's gym-toned body, but wax satirical over the "bin-loads of rubbish" that get "tipped out" onto the stage, the mix of high and low brands of music, "sexual scenes, nudity, gun shots, and (worst of all) cigarette smoking," and above all the dearth of "potent sexuality." There is doubt that the "box-like blank set" works for "a piece that is so sweatily soaked in realism" (Cavendish 2017; Taylor 2017; Treneman 2017). The stripping away of traditional realism the London critics so appreciated in *View From the Bridge* is now found incompatible with the source material. Some even dismissed Jude Law's performance:

> [Van Hove's] latest production, 'Obsession' starring Jude Law, carries his unmistakable visual flair, but it's a disjointed affair, filled with gambles that don't quite pay off, not quite up there with his best work. One of those gambles is Law himself, upon whose broad

shoulders is placed a vast weight of expectation. Law brings a shouty physicality to the role, but his delivery is often one dimensional, lacking the deftness of touch to make his character's slow-motion breakdown plausible, and he's badly outshone by his excellent co-star Halina Reijn.

This reviewer allows that projections, music, and "surreal moments" are all effective, but that:

> other conceits work less-well, such as the tread-mill. . . . in the end, there are too many clever pauses that lead nowhere, too many dud lines that highlight the lack of chemistry between the two leads. Van Hove could make drying paint into riveting theatre, but we've been trained to expect more of him.
>
> *(Dinneen 2017)*

Really, it's like a honeymoon gone sour. It isn't certain if the short rehearsal period was to blame, as much stage business lacked the polish of other shows, or if working with a star this time was too intimidating. Was it that the chemistry between actors and director didn't gel due to time or lack of affinity, that van Hove is simply applying his system too mechanically to each successive project, or that it has consolidated into a recognizable *system* and is yielding diminishing returns in dramatic surprise, and therefore power. Only time will tell whether the London theatre scene will give van Hove the chance to reprieve himself, although he has certainly experienced similar career-cycles before both in Belgium and Holland.

The highest form of flattery

One barometer of an artist's impact is the quantity and quality of their imitators. I had the pleasure of seeing a 2014 production of *The Oresteia* at the famed Almeida Theatre in Islington, north London, by Robert Icke. This was not a translation, but a reworking of Aeschylus' trilogy with the plot of Euripedes' *Iphigenia in Aulis* added as prefix. This powerful production, its many virtues notwithstanding, bore a striking resemblance to a van Hove. Its catalog of features, as we will see, could be mimicking any number of van Hove's signatures: the physical space, minimal, but divided by several horizontal plexiglas panels that are transparent and opaque by turns, with a ritual bath upstage; the occasional use of a live camera feed to magnify the actors' faces even as we simultaneously watch the live version; the costumes, simple business suits, jeans and tee shirts for the men, sober dark-colored, clean-lined pant-suits for the women; an acting style that is initially terse, understated, and direct, but when at the height of the dramatic arc as though drilled out of the actors' guts and souls in howls, spasms, and grunts; a polished aesthetic surface initially, with a literal tempest, ulteriorly, unleashed across the stage; a radical reduction of props and set pieces into a small essential assortment with a single, unadorned table serving multiple purposes, both quotidian and ceremonial being the sole furniture in a domestic setting; a political motif of war and social power conjoined with a single family's most intimate dynamics, are hallmarks of Ivo van Hove. If one were to examine van Hove's production of Eugene O'Neill's *Mourning Becomes Electra*, another attempt to modernize Aeschylus's same classic work, one could easily draw a strong comparison between the abject, involuted performance of Eelco Smits who plays Orin, the modern counterpart for Orestes in van Hove's show, and that of Luke Thompson who plays Orestes in Icke's.

This observation is in no sense an attempt to diminish Robert Icke's achievement. His *Oresteia* stands on its own as a remarkable and powerful artistic achievement. There were several scenes that imprinted themselves indelibly on my memory, so great was their dramatic power—notably when Agamemnon administers poison to his young daughter, Iphigenia. The final image of Orestes sitting downstage turns him into a voyeur staring into a tableau of his formerly united and stable family. The digital clock that marks the seconds until his death meanwhile whirs away above the stage. While this smacks of van Hove, and is an iteration of a technique we have seen in *The Roman Tragedies* for example, it is also all *echt* Icke.

One of the stars of contemporary German theatre, Thomas Ostermeier, staged a version of *Hedda Gabler* in 2008. The onstage furnishings were limited to a single austere art-deco style sofa and table. The surroundings that comprised the semi-transparent setting were a concrete wall on one side and a glass one in the rear, forming a t-shaped structure. The glass wall affords translucent images of characters passing by it, morphing into mirrors when the lighting changes and changing from reflections into shadows. In other words, the visual life of the production is hauntingly similar to van Hove's *Othello*. Given Ostermeier's reputation for originality, it is tempting to draw the conclusion that van Hove must have plagiarized his German counterpart until it comes home that *Othello* premiered at Toneelgroep Amsterdam as early as 2003, five years earlier. Ostermeier ironically interjects a pop-music song that plays as Hedda smashes Eilert's laptop (i.e., burns his manuscript) with a hammer. Also, an overhead mirror hangs, while occasional projections of live film disclose the charactes' actions even when they are off-stage. Ostermeier was later an invited guest director at Toneelgroep Amsterdam both in 2011 and 2013, and van Hove evinced great pride in interviews to have snagged this star of the German theatre.[97]

Another former guest-director at TGA is the American, Sam Gold. Ben Brantley's suspicions were aroused in his *New York Times* review of Gold's spring 2017 Broadway rendition of *The Glass Menagerie* with Sally Field:

> Oh, yes, that [indoor] rainstorm. It may make you think about a similar downpour last season in the Belgian director Ivo van Hove's stunning interpretation of Arthur Miller's 'A View From the Bridge,' or about the ferocious wind that blew through his other Miller production on Broadway, 'The Crucible.' This probably isn't a coincidence. . . . This is a production in which subtext elbows text out of bounds.
>
> *(Brantley 2017)*

There are other items Brantley describes that put one in mind of van Hove productions: "We have Tom pulling Amanda into his lap, as if she were a cuddly doll" (c.f. *Things That Pass* and *More Stately Mansions*); radical interpretative revisionings of several roles (c.f. Stanley in *Streetcar* and Torvald in *Hedda Gabler*); "a bleak, nearly naked, fully lighted stage, with a metal cart of props,"; and the sort of metal and wood chairs associated with elementary school (Brantley 2017). The list of Hoveisms goes on. Many others too are jumping on this stylistic bandwagon. It really does seem to be a bandwagon, as Gold has taken to the road along with Ostermeier and Icke to direct at Toneelgroep Amsterdam.

Richard Schechner, who discerned that the avant-garde had recently subdivided into five avant-gardes, which he subsequently christened "Niche-garde,"[98] hadn't yet divined the force of van Hove, whose example may single-handedly have led the way to a sixth. In the arts, it is altogether normal for artists to borrow from each other. At least Ivo van Hove seems to think so. He is as emulated, it seems as he was ever emulating, rising above the current litigious and accusatory trend to regard all creative choices as privately owned "intellectual property."

For him, it has been a necessary and fertile conversation with his peers. Ben Brantley, in his rave review of *Kings of War*, dubbed van Hove, "perhaps the most influential director of his generation in international theatre" (Brantley 2016). Although van Hove may have been in the actual vanguard of a new avant-garde style, the rest have assimilated themselves into his niche, an unmistakeable sign of his prominence in our theatres.

At present

More stately warhorses

As has been noted, Ivo van Hove belongs to the generation of young Flemish directors who came into their own through the dismantling of the calcified repertory system that had dominated Flanders's major urban theatres since before World War II. Discarding their civil service-minded troupes performing a standard repertoire that had stagnated somewhere in between Feydeau and Brecht, the state theatres of Brussels, Antwerp, and Ghent dove headlong into radical experiments. Luk Perceval, Guy Cassiers, Johan Simons, and later Jan Goossens were among the avant-garde radicals who replaced the former artistic directors with their bold new models for institutional, large-scale theatre.

In 1990, van Hove was invited to Holland, whose theatres had undergone restructuring even earlier, and established himself as a radical *within* the context of a traditionally-structured repertory company in Eindhoven, Zuidelijk Toneel. Since then he has practiced a balancing act between a traditional approach and pursuing his iconoclastic career, all the while supported by the infrastructural security and substance a firmly established state theatre affords. A certain number of van Hove's productions remind us that he is the director of a major European resident company that must keep pace with its counterparts in various English, French, and German capitals, whose artistic directors are all keeping an eye on each others' repertoire choices.

In a recent interview, we find van Hove pugnaciously asserting his autonomy of choice and direction in all he does artistically: "Nobody, come what may, can buy me or impose anything on me: I'm only capable of doing what I want to do" (Pascaud 2016a). And in the same interview, he also confided: "I like to be included, not excluded" (Ibid.). Juxtaposing these two dissonant statements reveals a great deal about the juncture of van Hove's current career position, and it is perhaps through this Janus-lens that we should consider it.

Without suggesting that he has ever selected plays that disinterested him entirely, it feels at times that van Hove has staged plays simply to show that he is up to the challenge of a full range of prominent plays from theatre history. We see him two years ago undertaking a perfectly presentable *Mary Stuart* by Schiller, that perennial showcase for two diva actresses to unleash their personal pyrotechnics. It did not, however, exceed in inspiration, innovation, or stirring performances like the 2009 revival on Broadway with Harriet Walter and Janet McTeer. It proved not to be his strongest suit, nor that of his actresses, all of whom put in workmanlike turns, but no more.

So, also, did he produce *The Russians* several seasons back. Merely pairing and interweaving two massive plays, *Ivanov* and *Platonov*, setting them on the roof of a former factory-cum-loft building, and throwing in a few shots of flashy visual technology didn't disguise the sense that Chekhov was being undertaken more out of obligation than personal bent. We have noted that van Hove creates theatre by way of "writing in a personal diary." When he violates this principle of the personal, instead selecting a show from some professional imperative, the work tends to suffer.[99] The heart wasn't in it. The same holds for the Goldoni offering, based on the *Villegiatura Trilogy* (*Summer Trilogy*) where, despite the modern-seeming scenic space and costuming together with some post-modern casting, the traditional laws for playing farce comedy were laid on thick: the actors going for loud monotone line readings; closing in all pauses; topping each other's intensity; and starting higher than the one before. There was also a lot of arbitrary throwing each other to the ground, but it all added up to neither great hilarity nor remarkable innovation. But Goldoni is one of those standard playwrights a European municipal theatre is obliged to put on the bill now and then.

Gorky's *Children of the Sun* also feels like an awkward fit. On the printed page it is an unabashedly, early twentieth century naturalistic comedy/drama play of personalities with a serious social theme embedded, a surprising choice all round. Again, van Hove does certain things that prove that he is up to the entire play repertoire expected of, in his own words, "the official theatre." It also pits his actors against the challenge of playing three-dimensional characters. It is, in a broad sense, a play centered around ethics and the large social question of where science is leading society, which reflects van Hove's recent inclinations. With all the will in the world, however, neither the genre of dramatic writing nor the subject lent themselves terribly well to the van Hove approach.

Even the much vaunted *Angels in America*, where van Hove's main innovation was to remove the trademark gimmick, an oversize angel, missed the mark. Held in greater reverence than any American play written in the past twenty-five years, this one has made it into the canon of classics in the United States, and is esteemed on a par with *Death of a Salesman* and *The Glass Menagerie*. It is frequently anthologized and is a staple of university theatre departments; its shocking aspects having accrued a patina of tameness, even honor, and been steadily digested into the ambient culture of political correctness. But despite the obvious opportunities for bravura acting it offers, Tony Kushner's script doesn't leave much room for directorial invention; such theatrical coups are embedded in the play's structure by the author. So any chance for van Hove to positively transform *Angels in America*, in this case, had already been removed by the imaginative playwright from the outset.

Van Hove's rendition was a large, portentous show, aspiring to an epic scale. To compensate for the play's diminished power to shock and the reduced wiggle room for conceptual innovation, van Hove weighted it with a bric-a-brac of discordant acting styles. Some actors were able to evoke the pathos of the dawn of the era of AIDS, and others less so. Marieke Heebink had the unfair burden of representing such New York denizens as a local Bronx rabbi and Ethel Rosenberg, characters New Yorkers of a certain generation harbor beneath their own epidermis like household gods. She was also assigned to play the uptight Mormon mother, the only character whose vibe corresponded to her own Calvinist Dutch flavor. As for the two Jewish characters, rather than making them recognizable or believable, she opted to portray each of them with a stripped down Grotowskian ideogram, an abstracted and distanced broad stroke of presentational panache. Thus for Ethel Rosenberg, Heebink strode across the stage with one arm bent straight up in a rictus, legs stiffened, and staring out directly at the audience, announcing rather than saying her lines. How could a New York audience, which fully expected Ethel Rosenberg to resemble nothing other than a familiar *kneidel*, an ethnic babushka who could be your own grandmother, accept such an interpretation? As Frédéric Maurin noted: "van Hove's production levels the realism and the fantastic elements, annulling both referentiality and the spectacular, producing an abstraction which, according to the author himself, 'strips the play to the bone'" (Maurin 2016: 220).

Even when playing the Mormon mother Hanna Walter, for whom she was best suited, Heebink's approach was to strike a single unchanging tone and stance and hew to it without variation. One wonders why van Hove burdened one actress with all these roles when he had a large stable of other actresses to draw upon? Perhaps some were retained in Amsterdam to keep the repertoire going. But the great problem with this show was that, although there were powerful performances from Hans Kesting as Roy Cohn and Eelco Smits as Prior, the cast as a whole didn't cohere into a unified ensemble; which is self-contradictory for an established repertory company.

In the German version of *Long Day's Journey Into Night*, none of the actors worked up any vividly defined characters, overlooking the magnificent histrionic opportunities to reveal complexities and quirks. Instead, they were projected as an unremarkable, generalized European family. So much of the potential delight of the play is contained in its fascinating character studies, juxtaposing the ludicrous with the noble, including the pompous pluming of the ego on display by the aging ham-actor Tyrone, to which O'Neill lends a comic dimension; but this was pretty much ignored or left out. Everyone just spoke to each other reasonably.

We also see a similar approach in O'Neill's *Strange Interlude*. The set is a square of sand in the midst of which the actors strike a stance and declaim their lengthy monologues for the six or so hours of playing time. While the scenic approach is unquestionably descended from Peter Brook's concept of the "Empty Space," it should be remembered that Brook's purpose in clearing out the unessentials was to take theatre back to its primal roots. With epic shows like *The Mahabarata*, a wide and deep space was defined only by a river running laterally across it, so that fresh, inspired acting and images might emerge out of the clean sweep. This technique of late van Hove is more like neo-classicism in its austerity, thorough unity of character impersonation and tone; a form of what theoretician, Peter Szondi, has called "absolute drama." It is a reversion to a theatrical experience he characterize[s] by the following:

> the dominance of dialogue and interpersonal communication; the exclusion of anything external to the dramatic world (including the dramatist and the spectators, who are condemned to silent observation); the unfolding of time as a linear sequence in the present; and the adherence to the three unities of time, place, and action.
>
> *(Lehmann 2006: 3)*

Plenty of directors can do that. Van Hove looks like he is treading water when he does, and it may ultimately come under the law of diminishing returns.

Another issue is his artistic home. When directing in the Netherlands, van Hove has a traditional repertory company of actors contracted for the season to work with, and has had for many years.[100] Most stay under the TGA roof for decades, although there is a continuous natural process of light attrition and new arrivals.[101] The obvious upsides of the traditional European repertory system where a consistent stable of actors is retained—that they cohere into a stylistic ensemble, that their steady salaries reflect respect from society for the art-form and the artists, that they will be less tempted by glitzy outside work—are counterbalanced by some disheartening downsides. While the acting and directing is often strong, so much depends on how well the casting needs of each play selected align with the abilities of the particular actors in the pool. They may be cast in roles for which they are not ideally suited. They are on the payroll and must perforce be given work. A perfunctory civil servant attitude toward performance may set in at times, and the temptation to fall into a kind of journeyman sufficiency is ever lurking.

Actors develop tricks to conceal want of inspiration for, or connection with, a given work. Brio, earnestness, and efficiency sometimes masquerade for emotional heights, wit, and vulnerability, though these tendencies vary from actor to actor. Also, because they are expected to keep to an intense schedule of learning and playing diverse roles in a compressed time-frame, there is a temptation to grab a basic characteristic of each role in their portfolio, and reduce it to a silhouette rather than developing fuller, more complex, and layered renditions. Undoubtedly, every repertory company suffers from these ills at times.

The director will also select a play from the mandate to either balance out the season or to keep in step with the other repertory companies of Europe. When he also brings this journeyman sufficiency to the work, he falls short of the expectations he has raised. At this juncture, the TGA tilts dangerously close to the quality on display in Flanders before the Flemish Wave swept away the municipal office-worker mentality. All these flaws may be seen to affect van Hove's repertoire over time, if he remains artistic director.

As for the London and New York hit, Arthur Miller's *A View From the Bridge*, van Hove transformed the kitchen sink naturalistic drama into yet another neo-classical tragedy. As the rave review in *Le Monde* expressed when it played in Paris:

> Arthur Miller's back again, but in a way we've never seen before, relieved of his Actors Studio straitjacket, of the trappings of the theatre of denunciation, to get back to the bare bones of his oeuvre: the role that this relationship with tragedy plays in American history.
>
> *(Darge 2015)*

And further on, it revealingly exults: "No need of any scenery to evoke the story of Eddy Carbone" (Ibid.). It is hardly surprising that the French would adore an approach that brings Arthur Miller in line with their own tradition for mounting the adored Racine and Corneille; nor is it surprising that the English have taken to Miller now that he's produced just like Shakespeare. Apart from an obvious effort to get the English actors to speak an acceptable version of Brooklynese, van Hove stripped *View From the Bridge* of all American signifiers:

> There are no props, but that was not my original intention. I had all the props ready next door—a roomful—and I said, 'Whenever we need something, we'll bring it out.' We ended up with two props: a cigar and a chair.
>
> *(Newton 2015)*

Gone were the checked tablecloths and fire escapes visible through windows; gone also the faded wallpaper, brooms, and sheets being folded. Devoid of the usual physical life of this naturalistic mainstay, what remained for the actors was the language and dramatic tensions to work with on an open stage space analogous to the Globe. In rendering the play Shakespearean, van Hove played to the British actors' strongest suit. While it may have looked experimental, it had actually become classical in the way the actors have been trained to perform. This meeting of alien minds in a common comfort zone may partially account for this production's notable success.

The postage stamp of sand ringed by a rectangle of benches is cribbed from the earlier German production of *Long Day's Journey*. More than anything else, this conception of theatre follows the precepts David Mamet advances in his acting textbooks: in essence, actors should just stand there and say the lines accurately and clearly. As David Savran truculently foresees though, Ben Brantley, the oracular first critic for *The New York Times* was certainly going to be swayed. This ultimate arbiter of "upper middle-brow taste" is in search of "serious" theatre that functions on "the imagined site of authenticity," (Savran 2003: 47) one that in Marianne Conroy's words is "'at once politically effective, morally responsible, commercially successful, and culturally respectable'" (Ibid.: 17–18). The current van Hove trend ticks all these boxes, winning both the hearts and minds of the Broadway and West End audiences, as well as their respective leading critics.

This particular current of van Hove's work stakes its claim at a point of intersection between various forms of respectability: that of the recent Shakespearean and Racinian traditions of the empty space, and that of the revered modern American classics. So van Hove, who had burst on to the scene as "a bad boy," has been paving a way toward middlebrow acceptance, and his strategy has paid off. You might say, along with David Savran's caustic citations of Edwardian period impresario Charles Frohmann, that van Hove is at present aiming for "an impossible ideal" as he works "'through' the 'white heat' of the commercial to reach 'the artistic,'" and engages in the "familiar task of balancing the 'meaningful' with the 'profitable'" (Ibid.: 24, 36).

From one point of view, van Hove is simply persevering with and expanding the project he announced in an interview twenty years earlier: to clear the naturalistic "bells and whistles" out of the habitual American stagecraft in approaching its own modern classics.[102] It is, as he repeatedly said, a straight "text" approach, although—in its present configuration—a few pyrotechnical visual features are injected at crucial moments, most often as a spectacular coda at the very end of a show. The blood that rains down over actors and set alike in *View From the Bridge* is just one example of several that could be named.[103]

When placed on the Broadway bill, audiences can congratulate themselves that they're seeing the latest in cutting edge theatre (*The New York Times'* critic told them it was), and it doesn't make them feel too uncomfortable, even though the director has a reputation for being really far out! It's certainly competent, well spoken, soberly staged, and yet it looks different from the other productions of the show they've seen, and makes the spectator ask questions about the play. At various points during his earlier career, van Hove has been burnt by bad or mixed reviews as well as by lukewarm audience responses when he's stepped out of his or their comfort zone. Yet his most brilliant endeavors always involved taking artistic risks, including the risk that the audience and critics wouldn't like the result.[104]

The current phenomenon of van Hove's success in New York and London can be explained in part by Dwight MacDonald's description of audience reception in American theatre back in the 1960s, as cited by David Savran:

> 'We have,' Macdonald wrote, 'become skilled at consuming High Culture when it has been stamped PRIME QUALITY by proper authorities, but we lack the kind of sophisticated audience that supported the achievements of the classic avant-garde, an audience that can appreciate and discriminate on its own.' So even highbrow plays fall as pearls before Midcultish swine. Moreover, the very structure of theater's system of production, distribution, and consumption—as well as its heavy reliance on the 'proper' authority of the daily critics—would seem to guarantee its middlebrow status in perpetuity.
>
> *(Savran 2003: 17–18)*

Savran, who neither goes along with Macdonald's contempt for the audience nor harbors the same exalted opinion of the avant-garde, goes on to say that "middlebrow culture must evince an unstable, unpredictable, and anxious relationship between the commercial and the artistic"

(Ibid.). His discussion of the anomaly of the avant-garde and its highbrow audience catches the van Hove phenomenon neatly in the net of his analysis, adding pertinence to this discussion:

> But with the institutionalization of what used to be called the avant-garde by the early 1980s [exactly when van Hove was launched], there is very little theater left in the United States that amasses the kind of cultural cachet or enjoys the prestige of what passes for elite culture. Work by the likes of Richard Maxwell and the Wooster Group that continues to be performed in tiny venues perhaps qualifies, but certainly not the mammoth productions [cf., van Hove's] that fill the Brooklyn Academy of Music during the ludicrously misnamed Next Wave Festival [precisely where his works are shown].
>
> *(Savran 2003: 17–18)*

I have to wonder whether the kind of work van Hove has long staged at New York Theatre Workshop, a smallish venue, is qualitatively different from what he has staged for the Next Wave Festival at BAM, where more people have seen it. The BAM venues, the Gilman Theatre and the Harvey, are substantial in seating capacity; the typically limited, week-long runs perforce rule out really massive audiences. Still, NYTW arguably draws a somewhat more adventurous, cutting edge crowd and BAM a more conservative one. Savran continues:

> Moreover, with the increasing dependence since the 1970s of the major non-profit theaters on profit-making ventures (beginning with *A Chorus Line* in 1976), the growing number of collaborations between nonprofit and commercial producers, the line between art and commerce has become all the more indistinct.
>
> *(Savran 2003: 15–16)*

Is van Hove now part of what Savran sarcastically describes as, "the . . . kind of elite culture [that is] supported by big money and prestigious foundations [that] caters to the champagne and caviar crowd and "imagine[s] high art as being either sacred and wrapped in mystique?" (Ibid.).

Is van Hove's present New York audience middlebrow or highbrow? Whatever the answer, it is inarguable that the audience coterie has now expanded from that limited population to encompass a much larger, more heterogeneous public for *View From the Bridge* and *The Crucible* on Broadway, radically "commodifying" it (Ibid.: 36–37). Even the recent production of *Lazarus*, staged within the relatively confidential margins of NYTW, drew exceptional notoriety largely due to the renown of van Hove's late collaborator, David Bowie. Analogously, Savran cites the destiny of the British playwright David Hare, who had three plays running on Broadway in one season and who "achieved commercial success only by forsaking his class-based critique of British society, his formal experimentation, and the corruscatingly edgy style of earlier works" (Ibid.: 51). Will a similar of loss of pioneering spirit befall van Hove? Has it already?

While intermittently continuing to innovate in "corruscatingly edgy styles," van Hove has also recently evinced a tendency to forsake formal experimentation in favor of his neo-classical approach as well as connecting his work with media stars and imported British theatre, which tends to be received so well with the New York public. He is not one to disdain mass popularity if obtaining it does not entail adulterating his work. In an interview, Randy Gener asks: "So has the public caught up with him?"; and van Hove responds, "that's my mission as a theatre director.

I want to make the most extreme work possible, without compromise, shown to as many people as possible" (Gener 2009).

It remains to be seen whether those two aims can be realized in one and the same performance. Either the audience might reject unadulterated extremity and true novelty, or the artist wittingly or unwittingly may curtail it in order to render it palatable to the wider public. In his international work, especially on Broadway, van Hove is subject to the American star system. No stage director's name alone, except maybe those of Mike Nichols or Harold Prince, will bring in the crowds as a well-known director's might in Europe. To fill the house, he must cast big name actors, hoping that the crowd-pleasers, often drawn from the world of film and television, will be competent onstage as well. This vital necessity, combined with a truncated rehearsal schedule the Actors' Equity Association mandates, and mediatized performers' heavy obligations are other debilities that surely hamper van Hove's exploratory bent.[105] His German productions, such as *Edward II*, *The Miser*, and *Ludwig II*, which I count among his best, were rehearsed over six weeks at a minimum. In France, he is now accustomed to a three-week rehearsal schedule, and claims to like it that way. He also claims to confine rehearsals to "a few hours in the afternoon." "'How do you work?' the interviewer asks. 'Fast,'" is the pithy answer.[106] Although he has balked at the notion that the creative process in film and theatre are alike (Takken 2009), he has de facto adapted a film-making calendar for theatre rehearsals: a protracted, detailed stage of contemplation and preparation with dramaturgs, designers, and composers, followed by a short, intense work period with the actors themselves. The early rehearsal phase of gaining actors' trust is obviated by the director's arrival on the scene in a glow of established prestige. He comes to town, they put themselves into his hands totally from the first, and they knock the show out. This formula worked very well for *The Damned*, performed at the Comédie Française during the subscription-based Avignon Festival. In America, the financial pressures of the free market, when a producer needs to recoup the show's investment, and where van Hove is in so much demand he's always off to direct the next one, introduce a brake on risk-taking. Can van Hove still claim, as he did shortly after taking over TGA in 2002, that "he still makes subversive theatre?" The answer appears to be yes *and* no (Meijers 2005).

His spring 2017 London stage adaptation of Visconti's 1943 film *Obsession* offers a cautionary tale. It should be remembered that van Hove has had rather a charmed existence with British audiences and critics. His 2006 TGA production of *Scenes From a Marriage* was very well received (Billington 2013). *The Roman Tragedies*, *Song From Far Away*, *A View From the Bridge*, and *Kings of War* all seemed to entrance London. Bringing Shakespeare to England in Dutch with super-titles had the same kind of chutzpah as bringing American classics to New York, and encountered much the same success. *Kings of War*, his second trilogy of history plays, although less iconoclastic than *The Roman Tragedies*, was universally admired: "When the Brits revive these plays – as Trevor Nunn did recently – we tend to do so with fusty pomp and circumstance, but even with a conventional staging, Hove's take feels thrillingly modern" (Lukowski 2016). Lukowski was not the only reviewer to make that comparison, one so unflattering to the British. Only with *The Antonioni Project* did he seem to falter in their eyes (Gardner 2011; Taylor 2011). But that was the exception that proved the rule: van Hove had achieved a special status in the London theatre scene. "In the last few months it feels like Belgian director Ivo van Hove has gone from being one of those distant European geniuses whose work could only be seen in brief surtitled stints at the Barbican, to one of our own" (Lukowski 2016).

That infallibility has started to be challenged, first rather hesitantly with *Hedda Gabler*, and more emphatically with *Obsession*. The source material for *Obsession*, like *Rocco and His Brothers*, is a classic neo-realist kitchen sink venture: full of Latin local color, with both the environmental detail and rounded character definition typical of the genre. The plotline, cribbed from the 1934 American novel by James N. Cain, *The Postman Always Rings Twice*, is about a drifter, Gino, who winds up at a gas station-cum-cabaret in the middle of nowhere. He makes himself useful and is hired by the affectionate, openhearted owner, Johnny. The drifter immediately falls in love with Hanna, the owner's frustrated wife. The two discard the notion of running away together, opting instead for killing Johnny. They do so by staging a car accident. The drifter then takes the man's place as boss and man about the house. The couple initially seem to get away with the murder. Ultimately, guilt undermines the relationship, especially when it comes to light that the victim had a life insurance policy the wife had counted on collecting. The drifter, who has in the meantime been tempted to go off on the highroad with a buddy from the past and a younger woman who happens onto his path, instead resolves to stay and ends up killing his mistress and partner in crime. In doing so, he seals his fate as a condemned murderer.

Van Hove chose to premiere his stage adaptation in England, at the Barbican, scene of numerous prior triumphs. He combined several Toneelgroep Amsterdam company stalwarts, notably Halina Reijn in the role of the wife, Gijs Scholten van Aschat as the husband, Robert De Hoog as the buddy, with a few British actors in secondary roles, and induced the film star Jude Law to play the lead role of Gino, the drifter. The entire production syncretizes a multiplicity of elements that van Hove and Versweyveld have used often in previous productions, and in that sense, represents a stylistic culmination. The love triangle has echoes of many such from the decades-old repertoire, but especially *Desire Under the Elms*, while the revenge/guilt motif was reminiscent of the *Macbeth* production as noted by several critics. The casting is classic van Hove. Whereas the actor who played Johnny, the husband in Visconti's film, was a corpulent, ungainly slob, van Aschat is a trim enough and presentable middle-aged man, plausibly mildly senior to the compact, feline Halina Reijn who visually complements both him and Jude Law, whose gym-fit body was considered by many critics as one of the prime draws of the occasion. In contrast, the casting in the movie aspired to the crude, the unremarkable: plebeian recognizability of a rural Italian gas station verging on cinema vérité in both locale and character portraiture; van Hove here favors the idealized.

Yet again, van Hove removes many cues of the local and time-specific, leaving only the characters' Italian names and a passage of Italian opera, sung by Johnny who enters a singing contest in the story. The set was once more conceived by Jan Versweyveld using the empty space principle. On a wide, deep proscenium, there is an unaccoutered café counter to one side, a few atmospherically lit exit doors set upstage, one within a glass cage, and a pillar in front of which is a covered metal tub. Nearby is a stand-pipe that gushes real water as needed. Hanging over the space is an exposed car engine, which can be flown in and out, that is ignited by means of a remote attached to a thick black cable running down from the flies. Running across the far upstage end is a giant projector screen, and concealed in the floor in front of it is a treadmill that is set in motion each time one or two characters attempt to flee, facing upstage and running in situ, with their faces projected in large scale on the screen. The space is stripped of identifying characteristics other than bare function, and time markers are also removed. We are in a universe governed by Zygmunt Bauman's "Liquid Time" that flows undifferentiatedly forward. Indicators such as blackouts and fresh costumes that normally divide dramatic sequences—which in the movie had been typical editing cuts and dissolves to indicate time passage—are reduced to a minimum. A very few overlapping transparencies are managed by having simultaneous action in different parts of the stage space. We may, from the dialogue, deduce that a day or several months may have passed, but the lack of emphasis on time comes through; rather, it is the archetypal, even mythic, evolution of the human relations that are foregrounded.

With this, van Hove introduces a visual intertextuality having more to do with theme and inner dramatic life than verisimilitude that goes hand in hand with his heterogeneous musical choices. One critic notes that the café has a hint of an Edward Hopper painting in spaciousness and nostalgic lighting. The car crash is represented by a typically objective correlative image, in which the hanging motor, now virtually the sword of Damocles, switches on and, growling and flashing, comes pressing down on the three lead actors from above. They intertwine all the while, coiling in a serpentine pattern and segueing from standing erect to lying supine on the stage floor (see Figure 1.17). This choreographic vignette, executed in a strictly confined area, recalls the excruciating three-character image of the classic Rhodian sculpture "Laocoön," which stands in the Vatican and upon which Lessing based his aesthetic theories. A third example of pictorialization occurs toward the end of the show, when Gino makes one more attempt to break away from Hanna, the gas station, and his past: as he stands with his silhouette plastered before a giant video image of a rough sea, that seems to me an evocation of Caspar David Friedrich's famous painting "Wanderer Above a Sea of Fog." The latter citation particularly re-frames the production, lifting it beyond a squalid anecdote of sex and jealousy, and into the grand romantic tradition, of an individual's quest for existential freedom in the face of an indifferent, savage, and enticing universe. The diverse snatches of music—Italian opera arias to French torch songs from the heyday of Juliette Greco, that Halina Reijn lyp-syncs, juxtaposed with Woodie Guthrie singing "This Land is My Land,"—play with the audience's associative memory, beckoning from the post-war smoke-filled cafes of Continental existentialist gatherings to Whitmanesque hoboing,

FIGURE 1.17 *Obsession*

© Jan Versweyveld

or hopping freight trains across America's wide-open heartland spaces. These motley selections, again typical of van Hove caprice, detach us from the purported setting and invite us into a universal, abstracted super-reality.

Once more, the buddy-drama trope embedded in the movie, gets revisioned as latent gay longing made manifest. The repair shop owner Johnny's impetuous hiring of the stranger Gino, as well as his generous offering up of his wife, all clearly issue from a hard crush he knows and does not know he's going through. He removes his own shirt, and urges Hanna to remove Gino's shirt. The three, the two men shirtless, hunker down on a cozy ledge together, the resultant tableau full of suggestibility. The buddy character who first deposits Gino at the gas station, and then compulsively returns to lure him off into a fancy-free, open-ended road trip, is clearly motivated by sexual longing. His hand hovers over the sleeping Gino and finally makes contact; the latter shoots to consciousness and warily rejects the unmistakable overture, leaving doubt in the air. The central macho figure, Gino retains the right of denial throughout, all the while leaving space for eventualities. Going off with this friend would represent a radical kind of disentanglement from the world of convention into a brand of freedom he is ultimately not prepared to make. Instead, gentle intimacy turns to hothouse wrestling in a twinkling, in a sequence of counterintuitive emotional logic we've often seen before. And speaking of emotions, the detective investigating the case, in the midst of speaking neutrally and rationally, goes off into a high decibel hysteria for no apparent reason at the drop of a hat.

Other van Hove ritual trademarks are legion. In every case where someone is stripping or being stripped of clothing, the naturalistic rhythm of a banal daily activity gives way to one of ceremony—a slowing down of time and gesture so that attention is drawn to the inner transformation that the outer shell represents. Once the black oil from the hanging car motor has inundated the murderous couple, they strip, Reijn entirely and Law mostly, and wash each other off in the little tub, in gestures that are both sensual and emotionally symbolic. Elsewhere, in a fit of pique, Reijn strews several containers of garbage all over the space, and there the trash stays for the duration constituting a characteristic van Hoveian objective correlative—scenic evidence of the dislocation of relationships and morality that has transpired: the inside turned outside.

On the vast playing area with its minimal definition and austere appearance, which one critic compared to the lobby of the Barbizon itself, the actors employ a bare minimum of props, and those that they do use have emblematic or symbolic resonance. The way van Hove handles food, for example, defies any realistic expectation, but rather creates a dissonance. Hanna throws a thick piece of bloody meat down on the counter, which is never cooked or eaten. When the time comes for a meal, three empty white bowls get placed on the counter, the actors make no pretence at eating although one complains of the lack of salt in the food, and Hanna peremptorily clears the plates shortly thereafter. The young girl, who attempts to draw Gino out of the tangled web in which he finds himself, drinks from a bottle of milk that he shares with her.

Safely subversive

The New York audience thrilled to the steady drum-beat of van Hove's contributions to the 2015–16 season; his *annus mirabilis*. He began at BAM with his imported production of *Antigone*, starring Juliette Binoche; then rolled out his Broadway debut with the British transplant of *View From the Bridge*; third came the highly anticipated original staging of the David Bowie musical *Lazarus* at his old fringe haunt, the New York Theatre Workshop; finally, he wrapped up the season with an original American staging of *The Crucible*, albeit with a much vaunted international cast, again on Broadway in March, 2016. As he said, without exaggeration, "The 2015–2016 season allowed me to live ten years in one. I love that" (Pascaud 2016a). The almost universal approbation *A View From the Bridge* garnered illustrates what a safe choice it was for Broadway consumption, as detailed above; it came in the wake of a series of other stylistically circumspect productions abroad—including *Maria Stuart*, *Long Day's Journey Into Night*, and *The Fountainhead*.

The Crucible belongs to that recent cluster of shows. While van Hove again took on a revered American classic, this time, his interpretation did not jar with it dialectically as had happened with earlier shows like *A Streetcar Named Desire* or *More Stately Mansions*. To cite an antecedent, the Wooster Group's radical deconstruction of *The Crucible* that they called *L.S.D.: Only the High Points*, incurred Arthur Miller's wrath to the degree that the celebrated author tried to shut it down. Van Hove rather took the approach, now bordering on a personal formula, of de-historicizing it by stripping down sets and costumes; banishing long-held preconceptions of the characters and through both casting and interpretation building them back up from zero; making sweeping changes to traditionally charged line readings; eliminating whole scenes and characters, and stripping other scenes of generationally accreted melodramatic heightening; plus adding a few spectacular meta-dramatic touches, including restrained use of video and an animal presence. All of these innovations that refresh the play, without rendering it unrecognizable, are subtle enough to pass muster with a Broadway public that likes perhaps to consider itself as open and liberal. Added to the recipe is the usual inducement of mediatized stars playing principal roles in order to ensure the consistently sold out houses required by the absurd Broadway economy to recoup its investment on a rare occasion such as this when it allows serious drama to be produced in its precincts.

The audience at the Walter Kerr Theatre is presented with a capacious, but enclosed space, evocative of some disused junior high school gymnasium or lunchroom, but clearly the kind of place where Americans in small towns go to cast their ballots in local and national elections. There is a large blackboard up center, and the floor has a gray and black chessboard design. The upstage wall, which one suspects is the actual theatre wall, is charcoal gray with a hanging piped heating unit sticking out from it, as well as a slops sink. The stage right contains three vast windows, and stage left a door, the only means of egress. In a customary staging, as indicated in the script, the setting varies between Reverend Parris's house, Proctor's house, the local dungeon, a courtroom, and so on. In van Hove's production, however, all scenes appear in succession on the same set effectively containing all those functions without much alteration. Locales are differentiated within the overarching master space in the most minimal way, largely by redistributing, clumping, and overturning chairs in new configurations.

This box set, while much larger than usual, follows the established van Hove scenic pattern of Isolation in an enclosed rectangle that we have seen in *Hedda Gabler*, *Children of the Sun*, and others. Fire is used sporadically, as with a series of candles accompanying the watch kept over Betty Parris in Act I, and a live brazier that flares up later in the show. Certain anachronistic props are inserted and unobtrusively coexist, such as highly modern thermoses and paper cups.

The blackboard is put to plentiful use to crudely embody, through pictograms, the progressive unmaking of the community; to give visual, graphic life to howls that issue from the characters' guts. Blackboard writing, of the kind we've previously seen used in *Ludwig II*, graphically charts the growing hysteria engulfing the community. At first, there is only a big tree and small house chalked on the board in a child-like manner, depicting the sedate life of the sleepy town. When John Proctor is made to repeat the Ten Commandments, to test his piety, he writes the key words on the blackboard in addition to speaking them. At the point when the servant Mary Warren is clinging to her resolve not to inform on her master and mistress, she repeats the word "cannot," and also repeatedly writes it on the board. In Act III, the accumulated chalk marks on the blackboard start moving and cohering into tiny bifurcated icons. Through video wizardry, this flock of winged squiggles starts to detach itself from the blackboard frame, grow larger and more numerous, and swarm over the entire back wall of the space. As this is the only use of video in the production, it evinces both restraint and yet has theatrical power.

All the actors wear nondescript gray and black clothes, which while decidedly not period Puritan garb, retain an air of sobriety and modesty, at the same time as allowing for greater universality. The aged Rebecca Nurse and several other female characters, including Elizabeth Proctor and Tituba, wear pant-suits, an anachronism that doesn't jar particularly. Once established, it may be assumed that the audience simply forgets we are meant to be in seventeenth century Massachusetts. As is usual for van Hove, we are in no locality or point in history.

The first segment is a brief and silent tableau of the girls working at their school desks facing away from the audience, a briefly glimpsed image on which the act curtain shortly comes down. It reminded me of the mise en scène for German director Christof Marthaler's production, *Maeterlinck*, at the NTG in Ghent some years back. The leitmotif of such non-verbal tableaux, however, is used most sparingly. Another departure from the text that occurs early on is that Betty Parris briefly flies high above the stage floor at the end of Act I.

Later, a wolf or wolfhound stealthily prowls on, stares at the audience, and then runs off. This latter, startling, unexplained image must derive from a reference in Miller's postface to the published play wherein he writes of farms abandoned by their condemned owners, left for the wolves to pillage. The animal, for those who haven't read that text, will remain semiologically opaque, yet resonant and striking: an unforgettable if difficult to decode moment of theatre. Another gratuitous image later in the action comes in the form of a veritable storm of garbage that blows through the large side windows, leaving the stage floor littered in muck, accompanied by lightning flashes and thunder that cause an air duct (actually a giant overhanging batten) to shake loose and dangle from the flies. That disconcerting infrastructural fracturing is a bit of stage wizardry we've seen van Hove use before in previous productions, as recently as in *Antigone*. These visual statements of decomposition and soiling are more readily legible than the wolf-hound, as implying that the community has been engulfed in the filth from the girls' imaginations. Their mental slime has led to the town's ruin. Is it also an intimation of the existence of a divine presence making its opinions felt? The image is open enough to allow for such an interpretation.

In one of Versweyveld's masterly strokes of unconventional lighting, a medium-sized, rectangular fluorescent instrument that casts a ghastly, harsh glow is laid upon the floor stage right. All other light sources fade to zero. As circumstances begin to close in on John Proctor and force him to his ultimate moment of tragic choice, the four compromised representatives of the local power structure debate in front of this lighting instrument, casting shadows that project like souls in hell. Later, Proctor squats before the fluorescent unit, morally squirming before the light of truth, as it has clearly come to be, grappling with his impossible decision.

While there is no actual nudity, in a modification of van Hoveism and a concession to the Puritan society depicted, the audience is treated to Ben Whishaw removing his shirt only. Another unusual feature is that Philip Glass has composed extensive incidental music for the occasion. His famously minimalist drones simply and pleasantly underline growing tension, although at times they become more obtrusive as when a leitmotif of plucking strings accompanies Reverend Hale's intensifying rhetorical hunt for devils. Suffice it to say that there is a much greater quantity of music here, especially underlying the dialogue, than in most van Hove shows and most non-musical shows in general.

And so van Hove tastefully injected the energy of his personal theatricality into this shop-worn modern American classic, breathing new life into it, even though the individual performances were fairly underwhelming. The stars did their bit simply by having their names on the bills as audience draw. The real star of the show, whose name alone wouldn't have been sufficient to bring them in, was the director. Only Bill Camp gave a somewhat memorable portrayal as Reverend Hale, and Ciarán Hinds as Judge Danforth performed with concentration and inner logic. For all the innovative stagecraft added to the play, van Hove works with highly conventional stage groupings. When many characters are on stage at the same time, they stand bolt upright in fairly static geometric formations that are the hallmark of classical revivals as performed everywhere.

The Crucible has long been considered a historicized indictment of the McCarthy era in American politics. What were commonly characterized as "witch-hunts" arose from the post-war, anti-Communist fever played out in House and Senate hearings that ruined the lives of so many. Arthur Miller himself was called to testify, and he faced the same moral dilemmas as John Proctor, his anti-hero from the times of the Salem witch trials in Puritan New England, although, unlike Proctor or the Rosenbergs, it was not for him a matter of actual life and death, but of gainful employment. *The Crucible* is thus a canonical text of American progressivism.[107] This production puts that reading squarely on the back burner. In a recent interview, van Hove finds commonality between the two Arthur Miller shows and *Antigone*, all of which he did in New York in one season: "I consider *View* a modern Greek tragedy, and Arthur Miller did, too. *The Crucible* also has that feeling of fate, of the thing that you think is not changeable." He then elaborates on Creon's role in Sophocles's play, which brings him full circle: "When I think about it, it's the same in *The Crucible*. There is this whole fight between the word of the law and the right human decisions to be made" (Newton 2015).[108] His universalizing tendency takes McCarthyism out of the mix entirely, although for all the American baby-boomers with long memories that make up the bulk of the Broadway audience that association would have been inevitable.

Van Hove's rendering, while not absolutely subverting that generally accepted reading of the modern classic, fissures the production by having Betty mysteriously levitate from the stage when she's unobserved. Although the persecution of innocent victims by a juggernaut of hysteria and malevolent forces is unquestionably dramatized, Betty's levitation implies the presence of real supernatural forces at work—through actual witchcraft in the play's imagistic canvas—Miller's text renders the absurd accusation of witchcraft in colonial Salem analogous to that of Communist activities in 1950s America. By extension, van Hove would be applauding the feverish vigilante search for "Un-Americans." Betty flying confirms the malign omnipresence of such 'Un-Americans.'" If, on the other hand, no metaphorical meaning was intended and supernatural powers were meant to be taken literally, the play is stripped of its other customary political associations, and a totally different thematic balance is struck. While the witch-hunters are evil and misguided, it seems there actually are grounds for their suspicions. Young girls—only no one can see them—appear to be levitating in this town! Van Hove has muddied the moral universe by succumbing to his stronger instincts as a showman.

Van Hove can just as easily dignify this sacred cow of American progressivism by reviving it and see no contradiction in doing the same for Ayn Rand's reactionary *The Fountainhead*, as he did recently at the TGA. That work along with her other monumental novel, *Atlas Shrugged*, are taken by many as bibles of neo-liberalism (or neo-conservatism, as the case may be). Rand formerly hobnobbed with Alan Greenspan, former President of the American Federal Reserve Bank. Their shared ideas, prestige, and purported intellectual heft were behind the perilous monetary policies and deregulation that led both to the Crash of 2008 and promoted the present economic gulf where we talk about the hegemony of the "One Percent." While she has no particular profile in Europe, she's had a resurgence of popularity with many in America, and is regarded by others as the chief cheerleader for Social Darwinist supply-side economics. She is the hero of John Boehner, Paul Ryan, and Mitch McConnell.

When van Hove though, describes his first bedazzled reading of *The Fountainhead*, he instantly recasts it within the sphere of the highly personal:

> Chief character is Howard Roark, a young architect who refuses to engage in compromise, and obstinately opts for modernism, who's allergic to each and every reference to classical antecedents. His fellow student Peter Keating, however, promptly chooses to go to work for the top architect of his day and rapidly goes up the career ladder. The book is a tornado, and grabs hold of you. It situates the mental world of the artist in opposition to that of the opportunist. And so I thought, let me just for once be Howard Roark. Let it be today.[109]

In Johan Reyniers's interview with van Hove reprinted in this volume, he confides that the idea of putting *The Fountainhead* onstage hit him during a conversation with the American political scientist Benjamin Barber, whom he revered. It should be pointed out that Barber's writings reveal the scholar to be on the opposite side of the political/philosophical fence to Rand. Barber was known for propounding a cooperative vision of diffusely distributed responsibility that cuts across class and professional lines as prescription for society's ills. His writings are dedicated to analyzing the pressures that threaten extant democracies on a global scale and which prevent new authentic democracies from forming, whereby volition and responsibility are shared across the widest possible swath of the population. From there, he ventures to propose policies that could restore and expand democracy's initial intention and reach.[110] That is a profoundly egalitarian vision in sharp contrast to one of the elite geniuses being invested with all the power, and he surely didn't endorse van Hove's project; instead, he proposed Ibsen's *Brand* as an alternative with a similar theme (Barber 2012). The notion that van Hove would select Rand's politically loaded text for adaptation and presentation betrays either an indifference, or refusal, to confront what such political ramifications might signify for "*nous autres.*" I would say that this is a case of intense self-identification with the main character (and perhaps unconsciously with others in the narrative such as Peter Keating), such that the production text he wrought from Ayn Rand's polemical novel became, in effect, an entry into his personal creative "diary," thus obliterating its larger social statement and all the political reverberations it has in America. He brought the show to the Cour d'honneur in the Palais des Papes for the Festival at Avignon, but no political storm broke out in its wake. Still, it shows a certain discretion that he hasn't yet tried to bring *The Fountainhead* to BAM, where it risks being boycotted or booed.

Setting that issue aside, and grouping *The Crucible* and *View From the Bridge* together, it can be seen that van Hove and his producer Scott Rudin were positing a new model for how serious drama on Broadway could flourish economically without compromising artistic standards. Both were resounding hits. Perhaps it takes a European experimenter, who admires these works as "classics" but is not imbued with the sense of tradition, to show the way to American producers. This is van Hove at his most conservative, but Broadway at its most radical.

The impure

The musical theatre piece *Lazarus*, a collaboration with the celebrity rock star David Bowie, was at once highly publicized and confidential, the confidential aspect enhancing its cachet (see Figure 1.18). As it was performed at the relatively intimate NYTW venue for a limited engagement, only a select few could see it, and those who were not quick enough found themselves faced with a sold-out run very early on. Matters grew exponentially more dramatic in the midst of the show's run when Bowie shocked the world by dying, drawing that much more attention to the boutique event, and causing van Hove's stock to skyrocket. He, it transpired, was one of the tiny number of intimates who had been informed of the rock star's cancer. The secrecy to which he was sworn and by which he abided extended even to his partner, Jan Versweyveld (Coscarelli and Paulson 2016). It was in this highly mediatized context that the production came and went, and has quickly become the stuff of legend, especially as so few people were actually able to see it in America.

The show is a theatrical and theatricalist sequel to the 1976 Nicholas Roeg film in which David Bowie starred, *The Man Who Fell to Earth*, which, in turn, was based on a novel of the same title by Walter Tevis. Critic David Rooney encapsulates the action, providing exposition not

FIGURE 1.18 *Lazarus*

© Jan Versweyveld

necessarily extant in van Hove's cryptic show by adaptor Enda Walsh, completing the whys and wherefores from the book and movie:

> The extremely loose narrative . . . centers on Thomas Jerome Newton (Hall), a humanoid alien who came to Earth from his drought-stricken planet many years earlier. After amassing a fortune in business while attempting to build a rocket ship to take him home, he was experimented on by the government. . . . He's tormented by visions from his past and his imagination, which fuse in his memories of the blue-haired woman he loved, Mary Lou. As his assistant, Elly (Cristin Milioti), gets sucked deeper into Newton's world, she separates from her husband (Bobby Moreno) and remakes herself as Mary Lou, forgetting her own identity for a time. . . . There's also an ethereal Girl (Sophia Anne Caruso), sent on a mission that she initially struggles to comprehend but eventually deduces is to help Newton return to his planet. (She builds a rocket onstage out of masking tape in one of the show's simplest but most evocative images.) But it emerges instead that it's Newton's task to help free the Girl from her limbo state, a revelation involving dark deeds related by Alan Cumming in a video insert. Finally, there are black-clad figures, led by the enigmatic Valentine (Michael Esper), who appears to be some kind of agent of death. Audiences will make more or less sense of the show depending on their willingness to invest in its unrelentingly opaque and choppy storytelling.
>
> *(Rooney 2015)*

The audience member who expects to get a fully explicated narrative, such as that above, will be disappointed and frustrated by the show, as the characters who appear more or less out of nowhere are not generally identified and do little to advance the action. Such apparitions recall those from Richard Foreman plays and Strindberg's *To Damascus* rather than—say—*A View From the Bridge*. They are Jungian *animae* of interiority and subjectivity, which serve more as sounding boards for the central character's psychic torments than enjoying independent existence. *Lazarus*'s loose narrative is an armature that strings various classic Bowie hit songs together with some especially composed for the occasion.

The exposition gradually and elusively reveals that the central character is a being from outer space who is in a kind of containment cell until the mystery surrounding his mission can be ascertained. Indeed, as he is confronted by the various characters described above, the basic narrative premises can only be deduced through the interstices; that is if one hadn't boned up on them by watching the film and reading the novel before coming to NYTW. The fragmentary and incomplete accretion of circumstantial information, which resists easy penetration and intellectual access, is a key element in the performance's originality. I would maintain that its inconclusiveness is intentional. Walsh and van Hove never intended to make it clear; rather they were shifting the interest of the show toward the spectacular and away from the plotline.

For the production, van Hove again insisted on exacting an extreme renovation of the NYTW space, and as with the gutting and reinstallation he carried out for *Scenes From a Marriage*, artistic director Jim Nicola again indulged him; but ticket prices were raised to unaccustomedly high rates to account for it. The audience is greeted by a scenic arrangement on the proscenium stage with which van Hove aficionados would be familiar: a closed-off anonymous looking chamber in the form of an unadorned rectangular space. There is a large screen occupying the center stage portion of the upstage wall, set against a larger rectangular, recessed alcove that encompasses it. The screen at first simply looks like a rather unattractive patch, fronted by a ledge. Against the stage left wall is a refrigerator that provides strong, extra-terrestrial LED light when opened, and embedded in the stage right side, a door, and some very unobtrusive sittables. We are back in the scenic mode of Isolation, as the box the central character inhabits is cut off from any sense of an outside world. Suffice it to say that van Hove and Versweyveld had a ready-made handy, a pre-tested spatial strategy that matched up perfectly with the hermetic story line.

The central rectangular patch on the upstage wall is rapidly revealed and put to work as a screen, and the play starts with a barrage of video and audio. The main character, Newton, lying supine on his back on the stage floor center, is circumscribed by a projection of himself on the screen. This establishes the show's leitmotif of combining live feeds of the actors together with recorded images of them. He is surrounded on the floor by a line drawing of a spaceship, and that is projected onto the vertical screen, the image starting small, but zooming in for a tight close-up. His image is replaced on the screen by that of the Girl, who sings "Life on Mars." It is reported that he is a victim of amnesia, who has thus become disassociated from his past, and survives day-to-day on Lucky Charms cereal, gin, and Twinkies. Female presences, "Adolescent Girls" One, Two, and Three, dressed in black, but sometimes in blue with blue hair, function as a chorus. Newton sings David Bowie-like, slides across the floor, agilely hops up on the ledge, and slaps the glass that has covered the rectangular screen space, leaving greasy marks on it.

Behind the glass of the larger rectangular plaque we can dimly make out the live band that accompanies the singing throughout. Beyond them is another plane of window through which we can see cityscapes and watery cascades in the gaps. A Kabuki-costumed woman emerges from behind the video screen on which she also remains paradoxically as a video image, to torment Newton and dance around him. The chorus of three female figures, now wearing facial masks, sing backup as a blonde virginal nymph also appears on-screen then emerges from it as a live entity singing about America. We also see the heartland whizzing by on-screen, then as though seen from a car hurtling along. Newton and the blonde waif, who may be a figment of his mind, lounge in front of the careening cars of the thoroughfare.

The Little Girl divulges the full exposition in one fell swoop, making it hard to absorb. Videos of Potsdamerplatz in Berlin then fill the screen, showing footage of wartime and post-war Berlin, including monuments being mauled and torn down, walled up windows, student uprisings, and so on. This raised space upstage beyond the window is transformational. As the glass panel slides open, projected Berlin gives way to a three-dimensional café setting, along with a rear-projected video café environment.

Once the screen has again eclipsed this inner sanctum of surprising and ever-altering dimensions that lead into recesses of memory-space, we are returned to the circumscribed realm of the containment chamber. Newton sings in front of the screen in presentational, rock concert fashion, so the isolation chamber's fourth wall is frankly acknowledged to be absent. This blatant theatricalism, playing directly to the audience, renders Newton not so isolated after all.

The Three Adolescent Girls assist Newton in killing the girl, Mary, who might be an impostor stand-in or doppelganger of his daughter. The actor playing Newton sings in front of a neatly in-sync, congruent image of himself on the screen, an interplay of live and recorded selves in perfect symbiosis. Once that melding is established, it is then torn asunder as the video image of Newton separates, escapes the screen, and runs all over the surfaces of the room, finally filling up the entire back wall. The virtually-projected Newton yanks aside virtual velvet drapes, which open to reveal identical *actual* velvet drapes that the *actual* Newton also then pulls apart. So while the initial scenic arrangement had established an understated principle of Isolation, the electronic media layer on many witty, brilliantly executed stunts that lead to an expansion of the space in all dimensions, and synthesize Ramification both of the human presence and the space itself, the entirely morphed environment having become an extension of Newton's being.

As the action winds down a milky white viscous paste, like condensed milk, seeps in from unknown provenance and covers the stage floor. The dead Girl wakes up, and chats with Newton. He recovers his past and family through her. The Girl unravels masking tape, creating a schematic outline of a rocket on the stage floor. Newton lies down within the rocket, which fits snugly about his form. Both man and rocket are ramified on the screen and projected to the audience as a live video feed shot from directly above the stage floor. On screen, the rocket outlining the central character's body ultimately lifts off and sets out into the stratosphere via computer video technology, propelling Newton back to the planet he came from.

Some of the harsh criticisms dished up by reviewer David Cote in his pan give hints as to the show's innovative structure. He starts off by lambasting it as "cryptic" and for being "too weird and disjointed" and redolent of "self-indulgent stasis." It is the playwright/adaptor Enda Walsh who comes in for his worst barbs. Cote accuses him of specializing in "the static, repetitive and faux-existential: Beckett Lite. His fragmentary, banal dialogue frustrates any emotional or intellectual connection with the characters or situation." Cote admits to admiration, however, for the Bowie songs as well as their delivery, together with van Hove's "typical visual flair" (Cote 16–22 December 2015). By criticizing these creative choices, Cote, the epitome of the conventional, literal-minded sensibility, ipso facto implies his expectations and standards or critical "horizon" (which, like so many critics, he assumes the reader shares) for what he has no doubt are the right ingredients of a good theatre play: it must be dynamic and full of logical dramatic action; it must be clearly legible; it must be, in contemporary parlance, "relatable," and its parts must fit together in a tight causal dramatic line; its dialogue must flow and sparkle with originality. Indeed, if one only added likeable characters to that recipe it would be the play of his dreams. And it is also unsurprising though paradoxical that he thoroughly appreciates all the abstraction, fragmentation, and ambiguity typical of David Bowie's rock songs, the very qualities that he will not tolerate in a theatre production. This list would express the exigencies and prejudices of the average American middlebrow theatre-goer, and a play created from it would be the beau ideal of the "Culinary Theatre" that Brecht deplored and the "Dead Theatre" that Peter Brook condemned.

Lazarus manifestly violates every item on the checklist. But therein, for me, lies all its interest and the tipoff that van Hove hasn't lost his willingness to subvert, offend, and fly in the face of convention. For Cote is right that the play has cryptic situations, is weird, discontinuous, and static in structure, and has fragmentary, banal dialogue. These features taken together give it avant-garde bona fides, and betray a seeming indifference to pleasing and reassuring the audience. Writer, Enda Walsh, speaks without any embarrassment about the show's "opaque" and "disjointed" narrative, exulting rather that it's "hallucinogenic, drunken really." He freely concedes that the audience will have to conceive their own story as the show goes along (Van Hove and Walsh 2016). The concessions to commercial exigencies are the Bowie name, the crowd-pleasing musical numbers, and the stunning visuals, all of which do render the show (why even call it a play?) more palatable.

Thus a new van Hove synthesis is born. Dutch critic Herien Wensink calls it both "a total-artwork," and "a chameleon-like" artwork (Wensink 2015b). Ben Brantley's highly laudatory review betrays a greater tolerance for the show's forays into the new than Cotes' does, but finds some of the same issues to be troublesome:

> These [production] elements often meld exactly as they should, which means that they create a haunting impression of dividedness, of life as a perplexing jumble of puzzle pieces that can never be fully assembled. Unfortunately, that sense of dislocation extends more clumsily to the relation of the script to the songs. The spoken story line, when it's not opaque, brings to mind a young adult novel of the supernatural, featuring restless and winsome spirits longing to be put to rest.
>
> *(Brantley 2015)*

He goes on to note that Michael Hall, who plays Newton, "has mastered a perfect semi-anaesthetized style of speech," thus heralding a return to or continuation of van Hove's *More Stately Mansions* experiments in "Zombie Speech." Still, the director is absolved of any of the flaws the writing suffers from: "Van Hove's signature style—skeletal, shimmering and ominous—is as distinctive as Mr. Bowie's, and in many ways, a perfect match for it" (Ibid.). It is not necessarily the case that van Hove has embarked on an unpromising creative path, rather that he should be more careful which collaborators he chooses to take risks with.

The series of songs, many of which are hauntingly familiar from the various phases of David Bowie's long career, do not necessarily fit neatly into the narrative's ostensible episodes. They make commentary or are simply inserted without excuse or justification. This arbitrary connection of "numbers" is a throwback to van Hove's variety show, post-dramatic roots of *Wild Lords* and *Imitations* as well as his later forays into musical theatre, including *Carmen* and *True Love*; all examples of what he is proud to call "impure theatre" (T'Jonck 2002). The alienated central character together with all the doppelgangers and negative animae who manifest themselves as outgrowths of, or worthy opponents to, the central character's ego, take us back to the subjective, neo-expressionist world of *Rumors*, van Hove's first show. There he had another three-character chorus of specialists to provide pseudo-expert commentary on the aberrant central character Matthias's motives. And Newton—the quintessential outsider, the guinea pig, the cool hipster—is akin to that far off character of *Rumors* in more ways than one. Let us recall once more the favorable review Ivo received back in his artistic infancy in 1985: "Although the average theatregoer still swears by 'a story,' . . . van Hove's Concept is an associative sort of theatre through which the audience creates their own 'stories.' It isn't easy, but it can't leave you unaffected" (De Win 1985).

Lazarus is a return to his roots in the "associative" and the hermetic. However, this *mix* of two genres—the musical variety show and the expressionist montage—is something new for van Hove, resists easy commercial digestion, and perhaps represents a new and tantalizing road ahead for the future. As Raymond Loewy said: "Consumers are torn between two opposing forces: neophilia, a curiosity about new things; and neophobia, a fear of anything too new" (Thompson January/February 2017). Insofar as theatre is a commodity, it is a question of getting the right mix for people to "buy the product." Van Hove seems to understand and be guided in part by this principle, although the right mix may at times elude him.

The show seemed overly contained in the NYTW theatre, and could easily have a future life in much larger auditoriums or even stadiums, especially considering the David Bowie allure. It has the potential to expand into the proper scale for its rock concert dimensions, yet retain its introspective, ontological focus. Indeed, in Fall 2016, *Lazarus* was transferred to a larger space, the King's Cross Theatre, "a pop-up space five times" the size of NYTW (Hitchings 2016), in London with some cast changes to include British actors. While it played to sell-out crowds, the critics were similarly divided on the show's worth. Many of the same complaints surfaced regarding the narrative structure, and again, van Hove's directing generally escaped the barbs. Often he wasn't mentioned at all (Clapp 2016a; Shuttleworth 2016). Some critics praised the spectacularity of the show, one for example gushing that it was "stunningly staged" (Shenton 2016). Henry Hitchings, at the negative end, said that despite its "striking projections," it was "stuck in a mood of sophisticated solemnity" (Hitchings 2016). Michael Billington, in a trope that will feel familiar from the "War of Images," asserted that:

> while the separate ingredients are fascinating to watch in Ivo van Hove's kaleidoscopic production, I rarely felt moved. . . . Van Hove, his long-term designer Jan Versweyveld and the video designer Tal Yarden have created an engrossing spectacle. The deliberate plainness of the surround is offset by the profusion of images that pour from the central screen. . . Yet, for all the show's skill, I found myself more impressed by the visual sophistication than emotionally engaged by the story.
>
> *(Billington 2016a)*

Some critics didn't even grant the brilliance of the images:

> Belgian director Ivo van Hove has made a brave choice in giving us a beige (ugh!) set to look at for nearly two hours, with a less than lovely hinterland of blokey musicians looming behind the apartment windows. The video projections are surprisingly rudimentary given Bowie's avant-gardism.
>
> *(Cavendish 2016)*

And Ian Shuttleworth ominously noted that Versweyveld had "recycled" the same hotel room setting from his recent production of *Song From Far Away* (Shuttleworth 2016). The reservations expressed represented something of a reversal for van Hove from the run of frothy praise he'd garnered for such productions as *Roman Tragedies*, *View From the Bridge*, and *Song From Far Away*.

Acknowledging these London critics' caveats, *Lazarus* is still a potential paradigm for van Hove to follow and augurs a return to his avant-garde, riskier roots, while managing to retain his new-found larger audience. As van Hove had said some years earlier: "I even think that classical theater will continue to be in existence, and the backbone of theatre forms will also remain, but the future will be in the 'impure' arts" (T'Jonck 2002).

A second foray in a promising direction is embodied in van Hove's guest production of Visconti's 1969 film script, *The Damned*; a movie that boasted an international company of actors, who spoke or were dubbed into German (see Figure 1.19). Van Hove's version was acted live by the famed Comédie Française in French at the Cour d'honneur of the Palais des Papes for the 2016 Festival at Avignon. For van Hove, this assignment was exponentially more of an honor as, strangely, the Comédie Française had only been invited to pride of place in the prestigious annual Avignon summer festival six times in its 69-year history, the most recent being thirteen years previously.

At the center of this production were several themes that interested van Hove: the question of the nature of leadership over a big business through turbulent times and under a regime that exacts moral compromise; the pattern of an historical epoch depicted through a family struggle to

FIGURE 1.19 *The Damned*

© Jan Versweyveld

the death that has overtones of Greek tragedy as in *The Oresteia*; and the topos of decadence, as epitomized both in the character of Martin and the major sub-plot concerning the S.A. brown-shirts. All these are familiar from other van Hove shows. The first item is reflected in the memorable remark he made when explaining his interest in Shakespeare's *Roman Tragedies*: "I'm head of a company myself. I'm a manager myself. I know how decisions are brought to a successful con-clusion" (Arian 2007). While the company he's referencing isn't a steel-turned-armament man-ufacturer, but rather a highly visible, state-supported theatre company, the nature of compromise and political pressure operating within both may have analogies.

The succession of men who lead the Essenbeck Steel Works, a fictionalization of the Krupp empire that supplied Hitler with munitions for his military campaigns, reflects the downward spiral of CEOs. It starts with the aged patrician, Joachim, who saw his nation through World War I, the disarmament forced by the Treaty of Versailles, and rearmament, as Hitler began to violate the terms of the treaty. He abdicates in favor of his son, Herbert, not because he cannot tolerate serving the National Socialist cause, but because he has the aristocrat's contempt for the low-life Hitler, and never wants to find himself in a social situation where he'll have to shake his hand. His son, Herbert, is sensitive and rational, a virulent anti-Nazi married to a Jewess. In no time he is forced into exile so he never has a chance to lead the company. Herbert's place is taken by S.A. Commandant Konstantin, an out-and-out thug. But Martin, the pervert son, controls over fifty percent of the company's shares, and in a capricious fit, replaces Konstantin with Friedrich, his mother's lover, who is an unaffiliated technocrat. Ultimately, Martin himself, by then a willing tool of the regime, having donned the SS uniform, takes over the active running of the firm. Thus, Visconti provides at least five models of business executives, one more craven than the next. One can view them either as individuals or as a five-headed hydra.

It may be remembered that even the best Krupp CEO is supervising an industry whose purpose is to wreak death and destruction on mankind. But the moral dubiousness of engaging in the manufacture of weapons of mass destruction barely enters into either Visconti or van Hove's productions. The closest we get to the reality of the physical process and moral implications of weapons manufacture is a backdrop video of clean, efficient factory machines, gears, and pistons pumping and grinding away to create links for the long transition between scenes.

The show played in front of the magnificent medieval backdrop of the inner Cour d'honneur of the Palais des Papes; a vast stone wall inset with occasional Baroque doors and windows up to the highest level rises above and behind the spectacle. Recorded hard metal music stands in place of Maurice Jarre's memorable, pounding movie score. German lyrics are sometimes heard. There is also a live instrumental ensemble playing an original score of somewhat discordant modern music. The space is wide open. To stage right, leading directly from down to upstage, is a straight line of make-up tables with large round globes circling each mirror. In a parallel line are square, industrial black sittables. In a third layer of offstage reality, in fact furthest offstage, are compact risers on which sit black-clad S.S. men, their faces glued to the action. From a semiotic point of view, they are stationed behind everything. Symmetrically across the open expanse from these three lines on a raised platform, is a straight line, this time composed of coffins, parallel to the make-up tables across the stage from them. These, like everything else, are black and characterless. The coffins too are poised to get their chance to participate in the historical event, and indeed they get it.

The Damned makes one of the most sophisticated uses of video we have seen from van Hove, particularly for its multi-focus and monumentality on a vast screen matching the giant scale of the Cour d'honneur. Although there seems to be only one live cameraman moving about, an extraordinary variety of clashing realities are dizzyingly picked up as he circles the space. The effects go by so fast we have no time to analyze them, but can only, bewildered, try to absorb them on the run. The offstage area by the make-up tables is frequently in the frame, reminding us of the half made-up actors waiting in the wings, dispassionately watching either themselves in the mirrors or the action onstage. Beyond them are other actors in costume, mostly S.S. men sitting in rows, patiently awaiting their turn on the stage of history until the time is ripe. So the offstage spaces, which perpetually come into view either through the roving of the naked eye or directed to it by the hand-held camera and screen, force the audience to confront latencies and potentialities. The audience may not ignore what stands in wait—the takeover by the sinister S.S. not to mention all that the coffins imply—and is made complicit, and by extension shares in the responsibility for allowing unfolding events to become active, emerge, and take to the stage.

Once again, given the vast open central space, van Hove is working with the Reduction principle. However, the acting and staging style is no longer neo-classical as in other recent shows, but something at once less recognizable and more compelling. The family riches are embodied in an array of stainless steel goblets, plates, and bowls that litter a large side-table. Following Herbert's exile, the deviant scion of the family who controls the majority of stock, Martin, sweeps this landscape/still life of conspicuous consumption off the table in one fell clattering swoop, and it is clear that all dignity and tradition has come to an end for the Essenbecks.

According to the van Hove formula, the precise, authentic history being related has less primacy or verisimilitude than the pattern of which it is a paradigm. From the display, we are meant to make our own connections with present-day life. Some lines of dialogue jump out at us, mostly from the mouth of Herbert, the well-intentioned, altruistic son. As it becomes clear that Hitler will inexorably assume power following the crucial burning of the Reichstag, Herbert tells his family: "It's too late, too late for us to soothe our conscience." His family, like so many German industrialists, abetted the dictator's rise to power, and now they have only themselves to blame. Without detailing the ways in which they have enabled what happens, it is understood. And, if there were any room for doubt, the camera periodically zooms into the audience, capturing that mass on the big screen for their own contemplation as Herbert tweaks our consciences.

Then, once he recognizes that he must leave Germany to save his and his Jewish family's life (although they are already doomed), he says: "Every day thousands of people are forced to emigrate from our land. We aren't the least fortunate among them." And instantly the entire current immigrant crisis is invoked, and hits home; the rise of Nazism mirrors the present precarious state of Europe where the extreme right is presently clamoring for a bigger place at the table once more. There is no need to comment on how this show anticipated what is happening in America; we are living its ghastly progress all the time.

In the midst of all the political upsets the play depicts, laced with staid, sentimental tableaux of Herbert's classic two-child family, the presence of the young brother Martin insinuates itself as a disruptive element; not threatening political stability, for of that he is oblivious, but of the standard idealized image of the heterosexual family unit. During the initial family gathering, he grabs the mike and does a musical number reminiscent of the master of ceremonies in *Cabaret*. Whereas in the movie, Martin appeared on a little raised stage in full female regalia, doing a Marlene Dietrich imitation, here he merely performs before the staid spectators scantily dressed, resembling an Egon Schiele drawing, assaulting them all with the affront of his own exposed body. Following this shocking introduction, we assume he is gay, but even his queerness is stomach-churningly subversive as he sexually pursues both his pre-adolescent niece, and subsequently, his own mother.

Among the multiple, ingenious ways in which Ramification was employed in *The Damned*, thanks to the various domains established on this spare set, was the inclusion of an extended game of hide-and-seek Martin played with his young nieces, Herbert's daughters. The counting down before "Ready or not, here I come," does double duty as the countdown to the Reichstag fire. There is a hush as Martin hides in some dark closet, that is invisible onstage to the naked eye, with the older of the two girls; their silent, close confinement splayed out on the big screen. It comes to an abrupt crisis as the girl first casts her eyes around while her uncle kisses her hands. What then follows is off camera, and cannot be determined, as she suddenly and inexplicably screams for help. As the unnerving screen life goes blank, life on the stage is unleashed in a frenzy, the personal getting swamped by the historical moment. The whole family dashes about the stage in all directions, and there is a seamless morphing of one emergency into another, with the girl's father and mother forced to hustle their branch of the family out of Germany.

The show proceeds via a series of set piece confrontations between family members as outside events, which force the company to make constant adjustments, run their pre-determined course. One such memorable bit of business is the search for Martin by his mother Sophie. She receives notice, presumably from him, the chief but *fainéant* shareholder, of a special board meeting. But he has disappeared. She exits the stage to hunt him down through all the stairs, corridors, and horse stalls of the off-limits inner precincts of the actual Palais des Papes. We follow Sophie's elaborate movements throughout the building on live video feed only to find Martin, back on stage where the search began, cowering and crawling on his belly.

In the play, as in the film, the historical "Night of the Long Knives," whereby the S.S. (led by Goebbels) crushed its rival militia the S.A. (led by Erich Roehm), proves to be the splashiest and most extended segment. The massacre of one branch of Hitler's armed forces by another occurred as the entire corps of the S.A. indulged in a holiday orgy on an island in the Wannsee. Again, van Hove creates a special theatre language to substitute for Visconti's masterful cinematic rendition. Konstantin, the Essenbeck cousin with S.A. affiliations, enters with a young Aryan giant of a lieutenant. They are the only live-stage participants. They are, however, accompanied by a gathering of multitudes of virtual S.A. members on screen upstage of them, that sing a Heimat song. The lieutenant goes into a little jig, with Konstantin circling him. On screen, shot from far above, the S.A. troopers strip and launch into an orgy. Downstage, meanwhile, Konstantin and his lover drink big steins of beer. They then strip, dump a keg of beer on the stage, and literally breast-stroke through the lake of beer they have made. The onscreen orgy of sex and noise intensifies. Konstantin and the lieutenant attack a bargirl and strip her of apron and garters with which they adorn themselves. All the soldiers, onscreen and off, circle and do the cancan, ultimately dissolving in drunkenness. The two then awaken from the debauch onstage. On screen, the men are picked up in the orgy's aftermath suddenly, lying, littering the ground in drunken stupors, still seen from above. A contingent of S.S. men silently enter, stand over them and shoot them one by one. With each blast a blood stain instantly appears around the body. Finally, two others, including Friedrich, president of the company, come out and toss a bucket of red blood on Konstantin and the boy lieutenant, a ceremonial gesture signaling their death. The two dead victims then stand and are led off into their inevitable coffins. Following this segment of the Night of the Long Knives, which terminates Act I, the brown dance floor is rolled up. Brown was the color of the S.A. Everything on stage is now uniformly black. Black, the color of the S.S.

Four parties, who at present constitute the mutually mistrustful leadership of the Essenbeck manufacturing company, sit at an industrial-style dinner table while it is being set by S.S. men, with an array of pristine stainless steel plates and settings. This silent segment is focused entirely on a choreography of eyes, as the four company directors exchange and conceal visual messages. Later in the scene, the four rise, and stare offstage. A full minute of silent stage time goes by before it is revealed that they are looking incredulously at Herbert Essenbeck, the sacrificial lamb returned from exile.

These scenes described above are intercut with a parallel series of ceremonial segments. Thus, the balance between the addressing of "questions" and the penetration into the irrational, the twin elements that van Hove has identified to be at the heart of the theatrical experience, are both mined.

There is the ceremony of assassination. Many characters die throughout the show. Most of their deaths occur without preamble or explanation. They are voluntarily escorted by a squadron of Black Shirts up onto the platform where the coffins are lined up. A gun is pointed at the head and silently explodes. The victim, often relieved and smiling to surrender a difficult life, is formally led into the coffin and there lies down. The lid once closed, the "corpse" is shot by camera from within the coffin. Invariably the victim appears on the great screen in sepia close-up, suddenly horrified at their situation, silently protesting being left in that coffin. This protest continues at length on the great screen while the life of the onstage actors moves on obliviously apace in front of the giant, grimacing, pleading face.

A variation on this ceremony occurs when Martin, during the recurring game of Hide and Seek, secretes himself in one of the coffins. There his young niece comes upon him. He tricks her into taking his place in the coffin and shuts the lid on her. She, like all victims, appears fighting against the reality of death on screen. Her nanny arrives to rescue her from the coffin. Unfortunately for the little girl, her Jewish mother is later reported to have been intercepted in their attempted escape from Germany and to have perished in a concentration camp. Her father has to trade his own life for his daughters' so they may survive.

Yet another variation occurs when the dignified and sensual family doyenne Sophie ultimately gets tarred and feathered by her own son Martin, which is in itself a ceremony of defilement linked to her belated marriage with Friedrich, the technocrat. Covered in bird feathers, she is then dressed as a bride and escorted by her paramour Friedrich, who'd run the company, into twin coffins, where—in a sign of suicide—they lie down, and voluntarily resign themselves to their fate.

There is also the ceremony of going into exile, which Herbert effects by simply stepping down off the stage. His pronouncements from that exceptionally used part of the space nearer the audience and outside the rectangle of the Essenbecks' comfort zone, have a Brechtian flavor, the off-stage area being indicative of broader consciousness of the historical significances regarding the events they are living through.

And finally there is the ceremonial preparation for mass annihilation that constitutes the coda to the performance. Martin stoops before the great steel bowl down center, gathers up and covers himself with white powder, crosses to the platform up center, picks up a machine gun, and guns down the audience. The preparations for this show went on in the wake of terrorist outrages in Paris and Brussels. As the actors convened for the first day of rehearsal, they learned of yet another such attack in the airport of Istanbul. The perhaps too facile and specious equivalence between Martin's conversion to Nazism with present-day Islamic terrorism grows out of that immediate context.

Still, all in all, *The Damned* represents an extremely positive new direction for van Hove. The images of this epic show are stunning, the stage life layered, dense, and continually surprising. He has found a convincing "stage language" he always seeks when adapting film scenarios. The French actors, despite their various lapses into maudlin tropes, are well-suited to conform to the brittle aesthetic surface of this unsentimental, decadent rendition of the Nazi period.

A third promising recent departure is represented by the TGA production of *The Hidden Force*, an adaptation of a turn-of-the century novel by revered Dutch author Louis Couperus (see Figure 1.20). This is a tale of the Netherlands' colonial past in Indonesia, and van Hove retains its highly narrative quality, taking great advantage of the cultural atmospheres and artifacts of the Javanese environment. The deftly managed clash and intermingling of the two cultures' performance modes, which echo the key dramatic confrontation in the subject matter, injects a great richness into the production.

It is set on a radically stripped stage space, with loose floorboards. Almost all physical objects— costume racks and racks holding indigenous musical instruments—are pressed up against the three solid encasing stage walls. The sparsest of furniture elements are added and subtracted as needed. This is a ceremonial space and a story-telling space, with a strong bow to Peter Brook, which nonetheless advances the way imagery may be produced further into the twenty-first century. There are periodic washes over all three walls of video imagery of sea, storms, and the ambient natural elements that engulf the lives of the Indonesian and European characters alike. These screen images are filled out by occasional infusions of thick fog that pump up through the floorboards. The mist becomes so thick that it defines the space like ever shifting panels. The image is intensified when dense, tropical rain drenches the stage space from the flies in a convincing rendition of a typhoon in the rainy season.

FIGURE 1.20 *The Hidden Force*

© Jan Versweyveld

The stage imagery generally fortifies two-character scenes of dialogue with additional characters that move in counterpoint, sometimes dance-like, others in still tableaux, giving a shorthand complexity to the picture. The cast has likewise been enriched with a more multi-cultural variety of actors than Ivo's usual, as the stage is infused with ethnic dance and ethnic music. The costumes, which include some typical van Hove business suits for the Dutch bureaucratic official, the Resident, nonetheless, are expanded in range to include skirts and other looser, more colorful body drapings and wrappings, again borrowing from Indonesian styles. So, the whole staging takes on a looser, more free-form, novelistic feeling that has scenes blending into each other, than van Hove has generally permitted himself of late. Despite the empty stage, the infusion of natural elements provides the actors with more of a sense of altered environment, and so affords their performances a greater sense of visceral support and hence authenticity than has been seen in other recent productions, notably *View From the Bridge* and *The Crucible*. In such simple actions as standing and sitting, but also in the release of intense passions, they are manifestly more at ease in their bodies due to the embrace of the surroundings, the introduction of so many guest performers from other cultures, and the performers' granular familiarity with Couperus's distinctively crafted Dutch idiom.

The Hidden Force is the first of an anticipated Couperus trilogy on van Hove's roster. The second and most recently produced adaptation of one of his novels, *The Things That Pass* (*Oude Mensen en de dingen dat voorbij gaan*, 1906), was presented in fall 2016. In the fall of 2017, the third entry will be Couperus' *Small Spirits* (*De boek der kleine zielen*, 1901). Written five years after Thomas Mann's *Buddenbrooks*, *The Things That Pass*, which it resembles, is a chronicle of a colonial family residing in Java, repatriated back to their native city, The Hague. Although virtually unknown in English-speaking realms, *Old People and The Things That Pass* (van Hove has eliminated the first part of the title) has long been considered a classic in the Netherlands and required reading for generations of Dutch schoolchildren. Contrary to a play like Ibsen's *Ghosts*, another roughly contemporaneous work dealing with a deep dark secret from the past that seeps into and despoils the present, this adaptation ambles with novelistic looseness. The characters, the two oldest of which are approaching their centenary, are like the living dead, their existences stretching out in a limbo-medium. For despite their remarkable longevity a great shameful secret has infected the quality of their inner, secret lives. In various ways it puts one in mind of Proust's *Time Regained*, Strindberg's *Ghost Sonata*, Victor Hugo's *The Burgraves*, Ionesco's *Journeys Among the Dead*, and even Kantor's *The Dead Class*. "A little like Chekhov, but without the humor" (Hillaert 22 October 2016), wrote one Flemish critic. And yet I detected a fair amount of very special humor in it. It is written in the masterful naturalistic prose of the Belle Epoque that is yet decidedly tipping into modernity with outrageous, insistent repetitions and near-streams of consciousness that leap forward to the styles of Proust and Gertrude Stein.

The Dercksz family, though well off and outwardly respectable, are shunned by society due to the scandalous ways in which several of them have comported themselves: one woman is twice divorced and now married to a man twenty years younger than herself; another, who has no intention of ever marrying, lives in sin with a lover in the south of France; and one of the men is a serial pedophile, who has had to be repeatedly bailed out for his infamous dalliances with servant girls; and yet another has converted to Catholicism (scandalous in this ultra-Protestant milieu!) and become an overzealous lay sister in a French convent.

The superannuated matriarch of the clan, Ottilie Dercksz, is visited every day by Mr. Takma, the man with whom she had been lovers over a half-century earlier back in Java and together with whom she had murdered her odious husband—the dread secret they've been harboring. Their relationship, which has long since hit an impasse, is juxtaposed with a new relationship between two youngish first cousins Lot and Ellie, and it is on their love that the plot turns. Their impending union, while vaguely incestuous, embodies the hope that the family can turn a corner. But first "the thing," the evil homicide from long ago, must finally "pass," and a cleansing occur. But it passes ever so slowly! That mantra, oft-repeated like a tocsin in the book, is the trope that permeates the proceedings. Also, a series of misadventures conspires to inform one family member after another of the long-ago murder, although the perpetrators to the end are convinced that they alone are in the know.

Performed in the massive Rabozaal in the Amsterdam Schouwburg, there is a deep, open proscenium space with a very high ceiling overhead. The stage gives an impression of emptiness once more, although ordinary chairs are lined up facing each other on the two sides of the space, going all the way back. Behind each row of chairs are sets of transparent glass units on which are carelessly smeared primitive, horrifying masks in white soap; talismanic fetish effigies. Far upstage is a giant mirror which offers the audience a reflection of itself. In front of this mirror is a modern rendition of a grandfather clock: a square metal and glass stand with little rectilinear tinkling clocks perched on top.

The action transpires in a cinematic rhythm, with characters meeting in the vast open space in the center to play out scenes from the book. They drift in at random and settle in the peripheral chairs to watch the show—transforming the space to a great waiting room, "a transit-room toward death" (Hillaert 2016)—and join the action as needed. Behind the

FIGURE 1.21 *The Things That Pass*

© Jan Versweyveld

other chairs and far downstage, Anna the Maid is seated, stationed as both silent commentator and intermediary (like Berthe in *Hedda Gabler*) between the other characters and the audience.

This theatrical rendition, with its naked stage and uniformly black, denatured costumes, strips the original novel of its local color and period quaintness, leaving a stark universality (see Figure 1.21). It is also typical of van Hove that he introduces Couperus's subtextual suggestions of semi-conscious longing into the plane of the corporal, even gross. Ottilie's twice-divorced daughter who is also called Ottilie—as is one of *her* daughters making three Ottilies in the show creating a situation not only confusing, but perhaps absurdist in the fashion of Ionesco's *Jack or the Submission*—not only never tires of sex with her young husband (who has long since tired of sex with her), but also entertains feelings that border on carnal for her two sons, each a child of a different husband. In the show she leaps at them where they stand, locking her hands behind their necks and her legs around their waists, pressing her crotch into their torsos. Lot, the young central character and the first of Ottilie's sons, also bears many resemblances to Couperus himself. He's a writer and dilettante, besotted with beautiful aesthetic surfaces. In the book, while on his honeymoon to Provence with his newly-wedded Ellie, he speaks with submerged admiration for his scandalously liberated aunt's hunky Italian husband. In this theatrical version, he goes so far as to approach the shirtless paragon and caress his washboard chest. The body-builder, meanwhile, stands smiling the while, oblivious to the transgressive touch. It is clearly the enactment of an unrequited fantasy, but one which the bisexual Couperus didn't include in his novel.

While the visual aspect of this show is predominantly austere, in following Lot and Ellie to the south of France, the transition between the two empty spaces is positively virtuosic. The gigantic upstage mirror whirs into action and slowly starts to revolve horizontally. As it tilts upward, the image of the audience that is reflected on it starts to rise too, grows attenuated, and then disappears to be replaced by brilliant white light; as in fact the mirror reflects all that is on the ceiling . . . the plethora of lighting instruments. Then a vast shadow runs uncannily along the stage floor from up-to-downstage as the mirror tilts away from the ceiling. It is then replaced by a large video screen—on the mirror's obverse side—and footage of Italy is shown as we follow the newlyweds on their itinerary. Eventually the apparatus revolves once more to bring us back to the mirror, when Lot and Ellie arrive at their final destination. This complete sequence reverses once that interlude is over and they travel back north to Holland.

Another striking tour de force is the exit and return of the whole cast in between intervals. What might generally be a simple, perfunctory operation of getting actors on and off stage, here is like a balletic dance of death. They move ever so slowly—in fact like the "thing" that refuses to entirely "pass"—and evoke in as simple an image as possible a realm of ghosts or zombies. It is reminiscent of, although in a different key and tempo, the repetitive revolving of the ageless pupils in Kantor's *The Dead Class*. Among other theatrical ghosts that haunt this stage are Nagg and Nell from Samuel Beckett's ashcans. For when old Ottilie and Mr. Takma uncharacter-istically break the silence of stoic protocol during one of their quotidian tête-à-têtes, and bring up the murder they'd collaborated in, their shrieking verbal duet recalls the strident grotesquery of Beckett's *Endgame*. And speaking of games, the Toneelgroep Amsterdam ensemble is at the top of theirs with this native Dutch masterpiece. Although many were cast against type (most are perforce too young, for one thing) and defied the description of their character given in the novel, they inhabited their roles most credibly nonetheless. It is as though this obligatory book was running in their veins and they were merely channeling the masterful dialogue they'd been nourished on since a young age. For once, it was Dutch actors playing the very best of Dutch poetry, and it fit them like a glove.

I would adjudge that this family chronicle is just that, with an emphasis on karmic debts that can only be expiated across the generations, thus framing it in a cosmic space rather than a political one. And yet, Wouter Hillaert perceives a certain political dimension as well:

> The great auditorium looks itself in the face in a giant rear mirror: old Europe that has given up on its striving toward a better future and is aestheticizing its downward spiral for a sweet swan-song. The standing ovation for it is one of lost souls.
>
> *(Hillaert 2016)*

This, as van Hove says, is text theatre, whereby a great writer's words are transformed to unforgettable three-dimensional images.

Key productions

In this next section, I will present detailed descriptions of salient productions that either changed van Hove's course over time or were a strong paradigm for a given kind of approach. Taken together, they reveal an amazing virtuosity. Many are productions that today's theatre-goers, some of whom are only now discovering van Hove, will barely have heard of, if at all.

My main aim here is to bring these shows back to life with words, so that the reader may vicariously re-experience the long-dead theatrical event in some small measure: that is, to present a précis of the "production text," the director's contribution, and only to summarize the plot where absolutely necessary. My model for presenting van Hove's contribution is what Edward Braun did so lucidly for Merhold's famous production of Gogol's *The Inspector General* in his book *Meyerhold on Theatre*, with descriptions so vivid they make the reader feel as if they had been there watching (Braun 1969: 209–254).

Wild Lords, *one of three defining oeuvres de jeunesse, AKT/Vertikaal, 1984*

Van Hove burst onto the scene with *Rumors, Disease Germs*, and *Like in the War* as a true *auteur*—both writing and directing his shows. Then he veered off to direct a few extant scripts of small-cast plays by Pinter and Marguerite Duras, but traded in that traditional method for yet a different, collaborative process of theatrical creation. While in numerous interviews he has been insistent on the point that he is, "a text director," it was not always thus, nor is it entirely the case even today. As he was searching for his artistic identity early in his career he fashioned shows with rudimentary and incidental verbal texts; productions that were sprawling, undisciplined, and even self-indulgent. In *Wild Lords, Imitations*, and *Wonders of Humanity* he engaged in a method of ensemble creation, more or less equivalent to what today is called "devised theatre." They served a significant purpose. With them he was to introduce much of his stock imagery, theatrical ideas, and thematic material that he would later employ time and again, marbling it into extant texts written by others. During this delimited phase, rather than writing a text himself or staging another author's text, he assembled a group of actors and hit on a governing idea, using some inspiring author's work or themes as jumping off points. Then he would embark on improvisational explorations that eventually were given some modest shaping, finally to be performed to an audience. Subsequently leaving such group explorations behind, he returned to staging a series of extant plays by modern authors.

This was more of a process of creation than a performance style in itself, developed in the 1960s by the Living Theatre, the Open Theatre, the Performance Group, and a slew of other American experimental companies. It was later picked up in Flanders by collectives such as the Internationale Nieuwe Scene, De Trojaanse Paard, Maatschappij Discordia, and others. A certain set of transitional collectives that flourished in the 1970s, and with whose work van Hove was certainly familiar, such as Theater Antigone from Kortrijk, Belgium, 't Barre Land based in Utrecht, and Dood Paard from Amsterdam, also made an impact. The German theoretician, Lehmann who has studied these particular Dutch-language companies, relates that their performances were:

> characterized by a peculiar mixture of school theatre atmosphere, party mood and folk theatre. The players saunter in leisurely fashion onto the stage, chatting, glancing at the audience, muttering things to each other, seemingly agreeing on something. Then it may gradually become clear that they are in the middle of allocating roles. Jokes, within the play or outside of it, private conversations and a mode of acting that does not want to cover up the lack of professionalism: all this converges into scenes that can in turn be interrupted again.
> *(Lehmann 2006: 121)*

They all produced what more recently has been termed "post-dramatic" works in the sense that they embraced, "the unfolding and blossoming of a potential of disintegration, dismantling and deconstruction within drama itself," performances in which a "staged text (*if* text is staged) is merely a component with equal rights in a gestic, musical, visual, etc., total composition" (Lehmann 2006: 44, 46). In coopting the group developmental method, van Hove was perforce exploring the same sources which had inspired the immediately earlier schools and artists whose work had so moved him—Artaud and Grotowski.

While shows from van Hove's mature period largely don't work with this aleatory aesthetic in the way, for example, that the Belgian company TG Stan continues to (Willinger and Van Belle

2014), one does pick up on flashes of it here and there; an arrow to be plucked at will from the artist's stylistic quiver. But his three early ensemble pieces manifestly leaned heavily in this direction.

The first of the three, *Wild Lords* (presented under the rubric of AKT/Vertikaal in 1984), is a meditation on manhood, and an explicitly gay, even homoerotic piece—van Hove's most explicit coming out statement (see Figure 1.22). It can certainly be characterized as post-dramatic, as in contrast with his later productions, dialogue takes a back seat and the original source material disperses almost to the point of being unrecognizable.

While he claims to have used William Burroughs's daring and outlandish 1971 novel *The Wild Boys* as a jumping off point, it is no more than that, for *Wild Lords* can't really be regarded as an adaptation at all. At most, the novel and show are both epic explorations of homoerotic longing, but there the similarity ends. None of the narrative segments from the van Hove piece match up with any from Burroughs's novel, which imagines international herds of feral boys going up against nation states' heavily armed battalions, and obliterating them using various fantastical weapons of mass destruction in a quest to wipe out the institution of the nuclear family, and by extension, civilization as we know it.

The book also indulges in endless ritualistic episodes of surrealistically sensational sexual encounters, but they bear little resemblance to relationships found in van Hove's play. Burroughs's book obsessively repeats certain scenes of seduction, suggesting the existence of a coordinated international network of squalid, but mythopoeically grandiose homosexual encounters. They are set variously in Mexico, North Africa, Alaska, and St. Louis, whereas van

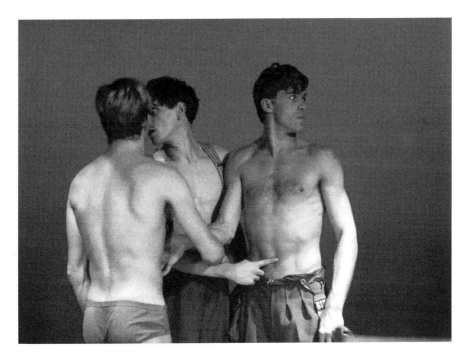

FIGURE 1.22 *Wild Lords*

© Luc Peeters (Keoon)

Hove's show contained no requited sexual acts at all. Burroughs resorts to multiple scenes of anal sex, revisiting this leitmotif over and over in various dream permutations. While Burroughs' emotional tone is seamy, daring, straightforward, and always fulfilled, van Hove's is coy, embarrassed, and unconsummated. The show, rather, derives from guided improvisations springing from his actors' experiences, points of reference, and imaginations. *Wild Lords* ought to be taken on its own terms as an original work, a piece of devised theatre, a case of van Hove wading into the post-dramatic.[111]

The cast consists of three appealing, slender young men. The performance had a variety show structure without a traditional unifying plotline. It allowed for the willy-nilly addition or sub-traction of any idea introduced along the way.[112] It is a structure Bernard Beckerman called "extensive," in that it relies on "the juxtaposition of parts," as opposed to an Ibsenian or "intensive" dramatic organization "which depends on the accumulation of parts." (Beckerman 1979: 195) This free-form armature is laden with influences from gay culture performance traditions—that is, lip-syncing, posing, transvestism and multiple others—such as Commedia, mime, gesture, cabaret singing, and so on.[113] Even in performance, it remains heavily improvisational, some sections only using words when absolutely necessary, relying more on non-verbal idioms.

In other sections, dialogue is derivative of pop-culture sources. One such segment is based on some British TV show where "ordinary people" tell of their lives, another a send-up of Noel Coward's *Private Lives*, all tropes of ridiculing conventional heterosexual existence. Flemish critic, Klaas Tindemans said of this phase of van Hove's work: "I can't rid myself of the impression that I'm looking at a post-modern revue" (Tindemans 1984). While later in his career, van Hove has come to lean on actual electronic multimedia onstage, here he introduces a different, non-technical, form of mediatization that Lehmann defines as,

> its very opposite: theatre on a bare stage with minimalist, pared down aesthetics, which nevertheless can only be understood by being related to life in a 'mediatized' society. Whether or not media technology is actually being used on stage, as Etchells says, 'technology will move in and speak through you, like it or not.'
>
> *(Lehmann 2006: 10, 13)*

Both content of the various segments and the space between them are determined by a principle of randomness, extreme spontaneity, and refusal to shape dramatic time into minimally significant moments or even much of anything for long periods of stage time.[114] There is a bare stage with mikes, which allows for a presentational style, and long uneventful transitions as the performers change in and out of costumes right in front of the audience.[115] "Rebel Soul" is the first song they sing. A few other melodic and uninhibited rock songs from Bad Company, The Sweet, Engelbert Humperdinck, Samantha Jones, and Johnny Halliday follow, but after throwing themselves into the singing, the performers look at each other as though embarrassed. Next, they take off all outer garments and come back to the mikes. They finger their elastic waists or pockets and look at each other uneasily in silent sexual tension, and, potentially, attraction. The initial unease evolves into a silent power game, in fact a "Mirror Game," one of Viola Spolin's basic exercises. Shuffling shoes develops into a dance evolving with varying degrees of speed and force into a Rockettes number before it breaks down entirely. Phrases of abstract sound and movement are repeated, picked up and explored; yet another Spolin or Living or Open Theatre game.[116] One actor steals another's shoes, which morphs into a lengthy exchange of shoes and socks between the three to see what difference it makes. Attraction leads to emulation.

Following these preliminaries, the major segment of the play consists of the three actors departing from their own interrelationships and incarnating various harshly satirical renditions of straight people, all very unflattering. They start by lip-syncing and impersonating Serge Gainsbourg and Jane Birkin, father and daughter French celebrities, singing at each other lasciviously. This marks van Hove's second exploration of several into incest, the first being his 1983 adaptation of *Oedipus at Colonus*, *Like in the War*.

The song once over, the third actor, wearing a long orange wrap-around skirt and white towel over his head, takes the focus and turns the skirt into a Commedia curtain. The other two run behind the skirt, which is now held aloft. Then all three clown around behind it like Punch and Judy, donning pointy gold hats and telling coarse jokes. One plays a raucous out of tune sax over the top of the curtain. They dissolve into raucous laughter as they ever so gradually transition out of this segment. The long transitions between segments bespeak an intentional defiance of professional discipline, but introduce a lax rhythm familiar from Happenings and Performance Art, one that refuses to bow to the audience demand for constant sensation. Van Hove, in later productions, faithful to his early performance art aspirations, often interposes segments that slow down action, that disorganize the forward-moving plot, that tend toward randomness and indiscipline, though always within a framework of much tighter structures than in *Wild Lords*.

Next in *Wild Lords*, there is a long segment borrowed from generic British TV shows, where ordinary people turn out to parade the seamy underside of their lives before the audience. The first "volunteers from the audience," are obvious plants, a married couple and their friend Amanda, "the other woman." They are none other than the same three cast members, two of whom thus appear in drag. They play out heterosexual roles of mutual degradation riven with alcoholism. The many scenes of domestic violence, here played in the distanced style of brutal clown shows, forecast later examples of van Hove's widely disparate script choices, such as *Othello*, *Desire Under the Elms*, *Faces*, and *Rocco and His Brothers*. We will see in all of them that he imposed or seized upon potential for abrupt, intense, and unanticipated physical violence to break out between heterosexual domestic partners.

Discarding those tropes, the three performers parade around the stage to a James Brown tune. This section is almost entirely physical and non-verbal. No longer playing assumed roles, the three actors are left simply with each other and themselves. Their movements are governed by leitmotifs of contradictory impulses: abandoning themselves to their attractions for each other, arising self-consciousness at having gone too far, and each projecting their own self-censure on the others. They're all clearly working from the Grotowskian/Artaudian tenet that they are to go to extremes of physical exertion in order to break through to a form of psychic self-confrontation and exposure.[117]

This show demands a lot of patience from the audience. It periodically coheres into high points of some interest. But much is dross, where the actors wander around, dance, and search for an impulse to follow. The dancing finally rises to a sweat-bath of Dionysiac frenzy that resolves into a one-man dance in self-abandon as the other two watch him lose himself. As the two "spectators" drift away, the exposed one finally stops, conscious of the self-spectacle he's been making that lost him an audience. All three are embarrassed. They then wipe the sweat off each other in silence, poke each other in the navel, forage in there with their fingers, but then look around as though worried they had been seen doing something illicit. This scene struck one critic as the most original in the show.[118]

The entire trio, having worked themselves into a state of liberation and self-abandonment to a showy Motown number, are again reduced to one alone forging on to the end, singing and dancing by himself as the two others drop out of the revels. Meanwhile, the two others light a real campfire upstage, evoking one more trope of acceptance and abandonment. The third leaves off dancing and joins them. One sings "House of the Rising Sun" accompanying himself with a soulful acoustic guitar. This segment is very relaxed, formless, and unpretentious in contrast with the glitzy, campy one that precedes it. A half moon is flown above their heads as the stage lights fade out on them. Nonetheless, they sing on into the gathering darkness. All of a sudden, many stars are hanging over the stage, and the three stand staring at them in wonder, grabbing each other's pants—in a half-sexual, half innocent spirit. That's how the show ends, with innocent images of boys together.

It's all very outré, and tedious too, if judged by the criteria of traditional theatre. But, if seen through a post-modern or post-dramatic lens, the same criteria do not apply. It was material that took courage to present in a homophobic culture with strong, strict Catholic traditions such as Belgium, and it had a kind of take-it or leave-it insolence throughout. In the long view, one might consider it a theatre of incubation, one of the artist's way stations on the path to finding his voice.

The next piece during the same early period was Calderon's *The Constant Prince* from the Spanish Golden Age, calling it instead *Wonders of Mankind* (*Wonderen der mensheid*). Grotowski did a famous production of this play as well. Apart from that, we never seem to hear of it, and it is seldom anthologized. But here, Calderon, like Burroughs before him, proves to be largely incidental. *Wonders of Mankind* was rather an attempt to do another post-dramatic show in which music, movement, and image supersede text and leave it behind. This was a creative path heartily embraced by Jan Fabre, but ultimately scrapped in large part by Ivo van Hove.[119] The freedom from text that van Hove achieved in this production, however, accounts for the insouciant departures and liberties he later takes in his text-based theatre. One example that recently jumped out at the audience occurred when Hans Kesting as Richard III in the midst of *Kings of War* suddenly drops the Shakespeare text, picks up the receiver to a red telephone on his desk, and says, "Hello Barack." Next, he picks up a white telephone receiver and chats in German with Angela Merkel. And finally, via a green receiver, he speaks with Vladimir Putin in Russian, then goes back to Shakespeare, but not not before announcing that Putin is "a fag."

Wonders of Mankind is a series of non-verbal études between the four men and one doll-like woman. One may look to Peter Handke's *Offending the Audience* or even further back to the happenings of the 1950s and 60s, or Marinetti's Futurist *Serate* from the 1910s for antecedents. Van Hove credits the performance art tradition he witnessed when young, particularly the work of Marina Abramowic, as a personal, direct influence,[120] but a whole slew of other historical performance movements crowd behind it too. It is not clear that the show has a subject.

Body movement sometimes galvanizes into traditional dance modes such as tarantella, flamenco, the dancing of Fred Astaire in 1930s movie musicals, and so forth. At the same time, there is a wild mix of music, from opera (*Trovatore*) and other classical music selections including "The Blue Danube" and "Thus Spake Zarathustra," to well known and easy to make fun of 1970s pop songs such as "Angie," "Happiness is a Warm Gun," and "Yellow Submarine;" from period dance music like "Put on Your Dancing Shoes," bossa nova, other latin music to some German Heimat song round the campfire—in short, an unrelated smorgasbord of familiar music that make for easy, often kitschy, commentaries on the action. Here then is established the precedent for van Hove's idiosyncratic use of the music of bad taste—the content of any extant musical piece literally echoes the themes of any given dramatic moment.

One recent use of this approach by van Hove is in the 2014 NYTW production of *Scenes From a Marriage*. In it, we hear the easily recognizable introductory chords from Paul Simon's "Fifty Ways to Leave Your Lover" just as the main character, Johan, has announced he's leaving his wife of twenty years, Marianne. Then Marianne puts on an LP of Leonard Cohen singing "Hey, That's No Way to Say Goodbye"—a tune sure to bring tears to the eyes of superannuated hippies—in a ploy to keep her husband from leaving. Even kitschier, "Windmills of My Mind" plays at the end of the show. The apogee of this over-obvious use of golden oldies is van Hove's insertion of a particularly cloying rendition of "Some of My Favorite Things," from *The Sound of Music* for Jon Fosse's portentous, Pinteresque *A Summer Day*, in which a husband goes out on a boat and doesn't return. It's like putting a garish statue of a leprechaun in the middle of a Japanese rock garden. We see van Hove doing this again and again. It is well understood that music can often touch emotional chords that would support the dramatic action. Sometimes it brings a smile; often it evokes a nostalgic wave.[121]

Desire Under the Elms: *cows without borders, Zuidelijk Toneel, 1992*

Julian Green's 1957 play *South* started van Hove on his practice of unearthing American twentieth century playtexts that, however revered, would be tricky to revive in an American context and seldom have been. Eugene O'Neill became an especial favorite of his,[122] but Lillian Hellman, Green, Tennessee Williams, and Arthur Miller all eventually undergo van Hove revivals. *South* is a most peculiar play by a peculiar writer. Its sole British production was put on shortly after it was written, but was banned by the Lord Chamberlain due to supposed gay content that today would seem extremely tame. Green was born and educated in the American South, ancestral home to his mother's family, and then spent his entire adult life in France, where, apart from this play and a few other works, he wrote primarily in French. He was accepted into the pantheon of great French writers and even elected to the Académie Française, while he remains little known in Anglophone countries.

The play is set on a plantation in South Carolina, during the American Civil War, in the three days leading up to the bombing of Fort Sumter, which lies just a few miles away. The gay plot thread concerns an extremely bottled-up but charismatic Polish transplant to South Carolina, Lieutenant Wicziewsky, who falls in love with the scion from a neighboring plantation, Eric McClure. After trying and finding himself incapable of confessing his love (although it is divined by several other characters), he fabricates a conflict with his beloved Eric. Doing so boxes McClure into a corner where Southern honor requires that he challenge the Pole to a duel. The latter dies in the contest. Throughout, other characters, notably Regina, a stiff-necked cousin from the North, and McClure as well, also seethe with unexpressed libidinous longings. These rise to the surface as van Hove has her striking poses while singing Billie Holiday's "I'm a Fool to Want You."[123] This is all set against the backdrop of a beneficent plantation where the land-owner Edward Broderick prohibits his family from raising a hand against the black slaves.

While the gay theme may have come to be acceptable, some of the sentiments from the black slaves would be extremely difficult for a contemporary American audience to swallow. Green, who exiled himself from Virginia to Paris, always considered himself a "*sudist*," and maintained the family loyalty to the Confederate cause, even from far away France. When he writes a play about antebellum South Carolina these sympathies seep through. Many of the slave characters have run away from the plantation, but returned because the life there agreed with them. The old blind black seer Uncle John says to his white mistress without irony:

> You've been very good to me. You freed me twenty years ago, or more. You gave me a
> little house and a cornpatch by the roadside. We stayed on the plantation because we love

you, and it's because I love you that I got up this morning when I heard the children, and came to see you.

The female house slave Eliza has a long soliloquy in which she fantasizes about being white as she looks in a mirror. This type of regressive longing for a change of racial identity may pass muster in an Adrienne Kennedy play, but is hard to digest in a play written by a white male with Confederate sympathies. It wouldn't be surprising if the affectionate and loyal attitude of the slave characters toward their masters in the South Carolina of *South* accounts for how seldom this fascinating play gets revived.[124] It seems that what attracted van Hove to *South* is the gay theme, as well as the generalized undercurrent of intense sexuality that the director once again dislodges from the subtext and physicalizes with stark brutality.

But it was with van Hove's production of Eugene O'Neill's neglected American classic *Desire Under the Elms* that he was firmly established as a director to contend with on the Flemish/Dutch landscape (see Figure 1.23). The showman in him came to the fore when he captured headlines by employing eight cows. It is certainly noteworthy that *Desire Under the Elms*, like *South*, is also a play about incest, albeit incest between non-blood relations. O'Neill has written a play about the intersection between material property and sexual potency:[125] "Whose farm is it? Whose woman?;" O'Neill has the two dramatically intersect, and it is from this capitalist-materialist starting point that van Hove jumps in.

His production places insistent emphasis on low, appetitive, repellant daily behavior, appropriate to the farm milieu being depicted. In the more immediate past it's surely related to the New German Realism of Francis Xavier Kroetz of the 1970s, and in some measure to Fassbinder films such as *Merchant of Four Seasons*, which specialized in uncovering the maggots beneath the rotting flesh of daily life.[126] There are real animals onstage, and the humans act and

FIGURE 1.23 *Desire Under the Elms*

© Luc Peeters (Keoon)

sound like animals. It also bears resemblances to American productions not available to van Hove such as Sam Shepard's *Curse of the Starving Class* and Irene Fornes's *Mud*.

O'Neill's resuscitated modern classic gains force by having its antiquarian, ponderous New England dialect—transcribed so thickly as to make it difficult reading in English these days— translated and adapted by a master of local Flemish dialect, Arne Sierens. Just as van Hove could afford to be unaligned regarding the American Civil War politics in South, so too the clumsy dialect of O'Neill's New England farm-folk presented no obstacle, as it would in America. He was able to envision it unaccoutered and breathe new life into it, as he has done so often since. Sierens replaces the muddy American palaver with a lightly archaized Dutch in a facsimile of rustic Flemish peasant jargon. Sierens's artificial lingo in Dutch has a directness of expression and simplicity that is more analogous to the stripped-down visceral English of Shepard or Fornes than to O'Neill's sometimes wooden cadences. According to some critics, it is wonderful and to others impenetrable:

> O'Neill set it in 1850 New England and gave it a jagged dialect in order to tap into the same sort of feelings. For Zuidelijk Toneel Arne Sierens translated that blunt instrument into an unfathomable sort of Flemish that has much in common with the set designer, Jan Versweyveld's, cows. It is a language cobbled together out of scraps, out of dissonances, designed only to express the most urgent of feelings. Reflection and thought are made redundant through an unwavering tradition. The which gets channeled into action, but scarcely into language.[127]

The critic overestimates the original English dialect's intelligibility. For another critic, this approach to language brings the characters on a par with the animals, bringing out its primal energy:

> The characters open their mouths, and what comes out are tatters of ruminations, in a mix of diverse Flemish dialects specially prepared for this production. The almost animal sounds obviate all misunderstanding: They are illiterate, linguistically impoverished suffering people.
>
> *(Van der Harst 1992)*

Van Hove and Sierens' relationship to Naturalism is to refer to it, but actually betray it, creating a poetic space in which the concrete accrues metaphorical life through overkill. Eight cows onstage particularly create a sense of clutter and false verisimilitude. For while they are pure aleatory agents, standing, sitting, urinating, and defecating in defiance of dramaturgical imperatives, they are bearers of unimpeachable semiological authenticity. They make it hard to forget you're watching a play, thus theatricalizing a manifestly "real" element. The animals also provided enormous sensation for the show, and they were headlined in all the press reactions.[128]

The play begins in murky, reddish glow lighting, suggesting a pre-dawn hour, which picks up here and there on some details and only gradually brightens to reveal the entire stage, with isolated pinpoints highlighting intriguing figures. Stage right a real cow is being milked, the rest calmly ruminating. They are animate space-fillers, but there is a great deal more inanimate farm implements and furniture proliferating in seemingly chaotic fashion. This farm culture, deeply imbued with primitivism, is devoid of privacy or the niceties of civilization.

In all, there are four cows stage right and another four are later revealed stage left. The four men of the family are dressed in drab farmers' outfits—that are clearly the standard European and not the American farmer garb—gray-blue jumpsuits. Once their dialects confirm them unmistakably as Flemish farmers, that confirmation is further driven home by the fact that they chug Belgian Genièvre and not the American whiskey (or "likker") indicated in the play. The older sons, Simeon and Peter, are slobs, their shirts partly hanging out of their pants and their hair slicked down unappealingly.

A special grim humor of human and animal fluids, functions, and excreta is firmly established and plumbed in this show. Milk spurts into a can before our very eyes by hand. The younger brother and hero of the play, Eben, is cooking thick slices of ham over a real open fire right on the stage floor. Peter, having washed in a bucket, now shoves food into his face. The third brother, Simeon, holding a coffee cup, forages deep and long into his nose.

Prominently situated between the now well-lit cows is a long table. Simeon takes a long, long pee, which gives every indication of being as real as the fire, into the cow pen. Halfway through, he spits in the same direction as the pee for good measure. Numerous pots and pans simmer away. An older man playing his father, Cabot, a noted Dutch actor Gerard Thoolen, in what was to be one of his last major roles before dying, stands rubbing his crotch. In short, we are treated to a lot of vulgar, low activities involving the elemental and appetitive, absorbing us into the groove of what purports to be real farm life in rural New England-cum-rural Flanders. The veneer of civilization and specificity of place fritter away.

As Simeon and Peter go off to prospect for gold in the west, they sing "California, Here I Come" in a rock and roll-like riff—which is anachronistic in every sense. It's an excellent example of how van Hove embraces the "impure" and post-modern. Cabot, when he sees his sons are leaving the farm for good, has a conniption on the floor—which is nowhere to be found in the original playtext—screaming about using a knife on them and beating the floor. The excellent acting is here and there mixed with such arbitrary incursions from other "codes." In van Hove's earliest work, all was improvised. In his mature work, improvisation can always be resorted to, to violate or amplify the main text as it does here, although with greater or lesser justification.

Abbie (played by Hilde van Mieghem), the woman Cabot has just married, arrives in a blue polka dot skirt, unbecoming high-heeled shoes, and a gray jacket. Her low white bobby socks, suggest some indeterminate period of the past—the 1940s or 50s? She is unfashionable and plain, but possessed of a dominant personality. Her arrival is instance to a lot of fooling around by the men, splashing water out of a large tub, throwing hay around, all intended to impress her. Eben, responds to her friendly overtures by spitting a mouthful of food across the stage at her, accusing her of trying to take over the farm, which belonged to his dead mother, and thus by rights, to him. While in the text, O'Neill has her responding to him with calm forbearance, in this production, they—typically for van Hove—have a violent, loud argument. She comes to get the upper hand in the dispute, and he takes refuge under the table; he's obviously smitten with her. Still, she is a plausible young wife to the old man, who has now donned a bright red shirt and is bent on showing he's vigorous for his age.

Abbie changes into sneakers and adds an apron, ready for work, in an almost ritual transformation from big city woman to farm woman. Eben, in his turn, strips down to his skin upstage, and settles down into the water in the big tub to wash himself, presaging the famous van Hove bathtub in *A Streetcar Named Desire*. As he takes his time washing himself, she washes the floor immediately around him on her hands and knees. Both Eben and Abbie maintain silence in their shared space. She even dips a pitcher into his dirty bathwater to get more floor washing water. He dries off naked in full view of the audience, as she cleans and sets the table and starts peeling potatoes. He pats his hair down using the soiled water out of her tub. Again, a ritual is at work—a courtship ritual.

Whereas in the O'Neill play, Abbie drops subtle, cautious hints as to her attraction for the son, here she promptly lays down on the stage floor her arms splayed out, an unmistakable gesture of invitation. He lies down in a similar pose, across from her. Their projects have thus come into sync. Father Cabot, on the other hand, approaches her grossly, brutally sticking his hand in her bodice by way of taking possession; she rejects him. Vexed, he starts ordering her around in a bestial dictatorial way, and then makes another attempt on her body. When she tells him she wants to make a son with her new husband, he buries his head in her crotch.

Turbulent lovemaking is depicted as a series of sudden shifts in power, and just as sudden alternations between violence and tenderness. As the father goes off to sleep in the cow stables, the boy and girl throw themselves at each other, and make passionate love on the table. The lovemaking dissolves into shouting and violent abuse, both parties sneering at each other. When she exercises the ultimate weapon of abandonment by finally walking out on him at the end of the scene, he is left literally howling in uncertainty and pain.

What starts as an argument between the old and young man transforms into a downright physical battle during which the verbose dialogue is mostly suspended. The stronger father, goaded by the boy, is finally drawn into the fray and defeats the younger, weaker one. The "fistfight" is here depicted as a series of open-handed slaps showering the head and body, which is a typical van Hove physical fight. Once Abbie is lying on the ground, trounced, Eben spits a big clod of spit into her face as a coup de grace. Van Hove permits and encourages these lengthy non-verbal, physicalized passages in violation of the American tradition for continuous, uninter-rupted dialogue that predominates in the canonical plays he favors, though O'Neill's prolix monologues also occupy long periods of stage time.

The boy and girl end wrapped up in each other lying on the stage floor, asleep. Cabot walks around upstage clapping, slowly, then faster. He is applauding them, then rages at the sight of them together; he then sits down at the table, and talks incontinently. The young man eventually overturns his bowl, splattering his face with mush. He goes into a violent, rageful sea ditty, as he stomps around the stage. Suddenly an upstage area that had never been used or noticed earlier, appears, revealing a male figure with a wide-brimmed hat silhouetted in a door opening. And the play is abruptly over.

In this production, van Hove succeeds in integrating his earlier experimentation—dialogue, movement, image, committed acting, and post-dramatic innovation—at the unlikely point at which Zola intersects with Artaud. Both the slice-of-life, which wallows in materialiality, and the breakthrough beyond the material level to extremes of the spiritual sphere, now coexist and reinforce each other.

> Van Hove takes realism so far out here that it becomes poetic, unearthing the ritualized and imagistic life from under the surface of dull, fetid farm routine, despite the fact that O'Neill's copious stage directions make no mention of them. . . . The production transcends the indications of reality in many ways and successfully seeks out a congenial representation of O'Neill's text which incorporates all human existence.
>
> *(Bobkova 1992: 13–14)*

In this play about potency, van Hove unearthed his own directorial potency through synthesizing his earlier forays together into a united whole of theatrical dazzlement. The unprecedentedly strong, heartfelt acting he elicited from the actors in this show paved the way for a similar coup years later in *Cries and Whispers*.

Splendid's: *Artaud resplendent, Zuidelijk Toneel, 1994*

In this play, Van Hove veered to an obscure example of French Theatre of the Absurd, which was also an explicitly gay play by an openly gay playwright. A reading of *Splendid's'* written version reveals a sketchy, even half-baked text in which character development is meager and the narrative blurred. Genet wrote it in 1948, but requested that it only be published posthumously. It finally was in 1993. The Berlin Schaubühne gave it its world premiere in German translation that same year. And van Hove staged it in Dutch the following year, apparently before it had ever been produced in the original French.

It is not, by any measure, on a par with Genet's best-known works—*The Maids*, *The Blacks*, or *The Balcony*. It is, though, his most blatantly gay play, and the only Genet that van Hove has been moved to put on thus far. Van Hove saw in it an opportunity for theatrical fireworks and

FIGURE 1.24 *Splendid's*

© Deen Van Meer

a machine or pretext for working out directorial experiments that ultimately justify belief in the work's potential value. He invests it with much of the baroque imagery of sexual assault coupled with ecstatic devotionalism that characterize Genet's novels—*Our Lady of the Flowers*, *The Miracle of the Rose*, *Querelle of Brest*, and so on—which, in encapsulated form, it strongly resembles (see Figure 1.24).

It depicts a closed world on the margins, that of homophilic French street toughs. The production marries the verbal outpourings of a petty criminal—Genet—with the realization of Artaud's theories for ideal theatre production practices. The text opens the door on a mix of bathos, sexuality, and exaltation through crime and voluntary humiliation, and van Hove elicits extreme wallowing in all of them from his collaborators. This show is a culmination of an Artaudian approach to voice and gesture, and deploys a mode of acting and production values van Hove has dubbed his "primitive manner" (Laveyne 2010).

The site-specific cellar in Ghent recalls the warehouse used in *Disease Germs*. But when it was done at De Singel, a major cultural center in Antwerp, it had to reproduce that same ambiance in a conventional theatre space.[129] Metal grills surround the stage and enclose a series of individual, separated platforms that comprise the playing area, behind which is the corrugated metal wall of the warehouse. It is a raw, makeshift environment. The play opens with a cacophony as the audience assembles, and there is a lengthy period of time, which constitutes a prelude, for the atmosphere to be established before the dialogue begins.

A middle-aged bald figure, Scott, who resembles Genet, presides in a swivel chair, enjoying all the noise and pluming himself up. A policeman character, wearing a tight-fitting uniform and no jacket who looks more like a member of The Village People than an actual cop, bops to the raucous music. He surveys the scene, patrols through it, and brandishes his gun. Another guy wearing tails compulsively beats and brushes the wire metal enclosures with a big shovel. Another runs around in a frenzy. The audience is greeted with lots of screaming and incomprehensible babble, priming them for something menacing to follow. The want of seats forces them to stand or else try to assuage their discomfort by milling. A bell announces the start of the play proper, and the spectators are then momentarily stuck where they happen to find themselves at that moment. One critic starkly relates how it felt to be an audience member at the top of this show:

> We stand in the half-light on a mound, encircled by the seven performers. Because director Ivo van Hove sides with them, he works it so that we have to look up at them. They tower over us on shoulder-high moving platforms made from steel gratings, kicking up a rumpus, each showing off their crotches, groping around in each other's pants. The stark platforms exercise their own terror depending on their respective placement, fast or slow, angular or smooth, swooping towards or away from each other. It is a good idea to change your position frequently. Not only because fleeing becomes mandatory from time to time, but also because from each new vantage point you get a different show, with the focus on a different character and a new vision of the unfolding violence.
>
> *(Roodnat 1994)*

Hana Bobkova saw a relationship between this dynamic audience configuration and Luca Ronconi's famous production of *Orlando Furioso*. The sinister space recalls, "a haunted house, a creepy disco, an s 'n' m basement" (Bobkova 2007/2008). Throughout the play, the actors remain in their harshly delimited spaces, separated from each other by the audience members below, only joining another actor on a different platform at crucial moments when alliances get redrawn.

This static arrangement forces the actors into circumscribed, fascinating movement choices on their own islands, as it were. They dredge up otherworldly voices and a convincing gestural language that is hieratic, resonant of secret forbidden ceremonies of sacrifice and self-immolation, and transcend the bounds of the everyday. The total conviction with which they perform creates an illusion that what is being said could be intuitively understood, even though it is vertiginous and hermetic. Genet's text is highly emcrusted with imagery in a practically incomprehensible private language. All the gang members, through casting and costuming, are made to appear beautiful and grotesque at the same time. They are dressed in the awkward, angular lines of the clothing that would have been worn in the 1930s street culture Genet grew up in.

A radio announcer reports a crime, a getaway, and a series of expository facts: that seven young criminals are occupying the seventh floor of the luxury Hotel Splendid's, where they are holding a policeman and American millionaire's daughter for ransom. Armored vehicles have the hotel surrounded. Several in the crowd have fainted and have been taken away by the Red Cross. The public is informed that in a moment of distraction the girl has been "accidentally" murdered and that the "cop" has chosen to take up sides with the criminals. The radio announcer's incursions, as he purports to keep the audience up-to-date with the developing police drama outside the Hotel Splendid's, demarcate the parts of the ritual.

One of the thugs, the gang leader Jean, often called Johnny, holds a large dangerous looking gun—an Uzi. He is crude, and wears a jacket with a stiff looking, white shirt, open down to the navel and with an open celluloid collar. He has a primitive, impassive facial mask in the Grotowskian sense of mask—that is, a mask-like face—and a gruff, surly way of speaking. He barely moves when he speaks, and so exercises convincing authority over the others.

He gets into dialogue with a blonde kid of Adonis-like beauty, Bravo, who wears a leather jacket, stiff and starched hanging down behind him, and a white vest. Bravo is ecstatic, but shifts very quickly to hysteria, weeping in self-pity. He whips himself up into an overwrought state that brings him to his knees. The silences in this play can be excruciatingly long, every bit as long as the verbal passages, while the criminals await an invasion of the hotel by the police and their own inevitable annihilation.

Each time the sound of a machine gun is supposed to go off, they make the sounds themselves, including by waving papers around. The company came to this choice through necessity. They had initially intended to use Uzis—real machine guns—but ran into a judicial roadblock while on tour through Belgium. After mounting a concerted legal appeal, which they lost, they made the interesting compromise of using toy guns and yelling out bangbangbang so the show could keep performing (Horsten 1994). So, a case of institutional oppression led van Hove to an even better, and riskier choice in which the highly amused audience is made co-conspirators to the ruse.

Riton is shirtless and wears a blank mask-like face with a mop of Rastafarian coiled hair standing on end. He has a washboard chest and highly developed muscles that give an impression of almost being molded from plastic. His head hangs down and he drools saliva liberally onto the ground. He is treated as a god-like sexual idol, the unattainable object of adoration, by the rest of the gang. When he ultimately looks up he seems to be sightless. Jean announces, "We don't have long to live," and Bravo jumps onto Riton's platform and presses his lips against the other's. As Bravo struts his triumph and heroism, then dissolves once more into hysterics on the ground, the blind Riton palpates the wounds in his pelvis and sexual parts that were inflicted by the police or his comrades. Or is he actually masturbating slowly? The former implies the latter. In the extremely terse stage directions that introduce the script, we are informed that the criminals "never touch each other." However, this proscription is not strictly adhered to in this production.

Suddenly, a miraculous female appears on one of the platforms, alias the Holy Virgin, alias "the American woman," alias the hostage who was reportedly killed. The Policeman below orders them not to proceed with this ritual, but miraculous religious music plays as gang members defy him and wheel the "mansion" platform through the house like an icon. After the solemn procession, Riton unmasks the female figure to reveal that the "American kidnap victim" is actually the gang leader, Jean, who had put on drag. He jumps on Riton, throwing him to the ground, and beats him up unmercifully, in what almost seems like a rape. Back on his platform, Bravo performs a hopping, pounding rhythmic dance in accompaniment to the violence. This grotesque, but exalted segment comes to an abrupt stop as a shot rings out, and then Bravo falls. He writhes and moans pathetically on his platform. Jean in his dress staunches Bravo's wounds in horror.

The Policeman, now up on one of the platforms, brandishes his gun and strikes flattering poses to show his body off to greatest advantage. Scott, in his swivel chair, and the policeman then join in a lengthy philosophical disputation, somewhat in the spirit of the dramatized debates between the title characters in Peter Weiss's *Marat/Sade*. The Policeman grabs a flower, eats part of it, then drops it on the body of the devastated transvestite who is really Jean, the gang leader. The transvestite protests as the Policeman prepares to administer the coup de grace. Just before it happens, the Queen of the Ball sits up and, with great, lofty emotion, lambasts all the others. The Policeman lays his head affectionately on her bare breast in a Pietà tableau. Then he proceeds to "electrocute" her with a few brusque gestures and a sound effect. A shiver goes through her body. She is dead.

All the actors then gather on the center platform, the first time in the show that they congregate together, and strip off their clothes, replacing them with simpler, more modern-day garb. They intend to just walk out of the former reality and escape unharmed from what had been established as a hotel surrounded by law enforcement. The tenor of the acting changes from here on, as though it's all been one big joke, so they can no longer take anything seriously. One of them sprays the space with water as though firing a machine gun. But then, the Policeman reveals that he has been working undercover in their midst all along. He has them cornered with his prop gun. But the more he has them cornered, the more helpless he becomes, until he finally grabs a bag and playfully throws feathers into the air. After this explosion of silliness the show ends in darkness and silence.

The press was less than enthusiastic, but blamed the shortcomings on Genet's slack dramaturgy. On the other hand, they acknowledged van Hove's enterprise, sexual daring, and compelling directing, which they claimed still fell short of overcoming the weakness of the text.[130]

Faces (Koppen): *poor theatre for suburban marriages, Zuidelijk Toneel, 1998*

John Cassavetes's 1968 cinéma verité movie is the basis for this show, which could be considered the heterosexual answer to van Hove's own production of *Splendid's*. It was the first time that he had used a film script as a basis for a live theatre production. Van Hove purports not to have consulted the finished movie, only the scenario, and evolved a scenic world from that source:

> Theatre is a sponge that sucks up all the various influences from other art-forms: video, visual art, performance, music. Theatre seeks out the other genres in order to ultimately produce a new language. Film came into the mix because my generation was brought up on film, with the great auteur films of the sixties and seventies. Before that the genres had been more separate, and theatre was an extension of literature.
>
> *(Takken 2009)*

He is one of the first stage directors to take this route, and it is one that has since proved most fertile for him.[131] Once van Hove discarded writing and developing his own scripts, he instead sought extant texts that said what he wanted to say himself, or that could be made to say it. In contrast with Shakespeare plays, which van Hove maintains are too sufficient unto themselves, film scripts are susceptible of being subsumed by the over-arching meta-dramatic narrative within which he wants to embed them.[132]

The source film puts the audience in the position of voyeurs peeking in on something unsavory, but extremely human and detailed—almost a sociological cross-section of a certain type of suburban middle class society. Thus, we enter into scenes that are already in progress without knowing how these particular characters came to be together or what their specific agendas are. We may glean or guess, but the full conscious and unconscious truth is hidden from us. There is an overwhelming sense that the characters are themselves semi-conscious, careering through their lives propelled by unbridled impulses that hit them from who knows where at unexpected moments, their ensuing behaviors wreaking havoc for themselves and their intimate friends and family members. They seem to be textbook illustrations of the pioneering gay theorist Edward Carpenter's analysis of the married couple, as expanded on by John Clum:

> Men are crippled by their education, which teaches them to dominate but does not teach them self-consciousness or spiritual development: They really have never come of age in any adequate sense. Men create society in their image: 'In consequence of which we naturally have a society made after his pattern—a society advanced in mechanical and intellectual invention, with huge passional and emotional elements, but all involved in whirling confusion and strife—a society ungrown, which on its material side may approve itself a great success, but on its human and affectional side seems at times an utter failure.' Part of the male-created capitalist order, built on his 'craze for property and individual ownership,' is the enslavement of women. As a result, there are only three roles for women: The upper-middle-class lady who is basically an ornament, the lower-middle-class household drudge, who is free domestic labor, and the prostitute.
>
> *(Clum 2012: 20)*

The Cassavetes characters are respectable, supposedly heterosexual married people, who bring disreputable individuals into their orbit in order to experience both thrills and relief from the enforced conformity and high financial and social pressures of their lives. We are not supplied with enough exposition to know whether these forays into infidelity are regular rituals or one-offs. But what starts as controlled experiments in having a little illicit fun, wittingly or unwittingly cause major disruption in their official relationships. It is my distinct impression that van Hove has added numerous lines to the Cassavetes script, lines that often clarify a layer of motivation that the film rather keeps hidden or ambiguous. One example is when an actress, distinctly declares, "I want a baby," a bit of additional, character motivation the movie never revealed.

Connecting the dots between the set of loosely strung together scenes we spy on, the plot of the narrative is as follows: after his late afternoon tryst with Jeannie, a self-employed prostitute, to which he is accompanied by his buddy Fred, Richard Furst goes straight home. The encounter with Jeannie ended on a sour note, but within minutes of arriving home, he tells his wife Maria that he wants a divorce. He then recontacts Jeannie, and eventually extracts her from the clutches of another pair of johns. He spends the night at her place during which they make love. Meanwhile, Maria, Richard's wife, goes out on the town with three girlfriends to a nightclub. They hook up with a certain Chet, a guy on the prowl. After luring him back to Maria's home, their hostess finally manages to get the other three women out the door, and Maria gets to have sex with Chet. When Richard comes back in the morning, Chet escapes out the window, leaving the unhappily married couple in a face-off. Maria tells Richard she doesn't love him. As one of van Hove's actors in the project, Bart Slegers, perceptively remarked to an interviewer at the time, the film had no beginning and no end; it seemed as though the camera could come to rest on any random point of focus by total accident (Kottman 1997).

Cassavetes's movie is unmistakably anchored in its own time—the late 1960s—while evoking a world that feels more like what we think of as the repressed 1950s. This is the milieu of businessmen husbands and stay-at-home wives with two cars in the garage. But van Hove eliminates that specificity through costuming. The men wear nondescript jackets, pants, white shirts and narrow ties, and the women unobtrusive though flattering dresses, skirts and blouses classically a-temporal, but which could plausibly be worn today. We are therefore, then, now, and in no particular time all at once.

The movie fluidly transports us into various rooms in the affluent home of Richard and Maria Forst, a successful CEO and his wife; the home of Jeannie Rapp, an upscale callgirl; two bars; tumbling outside onto streets and in cars, and so on. The movie moves chronologically, although disjointedly, through the course of a single late afternoon through to the morning of the following day. The original film of *Faces* has a grainy, homemade look, full of unscripted scenes that came about through improvisation. Many of the elements of exposition are incomplete. In the movie there are two bars—The Loser's Club—where Richard goes looking for Jeannie (and where she is not), and the unnamed one where Maria and her girlfriends pick up Chet. In van Hove's production, there is only one undifferentiated club, an overarching meta-environment, that contains all the scenes (see Figure 1.25). The spaces lack the identifiability of the movie's realistically depicted locales, therefore registering as more abstract and emblematic. It also makes the individual character arcs harder to follow. Instead, it foregrounds states of being over action, underlined by the meandering jazz ambiance.[133] The Cassavetes trademark kitchen sink naturalism has been given a strong infusion of the post-dramatic.

The audience is greeted by a deliquescent, maudlin atmosphere. The actors move about serving drinks, dancing randomly, shedding inhibitions, all of this setting the stage for some sort of Dionysian revels; 1950s and 60s-style live jazz plays throughout. The show too ebbs in and out of "organization," like a piece of jazz music. In the movie too there is a jazz soundtrack, and characters break into singing and extemporary pseudo-performances put on for other characters' amusement in a strictly amateur way. Van Hove has expanded the musical dimensions. When the live Dutch and Flemish performers sing they have a more professional delivery than do those in the film. Freddie and Jeannie sing "White Christmas" discordantly and obnoxiously. She

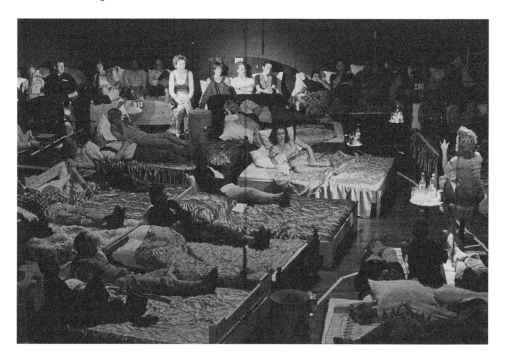

FIGURE 1.25 *Faces*

© Deen Van Meer

makes herself up and performs a pseudo Russian folkloric song and dance. Jeannie gets serenaded with "I Dream of Jeannie," with which she joins in. In all these cases, they turn the film's feeble, almost poignant attempts at performance into full-blown cabaret numbers, backed up by the live jazz ensemble under the baton of the gifted musician, Harry de Wit. They also do the rousing "Limbo Rock," a participatory West Indian number from the same period that wasn't in the movie. They weave in a line through the audience, infecting it with their sense of fun.

Three characters, Richard Furst, his old school buddy Freddie, and the call girl Jeannie, are widely deployed throughout the space, their acting in keeping with the boozy keynote that establishes the performance style and atmosphere. They crouch and stand swaying to music, singing drunkenly, and acting the fool. They have obviously already had a few lubricating drinks, and all the characters keep up this uncontrollable swilling right until the end. The singing builds to shouting into hand-held mikes as they crow out their songs raucously.

This prologue segues into the first scene—clearly a little party, a gathering among friends. Freddie tears his shirt open, and starts coming on disgustingly and aggressively to Jeannie, who freely accepts his hands all over her. She then walks away and settles into a double bed in the center of the café space, leaving the audience uncertain as to whether she has gone to another part of the room, another room in the house, or a different time/space zone entirely. Meanwhile, Richard is sitting at a far remove in his suit, observing and drinking. The free-flowing peripatetics of the Dispersal principle frequently engender narrative discontinuities and ambiguities of which this moment is a paradigm. Richard, located at a far remove from the others, is very much a voyeur of Freddie and Jeannie's dance of approach and avoidance.

They add impersonations, as when they play at "cowboys and Indians," mock-shooting each other, and then perform feats of prowess as if they were in a circus, backed up by drum rolls. These attempts at hilarity dissolve in failure, with Freddie and Richard getting into a shoving match. As Pieter Kottman described this recurring romp that takes over the entire environment:

> The actors from the Zuidelijk Toneel court physical danger, in chasing each other around through rapacious territorial combats, all of them actually the same character. The orgy of violence, in voices and moods, in sound and light, goes on for a long time, maybe even too long.
>
> *(Kottman 1997)*

All the frolicsome and comical pieces of business invariably turn aggressive and hostile, as though the men's competitiveness were just below the surface of their amiability champing to burst out; a pattern that is repeated throughout the show. Every time the actual anticipated sex is on the point of being realized, one of the three veers away from it, as when Jeannie performs Kama Sutra calisthenics to invite Freddie to sex that doesn't lead anywhere.

While Cassavetes never uses the cinematic "split screen" to relate Richard and Maria's parallel plot lines, as they disport through the night in different places, van Hove does just that in a live theatre equivalent, keeping simultaneous life going in several areas at the same time—once more applying his oft-used principles of Ramification and Dispersal. Individual actors, couples, and groups go about their lives at the same time, creating multiple foci for the audience to keep following, putting them in competition with each other. This contrapuntal approach reinforces the dominance of jazz, as though the actors were various instruments and voices riffing with each other through successive waves of dissonance and harmony.

The next scene starts long before the previous one has run its course, as Richard's wife Maria makes phone calls to her mother and her friend Louise in a different part of the space that acts as a "split-screen." Eventually, the first scene tapers off, and is replaced by a four-way phone conversation between various women at extreme ends of the stage space, and at a variety of voluble levels, speaking simultaneously and overlapping. They barely hear each other, if at all, as they gab about available men, marriage, and so on. Most of this dialogue is invented and wouldn't have been in the film script. It develops into a very long segment of aimless chitchat that works with a rhythm of formlessness and randomness, mirroring the jazz ensemble that meanders along without any discernable organizing principle. Each part of the audience that is closest hears more of one conversation than the others.

All the men enter the space insinuatingly snapping fingers, circulating freely. Their peppiness interjects a new sense of forward motion and intentionality, the intention of having a good time that would ideally include transgressive sex. The on-stage violence, hostility, and sexual assaults throughout the dance club scenes are much more explicit and extended than those in the movie, where conflagrations are generally muted and quickly stifled. Chet starts to casually flirt with one after another of the women; now poking his hand into décolletage, deep-kissing another—that is Florence—who responds by feeling him up, and humping him in order to distract him from the others. One of her lady friends, trying to lure him away, draws him into a dance whose steps require the partners to kiss. The women friends' vying for Chet's attention resolves into a three-way dance that is just as much a clinch as a dance. When Chubby Checker starts singing "Let's Twist Again!" the triad collapses onto a bed, as other actors twist elsewhere. Then Chet breaks out, chasing all the women around the space in incoherent pursuit, as the women scatter, screaming.

The unpredictably violent character Joe Jackson camps it up, pretending to be gay, and then, on a whim, smashes a bunch of glasses. Low-level disputes break out everywhere. The guys start taking off their jackets and preparing to fight. This leads to clumsy jumping on, rolling about, and drunkenly pummeling each other right into the laps of the audience. Everyone is screaming and hurling accusations indiscriminately. Each time Joe Jackson is subdued briefly, he breaks out again, with periodic spates of glasses shattering, as the women stand off to the side editorializing with Chet. This long section is an elaboration of certain extremely minor moments in the film that van Hove gives scope to expand and explode.

This intentionally anarchic segment comes to an abrupt stop when McCarthy proclaims contempt for his son's affinity for the game of tennis, which he implies is effeminate. Richard in response falls out, laughing uncontrollably. Richard and Jeannie are now left alone, the atmosphere turning confidential and even tender. While a lazy jazz piano riffs behind them, she starts undressing him slowly as they talk low. She kisses his toes and moves up his body, singing "Dry Bones"—"Your shoulder bone's connected to your neck bone," and so on—and playfully feels him up all over, just as in the movie.

No actual sex has come to fruition between them by the time a conga line starts up; the café and the "community" once more ritualistically invading and taking possession of the space, ultimately snuffing out their tender moment. Richard and Jeannie get more violent and explicitly sexual, grunting the whole time, not actually making love, but engaged in a protracted struggle that stands in the place of copulation.

At this point in the film, Cassavetes uses a jump cut, so we never actually see the two leads in the sex act. Neither do we here, as Jeannie finally stumbles away from the bed. Clearly it's the wee hours and everyone has more or less subsided. Soft, subliminal music, with random song phrases in English, plays as "dawn" lighting comes up. Chet meanwhile hauls Maria off the floor and into bed, does some vague CPR maneuvers and stumbles to a phone to call emergency medical services. He tries to get Maria, who now gives every impression of being a corpse, to stand and walk, trundling her lifeless body around. When he slaps her hard she comes to, much to his delight. She tells him she's cold and he wraps her in a blanket, pulling it out from under some surprised audience members, discomfiting them in the process.

General lights come up throughout the space; this in contradistinction to the film, which highlighted only one couple, the married Richard and Maria, who have to face each other after their separate revels of infidelity. In van Hove's theatre version, the focus is hereafter scattered among various couples having conversations and doing random things in all the beds. Chet is smooching with Maria, while Jeannie roves around the café smashing bottles into garbage cans as she cleans up. This provides a harsh counterpoint to the moody jazz. Now all the cast members pull themselves together, the men putting on their jackets and roaming around the space. The final scene of recrimination between Maria and Richard in which she tells him she feels nothing for him, that she hates her life with him, is extremely low-key and anti-climactic. So, the central action trails off rather than resolving itself. Both the film and the play end on a dying fall, each using its respective means, cinematic and theatrical. Reminiscing about it, van Hove saw his show as "a great impressionistic fresco" (Stuivenberg April 2002). And so it was.

A Massacre at Paris: *exercise in style, Toneelgroep Amsterdam, 2001*

This production is yet another convincing proof of the prominent place Artaud holds in the van Hove aesthetic, and of how fruitful that influence has been for him. There is a very heavy

FIGURE 1.26 *A Massacre at Paris*

© Jan Versweyveld

emphasis on ritual and atmosphere (see Figure 1.26). The sound tapestry, visual life, and daring approach to voice and movement all dovetail to radically alter the very stage air, making it thick, heavy, and redolent of a perverse hallucination that manages to be sacred and profane all at once (Janssen 2001b).

> Alongside the rhythm and edifice of the word, there is in the theatre a rhythm and edifice of movements . . . of a sort of perfectly aerated support, bathed in air and space, by whose lines, proportions, and general spirit an entire psychology is spiritually clarified. This edifice is triple. It contains the text and its plasticity (intonations, etc.), then the plasticity of the movements, all ordered and placed on stage. (Letter to Jean Paulhan, 1932). 'The staging that displays the play will function like a well-mounted machine. And everything, the entirety down to the tiniest details, will answer to it. The characters' evolutions, their entrances and exits, their conflicts, their stage crosses will be regulated once and for all with a meticulous precision which will foresee if possible even chance occurences' (Plan for a production of Roger Vitrac's *Coup de Trafalgar*).
>
> *(Dort 1979: 260)*

Artaud's visions, traced out above, could be accurate descriptions of van Hove's's *Massacre at Paris*. This is "Theatre of Cruelty" with a shiny brittle surface concatenated from complex and daring design choices. It is van Hove's one and only venture into extreme Mannerism, with a whiff of Peter Greenaway in the air, and so represents a road not ultimately hewn to.

Christopher Marlowe's Senecan drama is drenched in resigned foreboding, as though the characters have no choice but to be dragged into a preordained bloodbath of cruelty and intersecting revenge plots. This 1579 play is rarely performed, and with good reason. Its weak points are manifest and legion. Seemingly Marlowe's last work, it is set in the Counter-Reformation that depends for its narrative on an event from then recent history. The Massacre of Saint Bartholomew's Eve had convulsed France in 1572, only seven years before Marlowe wrote the play. This was a plot by which the Catholic Duke of Guise orchestrated the slaughter of many of the prominent Protestants of Paris, a move that incited similar popular massacres to spread like wildfire through more than seven other French cities. The massacre was pre-cipitated by the marriage of King Charles IX's sister Margaret to the Protestant Henry of Navarre, the culmination of a series of failed attempts by Protestants to come into their own at the time of the religious wars of the sixteenth century. This bloodbath, in which between ten and twenty thousand died, led to the Day of the Barricades, and thence to the reactive assassination of the Duke of Guise and coronation of Henri Navarre; all events obliquely dramatized in the play.

Marlowe's truncated play seems to be an unbroken series of murders, with only the most peremptory lead-up and ulterior reflection appended to the deed. The relentless *fougue* of butchery is evoked with a minimum of linguistic elaboration or interest, depriving the work of one of the virtues of contemporaneous revenge and history dramas, a *Richard III*, for example. The slenderest of character development is packaged in a truly clunky, almost apathetic, dramaturgy. As Marlowe scholar J.B. Steane puts it, where some might see "terrific pace" in the flow of short scenes, "other people may find a sort of scrappiness, or a sense of over-compression" (Steane 1969: 28). The episodes are indeed so ragged and mechanical as to remind one of *Ubu Roi* by Alfred Jarry, rendering the bloodshed distanced if not downright ludicrous. Scholars think parts may be missing, that it can't possibly be the finished version, or that no finished version was ever written. Indeed it is rarely produced, and was a perverse choice for van Hove to have begun his stewardship of the TGA.[134]

His production endeavors to bring fluidity and coherence, and generally succeeds. Whereas the actual historical events depicted played out over the breadth of France, Marlowe delimits the drama to a virtual royal closet within which the luminary presences float through like so many balloons that get pricked and pop. It is this quality, at once claustrophobic and fore-doomed, that van Hove captured in his production. One gets a powerful sense of what Jan Kott called "the Grand Mechanism" of history (Kott 1966: 3–56), and by intensifying this quality to the nth degree, van Hove turns the play's weaknesses into performative strengths.

Van Hove's adaptor, Hafid Bouazza, was at pains to make the complicated historical dynamics clearer than Marlowe did. It is evident that his Dutch translation is really an adaptation where so many liberties have been taken that it might be deemed an entirely separate work, one actually superior to Marlowe's.[135] Lines are added, others suppressed, still others assigned to different characters than Marlowe indicates—especially to beef up the women's roles, to take advantage of the marvelous actresses who are playing them—or are simply interpolated freely. Yet the jumps from Marlowe's lines to Bouazza's are seamless and the quality of the Dutch, whether it be Marlowe's or Bouazza's, is gutsy and powerful.

There is something clownish about the costumes: they are outlandish and unflattering, with odd angles and exaggerated ruffs for the old queens, and sexy, sinuous clinging outfits for the men. The actors' humanity is reduced and disguised by the strangely shaped, cumbersome costumes and hairstyles they're accoutered with. As the female characters place themselves immediately behind the big shimmery spheres that litter the stage it is as though the human parts had become extensions of them, completing elements in the preexisting landscape. To exit, the actresses simply face upstage as the lights around them dim and, to all intents and purposes, vanish. In contrast with the stately immobility of the females, many of the male subalterns, in their slinky body suits that make them look reptilianly scaly but virtually undressed, are quite athletic, recalling early expressionist dance by Mary Wigman. The Cardinal is depicted as a serpentine and sensuous figure in white leotards, with flowing blonde hair and a bared chest. There are also shadow characters in tight-fitting, space-agey outfits in blue, red, and yellow, sculpting their svelte figures. These control the movements of certain others, slowly molding them into strange and exaggerated postures, lending an echo of Japanese theatre. They carry their charges off, like puppets or lifeless dolls, after they have been slain. As the Duke of Guise, the central male character, speaks various electronic contraptions go on and off upstage of him, lighting up and flickering off—like a twinkling, glimmering technological firmament, or suggestive of the neural pathways in his scheming mind. This stately river of sound/image-scape flowing by, where humans and set-pieces blend into each other even as voices and instruments also meld, makes for a unified aesthetic, different from those found in virtually all of van Hove's other shows.

Through this period of van Hove's work, which includes *Desire Under the Elms* and *Splendid's*, it is clear that he placed a high priority on exploring the actor's vocal potential in daring ways, more than before or after. The composer and conductor, Harry de Wit, comes downstage and conducts, his ensemble producing a strong percussive stroke that segues into mysterious and premonitory music. His presence blends seamlessly with those of the actors. Hard tones combine with lengthy bell-like chords, as various characters move about and assume their place.

The primacy of King Charles of France is established on his first appearance. He is first seen wrapped in a banner by two lithe, reptilian subalterns, as though from *Mummenschanz*, dressed in clinging white. The King steps forward, and exposes the interior side of the rectangular banner by extending his arms. On it is stitched a giant target, and he is at its center, revealed as principal candidate for sacrifice. The unwrapping of various characters and display of their respective banners just behind them, like sets of rectangular wings, becomes a ceremonial leitmotif throughout the production.

Following Navarre's devout wish that the French people protect the Protestant minority, loud clanking music rings out, accompanied by a sharp light change and reconfiguration. It is not exactly a kind of Brechtian alienation, but rather a melancholy irony that permeates the proceedings. As characters die, most often by simply saying "I die," the head lowers, and the bodies are dragged off. It is a narrative technique that telegraphs the regrettable, almost-preordained wheel of history's turning.

Yet sometimes it rises to crescendos of violence. The Queen Mother Catherine who witnesses, and had indeed instigated the murder of the king, comes out from behind her giant tomato. The chief villainess' dress is ridiculous, with side bustles, but with her calves exposed. At her instigation, the Duke of Guise directs that the Protestants be massacred, the nub of the play. He yells in repeated refrain "Push, push, push, die, die, die!" which, as with so much other text in this performance, cannot be found in Marlowe's laconic script. It is because of additions like this that an unprecedentedly brief Elizabethan play here stretches out to a full two and a half hours.

The meandering flow is broken as *Phantom of the Opera*-like organ music pumps out. The lost, melancholy King Charles, while seated on the throne, places a favorite on his lap, who in his turn, caresses the king's hair. The speech becomes a paroxystic Senecan tirade about the rot in his body, which resolves into a grotesque groan of liver or kidney pain. Has he been poisoned? As with so many things in this production, the historically precise fact of the matter is sidelined in favor of a theatricalist effect.

The play's direction now changes drastically once more leaving the violence behind. A child's face appears and fills one of the tomatoes, which now functions as a holographic image-bearer. Imagistically the tomato has morphed into a womb that contains this otherworldly presence. So, the element of video is added to the organically designed environment, albeit unobtrusively integrated with the undulating whole. In that same womb appears a woman garbed in white who chants Dionysically and a male bacchante. These virtual figures dance within the womb shape, suggestive of a happier potential future for France. The play thus ends on a celebratory and optimistic coda to the convulsive disaster that initially gripped this corrupt, imploding world that is now dead.

Both the audience and critical reception were tepid, making van Hove's debut at TGA an initial deflation and the future of his tenure appear precarious.[136] This partially accounts for why van Hove, who survived the critical debacle, never followed up on this baroque-mannerist style, and considers the show both a one-off and a dead end he'd rather forget (Willinger 2016b). Looking back, van Hove says that it failed through being "over-designed," with too many visual and aural artists larding the show with their contributions (Willinger 2014). Indeed, the reviews tended toward that point of view, with a further accusation that all the design was a waste of the government's money, putting the new artistic director who was simultaneously trying to prove himself artistically and administratively into an awkward spot. To me, *Massacre* was quite unified and controlled, a masterpiece of ensemble work. It was an impressive instance of all production elements blending seamlessly with an uncanny acting style. Its atmosphere is so encrusted one could cut it with a knife, in a manner most compelling, nay, hypnotic.

A tale of three Hedda Gablers: New York Theatre Workshop, 2004, Toneelgroep Amsterdam, 2006, and The Barbican, London, 2016

Elinor Fuchs singles out *Hedda Gabler* as *the* play from the modern canon whose "mythic structures of imagery and action" offer the director a post-modern opportunity par excellence, opening up vistas of multiple re-interpretation. It is perhaps not coincidental that van Hove's approach to it is among his most explicitly post-modern, with many clashing and illuminating departures from tradition (see Figure 1.27). It is also a fascinating case study of the cultural cross-pollination that has transpired as a result of van Hove's trans-Atlantic forays. He first directed *Hedda Gabler* at NYTW with American actors in English in 2004, then revived it in Dutch for TGA in 2006. Ten years later, working with mostly English actors, he again revived it for the National Theatre at the Barbican. While departing from the same general idea in all three productions, there were so many crucial alterations that it makes it worthwhile to juxtapose them in detail. Fuchs's call to "de-classicize the works of 'classical modernism'" is fulfilled onstage by van Hove's three *Hedda*s (Fuchs 1996: 62–63).

FIGURE 1.27 *Hedda Gabler*

© Jan Versweyveld

From the outside it appears as though he had a very willing cast of American actors at NYTW, a group that was looking to try a new approach and give him what he was asking for. But the chemistry failed to gel this time around, a rave review in *The New York Times* by Charles Isherwood notwithstanding. Isherwood, the second-string critic on *The New York Times*, had resisted van Hove up to that point, panning him. But *Hedda* won him over. He called it "strange and strangely enthralling," "a refreshingly daring revival" that "instantly slips the fall theater season into a higher gear," and "remarkable" (Isherwood 2004). Van Hove, Isherwood continued, "is an artist seeking, as Ibsen once did, to illuminate the world around him." Isherwood also compliments Christopher Hampton's translation/adaptation, but to my ears it's as stiff and inorganic as most English translations of Ibsen tend to be. Nor did the actors get it to sound any more natural.

Van Hove revisioned a new sort of scenic world for the Victorian-Age period piece as more open, modernized, or alternatively simply stripped of character; in a similar style as he employed for *South* and *Children of the Sun*. The set was a tasteless and characterless white box with a sterile Ikea sort of look. Contradicting the text, in which Judge Brack is thanked for taking responsibility for thoroughly furnishing the house while the newlyweds were on their extended grand tour, the place actually appeared quite unready for the return of the honeymooning couple or for any habitation. The actors addressed the text with the same matter-of-fact simplicity, but were impeded by vestigial traits of Victorianism in the translation. Van Hove also worked hard to sweep aside the usual "typed" casting we expect from a revival of this well-known work. "The familiar personae of Ibsen's drama are turned into nasty but undeniably interesting new creatures" (Isherwood 2004). The performances from the start were loud, shrill, and pushed comic readings and timing, often going for laughs in a script where dry irony is usually the closest it gets to humor.

The play starts with Hedda sitting at an upright piano upstage with her back turned to us while the audience enters. She diddles with the keys, as she doesn't have the skills to actually play, and this is expressive of her aimlessness within her newly wedded and bottled-up state. The piano is a wreck, with its guts of wires and wood exposed. The melancholy song "Blue" by Joni Mitchell plays, redundantly reflecting Hedda's mood. One of the first characters we meet is Berthe. In all versions, van Hove went to great lengths to build up this marginal role. He keeps Berthe onstage throughout the production and attempts to make her a conduit between the audience's world and the other characters'. In most productions, she is a functional and marginal figure who enters rarely. Here we watch her sitting on the sidelines throughout, spying on the spectacle of her employers' lives and forming both silent and sometimes highly vociferous judgments. The late Elzbieta Czyzewska played Berthe's role at the top of her lungs, pushing for volume and emotion.

Aunt Julie shows up in a leopard skin dress, and takes an arrogant and cold approach. Tesman's aunt is usually portrayed as a timorous, mouse-like presence, needy for any sign of acknowledgment from George and Hedda, whereas, in this case, the image she presents is outspoken and sure of herself. She is dressed to the nines, if in bad taste. In a further flip of custom, Hedda, by contrast, appears looking quite dowdy when we first see her, in faded pink housedress with a brown coat thrown over it and barefooted. So the usual visual balance between the two characters is turned on its head, with Hedda placed at a power disadvantage, styleless before this paragon of fashion.

Hedda's new husband, Tesman, is generally depicted as an introverted, socially uncomfortable and pedantic man without physical attractions but, in van Hove's production, he enters as a hip and self-assured young metrosexual with a strong gay affect, or as Isherwood euphemistically says in his review—"a slacker brat" (Isherwood 2004). Thea Elvsted too has a mod vibe, with backpack and shirt that lets her belly show, and culottes—contrary to the usual introverted, insecure portrayal. She is presented more like the prototype of the mischievous, outgoing, and venturesome Hilda Wangel from Ibsen's *The Master Builder*. During the famous tête-à-tête scene with Hedda, in which most productions place Thea primly in the middle of an overstuffed sofa, in this she lies on her back splayed out on the floor to recall her wonderful days with Eilert. It's a bold move that sweeps away all vestiges of Victorian convention and American and English performance tradition, which in itself could have been a good thing. But in the event it was unfortunately not well acted.

All that is traditionally understated and implied is brought extrovertedly out into the open. For example, the minute Hedda and Eilert are alone onstage they start unmodulatedly shouting and when they wind up on the sofa together it veers immediately into explicit sex play. We learn that all the various men in the play convene in a whorehouse on the edge of town, where they drink immoderately and engage in all manner of scandalous behavior that must not be referred to in polite parlors. The same characters, when they actually come before the audience in a group in traditional productions, generally stand or sit in uncomfortable clusters acting like they barely know each other. Van Hove sweeps this stiff formality away. When Eilert arrives on stage, he and Tesman exchange a long tight clinch, which can either be interpreted as homoerotic or as heterosexual male bonding. Later in that same scene, Eilert, Tesman, and the Judge play ringolevio with Eilert's famous manuscript, and scrimmage on the floor, bearhugging like football players.

The Dutch version of the show two years later was far superior, so that one must assume either van Hove didn't believe he could get the same types of performances from his TGA actors as those he managed in New York, or that in the interim he had rethought the New York production and subsequently strove to leverage very different qualities out of the play.[137] While superficially it was the same show, he in fact only retained certain aspects and made many subtle, but important alterations. The chief distinction was that the Dutch production took more time getting off the ground so that it insidiously got under the audience's skin, which paid off when the climax came more, so than in the New York version.

We find essentially the same proscenium box set arrangement as the NYTW production, three imposing unadorned white walls faced with commercially stamped insulation material, although the horizontal aperture of the TGA stage is much wider than the more diminutive Off-Broadway one, rendering the production that much more monumental and less intimate. There is yet again an upright piano plus a white sofa. And instead of the plethora of flowers suggested in Ibsen's stage directions, which lend the box set parlor the aspect of a coffin or funeral chapel, there a very few austere bouquets. The flowers, then, are typically Ibsensian signifiers— ostensibly gifts honoring the honeymoon couple, but deeper down, funereal blooms. Her marriage is the penultimate nail in the coffin of Hedda's spirit.

A deceptively simple window with vertical venetian blinds has been added, intimating an outer world that the American production did not signal. Here the blinds and window hint at an alternative for Hedda beyond the finite box she lives in, and an opportunity for the play of light that Versweyveld is so good at.

The text is preserved and has the ring of more or less normal spoken Dutch. The transfer from Norwegian to Dutch is much more gentle, as the two languages are more closely related than are Norwegian and English. We still have unconventional casting and impersonations of the characters, but they sit more appropriately here. For example, Judge Brack is a young vigorous and perfectly attractive guy in a suit without tie, not the usual old decaying roué of tradition. Thea, as in the New York production, is again a sort of hippie in tanktop with a knapsack. This Tesman is just a grown-up boy—not sexless and unappealing but a lively, naturally affectionate guy. He kisses the Maid. Might he be having an affair with her? And as the play moves toward its conclusion, he seats himself in front of Hedda, who kneels before him. It has been the norm in college English classes to allege that she only has sex with him under duress. But in front of our eyes, in the most matter-of-fact way, Tesman seems to be happily claiming his marital rights, and she automatically complies. It is clear, as Thea too gets on her knees in front of Tesman that she and he had been intimate in the past, normally a muted subtextual detail easily overlooked entirely, but now blatantly illustrated. These, and so many other new ideas jump out at us and make us see the play afresh.

Julie is handled significantly differently from the NYTW rendition. She is once again made crucial to the action, which is in itself a radical departure from what tradition dictates, but deployed here with measure and coherence. Tesman enters, throws himself onto the couch, and chats with his Aunt as the dark presence of the maid at the extreme other end of the stage remains poised in alert silence. Her silence and stillness carry equal weight with their chitchat, her mere gaze being sufficient to call all they say to each other into question.

The doorbell buzzes periodically with an inordinately loud and unrealistic electric sound that has the dramatic function of announcing visitors, separating segments, and introducing ominous elements. Hedda, in shocking violation of Victorian manners, howls, "Come in!"

Julie and Tesman shout for Hedda, and she pops out from behind the piano where she was all along, rather than making a conventional entrance through a door, signaling subversion of any naturalistic expectations. The surprising mode of entrance also establishes the area behind the piano, again, both as an emblem of Hedda's stifled creative life, and as a private refuge. Her present survival strategy is to conduct a furtive parallel existence in the circumscribed space behind the piano.[138] Eilert later makes a bold move, pulling the sofa away from the wall and inviting Hedda to sit on it with him. This places their backs to the audience, carving out one more private area within the larger exposed one.

Hedda, in a revealing teal dress covered with some black over-wrap, fiddles nervously with the window blinds so the light changes and shifts wildly all over the stage—shadows and glaring light in alternation, the tempo of the window blind shifts restlessly building to a climax when her alarmed husband runs back onstage, and she desists. The lighting and these physical actions, in signature van Hove fashion, exteriorize Hedda's state. The Maid in her chair off to the side, is eyewitness to her wild, alarming business with the window, as well as everything else.

This production takes a very long time to heat up. The whole first act is uneventful and unrewarding, but the groundwork for the pyrotechnics in Act II is patiently being laid. The actors in general speak in believable, unforced conversational tones. Unlike their American counterparts, they don't push emotions they don't feel. In other words, van Hove brought contemporary American acting technique back with him to Holland! The acting is thus generally quite conventional, although when violations come they are all the more unexpected and destabilizing.

But that doesn't mean the production is not without a large number of striking, even startling choices, bordering on vulgarity, as when Tesman describes how Hedda's "filled out so." He holds his hands wide out, bends his knees and emits a Bronx cheer. When the Judge leaves after a tête-à-tête with Hedda she literally flings all the plants—vases and all—all the way across the stage, hitting the hated walls that hem her in, and littering the floors. Eilert picks up a glass, downs the liquor, and then sends the glass flying against the walls to shatter. He follows this up by flying into a rage and slapping Thea.[139] His drinking and whoring are enveloped in unnecessary mystery in the script, typical of the Ibsenian (and perhaps all Victorian) drama, that went on, after all, under the watchful eye of the censor. It is refreshing to have his alcoholic unreliability enacted before our eyes.

The Judge is more forwardly sexual than usual, and Hedda bends over in front of him, sticking her rear end directly in his crotch. She enjoys sex play with the Judge and even lures him into it, causing the impulsion to end her life, to lose force and logic; it is one of the few really inappropriate choices (see Figure 1.28). When Eilert bustles in, passing Hedda without a glance, he grasps Tesman's hand warmly. In this Dutch rendition, the friendship between the two academic competitors is not at all feigned, but truly warm-hearted, indicating that their long-term friendship has a real affectionate basis.

The curtain goes up on Act II, and the minimal enclosed space has gone through a major transformation by altering a few simple elements. A big red table lamp has been placed directly on the ground, down center stage. The blinds have been closed and it is dark. The piano has been shoved out of the way upstage and is facing sideways. The ladies have been waiting for the men to come back from their revels. Hedda is on the ground. The Maid lights a real fire in a pit not previously noticed burrowed directly in the ground down center: a primeval stand-in for the highly civilized Victorian ceramic or cast iron stove we would expect. The pit's rawness reinforces the play's savage and allegorical underpinnings, turning the home into a shaman's or gypsy's cave.

As Judge Brack starts blackmailing Hedda and proposes his contemplated arrangement for securing her under his sexual power, the dynamics between them become highly physicalized. Hedda flees from one side of the stage to the other, trying to elude him, but the Judge succeeds in

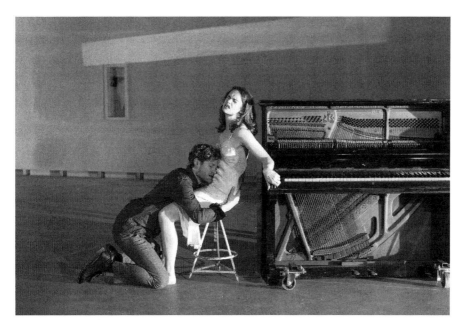

FIGURE 1.28   *Hedda Gabler*

© Jan Versweyveld

cornering her at each sidewall. He finally closes in on her and savagely throws her back at the wall repeatedly, till she sinks. So the blackmail, ever so gently implied in the text, is made explicit and brutally forced upon her.

The moment comes for Hedda to burn the manuscript over the fire, and she does so in a very subdued way; the Maid in this case becoming her accomplice. When Tesman and Thea go off to work on the manuscript by the window, they transform into a pair of mobile shadows engaged in something the lighting and their position renders ambiguous, but suggestive. Whereas in traditional productions the possibility of their romantic future remains very much sub-textual and rather a meeting of intellects, here it is blatantly physicalized for its sexual potential. They, like the Maid who lingers as mute observer to all that happens with her back to the audience, are ramified into Hedda's shadows or doppelgangers.

Judge Brack throws his jacket down on the ground and stands over Hedda. He opens a can of beer, chugs some, pours the rest over Hedda's head, and forces her to the ground. It is clear that the sex he has in mind for her is debasing sadomasochism with him in the domineering role. He dribbles sputum onto her face from above. Then the Judge kicks at a light down left that suddenly plunges the stage in darkness, presumably preparing to taking his sexual plot to its consummation. The only illumination left comes from a thin line of fluorescents lit all along the upstage line as well as the red-shaded practical table lamp stage right, that leave Hedda and the maid in silhouette.

Hedda emerges into the light of the table lamp and is seen picking up a gun. She bangs out some random music on the piano, aims the gun every which way in a reckless and dangerous fit, and finally winds up shooting herself. The other characters come and stand in profile as silent witnesses to her death.

Despite the decade-long hiatus, the London production was in most important ways similar to the Dutch one, although it was livened up in the first act, mostly through the brazenly comedic portrayal of Thea Elvsted. But the crucial change from the American production was the choice of text. In contrast to the wooden Christopher Hampton version used in New York, here, van Hove commissioned a lean, colloquial, tight adaptation from the clever, fashionable British playwright, Patrick Marber. Almost as soon as Thea arrives, Torvald asks if Lovborg is "employable," and "is he sober?"—a radical change from the endlessly evasive euphemisms used in more faithful translations. The dialogue has been edited down to its core, removing *longueurs*, so the play moves between the French scenes with sound-bite alacrity. It is an improvement on Ibsen, probably without betraying him.

Apart from that, the production generally follows the template of the Toneelgroep Amsterdam version. There are the same music choices: Joni Mitchell sings "Blue," while Nina Simone's "My Love is Like the Wind," and Leonard Cohen's "Hallelujah" also feature. The shallow rectangular encased space is, if anything, even more stark than in the other two productions but provided with a few pieces of the same sort of furniture. The prominent actress Ruth Wilson as Hedda opens the proceedings playing on an eviscerated upright piano with the Maid, down right, watching silently throughout the entire first act like a shade of doom, just as in the Dutch version. There is the same fire pit in the ground; the same splattered blood; the same gamut of hews in the lighting and play of shadows on the wall; the same loud buzzer. There is also a similar arrangement with the lights and vertical blinds at the stage right window.

Aunt Julie is as ordinary as possible, not glaringly fashionable or dowdy. She is just dressed in a simple black raincoat and black sensible high heels; and her supposedly hideous hat, is merely black and simple as well. Hedda is initially just as slatternly and carelessly dressed as in both other productions. Kyle Soller as Tesman is a slight, wispy, lightweight, faun-like presence with a neat little beard. He is very plausible as a post-graduate academic. All the actors are English, but Torvald is a London-based American and has unpleasant squeaks in his voice when he's attempting emphasis. Chukwudi Iwuji as Eilert wrings all the melodramatic possibilities out of his scenes with Hedda and Thea, as do they. As with so many recent van Hove shows, the actors are comfortable adapting the superimposed "thrilling voice" so explicitly discouraged by Stanislavski. Sinéad Matthews' Thea is a forthright, voluptuous, brassy, and uninhibited woman of unquestionable strength and force, with the consummate delivery of a born comedienne. In fact, she adapts the brassy, baldly presentational delivery of an Alan Ayckbourn farce. The major change in this version is all the easy, frank comedy. Eschewing the dry, somber tone laid down by Ibsen and exploited with all its shades of gray by the Dutch actors, here, the Elizabethan tradition of the mixed genre is brought to bear. The English audience delights in the music-hall timing and punch. Ruth Wilson as Hedda too gets her laughs, as when yelling at the top of her voice: "Academics are no fun!"

Certain of Van Hove's fetish moves have been ingrained as when Thea rains down slaps on Eilert's head after she learns he has "killed their child." Hedda, again, flings trash all over the stage. When he knows he has her in his power, Judge Brack dribbles bloody cocktail juice from a glass down onto Hedda's head. This is part and parcel of the same explicitly sexual relationship with Judge Brack; here he goes to the point of laying her hand on his crotch and holding it there. Just before helping Hedda burn the manuscript, the Maid, who remains the sober, totally silent, symbolic figure from the Dutch production, stands in front of the glass side door, her image reflected and ramified. A shadow becomes a split image, conveying the internal and understated onto the plane of the manifest.

Hedda manipulates Torvald into getting her own way by insistently rubbing her hands over her midriff. He, getting the intended message that she is pregnant, unleashes a gigantic howl of pleasure. One significant new idea that is added to the Dutch production comes before the final act: stagehands come on stage and, using electric screwdrivers, fasten plywood strips in front of the glass door, depriving Hedda of the only opening onto the outside world and brutally imagizing the closing down of her options. Next, the furniture is stacked up in front of the plywood, further barricading Hedda inside.

This production consolidated the British adulation of van Hove, which had been steadily building since *Roman Tragedies* and *A View From the Bridge*. Nevertheless, disapproval can be discerned emerging from the former positive unanimity. More than one critic wrote explicitly of the show that it required a "mental balance-sheet, recording its pluses and minuses" (Billington 2016b; Clapp 2016b). Three "pluses" were Ruth Wilson's performance, one of such complexity that it seemed to resist any easy single interpretation, and the fresh revisioning of other characters, especially Torvald, and Marber's adaptation. But there were complaints about the music choices being "over-insistent," not offering enough variety in dramatic rhythm, and what several took to be an "aestheticizing" tendency in the production values. The ground was being laid for future abandonment of the rapture.

A remarkable amount of visual life and physical business was retained but, because the actors played the comedic potential to the hilt and the melodrama with unabashed gusto, in a sense Shakespearianizing it, the whole seemed quite transformed from the English and Dutch versions. The juxtaposition of these three renditions, which shared a highly uniform template, shows that even by adjusting any small set of a thousand variables, the overall tenor of a production can shift significantly.

True Love: *scabrous and skittish, Toneelgroep Amsterdam, 2002*

This performance, which marked prominent American playwright Charles Mee's debut in Europe, was a reworking of material both from the ancient Greek tragedy *Hippolytus* and the French Neo-Classical tragedy *Phaedra* by Racine. Both are concerned with incestuous and adulterous love between the same mythological stepmother and her younger stepson. Van Hove commissioned Mee to write the play for the TGA, which then had its premiere in Dutch translation.[140]

True Love assaults the audience with various uncomfortable subjects and jagged energies as van Hove observed:

> My productions are often characterized by extremity. They can be very hard and aggressive. But also super tender and very romantic. I always try to allow feelings of compassion to come through. That's the way I directed *True Love*. To the consternation of many. Gang rape, incest, and adultery all found their way into the show.
>
> *(Smith 2002)*

The entire first third is a tendentious session, often embarrassing, often aimless and tedious, littered with harsh, provocative displays of sexually transgressive behaviors that push the limits of audience toleration. As it progresses, though, it resolves into a highly tender, revealing passage into the human soul that brings the audience along after all. Like many of van Hove's best shows, it manages to be a Stanislavskian and Grotowskian performance at the same time, with the actors taking their time to unaffectedly drill down to points of deep emotionality.

Mee re-set the ancient tale in a modern–day, lumpen proletariat suburban family of the most ordinary kind. But he retained the lengthy rhetorical monologues from the source texts in which the main characters, most especially Phaedra, examined their passions from all sides. Elinor Fuchs described another of Mee's re-workings of a different classic, *Orestes*, constructed along some of the same patterns as *True Love*, in this way:

> plot and character are rhetorical surfaces in precisely the way that ethics and personhood function as emptied-out simulacra in the world of his play. . . .vertiginous moral prospects are presented as objects of contemplation in a series of stand-up production numbers—monologues, occasional dialogues, and song and dance routines.
>
> *(Fuchs 1996: 105)*

The author laced the play with passages from Andy Warhol, Wilhelm Reich, and Valerie Solanas, as well as grabbing stray sentences off the internet. For van Hove, the show constituted a new opening, but also a reversion. It was not as loosely strung together as *Wild Lords* and *Wonders of Humanity* were, having a unified story to tell, but it still revived that music hall or vaudeville open structure. The text of *True Love* works with discontinuous time, and we are never quite sure where we are on the past/future continuum. Scenes don't complete; they just morph. Whenever the protagonists arrive at a crucial moment of catharsis they are interrupted by groups in the guise of line dances, kitsch songs, and even a circus or amusement park-ambiance segment. In any event, it is a pastiche, with the narrative lurching forward in fits and starts—a shared balance between plot and spectacle, dramatic and post-dramatic, maintained. This play gets right in the audience's face through the characters' neuroses, and heroic attempts to go beyond the internalized social boundaries that presumably hem in their behavior.

The ubiquitous choric figures have interest as paradigmatic prototypes of more or less intriguing personae. Though many of them seem recognizable, there is no discernible motive for why this particular cross-section of the human menagerie has been selected. Although each member of the ensemble is given a name and definable character silhouette, they are never really identified or possess any causal link to the main narrative. Each of them is thrust into the limelight at different points, but are ultimately just random people in society who participate vicariously in the central story. In some elusive way, they refract the central *Phaedra* characters back upon themselves. Character here is not, according to Elinor Fuchs's formula, dead, only flattened and recycled.

True Love was an environmental show, as was also true of *Faces*, *Splendid's*, and *Roman Tragedies*, where sections of the audience sat or stood facing each other. It featured a fragmented physical arrangement aimed at a "refusal of separation" (Ben Chaim 1984: 89). At the beginning there is a sense of dispersal and simultaneously, enigmatic presences going about their business. One actress sits in the center with a headset on; the rest are widely scattered—chatting or fighting. An outrageous middle–aged transvestite sucks on a popsicle. At least one live chicken is wandering around. What we are watching is a mosaic of a social background (see Figure 1.29). Suddenly, a pre-teen boy wildly wheels in on a scooter. He darts behind and in front of the audience at breakneck speed. He takes off his shirt and falls on the floor crazily; then takes off again, zooming around on the scooter. We don't get to identify him at that point, but do wonder.

The central female character, the Phaedra figure named Polly, with the costume and demeanor of a young suburban mother, goes into such an exceedingly long philosophical monologue about sex that the audience's eyes start glazing over until she starts, in their very

FIGURE 1.29 *True Love*

© Chris Van der Burght

midst, to masturbate and climax as she keeps talking. The scene evolves into a tickling match with the boy on the scooter, who we now discover is her stepson Edward, a Hippolytus who is really *very* young (twelve?). That dyad evolves into an ensemble orgy-like scene, as the chorus starts to pitch in, then transitions into a series of synchronized dance steps before it finally breaks up.

Once it is over, a prominent goofy male character in the chorus (who has no lines, but stands out through Roeland Fernhout's charismatic performance) unwraps a big cream cake, pulls down his pants, and hands the cake to the transvestite who smears the cake on the guy's naked behind and penis. The Fernhout character, we may speculate, is the mature adult Edward, although it is never explicitly confirmed. An alternative possibility may be that the mere contemplation of sex occurring between a boy and his mother unleashes a universe of ambient perversity in the chorus members' heads or projected into the external world; it is hard to say which (see Figure 1.30).

In this American script, the acting takes on an American influence as well, and the Dutch audience appeared to be intensely moved by it. From the middle of the show onwards, most of the acting, once it has found its footing, becomes very genuine, vulnerable, spontaneous, and unaffected. The mother, after confessing to her infatuation for her young stepson, impersonates a chicken that ultimately gets slaughtered; this identification of Phaedra explains why actual chickens are set loose in the space. The entire cast then builds a tall tower out of the modular blocks, as they sing the cloying pop song "I Will Always Love You." They then climb up and hang off the new construction. The mother, Polly, holding a big white balloon close to her, recites the spoken, syrupy "break" in the song.

Edward chases a young girl who then massages his body, lustily confessing her love. It is all very tender right up until he rhythmically and repeatedly spanks her, to jarring percussion

FIGURE 1.30 *True Love*

© Chris Van der Burght

accompaniment, and she screams. He goes into a tirade denouncing sex, backed up by abstract movements by Roeland Fernhoudt, who I believe to be his older self, and a woman singing gently in the background. Having turned away from love with a girl who is closer to his own age, the boy now confronts his stepmother, and they admit their love for each other in extremely passionate terms. In the most shocking moment of the play, he tenderly picks her up and carries her toward a safe haven. The saccharine strains of the Barry White disco tune "Love's Theme" burst out, while the company reconfigures the tower into a cocoon of modular blocks around the lovers, hiding them from the world.

At this point, shattering the romantic mood, the ensemble members repossess their benches, which are made according to the same design as the platforms, grabbing them out from under audience members, which forces them to stand. This is the beginning of a wild Dionysian rite, as the ensemble's energies turn from sentimental to savage, dancing and dousing both the floor and each other with water. Then, recovering from this anarchic mood, the cast forms into a line dance, with its characteristic regimented movements. All this leaves the audience both spatially and psychically displaced. Things morph into a circus atmosphere, as the audience is now channeled into the role of fairgoers: standing, milling around, observing. Observing morphs into peeping, as the Arab jock soaps up his body, and the transvestite rubs him down, to cite only one such dissident activity amid the general pansexual disporting that goes on. A rain of confetti comes down as the transvestite performs a spectacular fire-eating act! A huge plume of white foam is shot out over the space, spattering the audience. This segment ends when a silent firecracker is placed burning and sputtering in Edward's behind.

Enter a new character—Richard, the woman's absent husband, based on Euripides's and Racine's Theseus, who surveys the scene of debauchery, douses the flame, and then starts to lace into the two other family members. Edward, whom Richard had overtaken totally naked, reciprocally berates his father. As the wife and her husband have it out so no unpleasant truth or resentful passion is held back, they inhabit a devastated landscape of randomly strewn platform units. The space exteriorizes the chaotic, jangled state of their marriage. The floor is covered with white foam, like spent sexual juices spread across the playing space. Little by little the standing audience members find new places on the newly configured benches from which they view the rest of the show. Spectators are forced to grapple with finding a new seat at the same time as the actors, representing the family, struggle to see where they stand in their radically altered situation. When Richard ultimately shoots his wife, son, and himself, it is done as a ballet.

The audience—by now having been thoroughly integrated into the play's action—finally showed themselves to be pretty enthusiastic, but drained. They had been dragged through the mud of the tawdry, but very human story, and a roller coaster of theatrical events. Not only did they have to physically move around as the action dictated and virtually take part in it, but they could not help but make moral judgments. And that, in addition to doing the work of mentally reconstructing a disjointed narrative as it careered in all directions through time. They applauded wearily as the pop songs "I Put a Spell on You," and "No Messing Around" droned on in obvious commentary about what has gone before. But the truth is that through all the theatrical hocus-pocus and endless rhetoric, which took everyone out of their comfort zones, *Ivo van Hove* put a spell on *them*!

Rocco and His Brothers: *taking the gloves off for love, Toneelgroep Amsterdam, 2009*

The van Hove scenic version and the Visconti film version of *Rocco and His Brothers* were both major and successful autonomous works of art, though a comparison between the two may serve as a very instructive primer as to how the mediums differ.

The Visconti film, a masterpiece of 1950s Italian cinematic Neo-Realism, starred the French actor, Alain Delon, whose part was dubbed in Italian. The gritty, evocative settings, the rambling, but compelling script, the dynamic camerawork, and bold editing all militate to make this one of the most important films in history. The plot is extremely intricate, with many reversals and complications. The common narrative of both movie and play adaptation centers on a large, working class Italian family, the Parondis, who move to the city of Milan. It is a way for the five sons of the fatherless clan to escape from the lack of economic opportunity back in the countryside. They succumb to the various temptations and pressures of city life, even as they repeatedly exhibit nostalgia for the rural land of their formative years back in the south. Several are talented boxers, and the scenario charts their rises and falls, competitions and betrayals, both professional and romantic. The character Nadia the prostitute, whom one of the brothers introduces into the bosom of the family, plays a corrosive role and is a catalyst for domestic discord and dissolution. She becomes the film's sacrificial lamb.

The family members in the film, and those they bring into the family circle, interact with tactile, uninhibited passion, equally so between men and men as between women and men. The males assert their machismo in ways that suggest their ambivalence toward both sexes. The boxing, which forms the heart of the image-life of the movie, is where men work out their love-hate for each other in a ritualized arena; demolishing or submitting to annihilation by the loved object. What they can't love, they pound to smithereens. When Simone, the ne'er-do-well brother, breaks up a merry family gathering with the news that he has killed the prostitute that three of the brothers had shared, Rocco and Simone first wrestle and then wind up in bed together sobbing while holding each other like two bereaved lovers. After quite a long time, the mother's claw-like hand enters the frame and hovers over their writhing bodies. It is as though death, incarnated in the mother's hand, were hanging over the two male lovers. Both are now in effect widowers who can be reunited only in death.

It is easy to see why van Hove, who so often problematizes heterosexual male identity, was drawn to this movie. However, he eschews simply duplicating Visconti's imagery, even some of the movie's most compelling shots. He restricted his borrowing to the script itself, and entirely reimagined the physical life. Compared to all his theatrical adaptations of screenplays, the memory of the movie, remote but indelible, hovers like a ghost over the stage, regularly demanding comparison for better or worse.[141]

Van Hove's *Rocco* retains a byzantine dramatic structure, despite having simplified the action of the movie to a degree: eliminating, for example, a major subplot surrounding a brooch that Simone steals. The numerous secondary characters and crowd scene extras, including the multitudinous neighbors in the building who congregate on balconies around a central court-yard sticking their noses into the private business of the Parondi clan, form a representative social background in the movie. So do the crowds of spectators at the boxing matches. They are all gone. For the purposes of theatre, the actual audience serves as substitutes for these crowd-witness groupings. The kitchen sink realism of the movie, with the detailed multiple locations through urban and exurban Italy, are also excised and re-set in a generalized unit, meta-theatrical environment with a large bare platform in the center and four scaffolded towers at the four points of the space. Physical, detailed verisimilitude gives way to evocative suggestion through simplified objects and playing areas.

The acting aspires to roughness and naive exuberance, as in van Hove's *True Love* for example, not to the sleek, cool approach that typifies van Hove's later works. In fact, there is a rugged, artisanal feeling bordering on conscious sloppiness about the whole show that has a welcome warmth and humanity. Veteran actors like Fred Goessens, as the boxing coach, and Celia Nufaar, as the family matriarch, are let loose to sink their teeth into savory characters and play their scenes to the full in performances that aspire to an Actor's Studio flavor. Others betray an incapacity to act with the depth and multi-dimensionality that Visconti's film actors achieved. Instead, they strike a keynote for themselves replete with character mask, and allow those to stand in for character portrayal from beginning to end. The latter were not bad performances, just a little thin and overly efficient.

The show was made to mark the launch of the new Rabozaal of the Amsterdam Schouwburg, a barn-like flexible seating space, newly constructed as a secondary auditorium for Toneelgroep Amsterdam; it lends an epic scale to this production. Van Hove deployed a wide gamut of directorial and narrational tools including: disparate scenes were played simultaneously in different parts of the space, beginnings and ends of scenes overlapped, while other scenes surprised us by starting suddenly in a forgotten or never-used-before area. Prop chairs were spread alongside the center platform on the theatre floor. Plates, fruit, and a pot are strewn on the center platform's horizontal surface. The family members then take their places at the "table," even as the oldest son Simone lies right in the middle of the platform surface; to him, it's a bed in another part of Naples.

The Parondi family is introduced at the very start with cast members arriving in Milan carrying trunks and suitcases, boxes, and potted plants to one end of the space adjacent to the central raised platform. Rocco's family congregates around this cumulation of personal effects, encapsulating an eternal image of displaced persons huddling in alien surroundings. The mother sits there on a suitcase and waits. Her sons sit on the edge of the center platform. These pieces of baggage continue to be redistributed and repurposed throughout the show, as do various pieces of furniture. Once established in an "apartment," they all clamber onto the one camp bed so that an instantaneous image of cramped family life in reduced circumstances—tight, incestuous, intrusive—is suggested.

Nadia makes a first appearance in her emblematic revealing streetwalker's gold lamé dress and spiked heels and outrages the mother. The rest of the family members—indeed all the brothers—look down on her from the height of another scaffold at the other end of the space. Distributing elements of the family domicile to extreme ends of the playing space, as van Hove does here, is indicative of the free way he pictorializes functional locales, without respect to literal space relations.

A private chamber is evoked by the simple means of hitting an upper segment of a tower with a bright green light—a certain shade of green that somehow reminds us of Italy. The spare device of a small old-fashioned TV, flashing silently inside the otherwise unencumbered chamber, is all it takes to suggest rather than illustrate a lower class, cramped apartment. The windowsill of an Italian tenement is evoked by a crude horizontal wooden beam fastened to the naked metal scaffolding. All the brothers poke their heads out over it and the illusion is telegraphed. As with the windowsill device, van Hove often substitutes an appeal to the imagination in preference over naturalistic concreteness.

Whenever a big boxing match is in progress, lights, roaring crowd sounds, a clanging bell, and an amplified announcer's voice stand in for the Viscontian film reality of an actual boxing rink. The contestant boxes against an unseen opponent, and imaginatively mimics being struck himself. Each time one of the boxers strikes a boxing bag, there's a sound effect to accompany the impact. When Simone or Rocco connect with an imaginary foe's chin and knock him out, as they do, it's accompanied by a loud electronically produced thud. Simone lies down on a massage table and, though there is no masseur, he acts as though he's being worked on.

Images of greatest tenderness are reserved for moments when the brothers allow themselves intimacy and vulnerability with each other. Luca, the youngest son, cradles Simone, the elder's head in his arm, consoling him when he loses a fight. In yet another scene, most of the brothers are sleeping wrapped in each other's arms when Rocco storms in to throw his brother Ciro out so he can talk to Simone privately (see Figure 1.31). Simone listens silently and then gets back into bed with his three other brothers who are lying in one single bed like sardines, front to back, and goes back to sleep.

The scene of the two brothers locked in love and hatred after Simone murders Nadia is handled beautifully, but differently than in the film. Rocco, out of his mind with grief and rage at the senseless act, topples Simone on to the platform/birthday party table. But then they lie there, Rocco inert on top of Simone, like lovers. Rocco sobs, saying the murder is his own fault, caressing his brother and kissing him. Simone, numb, pats Rocco's back. Then he goes to sit and eats voraciously like a pig, upon which the murderer Simone too starts to sob uncontrollably before Mama leads him lovingly away. The rest of the family breaks down into antagonistic camps, screaming at each other from opposing towers across the vast space. Ciro announces that he's going to get the police to turn in Simone, and the others plead with him not to. The youngest brother Luca sits at the table in silence for a long time. He injects a coda into the play by simply stuffing his mouth with very real spaghetti.

FIGURE 1.31 *Rocco and His Brothers*

© Jan Versweyveld

Cries and Whispers: *unbridled pain, Toneelgroep Amsterdam, 2009*

Although it was later brought to BAM in Brooklyn, I originally caught TGA's adaptation of the Ingmar Bergman film *Cries and Whispers* (*Kreten en Gefluister* in Dutch) at the performing arts center De Singel in Antwerp, and it's that earlier version that I describe here.[142]

The original movie opened with the delicate tinkling of various gold-gilded clocks. We are treated to a series of opulent red-wallpapered interiors of the Belle Epoque in Sweden, which are impregnated with prosperity, complacency, and good taste. The central character, Agnes, writes in her diary, and it is through the medium of her highly private and hushed voiceover that the exposition regarding her illness emerges. While using the tropes of naturalism, the quietist film is structured by alternating between scenes that reflect outer reality with confessional monologues. Bergman makes abundant use of close shots of individual characters isolated from their world, set against a monochromatic background. Further, there are segments that start as though they were objective reality, but then transmogrify into grotesque fantasy, bespeaking a kind of Magic Realism; even these tend to occur in a hush.

Van Hove made extremely fundamental changes to the prevailing mood for his stage version. Whereas the lighting in the film is softly filtered, as though emanating from the bulbous oil lamps that adorn the discreet, lush interiors, onstage the light is harshly white, generalized, and clinical. Also, from a dramaturgical point of view, van Hove readjusts Bergman's multi-focus plot to an essentially uni-directional one so action gets heavily centered on Agnes's life and mortal illness; whereas in the film it's evenly divided between the sisters, as well as the loyal family servant Anna. The theatre version removes the narrative complexity from the beginning and downgrades the other characters' plot lines to vestigial add-ons, incommensurate to Agnes's calvary.[143]

De Rode Zaal in De Singel is a very large house with a gaping proscenium arch. It's a space that renders privacy moot. Yet as the personal drama comes over the footlights, it penetrates one's very marrow. Overhanging and encompassing the entire depth and width of the stage is a high rectangular canopy. The stage space below it is divided into a series of rectilinear compartments formed by industrial metal and glass dividers, by now familiar rudiments of the Ramification principle. We can see through and past most of them, thus reducing the possibility for privacy, but allowing for much simultaneous action. Video monitors are scattered throughout the space. The further into the narrative we penetrate, the more the event gives way to pure live action.

When the lights come up, the first things we take in are a hospital bed downstage to one side and another chamber to the other side where Anna, the servant, prays. Following this moment of illusory calm, equivalent to the filigree tinkling of Bergman's glass-faced clocks, snatches of frenetic cartoons of Tweety Bird, flashing faces, and high speed, abstract patterns whizz across the video screens. This feverish montage accompanied by hectic recorded sounds represent the last moments of troubled sleep for Agnes, the main character, as she snaps into waking consciousness. She is an artist now fatally ill, seemingly in the terminal stages of ovarian or cervical cancer.

Once she wakes up, we are dragged through a series of excruciating scenes, which do anything but sugar-coat the real ordeal of the patient. From when she sits on the toilet and removes her soiled underwear, to when she pounds her haunted, treacherous midriff in order to drive home to the impotent doctor how unremitting her pain is, the seamiest sides of horrifying illness are thrust at us. It is hard to imagine how Chris Nietvelt, in the role of Agnes, could volunteer to go through this agony performance after performance. But there are no holds barred in her expansive portrayal of a woman losing control over her bodily functions and facing implacable death. In the first act, Anna and the sisters are compelled to change the sheets on the hospital bed no less than three times.

As is typical of van Hove, so much that is expressed happens in the spaces between the dialogue, as he elaborates action that Bergman only implied or hinted at in his discreet film classic. It was mentioned in the film that Agnes is an artist. A small, framed oil painting by her bedside is briefly flashed on, and we see that she did indeed dabble in painting. But onstage, Agnes streaks the very glass of the stage partitions with bright blue tempera. As her pain peaks, Agnes unrolls a huge strip of paper and throws a bucket of the blue paint on it followed by her chamber pot full of slops, then rolls about in the mess, shrieking. While pain is crippling her, she crawls over to her paint pots and makes drawings all over the stage floor. At the height of her agony, the paint gets splashed and spattered all over the walls—a Rohrshach of suffering (see Figure 1.32). Her art thus detonates, or following the imagery of the play, metastasizes throughout the entire theatrical space. Where Bergman whispered, van Hove howls.

A master of suddenly shifting ambiance, van Hove periodically lowers the vast rectangular canopy in front of the set to conceal the stage action. What promises to offer relief from the

FIGURE 1.32 *Cries and Whispers*

© Jan Versweyveld

relentless catharsis proves to simply be a shift of medium, not of misery. For the canopy, once lowered, is actually a screen on to which is projected imagery showing reality being distorted, ramified, and transmogrified. The actors become Bunraku shadow puppets projected onto the canopy-now-vast screen, as Agnes's face, caught by a video camera upstage, is superimposed gigantically over those shadows. An entire arsenal of ingredients is thus enlisted to evoke the disordered inner world of the dying patient. This is the grandiose theatre of Gordon Craig consummated; the one he dreamed of but had not the means to realize.

Agnes' death does not mark the end of Chris Nietvelt's performance. We see flashbacks of the lives of her sisters with each other and their husbands; all fascinating, all harsh. These scenes that made up the main action of the movie have been displaced from the central action and back-ended to this aftermath, where their impact is mitigated. While the flashbacks play, Nietvelt appears upstage through the dividers, almost incidentally, tromping around casually; now either a ghost or simply an actress going about her offstage business.

The performance of her death, which dragged the audience through an emotional blizzard leaving them drained, contains its own antidote. We later rediscover Agnes casually seated downstage, and watching as her family members finally abandon their childhood house. They coldly leave behind the servant Anna, who had devoted years of her life to their now dead sister. Evicted, she is left to wander the high road.

Out of the blue, Agnes breaks through the fourth wall and starts chatting casually, directly to the audience, reminiscing about her earlier years spent with her sisters and mother. She speaks sitting behind a window cut into the canopy, which is lowered once more, reverting to its function as a giant screen. She says that she would dearly love to be reunited with those she had loved, those who had meant something to her. She then comes out of a door that is also unobtrusively cut into the canopy, and watches the images pass by on the screen. The canopy, through a simple but clever sleight of hand, has turned into the outside of her house.

Then, it becomes clear that all the forms before us on the screen are an artful video of the very people she just alluded to; those very loved ones with whom she had wished to be reunited. One by one, they playfully congregate and lie down, forming an amoeba shape. As the camera pulls back, they grow smaller. We lose sense of their integrity as individuals and re-perceive that the large shape their scattered bodies form is now a single human body. Thus, a second sleight of hand, performed through this virtual imagery, transforms what was an individual's house into the house of all human existence—a great all-containing human body—everlasting. Agnes walks back inside the canopy and in virtual existence assumes her position superimposed over the video image of her loved ones, finally merging with them. Their little bodies fill her large one and fit within its contours. Van Hove leaves us with a plausible and dearly hoped-for image of harmony in life-after-death and immortality, which we eagerly gulp down, children once more, hopeful and credulous. There is no denying that this play ranks among van Hove's masterpieces.

The Antonioni Project: *formal intricacy, Toneelgroep Amsterdam, 2010*

When the three Antonioni movies, *La Notte*, *L'Avventura*, and *L'Eclisse* were released in quick succession between 1960 and 1962, they were announced as a self-contained series. While they shared no characters or incidents in common, they were similar in atmosphere, rhythm, and theme. They all feature couples whose respective partners have great affinity, but whose integrity as couples is threatened by existential traps. The members of the couples misbehave, stray, act on caprice, and muse whether there's any point to throwing in their lot with this or that person for a lasting relationship. The films were made under the influence of the existentialist philosophy that was then in vogue. The anti-heroes and heroines of these films are riven with equivocation and moral outrage at their own responses to events, and those of their circle as well. All human action is subject to doubt as to its significance or validity. In existential cinema as much may be deduced from silent glances as from explicit verbal expression.

The reigning atmosphere is one of malaise. The characters are bourgeois or wealthy, insouciant as to getting their daily needs met. They interact with each other socially but without penetrating each other's lives in satisfying ways. The physical landscape is desolate. Certain characters may gain momentary thrills by betting on the stock market, going for a sexual quickie, or taking a luxurious boat ride. But even caught up in the swing of these distractions, they remain blasé, and some ruin themselves forever through an impulsive leap of a moment's duration. The slack, meandering sense of time in Antonioni is what most characterizes these films. Conversations have an aimless feeling about them. Entropy is the determining energy at work in Antonioni's modern classics, and many thought he had captured the zeitgeist of the mid-century. Others found it pretentious, self-indulgent claptrap.[144]

Van Hove's production is much more about states of being rather than political or social issues. Its originality is greatly enhanced by its disjointedness, its foregrounding of mood over dramatic eventfulness. It's quite a trick to throw these independent casts from three separate movies into one theatrical fishbowl, and retain clarity. This production is dependent on, as well as being about, electronic media. The live characters' proceedings are always under the scrutiny of a camera, and are performed as though on a sound stage (see Figure 1.33). Indeed, the stage is fitted out to resemble one. Technical paraphernalia and cinema lighting equipment—instruments,

FIGURE 1.33 *The Antonioni Project*

© Jan Versweyveld

reflectors, and filters—litter the environment. One technique we've seen used skillfully elsewhere in the Benelux by Guy Cassiers, for example,[145] employs a green screen with actors being filmed live offstage. It also has the capability to accommodate pre-shot footage along with the live feed, placing the very actors we see on stage as if they are there, having been filmed against a realistically shot offstage environment. So the audience can be both in the theatre with live actors and transported elsewhere to a completely fictional environment that looks real or as real as can be on the screen.

In this case, cameras are placed directly downstage, just off the proscenium arch. In the many screen close-ups projected onto a giant screen overhanging the stage, only the upper bodies are visible.[146] French critic Edwige Perrot adjudges that the introduction of live-feed video, renders the artificiality of relationships—behind the "mask of bourgeois well-being" and amidst "the ambient materialism"—more palpable than in the Antonioni film (Perrot 2016: 118). There is a lot of free-form movie music, largely piano, playing aimlessly underneath the action.

The first three scenes establish the three films' narratives before they start to intertwine:

(1)   Tomaso, a patient in a hospital, is pushed onstage in a wheelchair, accompanied by his two dear friends and acolytes Giovanni and Lydia. He's a well-known author, and is obviously fatally ill. The three are merely standing on a barely defined stage but, captured in live feed by the camera, the image is projected onto a green screen. So above the live actors are their virtual selves placed in a high defined setting: hovering not over the stage, but above the city, caught between two sets of the glass walls of one of those all too familiar corridors of a major urban hospital that connects two separate pavilions. This is a

character grouping from *La Notte*. The live actors are puny in relation to the stage space and to the monumental film images of themselves on the screen hanging high in the air.

(2)   A couple, whose story forms the core action from *L'Eclisse*, Piero and Vittoria, had formerly been lovers, and are in the midst of ending their relationship. Picked up by a different camera, they are standing in front of a background showing an urban landscape of office buildings.

(3)   Then another pair, two chic blonde women, Anna and Claudia, enter. Claudia's image is then displaced on the screen by the leading man, Sandro. This is the love triangle from *L'Avventura*.

By starting off with the triangle from *La Notte*, and in particular the scene in the hospital room, van Hove places the entire enterprise in the context of impending death. Not just the *La Notte* plotline, but it places the death of the esteemed professor at the center of the entire show; thus, in effect, de-centering the other two plots.

The illusion of the famous master scene in a boat sailing out to an island from *L'Avventura* is evoked: a whole group of actors wearing swimsuits are lolling on a blanket downstage backed up by a couple of low screens. Through the magic of green-screen, the screen background above the stage is all sky and sea, rising and falling. A cameraman kneels center stage facing stage right, thus capturing them all. This allows us to see the mechanism behind the illusion as well as the created illusion at all times. The audience's focus goes back and forth between the live and screen version at will, which makes for perceptual complexity and paradox throughout.

The bucolic, languorous idyll on the boat is suddenly disrupted as a live jazz band blasts out offstage, and the huge technical crew dashes about amidst a slew of monitors, as battens drop into view from the flies above. A jazz trumpet blares out in the midst of all this chaos, and we are meant to understand that we are now at the stock exchange from *L'Eclisse*. The stock exchange, where Vittoria's mother spends her days, was unforgettably executed in the Antonioni movie as a masterpiece of impossibly intricate choreography in which the brokers careen aimlessly in a pattern of shoving and near collisions.

A tumult of simultaneous dialogue, with many actors on cell phones and hands pointing in all directions, is meant to evoke the roiling stock exchange. The sense of a crowded public locale is achieved by focusing on the technicians of the show, revealed in the midst of all their multiple front-of-stage tasks, as the jazz trumpet once more blares out feeding the cacophony. The wagon camera running along the downstage track shuttles back and forth, its footage intercut with another camera's, creating a series of quick cuts back and forth, doubling and tripling-up on the chaotic on-stage movements.

An actor with his back to us, but whose face is captured on screen, suddenly announces the heart attack of a fellow stockbroker. The announcement, breaking the hubbub of the frenzied stock deals and forcing the driven stockbrokers into a taciturn moment of silence, is yet another sharp reminder of mortality at an early point in the show. One of the actors is picked out studying his cell phone, instantly causing a sharp drop-off in the stock value of the victim's life. The second the silent moment is over, business goes back to normal. A dizzying montage of the various actors and technicians shouting into cell phones flashes by, as the camera suddenly zooms in and out, from close to long shots, in sharp jerks.

In the film of *L'Avventura*, the two friends, Claudia and Anna, performed a scene of trying on dresses, where Anna hands Claudia one of her own. There is the gentlest suggestion of lesbian attraction between them. But later, when Anna has disappeared and Claudia replaces her as

Sandro's mistress, it is more that they are somehow existentially symbiotic, and then become interchangeable. The sexual tension between the two in the play is suggested even more strongly than in the movie, although what they mean to each other is left hanging. Are they sisters? Lovers? Friends? For the second time, Claudia leaves Anna and is replaced by Nico.

We're back to the *L'Avventura* boat. We only see the sea rising and falling on the screen, whereas below the live actors walk around and speak, very much as though they're on dry land. It is clear, as one calls "Anna!" that the crucial event of the film—Anna's mysterious disappearance—has just occurred in our absence.

Anna's Father appears in the middle of the curved track on the floor, as the camera circles him on it, accompanied by a mechanical sound. This sound is meant to give the impression of him landing in a helicopter whereas, in the film, he equally impressively arrives on the island on a catamaran. He talks of his daughter, who has disappeared. At the end of the conversation Sandro strides purposefully all the way across the wide stage. His movement is tracked lockstep by the traveling camera, so our eyes are glued to him on the screen. He arrives at the far left end of the stage to kiss Claudia, who has replaced Anna in his affections, now that the latter has disappeared. From hereon van Hove interweaves all three discrete couples, who in a certain sense become interchangeable.

As one scene winds down and the other begins, the characters from the two independent film narratives stare at each other and take each other in across the vast stage space (across the gap between the two dramatic plots as though the films were laid over each other like two transparencies) before pursuing their own stories once more. Discrete groups of characters from different movies cross each other's paths without the two stories becoming one. The act ends with an outburst of jazz music that lasts through the intermission.

At the start of Act 2, a new stage set-up reveals an L-shaped white platform dominating the central area surrounded by an ambient blue kidney shape on the floor, representing a swimming pool. Actors are lounging languorously here and there on low-slung modernist easy chairs. Onstage we are at the party at Patrizia's sumptuous home centered around a pool in *L'Avventura*. But later, two party scenes from two different movies—*L'Avventura* and *La Notte*—meld into one. This marks the beginning of a major shift in which characters from two different movies interact with each other.

There is a camera on a pivoting boom center stage, which can turn around and focus on subjects on opposite sides of the stage and also peer into corners. In fact, van Hove is recreating a voyeuristic audience/actor relationship we have seen in other shows. But instead of transparent walls or tight compartments, he uses the camera to invade spaces that are so private, they aren't even available to the audience's gaze any other way (see Figure 1.34).

Sandro, dressed in the bedroom, prepares to wander through the hotel but Claudia asks him if he loves her. He offhandedly says he does. In a slick transition, the camera follows him turning the corner to a flat. There, just on the other side of the wall from the bedroom area, the camera discovers another vamping female character—Vittoria from a totally different movie—to whom he offers a light. So he has literally left his new mistress in bed to come on to yet a third love interest. The camera, supreme voyeur, has captured the entire pattern of symmetrical infidelities.

The style now shifts to a long, grotesque, and alienating sequence depicting society as a James Ensor mosaic of mocking mask-like faces. Many secondary members of the cast, most of them masked, are panned in a line slowly and pass before our eyes, upside down on the screen. Once we scan the space we find that they are actually standing against a wall far stage left, in an out-of-the way spot, looking into a mirror. The masked actors then form themselves into a procession

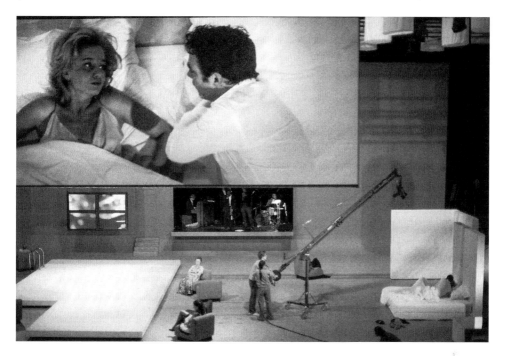

FIGURE 1.34 *Antonioni Project*

© Jan Versweyveld

and stride out center stage, arraying themselves around the pool, as though they were now statues. The lights go down on this oneiric tableau, and the screen immediately flies up and out of view, as a series of large red cylindrical lights descend from the flies and hang over the stage. It is as though certain human dramas are announced by the appearance of selected lighting fixtures of prescribed shapes and colors. As we hear Lidia's voice inquiring after the condition of Tomaso—the dying man from the first scene, whom we had all clearly forgotten, just as Lidia had—and the reply comes that he had died ten minutes earlier, the red lamps slowly move up and out of sight. A mirror ball effect is spinning very slowly over the stage, dappling it with reds and blues. For once, no music is playing.

Following the silence, Patrizia, the patrician hostess, seen both on stage and on screen, joins the band and sings "My Funny Valentine," a passage which did not appear in the film. Her performance starts off rather poignantly. Then, after a while, many join in singing harshly and discordantly as the band crescendos shrilly. The cast starts running around frantically, and hundreds of blue balloons drop down onto the stage. This signals another total and sudden switch in tone and modality, as the giant screen descends again from its high perch and for the first time entirely occludes the downstage playing area. There is no more live theatre, only film image filling the giant proscenium frame.

We see a montage of scenes of modern disasters—war, emergencies, mass killings, crowds of people on the move, police actions—with resonant, portentous orchestral music playing in the background, all of which goes on for an extended period. It is cataclysmic and grand at the same time. None of this prominent footage appears in any of the three Antonioni films. The live actors are entirely eliminated and displaced by huge, projected movie actors, though they are probably simply the same actors being filmed backstage. The live action that had shared the stage with video, via a Ramifying principle, is now entirely edged out by it:

> From a scenic standpoint he deprives the spectators of the access they had had up to that point to the stage, to the actors, and to theatre itself. But more than that, in using the screen to close the stage off van Hove opens another: that of the human condition, of relationships between the subject to the other and to itself. . . . the screen becomes the actor in the play.
>
> *(Perrot 2016: 118)*

Today, reality has become mediatic and magnified—put under a microscope. They are talking partially about a certain film they had seen in a movie theatre or on television. Life is a series of such conversations.

Claudia has lost track of Sandro's whereabouts and is frantically searching for him. After getting reassurances from the older women, she keeps walking in the darkness and comes upon Sandro making love to another woman. In the movie, *L'Avventura*, this desperate search for her lover, whom she feared had come to some dreadful accident, takes place in the brightly lit realistic spaces of a luxury hotel. Here it is visualized as abstracted faces emerging from the dark.

Lidia and Piero, appearing tiny on the very edge of the stage, then have a long scene right in front of their correspondingly gigantic screen images. This section moves out of realism and into a kind of expressionism: imagery with fluid, blurred contours, a penetration into extreme uneventfulness, a stream of dreary, going-nowhere images and action. Entropy dominates more and more, as the images deliberately lose intention and direction. And then almost imperceptibly we slip back into the drama that had gone into suspension. Lidia and Giovanni are lying together among the balloons and detritus left over from party. She says she just called the hospital and heard that Tomaso has died.

At that point, the screen goes up to reveal the live actors and the rest of the set once more, returning to their initial scale and medium. There is a composition of scattered empty chairs that had previously been occupied—the poetry of loss and death encapsulated in the image of disordered unoccupied furniture. Lidia leaves the balloons behind, crossing the stage. Only Giovanni remains in close-up on screen above as Lidia reads a letter she had received from someone long ago—including expressive and eloquent insights into the fleeting nature of life. At the end of the long letter, Giovanni asks who wrote the letter. She replies, "You." She screams that they don't love each other as he tries to comfort her.

The screen re-emerges and we see the jaded, matriarchal hostess Patrizia having breakfast in bed with her industrialist husband Ettore. He kisses her. They talk about sucking the juice out of a particular kind of egg. He asks: "What do you feel?" She replies: "Not much."

Although we see many of these characters over and over, the intertwining of the three stories dilutes the importance and specificity of each. The characters literally float in a medium of blue without much focus on the concreteness of their lives. The philosophical issues of connection and existence are foregrounded to the detriment of particular stories. It is hard to take in or absorb much more than a few facts about each character, other than that they fall in and out of love, betray each other, and wonder what's worth bothering about. They have become prototypes of people far more than individuals. This is a show of atmosphere, aesthetic surface, and floating ideas. The low-key acting that is called for in this essentially cool, understated piece suits the Dutch actors' temperaments quite well, regardless of the show's Italian roots. Again, this is a show where scenic dynamics are foregrounded over dramatic incident, charting a sea-change of subtle *states* (Lehmann 2006: 68).

By providing constant, unpredictable shifts in mood, alternating plots, and startling use of video and lights, van Hove is able to keep seemingly subdued and subtle, almost undramatic scenes, gripping, full of originality and compelling interest. It is not so much dramatic interest, as no character or set of characters retain our attention for any unbroken period, but aesthetic interest in the strategic shifts in music, lights, spatial shape; in other words, our attention is directed to the theatrical means themselves.

Recently, van Hove made this regretful assessment of the Antonioni tour de force: "the film scenarios were too weak, and the production I made was technically too complicated for the actors, too difficult to master onstage. An error" (Pascaud 2016a). Much of the press at the time found it an error. Van Hove today considers it to have been a useful "prototype" production with discoveries he made in the process improved upon in later ones. But I, finding it satisfying and fascinating in and of itself, beg to differ strongly.

Persona: *personal intimacy, metaphysical expanse, Toneelgroep Amsterdam, 2012*

Persona, together with *After the Rehearsal*, formed two halves of a double-bill of Bergman film scripts that van Hove adapted to the stage. It is of a spareness, understatement, and mystery to match the Swedish film classic. The dramatic text follows the film scenario in lockstep, but uses extremely different means. It deviates from van Hove's sprawling spectacles, with a canvas restricted to only four actors; of those, only two occupy the lion's share of performance time. It is subtle and sober, its meaning a deliberate puzzle permeated with mystery.

The show starts in a simple gray box set. There is almost nothing on stage, except an illuminated hospital bed center stage with a naked woman's body on it—Elizabeth Vogler—whereas all around it the stage space is dim. The Doctor is downstage in the dim light talking to the nurse Sister Alma. She spills all the exposition in one go revealing that a famous actress, their patient in the bed, had stopped talking right in the middle of a performance. Two such narrative passages frame the play symmetrically, although the main protagonists have lengthy, subdued monologues throughout the show as well.

All movements are kept to a minimum, and the acting is restrained, but charged. Sister Alma is enlisted to lead her catatonic patient back to her normal life. This entire section of the play has a very clinical tone, and all actions are performed with a medical precision. The music that plays, a monotone single electronic note, supports this sterility.

Sister Alma turns on the radio, and the recording that plays is of a radio drama—could it be Vogler's own voice of her acting in a show? The patient starts laughing wildly at hearing the lines. Then the nurse sits down left and wonders out loud about the source of Mrs. Vogler's malady. Spooky voices close in from all sides as in a horror movie. The patient starts stretching and moving, and assumes a hieratic statuesque pose, holding a letter high in the air. The nurse shows a photo of a nice little boy to Vogler, who rips it up. Then, for the first time, a brief video scene of Vogler's face in the role of Electra, silent but animated, plays.

Back on the live stage, the Doctor returns to propose that they take a trip to the seaside together. This preliminary scene ends as the Nurse gives Vogler her handbag with finality.

Music starts. Sister Alma rearranges the room as the three walls, that had so solidly manifested a hospital room, silently and suddenly fall. As though by magic, Sister Alma and Elizabeth Vogler are now on a platform—in effect a rectangular wooden float—adrift in an immense rectangle of real water; the greatest expanse of it is in the deep upstage area with a narrow channel downstage, which is where Vogler and Alma dip their feet.

Sister Alma reads a passage from her patient's diary, about each person being a closed book with its own series of hidden secrets, in effect trespassing on the patient's most closely guarded secret self. This betrayal was a turning point in the film, where Alma temporarily lost her patient's incipient trust. Van Hove theatricalizes the enormity of the betrayal: a machine starts up and water is spewed through the air at the two women sitting on the raft, an effect representing a great storm. They run about in it, throw off their clothes, luxuriate in the storm, and embrace each other passionately. The whole extended segment without words is sensual and unguarded. As the water lets up, in a moment of growing intimacy, they dry off and don white virginal dressing gowns to reassuring music. As the evening progresses and to fill the silence caused by Vogler's loss of her speech faculty, Alma confides many extremely private matters to her patient, who absorbs everything attentively and in silence. Alma jokes that she's not used to being listened to and it is clear that her patient has become a kind of spiritual doctor to her. Fog is pumped out from a fog machine that is within the audience's line of vision. Vogler stands staring at it, then back to us.

All of a sudden, the lights that were amber turn totally blue, and in a dream-like voice Vogler suggests that Alma had better go to sleep. Both are now in silhouette in the blue light. A recorded voice speaks, as Vogler caresses her back with a shawl. Once this lovely, static segment is over, the lights rise as though dawn had broken; so a series of days are compressed into what seems like one continuous segment. This is certainly a vision, dream, or inner fantasy, as Vogler has not yet recovered her power of speech.

With the new "day," Alma makes more direct attempts to get Elizabeth to speak. Elizabeth works herself into a state and rips the dark glasses Alma is wearing off her face. All of a sudden, the sweet nurse turns on her patient with extreme cruelty, threatens to strike her with a thermos, drags her around by her jaw, and pins her to the ground. Then Elizabeth wades out into the water, terrifying Alma, who follows her out into it. Elizabeth lies prone in shallow water down left. Alma sits in deeper water up center, all this action the stuff of dream and nightmare. The lights fade downstage as a male voice calls out imperiously "Elizabeth, Elizabeth!" Reflections of ripples in the water play over the upstage cyclorama as Alma creeps downstage to make sure that Elizabeth is alright. But she's drowned. Alma describes her—swollen lips, empty, sleeping— blurting out that she'll be "nothing more than a piece of meat."

And then out of nowhere from the remote upstage, breaking through the fog, a man in a suit appears: it is Alma's husband, wading his way, knee-deep through the water, trying to make contact and reawaken the broken relationship he'd had with her. The couple kneel in the water holding each other (see Figure 1.35). Elizabeth stands up, circles them, then stands over them. Alma leaves him. He stands, walks onto a little dock/step unit upstage center, opens the cyclorama and vanishes. He had been a dream. Alma and Elizabeth are now back on the main float in a bluish dawn light.

Elizabeth sits on the downstage end of the float on a chair while Alma sits on "shore" (on the ground) at the far end of the downstage area, with her back to us. Alma tells the story of what she'd heard about Elizabeth before she'd ever met her. "Elizabeth Vogler has everything she could possibly wish for as an actress and a woman, but she's not motherly." She tells the story of how Elizabeth Vogler looked at her newborn baby and said, "Why don't you die?" She'd tried to

FIGURE 1.35   *Persona*

© Jan Versweyveld

kill it, but the baby survived. In this remarkable speech, it appears very much as though Alma has assumed Elizabeth's identity and was speaking in place of her.

Then the nurse finally takes one of the chairs, sits alongside Elizabeth, and explains that the two of them are different people. A heavy pause ensues. Finally, Elizabeth answers—"Nothing," which, if the moment were interpreted as "real life," would mean that this was the first actual word out of her mouth since her trauma. She is cured. The Doctor comes back onstage and narrates Elizabeth's return to normal life as an actress, thus framing the action and ending the show.

This production works with both a small number of actors and just a few simple, but striking production elements—falling walls, water occupying the space creating an oneiric island, some minimal video, and fog. It is an environment that is extraordinarily visually open, but is in fact yet another isolation chamber. The initial isolation chamber of the hospital room was obliterated once its walls fell down to give way to a floating raft. But that too was cordoned off from the outer world, in its way, by the water that surrounded it. Once there, the healing of both women transpires through dream, fantasy, role-exchange, exorcism, talk therapy, and so on. Both the therapy and the show are remarkably effective.

Ludwig: *signs of madness, Münchner Kammerspiele, 2011*

This production in Munich was based on Luchino Visconti's 1972 movie about the "mad" nineteenth-century king of Bavaria, who spent his time building a slew of fairy tale castles that no one lived in. Almost bankrupting the state in the process, his other great project was to become chief patron to Richard Wagner, thus enabling him to write his great opera cycle, *The Ring of the Nibelung*. He ultimately shut himself away in a remote castle, deep in the forest, with a large band of young male assistants, avoiding all royal responsibilities. As his state was in danger of crumbling from neglect while he pursued these chimeras, he was forced to abdicate and was interned in a mental asylum. Shortly afterward he drowned in mysterious circumstances.

Both the film and stage productions are significantly marked by claustrophobia, but the respective mise en scènes radically create this closed-in feeling in different ways. One of the film's delights was that it took us to a plethora of palaces between which the Wittelsbach royalty flitted in their hothouse existence. Most of Visconti's prolix scenes took place inside rooms of the various palaces.

The live show went in a very different visual direction. It established a clear stage geography to distinguish between public domains, private domains, and those of a disordered mind. The stark, unadorned walls in the downstage area hem Ludwig in. He is trapped in the unwished for kingly role at the unfortunate moment when the historical Ludwig II inherited the Kingdom of Bavaria. This coincided with a militarized, dominant Prussia assuming suzerainty over his realm. Bismarck rendered him a relatively powerless, figurehead potentate, which aligned with Ludwig's aversion to the business of governing.

As the play proceeds, social isolation increasingly gives way to a psychic *cordon sanitaire*, and Ludwig sinks ever deeper into insanity, shut off from his few familiars and even alienated from his former self. The subjectivity of the stage space is ever reinforced as Ludwig compulsively scratches chalk symbols on the black walls that are ultimately overrun by these incoherent doodles. At times, the jottings indicate actual places in which the action is set—the underground cavern, a palace, the hunter's lodge. The camera picks up on each pictogram and enlarges them on the overhead screen. Ludwig's entire domain is overtaken up by his own hermetic jottings.

The video screen covering much of the stage, by contrast, generally allows the audience confidential views of the inner room of official life placed upstage, whose white walls are thickly encrusted with gold curlicue molding—signifiers of the pomp-ridden German court life. The actual space, seen from the audience's point of view, is a thin sliver, barely glimpsed through the cut out open door in the middle of the upstage screen. In the van Hove production, the single inner ceremonial chamber or receiving room emblematically encapsulates what, in the film, were many spaces within many palaces, as they actually were historically.

Then there is the administrative domain in front of the stage at audience level where bureaucrats make decisions and get papers signed. The area reserved for the Wagner sub-plot is also an audience level space in front of the stage. In between scenes, a narrator's voice describes the next setting and whatever has transpired in the interim over a loudspeaker. This is accompanied by a ticker tape: a moving written caption version of the same text travelling across the base of the upstage screen, together with a buzzing electric sound. One of the film's conceits was that it periodically interrupted the action to isolate a given character, who provided answers to unheard questions from an unseen committee of inquiry. Though not explained, it is understood that these witnesses have been called to clarify aspects of Ludwig's life and death and the role they played in it. Plainly, this inquest occurs, following Ludwig's abdication and demise, to get to the bottom of the mystery surrounding his death. Van Hove retains only one final character; that of a court official at the denouement of the drama; the rest are eliminated entirely, and with them much of the exposition.

Although this was a German production, van Hove as guest director imported Jeroen Willems, an extraordinary Dutch actor, to play the role of Ludwig in German. The entire cast's acting was intense, particularly Willems who convincingly clung on for dear life to his highly focused, involuted mental world.

FIGURE 1.36 *Ludwig II*

© Jan Versweyveld

The ritual of Ludwig's coronation is broadcast large against a background of stenciled wallpaper on the screen. There is then a great coming and going of young men through a door cut into the screen. With Ludwig's image displayed across the screen, it appears that the young men seem to be walking through the seam of his jacket (see Figure 1.36). Duchess Elisabeth of Bavaria, with whom the historical Ludwig (and Visconti's film Ludwig) maintained an intimate, but essentially platonic friendship, spins onstage, dances a bit, and plops down on the floor.[147] The live Ludwig enters through the screen's cut out door. She spins over to him brazenly and grabs his arms, but he is at a loss for how to respond to her frank advance. He opens his jacket and confronts her almost like a flasher, an awkward overture she amusedly brushes off. He takes up a position, standing up against her, his front against her side. Seemingly oblivious to the gaucherie, she simply keeps talking and walks away.

The sub-plot involving the Wagner love triangle is introduced and is interwoven with the scenes concerning Leopold's own plotline. The periodic Wagner scenes depict the great composer with his mistress Cosima Von Bülow and her husband Hans Von Bülow. Just downstage of the stage is a grand piano, and these characters are confined with it on that plane. Most of the rest of Act I's plot consists of depicting Leopold's obsession for building an opera house for Wagner and the dreadful realization that his beloved younger brother, Prince Otto, is sinking into the long wasting illness that eventually kills him.

As Otto, Leopold's male confidant of his younger years, is removed from the action, a new figure is introduced to play that role. It is Joseph Kainz, a young courtier, who sneaks through a side door in his underwear, chuckling and scuttling away, his clothes in hand, as though he and Ludwig had picked up in the middle of some forbidden game. Ludwig closes in on him, while Kainz cowers up against the wall. Ludwig pins him there by attacking the wall with chalk and draws watery images around him. This leads to a strange erotic scene where Ludwig too strips down to his underpants as the sounds of water burble. In the film, Visconti led the viewer into a fanciful underground grotto the historical Ludwig had constructed, replete with swans, a swan boat, and arched stone ceilings—a theatre designed for sexual scenes that are never quite consummated. Here onstage, the far more restricted means of the sound of water together with the actors' facsimile of swimming evoke this setting theatrically and abstractly. More like a game of imagination, they physicalize walking through a watery realm together, and almost drown. Ludwig puts his clothes back on as Kainz keeps "swimming" both onstage and on screen against the chalky waves Ludwig had schematically drawn on the walls. One way of reading this suggestive scene is that Ludwig entertains consummating a sexual relationship with his alluring companion, only to reject it, leaving the other to swim on in the watery element alone.

The next segment in the show again involves Ludwig, but only on screen within the gilded inner chamber. We see him close up, his back to us, beating the floor with his shoes as Kainz, in his underwear, screams. It is an image of vicarious sadomasochism, as no one is actually being assailed. Kainz turns onto his side and the image fades. Is it merely an unfulfilled fantasy in Ludwig's head or a sexual episode he actually lives out with Kainz? All these scenes are stylized in such a way that their ontology as reality, dream, or fantasy remains indeterminate.

The characters are juxtaposed to themselves by means of a small stage-self against a large screen-self. The paradoxical variations of the scale of the characters in conjunction with the elusive size of the door that leads to the royal chamber bring about the most uncanny design aspect of the production. In many offstage interactions viewed only on screen, no faces are seen, only the lower parts of bodies. Van Hove reserves this disorienting technique for Ludwig's scenes of flirtation with Sophie. We only see their bottom halves as she attempts to perform fellatio on him. But before it's consummated he stands her back up and drags her back downstage. The historical Ludwig and Sophie's protracted engagement ultimately proved abortive, and he remained a bachelor.

Ludwig sketches a little hut on the side wall. This stands in place of an actual hunting lodge, which in the film, based on historical fact, is where the king brings his young subalterns. Kainz builds a "fire" down right of the stage—in point of fact, represented by a red-orange light that comes on—before which he stretches out, and Ludwig lies down next to him. They embrace on the floor, but the sex goes no further.

A series of discordant chords announce the entrance of a group of boys pouring onstage as they track another boy as if they were hunting or a lynch mob. This is also captured on screen as well, the camera positioned to show it from above, which renders the cruelty of the pursuit more harrowing. Ludwig succeeds in chasing the malevolent boys away and cradles the victim on the ground. Act I ends with Ludwig returning to draw on the upstage wall with his chalk as the young boy remains lying there. All these scenes follow a uniform pattern of the promise of some sort of human connection for Leopold from which he turns away, unable to complete the circuit.

When the audience returns from the intermission, Ludwig is still on his knees on the floor drawing with chalk on the floor, the screen having been raised two thirds of the way above the stage floor. Several other alterations have also been made to the set. The unitary flat arrangement has subdivided into many smaller flats facing in various directions upstage, and Ludwig has compulsively covered most of them with his scrawlings. The new arrangement is a scenic representation of the degree to which court life has receded from Leopold's fragmented psyche to be entirely displaced by his inner obsessions and of the loss of cerebral coherence.

Ludwig now responds to Richard Hornig not in words, but in jerky, spasmodic hand gestures. When he does finally speak, he stammers more than he had in Act I. His lover berates him, backs him against the sidewall, and grabs his penis as though pushing him to the fulfillment of a sexual act, which again, is frustrated. The screen periodically flashes white, goes dark again and a video flicker of the gold room, sputters out. The disjointed screen imagery seems to visualize Ludwig's deteriorating, short-circuited brain just as the graffitied stage flats exteriorize his descent into madness. As Ludwig exits, dark, murky, ominous music with weird, grinding effects plays.

In the film, Visconti takes us to the remote hunting lodge that Ludwig has staffed with a bevy of young men who live in perpetual orgy, all of which the king observes but does not participate in. Van Hove handles this segment differently. With every flash of light comes video imagery: large, but fragmented on-screen images show many boys, whom we assume are on a backstage live feed, taking part in an orgy. Mostly we see only their midriffs, but sometimes faces too. Is it Ludwig's fantasy world unleashed and running amok?

A spinet is now upstage in the white rectangle, the only white part of the stage floor. Ludwig bangs on the keyboard, removes the lid, and shakes up the piano's innards, then shoves it about so that its legs collapse. As soon as the spinet is lying incapacitated on its side, the horrid music stops. Ludwig freezes there over the destroyed instrument and Richard Hornig lies down right next to him on the floor with his back to us. One could read the assault on the spinet as the deliberate exhaustion of his creative juices or life force. This tableau lingers as cold light, as depleted as Ludwig, now rises on the environment. He is now given over to the hands of the legal and clinical powers.

Ludwig agrees to abdicate after being playfully cajoled into it by Hornig. Professor Güdden then changes the tone abruptly, addressing Ludwig in a harsh, official manner from downstage, informing him of the details of the internment he has just agreed to. Ludwig climbs onto the tabletop and stands over the doctor and the severe official Von Holstein, also seated at the table. The doctor, in a black frock coat, now joins Ludwig onstage and jollies him down from the table. Ludwig joins the doctor in exiting the stage. They keep chatting, after they have stepped down to audience level, and head to the back of the theatre.

The sound of dripping persists. Then silence. We now see Ludwig and the doctor, large on screen, at the coat check of the actual theatre, where they are handed their coats before moving through the theatre lobby and out through the theatre's front door. We follow them walking down the real street beyond, presumably on live feed. Ludwig and the doctor are viewed on screen, as though it were a continuation of the earlier video, approaching and penetrating a closed white castle or asylum.

Van Hove has referenced the twelve-week rehearsal schedules that are the norm in German state theatres. This remarkable production was the fruit of such a lengthy and deep process, as were his productions of *The Miser* and *Edward II*, the next play up for discussion. These three productions are among his most structurally complex and satisfying, and the acting is certainly uniformly compelling. There is nothing like them for strong, integrated ensemble acting and originality of style in his oeuvre.

Edward II: *how the other half lives, Berlin Schaubühne, 2012*

This production reset Marlowe's historical drama of a gay English king in a jail cellblock. Without altering references to kings, earls, or the English throne or realm, the text was nonetheless cut to ribbons, refocusing the story on the power, sexual peripeties, and struggles among a select group of prisoners who inhabit a line of cells.

Johan Callens, in his review of *Edward II*, reminds us that van Hove had previously undertaken yet another Marlowe play with *A Massacre at Paris*, the Elizabethan playwright's other most cruel and perverse play (Callens 2012: 601). Van Hove again infused a Marlowe play with Artaudian sensibility, charging the theatrical air. Like Genet's *Spendid's*, this is yet another homoerotic world of criminals inexorably thrown together, both longing for each other and nosing around each other with instinctive hostility. The heady homoerotic atmosphere, the wrenching of guts, primal voices and imagery, and the trope of human sacrifice signals with the clean lines of the set and video that the director has sought and achieved a synthesis of two antipodal ends of his range.

Scenically, *Edward II* is a return to the Ramification principle. There is a series of six isolated chambers in which Florence March sees a version of Jeremy Bentham's Panopticon (March 2016). In this case, they aren't lined in clear plexiglas, but bars, on the front and back of each cell as well as the top, with thick, impenetrable walls in between them. There is one horizontal corridor running downstage of the cells and another upstage. Along half of the upstage corridor a series of working showers is installed. The audience can see the overhanging shower heads, but not the stalls, which are blocked from sight by the cells. The opposite upstage end is occupied by the sort of gym equipment that may be found in a prison: barbells, bench presses, and the like. The line of cells is bifurcated by a tall rectangular tower, at the top of which sits an omnipotent technician who appears to be operating the video, sound, and lights. He frequently obtains focus as a detached observer, providing a cool, objective perceptual filter, particularly in highly passionate or eventful scenes. But, he also periodically takes part in the action when he performs as a guard and is assigned several of Marlowe's minor characters' lines.

There is also, importantly, a large horizontal video projection screen hanging over the stage, subdivided into some twelve parts separated by black lines. The screen is akin to the multiple, split-screen monitors with which department stores, grocery stores, and office buildings survey many locales at once, so that any malefactors can be captured for their misdemeanors on the premises. So the ramification of prisoners in the six cells, each a mirror of the neighboring one, is repeated on the flat screen where surveillance cameras track each of the prisoners, and yet *again* visually isolate them in boxes. The screen simultaneously displays many different images as it projects live feed of various parts of the stage—mostly peering into discrete cell units to reveal intimate moments within them from angles the audience can't access from the front. Just as often, they present one large, unified image that swamps all the little boxes in the screen, generally close-ups of a few characters, including the face of the technician high up, or on occasion, pre-recorded material.

The prison block setting is a perfect analogue for a divided family, albeit a highly unconventional and transgressive one. Each prisoner suffers in isolation: they are brought together during recreation periods but otherwise forcibly separated. In the highly charged homoerotic space of this van Hove rendition of an already passionately abject text, the characters' longing for tactile contact is greatly exacerbated. They make love to the wall, on the other side of which is the personification of their love, visible to the audience, but not to the lover. Sometimes, two men unwittingly make love to either sides of the same wall, creating a mirror image. The action is relentlessly punctuated by shrill whistles that force the men back into their cells, the gates clanging shut on them, with their arms held high in the air in a gesture of capitulation to the higher power of the prison system. Here, all royals are uniformly reduced to being prisoners, imbued with the higher or lower status a prison's hierarchical structure accords, based not on hereditary advantages, but on criteria such as charisma, brute strength, persuasive abilities, and so on.

There are nine actors—all male—with some doubling of roles. In keeping with his usual method, van Hove cuts a fair amount of text—specifically, whatever is superfluous to the central story he wants the play to tell. Abrogations of the narrative complexity, native to Elizabethan drama, to facilitate streamlining cause secondary characters to be cut as well. But even major roles, such as the Archbishop of Canterbury, who in Marlowe's text is humiliated and stripped of lands, are eliminated. What remains of Marlowe's action is powerful, compelling, and is impregnated with enormous dramatic power. Van Hove has traded the play's *dramatic* complexity for a *theatrical* intricacy of production values. Van Hove divides the play into suddenly arising and ending segments that are introduced by large captions popping up on the screen, such as "Homosexuality," "Underlayer," "Conspiracy," "Love." These words, reminiscent of Brechtian placards that frame each segment conceptually, suddenly interrupt whatever's going on and signal a shift in tempo and mood with which the lighting, acting energy, and stage imagery work in concert to evoke.

The play starts with Gaveston's long monologue, reading the letter in which Edward tells him that his father, the king, having died, Edward is now king, and summoning him back from exile in France to be by his side. At first, Gaveston is concealed, taking a shower upstage behind the cells, as he contemplates the panacea awaiting him on returning to his lover. Still speaking, he emerges from behind the cells, naked and dripping. He addresses the half-naked Edward, who is lying supine in his cell, unaware that his lover Gaveston is standing right outside his cell . . . because he is not literally there at all, one in "England," the other in "France," together only in imagination. Gaveston scales the outer bars of Edward's cell, and speaks to him, that "him" perforce being the Edward in his mind. The Edward, seen by the audience in his cell, is oblivious to his lover sitting perched on top, reaching down between the ceiling bars.

Edward, both inside his cell alone and with his underlings when in the common space, indeed, throughout the play, wears only a white breechcloth. In Edward and Gaveston's first love scene, after knocking on the cell wall to signal their presence, they first embrace the metal wall that separates them, then grope each other from their separate cells through the bars and across the wall. It is a scene that is both explicit and frankly erotic.

Revenge, lynchings, and prevailing violence are the stuff of prison culture. In the next scene where the various nobles plot Gaveston's demise and then argue their plan to the king, Edward warns: "Lay hands on that traitor Mortimer!" to which Elder Mortimer responds "Lay hands on that traitor Gaveston." That is the signal for the nobles to turn and set upon Gaveston, who is sitting in a hoodie on a downstage stool. They beat him up, just as a cabal in a prison might. As the savage fighting ensues, the video camera picks up on the technician in the tower, his image magnified, viewed in an aerial shot, adjusting his dials and eating a big salad with consummate detachment.

Van Hove transfigures the character of the spurned Queen Isabel, Edward's historical wife, into another male prisoner—a flaming queen in a different sense, with high status in the prison population—who burns for the love of Edward and sees Gaveston as competition that must be eliminated. This role is played by a very fine German actor, Kay Barthalomaus Schulze. Edward promises "a second marriage 'twixt yourself and me," to which the Queen assents: "And may it prove more happy than the first." The king then urges "revels" upon them, at which point the prisoners frolic about, kiss, and embrace each other. They spin and bounce about the stage as buoyant soft reggae music plays. The camera slowly pans the entire stage, the actors only seen from the waist down (a technique we had seen used recently in *Ludwig*), capturing the entire row of cells and the men's legs in action. Their hilarity is unexpectedly extinguished by the high decibel prison siren going off, the prisoners' sudden return to their cells, and the gates all decisively slamming shut.

FIGURE 1.37   *Edward II*

© Jan Versweyveld

In Marlowe's text, Gaveston's chastisement is described verbally and allusively. But not so here. As Elder and Younger Mortimer casually pass the time of day, the others strip down entirely and line up to take showers upstage. Their naked bodies can be half-seen between the upstage bars. Gaveston is now returned "from Ireland," and the conspirators waste no time in teaching him a lesson. As the showers liberally douse the actors with hot water, Gaveston, who is also naked, is suddenly seized upon by the lot of them and—seen from above on the screen only— skewered up his fundament with a long wooden rod. Dripping blood, he is unceremoniously dumped in his cell and covered with a blanket (see Figure 1.37). This scene is truly blood-curdling. The men who perpetrated the outrage scurry back to their individual cells and quickly and furtively get dressed, disassociating themselves from the attack.

Before the crime is discovered, the King lies back down on a benchpress upstage right of the cells, slowly lifting heavy barbells while Mortimer and Lancaster, the chief ringleaders in the lynching of Gaveston, lean in on him, giving him urgent advice about how to salvage his reign. When the time later arrives for the conspirators to complete their plan and decisively put an end to Gaveston's life, they pinion his spreadeagled hands and feet to the rear of Edward's cell where he hangs with a bloody, horrified mask-like look on his face. In fact his face is enshrouded in a red plastic bag that suffocates him, the image of which is broadcast and frozen on the great screen above. Presumably using SFX, the onscreen face changes very slowly from horrific red and livid to white, washed-out, finally flattening into two–dimensionality. No sooner has Gaveston's face gone white and schematic, like a mask, than Edward falls in love with his successor, Young Spencer.

When Edward and his adversaries "go to war" against each other, van Hove is left in a bind. Does he stage war as an historically accurate Elizabethan armed struggle or in the visual language of a modern prison riot? He charts a middle course halfway between civil war and prison break, but finally more of an objective correlative than either. Fog sweeps the stage; horses gallop across the screen; the technician dumps white pillow feathers from his tower, and various characters clamber up and over the jail cells. The Allman Brothers' "Midnight Rider" plays over the general pandemonium of shouting. The overhead screen depicts close-up images of the same tufts of white fog, captured in live feed, that are rushing in and covering the stage. Finally, the technician, now functioning as a guard, climbs down from the tower, intercepts Edward, and shoves him back into his cell, thus putting the genie of war back in the bottle.

After the Queen has a temper tantrum over her son Edmund's rights, the word "Underlayer" appears, and a blue light envelops the stage. Two figures are then seen moving about Edward's cell in near darkness. But on the screen they are paradoxically large and fairly well lit. It is Edward and Young Spencer, making love. In the midst of this idyll, an assassin reaches through the bars and slips Spencer's head into a red plastic bag. Captured on the screen then, large and grotesque, Spencer's face is now deep red, frozen in a death mask, just as all death is represented here.

In the playtext, Edward imprudently spares the traitor Mortimer's life, imprisoning him instead. The rebel then escapes from captivity and sails to France to make common cause with the Queen. On van Hove's set, Mortimer swears his affections to the male prisoner Queen, who stands with his belly pressed against the bars of his cell while Mortimer mechanically and rhythmically pounds away at him, midriff to midriff. It is uncanny how, through modern technology, as the stage remains extremely dimly lit and bathed in deep blue light, the same characters that can barely be made out on stage are seen picked out in glaring white light, via live feed on the giant screen above.

Toward the end of the play, the technician descends from the tower to play various small roles combined into one. The King reclines, head on his confidant's lap, just as Edward in the text asks if he may lay his head on the lap of the Welsh friar who takes him in once he has lost the battle and fled. The technician asks him to give up his crown. The crown in question is a thick plain black cylinder—what a diadem of a modern prisoner might plausibly look like if such a thing existed.

During Edward's lengthy monologue in which he entertains giving up the crown and spiritually detaching from the exigencies of the material world of status and struggle, his face appears large on the screen. It is shot from below against a sky-blue and white background that, while unseen by our eyes when looking at the stage figure, is preeminent on the video screen. This depiction, his face set angelically against an infinite azure, suddenly restores to Edward an exalted stature: an almost angelic quality that he had lacked through many previous scenes.

When the time comes for Mortimer, Edward's principal and longstanding opponent, to pay the price for his treachery, the actor is taken behind the technician's tower. The well-built, sturdy actor is dragged on screen, filmed overhead through a fish-eye lens that distorts his body, transforming him into a dwarfish gnome with giant head and tiny, spastic limbs. In this guise, his shadow self is unmasked, as it were, and shown to be paltry, grotesque, subhuman. He pleads his case, to which a subaltern answers by slicing his neck from end to end.

Shortly after, Edward is discovered in his cell entirely naked, in pain, and smeared with excrement—the technician soothes him, offers him water to wash with and drink. This is an image of the extreme wretchedness to which Edward has, through circumstances and his own defects, sunk; but one that also evokes all victims of war and political dislocations. As the bathetic end draws near, the Ramification effects are dispensed with, leaving simplicity and unity in their wake. The stage is littered with the white feathers tossed out during the battle, giving a sense of devastation to the realm. Edward, who is still totally naked but bears traces of excrement on his skin, takes part in lengthy, quiet, measured, and unhurried colloquies with the technician, as they simply sit and talk together on the down center bench. The contrast with all the foreground cacophony evokes a welcome inner peace Edward only achieves by way of extreme humiliation and loss. The King's death is very quiet and sensual. The technician, turning his back to the audience, squats on the fallen king's lap, and embraces him long and intimately. This embrace is the execution. Edward rolls off the bench and is dead.

When young Edward, the prince who has inherited the throne from his father against his own will, appears to eulogize his father, he deposits a large red bag containing smaller red plastic bags by his head. He voluntarily walks into the cell that had been his father's, closes the door on himself, and raises his hand in the gesture they've all been using as a sign of acquiescence to prison authority. This image succinctly captures the essence of kingship: it is equivalent to voluntary imprisonment. The Ramification effects used throughout leave us with a strong sense that the prison has much more metaphorical than actual significance, and that Edward's journey is one of "Everyman," with supplemental resonances concerning those who enter the political sphere.

Now and into the future

The Reduction approach van Hove has lately relied upon in multiple productions has, in its stripping away of inessentials, an intrinsic authenticity. But it has grown to be a concern, as it begins to seem merely non-committal. When Peter Brook introduced his concept of the "Empty Space" in theory and practice, it revolutionized the theatre, at least for a time. But the avant-garde is imbued with a natural assumption of timed obsolescence, and a new idea either gets absorbed into "the culinary theatre" or becomes old hat. But at this point, some sixty years after its inception, van Hove is re-tooling the "Empty Space" with new accoutrements. Thus far, in London, Paris, and New York, it has garnered him lavish praise. With an unorthodox injection of media, he has shown that a fundamentally empty space can open up numerous possibilities and variations. But how long can this particularly fecund path continue without it, too, getting tired?

Van Hove repeatedly makes the distinction between "little theatre" (*klein zaal*) and "large-scale theatre" (*grote zaal*), associating the "little" with his sincere, early fumblings toward a given vision. He left that sort of experimentation behind a long time ago, after he departed from Zuidelijk Toneel in Eindhoven, opting for the showier venues that liberated and matched the scope of his vision. But large-scale theatre entails constraints of other sorts. The twenty-first century audience may have to content itself with a mere simulacrum of "the real thing." The ensemble members may be individually disciplined, and one assumes sufficiently trained. But when they stand still on stage and "simply speak," it sometimes starts to reveal an insufficiency. Neutral only goes so far.

On the other hand, this minimalism is not an offensive style and it *is* one that manages, as we have seen, to attract audiences. It has been proof positive that serious theatre can be a draw on Broadway, provided that there are some big names attached to the show. "Not to be adulterous,"van Hove recently said, "but you can do different things in different circumstances, as long as there is an audience to see it" (Newton 2015). In a very real sense, it is the ultimate fulfillment of the project the Flemish director set out to accomplish when he first came to America: to shake up the literal way American classics tended to be produced here. With such productions as *Antigone* and *The Damned*, he has also, it seems, been given his lead and shaken up theatre in France in a different way. He has been so successful that his initially defiant quest on two continents has lost its controversial tension.

Van Hove, thus far, has moved on parallel tracks, bi- and trifurcating his efforts. He is both Broadway and Off-Broadway when in New York. He is official repertory theatre back in the Netherlands. Who knows how he might again reinvent himself over time? If van Hove doesn't restrict himself, but finds venues and opportunities to keep experimenting and growing on a parallel track in *klein zalen*—with *Lazarus* standing as exemplar for this possibility—then there is great hope for a continued, highly fruitful career and numerous fascinating productions ahead. To give him the penultimate word:

> Our first productions, *Rumors* and *Disease Germs*, signified a rupture: with the theatre tradition in Flanders. There were vehement proponents and adversaries. Our work has virtually always provoked controversy. In New York they call me a bad boy and an iconoclast, for the way I direct Molière and Ibsen. It's never been any different. And I feel just fine with that. It means something. If you rub everybody the wrong way then you've got something worth talking about, I say.
>
> *(Heene 2007)*

And the last word:

> I see life as one continuous failure, so that afterwards you might rise from the ashes like a phoenix. I am still, every now and again, liable to fly off the handle.
>
> *(Van de Grift April 2008)*

Notes

* Total Theatre pieces, in Richard Wagner's formulation.
1 Quoted respectively from: Charles McNulty, "Meet Ivo van Hove: The Most Provocatively Illuminating Theatre Director," *Los Angeles Times*, 18 March 2016; Fabienne Darge, "'Vu du pont,' la piège tragique d'Arthur Miller," *Le Monde* (Paris), 16 October 2015; Andrzej Lukowski, review of *View from the Bridge*, *Time Out*, London, 17 February 2015 and Andrzej Lukowski, "Revered Belgian Director Ivo van Hove," review of The Young Vic Production of *A View From the Bridge* at the Wyndham Theatre, *Time Out*, London, 14 November 2014. Oracular kudos bespeak his new-found critical beatification, such as: "Mr. van Hove brings us so close to a work's emotional white-hot center that it burns as never before." [Ben Brantley, "A Universal Heart, Pounding With Hope," *The New York Times*, 24 October 2014b.] On the Continent, as far back as 2001, he was locally being touted as the "most powerful man in the Netherlands" [Trudy Van der Wees, "Machtigste man van Nederland," *Haagsche Courant* (The Hague), 27 January 2001], and "the director who dares it all." [Margriet Marbus, "Dus dit is de regisseur die alles durft," *De Theatermaker*, June 2002.] As early as the mid-1990s, he was being called such things as "wonder-boy" of the Flemish theatre in the Benelux press. [Ariejan Korteweg, "Ivo gebruikt geen woord te veel," *De Volkskrant*, 22 January 1997, and Max Arian, "Het van Hove Festival," *Het Groene Amsterdammer*, 17 June 1998.] Now his ship has come in globally. In a recent French press release, he has been referred to as a "super-star." He is "Broadway's man of the moment!" Peter Marks, "Broadway's Man of the Moment," *Washington Post*, 12 March 2016.
2 Was that not also the founding philosophy of the National Theatre in London that William Archer and Granville Barker envisioned as, "visibly and unmistakably a popular institution, making a large appeal to the whole community?" [Richard Findlater, "The Winding Road to King's Reach." In *The National: The Theatre and Its Work, 1963–1997*. Edited by Simon Callow. London: Nick Hern Books, 1997.] Joseph Papp in New York was animated by the same idea.
3 "The play's [*View From the Bridge*] transfer to Wyndham's Theatre elicits a wry remark: 'Until yesterday I was considered an avant-garde director. But I am really happy that the West End is open to receive this kind of work.'" [Sarah Hemming, "Ivo van Hove brings 'Antigone' to London," *Financial Times*, 6 March 2015.] In London in 2015, he was given an Olivier Award for directing over three British

nominees for *View From the Bridge* and, as of June, 2016, he was awarded a coveted Tony Award for Best Director for a non-musical. A *View From the Bridge* was named Best Play of the season as well, the highest honors bestowed in New York, and by consequence, American theatre. He won the French theatre's 2017 Molière Award for Best Director for his production of *The Damned*.

4 Regarding auteur European theatre directors see: Maria M. Delgado and Dan Rebellato, Introduction, *Contemporary European Theatre Directors*. London and New York: Routledge, 2010, 2. The French are best at honoring their stage directors with full-length books. They go further: they honor foreign directors who achieve renown in France with books as well—most recently the Flemish Belgians Guy Cassiers and Ivo van Hove. Flemish Belgians, Geert Sels, Christel Stalpaert, and Luk Van den Dries, have dedicated books to Luk Perceval, Jan Lauwers and Needcompany, and Jan Fabre respectively.

5 The progressive shift in valorization from the playwright to the director as "the dominant creative force" in the theatre, while certainly not endorsed by all and actively opposed by many, was initiated by Gordon Craig in theory and Meyerhold in both theory and practice. Artaud's theories gave the concept a radical boost which impacted on a plethora of practitioners and theoreticians from the 1940s until today. Bernard Beckerman propounded a theory of the interweaving of all the elements which would also abrogate the traditional scale of values attached to them. Richard Schechner made undoing the traditional Aristotelian hierarchy into a personal cause from his platform as editor of *The Drama Review*, during the 1980s and 90s based on, "the conviction that the text/narrative/character-based theatre of the mainstream Western tradition is moribund." See Gay McAuley, *Space in Performance: Making Meaning in the Theatre*. Ann Arbor: University of Michigan, 1999, 213–214.

6 It is neither a libel nor a surmise to make such a statement, as he frankly avows that he and his Flemish contemporaries in the Flemish Wave have been doing just that—imitating each other—all along. Ivo van Hove, interview with David Willinger (Upper West Side, New York City, 17 September 2014).

7 My research has uncovered allusions by van Hove to this long ago accident that brought me to their debut as director and designer in several interviews: Ivo van Hove, interviewed by Paul De Bruyne, "In de jaren zeventig is niets gebeurd: Ivo van Hove als regisseur," *Knack*, 1 December 1982 interview; Erwin D.A. Penning, "Vertikaal onderweg met Ivo van Hove," *De Scène*, December 1985; Jan Versweyveld, interview with Johan Thielemans, "Jan Versweyveld: 'Ik ben van toneel gaan houden door aan toneel te doen,'" *Etcetera*, 1988, no. 23; Ivo van Hove, interview with Paul Kraijeveld, "Ivo van Hove blijft loyal aan z'n idealen: 'Ik ben een trouwe Mechelse hond,'" *De GAY Krant*, 22 February 1992 (interview); Rebecca Mead, "Theatre Laid Bare: A Radical Director's Raw Productions," *The New Yorker*, 16 October 2015, 56–57; Geert Sels, "Ivo van Hove werpt het masker af: een terugblik met onze meest gelauwerd theatermaker," *De Standaard*, 10 August 2016, Culturele Bijlag [Interview on the occasion of van Hove receiving of the prestigious Flemish Prize for Cultural Achievement]. The most detailed and accurate version is as follows:

> There was a man who was researching the theatre in Belgium, a professor, David Willinger. I'll never forget his name. In *De Standaard* an article by this man appeared, a few weeks after we'd been performing, and he announced that the production of the year as far as he was concerned was *Rumors*. Then naturally it all started, and Pol Arias came straight to us. He was one of the very few journalists who saw that show. Kaaitheater also came immediately, because they thought: this is something we'd better not miss. But it's a production about which not one single review appeared, except in New York in *The Drama Review*, in other words, one of the biggest theatre periodicals in the world. And so it came to have a kind of cult success.

Ivo van Hove, interview with Wouter Hillaert at the Monty, *Belgium is Happening* (University of Antwerp, 2009), 6. The article in *De Standaard*, one of the principal daily newspapers of Flanders, was actually a two-page interview with me conducted by their lead critic. In it, I named *Rumors* one of the three most interesting theatre pieces I'd seen throughout my fellowship time. David Willinger, interview with Jef De Roeck, "Toneel in Vlaanderen '80-'81: Niet slechter en niet beter dan elders," *De Standaard* (Brussels), 25–26 July 1981.

8 For definitions of The Flemish Wave and discussions of certain of its members, see: Gino Coomans, interview with Luk Van den Dries, *Belgium is Happening*, 2 March 2009; "Editorial: Border Collisions—Contemporary Flemish Theatre," Peter M. Boenisch and Lourdes Orozco, Special issue of *Contemporary Theatre Review*, eds., Peter M. Boenisch and Lourdes Orozco, 20, no. 4 (November 2010): 397–400; and Thomas Crombez, "Canonisation in Contemporary Theatre Criticism: A

Frequency Analysis of 'Flemish Wave' Directors in the Pages of *Etcetera*," *Contemporary Theatre Review*, 24, no. 2 (April 2014): 252–261. Van Hove himself recounts his personal experience of living through the Flemish Wave as follows:

> At the start of the 1980s Jan Versweyveld and I began to make theatre, but in the same year Anna Teresa De Keersmaeker for example also began creating theatre. A little later Luk Perceval tore himself away from the KNS [the major state theatre in Antwerp] as it was then called. There was Sam Bogaerts and the Witte Kraai company, a fringe group, but with extremely good actors like Warre Borgmans, Johan Van Assche and Lucas Vandervorst. Jan Lauwers was also there of course. Jan Fabre, who came out of the visual arts, same as Jan Versweyveld. That was the kind of generation of people it was. They all actually wanted to make their mark, and we all did just that, not so much in institutes or in large institutions. We each went our own way and didn't request any subsidies. We didn't even give a moment's thought to it. Thus that particular generation rose up, but not without a great many stresses, because there was, naturally, a lot of competition. And when you start off without any money you naturally want the attention to go to you, and whoever gets more attention you get jealous of, and at the same time not necessarily because you have their best interests at heart. . . . After my first triumph came a sort of 'waste land': there was only old, moldering, outdated theatre in groups that were static, which rubbed no one either the wrong way or the right way, which had an obsolete hierarchical structure, and which hadn't the slightest interest regarding what was going on beyond the theatre. Who wouldn't look beyond their own side of the border, you see? Something had to give. It was a kind of in-between time: it's very quiet and then the birdies start to wake up, and those little birdies were us. I think that really sums it up. It was a new time with members of a new generation who by that point had very tight connections with each other.

Ivo van Hove, interview at the Monty, op cit.

9 For an in-depth chronicle of the adventure of De Tijd see: Fred Six, "Het dubbele theaterspoor van De Tijd," *Ons Erfdeel* (Rekkem, Netherlands), 6 (1993).
10 "'I led small groups in Flanders for nine years. Nothing but financial constraints. That's why I finally left. Here [in Holland] I hardly have to give it a second thought. It's nice being an artistic director. I'm free to choose. I can balance out a season. If one play selection turns out to be more expensive, then I can balance it out with something else. I have yet to be presented with a financial reason for being kept from realizing a wish.'" Quoted in Eddy Geerlings, "Ivo van Hove houdt niet van klagen," *TT*, 6 June 1993. His material conditions changed substantially for the better once he crossed the border to the north. As artistic director of Zuidelijk Toneel, he boasted a company of six contract players and many other benefits:

> As producing director of Zuidelijk Toneel, as per the new planning rules for the arts, he managed an annual budget of around 83 million Belgian francs [this was before the Euro], that would go toward putting on a minimum of four productions to be performed throughout the southern end of the nation [Netherlands]. And Zuidelijk Toneel exceeded that mandate: The production of *Desire Under the Elms* managed to put on 57 performances for 30,000 spectators, and *Thyestes* went great guns with 53 performances for around 20,000 people.

Luk Van den Dries, "Moord op onschuldige kinderen," *Etcetera*, 11, no. 40 (February 1993): 44–46.
11 Toneelgroep Amsterdam (TGA) is the largest theatre company in Holland, with one hundred permanent employees, including a stable company of approximately twenty-five actors on salary. It has intricate design, education, literary, and publicity offices. Visiting it, one feels very much that it is a considerable national and municipal institution provided with an abundance of amenities. Apart from enjoying pride of place in the Gothic style Amsterdam Schouwberg edifice in the heart of the city, productions also show at the more open and spacious Joop Admiraalzaal. It receives sizable subsidies from the Dutch Ministry of Education, Culture, and Sciences and the city of Amsterdam. Like most theatre companies in Europe, they regularly take selected productions on tour throughout the Netherlands and Flanders, to the presenting auditoriums and cultural centers that proliferate, even to some of the tiniest, most far-flung towns.
12 Hans-Thies Lehmann cites Jean-Pierre Sarrazac's theory of theatre of "the second degree." *Post-Dramatic Theatre*. Oxford: Taylor & Francis, 2006: 116. In a "logocentric philosophy of theatrical

art," such as that which prevails on the vast majority of America's naturalistically inclined stages where productions go no further than "the first degree," "the mise en scène seems to do nothing other than confirm what the text has already suggested or replace what the didascalia communicated to the reader." Patrice Pavis says more or less the same thing using different terms. Patrice Pavis, *Analyzing Performance: Theater, Dance, and Film* (David Williams, trans.). Ann Arbor: University of Michigan Press, 2003: 145.

13 Of course, later on in his career, van Hove did a great deal of adding, subtracting, and at times, parodying of texts. This observation, bear in mind, dates from 1993. Six, "Het dubbele theaterspoor, op cit.

14 "American audiences often . . . think of van Hove . . . as an experimental theatermaker—a provo-cateur bent on re-authoring classics. But don't be fooled by the video cameras or perfume-ad visual sophistication. In Europe, van Hove is considered conservative, even conventional." Tom Sellar, "The Dark Secrets of the Belgian Avant-Garde," *Village Voice*, 18 September 2007.

15 "Sick mind" is stated in English in the Dutch-language anecdote. Paraphrased from: Mieke Zijlmans, "Toneel als Boze Droom," *HP De Tijd*, 16 September 1994 (Kunst & Genot).

16 Of course, one must be wary of making generalizations. Many of his experiments in Europe have come in for criticism from all sides. One notorious review crossed the line with the shocking, homophobic statement: "If the Holland Festival were to really get rid of him in the near future, and Toneelgroep Amsterdam also started casting about for another artistic leader once more, he could always open a bordello for boys." Hans Oranje, theatre critic from *Trouw*, quoted in: Richard Stuivenberg, "Ik zit aan mijn botten om aan te rukken," *De Theatermaker*, April 2002. Van Hove, incensed, responded that he was still waiting for an apology.

17 While van Hove generally denigrated the directing training he received at De RITCS, still, he paid tribute to his directing teacher at the time, Alex van Royen, a veteran actor/director, whose cur-mudgeonly dished out expertise Ivo found useful in laying down some basic concepts, particularly concerning rigorous analysis of text. Van Hove's interest in theatre actually began at the boarding school he went to from a very young age. There, when given an option for an extra-curricular activity, he chose the drama class six years in a row. He acted and directed, and even once had a leading role. Ivo van Hove, interview by Elisabeth van de Grift, "Op de divan—Ivo van Hove," *Red*, April 2008; Ivo van Hove, "Het misverstand van die éne tekst," *Trouw* (Amsterdam), 2 July 2005.

18 One example:

> Provocation in some crude sense has never thrilled me. Last summer I put on a performance of a Molière in New York. The papers were crammed with news of my provocation. That's all to the good: when people are given something to see that they weren't expecting. It shocks you, but it wakes you up too. In that sense I'm all for provocation.
>
> *Quoted in: Ivo van Hove, De Grift interview, op cit.*

19 As well as by such established European directors as Peter Stein, Ariane Mnouchkine, and van Hove's hero, Patrice Chéreau, for a time. David Bradby and David Williams, *Directors' Theater*. New York: St. Martin's Press, 1988: 196.

20 "You can undoubtedly see influence [in my work] from Karl Ernst Hermann, Richard Peduzzi, and Gilles Aillaud." Quoted in: Jan Versweyveld, interview by Wouter Hillaert, "De Toneelvloer is een Metafoor voor het Hele Bestaan," *De Morgen*, 25 March 2006.

21 Van Hove, who rarely tries something only one time, used a moving car again in his show *The Unbeloved*.

22 Van Hove: "Although I never saw it, I know he did it; that's why I did it." David Willinger 1 May 2017a.

23 Benhamou, 47, 84, 97; Dort, *Le Théâtre en jeu*, 154; Marie-Françoise Lévy and Myria Tsikounas, "Avons-nous besoin d'un lieu qui ne serait qu'un théâtre? Patrice Chéreau à Nanterre," Marie-Françoise Lévy and Myria Tsikounas, eds., *Patrice Chéreau à l'oeuvre*. Rennes: Presses Univérsitaires de Rennes, 2016, 194–196.

24 Van Hove: "I have a very specific take on O'Neill, and it is not psychological." Quoted in: Gener, op cit. We shouldn't be too hard on van Hove when he contradicts himself in a different interview: "My theatre is based on psychology," he confides to Tom Sellar, "but not only on psychology. I try to make an X-ray of a character, to bring the subtext out where it can be seen. American actors learn to keep it hidden." [Sellar, "Dark Secrets," op cit.] And indeed, one critic said of his *Desire Under the Elms*, "that it's actually Freud for Beginners, gussied up in a curious mix of domestic tragedy and confessional

literature." [Hein Janssen, "Met overgave de valkuil in," *De Volkskrant*, 4 June 1994.] Perhaps it's just an inevitable booby-trap that words like "psychology" can mean such different things in various contexts, so that they cease to mean anything finally.

25 "No Law in the Arena." In *Sexual Personae*. New York: Vintage, 1991: xiii, 12, 12, 19, 22, 23, 26, 34, 41, 46, 81. She argues that, "our dream life itself, as Freud has shown, is both power play and passion play." No wonder that an artist like van Hove can find applicability for such simply and vividly expressed ideas, although she tends to be marginalized by the critical community.

26 Which simply means, in the conventional theatre, that a director will pressure his or her cast to speak fast without any pauses between lines; so pacing means to apply a single kind of rapid unbroken rhythm.

27 Ivo van Hove interview by Pieter Bots, "Ivo van Hove: Ik vindt dat ik nog steeds subversief theater maak," *De Theatermaker*, October 2005. Several critics on viewing his 1994 Dutch version of O'Neill's *More Stately Mansions*, while voicing reservations about the author's text, both called attention to the show's unusually long running time and yet heralded the director as the new hope for the Dutch theatre. And:

> They ought to ban shows that last longer than three hours. Seldom is such a long duration justified. Seldom are there any exceptions. Take *More Stately Mansions*, such an exception that is now on view in the Holland Festival. It lasts around three and a half hours, but has such an unusually high level of acting and they're so deeply intertwined that there is no opportunity for the spectator's attention to slacken.

Nicole Bliek, "'Rijkemanshuis' boeit drieenhalf uur lang," *Algemeen Dagblad*, 4 June 1994. As well as:

> There are two intermissions, you're back on the street around midnight, but after the premiere in the cafes around the Leidseplein [where the Schouwburg of Amsterdam is located] there was a lot of people talking late into the night. Something had really happened. It was high time.

Gerben Hellinga, "'Rijkemanshuis': een wreed schouwspel van grote schoonheid," *Vrij Nederland*, 11 June 1994.

28 As, for example:

> Bots: 'As one of the foremost directors you rediscovered large theatre spaces in the mid-eighties. Why did you opt, after all the rented and small venue performances that you did with AKT/Vertikaal, to work in large theatre spaces?'

> Van Hove: 'It was a logical next step for me. Patrice Chéreau is my greatest idol, and his staging in large theatre spaces has had a profound influence on me. The way he devises his mise-en-scènes! For example, I'll never forget Laertes's first entrance in his *Hamlet*. I admired his large-scale productions, and I too wanted to create such wild shows. That goes just as much for the directing of Peter Stein, such as his *Oresteia*, that I saw on television back in those days.'

Ivo van Hove interview by Bots, op cit. At each new juncture of his spectacular career, van Hove appears to have been honest with himself as to his ambitions and done what it took to fulfill them. He has asserted that he doesn't "do career planning," [see Geerlings, op cit.] and we have no reason to doubt this, but at the same time, through his latter formative years in Flanders, he put out ample signals that he was champing at the bit to do "*grote zaal*" productions, that is, shows on a grander scale with more munificent resources.

29 This tendency did not go unremarked by the critics:

> De Tijd's planned debut production resulted in fireworks without festivity. Ivo van Hove as director conjured up one effect after the other from the lightboard, merrily set the wind machines blowing, and both literally and figuratively sent the actors into an artificial fog.

Ria Breyne, "Shakespeare bij De Tijd: 'Macbeth' tussen lichtbundels," *De Standaard*, 10 September 1987.

30 Martin Schouter, "Chris Nietvelt draagt Macbeth in grandioos opgebouwde rol," *De Volkskrant*, 4 September 1987. And:

> Macbeth is perched on top of that horse like an equestrian statue when he hears of his wife's suicide and thereupon utters his greatest speech about life being nothing more than a tale told by an idiot full of sound and fury. But according to a time-honored theatre adage ('don't let yourself to be caught on the same stage with children or animals') you sit staring at the horse the whole time and not at Lucas Vandervorst who's playing Macbeth. The horse poisons the well ever so slightly, however pretty a picture it makes, eliciting an 'ooh' and 'aah' that waft up from the auditorium.
>
> *Breyne, op cit.*

31 Alex Mallems attributes the grab-bag feeling that characterized this production to the fusion of two separate companies—AKT/Vertikaal and De Witte Kraai—each with its own aesthetic, into one, De Tijd:

> the somewhat nonchalant, off-handed acting style of De Witte Kraai and the more stylized, expressive approach of AKT/Vertikaal had succeeded in generating a confrontation.
>
> *Quoted in Six, "Het dubbele theaterspoor," op cit.*

32 A reference to Brabant in the Middle Ages would have a different nuance to it in a Flemish or Dutch production, as Brabant is a neighboring province in the Lowlands, the one indeed that houses Brussels.

33 Ben Brantley picked up on this novelty:

> But that willowy sensitive plant Ben Whishaw as the strapping, rough-hewed farmer, John Proctor? Really? . . . John Proctor has often been portrayed (by the likes of Liam Neeson and Daniel Day-Lewis) as a stalwart Gary Cooper type [in large part because Miller expressly describes him that way both in stage directions and other characters' descriptive dialogue], and part of the tragedy in that context is seeing a big man brought to his knees. The slighter-framed Mr. Whishaw looks more vulnerable, and we fear for his safety from the beginning. . .

"In Arthur Miller's '*Crucible*' First They Came for the Witches," *The New York Times*, 31 March 2016.

34 Although there has been disagreement on this point.

> Whoever labels this as gay theatre is mistaken. It's about relationships, plain and simple, between people and about the prejudices which take hold of us.

Ronny De Schepper, "Een kijk op de wereld van literatuur, wielrennen, muziek, film en zoveel meer Ivo van Hove, "Dagelijks iets degelijks," 26 April 2012.

35 Brantley's initiation to van Hove was the 1997 production of *More Stately Mansions* at NYTW, and his response was irritable and caustic, a stance he maintained through several more shows. He called the rendition of the O'Neill classic "a comic-strip version":

> Mr. van Hove brings a lot of sensational flash and deconstructionist tools . . . but the overall effect is to accentuate the obvious, in the manner of a student highlighting a study text in bright Magic Marker. . . . Much of this feels like acting-class exercises that were never developed into integrated performances. . . . But as far as achieving the sense of a haunting concert of voices, this production falls way short. (It makes you realize how accomplished the Wooster Group's interpretations of O'Neill are.) [It had taken him some time to be so converted to Elizabeth Lecompte as well. Ed.]
>
> *(Brantley 1997)*

The above pales beside the out-and-out pan from *The Westsider*'s uncredited theatre reviewer: "It's only early October, and we already have a front runner for Bomb of the Year. . . . His directorial choices make Anne Bogart's look like the picture of clarity and restraint" (Unattributed, *The Westsider*, 16 October 1997). And then there's the review by the venomous John Simon whose title says it all: "Unmansionable," *New York Magazine*, 20 October 1997. Still, quite a few other critics were impressed by van Hove's American debut, including those from the *New York Post*, *Newsday*, and the *The Wall Street Journal* at a time when there was still a variety of newspapers that reviewed theatre in New York. Consider how far Brantley has come to virtual infatuation. Regarding the 2015 *A View From the Bridge*: "This must be what Greek tragedy once felt like, when people went to the theater in search of catharsis. Ivo van Hove's magnificent reconception of Arthur Miller's '*A View From the Bridge*' . . . takes you into extreme emotional territory that you seldom dare visit in daily life. . . . You also feel ridiculously blessed to have been a witness to the terrible events you just saw." ["'*A View From the Bridge*' Bears Witness to the Pain of Fate," *The New York Times*, 12 November 2015.] For the recent *Crucible*, his rave review celebrates it as flawless: "The director Ivo van Hove and a dazzling international cast . . . have plumbed the raw terror in Arthur Miller's '*The Crucible*.' . . . And an endlessly revived historical drama from 1953 suddenly feels like the freshest, scariest play in town." ["In Arthur Miller's '*The Crucible*,'" op cit.] What can account for this evolution?

36 The multiple mirthful plays on words of the reviewers' responses bespeak their manifest contempt for van Hove's interpretation. Ben Brantley in the determinative *The New York Times* review wrote:

> If this production, which I will always think of as 'A Bathtub Named Desire,' sounds like an antic outlandish hoot, it really isn't. Mr. van Hove, who played similar (and marginally more illuminating) tricks with Eugene O'Neill's 'More Stately Mansions' two seasons ago, has the severe logic of the steely literature teacher who parses works of art into diagrams.

"A Brimming Bathtub as the Focus of Desire," *The New York Times*, 14 September 1999. Still and all, the critics were divided, even within certain reviews. James Hannaham in the *Village Voice* is one who comes down somewhere in the middle. "It's remarkable how bizarre the director's choices can get, but 'Streetcar' still rings out and soars above his vision of it. If you read the script afterward, many of van Hove's conceits appear completely logical, if overstated." Donald Lyons in the 14 September 1999 *New York Post*, under the derisive banner "Clean 'Streetcar' leaves Something to be Desired," admits, "This spring cleaning of an over-familiar play may have been too ruthless, too thorough, but it's never boring. On balance, I like this 'Streetcar' for its audacity, impudence and theatrical excitement." But Brantley and the vulgate's negative view found support from the *New York Daily News* of the same day with a blistering review entitled "An Undesirable 'Streetcar': Bizarre Staging will make Tennessee Williams Fans Blanch." The notoriously mean John Simon captured the prevailing mood when he wrote, "In this *Streetcar*, a functional bath is the only thing that works," calling it, "a downright nauseating 'deconstruction' that the Belgian charlatan Ivo van Hove has perpetrated." Still a minority of reviewers, such as Debra Jo Immergut in *The Wall Street Journal*, and especially the erudite, venerable (and more prescient, it seems) Robert Brustein in the *New Republic* so appreciated the effort that he wrote an extensive thought piece about it. He asserted van Hove's right to take the approach he did. Brustein frames his response by establishing that, "the challenge of Williams revivals, then, is how to make them surprising to people already familiar with their content while delivering the material anew to younger audiences." And he follows up with a measured analysis of why it worked (and what didn't work for him), summed up with the remark, "I found it deeply absorbing for most of its three-hour length." But, as anybody who knows American theatre can tell you, nobody reads the *New Republic* and everyone takes *The New York Times* as gospel. See: James Hannaham, "A Formalist Affair," *Village Voice*, 21 September 1999; Debra Jo Immergut, "Deconstructing 'Streetcar': A Bold Look at Williams's Timeless Southern Drama," *The Wall Street Journal*, 15 September 1999; Brustein, "Revisioning Tennessee Williams," *New Republic*, 25 October 1999; John Simon, "'Mud,' 'Drowning,' and 'A Streetcar Named Desire,'" *New York Magazine*, 11 October 1999.

37 As Richard Schechner said, "'Performance art flourishes but it . . . ought to be a sideshow,' he argued plaintively, 'not all the action there is.' The American avant-garde theatre could not survive, Schechner felt, if the introspective solo performer replaced the collaborative-creation model of theatre." Quoted in: Arnold Aronson, *American Avant-Garde Theatre: A History*. New York and London: Routledge, 2000: 181.

38 Van Hove recounts his harmonious working relationship with Joan MacIntosh:

> It was difficult at first to bring that off with American actors. I make a much more theatrical show out of his text. Also I treat O'Neill with humor—some critics couldn't accept that. Joan

MacIntosh was the catalytic agent who made *More Stately Mansions* possible for me. She really understood me. Because she was a member of Richard Schechner's avant-garde collective, she could connect with my extremity.

Gener, op cit.

39 "One has to distinguish the new forms of a heightened and reflective naturalism from what Theodor W. Adorno called the 'pseudo-realism of the culture industry.' What has been perceived as naturalistic in theatre productions since the 1970s, often under the impression of photo-realism, is also a form of derealization, not of perfect representation." Markus Wessendorf, "The Postdramatic Theatre of Richard Maxwell," 2003, University of Hawaii website.

40 Aronson, *Abyss*, ibid.: 17, and Edward Braun, *Meyerhold on Theatre*. New York: Hill and Wang, 1969, 253. For more on the notion of the theatrical, see: Tracy C. Davis, "Theatricality: An Introduction." In *Theatricality*. Edited by Tracy C. Davis and Thomas Postlewait. Cambridge: Cambridge University Press, 2003: passim. Johan Thielemans, for one, has directly remarked on the provenance of van Hove and Versweyveld from Meyerhold, particularly where his shows invaded the audience space, a radical innovation for the time. [Thielemans, "De totaal ontwerper," *De Theatermaker*, 9–10 December 2007/January 2008.]

41 See: Johan Thielemans, "De totaal ontwerper," Ibid. Baudrillard has already employed the term "hyper-realism," to mean something quite different. Wessendorf, op cit.

42 Langer applies this notion to the artform of dance, but as these interludes play out on the van Hove stage, they bear as much resemblance to dance as to theatre. Susanne K. Langer, *Feeling and Form*. New York: Scribner's, 1953: 169–187.

43 Jan Versweyveld states that he became attached to this chilly aesthetic after seeing a production of *The Children of Herakles* by Peter Sellars. It premiered at the A.R.T. in Cambridge, Mass. in 2003, but then toured in the Netherlands. Versweyveld describes his impressions:

It was done extremely clinically, without any frills, with just a pail of red liquid. There was no illusion or forcing, and it wasn't acted. . . . That's why in recent days Ivo and I are allowing more and more of what goes into the production to be in general view, as much onstage as off. Nothing is left secret.

Quoted in: Hana Bobkova, "De ontedekking van de schouwburg als locatie,"
De Theatermaker, *December 2007/January 2008*

44 In the event, the shells she refers to are "the partially-built aluminum stud structure[s]" often employed by Elizabeth Lecompte and the early Wooster Group. Bonnie Marranca, *Theatrewritings*. New York: PAJ Publications, 1984: 126. The same principle applies for Versweyveld's sets, which are inspired in part by Lecompte's, referenced above.

45 Quoted in: Bobkova, "De ontdekking," op cit. For the most in-depth discussion of Versweyveld's lighting concepts and practice see: Jan Versweyveld, interview by Johan Thielemans, op cit.

46 Quoted in: Wouter Hillaert, "De Toneelvloer is een Metafoor voor het Hele Bestaan," *De Morgen* (Brussels), 25 March 2006.

47 Several others have remarked earlier upon certain of these spatial strategies, although without expanding those insights into a full-blown study. For instance, Luk Van den Dries contrasts two of Ivo's uses of space in: *Desire Under the Elms* and his production of Edward Bond's *Saved*. Luk Van den Dries, "Moord," op cit.

48 Michel Corvin claims that the most adventurous of current directors (he cites Robert Lepage and Olivier Py) are opting for "rectilinear frontality." The time of "breaking out into omni-directional space so dear to Mnouchkine or . . . Ronconi is past." [Michel Corvin, "L'écriture théâtrale contemporaine a't-elle conquis sa liberté d'espace?" Marcel Freydefont, ed., *Etudes Théâtrales: Le lieu, la scène, la salle, la ville"* (Louvain-la Neuve: Centre d'Études théâtrales, 1998: 65.] With certain notable exceptions, this assertion applies to Ivo van Hove.

49 "[T]he Belgian-born Mr. van Hove applies his demolition devices to not one but two fourth walls in the course of this rambunctious evening, since he has not one but two separate audiences to consider." In this show, the audience had been split in two. Ben Brantley, "A Natural Cassavetes Woman," op cit.

50 Tom Sellar, reviewing the New York version, felt that the vast site-specific warehouse subverted any sense of claustrophobia and rather swamped the production. "Ivo Van Hove Stages Pasolini on Governors Island," *Village Voice*, 20 July 2010.

51 "The liberal-minded, middle class characters have entrenched themselves in their sparkling white house, their ivory tower, and don't enter into actual contact with the people outside the door—right up until the latter literally force their way inside." Herien Wensink, "Van Hove halt Gorki naar de politiek van nu," *NRC Handelsblad*, 30 November 2010.

52 Fuchs, op cit., 143. Arnold Aronson suggests that Heisenberg's Uncertainty Principle has become "the metaphor of choice" for the current age, "replacing Einstein's relativity principle." [*Abyss*, op cit., 112.] Perhaps it is precisely the rhythm governing such existential uncertainty that van Hove is expressing through these abrupt, destabilizing, mixed-media interventions.

53 This is a term Camille Paglia introduces in the course of advocating an embrace of the pagan: "What the west represses in its view of nature is the chthonian, which means 'of the earth'—but the earth's bowels, not its surface." "Sex and Violence," *Sexual Personae*. New York: Vintage, 1991b: 5.

54 Even when his characters come from the lower echelons of society in other productions, as with the farmers in *Desire Under the Elms*, the street toughs and cop in Genet's *Splendid's*, the boxers from Visconti's *Rocco and His Brothers*, and the marginals from Charles Mee's *Perfect Love*, who all hail from the lumpen proletariat, the economic and political facets of their plights are not especially problematized by van Hove.

55 "Roasted Tartar, crazy nicker, shiny stovepipe, Maghreber, sandnigger, Fattah, camel, desert rat, Saracen. In the terrific translation that the writer Hafid Bouazza has created from the tragedy *Othello*, he gives a series of loaded synonyms for Shakespeare's neutral indication, 'Moor.' Bouazza's Othello is more than ever discriminated against as an Arab. He's an alien who's never secure in his position." Wilfred Takken, "Arabische Othello als kippige Colin Powell," *NRC Handelsblad*, 2 February 2003a.

56 One reviewer elaborates on how this doppelganger effect was brought about:

> Iago (Roeland Fernhout) in this version becomes seen as the evil side of Othello, his phony, misleading navigator from the Western world, his false friend. He stands for eternal envy and resentment. To underline this mirror effect he wears the same uniform, and both of them have shaved heads.
>
> *Takken, op cit.*

57 Van Hove:

> Molière, unfortunately, is very rarely performed in the Netherlands. When I read his plays, I find them extremely relevant, even though that's a horrible word. . . . Zygmunt Bauman, the Polish-English sociologist, has written a series of pertinent books: *Liquid Society, Liquid Love*, etc. He says that our society has become fluid and all relationships of short duration. We no longer get into long-standing relationships, not in work, and not in love.
>
> *Quoted in: Ivo van Hove, interview by Max Arian. "Ik ben een onvermoeibare optimist,"* Het Groene Amsterdammer*, 24 August 2007*

58 The image of a society in the grip of anomie, embodied here and elsewhere in various productions, seems either to be based on van Hove's reading of Zygmunt Bauman, a Polish-English sociologist, as well as the Americans Richard Sennett and Benjamin Barber, or he possibly draws on such scholars' ideas because they confirm his own inclinations. He suggests that these commentators' visions of contemporary society as absolutely fluid, riddled only with short-lived relationships, as a consumerist orgy, together with its hypermediatized information and communications systems that distort all relations, conforms to what van Hove calls the "social choreography" he has concatenated to represent it as such. Ivo van Hove, "Ik ben," op cit.

59 For diagrams and photos of the pioneering set configurations, see: Jerzy Grotowski, *Towards a Poor Theatre*. New York: Simon and Schuster, 1969: 89, 99, 101, 158–164, 239–240.

60 Lehmann describes this craze as a phenomenon that grew out of "club culture." Op cit., 118. A journalist interviewed three of van Hove's performers from *Faces*, who said that, due to proximity with the audience, any "lie" in their acting would be immediately detectable. Pieter Kottman, "Orgie van geweld is een belevenis," *NRC Handelsblad*, 9 June 1997.

61 In so many of these productions, he seems to be desiring to awaken a "multi-conscious" response in the audience, one that is—according to Daphna Ben Chaim's definition—spontaneously and unconsciously on more than one plane at a time. [Daphna Ben Chaim, *Distance in the Theatre: The Aesthetics of Audience Response*. Ann Arbor: UMI Research Press, 1984: 88–89.] Although I am not directly

addressing the question of audience response to van Hove's productions, it could be a fruitful subject for investigation, particularly in these aforementioned productions.

62 Harley Granville Barker and William Poel in turn-of-the-century England (in their fresh approaches to Shakespeare) and Jacques Copeau in France of the 1920s and 30s had already done radical experiments with similar aims of physically purifying the stage. Oscar Brockett and Robert Findlay, *A Century of Innovation*. Boston: Allyn and Bacon, 1991: 109, 110, 128, 140.

63 In his chapter, "Density of Signs," Lehmann references an aesthetic of "*plethora*," which generally aligns with the term "Proliferation," as well as one of "*deprivation*," which correlates with the "Reduction" principle. Hans-Thies, Lehmann, *Post-Dramatic Theatre*. Oxford: Taylor & Francis, 2006: 89.

64 Who played a lead, René, in Ivo's very first production, *Rumors*, and then went on to become a pioneer in the use of video in theatre, perennially coming up with astonishing new ways to integrate stage and recorded performance throughout his illustrious career. He is currently the Artistic Director of the most significant municipal theatre in Antwerp, Het Toneelhuis.

65 Lehmann describes Needcompany's productions' use of space metonymic as opposed to metaphorical, and his observations could apply equally to this production. Lehmann, op cit., 151. Van Hove tries out this strategy in various shows, culminating in this *More Stately Mansions*, but ultimately discards it or waters it down so it no longer registers as such.

66 Note, for example, Polanski's 1971 film version.

67 Paglia writes:

> The female body's unbearable hiddenness applies to all aspects of men's dealings with women. What does it look like in there? Did she have an orgasm? Is it really my child? Who was my real father? Mystery shrouds woman's sexuality.

"Sex and Violence," op cit.: 22. Orin's fixations seem perfectly illustrative of her point.

68 Lehmann cites Marina Abramowicz as a salient exemplar of this practice, but many others as well; Ivo, it will be remembered, lays particular emphasis on being a disciple of hers. Op cit.: 140; and Ivo van Hove interview with author, 2014, op cit.

69 Dominic Johnson rejects:

> the popular belief that the mainstream had suffered such extensive assaults from the experimental fringes that people were now unshockable. The adage of the 1960s is one of the most persistent fallacies of cultural perception, even though it is consistently refuted by reactions in tabloid journalism, grievances over public funding of the arts, and popular outcries about the values (or lack thereof) upheld by artistic productions. The belief that nothing we see in art or the theatre can shock us is a decoy for the coincident fact that spectators are promptly offended by feminism, homosexuality, blasphemy, violence, death, prurience, and other images of extremity. Dominic Johnson, *Theatre and the Visual*. London: Palgrave Macmillan, 2012: 73.

70 "No Law in the Arena," op cit., 25. Van Hove found an echo for his attitude toward singular, savage divas from the classical canon in Camille Paglia's writings on pagan women.

71 Who still frequently works for Ivo, now in mature roles. He is a member of Toneelgroep Amsterdam and has evolved into a most impressive performer.

72 Flemish critic Eric De Kuyper closely analyzes the male body as fetish in Hollywood films from the 1930s through to the 50s. While he never exactly helps us to identify the precise image van Hove fetishizes, he does home in on many of the same traits of dress, physical traits, and stance that ultimately approximate the van Hove male prototype. Clark Gable, Tyrone Power, and James Dean are all in the ballpark, but the early Paul Newman comes closest. *De Verbeelding van het Mannelijk Lichaam*. Nijmegen: Sun Uitgever, 1993: 14, 15, 17, 39, 75, 97, 104, 110, 112, 125.

73 The gay-oriented Ka Theater of Amsterdam is an example of what the Netherlands had to offer which Belgium did not. Jan Versweyveld does attest to having stumbled on *Rose*, a play by Ka Theater when he was 18 years old, and that it changed his life. See: Thielemans, "Jan Versweyveld," op cit. This news belies a different interviewer's contention that Jan had never seen a live theatre play at all before he'd met Ivo. [Geert van der Speeten, "Waarom de ster van Ivo van Hove blijft stijgen," *De Standaard*, 25–26 June 2016.]

74   *Wild Lords*, a play for the theatre by AKT/Vertikaal, is an offensive evocation of the pink world in which all sorts of homosexual guys head underground and give themselves over to their

exuberant fantasies. An *Our Lady of the Flowers*, staged as a sloppily thrown together underground film, but with powerful images and unmistakable self-glorification. . . .the megalomania of the pink ghetto culture. Van Hove doesn't only settle scores, he romanticizes too, opens the way for sentiments. That makes *Wild Lords* a militant, kitschy production in which the Act takes precedence over artistic perfection. . . . It could have been an underground film, an ode to drag-queens. . . But *Wild Lords* is now generally amusing mostly because of the notion that half of the audience is getting annoyed at the over-exposure of a gang of romping butterflies.

Daan Bauwens, *"Amusante 'Wilde heren,'"*
De Morgen, *26 September 1984*

75 "That man [with whom he has lived and worked for many years] was Jan Versweyveld, van Hove's life partner and his secret weapon. . . . Randy Gener: 'Why have you stayed with one designer throughout your directing career?'
Ivo van Hove: 'Because I live with him.'" Gener, op cit. And:

'Why does he stay with you?' Van Hove: 'I'm very loyal. He stays with me for the same reason. He knows I love him tremendously.' 'And for what reason might he leave you?' Van Hove: 'I'd rather not even think about it.'

In the same interview and several others he avows that, "I'm Catholic, and so, loaded with feelings of guilt and shame." See also: Ivo van Hove interview with Van de Grift, op cit. and van Hove interview with David Willinger, 2014, op cit. Regarding his identity, as distinct from the nature of the themes in his work, he has become more insistent and open about his gay identity recently. Inasmuch as he is a gay man in the public eye, he feels he has a responsibility to be a role model to young gay people in difficulty, particularly because he perceives homophobia to be on the rise once more in the Netherlands. See: Sels, "Ivo van Hove werpt," op cit. In that interview, among other things, he goes into the way he came out to his parents and shares his inconsolable feelings of grief at losing his first lover at age 15 in a bicycle accident.
76 John Clum has effectively and systematically debunked Albee's detractors' arguments, which "reduce Albee's play [*Virginia Woolf*] to only one subject and reduce Albee to his homosexuality." [John M. Clum, *Acting Gay: Male Homosexuality in Modern Drama*. New York: Columbia University Press, 1992: 182–183.] Many of the same points can be applied to van Hove.
77 In the latter instance, Savran is writing about Sam Shepard's plays, and while van Hove has never been drawn sufficiently to Shepard to mount his plays, this treatment of gender is something the two share. David Savran, *A Queer Sort of Materialism: Recontextualizing American Theatre*. Ann Arbor: University of Michigan, 2003: 74, 146.
78 "In the Catholic boarding school he discovered friendship with other boys and homosexuality. In Shakespeare's *Richard II* [and later in *Don Carlos* and other shows we cite] he introduced a boy's world full of rollicking, sparring young men." Arian, "Het van Hove Festival," op cit.
79 The interviewer Pieter Bots sees, in the aggressive knot of male buddies in van Hove's *The Taming of the Shrew*, a commentary on specifically Dutch sports party culture, with its own rip-roaring xenophobic, misogynistic atmosphere, claiming that the recognizably boisterous "Orange Feeling" (The Dutch House of Orange) would naturally come into relief for a Flemish outsider such as van Hove; the latter admits that he may very well have been referencing that specific atmosphere. Ivo Van Hove interview with Pieter Bots, op cit.
80 If one is inclined toward biographical interpretations of theatrical choices, then anecdotes from van Hove's youth can explain this association, although one must make such connections with caution.
81 It's notable that American director Anne Bogart describes virtually the same experience of finding her earliest inspirations from leafing through *Theater Heute*. Preface. *A Director Prepares: Seven Essays on Art and Theatre*. New York and London: Routledge, 2001: 12.
82 The belief that there is such a thing as *non-political* art is, for Adrian Piper, pure ideology: art that is not explicitly political is implicitly political. Darmuid Costello and Dominic Willsdon, eds., *The Life and Death of Images*. Ithaca: Cornell University Press, 2008: 25.
83 Theorist and explicitly political visual artist Adrian Piper, explains:

implicitly political art is no less culturally necessary, significant or valuable than explicitly political art. A healthy and well-functioning society makes room for both. Most artists who produce implicitly political art are extremely fortunate to have the luxury of an inner, creative sanctuary in which the drive to produce such work can be nurtured. They are fortunate to be spared the necessity of grappling consciously and always, at all levels of their being, with the urgent social problems that often drive explicitly political art. Most producers of implicitly political art have reason to be grateful for the creative solace from such problems they are privileged to enjoy.

Adrian Piper, "Political Art and the Paradigm of Innovation." In *The Life and Death of Images*. Edited by Darmuid Costello and Dominic Willsdon. Ithaca: Cornell University Press, 2008: 126–127. Her liberality as concerns apolitical art is highly tinged with condescension; she clearly sees it as moral abdication; this viewpoint which essentially condemns nonpolitical art has permeated the cultural discourse for more than twenty-five years. It is highly unlikely that van Hove has read Piper's theories; it is equally unlikely that these kinds of ideas have failed to reach him and had their impact.

84 "[Since 9/11] The life of the image has been given urgent global political and cultural significance in the image wars" that have since ensued. Darmuid Costello and Dominic Willsdon, eds., Introduction, *The Life and Death of Images*. Ithaca: Cornell University Press, 2008: 18.

85 Again, this shift for van Hove is part of a much larger crisis in the arts.

> Though the idea of the autonomy of art may have been ascendant through the Minimalist moment, with the arrival of politicized post-modernism in the late 1970s and its consolidation in subsequent decades, it will be proposed, faith in the autonomy of art has become an artifact of the past. Art is no longer regarded as autonomous, nor is the ambitious art of the present self-alienated from the rest of the culture. It is patently engaged, primarily in social criticism.

Noël Carroll, "Art and Alienation." In *The Life and Death of Images*. Edited by Darmuid Costello and Dominic Willsdon. Ithaca: Cornell University Press, 2008: 99.

86 In 1992 with *Desire Under the Elms*, a strong production in which he was finally able to wed strong visual images with successful work on text, voice, and acting – van Hove thus fulfilled the prescription and prophesy van Gansbeke laid down in his 1983 review.

87 He began this cycle in 2004. It included: Alan Ayckborne's *The Norman Conquests*, and followed it up with *The Taming of the Shrew*, Bergman's *Scenes from a Marriage*, and Charles Mee's *Perfect Wedding*.

88 The public intellectual Jacques Rancière is an excellent example. Close examination of several of his books on the relationship of politics with aesthetics reveals that he resorts to highly recondite definitions of both, avoiding common usages entirely; in some way, he means aesthetic when he refers to the political and vice-versa. For one who asserts the importance of the accessibility of the "realm of the sensible" to all readers, his own rhetorical style closes out most but a select few. One exasperated Rancière specialist confirms this troubling contradiction:

> the acts of speaking and writing are moral and political acts because they display 'the intention to communicate,' to recognize 'the other as an intellectual subject capable of understanding what another intellectual subject wants to say to him.' . . . If equality is to be verified in action and in thought by finding the right sentences to make oneself understood by others, how come so many of Rancière's texts appear so abstruse and, indeed, as Badiou once nastily remarked, so afraid of drawing conclusions? . . . How can we relate Rancière's precise practice of writing with his quest for the verification of equality?

Jean-Philippe Deranty and Alison Ross, *Jacques Rancière and the Contemporary Scene: The Philosophy of Radical Equality*. London and New York: Continuum, 2012: 2.

89 Some felt his dual posts caused him to stint on his role at the Holland Festival as well. When he ultimately left, it was officially announced that it was simply because his contract was up. The minister of culture followed up by saying that he wished to restore the priority for music and dance, and less for theatre. Editorial Board, "Vertrek Van Hove is geen concessie," *NRC Handelsblad*, 2 July 2002.

90 Kesting returned later and has done many productions since.

91 As he did, for example, in a recent hour-long interview on Flemish television. "Alleen Elvis blijft bestaan," Interview by T. Vanderveken 17 December 2016.

92 Quoted in: Liv Laveyne, "De tijd is rijp om Tsjechov weer te spelen," *Knack*, 29 September 2010. But there was a time early in his career, with such a play as *Like in the War*, when the aesthetic qualities took

greatest precedence to the detriment of dramatic action and character. He was lambasted for this tendency, and, burnt, then veered away from it. The critic at the time took him to task for treating the actors as purely compositional elements on a par with set pieces and lighting. [See: Theo van Rompay, "Kroniek: Ook al doet de toneelcriticus: *Als in de oorlog*," *Etcetera* (Brussels), 1983.]

93 Maeterlinck, a Belgian, was the first successful practitioner of Symbolist drama in the 1890s, a school that rendered unseen powers theatrically palpable. At first essentially apolitical, he became attached to progressive socialistic ideas, but as World War II grew near flirted with fascist alliances. See: David Willinger, "The Missing Link of Modern Drama." In *A Maeterlinck Reader*. Edited by David Willinger and Daniel Gerould. New York: Peter Lang, 2011. He was not so atypical. The magnetic pull of right-wing totalitarian tenets for abstract, avowedly apolitical writers such as Céline, Ezra Pound, and Gertrude Stein proved so strong in the 1930s and 40s that they became spokespeople for that cause. As for the American school of Abstract Expressionist painters, as Serge Guilbault has demonstrated, their apolitical stance, fancying themselves autonomous artists, struggling with their own aesthetic issues and oblivious to societal upheavals, made them tools for a certain type of reactionary liberalism during the McCarthyite fever in the late 1940s and 50s. [*How New York Stole the Idea of Modern Art*, Arthur Goldhammer, trans. Chicago: University of Chicago Press, 1983, passim.] The world's political tectonic plates have shifted since then, however. In times in which the representative democracies of the Occident verge on teetering into totalitarianism, a spiritually free artist simply practicing daringly expressive art out in the open could be an important counterweight to the fascistic tide. It may be that, due to its exemplary *aesthetic* freedom, essentially apolitical work such as van Hove's may yet have a positive political impact.

94 According to Langer, "the concept of significant form as an articulate expression of feeling, reflecting the verbally ineffable and therefore unknown forms of sentience," forms the very basis of any work of art. In theatre specifically all the component parts of the event from the script to sets "delimit the 'world' in which the virtual action exists . . . [and] keep the fictitious history apart from actuality and insure its artistic abstraction." See: *Feeling and Form*. New York: Scribner's, 1953: 39, 312.

95 In a sidebar, he prefers to mount Shakespeare in Dutch and has never done so in English. He avers that doing so frees him from the tyrannical traditions of the English-language theatre for these canonical texts and allows him far greater freedom in reinterpreting them. Ivo van Hove, interview on *Leonard Lopate Show*, WNYC Radio, 3 November 2016. Indeed, Dutch translations as a general rule tend to streamline Shakespeare's lines.

96 One such prolonged slapping match occurs between Edward and Gaveston in *Edward II*, when Edward urges Gaveston to leave him and seek refuge in Ireland. Gaveston realizes he must give up his place even as Edward urges him to seek safety. In desperation at the potential separation, Gaveston picks a fight with him and beats up on his love, a typically hyper-physicalized rendition of emotional abandonment.

97 For a detailed description of Ostermeier's *Hedda Gabler*, see: Bilha Blum, "Looking at Postmodern Performances of Canonical Plays." In *Activating the Inanimate: Visual Vocabularies of Performance Practice*. Edited by Celia Morgan and Filipa Malva. Oxford: Inter-Disciplinary Press, 2014: 19. Adjacent to the article is a production photo that speaks volumes.

98 He makes this provocative, but prescient analysis:

> The current state of the avant-garde is of a circulating stasis. Not in advance of anything and more of a 'niche-garde' than an 'avant-garde,' this art has for a long time been settled in its various places geographical and conceptual 'Niche-garde' because groups, artists, and works advertise, occupy, and operate as well-known brands. The younger groups fall into line behind their forebears in a familiar pattern of tradition and marketing: take a lot, change a little, and make something old look excitingly new. . . . the brand avant-garde is not 'avant' but a tradition: replete with identifiable styles, themes, and lineages. . . . They premiere their work wherever the money is, wherever sponsors can be found. Like Lexus or Sony, the niche-garde has been tested and branded in the global market, acquiring a following in the press and public.

Richard Shechner, "The Conservative Avant-Garde," *Performed Imaginaries*. London and New York: Routledge, 2015: 19, 22, 27.

99 It wasn't so much earlier that, when asked if he cared to direct any more Chekhov, he had responded: "No. I wonder if Chekhov still has a whole lot of meaning for us. Whatever he has to say about people we've come to know little by little ourselves." [Ivo van Hove interview by Bots, op cit.] The statement, made in 2005, by 2010 had morphed into: "The time is ripe to stage Chekhov again.

But I find that those plays today, over a century later, once again are really significant." [Laveyne, op cit.] He justifies the play choice due to analogies with present-day Dutch and Belgian politics, but these reasons, however plausible, don't add up to a personal impetus. For, "the morose quality in Chekhov doesn't seem to be in van Hove's register." [Julie Phillips, "Ivo, Chekhov, No Nudes: Van Hove Tackles 'Three Sisters' at the Holland Festival." *Village Voice*, 24 June 2003.]

100 He is clearly ambivalent about the pitfall of becoming too institutionalized. T'Jonck, "Onpure," op cit. As always, it rankles with him every time he senses that someone is pigeonholing him into any one kind of theatre identity.

101 See, for example, Marion Florusse, "Complimenten maken me verlegen," *Elegance*, 31 January 2005. and Ivo van Hove, Bots interview, op cit. for anecdotes about how certain new actors have entered the company, and Kagie, op cit. about how some have taken their leave.

102 The missionary quest for which he was chiefly congratulated in *Foreign Policy* [cf, f.n. 215]. They celebrate him specifically for having, "revived classic American theater and sharpened its edges." David Rothkopf, "The Leading Global Thinkers of 2016," *Foreign Policy*, 14 December 2016.

103 In the 1970s, theatre artists like Robert Wilson, Ariane Mnouchkine, Meredith Monk, Ping Chong, and Richard Foreman with the "Theatre of Images" restored a theatre with visual primacy to the highbrow realm. Van Hove, for his part, manages to interject visuality that is often suggestive of popular imagery with relentless rhythms borrowed from "Grand Guignol" and melodrama into high art text theatre, one of the hallmarks of his method.

104 "I think, deep down, it is a hope to be loved by audiences all over the world." Maxie Szalwinska. "The Camera is Ruthless: Ivo van Hove's 'Antonioni Project," *The Guardian*, 9 January 2011.

105 In 2003, he reported that he required certain nonnegotiable elements in order to be in the right creative spirit for rehearsal:

> My theatrical imagination isn't conventional and that means I truly need a group of actors that are prepared to go on a creative journey with me and to be driven to the furthest extremes. That can only be done with people with whom I share a future and a past.

Quoted in: Kagie, op cit. But such exigencies didn't remain so fixed. As van Hove said when he had first been invited to direct in New York and was interviewed right before heading off to work at NYTW:

> It's thrilling that plays are produced totally differently over there. I've now got to fight for a rehearsal period of five weeks, and they find that terribly long [in New York]. In Germany it's the exact opposite. There you've got to rehearse at least for twelve weeks if you want to be taken seriously.

Hein Janssen, "New Yorks-theater vraagt Van Hove voor regie Rijkmanshuis," *De Volkskrant*, 5 December 1996. See also, Ivo van Hove, Bots interview, op cit.

106 See Fabienne Pascaud, "Ivo van Hove," *Télérama* (Paris), 29 June 2016. He enlarges on the point, saying that it now suits him to plan all the details so far in advance that the compression of face-time with the actors doesn't hurt the show. For the French production of *The Damned*, the actors arrived at the first rehearsal with all their lines pre-memorized. But recall that he earlier wrankled at the American system, where he was expected to have it all done within four weeks, insisting on an extra one.

107 In his review, Ben Brantley finds topical political signification in the production, and in its being done now, finessing the production's ambiguity thus:

> That its arrival also feels perfectly timed in this presidential election year, when politicians traffic in fears of outsiders and otherness, is less surprising. Miller's portrait of murderous mass hysteria during the 17th-century Salem witch trials was written to echo the 'Red menace' hearings in Washington in the 1950s. . . . Nazi Germany comes to mind. Certain pundits might even think of the United States today [Brantley already did.].

He later contradicts himself: "What makes Mr. van Hove's interpretation so unsettlingly vivid has little to do with literal-minded topicality." Brantley, "In Arthur Miller's 'Crucible,'" op cit.

108 Pamela Newton, "Ivo van Hove is Having a Moment," *American Theatre*, 11 November 2015.

109 Ivo van Hove, "9 punten voor een theater van de 21ste eeuw," excerpted from a speech given on the occasion of the opening of TF-1 Theater Festival, 31 August 2006, disseminated as a press release by TGA.

110 These notions in the interest of "securing global democracy," form the basis for his book *Jihad vs. McWorld*. New York: Ballantine Books, 1996: passim.

111 Van Hove confided that two out of three of the actors were straight; the only gay one, René Van Sambeek, who all pundits predicted would have a brilliant career ahead of him, tragically committed suicide at a very young age. Ivo van Hove interview with David Willinger, 2014: op cit.

112 And thus fulfills a stipulation for post-dramatic theatre that unified plot and action take a back seat to other theatrical elements. "In post-dramatic forms of *theatre*, staged text (*if* text is staged) is merely a component with equal rights in a gestic, musical, visual, etc. total composition." And: "Ostentatious kitsch, solidarity with the taste of the masses and a thirst for fun are combined." The post-dramatic has, "a tendency toward parody." Lehmann, op cit.: 46, 119, 120.

113   The conspicuous variety of postdramatic theatre often finds its inspiration in the patterns of television and film entertainment and makes reference (irrespective of quality) to splatter movies, quiz shows, commercials, and disco music. . . . the most forcible assertion of "fun" in the now' is a statement which captures the relationship between the blatantly performative elements and the anomie they cover up.

Lehmann, Ibid.: 118–119, 151.

114 Some of the negative reception the play received confirms its post-dramatic creds:

> With *Wild Lords* van Hove hasn't produced real theatre. A sloppy structure, no original images, terrific acting, but beyond that: everyone only plays themselves and tries to pull attention to themselves, limited and extremely thin in regard to contents. Twenty years ago it would have been avant-garde.

Bauwens, op cit. In Bauwens's denial that the show is even theatre at all he is by default advancing a claim that its something else. All he finds wrong would be right if seen through a post-dramatic lens, a term and praxis that were not yet in vogue at the time.

115 Again Lehmann observes that the "real" tends to intrude on and is not connected within the fictional frame, creating "an unsettling blurring of boundaries," a further condition for post-dramatic theatre. Lehmann, op cit.: 104.

116 Van Hove, whose directing training at Het RITCS seemingly didn't include practical work with actors, was probably not the initiator of these theatre games. The three actors in this show, as well as those in *Wonders of Humanity* that followed, were all graduates of the Studio Herman Teirlinck in Antwerp. In his review, Klaas Tindemans makes a snarky comment that the theatre games that appear are perhaps "tricks" or "stunts" inherited from Fons Goris, director and principal acting teacher at "The Studio." ["'Wonderen der mensheid': een bal van de poseurs," *De Standaard*, 13 December 1984.] The Studio had indeed been imbued with influences from The Living Theatre through the 1960s and 70s; apart from touring in the area, Living Theatre actor Rufus Collins settled in Holland and went far and wide in the region giving influential workshops. It is undoubtedly owing to that immersion that van Hove's actors introduced him to these games and warm-up techniques, and in a collaborative spirit, they became an integral part of the show. I am grateful to Dr. Jaak Van Schoor, professor emeritus at the University of Ghent and long-time theatre history teacher at The Studio Herman Teirlinck, for this intelligence. Interview with Jaak Van Schoor on 13 December 2016 and e-mails from Van Schoor, 2 and 3 January 2017.

117 One critic found cause to complain that the actors kept eluding the authenticity they started to expose behind and in between the satirical impersonations.

> You're initially expecting the potential authenticity to be realized for quite some time, until you [start to] feel that the show isn't going to go any further than showcasing it, for the sole purpose of bringing it into perspective. . . . Too bad from this perspective that the actors have taken on 'characters.'

He follows by calling it "non-committal theatre." Fred Six, "'Wilde Heren' breken geen potten," *De Standaard*, 30 September 1984 (Kultuur). Another critic was bothered precisely because he felt the actors were *too* authentic and unencumbered by characters:

> In most scenes meanwhile one or more actors are sitting onstage entirely visible, watching their fellow actors—who make a show of striding straight down to the audience—and have to laugh

heartily at it, or they seem to. Or they talk—practically unintelligibly—with each other about how they're doing: ordinary chit-chat, from the looks of it, but which looks inappropriate, because the audience is bound to grasp the performance principle that a theatre production at most may interpret reality, may imitate it, but isn't really the same thing.

Rudy Vanschoonbeek, "Akt-vertikaal: 'Wonderen der mensheid,'" *De Nieuwe*, 13 December 1984. Yet another, while admitting the show's flaws, was more positive:

> There are a few fragments that are too facile and turgid as to meaning; they drag the level of the production drastically downhill. The singing of 'Happiness is a Warm Gun' (The Beatles) as gospel, the way in which 'Angie' by the Stones is presented, it's all far too silly, and would have been better off being left out. Apart from those blunders, *Wild Lords* is a very exciting, somewhat pleasantly muddled event that once more shows that things can be tried out in Flanders that no Dutch theatre group would be likely to dare to venture into.

Jan Middendorp, "Aangename 'Wonderen der Mensheid' bij vlagen melig," *De Volkskrant*, 8 February 1985.

118 "One scene that leads straight into the most beautiful action in the whole production is where the three men poke around in each other's navels, shyly forming an hermetic fellowship. The inhibited camp-fire-romanticism that results is not entirely free of irony. It can even be found in the title." Six, "'Wilde heren,'" op cit.

119 Several critics saw resemblances between the shows from this phase of van Hove's work and those of Jan Fabre, but point out the disparities that exist as well. Tindemans, op cit. And:

> The movement style of AKT/Vertikaal is situated midway between dance and posturing, and is undoubtedly the result of a quest toward a contemporary theatre language. Cleaned up choreographic, virtually text-less, abundantly quoting other sources. Especially in the inauthentic use of 'real' physical reactions such as exhaustion or pain makes the show seem to be something of a polished up version of Fabre.

Johan De Feyter, "Ivo Van Hove toont de baltsende mens," *De Standaard*, 1 October 1985 (Kultuur).

120 Ivo van Hove interview with David Willinger, 2014, op cit. For an overview of how performance art came to Belgium in the early 1980s see Crombez, "Happening in Belgium," op cit.

121 For an in-depth essay regarding van Hove's use of music, see: Anaïs Bonnier, "'Du bruit qui pense': mise en scène, musique et musicalité." In *Ivo van Hove: la fureur de créer*. Edited by Frédéric Maurin. Besançon: Les Solitaires Intempestifs, 2016: 129–145.

122 "Do you have a favorite playwright? 'Eugene O'Neill is my all-time favorite. I'm doing *Mourning Becomes Electra* next season, for the second time. I just did *More Stately Mansions*. My production of *Desire Under the Elms* was on CNN because I had live cows in it. I love O'Neill because he is thinking about the catastrophe that life is.'" Julie Phillips, "Ivo, Chekhov, No Nudes," op cit.

> 'Why don't these plays get put on anymore, I wondered. I know of no other writer whose characters are allowed to come out so directly with what they say and feel. It may be that the plays are un-modern, because in the present day we're so accustomed to leaving things out and to double-entendres, but with O'Neill there aren't any double-entendres. . . . They lay their hearts thumping right on the table ever so theatrically, and that's what I love about them.'

Hein Janssen, "Hunkeren naar hetgeen niet te begrijpen is," *Volkskrant*, 27 May 1994 (Kunst & Cultuur).

123 One critic deemed that this technique was, "bordering on cheap." [Pieter Kottman, "Dat onuit-gesproken lijdzaam zijn," *NRC Handelsblad*, 9 March 1992.] It took critics a long time to accept this sort of post-modern use of music by van Hove.

124 This 1957 play was presented for the first time in the United States at Target Margin Theatre in NYC, directed by David Herskovits, as late as 1997. In the event, none of the critics raised the same objections I do.

125 Hana Bobkova calls it, "a drama of impotence." Hana Bobkova, Review of *Desire Under the Elms*. "Kunstkroniek: 'Begeren onder de olmen,'" *Het Financieele Dagblad*, 4 and 6 April 1992.

126 Van Hove, interview with Van de Grift, op cit. Hans-Thies Lehmann argues for the term *hyper-naturalism*, as applied to the 1970s and 80s works of Kroetz and Fassbinder, that seems applicable to certain of van Hove's productions. Lehmann, op cit.: 117–118.

127 Kottman, "Dat onuitgesproken," op cit. And: "Arne Sierens's translation was very effective (up to and including the word *'totteke'* for a kiss) but in the mouths of the Dutch actors, it didn't always come out sounding right." [Ronny De Schepper, *Dagelijks iets Degelijks*, 28 April 2012.]

128   Eight real live, red-hewed cows on stage, who throughout the performance do nothing more than eat, drink, shit and piss, and from time to time, blissful on account of their feed bags, just sack out in the hay and take a snooze. They were the real eye-catchers of the show. . . . During the first ten minutes of the show you can't take your eyes off of them, but after that the people get more interesting.

       Hein Janssen, "Het begeren onder de olmen door het Zuidelijk Toneel,"
       De Volkskrant, 9 March 1992

And in *NRC Handelsblad*:

       Desire Under the Elms (1924) was, as presented by Zuidelijk Toneel, defined by cows, real cows. Their roles consist of their presence, the manure on the stage floor, their lying down and standing back up again. They symbolize the connection with the earth, which is otherwise absent from the set design.

       Kottman, op cit.

129 Ilse Vandesande, "Engelen van het kwaad die schreeuwen om genegenheid: *Splendid's* van Jean Genet door Het Zuidelijk Toneel," *Etcetera*, 13, no. 48 (February 1995): 29–31.

130 "It's unfortunate, but the play isn't strong enough to keep the spectator engaged through to the end. Together with the slow and awkward unfolding of the story, the menace and consequently the tension trail off entirely. Yet *Splendid's* is a production that can't possibly leave you unshaken, inasmuch as it goes as far as it does." Vandesande, ibid.

131 He repeats it himself uncategorically and often: "I create theatre from film scripts, not from films." For a thorough consideration of how and why van Hove uses film scripts as source material for theatre productions see: Wilfred Takken, "Filmscripts zijn ideaal," *NRC Handelsblad*, 5 June 2009, Cultureel Supplement.

132 Van Hove: "The themes I wanted to take on, I didn't find in plays for the theatre, but did in film scripts." Quoted in: Takken, "Filmscripts" op cit.

133 "Effectively, the category appropriate to the new theatre is not action but *states*. . . .This does not preclude a particular dynamic within the 'frame' of the state — one could call it a *scenic dynamic*, as opposed to the dramatic dynamic." Lehmann, op cit.: 68. And indeed, the audience to van Hove's *Faces* is confronted more with *states*—states in the acting, states in the ambiance, and the ebbing and flowing of a *scenic dynamic* that is alien to the purposefulness of Ibsenian "absolute" drama.

134 There were productions of *The Massacre at Paris* in 1981 featuring Gary Oldman and one by the Royal Shakespeare Company in 1985 that was also done at Stratford-upon-Avon in October of that year. In fact, it has been done in recent years in New York in 1999, Sydney in 2001, and Dublin in 2002 with many cutting and adding freely to the script; 2014 saw the 450th anniversary of Marlowe's birth and a number of revivals as well. Thus, van Hove's production, however improbable, was part of an international renaissance for this obscure classic. See: The Marlowe Society website.

135   Marlowe wrote a fragmentary play on the subject for the theatre; Haffid Bouazza created a free adaptation from it. Of how mankind allows itself to play out its cruel power game in the name of religion—that's the story both Marlowe and Bouazza tell in flowery, bloody language. Bouazza's text matches the entire composition for excess. With Hugo Claus and Shakespeare as sources of inspiration, he's made up his own language throwing in both obsolete words and contemporary Dutch.

       Hein Janssen, "In 'Massacre' gaat vorm boven spel," De Volkskrant, 10 March 2001

136 Wilfred Takken claimed that, after assuming office as artistic director of TGA in the middle of the season, van Hove hoped to take the theatre by storm with a grandiose production. "The theatre critics

tore the play apart, the audience was bored to death, and many of the actors felt miserable." In an interview, van Hove later admitted he ought to have started with a more modest production and should have waited until the beginning of the following season to assume leadership of the company, but went ahead because, "this had been a dream of mine for twenty years, the staging for which I'd run over in my head a hundred times." ["Een koud bed," *NRC Handelsblad*, 19 December 2003c.] He'd been planning it as early as 1984. Tindemans, "Wonderen," op cit.

137 Acknowledging, without necessarily accepting my critique of the NYTW production, which, after all, garnered much praise from the press, van Hove told me that he often gestates a given text in between productions and welcomes the process of revision based on lessons learned. [Ivo van Hove interview with David Willinger, 2014, op cit.].

138 Van Hove himself refers to this piano's "fetishistic function." See: Bots Interview, op cit.

139 A van Hovian trope of slapping as first and last resort of frustration started with parodies of middle-class married men from Jerry Springer-like TV shows, as portrayed in van Hove's early work, the post-dramatic vaudeville, *Wild Lords*.

140 From an interview with van Hove from around that time:

> Van Hove programmed his own directorial work as the Holland Festival's opener: a production of *True Love* by New York playwright Charles Mee. (Van Hove had planned to direct a stage adaptation of Scorsese's *Mean Streets*, but the rights fell through.) Van Hove and Mee originally discussed doing *True Love* together at New York Theatre Workshop; instead, this last-minute substitution became Mee's European premiere. . . . 'Mee is writing a play for me now. I've been directing for 22 years and it's the first time I've commissioned a play. I was very afraid of that. He's in America, I'm in Europe, it's not an obvious combination. But we'll give it a try.
>
> *Phillips 10 July 2001*

141 As Marvin Carlson alerts us, these kinds of ghosts of past performances that hover over our theatre-going experiences can be absolutely determinant. *The Haunted Stage: The Theatre as Memory Machine.* Ann Arbor: University of Michigan, 2003: passim.

142 This passage is a reworking of part of an article: David Willinger, "The Current Belgian Renascence," *Western European Stages*, 21, no. 2 (Spring 2009): 70–72.

143 Van Hove undertook this project shortly after the harrowing death of his father in 2007, and he has made no secret that, in doing so, he was working out his feelings of mourning and rage. John Del Signore, "Ivo van Hove Talks About 'Cries and Whispers' at BAM," *The Gothamist* (New York). He recently confessed that his grief over losing his first lover to death at age 15, an incident that he had passed over in silence at the time, was also on his mind throughout work on this production. Sels, "Ivo van Hove werpt," op cit.

144 "For many Antonioni's films are an affliction: slow, empty, and enigmatic. . . . Enemies re-christened Antonioni as Antonion-Ennui. Fellow film director Alfred Hitchcock characterized his films as hot air: 'It's easy to make a pretentious film. Pop in quite unnecessary images to baffle people. Like that Italian chap, Antonioni.'" Coen Van Zwol, "Het geweer gaat niet af," *NRC Handelsblad*, 5 June 2009.

145 In his show *Blood and Roses*, written by Tom Lanoye. See: David Willinger, "Belgian Theatre Making a Comeback: Four Plays and an Opera." *Western European Stages*, (Winter 2004): 79–84.

146 The way this production uses video tends to support Philip Auslander's contention that, flipping our customary association of live theatre with the virtue of immediate *presence*, television's "essential properties as a medium are *immediacy* and *intimacy*." In this show especially, but elsewhere too, as for example *Roman Tragedies* and *Lazarus*, the stage set is comprised of a "cultural landscape" just as Auslander describes, either littered with the detritus from "'a trial run, a mock-up for work in television, commercial movies, or advertising.'" Philip Auslander, *Liveness: Performance in a Mediatized Culture*. New York: Routledge, 2008: 14, 32, 43.

147 She latterly became the eccentric empress to the Austro-Hungarian Emperor Franz Joseph.

Reference list

Arian, Max. "Het van Hove Festival." *Het Groene Amsterdammer*, 17 June 1998.

Arian, Max. Interview with Ivo van Hove. "Ik ben een onvermoeibare optimist." *Het Groene Amsterdammer*. 24 August 2007.

Aronson, Arnold. *American Avant-Garde Theatre: A History*. New York and London: Routledge, 2000.

Artaud, Antonin. *The Theatre and Its Double*. Translated by Mary Caroline Richards. New York: Grove, 1958.

Artaud, Antonin. *Artaud on Theatre*. Edited by Claude Schumacher and Brian Singleton. London: Methuen, 1989.

Auslander, Philip. *Liveness: Performance in a Mediatized Culture*. New York: Routledge, 2008.

Barber, Benjamin R. *Jihad vs. McWorld*. New York: Random House, 1995.

Barber, Benjamin R. "Patriotism, Autonomy and Subversion: The Role of the Arts in Democratic Change." *Salmagundi*, 170/171 (Spring/Summer 2011): 109.

Barber, Benjamin R. "Yes We Built This—We the People of the United States," *Huffington Post*, 31 August 2012.

Baudrillard, Jean. *Simulations*. Translated by Phil Beitchmann, Paul Foss, and Paul Patton. Cambridge, Mass: MIT, 1983.

Bauman, Zygmunt. *Liquid Love*. Cambridge: Polity, 2003.

Bauman, Zygmunt. *Liquid Times: Living in an Age of Uncertainty*. Cambridge: Polity, 2007.

Bauwens, Daan. Review of *Wild Lords* in Antwerp. "Amusante 'wilde heren.'" *De Morgen*, 1984.

Beckerman, Bernard. *Dynamics of Drama*. New York: Drama Book Specialists, 1979.

Belga news agency. (2008) Excerpts of a speech delivered for the Machiavelliprijs ceremony. "Politiek moet handen van kunst afhouden." The Hague, 29 January.

Ben Chaim, Daphna. *Distance in the Theatre: The Aesthetics of Audience Response*. Ann Arbor: UMI, 1984.

Benhamou, Anne-Françoise. *Patrice Chéreau: figurer le réel*. Besançon: Les Solitaires Intempestifs, 2015.

Billington, Michael. Review of *"Scenes From a Marriage:* Audience Becomes Eavesdroppers in Ivo van Hove's Gripping and Inventive Restaging of Ingmar Bergman's Classic." *The Guardian*, 15 November 2013.

Billington, Michael. Review of *Lazarus* in London. "Michael C. Hall is a Loving Alien in Spectacular Bowie Fantasy." *The Guardian*, 8 November 2016a.

Billington, Michael. Review of *Hedda Gabler* in London. "Ruth Wilson Lets Loose Ibsen's Demons." *The Guardian*, 13 December 2016b.

Billington, Michael. Review of *Obsession* in London. "Jude Law Channels Macbeth in Tale of Passion and Murder." *The Guardian*, 26 April 2017.

Bleeker, Maaike. *Visuality in the Theatre: The Locus of Looking*. London: Palgrave Macmillan, 2008.

Bliek, Nicole. Review of *More Stately Mansions* at Z.T. "'Rijkemanshuis' boeit drieenhalf uur lang." *Algemeen Dagblad*, 4 June 1994.

Blum, Bilha. "Looking at Postmodern Performances of Canonical Plays." In *Activating the Inanimate: Visual Vocabularies of Performance Practice*. Edited by Celia Morgan and Filipa Malva. Oxford: Inter-Disciplinary Press, 2014.

Bobkova, Hana. Review of *Desire Under the Elms* at Z.T. "Kunstkroniek: 'Begeren onder de olmen.'" *Het Financieele Dagblad*, 4 and 6 April 1992.

Bobkova, Hana. "De ontedekking van de schouwburg als locatie." *De Theatermaker*, December 2007/January 2008.

Boenisch, Peter and Orozco, Lourdes, editors. "Introduction." *Contemporary Theatre Review: "Border Collisions—Contemporary Flemish Theatre*," 20, no. 4 (November 2010): 397–400.

Bogart, Anne. Preface. *A Director Prepares: Seven Essays on Art and Theatre*. New York and London: Routledge, 2001.

Bots, P. Interview with Ivo van Hove. "Ivo van Hove: Ik vindt dat ik nog steeds subversief theater maak." *De Theatermaker*. October 2005.

Bradby, David and Williams, David. *Directors' Theatre*. New York: St. Martin's Press, 1988.

Brantley, Ben. Review of *More Stately Mansions* at NYTW. "Talk, Talk, Talk: O'Neill in the Raw." *The New York Times*, 8 October 1997.

Brantley, Ben. Review of *A Streetcar Named Desire* at NYTW. "A Brimming Bathtub as the Focus of Desire," *The New York Times*, 14 September 1999.

Brantley, Ben. Review of *Opening Night* at NYTW. "A Natural Cassavetes Woman, Theatricalized, Magnified and Multiplied." *The New York Times*, 4 December 2008.

Brantley, Ben. Review of *Scenes from a Marriage* at NYTW. "A Marriage in Trouble in Triplicate." *The New York Times*, 22 September 2014a.

Brantley, Ben. Review of *Angels in America* at BAM. "A Universal Heart, Pounding With Hope." *The New York Times*, 24 October 2014b.

Brantley, Ben. "*A View From the Bridge*' Bears Witness to the Pain of Fate." *The New York Times*, 12 November 2015.

Brantley, Ben. "David Bowie Songs and a Familiar Alien in '*Lazarus*.'" *The New York Times*, 7 December 2015.

Brantley, Ben. "Arthur Miller's '*Crucible*' First They Came for the Witches." *The New York Times*, 31 March 2016.

Brantley, Ben. Review of *Kings of War* at BAM. "Shakespeare's Take on the Game of Thrones." *The New York Times*, 4 November 2016.

Brantley, Ben. Review of *Glass Menagerie* on Broadway. "Dismantling 'The Glass Menagerie." *The New York Times*, 9 March 2017.

Braun, Edward. *Meyerhold on Theatre*. New York: Hill and Wang, 1969.

Breyne, Ria. Review of *Macbeth* in Antwerp. "Shakespeare bij De Tijd: 'Macbeth' tussen lichtbundels." *De Standaard*, 1987.

Brockett, Oscar and Findlay, Robert. *A Century of Innovation*. Boston: Allyn and Bacon, 1991.

Brustein, Robert. "Revisioning Tennessee Williams." *New Republic*, 25 October 1999.

Butler, Judith. *Precarious Life: The Powers of Mourning and Violence*. London and New York: Verso, 2004.

Callens, Johan. "Review of *Edward II* in Germany." *Theatre Journal*, 64, 4 (December 2012): 601–603.

Caris, Marijke. Review of *Agatha* in Brussels. "AKT: *Agatha*," *Etcetera*, 2, no. 7 (July 1984): 61–68.

Carlson, Marvin. *The Haunted Stage: The Theatre as Memory Machine*. Ann Arbor: University of Michigan, 2003.

Carmody, Jim. "Daniel Mesguich: 'Unsummarisable mises en scène.'" In *Contemporary European Theatre Directors*. Edited by Maria Delgado and Dan Rebellado. London and New York: Routledge, 2010.

Carroll, Noël. "Art and Alienation." In *The Life and Death of Images*. Edited by Darmuid Costello and Dominic Willsdon. Ithaca: Cornell University Press, 2008.

Cavendish, Dominic. Review of *Lazarus* "Bowie Lands in London, But Does It Really Make the Grade?" *The Daily Telegraph*, 8 November 2016.

Cavendish, Dominic. Review of *Obsession* in London. "Jude Law Flexes His Muscles in a Spot of Avant-Garde Theatre," *The Daily Telegraph*, 25 April 2017.

Chaikin, Joseph. *The Presence of the Actor*. New York: Theatre Communications Group, 1991: 152.

Clapp, Susannah. Review of *Lazarus* in London. "Not Loving the Alien." *The Guardian*, 13 November 2016a.

Clapp, Susannah. Review of *Hedda Gabler* in London. "Ruth Wilson Shines in Patrick Marber's Ibsen Update." *The Guardian*, 18 December 2016b.

Clum, John M. *Acting Gay: Male Homosexuality in Modern Drama*. New York: Columbia University Press, 1992.

Clum, John M. *The Drama of Marriage*. New York: Palgrave Macmillan, 2012.

Cole, David. "Abstract Spaces: A Workshop Approach," *The Drama Review*, 22, no. 4 (December 1978): 45.

Corvin, Michel. "L'écriture théâtrale contemporaine a't-elle conquis sa liberté d'espace?" In *Etudes Théâtrales: Le lieu, la scène, la salle, la ville*. Edited by Marcel Freydefont. Louvain-la Neuve: Centre d'Études théâtrales, 1998.

Coscarelli, Joe and Paulson, Michael. "David Bowie Allowed His Art to Deliver a Final Message." *The New York Times*, 11 January 2016.

Costello, Darmuid and Willsdon, Dominic, eds. "Introduction." In *The Life and Death of Images*. Ithaca: Cornell University Press, 2008.

Cote, David. Review of *Lazarus*. *Time Out New York* 1032 (16–22 December 2015): 45.

Darge, Fabienne. "'Vu du pont,' la piège tragique d'Arthur Miller." *Le Monde* (Paris), 16 October 2015.

Darge, Fabienne. "Au Festival d'Avignon, la Comédie-Française dans la cour d'honneur." *Le Monde*, 6 July 2016 (Scènes).

Davis, Tracy C. "Theatricality: An Introduction." In *Theatricality*. Edited by Tracy C. Davis and Thomas Postlewait. Cambridge: Cambridge University Press, 2003.

De Bruyne, P. (1982) Interview with Ivo van Hove. "In de jaren zeventig is niets gebeurd: Ivo van Hove als regisseur." *Knack*. 1 December.

De Feyter, Johan. "Ivo Van Hove toont de baltsende mens." *De Standaard* (Brussels), 1 October 1985 (Kultuur).

Delgado, Maria M. and Rebellato, Dan, editors. "Introduction." In *Contemporary European Theatre Directors*. London and New York: Routledge, 2010.

De Kuyper, Eric. *De Verbeelding van het Mannelijk Lichaam*. Nijmegen: Sun, 1993.

De Roeck, J. (1981) Interview with David Willinger. "Toneel in Vlaanderen '80-'81: Niet slechter en niet beter dan elders." *De Standaard* (Brussels), 25–26 July.

De Volkskrant. Unattributed interview with Ivo van Hove. "Kunst helpt ons angst te bedwingen." 30 January 2008.

Den Breejen, Maartje. "Carmen plooit zich niet, nooit, *never*." *Het Parool* (Amsterdam), 23 August 2002.

Den Butter, Els. "Ivo van Hove: 'Mijn eerste voorstelling was in een wasserette.'" *Rails Magazine*, September 2005.

Deranty, Jean-Philippe and Ross, Alison, editors. *Jacques Rancière and the Contemporary Scene: The Philosophy of Radical Equality*. London and New York: Continuum, 2012.

De Schepper, Ronny. "Een kijk op de wereld van literatuur, wielrennen, muziek, film en zoveel meer Ivo van Hove." *Dagelijks iets degelijks*, 26 April 2012. Available at: https://ronnydeschepper.com/.

De Schepper, Ronny. Review of *Desire Under the Elms* at Z.T. *Dagelijks iets degelijks*, 28 April 2012. Available at: https://ronnydeschepper.com/.

De Win, Linda "Achter de gevoelsvitrine." *Knack*, 23 January 1985.

Dinneen, Steve. "'*Obsession*' at the Barbican Review: Jude Law Struggles in Ivo van Hove's Adaptation of Visconti's Classic Movie." *City A.M.*, 28 April 2017.

Dort, Bernard. *Théâtre en jeu: essais de critique, 1970–1978*. Paris: Seuil, 1979.

Dort, Bernard. "Double tranchant: Patrice Chéreau." *Théâtre en Europe*, 17 (1988): 5–13.

Dort, Bernard. "Un 'personnage combattant' ou le paradoxe de Nanterre." *L'écrivain périodique*, (Éditions P.O.L: Paris, 2001): 318–331.

Drukman, Steven. "Tomatoes and Their Consequences: Dutch Theatre, the Fringe and the Mainstream are One." *American Theatre*, November 1997.

Editorial Board. "Vertrek Van Hove is geen concessie." *NRC Handelsblad*, 2 July 2002.

Elsaesser, Thomas. *Fassbinder's Germany: History, Identity, Subject*. Amsterdam: Amsterdam University Press, 1996.

Fancy, Richard. "Patrice Chéreau: Staging the European Crisis." In *Contemporary European Theatre Directors*. Edited by Maria M. Delgado and Dan Rebellato. London and New York: Routledge, 2010.

Findlater, Richard. "The Winding Road to King's Reach." In *The National: The Theatre and Its Work, 1963–1997*. Edited by Simon Callow. London: Nick Hern Books, 1997.

Fitzgerald, Jason. Review of *Teorema*. *Backstage* (New York), 16 July 2010.

Florusse, Marion. "Complimenten maken me verlegen." *Elegance*, 31 January 2005.

Fuchs, Elinor. *The Death of Character: Perspectives on Theater after Modernism*. Bloomington and Indianapolis: Indiana University Press, 1996.

Gardner, Lyn. Review of *The Antonioni Project* in London. *The Guardian*, 2 February 2011.

Geerlings, Eddy. "Ivo van Hove houdt niet van klagen." *TT*, 6 June 1993.

Gener, Randy. "Ivo van Hove Has a Passion for Extremes." *American Theatre*, 6 November 2009: 83–91.

Goldberg, Isa. Review of *Hedda Gabler*. *New York Press*, 6 October 2004.

Gompes, Loes. "Eeuwige trouw volgens Ivo van Hove." *Uitkrant Amsterdam*, February 2005.

Grotowski, Jerzy. *Towards a Poor Theatre*. New York: Simon and Schuster, 1969.

Guilbaut, Serge. *How New York Stole the Idea of Modern Art*. Translated by Arthur Goldhammer. Chicago: University of Chicago Press, 1983.

Hageman, Simon. "L'expérience sensorielle de la société médiatique." *Ivo van Hove: la fureur de créer*. Edited by Frédéric Maurin. Besançon: Les Solitaires Intempestifs, 2016.

Halstead, Jack. "Re-viewing Richard Foreman and Theater of Images." *Journal of Dramatic Theory and Criticism*, IV, no.2 (Spring [1992]): 61–80.

Hannaham, James. Review of *A Streetcar Named Desire* at NYTW. "A Formalist Affair." *Village Voice* (New York), 21 September 1999.

Heene, Steven. "Ze noemen me een bad boy en daar voel ik me goed bij." *De Morgen*, 3 November 2007.

Heller, Agnes. *The Time is Out of Joint: Shakespeare as Philosopher of History*. Lanham, MD: Rowman & Littlefield, 2002.

Hellinga, Gerben. Review of *More Stately Mansions* at Z.T. "'Rijkemanshuis': een wreed schouwspel van grote schoonheid." *Vrij Nederland*, 11 June 1994.

Hemming, Sarah. "Ivo van Hove Brings 'Antigone' to London." *Financial Times*, 6 March 2015.

Hillaert, Wouter. Interview with Jan Versweyveld. "De Toneelvloer is een Metafoor voor het Hele Bestaan." *De Morgen* Brussels, 25 March 2006.

Hillaert, Wouter. Interview with Ivo van Hove. *Belgium is Happening*. University of Antwerp. 12 February 2009.

Hillaert, Wouter. "Gezocht, Echt Theater: Introduction." In *Stomp niet af, stomp terug: Twintig jaar theaterkritiek*. Edited by Wim Van Gansbeke. Berchem: Epo, 2010.

Hillaert, Wouter. "Treurwilligtheater." *De Standaard*, 22 October 2016.

Hitchings, Henry. Review of *Lazarus* in London. "David Bowie Show is Disappointingly Earthbound." *Evening Standard*, 9 November 2016.

Hitchings, Henry. Review of *Obsession* in London. "Jude Law Can't Save This Cold, Disengaged Show." *Evening Standard*, 26 April 2017.

Horsten, Hans. "Zuidelijk Toneel voelt zich slachtoffer van bende van Nijvel." *De Volkskrant* (Amsterdam), 15 December 1994.

Horwitz, Simi. "Ivo van Hove: A Dutch Director Does O'Neill." *Backstage.com*, 21 February 2001.

Immergut, Debra Jo. "Deconstructing 'Streetcar': A Bold Look at Williams's Timeless Southern Drama." *The Wall Street Journal*, 15 September 1999.

Ionesco, Eugène. *Notes and Counter Notes: Writings on the Theatre*. Translated by Donald Watson. New York: Grove Press, 1964.

Isherwood, Charles. "A Hedda for Self-Absorbed Modern Times." *The New York Times*, 22 September 2004.

Jans, Erwin. "Alles wat ik meende te weten werd onderuigehaald." *Veto*, 25 February 1987.

Janssen, Hein. "De schouwburg als kathedraal, het podium als altaar waarop van Hove als De Schepper een hoogmis opvoert." *De Volkskrant*, 15 March 2001b.

Janssen, Hein. "Een gelatenheid die nauwelijks te verdragen is." *De Volkskrant*, 24 March 1997.

Janssen, Hein. "Een Hamlet met twee hoofden: Reportage Perceval en van Hove in Duitsland." *De Volkskrant*, 24 September 2010.

Janssen, Hein. "Het begeren onder de olmen door het Zuidelijk Toneel." *De Volkskrant*, 9 March 1992.

Janssen, Hein. "Hunkeren naar hetgeen niet te begrijpen is." *De Volkskrant* (Kunst & Cultuur), 27 May 1994.

Janssen, Hein. "In *Massacre* gaat vorm boven spel." *De Volkskrant*, 10 March 2001a.

Janssen, Hein. "Ludwig II! Ein Niederländer, Ludwigs megalomane leven." *De Volkskrant*, 8 March 2011.

Janssen, Hein. "Met overgave de valkuil in." *De Volkskrant*, 4 June 1994.

Janssen, Hein. "New-Yorks theater vraagt Van Hove voor regie *Rijkemanshuis*." *De Volkskrant*, 5 December 1996.

Johnson, Dominic. *Theatre and the Visual*. London: Palgrave Macmillan, 2012.

Johnston, Sheila. "Fassbinder and the New German Cinema." *New German Critique*, 24–25 (Autumn 1981/Winter 1982): 69.

Kagie, Rudie. "Ik kon alleen maar wenen." *Vrij Nederland*, 12 December 2003.

Kirkup, James. "Patrice Chéreau: Film, Theatre, and Opera Director Hailed for His Bayreuth 'Ring Cycle' and for 'La Reine Margot.'" *The Independent*, 9 October 2013.

Koller, Ann Marie. *The Theatre Duke: Georg II of Saxe-Meiningen and the German Stage*. Stanford: Stanford University Press, 1984.

Korteweg, Ariejan. "Ivo gebruikt geen woord te veel." *De Volkskrant*, 22 January 1997.

Kott, Jan. *Shakespeare, Our Contemporary*. Garden City, NY: Doubleday (Anchor), 1966.

Kottman, Pieter. "Dat onuitgesproken lijdzaam zijn." *NRC Handelsblad*, 9 March 1992.

Kottman, Pieter. "Orgie van geweld is een belevenis." *NRC Handelsblad*, 9 June 1997.

Kraiijeveld, P. Interview with Ivo van Hove. "Ivo van Hove blijft loyal aan z'n idealen: 'Ik ben een trouwe Mechelse hond.'" *De GAY Krant*, 22 February 1992.

Lampo, Jan. "Ivo Van Hove neemt afscheid van De Tijd met 'Jakov Bogomolov.'" *De Standaard* (Kultuur & Wetenschap), 3 April 1990.

Langer, Susanne K. *Feeling and Form*. New York: Scribner's, 1953.

Lauwaert, Guido. "Theatre: 'Song from Far Away' is puur, naakt en bloot." *Knack* (Roeselaere, Belgium), 21 August 2015.

Laveyne, Liz. "De Tijd is Rijp om Tsechov weer te spellen." *Knack*, 29 September 2010.

Lehmann, Hans-Thies. *Post-Dramatic Theatre*. Oxford: Taylor & Francis, 2006.

Lévy, Marie-Françoise and Tsikounas, Myria. "Avons-nous besoin d'un lieu qui ne serait qu'un théâtre? Patrice Chéreau à Nanterre." In *Patrice Chéreau à l'oeuvre*. Edited by Marie-Françoise Lévy and Myria Tsikounas. Rennes: Presses Univérsitaires de Rennes, 2016.

Lukowski, Andrzej. Review of the Young Vic Production of *A View From the Bridge* at the Wyndham Theatre. "Revered Belgian Director Ivo van Hove." *Time Out*, London, 14 November 2014.

Lukowski, Andrzej. Review of *Kings of War*. "Director-of-the-Moment: Ivo van Hove's Thrilling Mashes Up Three of Shakespeare's Plays." *Time Out*, London, 25 February 2016.

Lukowski, Andrzej. Review of *View from the Bridge*. *Time Out*, London, 17 February 2015.

Lyons, Donald. Review of *Streetcar Named Desire* at NYTW. "Clean 'Streetcar' leaves Something to be Desired." *New York Post*, 14 September 1999.

Marbus, Margriet. "Dus dit is de regisseur die alles durft." *De Theatermaker*, June 2002.

March, Florence. "Le regard au risqué du spectacle." In *Ivo van Hove: La fureur de créer*. Edited by Frédéric Maurin. Besançon: Les Solitaires Intempestifs, 2016.

Marks, Peter. "Broadway's Man of the Moment." *Washington Post*, 12 March 2016.

Marlowe Society. www.marlowe-society.org/.

Marranca, Bonnie. *Theatrewritings*. New York: PAJ Publications, 1984.

Maurin, Frédéric. "Les jalousies de l'Amérique." In *Ivo van Hove: la fureur de créer*. Edited by Frédéric Maurin. Besançon: Les Solitaires Intempestifs, 2016: 220.

McAuley, Gay. *Space in Performance: Making Meaning in the Theatre*. Ann Arbor: University of Michigan, 1999.

McConachie, Bruce A. "Report from the Netherlands." *Western European Stages* (Fall 1990): 53–55.

McNulty, Charles. "Meet Ivo van Hove: The Most Provocatively Illuminating Theatre Director." *Los Angeles Times*, 18 March 2016.

Mead, Rebecca. "Theatre Laid Bare: A Radical Director's Raw Productions." *The New Yorker*, 16 October 2015: 56–57.

Meijers, Constant. "Verschil Maken." *De Theatermaker*, 7 October 2005.

Middendorp, Jan. "Aangename 'Wonderen der Mensheid' bij vlagen melig." *De Volkskrant*, 8 February 1985.

Newton, Pamela. "Ivo van Hove is Having a Moment." *American Theatre*, 11 November 2015.

Okonedo, Sophie (2016) "Radio Interview with Three Starring Actors from *The Crucible*." *The Leonard Lopate Show (WNYC)*, 15 April.

Oranje, Hans. "Jaloezie en wraak in een koortsdroom." *Trouw* (Amsterdam), 16 September 1991.

Paglia, Camille. "No Law in the Arena." In *Sexual Personae*. New York: Vintage, 1991a.

Paglia, Camille. "Sex and Violence." In *Sexual Personae*. New York: Vintage, 1991b.

Pascaud, Fabienne. "Ivo van Hove." *Télérama* Paris, 29 June 2016a.

Pascaud, Fabienne. Review of *The Damned* at Avignon. "Festival d'Avignon 2016: 'Les damnés,' la pièce monstre d'Ivo van Hove." *Télérama* (Arts et Scènes), Paris, 8 July 2016b.

Pavis, Patrice. *Analyzing Performance: Theater, Dance, and Film*. Translated by David Williams. Ann Arbor: University of Michigan Press, 2003.

Pavis, Patrice. "The Director's New Tasks." Translated by Joel Anderson. In *Contemporary European Theatre Directors*. Edited by Maria M. Delgado and Dan Rebellato. London and New York: Routledge, 2010.

Peduzzi, Richard. "Faire de plusieurs mondes un seul monde." In *Patrice Chéreau à l'oeuvre*. Edited by Marie-Françoise Lévy and Myriam Tsikounas. Rennes: Presses Universitaires de Rennes, 2016: 380.

Penning, Erwin D. A. "Vertikaal onderweg met Ivo van Hove." *De Scène*, December 1985.

Perrier, Jean-Louis. "Au bout du texte." *Mouvement*, January 2012.

Perrot, Edwige. "Le vidéo en directe: pour une dramaturgie de la subjectivité et de l'intersubjectivité." In *Ivo van Hove: la fureur de créer*. Edited by Frédéric Maurin. Besançon: Les Solitaires Intempestifs, 2016.

Phillips, Julie. "Ivo, Chekhov, No Nudes: Van Hove Tackles '*Three Sisters*' at the Holland Festival." *Village Voice*, 24 June 2003.

Phillips, Julie. Review of *True Love*. "The Theater of Live Chickens: Van Hove, Mee, and Donnellan at the Holland Festival." *Village Voice*, 10 July 2001.

Piana, Romain. "La comédie: un art du déplacement." In *Ivo Van Hove: la fureur de créer*. Edited by Frédéric Maurin. Besançon: Les Solitaires Intempestifs, 2016.

Piper, Adrian. "Political Art and the Paradigm of Innovation." In *The Life and Death of Images*. Edited by Darmuid Costello and Dominic Willsdon. Ithaca: Cornell University Press, 2008.

Rancière, Jacques. "The Immobile Theatre." Translated by Paul Zakir. In *Aisthesis*. London and New York: Verso, 2011.

Review of *Kings of War* at Théâtre National de Chaillot, Paris. "Ivo van Hove, Superstar." *Télérama*, 27 January 2001. (Unattributed).

Reyniers, Johan. Interview with Ivo van Hove. "Toneel is de kunstvorm van de eenentwintigste eeuw: toesprak met Ivo van Hove." *Etcetera*, 30th Anniversary edition, 18 September 2013: 5–9, 17–19.

Roodnat, Joyce. Review of *Splendid's*. "Bij 'Splendid's' is vluchten nu en dan geboden." *NRC Handelsblad*, 21 November 1994.

Rooney, David. "Review of *Lazarus*." *Hollywood Reporter*, 7 December 2015.

Rothkopf, David. "The Leading Global Thinkers of 2016." *Foreign Policy*, 14 December 2016.

Savran, David. *A Queer Sort of Materialism: Recontextualizing American Theatre*. Ann Arbor: University of Michigan, 2003.

Schechner, Richard. *Environmental Theater*. New York: Hawthorne, 1973.

Schechner, Richard. "The Conservative Avant-Garde." In *Performed Imaginaries*. London and New York: Routledge, 2015.

Schlumberger, H. Interview with Rainer Werner Fassbinder. "I've Changed Along with the Characters in my Films: An Interview with Rainer Werner Fassbinder." *Performing Arts Journal*, 14, no. 2 (May 1992): 1–23.

Schouter, Martin. Review of *Macbeth* by De Tijd. "Chris Nietvelt draagt Macbeth in grandioos opgebouwde rol." *De Volkskrant*, 4 September 1987.

Scolnicov, Hanna. *Woman's Theatrical Space*. Cambridge: Cambridge University Press, 1994.

Sedgwick, Eve Kosofsky. "The Beast in the Closet: James and the Writing of Homosexual Panic." In *The Masculinity Studies Reader*. Edited by Rachel Adams and David Savran. Malden: Blackwell, 2002.

Sellar, Tom. "The Dark Secrets of the Belgian Avant-Garde." *Village Voice*, 18 September 2007.

Sellar, Tom. Review of *Teorema* in New York. "Ivo Van Hove Stages Pasolini on Governors Island." *Village Voice*, 20 July 2010.

Sels, Geert. "De Belg die Amerika richting geeft." *De Standaard*, 14 December 2016b.

Sels, Geert. "Ivo van Hove werpt het masker af: een terugblik met onze meest gelauwerd theatermaker." *De Standaard* (Culturele Bijlage), 10 August 2016a.

Sels, Geert. "Omspringen met beperken." *De Theatermaker*, December 2007.

Shannahan, Anna. "Making Room(s): Staging Plays about Women and Houses." In *Dreamhouse Anthology*. Edited by Jill Stevenson, Jennifer-Scott Mobley, and Emily Klein. Des Moines: University of Iowa Press, 2017.

Shattuc, Jane. "R. W. Fassbinder as a Popular Auteur: The Making of an Authorial Legend." *Journal of Film and Video*, 45, no. 1 (Spring 1993): 54.

Shenton, Mark. "David Bowie's 'Lazarus' Review at King's Cross Theatre, London – 'Stunningly Staged.'" *The Stage*, 8 November 2016.

Shuttleworth, Ian. Review of *Lazarus* in London. "'Lazarus', King's Cross Theatre." *Financial Times*, 8 November 2016.

Simon, John. "'Mud,' 'Drowning,' and 'A Streetcar Named Desire.'" *New York Magazine*, 11 October 1999.

Simon, John. "Unmansionable." *New York Magazine*, 20 October 1997.

Six, Fred. "Het dubbele theaterspoor van De Tijd." *Ons Erfdeel*, 6 (1993) (Rekkem, Netherlands): 322–335.

Six, Fred. Review of *Wild Lords*. "'Wilde Heren' breken geen potten." *De Standaard* (Kultuur), 30 September 1984.

Smith, Max. "Theatermakers: Verbeelden is het wezen van theater." *Leidsche Dagblad* (Leiden, Netherlands), 21 June 2002.

Steane, J. B, editor. "Introduction" In *The Complete Plays of Christopher Marlowe*. Harmondsworth: Penguin Books, 1969.

Stuivenberg, Richard. "Ik zit aan mijn botten om aan te rukken." *De Theatermaker*, April 2002.

Szalwinska, Maxie. "The Camera is Ruthless: Ivo van Hove's *Antonioni Project*." *The Guardian*, 9 January 2011.

Takken, Wilfred. Review of *Othello* at TGA. "Arabische Othello als kippige Colin Powell." *NRC Handelsblad*, 2 February 2003a.

Takken, Wilfred. "Iedereen vergadert, niemand praat." *NRC Handelsblad*, 24 November 2003b.

Takken, Wilfred. "Een koud bed." *NRC Handelsblad*, 19 December 2003c.

Takken, Wilfred. "Filmscripts zijn ideal." *NRC Handelsblad*, 5 June 2009 (Cultureel Supplement).

Taylor, Paul. Review of *The Antonioni Project* in London. *Independent*, 7 February 2011.

Taylor, Paul. Review of *Obsession*. "Jude Law is Muscular and Brooding but Wooden." *Independent*, 26 April 2017.

Thielemans, Johan. Interview with Jan Versweyveld. "Jan Versweyveld: 'Ik ben van toneel gaan houden door aan toneel te doen.'" *Etcetera*, 23 (1988).

Thielemans, Johan. *"De totale ontwerper." De Theatermaker, December 2007/January 2008.*

Thompson, Derek. "The Four-Letter Code to Selling Just About Anything." *The Atlantic*, January/February 2017.

Tindemans, Klaas. Review of *Wonders of Mankind*. "'Wonderen der mensheid': een bal van de poseurs." *De Standaard*, 13 December 1984.

T'Jonck, Pieter. "Toneelbeeld van Jan Verweyveld: Scenografie als autonome kunstdiscipline." *De Standaard*, 15 September 1988.

T'Jonck, Pieter. "Onpure kunst over pure driften." *Financieel-Economische Tijd* (Brussels), 11 September 2002 (Cultuur Bijlage).

Todd, Andrew. Review of *The Damned*. "'The Damned' five-star review: Van Hove's Chillingly Prescient Masterstroke." *The Guardian*, 10 July 2016.

Treneman, Ann. Review of *Obsession*. "Jude Law Adds Fine Fury to an Otherwise Passionless Play." *The Times*, 27 April 2017.

Vaes, Eddie. Review of *Don Carlos*. "'Don Carlos.'" *Toestanden*, 7 October 1988.

Van de Grift, E. Interview with Ivo van Hove. "Op de divan—Ivo van Hove." *Red*. April 2008.

Van den Dries, Luk. "Grotowski in Vlaanderen." In *Liber amicorum Jaak Van Schoor: Meester in vele kunsten. Studies in Performing Arts and Film* 5 (1988), 174–190.

Van den Dries, Luk. "Moord op onschuldige kinderen." *Etcetera*, 11, no. 40 (February 1993).

Van den Dries, Luk. Interview with Gino Coomans. *Belgium is Happening*. University of Antwerp, 2 March 2009.

Van der Elst, Angela. Review of *Angels in America*. "'Angels in America': AIDS als metafoor." *Winq Magazine* (Amsterdam), 31 May 2008.

Van der Harst, Hanny. "De acterende koe als ultieme theaterrcensent." *Trouw*, 1 September 1992.

Vandesande, Ilse. Review of *Splendids'*. "Engelen van het kwaad die schreeuwen om genegenheid: *Splendid's* van Jean Genet door Het Zuidelijk Toneel." *Etcetera*, 13, no. 48 (February 1995): 29–31.

Van der Speeten, Geert "De Tijd gript te hoog met 'Don Carlos.'" *Gazet van Antwerpen*, 6 August 1988.

Van der Speeten, Geert. "Waarom de ster van Ivo van Hove blijft stijgen." *De Standaard*, 25–26 June 2016.

Van der Van, Colet. "Elk mens is een xenofoob." *Trouw*, 17 August 2005.

Vander Veken, Ingrid. Review of *Disease Germs* by AKT. "AKT met 'Ziektekiemen' in Montevideo: De strijd tussen geweld en kwetsbaarheid." *De Nieuwe Gazet*, 24 March 1982.

Vander Veken, Ingrid Interview with Pol Arias. "Pol Arias: Alle mensen in hun blootje." *Apache*, 28 October 2016.

Van der Wees, Trudy. "Machtigste man van Nederland." *Haagsche Courant*, 27 January 2001.

Van Engen, Max. "Begin van de Aktie: De crisis in het theater leidt tot openlijk protest en acties van het publiek." In *Een Theater Geschiedenis der Nederlanden*. Edited by R. L. Erenstein. Amsterdam: Amsterdam University Press, 1996.

Van Heer, Edward. "Van naaldhak tot langdradig." *De Standaard*, 12 January 1988.

Van Hove, Ivo. Excerpts from a speech given at the opening of TF-1 Theater Festival. "9 punten voor een theater van de 21ste eeuw." Toneelgroep Amsterdam press release, 31 August 2006.

Van Hove, Ivo and Walsh, Enda. Interview with Ivo van Hove and Enda Walsh. BBC radio *News Hour*. 8 November 2016.

Van Rompay, Theo. Review of *Like in the War*. "Kroniek: Ook al doet de toneelcriticus: *Als in de oorlog*." *Etcetera*, 1983.

Vanschoonbeek, Rudy. Review of *Miracles of Humanity*. "Akt-vertikaal: 'Wonderen der mensheid.'" *De Nieuwe*, 13 December 1984.

Van Vierken, Pieter. "Het geluk bestaat niet." *Eindhovens Dagblad*, 23 November 2000.

Van Zwol, Coen. "Het geweer gaat niet af." *NRC Handelsblad*, 5 June 2009.

Vanderveken, T. Interview with Ivo van Hove. *Alleen Elvis blijft bestaan*. Flemish Television, 17 December 2016.

Versweyveld, Jan. "Het Toneelbeeld van Jan Versweyveld." *De Witte Raaf*, September 1988 (Unattributed; however the text appears to be drawn from a press release drafted by Versweyveld himself).

Wensink, Herien. Review of *Children of the Sun*. "Van Hove halt Gorki naar de politiek van nu." *NRC Handelsblad*, 30 November 2010.

Wensink, Herien. "Van Hove laat Bowies universum zinderen." *NRC Handelsblad*, 8 December 2015a.

Wensink, Herien. "Geen tijd voor grapjes." *NRC Handelsblad*, 20 December 2015b.

Wessendorf, Markus. "The Postdramatic Theatre of Richard Maxwell." University of Hawaii website, 2003.

The Westsider "If O'Neill Were Alive." New York, 16 October 1997. (Unattributed).

Willinger, David. "Van Hove's *Geruchten*." *The Drama Review* 25, no. 2 (Summer 1981): 116–118.

Willinger, David. "Van Hove's *Disease Germs*." *The Drama Review* 27, no. 1 (April 1983): 93–97.

Willinger, David. *An Anthology of Contemporary Belgian Plays: 1970–1982*. Troy: Whitston, 1984.

Willinger, David. "The Current Belgian Renascence." *Western European Stages*, 21, no. 2 (Spring 2009): 70–72.

Willinger, David. "Belgian Theatre Making a Comeback: Four Plays and an Opera." *Western European Stages*, (Winter 2004): 79–84.

Willinger, David. "Culture Clash: Some Notes on Flemish Theatre and its Critical Reception in New York City." *Contemporary Theatre Review*, 20, no. 4 (November 2010): 461–464.

Willinger, David. "The Missing Link of Modern Drama." In *A Maeterlinck Reader*. Edited by David Willinger and Daniel Gerould. New York: Peter Lang, 2011.

Willinger, David. Interview with Pol Arias. Brussels, 7 December 2016a.

Willinger, David. Interview with Ivo van Hove. Upper West Side, New York City, 17 September 2014.

Willinger, David. Interview with Ivo van Hove. *Skype*, 29 September 2016b.

Willinger, David. Interview with Ivo van Hove. *Skype*, 1 May 2017a.

Willinger, David. Email correspondence with Ivo van Hove. 4, 8 and 9 May 2017b.

Willinger, David. Interview with Jaak van Schoor. Ghent, 13 December 2016c.

Willinger, David and Van Belle, Régine Van Belle. "TG STAN Performs Modern Classics by Bernhard and Schnitzler." *European Stages*, Volume 2, 18 April 2014.

Winer, Linda. "A 'Streetcar' Laid Bare." *Newsday* (New York), 13 September 1999.

Zijlmans, Mieke. "Toneel als Boze Droom." *HP De Tijd*, 16 September 1994 (Kunst & Genot).

Zola, Emile. "Naturalism in the Theatre." Translated by Jane House. In *Theatre/Theory/Theatre*. Edited by Daniel Gerould. New York: Applause, 2003.

2

FROM *MOURNING BECOMES ELECTRA* TO *LONG DAY'S JOURNEY INTO NIGHT*: IVO VAN HOVE DIRECTS EUGENE O'NEILL

Johan Callens

Compared to most other directors, Ivo van Hove has a quite prolific track record of producing works by Eugene O'Neill (1888–1953). To the cutting edge Fleming, O'Neill is a writer of Shakespearean stature, extremely personal yet universal in all his variety, one who creates out of the need to fathom our existence and face its contradictory forces, much as van Hove purports to make theatre "out of necessity" (Törnqvist 2004: 276). O'Neill also "helps" van Hove "in [his] thinking." As he puts it, "Each time I read something by him, it grows along with my personal biography. The things that I struggle with, I rediscover in him. Both when it comes to content and theatrically too, he releases my demons" (Sels 2004).

The first time van Hove staged a play by the American dramatist was in 1989 with *Mourning Becomes Electra* (*Rouw siert Electra*), when he was still artistic director of Zuidelijk Toneel in Eindhoven, in a translation by Ger Thijs, the first Dutch version ever (Törnqvist 2004: 276). A few years later followed *Desire Under the Elms* (*Begeren onder de olmen*, 1992) (translated by Arne Sierens), and *More Stately Mansions* (*Rijkemanshuis*, 1994) (translated by Walter Van den Broeck). The latter was intended to appear on a double bill with *A Touch of the Poet* (*Een druppel dichtersbloed*) (translated by Janine Brogt), but unfortunately that production was cancelled when one of the male leads withdrew. Once van Hove moved to Toneelgroep Amsterdam, *More Stately Mansions* became a test case for his collaboration with the New York Theatre Workshop in the fall of 1997 (see Figure 2.1). At that point, he had no immediate plans for another O'Neill production, though a remake of *Desire Under the Elms* was a tempting possibility, and he expressed an interest variously in *The Iceman Cometh*, *A Moon for the Misbegotten*, and *Strange Interlude* (Ibid.). In the Low Countries, *Interlude* had just been staged both by Blauwe Maandag Compagnie (BMCie) and Noordelijk Theater de Voorziening (Groningen), as directed by Luk Perceval (1996). This might explain why that play title came up first. In May 2013, Johan Simons gave van Hove the chance to produce *Strange Interlude* (in German, *Seltsames Intermezzo*) at the Münchner Kammerspiele in a new collaboration with dramaturg Koen Tachelet, just three months before Toneelgroep Amsterdam premiered *Long Day's Journey into Night* (*Lange Dagreis naar de nacht*) (translated by Ger Thijs).[1] On that occasion, the company also revived their 2003 remake of *Mourning Becomes Electra* with a slightly different cast.

FIGURE 2.1 *More Stately Mansions*

© Luc Peeters (Keoon)

Mourning Becomes Electra

By his own admission, van Hove in the late 1980s was drawn to poetic realism rather than the more existential questions that preoccupied him during the period of his remake of the play (Sels 2004), a co-production between Toneelgroep Amsterdam and Toneelschuur Haarlem. Even so, the out-sized belligerence of the American response to the 2001 US terrorist attacks caused him to challenge the naive conviction that war can solve problems, given that O'Neill's play re-sets and updates the Trojan War to the American Civil War period as its social background. In light of this, van Hove saw to it that his first rendition of *Mourning Becomes Electra* became less tied to current events. The elevated circular stage was backed by a curving cyclorama suggesting the Mannons' Greek revival New England mansion, evocative of the play's seaport setting and its model, New London's Whale Oil Row. Yet, Jan Versweyveld's concrete fence posts, on which ever more pitch-black crows perched, could just as easily symbolize a magical circle in which the characters were trapped, regardless of whether the dramatic action took place inside or outside, in keeping with the changing props—armchairs and ancestral painting or Astroturf, fountain, and gravel. The latter two made for chilling sound effects, just as the poisoning of Ezra was underscored by an amplified heartbeat. After all, the earliest Mannon ancestor was said to burn witches, and the visiting of past sins on successive generations is a central theme in O'Neill's play as well as in its primary source, Aeschylus's *Oresteia* that is based on the myth of Atreus. Granted, O'Neill felt the need to change the ending in which Electra was left unharmed by the Furies, and in some versions even allowed to marry Pylades (O'Neill letter to Atkinson 1931). The name of the Mannon family's old gardener, Seth, also invokes Cain's murder of Abel, an analogue for the sibling conflict over a woman between Ezra Mannon's father, Abe, and Adam Brant's father, David. In O'Neill's trilogy, however, the classical sources become intermingled with Gothic touches recalling Hawthorne and Poe, and there is an equally strong melodramatic influence (blackmail, murder, revenge). This tendency would last until *Long Day's Journey*, and explains why critic Martin Schouten experienced van Hove's first *Mourning Becomes Electra* as a B-movie (Freriks 1989; Robinson 1998: 78).

FIGURE 2.2   *Mourning Becomes Electra*

© Deen Van Meer

In Versweyveld's lighting design, the performers' bodies cast huge shadows on the cyclorama, which extended the cylindrical cut-out of the mansion (see Figure 2.2). Like ghosts, these loomed up from the repressed subconscious and the inevitable past, whose compulsive re-enactments were incarnated, partly through the Niles's bike rides around the circular stage, and partly by the doubling of actors. Tom Jansen indeed played both Ezra and Adam, the child of Ezra's uncle and a "nurse girl." Her name, Marie Brantôme, a near homonym of the French *"fantôme,"* reveals the parallel with the adultery of Oswald's father in Ibsen's *Ghosts*. At the same time, Jansen's doubling underscored Lavinia's incestuous attachment to her father, just as Orin might have served as a substitute for Ezra had he not followed his father into war. In interviews at the time, however, van Hove opted to see the play more as dealing with pre-sexual longings, in line with Orin's comparison of his sister Lavinia with Marie (O'Neill 1988: 1041). The domestic servant's "Canuck" or Canadian provenance must have been instance to the Inuit songs heard on the soundtrack. These also tie in with the puritanism of the Mannons and their icy hatred, offering a strong contrast with the passion between Adam and Christine, supported by the crackling of destructive blazes. The costumes and make-up of Trudy de Jong (Christine Mannon) and Jip Wijngaarden (Lavinia) further enhanced their physical resemblance, in keeping with Adam's comment that each Mannon generation inherits its facial features from the previous one. In their amorous struggle over Adam, Christine and Lavinia also rely on the same arguments and formulations. In the end, Lavinia buries herself alive in the mansion, whose dark door opening in Versweyveld's set yawns like a tomb. This burial alive was portended when Wijngaarden froze on a tree stump, like a caryatid upholding the crumbling family heritage.

Van Hove's 2003 remake of *Mourning Becomes Electra*, which was selected for the 2004 Dutch Theaterfestival, was conceived of as a therapy session, each act being introduced by the performers' ritualistic removal of their shoes, an echo of his *More Stately Mansions*. The therapy concept was in keeping with the psychoanalytical influence on O'Neill's script, but also with van Hove's enthusiasm for *Capturing the Friedmans*, Andrew Jarecki's 2002 documentary on a 1987 pedophilia case, combining the filmmaker's own interviews with news footage, police records, court transcripts and the Friedmans' home videos and audio tapes.[2] Freud partly derived his conceptualization of the Electra complex from the *Oresteia* trilogy's mythical underpinnings. O'Neill, when writing the play, was thinking in turn of transference and projection as necessary stages in his characters' conscious overcoming of their psychosexual and war traumas, which the attendant repetition compulsion fails to do in a satisfactory or healthy way. What is more, according to O'Neill scholar Stephen Black, O'Neill saw his dramatic explorations of the human soul as a way of coping with his own traumas and modernity's existential crisis (Black 1999). This becomes evident in the playwright's admission to Brooks Atkinson that Orin's "'intellectualization' ... is the essential process by which he, being Orin, must arrive at his fate and view it so he can face it" (O'Neill to Atkinson 1994: 390). There is no need to bring in van Hove's own psychological make-up and family heritage in order to explain his ongoing fascination with O'Neill and especially *Mourning Becomes Electra*. The only thing he is willing to admit, despite his wish to be independent, is that he cannot deny his upbringing and blood bond.[3] Yet, for van Hove, the Greeks' notion of fate, the naturalists' determinism, or even O'Neill's modern psychological fate, all too often tend to be excuses for refusing to assume individual responsibility, without taking into account the plethora of real enough constraints that circumscribe human freedom (Törnqvist 2004: 276).

In the 2003 version of *Mourning Becomes Electra*, overhead projectors, chat sessions, and flip-charts more explicitly updated and extracted the play from its post-Civil War realistic setting, even if O'Neill (like Shakespeare) used that war as macrocosmic image for an internal conflict. Even van Hove's first staging contained anachronisms, such as the modern bikes, Adam's Drum tobacco, or Peter's car keys. The prominence of the technological devices allows Lavinia to record her family's doings for her "photo-album" or for Orin's inner thoughts to be translated into an animated clip. This directorial choice invoked not just O'Neill's attention to evolving technology in the never finished cycle, but also the Friedmans' home videos and audiotapes. In the latter case, though, the insets from the past tend to give the lie to the contemporary interviewees. In more conventional crime stories they expose the truth, much as in van Hove's *Mourning Becomes Electra*, where an inset movie exposes the murder of Ezra (Becker 2004: 148). To the stage director, the name of Seth Friedman, brother to Jesse, who, together with his father Arnold, was accused of molesting dozens of boys attending the computer classes organized in the Friedman home, must also have chimed with that of Seth Beckwith, the old gardener in *Mourning Becomes Electra*. Ironically, given the contemporary family's tragedy, the third sibling, David Friedman, used to be the most popular children's birthday clown in New York, a phenomenon that initially prompted Jarecki to make his documentary. Throughout and after the court proceedings, David remained convinced of his father's innocence, despite the child pornography he kept and the earlier pedophilia incidents he confessed to when pleading guilty. Jesse also admitted to the charges of sexual abuse, but subsequently tried to get his conviction overturned. By the time Jarecki embarked on his clown movie, both offenders were coming to the end of their prison terms. Instead of taking sides, however, Jarecki turned his movie into a reflection on truth's elusiveness, similar to the way Kurosawa does in his famous *Rashomon* (Denby 2003: 29). Apart from drawing on Jarecki's documentary, van Hove's 2003 remake of *Mourning Becomes Electra* was also more tilted toward a liberation of Electra. That is why he and

Ger Thijs in his Dutch translation of O'Neill's title, interpreted the "becoming" more in the sense of "adorning" than "suiting," that is, as a positive indication of the character's relative success by embracing rather than opposing her family's sins (Sels 2004; Törnqvist, 2004: 277). This relative triumph is supported by one of O'Neill's own statements —"She is broken and not broken! By her way of yielding to her Mannon fate she overcomes it. She is tragic!" (O'Neill letter to Atkinson 1994: 390)—and presumably explains why the program for the Antwerp showing of the remake of 21 to 22 November 2003 was introduced by O'Neill's denial of his alleged pessimism:

> I'm far from being a pessimist. I see life as a gorgeously-ironical, beautifully-indifferent, splendidly-suffering bit of chaos the tragedy of which gives Man a tremendous significance, while without his losing fight with fate he would be a tepid, silly animal. I say 'losing fight' only symbolically for the brave individual always wins. Fate can never conquer his—or her—spirit. So you see I'm no pessimist. On the contrary, in spite of my scars, I'm tickled to death with life! I wouldn't 'go out' and miss the rest of the play for anything!
>
> *(O'Neill letter to Clark 1994: 181)*

Institutional controversies

Unfortunately, van Hove's 2003 remake of *Mourning Becomes Electra* became imbricated in a double controversy, the first concerning his leadership among the contractual repertory performers of Toneelgroep Amsterdam, the second one surrounding an essay by theatre critic Marian Buijs. In mid-October 2003, the rehearsals were suspended for a week because the actors in a collective letter protested against their working conditions, van Hove's purported more formal and distant style of leadership, faltering communication, and the time-consuming combination of his multiple functions: those of artistic and general director of Toneelgroep Amsterdam while he was simultaneously serving as organizer of the Holland Festival. According to some sources, the vote of no confidence had less to do with the nature of van Hove's theatre innovations and artistic cross-over initiatives than with the rift between the younger and senior generation of performers, several of whom felt they had been bypassed. To complicate matters further, the technical team had its own grievances. The play nonetheless premiered in the Toneelschuur Haarlem, but veteran company members Lineke Rijxman and Pierre Bokma announced their resignation for the end of the season, as did Hans Kesting, though he later reversed his decision. Titus Muizelaar, another key actor/director of the Dutch company, left to join the artistic direction of Het Toneelhuis, Antwerp. Van Hove, for his part, gave up leadership of the Holland Festival, which had required that he spend great lengths of time prospecting the world for guest performances, thus freeing more time for his acting ensemble back in Amsterdam. What could not be remedied were the weighty and protracted responsibilities for the still unfinished new theatre building, which van Hove had also assumed when he moved from Eindhoven to Amsterdam.[4]

One of the alarming rumors that was rampant at the time, that his ensemble would fuse with Theu Boermans's De Theatercompagnie, invites comparison with the difficult period Zuidelijk Toneel Globe went through after Gerardjan Rijnders left it in 1985. At that point, Paul De Bruyne was appointed artistic director, assisted by Boermans and Kees Hulst, both actors at Globe, and another Fleming, Sam Bogaerts. In 1987, Bogaerts became part of the new company resulting from the fusion of De Witte Kraai with van Hove's own AKT/Vertikaal. Rijnders went on to found Toneelgroep Amsterdam with which Bokma was affiliated from its inception. But in Eindhoven, the new team, whose mission was to serve the Dutch province of Brabant, was met by the local theatre's refusal to book some of the more controversial productions on offer, like Bogaerts's staging of Heiner Müller's *Hamletmachine/Egofiel* (1985) (Heijer 1985). After a year, De Bruyne, who felt his artistic freedom needlessly constrained, was replaced by Ronald Klamer, who in turn gave way to Eric Antonis (former director of De Warande, a cultural center in Turnhout), who was instrumental in converting Zuidelijk Toneel from a regional company into a municipal theatre and brought van Hove on board. In 2003, history seemed to repeat itself when the name of Klamer, by then head of Het Toneel Speelt, once again circulated, this time as a possible candidate for the top job of Toneelgroep Amsterdam, which permitted van Hove to focus on his creative work (Van Maanen 1997: 175).

The crisis within Toneelgroep Amsterdam partly explains why Alexander Schreuder, the dramaturg of van Hove's 2003 *Mourning Becomes Electra*, publicly protested, using a rather polemical tone, against an essay by then reviewer for the Dutch newspaper, *De Volkskrant*, Marian Buijs, which had appeared in the influential periodical *De Theatermaker* a few months after the ill-fated premiere. For Schreuder, Buijs's essay was no less than a personal attack and populist-political move to help oust van Hove from the helm of Toneelgroep Amsterdam in the wake of the actors' and technicians' protests, a piece of pseudo-criticism infringing upon all journalistic ethical and theatre-historical standards. In hindsight, whether one agrees with some of its positions and assessments or not (i.e. van Hove's bent for extremes), the essay provides a not implausible bird's-eye view of van Hove's career between 1989 and 2003, though Schreuder prefers to disqualify them as a matter of subjective taste, devoid of substantial content-analysis and interpretative power. More questionable are Buijs's personal insinuations and instigations (regarding, for example, van Hove's lacking any sense of humor), which must have been too much for Schreuder, a loyal team member of the then beleaguered director, to stomach (Buijs 2004; Schreuder 2004). Compared to Buijs's persistent confusion of characters and actors, Hans Oranje's hypothesis in his review of the show for the newspaper *Trouw* in which he insinuates that the incestuous relationship between Orin and Lavinia mirrored that between Toneelgroep Amsterdam and its director comes across as twice as offensive (Oranje 2003). Instead of taking the moral high ground about the production's carnal excesses, Buijs and Oranje should have fleshed out the truly unsettling parallel between the power relations within the theatre as an institution, and those in incestuous families, the way Milo Rau ever so subtly explored pedophilia in his metatheatrical *Five Easy Pieces*, a show based on the child molester and serial killer Marc Dutroux, a subject surely as grisly as that to which Buijs objected.[5]

Buijs not only vented her low opinion of O'Neill's trilogy, and indirectly of the Greek classics on which it is based, by implying, somewhat preposterously, that they would have benefited from a bit of irony. She also took issue with the conceptualism and apparent detachment in van Hove's productions, abetted, as she put it, by Jan Versweyveld's set designs. Over the years, these seemed to have grown ever more abstract, despite (and hardly because of, as she argues) the strong influence of performance art that infused the early days of the two men's tandem career.

The performers in the second *Mourning Becomes Electra* appeared to strain toward identification, but must have failed on account of the unembarrassed nudity, which like the production's push toward intermediality, was undoubtedly a superficial way of attempting to cater to a younger public. The inspiration van Hove drew from *Capturing the Friedmans* tends to gainsay Buijs' harsh judgment, as does O'Neill's express intent in *Mourning Becomes Electra* as well as

Long Day's Journey, to bring repressed drives to the surface, even if he flirts with melodrama in doing so. And while the living room setting in van Hove's *Long Day's Journey* seems to confirm Versweyveld's stylization, consisting as it does of a minimalist staircase, empty table, and mock window, both productions contained heartfelt moments that challenge Buijs' reductive view.

Long Day's Journey into Night

Ironically, Ibsen's *Ghosts*, a crucial intertextual source for *Long Day's Journey*, was another succès de scandale from its inception in the late nineteenth century, partly on account of Captain Alving's and Oswald's philandering with the domestic staff. Van Hove in his 2013 production of the play removed the secondary role of Cathleen, Mary Tyrone's confidante, presumably because he counted O'Neill's servant as a distraction from the intense family conflict. As he focuses on the four remaining protagonists, Mary relives her overwhelming first encounter with the matinee idol in a lengthy monologue. In that scene, Marieke Heebink sat on the tall winding stair, which dominated Versweyveld's set and which at times stands in for the typical American porch, where many an American teenager in more puritan days was courted in safe proximity to her watchful mother. Versweyveld's winding staircase has also been interpreted as evocative of DNA's double helix structure (Delanoye 2013), through which the burdensome religious and artistic family heritage of the Tyrones acquires the forcefulness of biological determinism, whether Jansenism, Shakespeare and melodrama, or Chopin. Van Hove musically supported the emotionality of Mary's nostalgic backward glance with Randy Newman's "Dayton, Ohio— 1903," a 1967 song from his album *Sail Away* (1972), the first of several Newman songs that are used to augment O'Neill's text.[6] These songs function as pop counterparts to the canonical literature referenced in the play.

Newman's song conjures a lazy, pre-industrial Sunday afternoon conviviality, recalling O'Neill's real-life mother Ella Quinlan's fond memories of her family's residence on Woodland Avenue in Cleveland, Ohio, as the only true home she had (Black 1999: 29–30), one far superior to the sparsely furnished, forbidding Monte Cristo Cottage. Newman's rose-colored view of the past would have suited the optimistic mood of the play's opening, which is not unlike the mood in the play's comic, equally autobiographical predecessor, *Ah, Wilderness!* (1933). Instead of alternating the two plays in the same set with the same actors, the way Irene Lewis (1977) and José Quintero (1988) did, Peter Monsaert's intermedial production of *Long Day's Journey* for Theater Antigone, in Kortrijk, Belgium, that ran concurrently with van Hove's, frequently played for laughs and thus highlighted the tragicomic contrast within one and the same production. Van Hove worked more subtly, aided by Newman's trademark irony, whose songs dominate *Long Day's Journey*. Such musical unity is uncharacteristic for the director, because his soundtracks tend to combine different artists, despite exceptions like the 2005 *Scenes from a Marriage (Scènes uit een huwelijk)*, where he added Herman van Veen and Paul Simon music, and the 2006 *Opening Night*, which featured Neil Young's.

Still, over the course of several nights, including the 25 August 2013 premiere in Amsterdam's Stadsschouwburg, van Hove's *Long Day's Journey* was shadowed by that of the Utrecht actors' collective, De Warme Winkel, under the leadership of Marien Jongewaard. In a mysterious online message, they had first called for participants and then personally screened and processed them by phone and text messages. As their satirical running commentary proceeded simultaneously behind the backdrop of Versweyveld's living room set, it was fittingly billed as *Flip Side (Achterkant)*.[7] The backstage conceit may be familiar from plays like Michael Frayn's

Noises Off (1982). A yet more direct influence may be Alan Ayckbourn, whose *Norman Conquests* (1973) van Hove directed under the title *Kruistochten* (premiere, 22 June 2004). Ayckbourn's *House and Garden* (1999) indeed consists of two plays with the same cast running simultaneously on adjacent stages. The fictional premise from which De Warme Winkel began was a parody of Eugene's father, James O'Neill's lifelong sell-out in his cash-cow show, *The Count of Monte Cristo*. Thus, Vincent Rietveld and Ward Weemhoff pretended to be two down-and-out understudies belonging to Toneelgroep Amsterdam, van Hove's real artistic home, but projected into an imaginary future. For more than a decade now, the send-up has it, the company has been garnering standing ovations with *Long Day's Journey* and the average subscriber of the established theatre is supposed to have reached a "terminal" age. The Dutch title *Achterkant* literally translates as reverse, rear, or flip side, but the concept was extended to comprise the downside of repertory theatre and fame, the tricks of the trade, the composition history and dramaturgical treatment of O'Neill's play, even the never fully exposed "back" end of van Hove's very tongue.[8] His production and Marien Jongewaard's ghostly counter-production thus worked a further variation on O'Neill's tragi-comic double-take on his family history in *Long Day's Journey* and *Ah, Wilderness!* as well as on Lewis and Quintero's system of rotating the two plays on alternating nights. Even within the anarchic script of De Warme Winkel, the more hilarious first part after the break was relieved by pathetic self-criticism, jealousies, and regrets for the days before the imaginative alternative company supposedly degenerated into narcissism and ultimately folded. Thus, theatrical insiders as well as outsiders, those familiar with the fellow artists and those without a clue, were manipulated into assent or indignation with what may possibly have been heartfelt confessions or pitch-perfect mockeries.

Most ticket-holders of Toneelgroep Amsterdam watched O'Neill's play impervious to the spectral goings-on behind the scene. De Warme Winkel's shadow audience, however, capped at 35, was regaled with the antics of a wigged Rietveld and Weemhoff, as well as being given glimpses of the mainstage doings, whether seen from the back through the Tyrones' one-way living room window or relayed intermittently through speakers and monitors that provided a view from the house. As in *House and Garden*, one of van Hove's performers would occasionally cross the divide or at least seemed to, as when Marieke Heebink, still in a drug-induced daze, retrieved Mary's wedding dress, when Gijs Scholten van Aschat (who played Tyrone) exited to answer Rietveld's phone call, or when van Hove in person allowed himself to be briefly interviewed. Insiders of course attended both productions in whatever order, each metatheatrical experience thereby being further layered, whether by anticipation or recollection. The distance thus established far exceeded the irony of Newman's songs in van Hove's production, limited as that irony was to the musical intermezzos. But Marian Buijs, for one, must surely have liked this treatment of O'Neill's venerable classic, even if De Warme Winkel during the intermission appropriated the mainstage of the Stadsschouwburg for a burlesque dance number against the backdrop of a giant inflated vagina, sardonically exposing O'Neill's mythic-Freudian maternal symbolism. That van Hove at the end of *Long Day's Journey* graciously accepted the applause of both audiences, indicates the credit asked and received for hosting De Warme Winkel and for daring to have framed his own production in such a witty way. Thus, a full decade after the initial controversy hit, exploiting the occasion of the remake of *Mourning Becomes Electra*, he found a way to answer his former critics in a most professional and creative way.

As a prelude to his own *Long Day's Journey* van Hove has the four haunted Tyrones embrace each other underneath a warm amber light. Soon enough, however, this congenial atmosphere is undercut by the evening's first song, Newman's bitter "I Think It's Going to Rain Today" (1968) from his debut album "*Randy Newman Creates Something New Under the Sun*" (1974). In this way, van Hove creates a textbook case of the pathetic fallacy as the speaker's disillusioned and misanthropic mood perfectly matches his derelict and inhospitable surroundings. With this critique of O'Neill's characters' more self-pitying moments, van Hove sets the tone for his production, one filled with cynicism, loneliness, and lovelessness, but also with incontrovertible compassion for humanity's imperfections. Van Hove took his lead from O'Neill's description of *Long Day's Journey* as "a quiet play" (Floyd 1985: 2; Murphy 2001: 2). Newman's restrained, piano-based songs do nothing to detract from this quiet atmosphere and seem apt, though O'Neill's stage directions explicitly mention music only once. Toward the end of van Hove's production, before Mary evokes the nuns scolding her for being "all out of practice," we briefly hear the required waltz, "groping[ly]" but resolutely spinning out (O'Neill 1994: 823–824). The text suggests "one of Chopin's simpler waltzes." When Ella Quinlan graduated from the conservatory with a gold medal, it was one of his polonaises that she was playing (Black 1999). The shift to the music of Newman dislocates us in time and reminds us of how similarly dislocated the characters are.

If the prelude gives the impression that van Hove finds a sense of communion in the play, his directing and the costumes (Wojciech Dziedzic) also suggested the reverse. Whereas the men—Gijs Scholten Van Aschat (Tyrone), Ramsey Nasr (Jamie), and Roeland Fernhout (Edmund)—are dressed in blue, Mary wears black, which becomes a mother mourning for herself and her family, the living and the dead alike. Sometimes, the blocking follows suit, as when the men line up and assume identical poses in front of the upstage window, thereby distancing and contrasting themselves from Mary. Closeness between the mother and her youngest son is nevertheless evident. He is the only one she hugs. Van Hove's set designer also suggests contrast by placing the warm round table in the middle of an angular, dark gray set. For one reviewer, at least, the connotations of an altar were overly blatant (Thielemans 2014: 55), presumably because the director also worked with *pietà* images, as in *Cries and Whispers* (*Kreten en Gefluister*, 2009), van Hove's stage adaptation of Ingmar Bergman's 1972 film, which is also why De Warme Winkel denounced the stage image so vociferously (Arian 2013; Wensink 2013). Initially, van Hove's four performers never left the cold and empty space, suggesting that O'Neill's characters are unable to extricate themselves from their complex love/hate relationships. The seemingly chilly set and its dimness below one light bulb may have been presented as evidence of James's miserliness, but it also leant a certain expressionist projection to Mary's bitter alienation from the place.

Downstage on Versweyveld's set, to the far left and right, a turntable and glass drink-stand on slender supports formed two treacherous anchor-points for the drifting characters. Upstage left, the exit was hidden by a giant plant next to the enormous window, a cosmic black hole that never lights up, reminiscent of the black mirror in O'Neill's bedroom at Tao House, if also useful for hiding De Warme Winkel's alternative universe. What did light up, like a lighthouse in the fog, each time Mary thinks of morphine, is the opening at the top of the sleek, nine-meter-high winding staircase.[9] The turning motion of Mary's going up and down that metal stairway neatly conveys the endless cycle of loving approach and estranging distance. I thought of Yeats' gyre in "The Second Coming," because here too "the ceremony of innocence is drowned" (Yeats 1956a: 184). As the calming effect of the morphine dwindles, despite ever higher doses, and after the phone call confirming Edmund's consumption, the lure of the liberating light at the top of Mary's stairway to heaven goes dark, turning it into Yeats' nightly tower from "A Dialogue of Self and Soul" (Murawska 1982: 141–162).

Yeats develops the Empedoclean notion of the gyre in such poems as "*The Second Coming*," "*Nineteen Hundred and Nineteen*," "*The Gyres*,"[10] and out of anarchic turmoil. To him, the British atrocities in Ireland during the Easter Rising (April 1916), as well as the horrors of World War I, were indicative of that sort of chaotic reversal: the progressive ideal of the nineteenth century had given way to a more tragic vision of life, aristocratic values, and civilization having been degraded by commonness and base instincts.[11] Newman's "Dayton, Ohio—1903" may be heard as a remnant of the past optimism, which would be lost in the turmoil of World War I and family tragedy. In writing the play, O'Neill harked back to that lost innocence at a parallel moment when World War II was looming, notwithstanding the writer's denials that the play was "concerned with the present world's crisis, as the title might indicate" (O'Neill 1994: 506–507).

Van Hove and his dramaturg, Peter Van Kraaij, may have recalled that Yeats's mystic cosmology was fed by regular visits to the spiritualist Helena Blavatsky (1831-1891), the Theosophical Society, and the Hermetic Order of the Golden Dawn. In fact, Yeats' mystic concerns have been interpreted as a reflection of a modernist desire to balance tradition and innovation, high culture and low. This desire is evident in a morality play like *The Hour-Glass* (Yeats, 1904), featured on the program of the Abbey Players' controversial 1911 American Tour, as well as in his modernist fascination with automatic writing in *A Vision*, which has been tied to the lingering influence of Victorian spiritualism and mesmerism (Sword 2002: 113–117; Yeats, 1956b: passim.). During the writing of *Long Day's Journey* O'Neill frequently finished his day's work by seeking comfort in the recitation of Yeats' poetry, "as if, besides enjoyment, he wished always to have running through his head the sacred words of a real poet" (Raleigh 1965: 209). Who knows, but perhaps O'Neill was also trying to revive the spirit of Yeats, who had passed away 28 January 1939, a few months before his first sketch of *Long Day's Journey* would materialize.

Ostensibly Yeats and Ibsen stood for the "new" text-based drama, whereas the actor/manager Henry Irving epitomized the old theatricalist tradition, much as Eugene and James O'Neill stood on opposite sides of a divide that might have seemed wider than it was. The new theatre was trying to put distance between itself and the old, but was drawn inexorably back, and meanwhile the old had already begun reaching for the new. A melodramatic star vehicle like *The Bells* became a major success because of how Irving's acting prowess enhanced the text as well as the stage picture, and because the use of transparent scrims, sophisticated lighting, and moving scenery served a dramatic function in reviving Matthias's repressed memory of his murder of a rich Jewish merchant. The evocations of the innkeeper/burgomaster's subconscious self and the frightening dream of giving himself away under hypnosis fully exploited the then current craze for split personalities, the occult and macabre, spiritualism and séances (Mayer 1980: 2004). At one point, van Hove's cast, while gathered in a circle around the table, collectively intone Newman's "I'll Be Home," a 1970 song whose split narrative point of view fittingly reflects a restless wanderer and a distressed one at home. What to some spectators may have sounded like cheap sentiment or an attempt to lighten a dark play thus also forms a *mise-en-abîme* of *Long Day's Journey* itself, which is a cautious séance or conjuring of the living and the dead. The song momentarily materializes their dream of communion, much as the two "Wish You Were Here" evenings, which Toneelgroep Amsterdam in April 2012 and November 2013 devoted to O'Neill, were communal attempts to commemorate the artist.

Among O'Neill's models, the not-so-entirely-new dramaturgies of Ibsen and Yeats had to compete with the aesthetic of Irving and James O'Neill's repertory. The latter was epitomized by Dumas' *Count of Monte Cristo*, in Fechter's adaptation, which shared the contemporary stage with works like Gabet's *The Bells of Corneville*, turned into a comic opera with the aid of Clairville, who wrote the libretto, and Planquette, the score. For the comprehension of local audiences of *Long Day's Journey*, Gabet's *Gaspard the Miser*, was replaced by the equally mean-spirited Scrooge from Dickens's *Christmas Carol* (1843), who suffers a spectacular change of heart after visitations by several ghosts. Monsaert's interpretation of the brothers in *Long Day's Journey* veered toward nineteenth-century histrionics in order to expose O'Neill's debt to his father's tradition. Van Hove's cast was more balanced, and by adhering to a naturalist style he, to some degree, glossed over the script's melodramatic heritage, which is perhaps most evident in Jamie's occasional characterization as a villain. As Jamie, Ramsey Nasr shied away from exaggeration. At times, however, the tragedy of the split consciousness remains too much indebted to the polarized characters of melodrama and even the morality play, as is the case in O'Neill's earlier *Days Without End: A Modern Miracle Play* (1933), which plays off belief against disbelief within the soul of the divided protagonist, John/Loving. A similar encounter between reason and faith drives *Long Day's Journey* in the conflict between the sons and their parents. In that light, one sees the psychodramatic and allegorical dimensions of O'Neill's characters, who partly externalize the inner conflict and its resolution. That all characters in *Long Day's Journey* consider themselves failures echoes the allegorical nature of the play, as if all were alter egos of the failing playwright.

In van Hove's production, this generalized addiction to failure presumably inspired the use of Newman's "Guilty" (1973) from his 1974 "*Good Old Boys*" album, where several themes from *Long Day's Journey* converge: the all-consuming guilt but also the mask with which to disguise the failure, and the despair that calls for drinks, drugs, and comfort from the very ones who have been hurt. In O'Neill's play, the guilt and resulting self-loathing are both existential and due to specific causes: Tyrone's reliance on a quack doctor, Jamie's infection of Eugene with the measles, Mary's relapse into drug addiction, and Edmund's loss of faith. The extreme degradation of O'Neill's characters in this case is closely connected to the aforementioned Jansenist guilt (Porter 2004: 31–42). The greater the humiliation, the more exhilarating the salvation. In short, the spectacular mood swings cannot entirely be ascribed to the indebtedness of O'Neill's dramaturgy to nineteenth-century popular theatre. His religious upbringing and subsequent loss of faith equally account for it, as does his attempt to create a modern offshoot of classical tragedy, capable of transfiguring and uplifting the lowliest of lives (O'Neill 1994: 195). In that sense, van Hove's production of *Long Day's Journey into Night* gave full credit to O'Neill's tragic ambition, an ambition already evident in *Mourning Becomes Electra*.

The research conducted for this article is part of the "Interuniversity Attraction Poles" Program, financed by the Belgian government (BELSPO IAP7/01).

Notes

1 Tachelet also adapted Ayn Rand's *The Fountainhead* (premiere 15 June 2014) and Louis Couperus's *De dingen die voorbij gaan* (premiere 16 September 2016), both van Hove productions.
2 According to Törnqvist, op cit., the remake of *Mourning Becomes Electra* had already been conceptualized when van Hove saw *Capturing the Friedmans* in New York. The cast consisted of Pierre Bokma (Ezra), Janni Goslinga (Christine), Halina Reijn (Lavinia), Jochum ten Haaf (Orin), Hans Kesting (Adam Brant), Alwin Pulinckx (Peter Niles), Karina Smulders (Hazel Niles), and Hugo Koolschijn (Seth Beckwith).
3 See the report of the "Monday" gathering on 20 October 2003 excerpted in the program for the showing in De Singel, 21–22 November 2003.
4 On the controversy with Toneelgroep Amsterdam, see Geert Sels, "Ivo van Hove over de onrust bij Toneelgroep Amsterdam," *De Standaard*, 29 November 2003, and "Ivo van Hove onder druk in Amsterdam," *De Standaard*, 24 November 2003; Hein Janssen, "Vertrek oude garde slag voor van Hove," *De Volkskrant*, 22 November 2003. In retrospect, it is interesting to note how van Hove is currently being praised by his entourage for his organizational capacities, his time management, and his strong team spirit, off and onstage, where ensemble acting reigns. See, in this regard, Geert van der

Speeten, "Waarom de ster van Ivo van Hove blijft stijgen," *De Standaard*, 25–26 June 2016, a reflection on the bumper years 2015–2016, which saw the Olivier and Tony Award-winning British and American premieres of Miller's *A View from the Bridge* and *The Crucible*, the musical *Lazarus* (at the NYTW with David Bowie), and the stage version of Luchino Visconti's *The Damned* (*Les damnés*) at the Avignon Festival with the Comédie Française, not to mention the Founders Award for Excellence in Directing that van Hove received from the Drama Desk.

5 *Five Easy Pieces* premiered 14 May 2016 at the KunstenFestivaldesarts (Théâtre Varia, Brussels) with a cast of adults and children between 8 and 13 years old.

6 The lyrics for all Newman songs, for copyright reasons, are not reproduced but are readily available on the internet.

7 See Herien Wensink, "Hilarisch Gekanker: De Warme Winkel versus Toneelgroep Amsterdam: 1-1," *NRC Handelsblad*, 2 September 2013; Jasmijn Sprangers, "Door de ogen van De Warme Winkel kijken naar het theaterestablishment." *Cutting Edge*, 25 August 2013; Lorianne Van Gelder. "Loeren achter het doek." *Het Parool* 25 August 2013; Karin Veraart. "Een heel goed idee dat al evengoed is uitgevoerd." *De Volkskrant*, 27 August 2013; Max Arian. "De lelijke achterkant van het toneel." *Theaterkrant*, 25 August 2013; Hanny Alkema. "Spannend bedacht, maar als experiment mislukt." *Trouw*, 27 August 2013.

8 In idiomatic Dutch, to hold or bite one's tongue is never to show its back.

9 In van Hove's 1989 original *Mourning Becomes Electra*, the dockside meeting between Christine (Trudy de Jong) and Adam (Tom Jansen) after the intermission was accompanied by a lighthouse's rotating beam blinding the spectators. This may explain why for *Long Day's Journey*, Versweyveld came up with a more stylized version having a wider interpretative range.

10 William Butler Yeats. *The Collected Poems* (New York: Macmillan, 1956), 184–185, 204–208, 291.

11 Stuart Hirschberg. "The 'Whirling Gyres' of History." *Studies: An Irish Quarterly Review*, 68 (1979), 305–314 and "Beyond Tragedy: Yeats's View of History in 'The Gyres.'" *Research Studies*, 42 (1974), 50–55.

Reference list

Alkema, Hanny. "Spannend bedacht, maar als experiment mislukt." *Trouw*, 27 August 2013.

Arian, Max. "De lelijke achterkant van het toneel." *Theaterkrant*, 25 August 2013.

Becker, Snowden. "*Capturing the Friedmans* (2003)." *The Moving Image* 4.1 (Spring 2004).

Black, Stephen. *Eugene O'Neill: Beyond Mourning and Tragedy*. New Haven: Yale University Press, 1999.

Buijs, Marian. "Van Electra tot Electra: veertien jaar Van Hove." *De Theatermaker*, February 2004.

Delanoye, Jan-Jakob. "Scherven van geluk." *Cutting Edge*, 13 October 2013.

Denby, David. "The Current Cinema." *The New Yorker*, 2003, 29.

Floyd, Virginia. *The Plays of Eugene O'Neill*. New York: Fredrick Ungar, 1985.

Freriks, Kester. "Op incest rust een louterende vloek in *Rouw siert Electra*." *NRC Handelsblad*, 3 April 1989.

Hanny. "Spannend bedacht, maar als experiment mislukt." *Trouw*, 27 August 2013.

Heijer, Jac. "Omstreden Globe-voorstelling grof en toch intelligent." *NRC Handelsblad*, November 1985.

Hirschberg, Stuart. "Beyond Tragedy: Yeats's View of History in 'The Gyres.'" *Research Studies* 42 (1974): 50–55.

Hirschberg, Stuart. "The 'Whirling Gyres' of History." *Studies: An Irish Quarterly Review* 68 (1979): 305–314.

Janssen, Hein, "Vertrek oude garde slag voor van Hove." *De Volkskrant*, 22 November 2003.

Mayer, David. The Bells: A Case Study. A 'Bare-Ribbed Skeleton' in a Chest. *The Cambridge History of British Theatre, Vol. 2: 1660–1895*. Edited by Joseph Donohue, Cambridge: Cambridge University Press, 2004: 398–399, 403.

Mayer, David. *Henry Irving and the Bells. Edited and Introduction*. Manchester: Manchester University Press, 1980.

Murawska, Katarzyna Murawska. "An Image of Mysterious Wisdom Won by Toil: The Tower as Symbol of Thoughtful Isolation in English Art and Literature from Milton to Yeats." *Artibus et Historiae* 3, no. 5 (1982): 141–162.

Murphy, Brenda. *Long Day's Journey into Night: Plays in Production*. Cambridge: Cambridge University Press, 2001.

O'Neill, Eugene. Letter to Mary Ann Clark, dated 8 August 1923. *Selected Letters of Eugene O'Neill*. Edited by Travis Bogard and Jackson R. Bryer. New York: Limelight Editions, 1994 [1988]: 389–390.

O'Neill, Eugene. *Complete Plays 1920–1931*. Edited and annotated by Travis Bogard. New York: Library of America, 1988.

O'Neill, Eugene. Letter to Brooks Atkinson, dated 19 June 1931. *Selected Letters of Eugene O'Neill*. Edited by Travis Bogard and Jackson R. Bryer. New York: Limelight Editions, 1994 [1988].

O'Neill, Eugene. *Eugene O'Neill*. Edited by Travis Bogard and Jackson R. Bryer. New York: Limelight Editions, 1994 [1988].

Oranje, Hans. "Een grimmige *Rouw siert Electra*." *Trouw*, 17 November 2003.

Porter, Thomas E. "Jansenism and O'Neill's 'Black Mystery of the Soul.'" *Eugene O'Neill Review* 26 (2004).

Raleigh, John H. *The Plays of Eugene O'Neill*. Carbondale: Southern Illinois University Press, 1965.

Robinson, James A. The Middle Plays. *The Cambridge Companion to Eugene O'Neill*. Edited by Michael Manheim, Cambridge: Cambridge University Press, 1998.

Schreuder, Alexander. "Vertekend beeld *Rouw siert Electra*." *De Theatermaker*, May 2004.

Sels, Geert. "Ivo van Hove over de onrust bij Toneelgroep Amsterdam." *De Standaard*, 29 November 2003.

Sels, Geert. "Ivo van Hove onder druk in Amsterdam." *De Standaard*, 24 November 2003.

Sels, Geert. "Bijdetijd (8): Ivo van Hove." *De Standaard*, 3 September 2004 (author's translation).

Sprangers, Jasmijn. "Door de ogen van De Warme Winkel kijken naar het theaterestablishment." *Cutting Edge* 25 August 2013.

Sword, Helen. *Ghostwriting Modernism*. Ithaca: Cornell University Press, 2002.

Thielemans, Johan. "Ivo van Hove en Peter Monsaert meten zich met O'Neill, en van Hove is pas thuis bij Mozart." *Documenta* 32, no 1 (2014): 55.

Törnqvist, Egil. "Staging O'Neill Today." *Eugene O'Neill Review* 26 (2004): 276–277.

Van Gelder, Lorianne. "Loeren achter het doek." *Het Parool*, 25 August 2013.

Van Maanen, Hans. *Het Nederlands toneelbestel van 1945 tot 1995*. Amsterdam: Amsterdam University Press, 1997.

Van der Speeten, Geert. "Waarom de ster van Ivo van Hove blijft stijgen." *De Standaard*, 25–26 June 2016.

Veraart, Karin. "Een heel goed idee that al evengoed is uitgevoerd." *De Volkskrant*, 27 August 2013.

Wensink, Herien. "Hilarisch Gekanker: De Warme Winkel versus Toneelgroep Amsterdam." *NRC Handelsblad*, 2 September 2013.

Yeats, William Butler. *The Hour-Glass and Other Plays: Volume 2 of Plays for an Irish Theatre*. New York: Macmillan, 1904.

Yeats, William Butler. *The Collected Poems*. New York: Macmillan, 1956a.

Yeats, William Butler. *A Vision*. London: Macmillan, 1956b [1937].

3

IVO VAN HOVE'S CINEMA ONSTAGE: RECONSTRUCTING THE CREATIVE PROCESS

Serge Goriely

A gift to the world of research

Ivo van Hove is very generous. One priceless gift he has bestowed on those engaged in researching and studying the art of performance is to have adapted fifteen or so films for the stage, among them the most noteworthy of the 1960s and 70s. Furthermore, they were produced by several of the greatest creative *auteurs* in the entire history of cinema. Six of them, to be exact, all renowned for their mastery in the exercise of their craft and their capacity to explore the human condition, which has given them status as cultural points of reference; and for their originality, bordering on subversion, which has at times earned them abuse, not to mention the lawsuits brought against them. I am referring to Ingmar Bergman (in this context represented by *Cries and Whispers*, *Scenes from a Marriage*, *Persona*, and *After the Rehearsal*), John Cassavetes (*Faces*, *Opening Night*, *Husbands*), Michelangelo Antonioni (*La Notte, L'Eclisse, L'Avventura*), Luchino Visconti (*Rocco and His Brothers*, *Ludwig*, and *The Damned*), Pier Paolo Pasolini (*Teorema*), and Joseph Losey (*The Servant*).

From this cinematographic treasure trove, van Hove has fashioned a whole set of pioneering works, largely between the years of 2005 and 2012. This vein seems not to have dried up, as the Belgian director has only recently come out with an adaptation of Visconti's *The Damned*, created specially for the 2016 Festival of Avignon. Perhaps it may be averred that the quality of these adaptations is uneven. One might prefer one to another, or determine that not all have the same ambition as *The Antonioni Project* or the same powerful impact of *Opening Night*. But to do so would be overly picky and a slave to the fleeting critiques of the moment, for the shows only gain in hindsight. Viewed after exhaustive examination of van Hove's creation, the fifteen relevant productions are sure to buttress the reputation of an original artistic corpus in perpetual flux. Each example, taken individually, demands and deserves an extended analysis of its own, inasmuch as each of them evince singular characteristics, all the while reflecting a common creative approach.

So, it *is* in effect a bonanza for the world of research. On the one side, more than fifteen masterpieces from the history of cinema, and on the other, an ensemble of significant, at times even stand-out theatrical productions. Between these two poles, Ivo van Hove emerges as a transformer, through which the basic matter—film—is turned into a different form, a theatrical production.

It is not my intention here to review and analyze all the productions drawn from these films in detail but, instead, to tease out several broad lines of reflection on the entire adaptation process with the following questions borne in mind: to what extent do these films present points in common? What does this process tell us about van Hove's method of transition from screen to stage and, therefore, about his definitive artistic path? And finally, what does this process indicate about the eternal questions regarding the specific nature and relationship of cinema and theatre? First, the study will have bearing on the approach toward adaptation insofar as van Hove practices it. Second, I'll concentrate on the films that he has adapted and ask to what extent they already contain in them, in innate form, theatricality particularly linked to the "static theatre," which would predispose them to a transfer to the stage. And, in the third and final section, an explanation of the nature of certain of the challenges posed by these films will be advanced, as well as addressing the solutions resorted to by van Hove within the framework of his adaptations.

What Ivo has to say on the subject

Ivo van Hove has often expressed himself in detailed statements on his mode of operation. Thus, in an interview from 2009 in *Alternatives théâtrales* (Laubin), he emphasizes how he has been influenced by the cinema. The films he chose to adapt, he confides, touched him deeply when he saw them between the ages of 17 and 25. But he insists, "the only reason" he wanted to transpose them to the stage was their exceptionally rich material, material he laments that is nowhere to be found in the theatrical repertoire (Ibid.: 33). One such example he cites is *Cries and Whispers*. He claims he had never unearthed any other classical text "as extreme on the subject of death," and that it brought him inspiration at a point in time when he found himself forced to confront that particular experience, the illness and death of his own father (Perrier January–March 2012: 77). The same holds for the films of Antonioni:

> Antonioni's subjects are almost visionary. His characters are too. He writes about romantic relationships and the difficulties in living them out, difficulties in being and staying together in a rapidly changing society. At the start of the 60s, Antonioni takes industrialization and the advent of a new urban environment as the point of departure. Fifty years later we are still in a new society that is rapidly changing. That's what interests me: how the characters position themselves in society, how these positions intersect, what the tensions are that arise between them. That is the subject Antonioni is writing about and which I've never come across in any extant theatre play.
>
> *(Laubin 2009: 33)*

On this matter, van Hove underlines how crucial it is for him to liberate himself from the finished film itself and limit himself only to the scenario as a working tool, which in practice results in his giving birth to the equivalent of a theatrical text. "I always depart from the original text or the exactly quoted transcription of the film," he declares (Ibid.), adding that it's a method predicated on taking off from virgin material: "It's like directing *Hamlet* for the first time," he says.[1]

This way of working doesn't preclude him from transposing the original screenplay to another context. For example, in *Cries and Whispers*, the cosseted and highly codified bourgeois universe of Sweden at the end of the nineteenth century is dispensed with and replaced by the emancipated Dutch environment of today. Furthermore, as so often when dealing with passages from a dramatic text on stage, he proceeds to make cuts or a whole new edit altogether, the aim being to compress, particularly to remove situations that require a proliferation of settings or characters. In this regard, his ambitious *The Antonioni Project* should be singled out, as three Antonioni films were fused together within it to make one single production.

And yet, certain additions have also been in the cards. In *Cries and Whispers*, van Hove makes audible verbal passages found in the "manuscript," a sort of letter to the actors, for the movie that Bergman wrote. For *Faces* or *Husbands*, he restored certain scenes that had been cut out of the final print by Cassavetes. And, as for *Teorema*, he gives voice to the text Pasolini wrote parallel to the film, a sort of companion written narrative version.

Thus, in accordance with van Hove's comments, we would conclude that these films, or more precisely, scenarios, were chosen essentially out of personal taste. Struck by them in his youth, he admires their power and their pertinence, for they each address themes that are dear to him. The virginity of the process also matters: it's exciting for him to be the first to take a scenario of this quality in hand, the same as with an unknown play by Molière or Shakespeare, and to give it a sort of second life without having to worry about tradition and the often paralyzing imprint of prior incarnations.

Strong connections with the theatre

But can the point be stretched still further? Is van Hove's choice of using these milestones of the history of cinema to be explained exclusively based on his personal tastes and the opportunity they offer him to take on certain contemporary themes with pertinence, depth, and originality?

From the standpoint of form—setting aside content for the moment—these films may be less heterogeneous than one might assume at first glance, especially from the common perspective of having been being transposed to the stage. Our hypothesis is the following: once we get beyond first appearances, all these films originally present a strong connection with the theatre that would naturally dispose them to a transfer to the stage. Expressed in another way, they all evince a certain "theatricality." "Theatricality" is to be understood here as the theatrical dimension presented in the films, not so much by any readily recognizable traits, but more so by a global and constitutive echo that passes between works of cinema and theatrical art.

A first indication that would support this hypothesis is furnished by the personal stories of the six filmmakers in question. In almost all cases, they have lived through a substantial period of participation in live theatre.

For Bergman, the connection with the stage is blatant. Throughout his long life, he conducted a double career as cineast and stage director, when he wasn't also an artistic director of a theatre. The way it worked in practice was that he'd put on plays during the theatre season and films during the summer, a pattern that eventually caused him to remark, "The theatre is like a faithful wife. Film is the great adventure—the costly, exacting mistress" (Cinema Scandinavia).

For Visconti, this connection is no less, as parallel to his cinematic career, he had engaged in major theatrical activities, having been at the forefront of introducing a number of classical and modern playwrights (Chekhov, Cocteau, Miller, Williams, etc.) to the Italian public and directing great lyric works for the opera, notably featuring Maria Callas.

Cassavetes was also eminently familiar with the stage. A graduate of the Actor's Studio, he started off as a stage actor, taught acting, and at the end of his life returned to the stage as an author and director in Los Angeles while still pursuing his film career.

If Pasolini's experience with the theatre was briefer, it was nonetheless decisive. He wrote a number of plays and brought out a visionary manifesto for an influential new theatre genre (the "theatre of prose"). As for Losey, it should be recalled that he was strongly involved in political theatre and that he collaborated with major playwrights. He worked with Brecht (being the first to stage his *Galileo*) and later also with Pinter, who was scenarist for various of his films, including *The Servant*.

Of the six, Antonioni was certainly the least affiliated with the theatre. Nonetheless, traces of theatrical creation are possible to identify in his biography. When still a young man, and before declaring himself a filmmaker, the Italian director sought to find himself in the live theatre, leading a theatre company, first at university and later on a more professional level. He might even have kept it up if he hadn't achieved success in the cinema.

Most probably, for these six cineasts, this powerful experience in the theatre—if it did not lead to an unconditional commitment for most of them—contributed to create an original cross-breeding in the framework of their best-remembered artistic achievements. This manifested itself through adapting scenarios from plays, in their way of directing actors regarding certain subjects related to theatre, or else as a personal vision of their art. To fully appreciate the strength of the link uniting the two media in the minds of certain cineasts, one paradigmatic quote from Bergman will give some idea:

> My texts are written without being intended for this medium or that, a bit like Bach's sonatas for the cello. . . . I wrote as I'm in the habit of writing for more than fifty years—it may bear a resemblance to theatre, but may just as easily be film, television, or simply a text for reading.
> *(Bergman 1994: 14)*

These diverse points of convergence, mixtures, and intersections have been remarked on by the critical community. In certain cases, they have led to foundational works,[2] some of which are even major or exemplary. One may recall the major impact on the film-opera genre of Bergman's *Magic Flute* or Losey's *Don Giovanni*, as well as all the critical debates engendered by Pasolini's film adaptations from Greek tragedies, *Oedipus Rex* and *Medea*, or his own plays such as *Porcile*.

If, in light of these powerful and rich connections, we return to discuss the films van Hove picked out for adaptation, certain salient marks of theatricality become immediately apparent. For some, the reference to theatre is explicit: *Opening Night, Persona,* and *After the Rehearsal* all concentrate on the life of theatre professionals and the difficulties they encounter in the practice of their craft, as well as the profound crises they endure. But even *Ludwig* or *Rocco and His Brothers* are relevant to the extent that the former dramatizes the fascination of the King of Bavaria for the opera, and for Wagner in particular, and the second sheds light on boxing, a sport of combat, no question, but also a source of performative spectacle, personal esteem, and social promotion.[3]

Furthermore, it is useful to recall that certain films like *Faces* or *Teorema* had previously been imagined by their authors (Cassavetes and Pasolini) as plays for the theatre, and were originally meant to be staged in live productions. Likewise, certain of the works have anticipated van Hove's initiative to be adapted to the theatre. Bergman himself had previously staged *Scenes from a Marriage* in a live theatre production (München Residenztheater 1981). Besides, the latter together with *After the Rehearsal* were first conceived for television and not cinema. This is clear through their austere and rather conventional style, as well in the key role the dialogue plays. To a certain extent, the imposed framework of a televised drama had already pushed both creations in the direction of a theatrical type of dramaturgy.

Extremely static films

Film directors who have broken with the theatre, films that relate to the theatrical world, or which were initially imagined for the stage, television dramas that had previously been adapted for theatre . . . . all these signposts tend to reinforce our initial hypothesis, namely that there exists a presence in these films of a predisposition to be adapted for the stage.

At this point, it is incumbent upon us to go further and raise questions about the original nature of the final produced films as theatrical material. One might argue that it would be preferable to resort to this scenario. But is that really justified? In certain cases, such as *Teorema* and *Cries and Whispers*, the initial scenario doesn't even exist in written form. All we have in these two cases is a retranscription of the finished movie or the writings that are connected to it, in a form resembling a novel. Then it must be pointed out that the initial contact between van Hove and these works in fact occurred through the intermediacy of the picture, not the text. He was initially drawn by the vision he had of these films, not by what he could read, but what leapt to his eyes. Therefore, going back to reconstruct the creative process implies delving directly into the filmic material.

In doing so, one feature stands out in every one of these films without exception: namely that dominant, classic codes of dramaturgy are far from being followed. Whether it's in the films of Antonioni, Bergman, Cassavetes, Visconti, Pasolini, or Losey, the narratives tend, depending on the case, to become circular, to depart from clear dramatic progression, or to be stripped of any perceptible evolution for the protagonists. Enigmas are left hanging at the end in place of clear resolutions of puzzles that were planted in the beginning. Thus, by the end of their pathetic wanderings, Harry, Gus, and Archie, the three forties-ish *Husbands*, will have barely made the slightest progress in relation to the crisis in their lives brought about by the death of their mutual friend (see Figure 3.1). Similarly, in *Faces*, after a night of agitation shrouded in mutual infidelities, Richard Furst and his wife, Maria, are once more left only to themselves. All they have succeeded in doing at the end of the day is giving vent to their suffering, their interior contradictions, and to the difficulty they have in expressing affection for each other. The same type of impasse applies in *Cries and Whispers*, where Agnes's agony violates cinematic tradition and does nothing to bring Karin and Maria any closer together. Likewise, in *Scenes from a Marriage*, Johan and Marianne are ultimately shown to be neither capable of living happily together nor separating from each other. As for *L'Avventura*, by the end of the movie, nothing further will be discovered to resolve the film's central mystery, the disappearance of Anna on the rocky island, any more than one will be able to venture a guess as to what the future will hold for Giovanni and Lidia, the couple in *La Notte* or, for that matter, for Vittoria in *L'Eclisse*. Similarly, the reactions of the family when confronted by the mysterious Visitor in *Teorema*, like those of Tony and the *Servant* Barrett, if they reveal anything, it is that the characters' empty interior lives hold no convincing road-map toward fulfillment. Even Visconti's characters' enterprises, which seemingly bear more fruitful results, will disappoint in the final analysis. Rocco, will, it is true, win a number of boxing matches, but only by way of self-sacrifice in order to redeem his brothers. Likewise, even if Ludwig is King of Bavaria, his insane dreams will lead not to some chimera of glory, but only to his demise.

What may be concluded from all this? First of all, that in every one of these films, action yields its preeminent status to situation. Each protagonist renounces the determination to act or manages to produce nothing but vain gestures, which come back to haunt them later or appear in an insignificant light to the others. On the inside, however, all characters respectively live out and

FIGURE 3.1   *Husbands*

© Jan Versweyveld

bear witness to their solitude, neuroses, and incapacity to love or be loved. To lead their lives well and actuate their dreams appears impossible for them, and they seem to be separated by an invisible wall from others.

As a matter of fact, at the center of these dramaturgies, there invariably figures a character who becomes a projection of modern man entangled in his futile condition, and who, when all is said and done, is lost on confronting himself, when face to the outside world, and to any sense with which he might endow his life.

Now, it so happens that the refusal of conclusive action and the consequences to that choice on the interior psychic movement of these characters distinguishes the films from what is generally known as classic cinema of the sort that is invariably dominated expressly by action and movement. Viewed from close up or far away, these films belong even less to mainstream cinema, what we generally think of as Hollywood movies. They cannot be included within the rubric of a standard genre (western, detective, comedy, war movie, etc.) for which action is the determining factor that defines character, following tried and tested recipes that the preponderance of scenarists churn out in a never-ending series of novel variations.

Quite the contrary, this preference for situation over action echoes a common pattern of dramatic or scenic theatrical writing, especially within the modern forms which call the Aristotelian dramatic rules into question, and where the concept of the "static" has therefore enjoyed a certain efflorescence.[4] Theoreticians define the latter as "an alternative criticism of dramatic progression, traditionally founded on an evolutionary dynamic of interhuman relations" (Kuntz and Losco 2001: 120). It would constitute, according to some, one of the two major evolutionary tracks in theatrical art covering over a century.

The theatre of our century [the twentieth century], at least that which was attempting to demonstrate the inutility of theatre to theatre itself, has evolved either towards a theatre of the avant garde which was trying to impregnate the theatre in artistic and social action of alienated peoples, even if it meant embracing a theatre which renounced one of the art form's most necessary conditions, that is to say, forward movement.

(Asholt 1995: 240)

The attraction for the static may first be detected in work by authors such as Chekhov or Strindberg, but was openly established by Maeterlinck, who personally proposed the formula for "static theatre" to designate a style that reveals the weight of invisible forces behind human decisions. Later, it was picked up principally by Beckett, who placed the notion of waiting firmly at the center of his dramatic crafting, and followed then by other more contemporary playwrights such as Muller, Bernhardt, Koltès, Duras, and Mamet, to name just a few.[5] Stage directors, too, have been involved in cultivating it. Thus, Meyerhold at the beginning of the twentieth century was able to sing the praises of an "immobile" theater: "We've got to have an immobile theatre. . . . There is no psychological action, nor even any material action, nothing in fact that one calls a 'subject'" (Meyerhold 1973: 106). Or else, much later on, Antoine Vitez declared:

and during the rehearsal period a parallel production emerges: it's almost always like this; the other, the one doesn't dare to actually realize on stage perhaps. . . . I dream of creating an immobile theatre, well, practically immobile.

(Vitez 1991: 390)

It should be noted that "immobility" isn't intended to be taken in a literal sense. Static theatre doesn't preclude dramatic movement. Essentially, it proposes the idea that movement no longer be taken as the principal source in the action, but that a tension arises between the physical immobility of the characters and their psychic immobility. In this sense, "static," would rather imply recognizing "suspended animation" or "movement in potential." That it is not now in motion, but could start to be at some indeterminate point in the future. One way to picture this key notion is through an image of a stormy sky that is awaiting the first lighting flash amid a sort of natural hush. Essentially, the static includes a power for setting things and characters in motion, but it can't be seen, it's not certain the potential exists, nor can it be linked to verifiable actions. You may intuit it, though, and expect the movement to arise on that highly tenuous basis. You will need to wait and see.

Historically, the imminence of the static has been one key response by and within theatre to the inception of film,[6] and following that, television:

The contemporary theatre places more and more emphasis on the fundamental difference between means proper to it and those belonging to the electronic media. In that sense, the static, perhaps for reasons comparable to those at the end of the nineteenth century, are opposed to the tide of images and sounds propagated by the media. It represents a luxury that only an art for which communication is possible in co-presence with the physical, can still permit itself. By making way for a prominent place to be afforded the static in the form of 'movement in force,' the theatre shows precisely in that way to what degree the artificial spectacle of media impoverishes life and gives a trumped up image of it.

(Asholt 1995: 247)

In effect, in light of these statements and the manifest theatricality of the films in question, it would be fair to inquire whether the famous distinction between film and theatre established by André Bazin might not be pertinent to revisit in the case of this filmography, so marked by the tell-tale traits of static theatre.

Bazin, it will be remembered, has asserted that cinema is a *cache* whereas theatre is a *cadre*:

> The idea of a *locus dramaticus* is not only alien to, it is essentially a contradiction of the concept of the screen. The screen is not a frame like that of a picture but a mask which allows only a part of the action to be seen. When a character moves off screen, we accept the fact that he is out of sight, but he continues to exist in his own capacity at some other place in the decor which is hidden from us. There are no wings to the screen. There could not be without destroying its specific illusion, which is to make of a revolver or of a face the very center of the universe. In contrast to the stage the space of the screen is centrifugal.

(Bazin 2005: 160)

Now, one might realize that the writing in a number of films chosen by van Hove, presents or leads in the direction of "closed meeting" without opening to the outside world. This is particularly the case in Bergman's, but also in *The Servant* or *Faces*, where the situation keeps turning back in on itself, and the exterior world is drained of importance alongside that which is seen of the characters. Parallel editing or cross-cutting techniques, ubiquitous in the language of cinematic language since D. W. Griffith, are absent here, with a heavy reliance placed rather on dialogue. Just as in classical tragedies, Bazin recalls: "What is specifically theatrical about these tragedies is not their action so much as the human, that is to say the verbal, priority given to their dramatic structure" (Ibid.: 161).

For these films, priority is essentially placed on the characters, rendering their action almost insignificant in relation to their interior evolution. Even for the films where the dramatic settings (locus dramaticus) proliferate, as in *Husbands* or *L'Avventura*, movement in the outside world seems to have no genuine interest for the central characters. Are Harry, Gus, and Archie going from New York to London? Are Claudia and Sandro traveling across the south of Italy to Palermo and Noto, in principle going in search of Anna? Actually, it is of no importance. Wherever the character may be, the locus dramaticus seems to exist only to signify their own psychic state, which generally tends to be that of loneliness, alienation, or despair.

In consequence, one may wonder to what point Bazin's postulate is validated in these movies. Indeed, instead of being "at the center of the universe," does character not wind up being rather the focus of the drama. . . as in the theatre? As a matter of fact, Bazin's description of theatrical character which follows could easily apply to Harry, Gus, Archie, Myrtle, Lidia, Vittoria, Richard, Maria, Agnès, Rocco, Ludwig, Tony . . . in fact, to all the heroes of these films in question:

> It is because that infinity which the theater demands cannot be spatial that its area can be none other than the human soul. Enclosed in this space the actor is at the focus of a two-fold concave mirror. From the auditorium and from the decor there converge on him the dim lights of conscious human beings and of the footlights themselves. But the fire with

which he burns is at once that of his inner passion and of that focal point at which he stands. He lights up in each member of his audience an accomplice flame. Like the ocean in a seashell the dramatic infinities of the human heart moan and beat between the enclosing walls of the theatrical sphere. This is why this dramaturgy is in its essence human. Man is at once its cause and its subject.

(Ibid.: 105–106)

Imbuing immobility with movement

In the interest of avoiding ambiguity, we hasten to emphasize that the *theatricality* of these films does not render them any less *cinematic*. The talent of the six cineasts bears reaffirmation, insofar as it allowed them to produce cinematic masterpieces taking off from material, the basis of which was naturally adapted to the theatre, namely a static story, one focused on one or more characters and stripped of a conclusive denouement and resolution.

More specifically, how did this come about? One aspect is that each of them found their way to invest movement into the apparent immobility of the narrative the author elected to relate. Naturally, a movie in and of itself is movement, as the etymology of the word reminds us.[7] But beyond that, the directors have had to work with the entire panoply of means germane to cinema editing—composition of frames, camera movement, music, sound, directing of the actors, and so on—which in themselves would merit the kind of detailed study that would exceed the parameters of this article. We shall content ourselves here by emphasizing that, apart from the profundity of the message on the selected theme or the extent of the creators' talent, one could actually quantify the originality of their style as well as the significance of their contributions to the renewal of filmic language.

At this point, let us return to the analysis of the artistic proceeding of Ivo van Hove. As we have seen, these films provided him with an exceptional opportunity for dealing with certain themes that had special meaning to him, such as death, the impossibility of communication, existential suffering, or romantic disarray. But beyond that, it appears that behind their outer appearance they offered a strong predisposition to be presented on stage. Yet to do so, it was necessary for van Hove to distance himself from all language proper to cineasts and the cinema. In this respect, van Hove's insistence that he based his stage adaptation not on the completed movie, but on the script for the movie only—or by default from the retranscription of the dialogue in the film—becomes more understandable. His statement regarding *Rocco and His Brothers* is unambiguous:

> The text is magnificent. It's not the visual style of Visconti, nor that of Pasolini either when I directed *Teorema*. I work on those texts in a totally different optic from the original films, an optic in which one doesn't recognize the original films. And yet the text is there.
>
> *(Laubin 2009: 34)*

Likewise, van Hove's systematic refusal to refer to the filmmakers' directing work appears logical in the course of developing his creations,

> I try . . . to find the real subject of the film and that's what I bring to the stage . . . Of course I'm impressed with Antonioni or Visconti, but the minute I start working, I have to stop thinking of them and situate myself in relation to their work. Of capital importance is that

I have to ask myself the question what I myself can do with their material.

(Ibid.)

By doing so, van Hove retraces the creative process taken by the filmmakers to the stage right before the cinematic directing proper starts, and gathers all the primary means at his disposal, whether they be a scenario, a retranscription, a novel, side commentaries, and so on. Of course, this mode of working is bound to come up short. For isn't the mise-en-scène in some measure already contained in a scenario? Or confined to a construct of the mind and memory? How can one eliminate from consciousness a film one has seen? Or not hark back to it when you have the retranscription at your disposal? Even so, that's how van Hove proceeds, and one can appreciate the enormous challenge that lies in wait for him, which is not one whit less than that the filmmakers also confronted. Indeed, for them as for him, the objective is to fully realize that initial "static" quality, namely to represent that famous quality of "immobility in suspension," and so succeed in generating a semblance of movement within an apparent immobility. Only, as distinct from the filmmakers, van Hove has a stage and not a screen confronting him, and he is obliged to imagine the non-cinematic but theatrical means to get it to function.

Front and center: the character

At the center of van Hove's preoccupations will figure the character, the dramaturgical pivot, which by reason of the static principle, finds itself being for the most part disencumbered of the actions that in a classically Aristotelian drama would have been the stuff of its definition. It's a matter of concentrating the spectator's attention on it, of amplifying its presence; in short, to make of it, according to Bazin's formula, the "focus" of the drama.

From this perspective, one of the most effective and obvious ways is by simply drawing the audience physically closer to the stage in order to get them to enter the world of the characters the actors are portraying. That, in fact, is the course that van Hove chose when adapting *Faces* (*Koppen*).[8] In this show, using a totally immersive scheme for the action, the spectators are sitting or leaning on sofas or beds between which the actors develop their story lines without any firm barrier being established between the auditorium and the stage. They are thus transformed into passive and invisible accomplices, if not voyeurs of Robert and Maria's escapades, whether they're in the intimacy of their house, the artificial atmosphere of nightclubs, or the apartment where Jeannie arranges her dubious encounters. The fourth wall has disappeared, so the public is literally plunged into the stage, enabled to perceive the slightest of the actor's gestures and thus of following what this might reveal of the character's inner agitation. To a certain extent, such settings are reminiscent of the use of close-ups in the cinema. To that is added, as quite often in van Hove's directing, violent, crude acting in which there's no holding back and that makes no concession to prudery. It verges on performance art. What is more, the audience has the privilege of being given an enlarged vision of what's being concatenated, as illustrated in the two scenes of adultery that are shown simultaneously and parallel to each other, like a split-screen effect if it had been in the cinema.

With all his elements deployed, it is interesting to recognize that the mise-en-scène of *Faces* dovetails with the styles adapted by Cassavetes, which are characterized by extremely expressive acting, corporally, gesturally, verbally, highly concise and expressive editing, an extremely mobile camera that stays glued to the actors, alert to and capturing their slightest movements, a dramatic stripping away that forces us to zero in on both seduction games that are in play at the same time.

Van Hove's set purpose in drawing the audience physically closer to the actors in order to drag them deeper into the interior world of the character is perceptible in other productions, with, however, a less radical immersion. For example, he opts for a circular configuration in *Rocco* with a boxing ring as its center. A similar choice is to be noted in *Scenes from a Marriage*, with an original twist, as the couple is followed at three different points in their married life across three shows given by different actors.

Van Hove is also expert at using a completely different strategy on the technical plane in order to augment the character's presence on stage. It reposes in the use of live-feed video, one of his oft-used methods that recurs in numerous productions. And yet it is clear that it is there to grapple with the same preoccupations as the physical displacement of the spectators: "Video for me is a means of rendering direct contact even more powerful. I use video in an attempt to show everything in detail, that the audience may truly witness everything that happens onstage" (Laubin 2009: 32).

Cries and Whispers furnishes an illuminating example of the benefits that can derive from this technique. For his adaptation, van Hove opted for an extremely physical kind of action, that at times even becomes frenetic, and which strongly contrasts with the alternative discretion and buffered reserve evinced by Bergman in his own film direction. He too had recourse to a series of screens, modulated according to the scene in question. In this case, he had them display the images captured by three roving hand-held cameras, the most important being that in the hands of Agnes, the protagonist of the agony, around whom the other characters revolve. A major innovation was to transform her into a performance and video artist and adapt her personal hand-written diary into a video blog. This is also a means to construct her identity as a tool for a work of art in progress, as Agnes's engagement in artistic creation constitutes the final bastion of her struggle against illness and death.

To those are added two further cameras, one in the flies and the other upstage in the wings, the two of which segue back and forth with the live feed captures of Agnes. However much more objective they appear to be, they implicitly serve as a conveyance by which the other characters may take in, and experience, the death that is gradually laying claim to Agnes.

The use of live-feed video in van Hove's hands can thus be extremely fruitful.[9] On a basic level, the presence of the protagonist is clearly intensified as greater access is allowed in to her subjective self, in this case, also allowing access to her artistic process. On another level, the secondary characters are concomitantly deepened thanks to the evocation of their subjective glance. On a third level, the character also gains in power on stage as a creator of animated images, which identifies her as a performer—an analogy that is even more evident where the three protagonists are all provided with portable cameras. On a fourth level, the different subjective and creative points of view of the protagonists, however parceled out in small lots, find an echo with the overall vision as matters unfold and are made available. It works as though in a film with a long steady shot, supposed to give a general and objective view of a situation, enhanced by a series of closer shots, perceived as subjective glances at the same situation. Finally, it should be pointed out that for much of the time, all these points of view—subjective, creative, and global—are offered to the audience, altogether and simultaneously. This engenders an ongoing flux as to what can be seen on the stage that is therefore in perpetual movement. This rich and complex approach has been explained by Edwige Perrot as follows:

> Whether it be in *Cries and Whispers* or *Husbands*, the conjugation of live-feed images and
> the stage permit the director to cause the audience's glance to drift from an internal and
> subjective point of view so that they may experience the subjectivities at play in the most

singular fashion possible. Even though the spectators are sitting in the audience, from one visual point of view, their position in relation to the representation is in perpetual movement.

(Perrot 2013: 318)

We can therefore see that Hove's use of live-feed video strongly conforms to the givens laid down by the original films insofar as they were "static." The "movement in immobility," indispensable to the success of the adaptation, is infused in multiple fashions at different levels. It is made obvious with the addition of the postures and gestures of the actor as captured and projected on the screen, and finally through the glances of the spectators who are invited to do their share. They ought indeed to be active, as they are given much volition, and are constantly being confronted with questions such as: what focus to choose in order to adequately follow the unfolding situation? Objective or subjective? Seen through the eyes of a given character, cued to do so by the live video feed, or their own? Ought they follow a lead or secondary character? Grant focus and follow any given character's trajectory over any other's? And what to choose if different characters, whether they be leads or secondary ones, pull focus to them at one and the same time?

Let us add by way of conclusion—as we are struck yet again by the richness of this approach to directing—that even after attaining the level of complexity described above, there is still room for the presentation to become yet more complicated. Two examples will illustrate the extent of the possibilities available.

Van Hove had increased *Cries and Whispers*' potential by having Agnes starting off with the special identity of being an artist—and of being treated as such. But with *The Antonioni Project*, he

FIGURE 3.2   *Opening Night*

© Jan Versweyveld

went even further: the stories of the three films are blended together and the entire theatrical stage is transformed into a film studio in action, loaded with screens and cameras, in this case, not capturing the subjectivity of the characters, but offering the audience an even more intricate set of points of view, and a supplementary tension between the world of the characters and that of the roles they are playing. It is fully justified to the extent that it dovetails with the specific theatrical universe, charged with alienation and incommunicability, in which they play out, and so, characteristic of Antonioni's cinema.

Then, in his adaptation of *Opening Night*, van Hove imagines how to combine the use of live-feed (still non-subjective as in *The Antonioni Project*) and bringing the audience closer to the action, as he did in *Faces* (see Figure 3.2). Aggressive cameras constantly follow Myrtle around as impolitely as possible, capturing and seeing into and through her body and to an even greater degree her face, and projecting that image onto several scenes, the largest of which dominates the stage. And further, a part of the audience—in an intra-diegetic manner—is invited to incarnate the audience watching the play-within-the play in which Myrtle is constrained to act and maintain her image as *grande dame* of the theatre. This multiplicity of perspectives thus opens the attention and comprehension of the spectators to an unprecedented extent into what is brought in to high relief of the inner world of the protagonist, her public image, and the challenges facing her as an actress.

As in all these productions, there is a correspondence between form and content: the justification of the scenic choices reposes in the fact that the original Cassavetes film is dedicated exactly to depicting Myrtle's crisis as an actress threatened by advancing age, forced to call herself into question, but at the same time, operating under the pressure of others' eyes, those of her colleagues and collaborators, as well as the audience.

Notes

1   Quoted in: Randy Gener. "In New York: A Director in Blue Jeans." *American Theatre* 26, no. 9 (November 2009): 3–11. See also: Johan Thielemans. "Ivo van Hove's Passionate Quest for a Necessary Theatre." *Contemporary Theatre Review* 20, no. 4 (2010): 456: "It's as though I was offering the film a second première. It's just as exciting as putting on a new play."

2   By way of example, one may refer to various passages regarding theatre in such works as Thierry Jousse, *John Cassavetes* (Paris: Cahiers du cinéma, 1989); Jacques Aumont. *Ingmar Bergman*. Paris: Cahiers du cinéma, 2003; or on the reflections of Gilles Deleuze on the theatricality of the body in: Deleuze Article, 366, University of Paris website.

3   And it is precisely the boxing ring that will attract Ivo van Hove in his adaptation.

> For *Rocco and His Brothers* the central image, in my opinion, is boxing. The brothers go to a boxing school. I no longer know how it's handled in the film but for me it's become the maternal image.

Van Hove quoted in: Laubin, op. cit., 34.

4   Let us recall that for Aristotle theatre is founded first and foremost on the dramatic element of action, ahead of that of character.

> Tragedy, then, is an imitation of an *action* that is serious, complete, and of a certain magnitude; in language embellished with each kind of artistic ornament, the several kinds being found in separate parts of the play; *in the form of action*, not of narrative; with incidents arousing pity and fear, wherewith to accomplish its catharsis of such emotions. . . . [my emphasis].

The Poetics.

5   We note in passing that van Hove is familiar with the writing of Chekhov, Koltès, and Duras, all of whose plays he staged.

6   See Michel Autrant who quotes the text of a commentator from 1925:

> At the Marivaux Cinema we saw a Charlie Chaplin in *The Gold Rush*, and it was incredible. What theatre! You can have Molière. You can have Shakespeare. You can have Ibsen. Because from here on in people are going to get used to a whole different kind of action and movement.

"Conclusions," in Hélène Kuntz and Mireille Losco. "Statisme." Poétique du drame contemporain. Lexique d'une recherche. *Etudes théâtrales* 22 (2001): 120, 259.

7   From the Ancient Greek κίνημα (*kínêma*) = "movement") or *movie*, obviously derived from *move*.

8   We note that van Hove preferred to translate *Faces* with the Dutch word *Koppen* (meaning heads) instead of *Gezichten* (which would literally mean *Faces*), which reflects the physical aspect he sought to emphasize in the production.

9   On this topic read Edwige Perrot. "Des corps-caméras de *Husbands* au journal vidéo de *Cris et chuchotements*." In *Les Usages de la vidéo en direct au théâtre chez Ivo van Hove et chez Guy Cassiers*, doctoral thesis under the direction of Josette Féral and Christine Hamon Siréjols, presented to the Université Sorbonne Nouvelle – Paris 3. Ecole Doctorale 267-Arts et Médias. Institut d'études Theâtrales, 2013: 317–320. In a very interesting fashion, the author juxtaposes *Cries and Whispers* with *Husbands*, characterizing the actors onstage as "body-cameras" and comparing them to the "body-paintbrushes" of Yves Klein.

Reference list

Asholt, Wolfgang. *Le statisme dans l'esthétique théâtrale actuelle*. *Statisme et mouvement au théâtre*. Poitiers: Publications de la licorne, 1995.

Aumont, Jacques. *Ingmar Bergman*. Paris: Cahiers du cinéma, 2003.

Bazin, André. *What is Cinema?* Berkeley: University of California Press, 2005. Epub.

Bergman, Ingmar. *Femte akten*. Stockholm: Norstedts, 1994.

Fijn van Draat, Sandra. "Lanterna Magica: When Your Role Model Becomes Human." Cinema Scandinavia website, 4 September 2015. Available at: www.cinemascandinavia.com/ingmar-bergman-lanterna-magica-when-your-role-model-becomes-human/.

Gener, Randy. "In New York: A Director in Blue Jeans." *American Theatre* 26, no. 9 (November 2009): 3–11.

Jousse, Thierry. *John Cassavetes*. Paris: Cahiers du cinéma, 1989.

Kuntz, Hélène and Losco, Mireille. "Statisme. Poétique du drame contemporain. Lexique d'une recherche." *Etudes théâtrales* 22 (2001): 120.

Laubin, Antoine. Interview with Ivo van Hove. "L'art du compromis." *Alternatives Théâtrales* 101 (April 2009): 32–36.

Meyerhold, Vsevolod. "Du théâtre," dated 1912. *Les Ecrits sur le théâtre 1*. Lausanne: L'Age d'Homme, 1973.

Perrier, Jean-Louis. "Au bout du texte." *Mouvement* 62 (January–March 2012): 77.

Perrot, Edwige. "Des corps-caméras de *Husbands* au journal vidéo de *Cris et chuchotements*." In: *Les Usages de la vidéo en directe au théâtre chez Ivo van Hove et chez Guy Cassiers*, doctoral thesis under the direction of Josette Féral and Christine Hamon Siréjols, presented to the Université Sorbonne Nouvelle – Paris 3. École Doctorale 267-Arts et Médias. Institut d'études Theâtrales, 2013.

Thielemans, Johan. "Ivo van Hove's Passionate Quest for a Necessary Theatre." *Contemporary Theatre Review* 20, no. 4 (2010): 455–460.

Vitez, Antoine. *Le théâtre des Idées*. Paris: Gallimard, 1991.

4

LOVE STILL IS LOVE EVEN WHEN IT LACKS HARMONY: *ANTIGONE* AND THE ATTEMPT TO HUMANIZE TRAGEDY

Charlotte Gruber

In a time when the story of *Antigone* has gained astonishing new prominence on and off theatre stages and its relevance emphasized in connection with a multitude of ever increasing recent political struggles throughout the world,[1] expectations were raised in 2015 when Ivo van Hove announced his upcoming production of the Greek tragedy. This promising Europe-wide, large-scale co-production by the Barbican in London and Luxembourg's Les Théâtres de la Ville in collaboration with van Hove's own resident troupe from Toneelgroep Amsterdam as well as Ruhrfestspiele Recklinghausen, Théâtre de la Ville in Paris, and the Edinburgh International Festival would have recourse to a brand-new translation by Canadian poet and translator Anne Carson (who was awarded the T.S. Eliot prize in 2014). Furthermore, van Hove's *Antigone* would cast French-born, Oscar-winning actress Juliette Binoche as the rebellious sister who determines to bury her dead brother, defying the decree of the king, her uncle Creon (see Figure 4.1). When he announced the performance, the Barbican's artistic director Toni Racklin stressed that he was "thrilled" to have introduced the two artists to each other and to have "commissioned the eminent Canadian poet Anne Carson to write this new translation" (Barbican 2015). However, after the production premiered in Luxembourg on 25th February 2015 and subsequently toured London, Antwerp, Amsterdam, Paris, Germany, and New York, the initial excited anticipation, while echoing through some of the reviews, had dissipated in many of the retrospective press articles that were published.

In this chapter, I want to examine certain elements of this production that left the critics dissatisfied. My point of departure is based on the assumption that triggering a feeling of unease in spectators is a characteristic feature of van Hove's work. Van Hove himself has admitted on many occasions that he is aware that he is considered the kind of director "you love to hate and hate to love" (Toneelgroep Amsterdam 2007). Bill Camp, one of the performers whom van Hove had worked with at New York Theatre Workshop said regarding *A Streetcar Named Desire* (1995): "I didn't like it. I had one of those reactions people would have with Ivo's work. I didn't understand it. I thought it was too obvious in all sorts of ways" (Ivo van Hove performers interview 2013).

Taking into account some excerpts from the most critical *Antigone* reviews, I want to show that the unease experienced is no reason to dismiss the production's value in the least. Quite the

FIGURE 4.1 *Antigone*

© Jan Versweyveld

contrary: the production's rejection by much of the press reveals a hidden and modest challenge to theatrical expectations, which is capable of disassembling our world-views and especially the assumption that there is one single "right" one. This analysis is based on extensive research into a variety of performances of *Antigone* from around the world and the realization that Hove's staging differs significantly from other contemporary examples in its unique, explosive and yet—paradoxically—ostensibly unspectacular stance toward a holyholistic concept of classic tragedy.

The grave stage: grave is both an adjective and a verb

Let's start by taking a look at the stage setting. *Antigone*'s production design, including both set and lighting, was developed by Jan Versweyweld, who has worked closely with van Hove since 1981 (Thielemans 2010: 455–460). The pitch-black stage combines an elevated stage base down front with a narrow boardwalk connecting its rear section to a doorway set in the back wall. Hanging over this passageway a large round hole will later symbolize the Sun and the Moon, standing for day and night, but at the same time mirrors the volatile heat of Antigone's temper, her acts of passion, as well as Creon's coldness and the rigidity of his decree.

On the downstage section, several sets of stairs, a black leather couch, and shelf units have been integrated. As the shelves are filled with boxes, books, and VHS cassettes, they give the impression of being an archive of sorts, as has been pointed out in many reviews (Higgins 2015; Harvey 2015; Van den Berg 2015). This setting was often linked to a quote from the adaptation, made by Anne Carson, who translated the Greek word for ancient—*archaia* as *archive*—and writes: "the archives of grief I see falling on this house" (Higgins 2015). It has also been suggested that this scenery represents, "the surveillance of a paranoid state" (Trueman 2015), but in any case it most definitely sets the scene for a governmental office in which Creon gives the mere appearance of consulting with advisors. He invariably and ostentatiously demonstrates that he is the one in charge, who knows what's best, and that betrayal, bribery, or any other undermining of his authority—especially from within—will lead as a matter of course to a certain death sentence.

As in many of van Hove's previous productions, the back-of-stage wall is an important conveyor of meaning, springing to life as a vast canvas for image-projections, subtle plays of light and video, which, as for example with *The Little Foxes* (2010), *Edward II* (2010), and *The Misanthrope* (2007), were designed by Tal Yarden. In accordance with the lighting changes of the Moon (using colder pale colors) and the Sun (using bright warm colors) as associated with the appearance of either of the key figures, Antigone or Creon, the projections generally alternate between two different sets of minimally animated images. Strongly blurred black and white pictures of faceless people in the streets are juxtaposed with vast, deserted landscapes. Both add an outlandish element of exterior existence that seems both surreal and detached, and stands in sharp contrast to the office-interior-in-a-cubbyhole. Onscreen, hectic city and quiet nature clash. This imagery beautifully encapsulates the concept of the city wall so central to the tragedy by Sophocles. After all, Antigone's brother Polyneices, who attacked his home city, is branded a traitor by Creon. The tyrant deprives him of his citizenship, rendering him an *outsider*. To cruelly realize this degradation, Creon has the corpse removed to lie unburied outside the city wall, expelled and exposed in all possible ways. While the stage action of the original text by Sophocles remains within the city of Thebes, and all that happens outside is invisible and evoked only through speeches by messengers, van Hove, Versweyweld, and Yarden deconstruct the separation. When the guard confesses to Creon that someone had buried Polyneices unobserved, a shaft in the ground becomes visible in the very center of the stage. Before Antigone is caught by the guard, and during the famous "Ode to Men" passage, a platform rises slowly, revealing the maltreated corpse of Polyneices. The audience is then invited to follow the entire burial procedure, performed by Antigone from start to finish, replete with smoking frankincense, holy water-washing of the body, and an actual soil rub.

Van Hove has previously stated that he rejects illusionism and opts instead for the honesty achieved by using concrete materials as "a direct quote from the outside world" (Thielemans 2010: 458). On several occasions he has even used real animals onstage. The highly realistic burial on the surreal stage creates a hyperrealism (Ibid.), which might present a challenge for any audience member unfamiliar with van Hove's theatre owing to its estranging rupture between naturalism and abstraction. One of the critics thus complains: "Why, oh why, are we first situated in a desert town and in the end all of a sudden find ourselves in a typical Western office space, with the bonsai trees and typewriters of a present-day megalopolis?" (Van der Kooi 2015). The uncommon mix of the two elements irritates both spectators who are used to a modern post-dramatic approach *and* those who favor more traditional representational forms. Here we encounter the first hint of the unease in audiences that I will address further below.

Regarding the focus on the stage-setting, it is crucial to mention how—from the burial onwards, after which the corpse vanishes down into the shaft once more—the centerpiece grave-platform, though practically invisible at this point, subsequently becomes a functional element symbolizing the impending death inherent in every character conflict within this tragedy. The fight between Haimon and Creon, for instance, climaxes with Haimon being pushed so hard that he falls to the ground, exactly where Polyneices's grave used to be. This reminder also creates a causal link between the un/burial of Polyneices and all the deaths to come. In later scenes, Eurydice and eventually Creon creep up onto the platform when they are grieving the deaths of their loved ones. It thus demarcates not only the vicious circle of dying but also the painful experience of giving up on life, which is a crucial but generally overlooked element in *Antigone*.

The stage oscillates between interior and exterior and calls into question whether inside and outside exist separately or rather occur as intertwined. At the same time, this oscillation poses a potential for resolving the conflict between two forces pushed to their extremes, as Hegel has it with his idea/l of dialectical *Aufhebung* (sublation) resulting in a utopia: an undefined no-man's land, a non-existent space.[2] The set design, taken as a whole, works as an exemplification of a locale without definition. And the fact that the design consists of disparate elements, joined through a principle of collage, further makes it impossible for the performers to take in the entire picture at once. This gives the sense that Antigone and Creon act on opposing levels of a shared reality, which they are unable to wholly perceive as their focus has been reduced to their own particularity: first, because they fail to recognize each other as essential parts of that shared reality; and, second, because they fail to recognize their own respective positions. The two disparate mindsets both reinforce Creon and Antigone's differences, which engender their conflict, yet also contain what they have in common. The blurred faceless people on the video-projection, which stand for the unrepresented masses and a chorus that has disappeared, reveal that Creon sees citizens not as individual human beings, but as a general public, subjects objectified under his authority. He fails to listen to them. Antigone's lonely landscapes reveal that she has given up on everyone but the dead; of whom she believes she is a constituent part. She never listens to either.

Antigone's world is emptied of people. Creon's world contains a people emptied of identity. The two are blind vis-à-vis their fellow men, both the abstract concept of the public good and the concrete reality of relatives, partners, and friends. Although convinced that the opposite is true, *neither* actually cares—either about one another or about those beyond. Or rather, they do care a great deal, maybe too much, but they don't *take* their caring accordingly; that is they don't act accordingly. They *see*, but do not *recognize* the other—to refer to the ethics of Emmanuel Levinas. Their own and the audience's view of the world literally remain projections.

This distorted view is reinforced by the fact that the cast consists of a mere seven people. Each of them plays at least one main character, but at the same time, each one of them (not including Creon and Antigone) are also assigned lines from the chorus. Van Hove decided to divide the text so that "the chorus" never actually appears in a choric configuration at all. Furthermore, the entire cast generally remains onstage throughout the performance, becoming silent spectators relegated to the sidelines. As a result, family members like Haimon, Ismene, and Eurydice not only merge with the public, but seem wholly to disappear, palpable beings only from time to time. Disrupting the dramatis personae's linearity has been identified as one characteristic of postdramatic theatre by Hans-Thies Lehmann (1999: passim). In this case, the technique renders them unstable entities and shows that the way they are perceived by Creon and Antigone depends for the most part on the ethical and political stands they take. It also introduces a perplexing, new diversity of standpoints and, hence, injects more human vacillation and insecurity into the play's characters. This performance is not about Creon versus Antigone, nor even about either of them in particular. Thanks to Carson's adaptation, Creon and Antigone are both offered a variety of strong and beautifully crafted arguments with which to expatiate. But whatever they hear, they seem to listen to exclusively with a view to reducing any given rhetorical point to a position that either works "for" or "against" them.

The tragic in van Hove's *Antigone* is not so much rooted in the dialectic of binary oppositions, exemplified by Hegel's interpretation of *Antigone*, as it is embedded in the tension this exclusionary, filtered kind of thinking causes. It addresses the problematic of blind spots, which arise due to the reduction inherent in predetermining and imposing a binary structure to begin with. Van Hove's approach thereby seems rather to resonate with the philosophy of both Derrida and Levinas, as opposed to a Hegelian one; at least in their counter-ontological ethical points of convergence, which have been skillfully unpacked, especially by Simon Critchley, who in his reflection on Levinas points out:

> Ethics occurs as the putting in question of the ego, the knowing subject, self-consciousness, or what Levinas, following Plato, calls the Same. . . . Thus, the domain of the Same maintains a relation with otherness, but it is a relation in which the 'I', ego or *Dasein* reduces the distance between the Same and the Other, in which their opposition fades (Tel 99/Tl 126). Now the Same is called into question by the other (*l'Autre; to heteron*) or to use Levinas's word, the 'alterity' (*altérité*) of that which cannot be reduced to the Same, that which escapes the cognitive powers of the knowing subject. Ethics for Levinas, is critique; it is the critical *mise en question* of the liberty, spontaneity, and cognitive emprise of the ego that seeks to reduce all otherness to itself.
>
> *(Critchley 2014: 5)*

Creon and Antigone are deceived by their inner perceptions of that which is outside of them, of their bias against the *Other*. Their focus on their singularity does not allow them to see their shared reality. Yet, there is actually no center in such self-centeredness—only an omnipresent, implacably unchanging grave. The term *center* stands out as crucial to Derrida's theory especially in terms of deconstruction. As had been made apparent in his ground-breaking lecture *Structure, Sign, and Play in the Discourse of the Human Sciences*, the concept of the center can serve to clarify the integration of hierarchy and dominance into discourse, especially by means of assuming the privilege of one part of a binary over another (Derrida 1978: passim). To critically engage with the center in discourse (deconstruction) thus becomes an ethical act insofar as the hidden introduction and perpetuation of power structures into discourse may themselves be violent acts and result in violent actions. Opposition then manifests as oppression, marginalizing positions and muting voices. In van Hove's *Antigone*, in which both Antigone and Creon each privilege their position over the other, the center of the stage thus comes to represent death. They both facilitate death, and they both ultimately long for death: as the *center* especially—in its most intense rigor, as Derrida pointed out—is a very fragile thing.

But on van Hove's stage there is another exit available besides the grave. There is another outside outside of the self-centricity and outside death, as is suggested by the doorway leading backstage, out of the theatre and away from the play.

The most terrible conflict is a trivial one: overacting, underachieving?

The first conclusions that I drew from the stage set suggested that in van Hove's *Antigone*, a shift can be seen, from the common dialectical approach toward Antigone and Creon to a counter-ontological ethics of the *Other*. Such an understanding also differs from dialectics insofar as it refrains from either reducing or expanding the two characters into ethical constructs, and instead focuses on them as human beings who appear to each other, so reinvigorating the relevance of the relationships between them. In the following section, I will elaborate on this aspect further, considering the stage action and acting, as well as assessing the voices of certain critics who took particular issue with the acting and stage action, rather than with the scenery, in van Hove's *Antigone*. Although their observations may have pertinence to a certain degree, I deplore their failure to pursue the underlying basis of their criticisms. By limiting themselves to a light dusting of first impressions, they tilted in favor of indulging in superficial pronouncements rather than engaging in the difficult task of critical analysis. On the other hand, their observations serve as invaluable proof of how incendiary preconceptions of theatre can be, and of how successfully van Hove creates theatrical provocations.

What most stands out is how the critics cited below found fault with the fact that it was hard, in this production, to empathize with or feel for the characters. The first two voices from the Netherlands are a lot less harsh than the following ones from the United Kingdom:

> Binoche has a perpetual sob in her voice and generally speaks in a fairly shrill tone. 'Look at me suffering!' —That's what gets drummed into our heads. The other actors, particularly Kreon (Patrick O'Kane), follow in her wake in an acting style that may be technically fine, as far as a mellow acting style goes. Furthermore an underlying bond between the actors is missing; they float past each other like islands in the ocean. . . . Juliette Binoche is too earnest in her demand that the audience put all its attention on Antigone's suffering. Not even the beautiful scenery can make up for it. The performance stays too solemn; too distant. . . . As a result, it holds itself aloof and never arouses empathy, emotion, or compassion.
>
> *(Janssen 2015)*

> It's difficult to put your finger on why, but the abstraction that is so often one of van Hove's strong suits seems to really stand in the way in this particular performance. His directing is admittedly tight and bright and most actors independently of each other are just fine, but one still remains entirely unmoved by the suffering of the characters. Although tragedy after tragedy unfolds before your eyes, you are left completely cold.
>
> *(Kleuver 2015)*

The fact that a strong distance between audience and actors and also between actor and actor is created is true, but in such a startling way! Though the characters who desperately go to their deaths are in the throes of emotions, they still do not seem to connect with each other when they meet. Van Hove inserts a gesture of closeness into just about every scene, and between almost every character: Ismene and Antigone's intense hug at the beginning, Haimon snuggling up to his father in devotion on the couch, Haimon kissing Antigone at the burial of Polyneices. Yet it all stands in sharp contrast with how the speeches are delivered, as though there were another third wall installed onstage separating the actors from each other at that very moment, despite their physical contact. It is a strong way to articulate how they are never talking to or with each other, but merely preaching at each other, and hence lose any possibility for real contact. They have indeed lost all connection and that is the real tragedy here. Again, they lack what Levinas has coined *response-ability* to the *Other*. As a result, each character's stubbornness is delineated almost grotesquely, which renders them rather hard to like.

> [W]hat becomes clear quickly is that celebrity status is not the same as tragic stature. Binoche's shrill Antigone is a diminished figure, more hysteric than heroine—there is much hoarse screeching and high-pitched shouting and only intermittent pathos.
>
> *(Kellaway 2015)*

Creon comes across as an arrogant prick most of the time. Haimon, after first making a solid razor-sharp argument to his father, suddenly degenerates into a frustrated toddler. Antigone, every inch the French Oscar's diva, really gets on our nerves with her constant self-involved outrage that is both over the top, and at the very least, silly. There are moments in every conflictual scene that are almost painful to watch due to the precipitous, unmodulated, and over-the-top emotional breaks that appear fake and absurd yet—refusing theatrical norms— ostensibly very real at the same time.[3] The overly intrusive orchestral soundtrack further reinforces the artificial extremity of the acting. Similar to van Hove's idea of hyper-realism, this hyper-organic acting style rejects the illusionism of heroes and, instead, painfully presents all the characters simply as people. In the past, van Hove has stressed that he is "not so interested in good and evil" (Kellaway 2015). From his earliest work onwards, relationships, especially complicated ones, were his main source of inspiration (Thielemans 2010). Points of interest van Hove has mentioned that nag at him include "the impossible attempt to keep a relationship pure" (Ibid.), and that love is still love, "even when it lacks harmony or when it is destructive" (Ibid.). "One moment you sympathize with the person you hate, then in the next scene you hate somebody you love. . . . I love this ambiguity," van Hove once confided to an interviewer, and this ambiguity and paradoxicality regarding human affections are clearly to be found in *Antigone*.[4]

The director reveals how the seeming complexity of a thousand year-old insoluble ethical paradox to a conflict, and the focus on the question of who is acting heroically and who is to blame for the plight of the dead, blinds us to the other immense tragedy of human beings failing each other within their relationships. Indeed, van Hove stated that he had expressly intended to shift the focus of this tragedy in such a direction:

> That play [*A View from the Bridge*], which is a domestic drama, I turned into a Greek tragedy. Now, with a Greek tragedy, I am trying to humanize it.
>
> *(Higgins 2015)*

> When I make theatre, I always want to surpass what I did before. I think this is essential for art. . . . I do not want to play it safe. In every project you have to go to the outer limit and try to go even further.
>
> *(Thielemans 2010: 459)*

Once the characters are made more human, and reduced from their status of tragic hero, they are consequently rendered more responsible than they had seemed before. When in plain sight, they fail to act responsibly, and consequently lose their status of victimhood and finally become less likeable. Then all of a sudden, the audience no longer *wants* to identify with them, because they adjudge that they ought to have done better, and hence experience the critically lamented loss of empathy:

> Greek tragedy, when performed superlatively, is unmediated—nothing stands in the way of emotion. I was not even faintly moved by this version of the tragedy, and it did not help that the actors' voices were amplified, as if in acknowledgment of the production's lack of reach.
>
> *(Kellaway 2015)*

Even renowned classicist Oliver Taplin admitted in a BBC Radio 3 broadcast review on the performance: "I wasn't moved as much as I had hoped" (Ishiguro 2015). What is going on here, hinted at by the consistency of all these negative remarks by critics, is of almost revolutionary import. Van Hove's performance functions as a deconstruction, which confronts the audience with their expectations toward tragedy. There seems to be a demand for something sublime, which would then grant access to empathy, as if the sublime was the one and only element one could and should care to discover in tragedy, as if whatever entails the sublime is exclusively worthy of identifying with.[5] By deconstructing the theatrical experience of tragedy itself, the audience is cheated of their awaited catharsis. The dramatic conflict becomes so human, so worldly, that it turns irritating, even to the extent of overturning the ability to experience empathy, especially because a classic tragedy is expected. After all, it has been announced and advertised that it is Sophocles' *Antigone* that is on the bill. Does that not imply that the sublime, empathy, and catharsis will all be part of the spectating experience?

Some critics, as we have seen, react to this innovation by simply rejecting what they see. Just as Antigone and Creon fail to act responsibly toward each other, the audience, hesitant before the experience of a deconstructed tragedy, falls into the same trap of dismissing that which cannot be reduced to a known quantity. For that which cannot be reduced to the *Same* is condemned to elude the cognitive powers of the knowing subject.[6] In an article on Flemish theatre, Christel Stalpaert, though not addressing van Hove in particular, elaborates on the very approach to tragedy he has taken here. According to her, on Flemish stages, "the tragic heroes are no longer treated as traditional elevated characters where catharsis develops from a mimesis of pain, from empathetic identification with the hero" (Stalpaert 2010: 447). Stalpaert postulates that instead a transition takes place "from represented pain to pain experienced in representation" (Ibid.). So although van Hove has associated himself with the theatre of the Netherlands for several decades, first at Zuidelijk Toneel in Eindhoven and then at Toneelgroep Amsterdam, he also remains a Flemish artist, one susceptible to the trends in his Belgian homeland, this being an important one.

To move toward a conclusion, I would like once more to revert to the element of unspecific context addressed at the beginning, which was also targeted by the press:

> [*Antigone*] is one of the hottest tickets in town: it has been sold out for ages, will go on a world tour and get a BBC broadcast. There's no getting away from it, though: I'm afraid it's pretty lacklustre stuff. . . . Although he has talked about being influenced by recent headline events, such as the unburied victims of the downed Malaysia Airlines plane over Ukraine, van Hove opts for an any-time, any-place ambience. . . . [T]here's a hole at the heart of this 90-minute affair; that elusive ability to make us make care.
>
> *(Cavendish 2015)*

The critics fail to see that by deliberately not choosing a single specific context, van Hove is refusing not only illusionism, but also ideology. He is clearly differentiating his *Antigone* from other contemporary *Antigone* performances such as Volker Lösch's *Antigone Oriental* (2012) or *Alexis: A Greek Tragedy* (2010) by the Italian Group Motus. The latter used Sophocles' text as a pretext for addressing particular political issues with a specific message. Van Hove on the contrary not only challenges the theatrical expectations of audiences but also requires them to make sense independently. He is reaching out to an emancipated spectator; to use the notion of Jacques Rancière's, an open-minded one. He refuses to *make* them care (Rancière 2009). Johan Thielemans has addressed this very tendency in van Hove's work as a whole:

> [T]hey offer an opportunity to go beyond the portrayal of lifelike psychological characters and the textbook display of emotion. The audience is thus not affected by emotional identification, but is kept in a state of detached witnessing.
>
> *(Thielemans 2010: 455)*

It is striking how van Hove's approach, though it is less imposing than some of these other classical renditions, actually winds up irritating the audience more. What is revealed as a consequence on so many levels is the tragedy of hostility toward the Other that is lurking behind the insecurity of all peoples. It is also at the basis of one of the biggest challenges we face in a globalized world: cultural clashes. According to David Willinger—who has followed van Hove from the very inception of his directing career—this aspect of inter-cultural provocation is one of the most outstanding characteristics of his work.[7] It is one of the goals of this anthology to show how van Hove's efforts, in working across the borders of Europe and the US and integrating contradictory styles into his performances, have not only led to outraged audiences and bad press, but eventually made him an important and prestigious director of world theatre.

With the (rather American) hyper-organic acting on the one hand, and the (rather European) hyper-realistic unspecific set on the other, van Hove's *Antigone* reveals the tragedy of an unspectacular and, human failure of responsibility toward the Other, a call to humbleness, which actually approaches closer to our lives than any of the recent sensationalistic news-story scandals. This might be exactly what creates unease: that he confronts us with ourselves and the fact that the most terrible conflicts are in fact the trivial ones that we confront day-to-day. This performance has the potential to make our world tremble when it counters the egocentric *cogito ergo sum* with the scepticist view and its modest *errare humanum est*, as when the adaptor ends Creon's final dirge with the following lines from The Velvet Underground's song "Heroine":

> I wish that I was born a thousand years ago
> I wish that I'd sailed the darkened seas
> On a great big clipper ship
> Going from this land here to that
> Put on a sailor's suit and cap
> Away from the big city
> Where a man cannot be free
> Of all of the evils of this town
> And of himself, and those around
> Oh, and I guess that I just don't know
> Oh, and I guess that I just don't know.
>
> *(Reed 1967)*

Notes

1   The author's dissertation, *The Other Antigone[s]*, focuses on the "Antigone Boom" from 2000 onwards and the increasing socio-political significance of the classical figure. It draws links between theatre productions and the subject's appearance in academic and public discourse. The dissertation includes a list of about 100 *Antigone* productions from the last 20 years. The dissertation was undertaken at Ghent University as part of the research-project "*Antigone* in/as transition" (2012–2016) supervised by Katharina Pewny. For other sources with a focus on the tragedy, see, for instance: Erin B. Mee and Helene P. Foley (ed.), *Antigone on the Contemporary World Stage* (Oxford: Oxford University Press, 2011); S. E. Wilmer, Audrone Žukauskaitė (ed.), *Interrogating Antigone in Postmodern Philosophy and Criticism* (Oxford: Oxford University Press, 2010); Tina Chanter, Sean D. Kirkland (ed.), *The Returns of Antigone. Interdisciplinary Essays* (New York: SUNY Press, 2014).

2   This addresses the popular understanding of Hegel having read Antigone and Creon as representatives of two necessary ethical concepts creating a clash, which, however, leaves the higher entity of solution by dialectical *Aufhebung* to the spectators. Following Hartmut Böhme, it has to be emphasized here that this iteration of Hegel's understanding of tragedy refers to late Hegel, especially to the publication of his *Aesthetics* by Heinrich Gustav Hothos in 1842 and its revised second edition (1976). Referring to Georg Steiner's *Antigones*, he further stresses that Hegel had been preoccupied with *Antigone* for decades, and that not all his interpretations coincide with this one. Cf. Hartmut Böhme, *Götter, Gräber, Menschen in der "Antigone" des Sophokles* in: Gisela Greve (ed.), *Sophokles. Antigone* (Tübingen: Kimmerle, 2002): 93–124.

3   To play emotional breaks and changes organically, so that the change can be followed and fathomed by the audience and appear more natural to them is one of the main first precepts of professional acting. It is the basis of creating a stronger theatrical as-if experience, in which audiences can forget that the actors are just playing roles. Emotional changes in offstage real life might very well take on a different cast altogether.

4   Cited regarding *A View from the Bridge* (2014) in Kate Kellaway, "Juliette Binoche is More Hysteric Than Heroine," *The Guardian*, 8 March 2015.

5   For an early account (1st Century AD) on the notion of the sublime in relation to affect, the art of writing and its aesthetics, see, for instance, the manuscript "On the Sublime" by Longinus, trans. W. Rhys Roberts (Cambridge: Cambridge University Press, 1899). Arthur Schopenhauer then made a connection between tragedy and the sublime as experience of resignation in the face of inescapable and inevitable fate. See: *The World as Will and Representation Vol. 2*, trans. E. F. J. Payne (New York: Dover Publications, 1958): 433.

6   The notion of "the Same" refers to the writing of Emmanuel Levinas. See, for instance, Emmanuel Levinas, *Totality and Infinity: An Essay on Exteriority* (Pittsburgh, Pennsylvania: Duquesne University Press, 1969): 21.

7   See, for instance: David Willinger, "Culture Clash: Some Notes on Flemish Theatre and its Critical Reception in New York City," *Border Collisions: Contemporary Flemish Theatre,* eds. Lourdes Orozco and Peter M. Boenisch, *Contemporary Theatre Review,* 20, no. 4 (November 2010): 461–464. The relevance of theatre for politics, applying the example of van Hove in particular as an artist who successfully interconnects cities, has also been raised by American political theorist Benjamin Barber in his latest publication *If Mayors Ruled the World: Dysfunctional Nations, Rising Cities* (New Haven, CT: Yale University Press, 2013).

Bibliography

Artform News. Unattributed article. Barber, Benjamin. *If Mayors Ruled the World: Dysfunctional Nations, Rising Cities*. New Haven: Yale University Press, 2013.

Barbican, The. "Juliette Binoche to Star in New Translation of *Antigone* Barbican Production and International Tour." Barbican website, 18 May 2015. Available at: www.barbican.org.uk.

Böhme, Hartmut. "Götter, Gräber, Menschen in der, Antigone "des Sophokles." In: *Sophokles. Antigone.* Edited by Gisela Greve. Tübingen: Kimmerle (2002): 93–124.

Cavendish, Dominic. Review of *Antigone* at the Barbican. "Lacklustre Stuff." *The Daily Telegraph*, 5 March 2015.

Chanter, Tina. "The Returns of Antigone." *Interdisciplinary Essays*. Edited by Sean D. Kirkland. New York: SUNY Press, 2014.

Critchley, Simon. *The Ethics of Deconstruction: Derrida and Levinas*, 3rd edition. Edinburgh: Edinburgh University Press, 2014.

Derrida, Jacques. "Structure, Sign, and Play in the Discourse of the Human Sciences." In: *Writing and Difference*. Chicago: Chicago University Press, 1978.

Harvey, Chris. Interview with Juliette Binoche. "We All Have a Secret. . ." *The Daily Telegraph* (online), 6 March 2015.

Higgins, Charlotte. "Death Becomes Her: How Juliette Binoche and Ivo van Hove Remade *Antigone*." *The Guardian*, 18 February 2015.

Ishiguro, Kazuo. Interview with Oliver Taplin. *Antigone Review*. BBC, 5 March 2015.

Ivo van Hove performers. Interview. "A Conversation with Ivo van Hove Performers." *Process in Performance*, Season 2, 19 March 2013.

Janssen, Hein. "Acteurs in *Antigone* drijven als eilanden langs elkaar heen." *De Volkskrant*. Trans. by Charlotte Gruber, 23 March 2015.

Kellaway, Kate. "Juliette Binoche is More Hysteric Than Heroine." *The Guardian*, 8 March 2015. Available at: www.theguardian.com/stage/2015/mar/08/antigone-review-juliette-binoche-is-more-hysteric-than-heroine.

Kleuver, Esther. "Wereldster Binoche valt tegen op toneel." *De Telegraaf*. Trans. by Charlotte Gruber. 10 April 2015.

Lehmann, Hans-Thies. *Postdramatisches Theater*. Frankfurt am Main: Verlag der Autoren, 1999.

Levinas, Emmanuel. *Totality and Infinity: An Essay on Exteriority*. Pittsburgh: Duquesne University Press, 1969.

Longinus. *"On the Sublime."* Trans. by W. Rhys Roberts. Cambridge: Cambridge University Press, 1899.

Mee, Erin B. and Foley, Helene P., eds. *Antigone on the Contemporary World Stage*. Oxford: Oxford University Press, 2011.

Rancière, Jacques. *The Emancipated Spectator*. Trans. by Gregory Elliott. London: Verso, 2009.

Reed, Lou and the Velvet Underground. *"Heroine."* *The Velvet Underground and Nico*. Verve Records, 1967.

Schopenhauer, Arthur. *The World as Will and Representation, Vol. 2*. Trans. by E. F. J. Payne. New York: Dover, 1958.

Stalpaert, Christel. "Something is Rotten on the Stage of Flanders: Postdramatic Shakespeare in Contemporary Flemish Theatre." *Contemporary Theatre Review* 20, no. 4 (November 2010): 507–511.

Thielemans, Johan. "Ivo van Hove's Passionate Quest for a Necessary Theatre." *Contemporary Theatre Review* 20, no. 4 (November 2010): 455–460.

Trueman, Matt. "'*Antigone*' Starring Juliette Binoche." Review of *Antigone*. *London Theater Review*, 6 March 2015.

Van den Berg, Simon. Review of *Antigone*. "De archieven van de smart." *Theaterkrant*, 11 March 2015.

Van der Kooi, Sarah. "Binoche niet scherp in ingetogen 'Antigone.'" Review of *Antigone*. *Trouw*, 17 April 2015.

Toneelgroep Amsterdam Website. (26 January 2007) Interview with Ivo van Hove about *Rouw siert Electra*. Website video.

Willinger, David. "Culture Clash: Some Notes on Flemish Theatre and its Critical Reception in New York City." *Contemporary Theatre Review* 20, no. 4 (November 2010): 461–464.

Wilmer, S. E. and Žukauskaitė, Audrone, eds. *Interrogating Antigone in Postmodern Philosophy and Criticism*. Oxford: Oxford University Press, 2010.

5

REALITY OVERTAKES MYTH: IVO VAN HOVE STAGES *DER RING DES NIBELUNGEN*

Francis Maes

During four successive seasons, from Spring 2006 to Fall of 2008, the Flemish Opera (known as the Opera Ballet Vlaanderen from 2014 onwards) entrusted a production of Wagner's *Ring des Nibelungen* to Ivo van Hove and his stage designer Jan Versweyveld, who were supported by the conductor Ivan Törzs. The Flemish Opera was a production organization that served two historical opera houses in the Flemish cities of Ghent and Antwerp. *Das Rheingold, Die Walküre*, and *Siegfried* were presented in Ghent, *Götterdämmerung* in Antwerp. Owing to urgently needed restoration works, the Antwerp Opera House was unavailable to host the entire cycle which proved unfortunate timing as it was admirably suited for Wagnerian performances. The Opera House, opened in 1907, had been deliberately conceived to meet the standards of Wagnerian music drama. At this time, the Flemish-speaking community of Antwerp aligned itself with Germanic culture in order to counter the dominant position of the French-language *Théâtre Royale Français* in their native city. As a result, Antwerp developed a veritable Wagner cult illustrated, for example, by the standing tradition of annual performances of *Parsifal* during Holy Week that were maintained with very few interruptions until 1993. The fact that the ambitious *Ring* cycle, which marked the centenary of Wagner performances in Antwerp, had to be partially diverted to the acoustically inferior Opera of Ghent was a serious setback.

Other strokes of bad luck affected the performances. Drastic budget cuts necessitated reducing the size of the orchestra to an absolute minimum; however, the most unfortunate development was that the production expired after its initial run largely due to the change of directorship of the Flemish Opera from Marc Clémeur to Aviel Cahn. The sets were dismantled.

Produced in yearly installments, though not as a unified production from the start, van Hove's *Ring* was never presented in the form of a veritable *Ring Cycle* spanning four successive days and, furthermore, was not permitted the time to grow organically: a prerequisite for every successful production of *The Ring*.

The production now exists only in memory and in the documentation of a video recording made by the Flemish Opera's technical services for archival purposes. Owing to these circumstances, it is no wonder that the van Hove *Ring* failed to leave its mark on the international operatic scene. However, there is every reason to treat it as one of the major *Ring* productions of the early twenty-first century. The international press coverage at the time leaves no doubt that the production was acknowledged as surprising and original by those who saw it. The impression of freshness, of constant discovery, was partly due to the fact that the production took an unusual amount of time to be developed. Van Hove has stated that he approached the *Ring* as four discrete operas, without the limitations of a rigorously preconceived concept for the whole. At the time of the *Rheingold* premiere, he declared:

> I approach each part on its own. Until now I have consciously kept *Götterdämmerung* in the background, although I know perfectly well what happens in it. But I did not want to allow myself to be overly influenced for *Das Rheingold* by how it ends. Wagner too prefers that we think in a linear fashion, because it's not until the fourth music drama that he gives everything away. I look at what the characters say and what drives them step-by-step.
>
> *(Playbill for* Das Rheingold *2006)*

The chief surprise about this particular production of *The Ring* was that it was greeted with almost universal enthusiasm and approval. Critics expressed their astonishment that van Hove's projection of the contemporary world, including the imposition of computer technology, into Wagner's mythic universe matched so well with the content of Wagner's drama. The most salient feature of van Hove's interpretation was its focus on the challenges engendered by contemporary computer technology and new media itself. The press reactions were mostly unanimous that "it all worked out well":

> Taken as a whole, the performance seems to work rather well. Images and text have achieved a complete unity.
>
> *(Jansen 2006)*

And:

> However uncanny and sober the atmosphere may be, the concept sticks. *The Ring's* start at the Vlaamse Opera is a brilliantly planned struggle for the power of the Media and the manipulation of knowledge.
>
> *(Fiedler 2006)*

Modern technology takes hold of Wagner's *Ring des Nibelungen* worldwide. The interest in van Hove's approach lies in how it integrates technology into the story as told. In most productions, computer technology is used as an instrument to create the theatrical illusion Wagner may have dreamt of, but could never achieve with the mechanical means of his day. This reasoning undergirds The Metropolitan Opera's *Ring* production directed by Robert Lepage. The technological means and know-how of the contemporary audiovisual industry are called into service for the realization of—as the title of the documentary film about the Lepage production calls it—*Wagner's dream* (Eisenhardt and Froemke 2012). The result is a theatrical experience that aligns the universe of the fantasy film industry with the high art aspirations of opera. Still, the imagery that results from the match doesn't stray far from Wagner's own mode of representation.

Although van Hove's *Ring* isn't in the same league as the Met's in terms of budget, audience attendance, or the longevity of the production, it has other things to recommend it such as the rapprochement between modern technology and Wagner's mythological imagination. In dealing with the technological world of today, van Hove goes straight to the heart of the matter in his representation of a contemporary world on stage. Laptops, computer screens, and media networks are completely at home in the world represented. In *Das Rheingold*, van Hove turns the mysterious ring that gives the cycle its name into a computer chip that controls a worldwide information network. The implication of this interpretative choice is clear from the start: gaining control over information systems equals power. The reactions from the international press and audiences alike indicated that Wagner's drama seemingly failed to offer the resistance such a radical reading might have led one to expect:

> Despite some of these oddities. . .it works. Why not possession of an all-powerful computer chip as a metaphor for world control? Certainly, at this performance (June 30), the idea seemed much less risible and far-fetched than a number of other modern takes on *The Ring*.
>
> *(MacCann 2006)*

And:

> You have to go a long way (not bothering to stop off in Bavaria en route) to encounter a more confident, audaciously original, more convincingly contemporary start to a *Ring* cycle than that launched by the Vlaamse Opera in Ghent this summer.
>
> *(Ward 2006)*

Finally:

> With this cogent *Walküre*, the Flemish National Opera's *Ring* cycle is well on its way. The Belgian theatre director Ivo van Hove is not the first person to bring a 21st-century vision with a twist of science fiction to Wagner's tetralogy, but his looks refreshingly new and beautifully thought through.
>
> *(Apthorp 2007)*

Especially for the younger segment of the audience, van Hove's contemporary take on the *Ring* appeared instantly recognizable. Indeed, his innovations facilitated their first encounter with Wagner's work. Many of the younger generation were discovering the *Ring* for the first time, without any grounds for comparison through Wagner's vast reception history. A representation of a world dominated by modern information technology was not only familiar in its own right, but combining it with Wagner's antiquated dramatic text caused no problem either. It made sense.

> Back in our country, these things would be booed off the stage before you could bat an eye by shocked Wagnerians of the old school. The audience of the Flemish Opera may be counted among the youngest in the world (with an average age of 35 to 40 years old) and looks with sympathy on how the director Ivo van Hove tells the story of Alberich, who steals the memory stick from the three ladies (in common language: Rhine Maidens) in the computer center.
>
> *(Goertz 2006)*

And:

> No matter that worshipful Wagnerians are not who's filling the orchestra and balconies in Ghent, the attention and excitement with which the uncommon performance on stage is received is remarkable nonetheless.
>
> *(Stuke undated)*

Perspectives on *The Ring*

Considering the richness of its contents, *Der Ring des Nibelungen* offers the stage director a number of lines of interpretation. All these approaches, however, can be reduced to two main possible perspectives. On the one hand, *The Ring Cycle* may be read as a family history, telling the story of successive generations: the marital tensions between Wotan and Fricka on the one hand, and the fate of Wotan's children on the other: Brünnhilde, daughter of Wotan and the goddess Erda, and Siegmund and Sieglinde, a pair of twins fathered by Wotan with an earthly woman. Siegmund and Sieglinde have a son, Siegfried, who represents the next generation. Wotan's craving for power leads to the destruction of the family. This dramatic line reveals that Wagner's inspiration originated in the *Oresteia Trilogy* by Aeschylus.[1] Both story lines possess striking parallels. In both cycles, the plot is set in motion by the conflict between a father/husband/king with his wife over his plan to sacrifice a young girl to his ambitions. In *Agamemnon*, the victim is Agamemnon and Clytemnestra's daughter Iphigeneia; in *Das Rheingold*, Freia, the sister of Wotan's wife Fricka. The ambition of the father/husband/king brings the entire family to ruin, with partial redemption at the end. In *The Eumenides,* the goddess Athena and the laws of Athens save Orestes and bring the family curse to a resolution. In Wagner's concept, Brünnhilde turns the death of all into an act of redemption of a more spiritual kind.

On the other hand, *Der Ring des Nibelungen* could also be approached as a metaphor for the history of the world. As Wagner's protagonists are gods, they may represent natural forces. In a mythic sense, their actions mark the history of the earth itself, from creation—magnificently invoked in the famous prelude to *Das Rheingold*—over the tensions between the earth's inhabitants, through to its apocalyptic end. The imagery of The Metropolitan Opera's production, directed by Robert Lepage, references the shifting tectonic plates and volcanic landscapes of Iceland with precisely this in mind.[2] The imagery links the story of the gods with natural forces and the movements of the earth. For the same reason, Wagner himself chose to set the drama in an Alpine setting, indicating both its transcendence of any historical locale and its mythical connection with natural forces.[3] The history of the human species is also present in Wagner's story, with its references to primeval innocence, the birth of sedentary life, the need for law and order, the emergence of the social contract to ensure the workings of society, the advent of capitalism, and the development of modern concepts of human freedom as a substitute for traditional religious beliefs.

What makes Wagner's cycle both compelling and difficult to stage are the ingenious ways in which both perspectives are intertwined. As is well known from musical analysis, the intersection between both perspectives is brought about mainly through the music. Wagner starts his drama with musical themes—the famous leitmotifs—that operate on a local level at first, but combine and develop gradually toward the end into a vast musical narrative that brings the drama to its transcendent resolution. At the end, music takes over from *logos*. Wagner chose not to set the final lines with which he ended the drama as a literary text, but transformed their Schopenhauer-derived sense directly into the realm of the inexpressible through the music. At the time when he composed the last act of *Götterdämmerung,* Wagner was immersed enough in Schopenhauer's musical metaphysics to give precedence to music over visual imagery as a means to reveal the metaphysical will that governs all existence.

The peculiar relationship between both perspectives gives stage directors cause enough for concern. Ivo van Hove solved the problem by cutting the Gordian knot, so to speak, by focusing entirely on the human side. The Gods and the Rhine Maidens are stripped of their mythological baggage and given recognizably human shapes. They are depicted as employees in an office. The gods are managers. The mythic fortress of Valhalla is a penthouse apartment. The Valkyries are nurses working in an emergency unit.

Das Rheingold begins in a realistic human environment. The realism set forth in the *Rheingold* prelude is maintained right through to the end of *Götterdämmerung* (see Figure 5.1). Instead of representing the ending as apocalyptic, van Hove's final image focuses on the human reactions to catastrophe. He noted that his ending reminded him of the images of people pulling themselves together after the destruction wrought by Hurricane Katrina in New Orleans in 2005. People gather, find each other, and search for ways to start over. Van Hove has turned the ending of the *Ring* into a paean to human resilience.

Ivo van Hove achieves the intertwining of the protagonist's family history and a narrative about the world-at-large through two interpretative decisions. Wotan's ambition, rivaled by the Nibelung Alberich, is world domination. The idea of global rule could be conveyed by two developments in the contemporary world: globalization and information technology.

FIGURE 5.1 *Götterdämmerung*

© Jan Versweyveld

Van Hove's reworking of the *Ring* is to a large extent a study of the theme of globalization. The director stated that he did not want to see the challenges of globalization in pessimistic terms: "It's not my intention to direct a *Ring* with a genesis leading to a vision of the future. The future no longer exists. Everything is there. In many places of the world. I want to think positively about globalization (Playbill for *Das Rheingold* 2006)." In van Hove's approach, *The Ring* may deal with the challenges and the dangers of the contemporary globalized world, but should not necessarily amount to a vision of doom:

> I have no interest in producing a *Ring* based on cultural pessimism. *Götterdämmerung* and the sacrifice of Brünnhilde may also be seen from a positive angle. Certainly not, as I see it, as a return to a primeval condition. We should ask ourselves whether it would indeed be such a good thing if nature ruled entirely. Extremists today often base their beliefs on an ideology of nature. Wotan, however, possesses an ideal of progress. He isn't drunk with power, because he uses power for creative purposes. I'm trying to make a *Ring* in which people endeavor to create an image of the future in a visionary way. Of course, it won't be a Hollywood vision with a happy ending. What matters most is the idea of the city: how can we all move forward together, and create coherence in a fragmented world?
>
> *(Playbill for* Das Rheingold *2006)*

Wotan's dream of a coherent world is projected onto the image of the city. Globalized culture is dominated by the contemporary mega-cities spread across the continents, from New York to Singapore. In *Das Rheingold*, the city is depicted with Wotan and Fricka's

FIGURE 5.2   *Das Rheingold*

© Jan Versweyveld

penthouse apartment as the center from which Wotan intends to rule the world (see Figure 5.2). In *Die Walküre*, the scene changes to the underground; the drug and criminal gangs that destroy the city from within. The famous scene with the Valkyries shows an urban world in ruin. Wotan's dream has failed. Above, young Siegfried's actions in *Siegfried* amount to a terrorist attack on Fafner's mansion.

Globalization also means technology, which transcends boundaries and has the ability to unify the world. The transformations caused by the contemporary technological environment are so far-reaching as to make all previous conceptions of world history and projections of its future seem obsolete. As technology surrounds and shapes every aspect of our lives, this transformation takes us practically unawares. The focus of this *Ring*, therefore, is to raise consciousness of the nature of and challenges facing our contemporary existence. In this context, the mythological foundation of Wagner's work may accrue new meaning. In his 1964 prophetic study, *Understanding Media*, Marshall McLuhan summed up our lack of awareness of technological innovation in these terms:

> In the mechanical age now receding, many actions could be taken without too much concern. Slow movement insured that the reactions were delayed for considerable periods of time. Today the action and the reaction occur almost at the same time. We actually live mythically and integrally, as it were, but we continue to think in the old, fragmented space and time patterns of the pre-electric age.
>
> *(McLuhan 1964: 4)*

However paradoxical it may sound, Wagner's nineteenth-century text may help to bring about that new awareness, precisely because the mythological theme dramatizes the extension of consciousness over the limits of space and time. The idea that technology makes us return to a "mythic" way of living—as opposed to the slow patterns of the mechanical age to which humanity has been accustomed for millennia—is a compelling entry point for analysis of a production in which technology replaces, and supersedes, myth.

When magic becomes technology

Richard Wagner based his dramatic vision on an abundance of fantasy and make-believe. A giant transforms into a dragon. Sipping from the same dragon's blood makes you understand the language of birds. The taste of the blood may even allow you to hear the villainous intent behind your adversary's words. As for Wotan outsmarting Alberich in *Das Rheingold*, the story of an apparently invincible sorcerer who is defeated by the cunning of his adversary who challenges him to change into a toad, it is a fairy tale classic. The invincible sword that awaits the divinely appointed hero who proves himself worthy of its power is a story line the *Ring* shares with Arthurian legends, among others. Armed goddesses fly through the sky on wild horses in many a mythological universe.

In *The Ring*, magical devices account for some of the least plausible plot turns. Mime's *Tarnhelm* and Gutrune's potion of oblivion steer the plot in directions that would be impossible in realistic drama. Gutrune's potion shares with Isolde's love potion the capacity to radically alter the destiny of the protagonists.

Standard Wagnerian interpretation holds that all these divine powers and magical devices are superfluous to the meaning of the stories that Wagner's music dramas develop. In most commentaries, they are hardly mentioned at all. A classical study like Simon Williams's *Wagner and the Romantic Hero* mentions the *Tarnhelm*, or the potion of oblivion, only in passing. In and of itself, the drink seems to have no impact:

> This (the drink of forgetfulness) does nothing more than indicate Siegfried's present state of mind when he meets Gutrune. His surrender to her charms displays an inner lack of resilience and shows him an instant victim of society rather than a hero who will transform it.
>
> *(Williams 2004: 95)*

The meaning of these magical devices is usually situated in the inner beings of the characters. John Daverio's assessment that we should give the magical element in the plot of *Tristan and Isolde* its due is rather the exception than the rule. He comments on the uncomfortable stance of many commentators regarding magical devices such as the love potion:

> The significance of the love potion is frequently downplayed. . . what the lovers happen to think as they consume the potion is immaterial compared to what they feel under its influence. . . Far from emerging from a process of rational thought, the lovers' latent ardor rises to consciousness as a result of a process over which they have no control—a process at least closely akin to magic.
>
> *(Daverio 2008: 123)*

Stage directors struggle even more with these magical devices than critics do. It is up to them, after all, to make their effects convincing. They therefore prefer to work out solutions that are based more on psychology than on magic. For his centenary *Ring* at Bayreuth in 1976, Patrice Chéreau explained Siegfried's downfall as a result of inner character flaws, not as the result of a magical trick:

> In Siegfried we find this capacity for forgetfulness. Out of the entire *Ring* he is the only hero who, intentionally or not, has no memory. He is neither the character out of Grimms' fable nor a revolutionary hero, but probably the two combined. (The truth was simpler, but I failed to see it: he is Wotan's right-hand man, from a dramatic point of view—the jack of all trades, the factotum.) The precursor of an instinctive fascism, a ludicrous figure, one ripe for forgetfulness, and therefore for multiple catastrophes.
>
> *(Boulez 1980: 101)*

The dramatic justification for the effect of Gutrune's potion of oblivion on Siegfried is a challenge. Its consequences for Siegfried's wooing of a disguised Brünnhilde on Gunther's behalf pushes every director to their limits. Both Pierre Audi and Willy Decker, in their respective Amsterdam and Dresden productions, brought the two characters of Siegfried and Gunther together on stage in their attempt to convince Brünnhilde of their deceit. Audi made the real Gunther lead the action, with Siegfried acting as a double, lending him only his voice. Decker made Siegfried perform the actual wooing, with Gunther peering over his shoulder, anxious that the trick might not work.[4]

The magical devices we find in ancient tales may be seen not only as psychological symbols: they could be considered the mythological forerunners of modern technology. Humans have always dreamt of extending the scope of their action outward toward domains that are physically out of reach. Modern technology makes this extension a reality. In the mechanical phase of its development, technology had already broadened the radius of human action. Contemporary information technology has gone much further, however. In its development "we approach the final phase of the extensions of man—the technological simulation of consciousness," were Marshall McLuhan's prophetic words, written in 1964, when the recent developments in computer science and I.T. had yet to emerge:

> After three thousand years of explosion, by means of fragmentary and mechanical technologies, the Western world is imploding. During the mechanical ages we had extended our bodies in space. Today, after more than a century of electric technology, we have extended our central nervous system itself in a global embrace, abolishing both space and time as far as our planet is concerned. Rapidly, we approach the final phase of the extensions of man—the technological simulation of consciousness, when the creative process of knowing will be collectively and corporately extended to the whole of human society.
>
> *(McLuhan 1964: 3)*

It is in this context of the contemporary technological world that van Hove chose to imagine the scenes of Siegfried's courtship of Gutrune and of Brünnhilde's wooing by the disguised Siegfried.

He tells the story in the following way: Siegfried approaches the court of the Gibichungs. Hagen recounts his exploits to Gunther and Gutrune, while they Google the hero and check his heroical deeds. When Siegfried arrives, Gutrune welcomes him not with a drink, but with a laptop. Siegfried enters the program of *Second Life* and starts a virtual flirtation with the image of Gutrune.

Second Life becomes the modern technological equivalent of the magical devices of the potion of oblivion and the *Tarnhelm* combined. At first sight, the equation may seem far-fetched, but on second thought it is plausible enough. What the combination of the potion of oblivion with the *Tarnhelm* brings about in the original comes down to a confusion of identities. Siegfried distances himself from his former self. Confusion of identity may be a result of the immersion in virtual reality, where one can assume different identities, and where common notions of identity and individuality may become uncertain and to a certain extent flexible. Through the use of virtual reality, we are offered the possibility of escaping from our normal selves and acting as if we were someone else. New ethical problems about individual responsibility arise when the self is capable of being divided into disparate identities. Van Hove's interpretative decision gives realistic credibility to a plot turn that would otherwise be unjustifiable on realistic grounds.

Technology may have a confusing effect on notions of the self. Technology may also be manipulated by those who strive for power over other peoples' lives. When Hagen remains alone on stage, singing that he'll be there to guard the castle, he takes the laptops, kisses them, and demonstrates through sardonic laughter that he is using the effects of technology for his diabolic plan. The encounter between Siegfried and Brünnhilde continues the same logic of virtual role-playing. Siegfried and Brünnhilde's love scene at the beginning of the first act of *Götterdämmerung* has been set in a closed space, which suggests the exclusion of surrounding society from their relationship. Wagner's idea that sexual love could supersede the power system of the gods and renew the world is suggested by a fleeting reference to John Lennon and Yoko Ono's hotel act, hinting at the naive optimistic belief popular in the 1960s in the redemptive force of sexuality. When Siegfried approaches Brünnhilde in the guise of Gunther, he drags her into the virtual universe he came to inhabit upon his arrival at the Gibichung court. By a simple push of a button, he makes the closed walls of their former love nest rise up to disclose the computer screens that are omnipresent in the Gibichung environment.

Narrated in this way, the director's decision to transmogrify the inexplicable story line of magic potions—a transformative helmet and a treacherous exchange of appearances—into the realism of the modern technological age may at first glance seem merely to be a clever director's trick way of finding a solution for a notoriously difficult knot in any production of the *Ring*. However, *Second Life* is the perfect illustration of the far-reaching effect that technology may have on formerly accepted notions of human individuality and identity. It is an idea that is justifiably linked to the content of Wagner's *Ring* because confusion of identity is a recurring theme: ranging from Siegmund's uncertainty about his real name, to Siegfried forgetting his love for Brünnhilde, and to Erda and Wotan's mutual denials of the other's identity, both reproaching the other for not being who they think they are.[5] Modern I.T. has brought such problems of identity confusion center stage. Technology offers possibilities of extending one's sense of self, living more lives than one, and crossing the borderline between the self and the virtual. Identity is no longer confined to a unified set of character features, motivations, and actions, as it has discovered a means to enlarge one's experience and divert responsibility for one's actions.

The computer technology referred to in the Gibichung scene in *Götterdämmerung* would not however be convincing were it not integrated into a larger, coherent interpretative system. In Wagner's concept, Siegfried's betrayal of Brünnhilde is a repeat of the fatal exchange of love for power, initiated in the *Ring Cycle* by Alberich's theft of the Rhine gold, but going back in time as far as Wotan's mutilation of the World Tree. In van Hove's production, Alberich's action is not the theft of mysterious gold, but of a computer chip. The Rhine Maidens are employees in an office that guards a powerful central computer that controls a worldwide information network. Knowing that no creature would ever exchange love for the possession of the central chip, they tempt Alberich with erotic computer images. Alberich becomes obsessed with the girls. In revenge for his unsuccessful attempts to seduce them, Alberich steals the central chip. The system then disconnects, and all data is deleted.

The decision to turn *The Ring* into a technological device is the starting point of the I.T. reading of the whole. It has the benefit of turning the elusive power of the Ring into a concrete effect. In the original story, one may argue, the object does not possess intrinsic power. It stands apart from the magical devices discussed above. The dreadful effects the Ring generates are due to the convictions that the characters have about its powers. What causes disaster is what the Ring stands for: the exchange of love for power. The towering tragic moment of the entire cycle, arguably, is the segment in which the Ring is almost once more turned into a simple token of love. Brünnhilde refuses Waltraute's request to give the Ring back to the Rhine, and in doing so to save the entire global power system. She refuses because the Ring represents what is most dear to her: Siegfried's love. This instance, in which Brünnhilde intuitively knows that love should transcend all political agendas, makes Siegfried's betrayal all the more tragic. The drama has reached its point of no return.

In van Hove's reading, Alberich's action joins the betrayal of love for power to the control over globalized information networks. By stealing the computer chip that governs the world's information system, Alberich makes a claim on global rule. His action is a serious threat to Wotan's attempt to rule the world from Valhalla, the global city controlled by information technology. Alberich's theft of the crucial chip causes Wotan to lose control. It becomes imperative for him to neutralize Alberich's technological dominance.

Once the mythological trappings have been turned into technological realities, the humanization of Wagner's characters could proceed further than in productions that preserve the mythological framework. I.T. provides almost everything that has ever been dreamt of in the mythologies of the world. The command over time and space offered by modern technology leaves mythic powers far behind. Time and space have been brought within human reach, to a degree that no mythology could equal. In this sense, van Hove could take Fricka's argument for Wotan's construction of Valhalla quite literally. She wanted a place where Wotan could remain at home, while maintaining his dominance over the world regardless. Modern technology makes it literally possible to know or even to rule the world from one's home.

In Wagner's concept, Alberich's gold treasure represented capitalistic exploitation of the masses. The possession of technology goes further than the command of the economic means of production. A single person may cause serious damage. That is how Siegfried is worked out. He stands for the unscrupulous young gamer, in full command of the latest computer technology, but devoid of any moral compass.

In van Hove's version of the story, young Siegfried turns the computer chip *Nothung* into a formidable weapon of mass destruction. Fafner is no dragon in van Hove's world, but a normal man. Siegfried destroys his villa. He encounters Brünnhilde, and discovers his manhood amidst the remnants of Fafner's world in ruins. Siegfried is a young computer nerd. His obsession results in an egotism that blinds him to the outside world. When such a character isn't kept within bounds by social forces or by moral priorities, the solipsistic gamer may lose all perspective and turn into a potential terrorist.

Van Hove isn't the first to be suspicious of the childlike naiveté of Wagner's hero. Patrice Chéreau did likewise in his suggestion of an anti-Semitic background to the relationship between Siegfried and Mime and in his mistrust of Siegfried's lack of memory. Van Hove's Siegfried drives the point to its radical conclusion. Siegfried is dangerous because he combines the most powerful of all weapons with a complete lack of knowledge, morals, and normal family bonds; while his first target in life—the murder of Fafner—isn't even his own idea. Someone else had breathed it into him, as Fafner knows.

The relationship between van Hove's interpretation and Wagner's original text can be challenged on several counts. To what extent does this production change Wagner's text? This question could be addressed in two different ways: what is the relationship between conceptual freedom and literalism, and how does the new context influence the way the music is perceived?

Freedom and literalism

Replacing mythology with I.T. enabled a fair amount of literalism in the reading of the text. Some lines from the text can literally be turned into stage action: for instance, the Norns calling each other to throw the rope—"*werfe das Seil.*" They do so in this production, not with mythological threads, however, but with computer wires. It is precisely this sort of literalism that makes the production work. The many screens in *Das Rheingold* project images that are directly related to the text. When Donner produces a lightning bolt, the effect is shown on a computer screen. The watery appearance of the original Rhine Maidens is present in the production through images of swimming women on screen as part of the computer games that the office Rhine Maidens play. When Wotan puts Brünnhilde to sleep, he induces her artificial coma with the use of advanced equipment and the help of an anesthesiologist.

This experimentation with literalism may yield surprising results. The representation of the *Ride of the Valkyries* is an example of how literalism may create unexpected surrealism. Van Hove reads the *Ride of the Valkyries* literally on two levels. The first level is the work the Valkyries

FIGURE 5.3 *Die Walküre*

© Jan Versweyveld

perform. Wagner's mythological Valkyries collect fallen heroes on the battlefield and bring them to their afterlife in the service of the gods. Van Hove's Valkyries do exactly the same. Only, their fallen heroes are not dead and do not enter their afterlife. They are merely gravely wounded. The Valkyries nurse them in an emergency unit akin to the field hospitals that are set up after a natural or man-made disaster.

The second feature of the Valkyries is the fact that they are Amazons; combative women on horseback. Wagner's Valkyries are presumed to fly through the air. This aspect is not followed in van Hove's *Ring*, but is compensated for by a very literal representation of their equestrian skills. They are dressed as modern-day Amazons with leather trousers and boots, and they ride horses— real horses (see Figure 5.3). Gerhilde's call, *"hier met dem Ross"* (*"come here with your horse"*), is literally answered by the entrance of a Valkyrie on horseback. The poetic image of Amazons on beautiful white horses—living horses that convey an overwhelming sense of natural energy— contrasts with the prosaic work of the emergency nurses and surgeons. Like a head nurse, Gerhilde records the presence of the Valkyries in her register. The Valkyries are not only nurses in a recognizably realistic sense, but the poetic luxury of riding horses in an otherwise totally prosaic scene gives a special twist to their actions: it reflects the Valkyries' otherness, just as the original Valkyries' flight on horseback represents their divinity.

If such a cluster of unrelated visual images might seem out of keeping with Wagner's vision, a reading of the music suggests that it makes sense after all. The scene of the *Ride of the Valkyries* is bursting with life and energy, but functions in its entirety as a static tableau. The world-renowned music performs a double function, mimetic as well as symbolic. The mimetic is located in the rhythm of the gallop, which faithfully imitates the sound and rhythm of a galloping horse. This principal mimetic feature is complemented by the representation of the atmospheric context of the scene: a stormy night over the mountains, with clouds chasing across the sky. The stormy atmosphere is represented by the continuous figures of sixteenth notes in the strings. The music avoids strong tonal development. There are no modulations to the dominant, no strong closure. Harmonic variation is mainly restricted to transposition. The static nature of the musical construction indicates that the Valkyries all perform the same, prescribed deed. Their actions serve one overarching purpose.

A more subtle symbolic level is written into the rhythmic measure that the music employs. The dotted figure that represents the galloping is mimetic enough, but the measure of 9/8 that structures the rhythm according to a bar in triple time, transfigures realism to a poetic level. The ternary structure of the metric pulse lifts the music out of the representation of a real, earthly gallop, and transposes the scene to the clouds. These horses are free from the laws of gravity. The choice of meter stands for the divinity of the Valkyries, the otherness of these mythological creatures. In Wagner's text, divinity is further suggested through their unearthly laughter. The Valkyries perform their duty from a divine perspective and with complete emotional detachment. They look down at the earth and its inhabitants from on high.

In van Hove's representation, the meaning of the music becomes even more perceptible. The stormy music indicates a situation of upheaval and disaster. At the same time, the poetic beauty of the horses and the detachment of the nurses from the activities they perform, as well as the suffering of their patients, synchronizes with the otherness of the characters, as constructed in the music.

Music and the construction of meaning

The viability of a radical opera staging depends on the significance that the music may acquire in its new scenic context. In the pre-Wagnerian operatic system, music was intended to duplicate the gestural and emotional qualities of the scenic action. Mary Ann Smart justifiably calls it a system of overstatement. Music mimed the gestural qualities of behavior or actions performed on stage (Smart 2004: 1–29). The principle of synchronization of music and action reached its end by the *fin de siècle*. Wagner's professed ideal of an invisible theater contributed to the dissolution of the age-long unity between music and action. Smart has demonstrated, however, that Wagner's comment should not be taken at face value and that his own system of leitmotifs preserved many traces of the former mimetic definition of musical meaning. The system of leitmotifs in *The Ring* occupies an interesting middle ground between the mimetic representation of bodily action, and the abstraction of the mental concepts that guide the drama and its perception as a whole. A radical staging defies the expectations that have accreted through *The Ring's* reception history. Such a staging automatically directs the attention of the listeners to the immediate and immanent qualities of the leitmotifs, rather than to their presumed conceptual function. The fact that they remain meaningful in a radically realistic setting may be attributed to this middle ground they occupy between the poles of mimesis and abstraction.[6]

The preparatory work of van Hove's musical dramaturg, Piet De Volder, was marked by a dual approach. On the one hand, the leitmotifs and vocal idioms were subjected to a process of close reading. This stage of analysis is meant to reveal what is really there in musical terms, free from all associations. On the other hand, the dramaturgical research explored the range of symbolical possibilities contained in the musical material. It is noteworthy that this method of analysis endeavors to transcend all anecdotal significance. Instead, Piet De Volder argues that the leitmotifs stand for the fundamental tensions of the power play that are at stake on stage. Leitmotifs should be understood in the context of the larger framework of the drama as a whole.

> I had been specifically asked to make a personal characterization of the motifs in Ivo van Hove's production, and then to check my own findings against the extant literature. In this domain, as in others, close reading is a method that bears fruit. The way Von Wolzogen and others have labeled the motifs is an attempt to get a handle on one of the many relationships between libretto and music. The first commentators were often satisfied with the connection between a specific melodic gesture and a given element from the text. The question why the separate motifs have such specific musical profiles is all too seldom asked. What does the musical gesture tell us? What is the relationship between the motifs amongst themselves?
>
> (De Volder 2011: 64)

The analysis of the giants' leitmotif offers a good example. The motif has a marked mimetic quality. It quite graphically illustrates the heavy step of the giants. According to Piet De Volder:

> the so-called Giants-Motif is not so much 'power music.' In the musical context of *Das Rheingold*, the motif appears to tell us more about the threat to Wotan's power that has been tamed by contracts. It relates to the latent aggression that Wotan is attempting to get under control. That is why the music of the giants references elements of motifs that are linked to Wotan: the spear and Valhalla.
>
> (De Volder 2011: 64)

The motif of Fafner in *Siegfried* retains the heaviness of the original giants' motif, but also gains in metaphorical potential. The ponderousness of the dragon motif indicates that Fafner literally sleeps on his possessions. Piet De Volder links this characteristic of Fafner's music with the sociological concept of "heavy power." This concept stands for the characteristics of power at the beginning of the sedentary age in human history. Heavy power means that power was clearly localized, connected to a place. Heavy power may rule over a large territory, but its main target is to keep that domain under control. Heavy power can be symbolized in the images of a closed gate, a city wall, a watchtower. Contrary to the standard examples of heavy power, Fafner displays no ambition to increase his territory. His power serves only to protect the status quo. His transformation into a dragon symbolizes his defensive attitude, his ambition to prevent the world from entering his realm.

Fafner is confident in his power because he's incapable of imagining any other way in which power could be used. His adversary thinks along different lines. Siegfried's ignorance has already been recognized in critical commentaries. His portrait in the first and second acts of *Siegfried* is very much tailored to Rousseau's ideal of "natural man." Siegfried is "bound by nothing; he has neither knowledge of the past nor fear of the future" (Williams 2004: 95). In sociological terms, Siegfried incarnates the principle of "light power" (De Volder 2011; Weyns 2006).

This kind of power is not bound by territory and doesn't operate from a center. It may be everywhere. Light power operates out of sight. There is no long-term planning involved. Light power acts as an instant operator. Its energies are musically symbolized in Siegfried's horn calls, with which he wakens Fafner to do battle with him, "old–style ruler versus gamer":

> In considering the confrontation between Siegfried and Fafner we notice that the most interesting aspect is not the battle in itself, but the last words of the dying giant, those with which he desires to open Siegfried's eyes. Fafner suspects Siegfried of being a hired assassin. Others are pulling the strings. In his death–struggle, he sounds surprisingly human, but his warnings to Siegfried are to no avail. Fafner's message could be summed up as: 'Welcome to a world of hatred and calculation.' But Siegfried is only interested in knowing more about himself. Nonetheless, the slaying of Fafner offers him an entry code into the world Fafner was invoking. Only now is he capable of grasping the essential information the Forest Bird extends to him.
>
> *(De Volder 2011: 64)*

The reason why Siegfried is able to kill Fafner lies not in his heroic strength, but in his lack of fear. In this new context, Siegfried's lack of fear is read as a manifestation of light power: the ability to be everywhere at the same time, to be invisible, to act on immediate impulse. Siegfried has no plan. Light power has no project. In this way, the contrast between the robust gravity of the Fafner motif and the energy of Siegfried's horn call serves as a musical metaphor for opposing principles.

Does it work on stage? The leitmotif of the giants in *Das Rheingold* does not duplicate the heavy step of giants. The characters of Fasolt and Fafner are represented as anything but grave. Indeed, they look quite ordinary. They behave just like ordinary modern businessmen. They shake hands with the gods in a merely correct, reserved but polite way. What the music conveys to the spectator, however, is an indication of the gravity of the situation. The moment has tremendous significance. The consequences of Wotan's treaty with the designers of his global city will be far-reaching, which is what the music adds to the scene. The music indicates that these businessmen are agents to be reckoned with, no matter whether their physical steps are heavy or not.

Fafner's power is visually located in his imposing villa. There is no need for a dragon. Siegfried's power is concentrated in an electronic chip he has planted into the skin of his hand. Even when he finds himself in front of Fafner's house, he continues to play computer games, surrounded by the music of the Forest Murmurs. His attempts to communicate with the birds are replaced by demonstrations of his computer skills to the members of a street gang. That is how he tries to communicate with them and how he gains their attention.

This *Ring* is set in a thoroughly urban environment, which stands for the global process of urbanization the world is presently undergoing. The social and political problems that van Hove's staging represents are specifically issues of the typical global city's ecosystem such as criminality, poverty, anarchy, and terrorism. *Das Rheingold* represents Wotan's dream of a world city as a system of justice and order. But even from the first act of *Walküre*, it is clear that the city failed to fulfill its promises. It has degenerated into a place of destruction. The city has been taken over by rival gangs. Siegmund's problem is exclusion. He is represented as a fugitive, torn between rival criminal gangs, a victim of the oppressive powers of the impersonal city.

Natural imagery is most prominent in the music and the text of *Siegfried*. Wagner conceived this drama as being entirely set in nature, from a hiding place in the forest to the divine heights, the "*wonnige Höhn*" of an alpine mountain. In van Hove's setting, nature has vanished completely

FIGURE 5.4   *Siegfried*

© Jan Versweyveld

from *Siegfried*. The bear he captured to terrify Mime is a computer game with which he assails Mime's efforts. In the scene of the Forest Murmurs, the birds are represented as members of a street gang. Siegfried's horn call is turned into a demonstration on his laptop. It elicits enough curiosity for the gang members to edge closer. They are interested in his technology. The vatic bird that instructs Siegfried after his fight with the dragon is a member of the same street gang (see Figure 5.4). The forest bird doesn't gain knowledge as a result of divine wisdom, but of direct experience. Street gangs are literally the eyes and ears of the urban jungle. They are ubiquitous and have seen and know all.

Wagner's *Tetralogy* begins, most famously, with nature imagery: pastoral horn calls over a pedal and tone painting that suggests the movements of the Rhine. The association with nature derives from a cluster of signifiers: the *creatio ex nihilo*, the natural scale, the acoustic phenomenon, the horn calls over a bourdon bass, the mimesis of the movement of the waves, and the pastoral theme of the *Weia* singing accompanied by *siciliano* touches.

In van Hove's staging, the first scene was crucial in establishing the codes with which the production should be seen and heard. Van Hove has the habit of enlivening visual tableaus with surface action. He usually augments the number of acting personae beyond those that do the actual singing. In this way, the storm music at the beginning of *Walküre* is worked out as the chaotic action of a violent underground gang. The mimetic function of the music is maintained, but the source of the violent motion is located elsewhere rather than in depersonalized nature.

The Rhine Maidens' scene at the beginning of *Das Rheingold* is represented by an office with a group of young female employees. They exercise a strong erotic attraction on Alberich. On first impression, the *Rheingold* prelude does not conform to this stage image, except for the idea of daybreak and a world that is coming to life. But there is more to it. The first visual image is an empty, dark office, with light concentrated in two video screens and in the computer unit that contains the central chip. The screens are usually blank, but on one of them we see a woman swimming underwater. The stage image defines the code by which the music instills meaning for the rest of the cycle. The swimming woman refers to the literal level of the story; the blank screens, and the computer lights to the signifying and fundamental source of the universe we are about to enter. This introduction makes it clear that the representation will oscillate between a literal reading and a specific definition of the worldview in which the drama will unfold. This worldview is dominated by the extended consciousness of modern information technology. Even at this point, the message is that the meaning of the music will act as a metaphor for the extended consciousness humanity established at the threshold of the twenty-first century.

Alberich is discovered on stage from the very start of the performance. He is interested in the computer technology and has a look around before the girls enter the office. The music of the *Rheingold* prelude defines the central computer as the seat of mystery; as the secret reality behind the world of appearances. The music loses meaningfulness as a symbol of nature. Alberich's action will be about the discovery and the usurpation of that mystery.

Where does this network come from? It could not have been the work of the gods. In Wagner's vision, the gods did not possess the gold before Alberich's action made them aware of its existence. The Rhine gold represents a primeval level of being. So what is the computer in van Hove's universe? It is a system of world control, but still untouched by the ambition for power. The music suggests as much through the pastoral codes in the singing of the Rhine Maidens.

When the Rhine Maidens come on stage, their actions underline the latent energy of the music. They play computer games. Images of car races and combat games visualize the energy of the figuration of the strings. When they explain to Alberich what the gold represents, the tranquility of the music is matched on stage by a stop to the nervous action. The meaning of their words is clarified on screen. News flashes from all over the globe indicate that the Rhine gold contains all information from all over the world. The pastoral *topos* of the singing, marked by the *siciliano* rhythm in which the girls sing their hymn to the Rhine gold, defines the Rhine gold computer system as the representation of a global status quo.

Later in *Das Rheingold*, the Rhine Maidens' music acquires a nostalgic connotation. Their voices are heard before the gods enter Valhalla. In this staging, they sing their pastoral hymn on stage, in the glass penthouse where Wotan and Fricka intend to set up housekeeping. The intimate setting enhances the nostalgic nature of the song. The Rhine Maidens are accompanied by diegetic harp playing on stage. It is this image of domestic music-making that gives their song its expressive quality of deep longing.

There are a few instances in the story to which van Hove's interpretative system has no answer relative to the mythological trappings of the text. One component of myth has no counterpart in modern technology: eternal life, represented in the story by the plotline around Freia. As goddess of love and fertility, Freia brings eternal youth to the gods. The director leaves this plotline undeveloped. Her divine power, however, is essential to an understanding of the hidden agenda behind the giants' request for Freia as payment for their work. Fasolt knows that she contains the secret of the longevity of the gods. To deprive them of Freia would turn them into vulnerable mortals. The moment when the gods seem to age, after the departure of Freia with the giants, is a blind spot in the production. The only visual clue van Hove can offer is a print of an apple issued from a large data printer. This blind spot has no consequences, however, as Wagner didn't develop the idea about the connection between longevity and Freia's apples any further either. Wotan immediately regains his energy to act. For the rest of *Das Rheingold*, the immortality of the gods is no longer an issue. This is probably the most far-reaching consequence of Ivo van Hove's interpretative strategy: by rendering the magical devices and mythological dimension as realistic, he was able to humanize the drama to an unprecedented degree.

After the catastrophe that brings the story to a close in *Götterdämmerung*, human life goes on. Van Hove employed news images of people gathering after the disaster of Hurricane Katrina as his reference for the closing scene. The computer screens indicate a new beginning by displaying a neutral test screen. The information network can be refigured. People gather around a tree to recover a sense of solidarity and endurance. The tree stands for nature, but not in the sense of an abstract force. In this final image, it is not nature that regains its force for renewal, but humans who discover in themselves a sense of endurance and solidarity. The closing tableau represents an attempt to humanize the most intangible moment in the entire work. In Wagner's vision, continuity of existence is only conceivable if the world returns to its natural state, which means that the world of appearances disappears and reveals the *noumenal* essence of existence. In van Hove's worldview, the continuity of life resides in the human sense for survival and adaptation. The mythic concept of love, which is regained at the end, distills to a propensity of humanity restored to its fundamental longing for atonement.

Two systems of hi-tech

Van Hove's universe works in tandem with Wagner's mythic drama, and both the press and audiences agreed. A possible explanation for the success of the match may be sought in the nature of Wagner's drama in itself. Wagner's *Tetralogy* is the product of an age of profound tumult. The storyline around Alberich hints at the then contemporary challenges of capitalist power, industrialization, and the exploitation of the working class. In her study on *The Persistence of Allegory*, Jane K. Brown has succinctly explained the special status of Wagner's *Ring* as the last stage in the history of allegorical drama, while demonstrating its demise. Allegory is a mode of representation that employs theatrical means to visualize what is invisible. In the Christian tradition, this invisible dimension was understood as the divine realm behind the world of appearances. Allegory needs a fixed cosmos in order to operate. Wagner retains many features of the allegorical mode while alluding to a cosmos that is no longer there. The haunting scene of the Norns at the beginning of *Götterdämmerung* is highly symbolic of the disappearance of an ordered universe that may justify existence. The system of meaning that ordered the universe in the divine perspective of the gods dissolves.

The invisible world that allegory should reveal becomes a fleeting one in Wagner's *Ring*. It is impossible to grasp intellectually. Its representation is no longer entrusted to *logos* but to music. According to Jane K. Brown, Wagner's attempt at allegorical theatre revealed its impossibility in the second half of the nineteenth century:

> The same stage practices continued, the same conventions continued to shape plots, but the kind of perspicuous dramatic allegory that really drove the development of Gesamtkunstwerk was no longer viable. Although the term became current in the wake of Wagner, he did not achieve it; instead, he revealed its impossibility. Music, dance, spectacle, and spoken drama were all integrated over the centuries in the service of a particular cultural structure that no longer prevailed in the mid-nineteenth century.
>
> *(Brown 2007: 230)*

Psychology replaced cosmology. That is what *Der Ring des Nibelungen* reveals, according to Brown. Ivo van Hove's production drives the point home in its radical humanization of the *Ring*'s characters and intrigues. His representation follows the laws of mimetic theatre—of Aristotelian as opposed to allegorical theater in Brown's dichotomy—and almost completely obliterates any metaphysical perspective. The metaphysical is replaced by the extension of consciousness epitomized by the information technology of the twenty-first century.

To realize his vision, Wagner employed the entire hi-tech apparatus available in his own time. Van Hove's production shows the hi-tech of the contemporary world on stage. The tension between the two systems adds a special poignancy to the experience. On stage, the hi-tech that surrounds us in real life is on display. In the pit, the live playing of Wagner's large orchestra represents the hi-tech of the nineteenth century. Wagner's enlarged orchestra represents the highest stage in the development and organization of music making in the ultimate phase of the mechanical age. Sound had to be made on acoustic instruments through live playing. Variation in tone color, volume, and density of texture could only be realized with the employment of some hundred live musicians, working together in strict discipline. Instruments were still conceived as extensions of the body, music as the result of corporal movement and energy.

In the experience of opera audiences, live orchestral playing is the norm, and therefore not surprising as such. The operatic system keeps the historical tradition of live musicianship and acoustic singing intact, whatever may happen on stage. In the world at large, however, manual music making is no longer the norm. The technological world represented on stage indicates that a sonorous world of comparable or even greater complexity may now be realized by a push of a button. The experience in the opera house demonstrates where we come from, and where we are, simultaneously. This *Ring des Nibelungen* reveals the transitional nature of Wagner's text, as a body of words and music that captures some of the dynamic perspectives that continue to shape our contemporary hold on the world.

Notes

1 "There was nothing to equal the exalted emotion evoked in me by *Agamemnon*; and to the close of *The Eumenides* I remained in a state of transport from which I have never really returned to become fully reconciled with modern literature." Wagner's reaction in *Mein Leben* on his study of the *Oresteia* in the translation and highly political interpretation of Johann Gustav Droysen is recorded and discussed in: Daniel H. Foster. *Wagner's Ring Cycle and the Greeks*. Cambridge: Cambridge University Press, 2010: 285–286.

2 Excerpt of interview with Robert Lepage:

> Eighty-five percent of the *Ring* is directly from the Eddas, and I became completely fascinated by that. If you want to do a fresh new *Ring* in this day and age, you have to go back to the very roots of it. I found this wealth of information just by digging into the Islandic myths. The inspiration for the set, for example, is the idea of tectonics. The reason why this story was developed out of Iceland is because it's a place that moves all the time. You see things that you can only see then in the *Ring*. You see these big glaciers and suddenly there is a crack and this lava coming out of the ice. It is the gods expressing themselves.
>
> *(Eisenhardt and Froemke 2012)*

3 See the chapter "The Search for a Visual World for the *Ring*," in Patrick Carnegy. *Wagner and the Art of the Theatre: The Operas in Stage Performance*. New Haven: Yale University Press, 2006: 76–81.

4 For an account of the genesis of both approaches by the dramaturg of both productions, see: Klaus Bertisch, "Wagner in tweevoud: hoe dramaturgie kan leiden tot verschillende theatrale visies," in: Francis Maes and Piet De Volder. *Opera: achter de schermen van de emotie*. Leuven: Lannoo Campus, 2011: 87–91.

5   The point is made, with a focus on the inherent untruthfulness of language and the instability of identity, in: Jane K. Brown. *The Persistence of Allegory: Drama and Neoclassicism from Shakespeare to Wagner*. Philadelphia: University of Pennsylvania Press, 2007: 226–228.
6   On the mimetic (i.e. gestural) basis of Wagner's leitmotifs, as applied to *Die Walküre,* see: Mary Ann Smart. *Mimomania: Music and Gesture in Nineteenth-Century Opera*. Berkeley: University of California Press, 2004: 171–189.

Reference list

Apthorp, Shirley. Review of van Hove's *Das Rheingold. The Financial Times*, 9 March 2007.

Bertisch, Klaus Bertisch. "Wagner in tweevoud: hoe dramaturgie kan leiden tot verschillende theatrale visies." In: *Opera: achter de schermen van de emotie*. Edited by Francis Maes and Piet De Volder. Leuven: Lannoo Campus, 2011.

Boulez, Pierre, *et al. Histoire d'un 'Ring': Der Ring des Nibelungen (L'Anneau du Nibelung) de Richard Wagner Bayreuth 1976–1980*. Paris: Robert Laffont, 1980.

Brown, Jane K. *The Persistence of Allegory: Drama and Neoclassicism from Shakespeare to Wagner*. Philadelphia: University of Pennsylvania Press, 2007.

Carnegy, Patrick. "The Search for a Visual World for the Ring." In: *Wagner and the Art of the Theatre: The Operas in Stage Performance*. New Haven: Yale University Press (2006): 76–91.

Daverio, John. "Tristan und Isolde: Essence and Appearance." In: *The Cambridge Companion to Wagner*. Edited by Thomas S. Grey. Cambridge: Cambridge University Press, 2008.

De Volder, Piet. "De witte raaf van de muziekdramaturgie: Der Ring des Nibelungen als case." In: *Opera: achter de schermen van de emotie*. Edited by Francis Maes and Piet De Volder. Leuven: Lannoo Campus, 2011.

Eisenhardt, Bob and Froemke, Susan. *Wagner's Dream: The Making of The Metropolitan Opera's New* Der Ring des Nibelungen. [film] Deutsche Grammophon, dvd 00440 073 4840 (2012).

Fiedler, M. Review of van Hove's *Das Rheingold. Das Opernglas* 9 (2006). Available at: http://archiv.opernglas. de/index.php?sid=1577178864864b226dbe11cd73c9ed2e&cl=details&anid=270771ed2bb357c081d 03700189caa98&listtype=search&searchparam=Das%2BRheingold%2Bvan%2Bhove.

Foster, Daniel H. *Wagner's Ring Cycle and the Greeks*. Cambridge: Cambridge University Press, 2010.

Goertz, Wolfram. Review of van Hove's *Das Rheingold. Rheinische Post*, 15 June 2006.

Jansen, Kasper. Review of van Hove's *Das Rheingold. NRC Handelsblad*, 15 June 2006.

MacCann, John. Review of van Hove's *Das Rheingold. Opera* 11 (2006): 1323.

McLuhan, Marshall. *Understanding Media: The Extensions of Man*. London: Routledge, 1964.

Maes, Francis and De Volder, Piet, eds. *Opera: achter de schermen van de emotie*. Leuven: Lannoo Campus, 2011: 87–91.

Playbill for *Das Rheingold*. Antwerp: De Vlaamse Opera, 2006.

Smart, Mary Ann. *Mimomania: Music and Gesture in Nineteenth-Century Opera*. Berkeley: University of California Press, 2004: 171–189.

Stuke, Franz R. Opernnetz.de—Zeitschrift für Musiktheater und Oper. Website for opera in Ghent.

Ward, Phill. Review of van Hove's *Das Rheingold. Opera Now* 11–12 (2006).

Weyns, Walter. *"The Ring:* Moderniteiten zwaar & licht." In: *Playbill* for *van Hove's Das Rheingold*, Janine Brogt, Piet De Volder (eds). Antwerp: De Vlaamse Opera, 2006: 87–96.

Williams, Simon. *Wagner and the Romantic Hero*. Cambridge: Cambridge University Press, 2004.

6

KINGS OF WAR OR THE PLAY OF POWER

Johan Thielemans

Ivo van Hove loves play marathons. Judging from his earlier productions, he has welded multiple plays together for more than one single bill in the theatre. Such was the case with *Ajax* and *Antigone* when he headed up Zuidelijk Toneel. That fed into the Shakespeare marathon *The Roman Tragedies* in 2006 and *The Russians*, an adaptation by Tom Lanoye of *Ivanov* and *Platonov* in 2011, both by Toneelgroep Amsterdam. In 2015, he returned to Shakespeare with a vengeance under the bill *Kings of War*, in which he brought three history plays together. Marathons have a special meaning for van Hove:

> I always feel that during the course of long productions people are transformed into a community. People feel as though they're very together watching them. . . . *Scenes From a Marriage* was four hours long, and by the end you could see strangers hugging each other. That's what can come out of a marathon, if it's good. You forget about time—you have the feeling like you're having a special experience.
>
> *(Bosanquet 2015)*

Even though *Kings of War* was a marathon, thoroughness was still required in scrapping a lot of the text. Not only does it comprise two full evenings' worth of plays, but one of the plays is comprised of a trilogy in and of itself, devoted only to Henry VI. It never would have occurred to van Hove to produce a reduced version of Shakespeare, but rather to seek out the themes that bind the three history plays together. In fact, it was a matter of creating an entirely new story that would overarch the three disparate history plays. Generally speaking, that new story is about power, a topic that van Hove finds uncommonly compelling.

The patterns of power: theme and variations

The critical jumping-off point for van Hove are the words of Henry IV, who on his deathbed gives advice to his son (the then Prince Hal) on how to proceed on the road to war, and about how to handle all the internal factions. Prince Hal, once he has become Henry V, follows his father's advice and throws down the gauntlet to France. This struggle and the ensuing victory are

FIGURE 6.1 *Kings of War*

© Jan Versweyveld

the beginning of a series of conflicts that Henry V never foresaw. Thus, we get to know Henry V as an intrepid king, who is past master at nationalistic rhetoric. It makes a victor of him (see Figure 6.1). But as he concludes a marriage of convenience with the daughter of his defeated enemy, he is depicted as clumsy and oafish. In contrast with the refined French princess, he has no idea how to advance a courtship stratagem. After a painful conversation, he grabs her hand without so much as a by or leave from the girl.

When we switch over to Henry VI, the "heroic" father is too soon dead. But this new Henry is cut from a very different sort of cloth. He is an intellectual who means well, but is incapable of dealing firmly enough with the nobles who surround him, all of whom are eager to steal his throne. He is also at the mercy of his ambitious wife—and we know that ambition for Shakespeare is a mortal sin. After much scheming and plotting, against which he is no match, he ends up paying with his life.

That ultimately leads to Richard III, the scion of the House of York, needing to eliminate a number of his family members before he can make a direct play for the throne. This Richard, misshapen and handicapped, turns out to be an unscrupulous intriguer to whom murder presents no obstacle. When he assumes the throne, his legitimacy is disputed, catalyzing one last war that eventually serves as the occasion for Henry Tudor, later Henry VII, to restore order. In this version of the facts, van Hove remains faithful to Shakespeare, and the Earl of Richmond is represented as a good king. He will bring peace and prosperity, beneath the beneficent eye of God. Or, in Shakespeare's words, "Now civil wounds are stopp'd, peace lives again. That she may long live here, God say 'Amen.'" (Act V, lns. 40–41). So ends this chronicle with a positive king in place.

A clash of characters

This summary doubtless reveals all that has been extracted from the plays. The polyphonic image of society, a major element in Shakespeare, is left out. The citizens and soldiery are absent. These interventions in the text are radical, so that the trilogy structure has been abandoned and the entire Joan of Arc sub-plot in *Henry VI* left out. Even the War of the Roses is barely mentioned. Our attention is entirely galvanized by the center of power. We see how leaders lead which, to a large degree, is a horrifying spectacle and that politics is viewed as a conflict between characters. One must admit that van Hove and his adaptors, Bart van den Eynde and Peter van Kraaij, have done an outstanding job. All that has been redacted serves no purpose in the governing production plan, and nothing that remains is superfluous. So they arrived at a logical, integral text that examines various aspects of what it means to be a political leader.

To play the three respective kings, van Hove has chosen three strong actors from his company, each with his own distinctive register. Ramsey Nasr is a resolute Henry V. There is not a trace of weakness or indecisiveness. He simply follows through on what his father had charged him to do. Only in the confrontation with the French princess (Hélène De Vos) does an entirely different person emerge, one that is clumsy and insecure. The contrast between the two aspects of personality accounts for a very comical scene, pretty much the only time any lightening of the tone occurs. It also allows us to see how brilliantly Nasr can handle such a variety of tones.

For Henry VI, the choice fell to Eelco Smits. This actor is short of stature and vulnerable. He is always useful for playing weak characters. That aspect is heightened by one extremely minor addition: that he wears horn-rimmed glasses. It is thanks to this attribute that he immediately stands out in this company. He is lost in the struggles of the court. He subtly acts out how this king is at the mercy of his environment. Impotent panic can be read in his eyes throughout. In opposition to him stands Bart Slegers, a competitor for power in the court, who exudes aggression. Fighting ensues all around Henry, but he himself is no warlord. In the text, it is indicated that he enjoys being in the company of sheep, which van Hove (with the help of videographer Tal Yarden) translated into a stark image: the king walks amidst a flock of sheep, from which the audience senses his ineluctable tragic ending.

With Richard III we have a comic character. In Hans Kesting's interpretation, he's just barely crippled, and barely has a hunchback. But on his face he bears a great red stain. In a company in which everyone is stylish and dressed in nicely tailored suits, he wears ugly clothes that are too small and tight for him. From his first appearance, it is immediately made clear that he is an outsider. Van Hove shows him to be a narcissist. As Kesting declaims his monologues, he avoids facing the audience. He talks to himself and looks in the mirror. In this way, the situation diverges from the traditional Shakespearean productions' device of direct address. This creates a tense and uneasy relationship as regards the audience, because Richard makes them an accessory to his plans and crimes—a technique that Shakespeare will later also use with Iago in *Othello*. This intimacy, which works so effectively at Shakespeare's Globe Theatre, is something van Hove has not sought. He respects the convention of the fourth wall so that the monologues become moments of introspection. It's a solution whereby Richard III becomes more than usually trapped within his own rageful self.

In the final scene, when Richard is settling accounts with the rebellious armies of Richmond, this is taken to an extreme. The large room gets entirely closed off. All exits have been eliminated. Richard is absolutely alone, entirely engulfed by his downfall. We see no armies or opponents.

The closed off room containing the desperate man has the same power as a scene from Beckett's *Endgame*. The image and the actor both exhibit the utmost individualism, an extreme narcissism that leads ineluctably toward his defeat.

But the production doesn't end on that nihilistic image. Once Richard is struck down, everything opens up once more, and a procession enters with the king and his "endless" train in tow. The court singer, who had previously performed, then sings the religious hymn, *Non Nobis*, a song that had special significance to the English court. In it, God is acclaimed as the only source of peace and mankind is humbled.

These themes are reiterated in the final soliloquy. Here we have Ramsey Nasr, now as King Henry VII, providing the entire marathon with a circular structure, as we move from bellicose monarch to the prince of peace. This new king is installed under godlike aegis, and requests spiritual help in eliminating all civil wars. Thus, these *Kings of War* come to an end; peace reigns once more.

Nasr delivers the monologue looking straight at the audience, and without the slightest trace of irony on the director's part. England, under the very banner of God, stands awaiting the next cruel civil war, which leaves the spectator with a broader historical awareness, but with just a hint of a sour aftertaste in their mouth. From the perspective of performance history, van Hove's choice to round things off with a "good" king naturally takes on a wider meaning. In previous decades, in which critical readings were under discussion, Richmond would be depicted as a savior summoned up from below (a typical Shakespearean motif) but not as a peace-bringer. He was introduced simply as the next successor, one just as dedicated to fighting, power-mad and ambitious. This approach was in tune with the age of skepticism, typical of the 1980s and 90s. But now with Henry VII undisputedly a good king, van Hove accepts Shakespeare's optimistic outlook, its ideological reasons typical of the Elizabethan age. This "faithful" reading is not innocent and has wider implications for the present day and for van Hove's view of politics and power.

Room and labyrinth

As well as an interesting reading, van Hove also sets off formal fireworks. In this, as always, he is supported by Jan Versweyveld in the set design and Tal Yarden in video. The action takes place in a large room with only a few furniture pieces. The model seems to be Churchill's war room. Versweyveld designs landscapes: stage left a bed, stage right, a chest of drawers and center stage a table; as well as a metal sink and stove unit hugging the upstage wall. They form a visual unity. But on the other hand, they're an accumulation of various places. They render scene changes superfluous. The style of the room is sharply realistic. But for Versweyveld, there is nonetheless a place reserved for an element that doesn't fit: off to the right is a balcony on which a brass quartet is placed that can be considered a subtle reference to a component part of Shakespeare's Globe Theatre, the "tiring house," and is a welcome addition. Through this element, the designed space is further characterized as a theatrical space, with its own laws, standing apart from realistic or photographic expectations.

Behind this large room are a number of white hallways, in which the actors are filmed. The hallways are a maze or a morgue as so many dead and dying bodies from the story appear there. That spatial arrangement in tandem with Tal Yarden's video work enables the action to flow. Time and place are neatly tampered with: now we're in France, now in England, even though the elements within the room are rarely changed. A simple switching of flags indicates a complete jump from England to France. Confusing? Absolutely not. This is van Hove manifesting himself as master storyteller. The accompanying videos play an important role. Thanks to close-ups of the actors, no matter how remote they are from us, the spectators, they are intensely present. Some images lend a sharp dynamic to the action; so, thanks to the camera, we get Bart Slegers's unforgettable conspiratorial look, a look that is stronger than any monologue could be.

The video screen plays an important role. It fulfills a number of functions. As we remarked above, it expands the space. It is also employed as a television screen on which official communications (which in traditional Shakespeare are expedited using public addresses) may be seen, or is an ideal medium for the periodic display of didactic material, such as historical data and maps.

The various atmospheres in the play are evoked in forceful ways thanks to Eric Shleichim's complex musical compositions. He runs through a broad gamut of styles: contra-tenor Steve Dugardyn sings songs from Shakespeare's time, party noises take on a disco feel and there's a real DJ onstage. The ceremonial moments, such as the coronations of one king to the next, are underpinned by the requisite music of a brass quartet. At times, trombone soloists slip in contemporary *glissandi* to underscore and color the text, and at those times, the musicians are in dialogue with the actors' words; it is as if music becomes text. All of it is top-notch work by composer Schleichim.

Anthology moments

In the course of the evening, there are a couple of scenes that are so telling they could make it into an anthology compiled out of "Great Moments in the Theatre": notably, the clumsy courtship scene between Ramsey Nasr and Hélène Devos, mentioned earlier, with all the hesitance, discomfort, and powerlessness lurking in Henry V's character. But the strongest scene is the one with the cherry pie in *Richard III*: the pie substituting for the famous strawberries Richard requests of the Cardinal in the text (because cherries are probably closer to the Dutch culinary experience). Friend and enemy sit in the salon eating pie together. It's an action that is performed in real time without a word being uttered. Here, the power brokers are reduced to mere upstanding citizens. Nowhere in the production is the mask of hypocrisy this strong. It all hinges on a trumped-up friendliness, masking their dark murderous designs. Van Hove here goes for an absolutely natural approach. The audience remains in a state of tension as they witness the innocent-looking tableau, because danger lurks behind the meaning of each banal gesture.

Another particularly strong moment is found in *Richard III* as well; it is a scene in which Gloucester, the aspirant-king, makes a speech to the citizens of London. But in van Hove's concept, there's no place for extras representing "the people" to appear. That is why Richard's dissembling is changed to a totally different clever theatrical strategy. Van Hove shows us Richard III and his accomplice, Buckingham, rehearsing the text in a private tête-à-tête before confronting the citizens of London, which Aus Greidanus as Buckingham executes as well as anyone. They try the text to test the effect it might make, and we see Richard practicing rhetorical tricks under the admiring eye of his accomplice. This scene in which the mechanism of political rhetoric is laid bare, puts one directly in mind of an analogous scene from Brecht's *Arturo Ui* in which Ui (the Hitler figure) learns how to apply all the tricks from the art of public speaking under the tutelage of a professional actor.

Van Hove's style is typically stamped by anachronism. His actors wear no period costumes but run around in tailored suits because actors who are too "dressed up" fail to speak to his imagination. Visual anachronism also leads to an a-historical view of events. Here, two epochs, the past of Shakespeare and the present of van Hove, merge, because, in essence, humanity is invariable. The image allows us to see the problems of yesteryear alongside the problems of today; furthermore, it shows us that the conflicts of the past have something to tell us about the conflicts of today, which may explain why this production drew commentaries contending that political theatre assimilated all contemporary world affairs. We submit to van Hove not so much out of interest in the past but, on the contrary, because Shakespeare's plays have real things to say about the world of power in which the spectator lives. One clear point is that van Hove refuses to encourage facile reception of the text. There are no prompts that give away any identifiable contemporary figures. With him, a tyrant like Richard III won't be found sporting a Hitler mustache. Van Hove would find such clichés from political theatre at once too literal and too limiting. He puts much more emphasis on stripping naked fundamental character interaction—an emphasis that was valid formerly and remains so even today—and putting the mechanism of power on display, which continues to be a highly instructive exercise for the contemporary spectator.

The conclusion is unmistakable: masterful theatre, a marvelous achievement on the part of all participants, and a director at the top of his game. Van Hove had previously delivered a superb production with *The Roman Tragedies*. This next set of history plays is yet another four hours' worth of Shakespeare in all his glory. The production once more dovetails the external and internal experiments of form that van Hove has fashioned as his trademarks during the course of his artistic trajectory.

Bibliography

Bosanquet, Theo. "I Can Really Kill a Darling." *What's on Stage*, 7 September 2015.

APPENDIX 1: *ROMAN TRAGEDIES*

The politics of distraction: spectatorial freedom and (dis)enfranchisement in Toneelgroep's *Roman Tragedies*[1]

Natalie Corbett and Keren Zaiontz

In the five-and-a-half-hour epic *Roman Tragedies*, staged by the prodigious Dutch ensemble Toneelgroep, Shakespeare's tragedies of *Coriolanus*, *Julius Caesar*, and *Antony and Cleopatra* are performed in a sequence that traces political history from the beginnings of democracy to the globalized world of international politics. The trilogy, billed as "Shakespeare that jumps straight from the headlines [. . .] hurled into the heart of the contemporary world," offers an updating that seeks to investigate the mechanisms of state power and the nature of "man [sic] as a political animal" (Festival TransAmérique 2010). Key to this twenty-first century interpretation of Shakespeare's texts is the production's encouragement of audience engagement, which implicates spectators as the absent public that bears witness to ongoing political turbulence. Audiences that attended the North American premiere at the 2010 Festival TransAmérique (FTA) experienced both exceptional physical duration and proximity to the event while circulating between (and within) the auditorium and the stage during timed breaks. Within the context of an international festival known for its contemporary theatre and dance, the dynamics of reception in *Roman Tragedies* (see Figure A.1) are the proud insignia of the "avant-garde" or experimental performance traditions. The production adopts slightly condensed versions of Shakespeare's dramaturgical structures, employs well-established conventions of disruption, and incorporates a realist mode of acting. However, the true experimentality of *Roman Tragedies* lies in linking the direct participation of audiences to a political commentary that dramatizes the dangers of (and desire for) distraction in a hypermediated world.

Jan Versweyveld's set design casts the play's epic actions within a modern, anonymous corporate environment, populated by blandly geometric Swedish sofas, potted plants, plexiglas, and ubiquitous television monitors. Modular configurations within the stage space function interchangeably as committee boardroom and private living room, highlighting the porousness between the public and private lives being staged. Camera operators relentlessly film the actors, whose images are projected onto the screens on stage and in the wings, simultaneously remediated as live news broadcasts. When actors exit the stage they often remain visible on the periphery; hair and makeup stations line the stage right wing, brushing up against one of the stage-side food vendors.

The dynamic of constant visibility created by this aesthetic of surveillance highlights the two most significant alterations to the original Shakespeare texts. Although nothing has been added, all battles have been replaced by extended spectacular sequences of flashing lights and violent bombastic sound, and all scenes in which the citizens speak have been cut. By collapsing the unfolding stratagems and defining events of major wars to their final outcomes—and by excising all record of public response to the momentous political events depicted—the edited script presents a narrative relentlessly focused on the psychology of those few individuals within the highest echelons of power. Stripped of the minutiae of developing action, the balanced causal chains of Shakespeare's tragedies are reshaped into contemporary portraits of political man-oeuvring, backroom dealings and press conferences, private scandals, and public obfuscation.

The increased biographical bent produced by this narrative condensation lends itself to the acting style of the piece, which is defined at once by the intimacy of filmic realism and by intense, even volatile, emotionalism. The unhinged displays by the ensemble, exemplified by group arguments and giddy encounters between lovers, deliberately risk a performance of excess. Certainly for those spectators on stage—standing or sitting beside the physical scraps that break out between politicians in *Julius Caesar*, or within arms' reach of the queen and her ladies as they swill champagne and dance boisterously in *Antony and Cleopatra*—these corporeal outbursts allow the audience to inhabit the tragedies in a way that exceeds the traditional prioritization of the word in Shakespearean performance. The intimacy of these encounters do not so much bring spectators

FIGURE A.1   *The Roman Tragedies*

© Jan Versweyveld

into contact with the politics of ancient Rome as with the politics of "personalized" media that feed our desire to be "up close and personal" with public figures, be they politicians or stars. Politics, separated from the lived consequences for the populace, and framed by the representational logic of the twenty-four hour news cycle, is displayed largely as a cult of personality.

What *Roman Tragedies* so deftly dramatizes is our insatiable need to come into proximity to, and accumulate intimate details about, the excesses of public figures. The spectacular performance environment shows this very act of accumulation to be mediated by continuous display. Thus, in mining Shakespeare's texts for their many private trysts and public betrayals, director Ivo van Hove lays bare the aesthetics of contemporary politics. Political power is represented through a disclosure of stagecraft in which theatrical and mediatized effects like make-up, recording technology, and cinematography are shown to produce public figures. As audiences witness how the images of politicians accumulate and circulate through the apparatus of the stage, the function of imitation shifts course. Van Hove expresses this refocused view of mimesis when he insists that the "*Roman Tragedies* are not realist theatre, but a theatre of reality" (FestivalTransAmérique 2010). The tragedies do not set out to imitate the spectacle of politics but to show how the contemporary political world is structured through imitation.

In a theatre of reality, the constitutive feature is a participatory culture that is permanently "plugged in" to the social world.[2] Scripted into the void left by absent soldiers and citizens, the spectators of *Roman Tragedies* function as a mute but networked populace, attempting to comprehend the machinations that shape their world. Ostensibly, the freedom to choose where to sit, to enter the stage space and be in close proximity to the actors, or to opt out of spectatorship, have a sandwich, check e-mail, or tweet updates to the outside world, suggests an enfranchised and flexible engagement with performance. Indeed, autonomous, individual contribution to the event was encouraged by the availability of public computers on stage, and even celebrated through the publication of spectators' Twitter comments on the overhead news crawler. Despite the variability of the configuration, however, participation, as such, is entirely proscribed. In the Montreal performance, rules structuring audience movement were explained via teleprompter and spoken announcement at the short break after the first scene: mobility was allowed during the breaks (the lengths of which were visible as a countdown displayed on all screens). Placement on stage was highly structured, generally limited to the sofas and a few additional boxes or stools in the offstage space. The implicit (and explicit) contract for the audience to be visible yet silent observers and not participants was quite rigid.

The separation of audience from the depicted action, manifested in their spatial complicity and visible passivity, is further emphasized by a number of traditional alienating strategies employed in the production. As the performance unwinds, the electronic ticker running above the stage provides updates as to the amount of time remaining until the death of each of the key characters. At the conclusion of scenes, spoken and visual announcements inform the audience of what will follow in the next scene, prompting individuals to make an informed choice about what perspective they would like to have on the event. The volume of narrative information presented and the duration of attention demanded by *Roman Tragedies* are almost overwhelming, and yet the devices that appear to support comprehension are suspect. At the top of the production, a lengthy history detailing the specific players and conflicts that have culminated in the events prior to the first scene scroll on both the projection screen and digital news crawler at breakneck speed. During battle sequences, a rapid summary of events competes with stroboscopic lighting and deafening percussion. The net effect is that of being witness to significant political events that are the products of a causality too complicated to understand either in the unfolding moment, or without specialist knowledge.

The disparity between the event and our understanding (or interpretation) of it is manifested, most compellingly, in the execution of stage deaths. Framing character deaths as facts that can be estimated, announced, and digitally archived, *Roman Tragedies* brings into focus our desire to master the finiteness of life through hard-boiled facts. Finitude is not grappled with, or even mourned, but is managed within the circuits of media as yet another image. Actors, at the moment of their stage deaths, are positioned (thrown, pushed, or voluntarily laid) on a sliding platform that, when thrust into place, triggers an overhead camera to photograph the corpse. The image, projected at the instant of death onto the main screen above the proscenium as well as the onstage screens, evokes an aesthetic of criminal evidence. The unmoving body, still and breathless in photography as no live performer can be, maintains the finality of death, even as the actor rises and walks off stage. The rupture between the liveness of the performance at this moment and the mediated image with its greater diegetic realism, emphasizes the contradictory multiplicity of informational tracks available to the spectator.

The distancing effects of *Roman Tragedies*, however, do not thwart engagement so much as serve to raise questions about what kinds of engagement are possible in an era of global accessibility, digital reproduction, and a higher degree of audience choice. Audiences in *Roman Tragedies* contend with scales of distraction that range from spectacular display to microspatial engagement: in the electronic ticker that scrolls across the proscenium arch, providing crucial information in multiple languages at almost unreadable speed; in the large screen above the ticker that projects a live feed of the stage action; in the sandwiches and refreshments served on stage between strictly timed breaks; and in the placement of computers to post updates just inches from the action on social networking sites like Twitter. Audiences witness state power as a dispersed event. The overproduction of the stage image onto multiple screens recharges the content of the tragedies so that state affairs are made to serve the consumptive habit of spectators. This reimagination of the tragedies as a visual display that is endlessly sensationalized—and appropriated into a twenty-four hour news cycle—does not belong to the "counter-traditions" in which the authority of Shakespeare's texts is tested. Rather, the authority that is challenged in *Roman Tragedies*, with the complicity of roving audiences, is that of mass media.

In Blog Theory, Jodi Dean's observation about online, participatory culture (by way of Giorgio Agamben's reading of contemporary spectacle), assists us in understanding how the public mirror the politicians and stars that dominate the media landscape by prioritizing individual "usership" online:

> We have been produced as subjects unlikely to coalesce, subjects resistant to solidarity, and subjects suspicious of collectivity. Central to this production is the cultivation and feeding of a sense of unique and special individuality. Every sperm is sacred, so began the story of our unique cellular lives. Or, every potential genetic combination carries with it the remarkable potentiality we locate in our individuated selves. Each voice must be heard (but they don't combine into a chorus). Each vote must be counted (but they add up to less than a movement). Each person must be visible (but then we don't see a group). Personalized "participatory" media is a problem not only because of its personalization of participation. More than that is its injunction that we participate ever more in personalization: make your own avatar, video, profile, blog, mobster, video, and app. Participation becomes indistinguishable from personalization, the continued cultivation of one's person. Leave your mark.

(Dean 2010: 82)

Notes

1   Originally published as: Natalie Corbett and Keren Zaiontz, *Canadian Theatre Review*, Volume 147, Summer 2011, pp. 117–120.
2   The Politics of Distraction: Spectatorial Freedom and (dis)Enfranchisement in Toneelgroep's Roman Tragedies.

Bibliography

Dean, Jodi. Blog Theory: Feedback and Capture in the Circuits of Drive. Cambridge: Polity, 2010.
Festival TransAmérique. Play Program. *Tragédies Romaines*. Ivo Van Hove by William Shakespeare. Toneelgroep Amsterdam. Montreal: FTA, May 2010.

Staging the Twitter war: Toneelgroep Amsterdam's *Roman Tragedies*[1]

James R. Ball III

On 14 November 2012, following an intensification of rocket attacks targeting Israel from the Gaza Strip, Israel Defense Forces (IDF) made their first formal announcement that military operations against Gaza had recommenced at 9:29 am Eastern Standard Time. The IDF's official Twitter presence (@IDFSpokesperson) tweeted, "The IDF has begun a wide-spread campaign on terror sites & operatives in the #Gaza Strip, chief among them #Hamas & Islamic Jihad targets" (2012a). Minutes later, @IDFSpokesperson tweeted their first target, the Hamas leader Ahmed al-Jabari, and within an hour had given what would become a week-long war its name: "The IDF has embarked on Operation Pillar of Defense" (2012b). The IDF Twitter feed soon became its own front in the battle as a locus for many of the speech acts that compose and surround war. Included in the declarations tweeted that morning were: "All options are on the table. If necessary, the IDF is ready to initiate a ground operation in Gaza" (2012c), and "We recommend that no Hamas operatives, whether low level or senior leaders, show their faces above ground in the days ahead" (2012d).

Hamas, the Palestinian political organization that has administered Gaza since 2007, returned fire in cyberspace via the Twitter account of its military wing, the Al Qassam Brigades @Alqassam-Brigade, which matched threat for threat, tweeting "Liberation of occupied #Palestine started. . .we are coming #IDF" (Alqassam Brigade 2012a), and challenged the IDF's characterization of events whenever it could. Responding to @IDFSpokesperson's message "Warning to reporters in Gaza: Stay away from Hamas operatives & facilities. Hamas, a terrorist group, will use you as human shields" (2012e), @AlqassamBrigade responded, "Warning to Israelis: Stay away from Israeli #IDF = #IOF [Israel Occupation Forces] and bases. IDF, a terrorist army, will use you as human shields" (Alqassam Brigade 2012b). Commentators would soon describe these discursive and narrative battles, playing out in volleys of 140 characters or less, as the world's first Twitter war. From 16 to 18 November 2012, a different Twitter war could be found onstage at the Brooklyn Academy of Music (BAM): Toneelgroep Amsterdam's *Roman Tragedies*, directed by Ivo van Hove. The nearly six-hour long, intermission-free spectacle cut together three of Shakespeare's Rome-set tragedies: *Coriolanus*, *Julius Caesar*, and *Antony and Cleopatra*. By reducing each play to as few as 90 minutes, van Hove emphasized interpersonal conflict and human intrigue (for instance, Coriolanus's fraught relationships with his mother, wife, and son, and Antony and Cleopatra's romance), allowing each play's political plots to emerge in abstractions (drums and strobe lights to indicate war), allusions (a uniform of suits and ties to suggest twenty-first century political classes), and the structures by which each spectator's gaze, body, and engagement were managed. A handy flyer distributed to playgoers at the outset contained a scene schedule marking the times at which each of the three plays' scenes (in their original sequence) would occur. It also featured the call to (digital) action, "You are encouraged to take pictures and tweet using the hashtag #RomanTragedies." Audience members could then follow the new media commentary from their devices or on an LED ticker that broadcast curated selections to those seated in the house. Many had already entered into this form of digital participation before receiving the production's blessing: as the audience waited for doors to open, user @cynthiayang tweeted, "Even the lobby experience is immersive: general admission can turn sextigenerians into gladiators #RomanTragedies" (Yang 2012). The flyer further identified set changes between certain scenes denoting the moments in which audience members could circulate from house to stage or back again, finding new vantages among the couches, televisions, and risers that were set on the stage. When the audience was first allowed onto the stage (soon after Coriolanus returned triumphant to Rome), the twitterati marveled at their access, "@natty_ijs we're on stage! Come to Rome! #RomanTragedies" (natty_ijs 2012), and bemoaned the new conflicts it sparked, "@planetaclaire apparently there's no more space in Rome #RomanTragedies" (Frisbie 2012). Those with the best views took on certain journalistic responsibilities, as did tweeter @sbishopstone who captured the "End of Coriolanus #Roman-Tragedies" (Bishop-Stone 2012a, 2012b and 2012c) pic.twitter. As the carnage mounted, photographic evidence proliferated. Twitter also became a venue for reflection and analysis. As Marc Antony wept over Caesar's corpse (a scene staged as a twenty-first century press conference), tweeters waxed philosophical: "Lessons Julius Caesar taught me: Don't try to be a god and people won't try to stab you." For some spectators, Twitter provided opportunities for *Roman Tragedies* to stitch itself into the fabric of the wider world. A few dutifully reported the moment the show spilled out beyond the opera house walls, Enobarbus running out through the audience onto Lafayette Avenue—"The cast literally moved out onto the street #romantragedies. Brilliant"—or offered their own analysis of the gesture—"Poor Enobarbus. It just wouldn't be Ivo van Hove if an actor didn't run out into traffic followed by a camera. #RomanTragedies." Still others on twitter drew attention to the ways the outside world encroached upon the staged history, as contemporary news briefs would also be featured on the LED ticker above the stage: "#RomanTragedies live news of Israel/Hamas during Coriolanus." Geoffrey Way identifies three primary modes in which social media have been integrated into live performance: "social media as a means for access, social media as a means for participation, and social media as platforms for dramatic performances" (Way 2011: 403–4). Way's categories mark several opportunities for theatre artists to use social media to encourage engagement with an audience from providing views of a rehearsal process, to promoting interaction between audiences and performers or characters, to serving as venue. Nonetheless, Way's examples offer scant evidence that the incorporation of such new media into live, stage dramas is or will become anything more than a fad. Yet for *Roman Tragedies*, Twitter proved essential: the play modeled a particular form of twenty-first-century spectatorship by incorporating the microblogging service, and by deftly navigating between the modes Way identifies. These modes further offer a conceptual apparatus that can clarify the formal similarities between the use of Twitter in war and in theatre. The IDF Twitter feed had long shown glimpses of the forces that would deploy in Operation Pillar of Defense and each tweet invited participation by others who could re-tweet or respond. Once Hamas responded, Twitter became a venue for the verbal spectacle produced by two political actors, and those following the feeds were once more spectators. As spectator to *Roman Tragedies*, I found myself a theatrical analog to this audience for global politics, an audience with fractured access to the spectacle of world affairs and an oscillating engagement with its players and events. Such spectators play a crucial role in piecing together the narratives that render geopolitical events meaningful, but feel largely powerless in spite of this capacity; I am immersed in the drama though I participate in it only rarely. This effect is not solely a function of the ways in which *Roman Tragedies* extends itself into digital realms. As the dramas onstage oscillated between an intimate private sphere and a broadly figured public sphere, so too did the audience's physical proximity with and visual access to those spheres. At *Roman Tragedies*, this public sphere was figured by a stage space cluttered with low-slung couches in minimalist Scandinavian styles of the sort preferred by the planners and policy makers who furnish institutional spaces in Europe and North America. Once the audience was allowed onto the stage, their bodies filled this space, and produced a new intimacy that suggested more private scenes. The plays were acted naturalistically in the same spaces the audience occupied, though the production also took pains to foreground its theatrical apparatus: makeup stations and concession stands were accessible and visible from the stage, serving the immediate needs of both actors and spectators and gesturing toward the work that goes into making real-world politicians camera-ready. The intimacy allowed to spectators did not always bring greater clarity or access as the stage featured dozens of flat-screen televisions and was embellished with a few well-placed ferns, one's view was often partial or indirect. The televisions offered live video of the play from several stationary cameras installed throughout the opera house and hand-held cameras whose operators followed the major players. The action I was trying to see might be blocked by other audience members or some furniture, or indeed be behind me entirely, requiring me to watch events happening inches from my back on a television a few feet ahead of me. When the televisions were not abstracting and doubling the audience's gaze, they served as breaches where the history of the twentieth and twenty-first centuries invaded that of Rome: historical and contemporary news footage (of John F. Kennedy, Barack Obama, the Olympics, etc.) complemented or contrasted individual scenes, cueing particular interpretations. Each new obstruction or mediation further alienated the spectator, ultimately materializing her acts of spectatorship onstage and submitting those acts to theatrical scrutiny. Every 20 to 30 minutes, the scene would change again and many audience members would shift to seek new vantage points onstage or back in the house. With each shift, the politics of engagement evolved as well; the form of spectatorship modeled by the *Roman Tragedies* was not solely visual and the play's representations went beyond the usual critique that contemporary politics has lost substance and authenticity as it has become increasingly mediated and theatrical. Being a spectator to the *Roman Tragedies* required physical choices and so had bodily effects. A particularly insidious game of musical chairs developed as audience members staked out their territory onstage. Some found an agreeable couch and refused to budge from it for the duration. Others became strategic, closely watching the countdown clocks that marked each scene change, waiting for an open seat to appear. Territorial maneuvering began to occupy more and more of the spectator's energy, and a zero-sum game of maintaining one's hold on a spot of turf developed: many shifted in place to optimize a changing view of the scene without relinquishing a claim to space or property. The political conflicts depicted found physical analogs in an audience that grew increasingly restless and divisive, clashing in subtle ways over an extremely limited resource. For the audience onstage, spectatorship became a battle: it required each spectator to stake her territory, assert a particular view, and maintain that view in the face of forces who would take it from her. The onstage audience was returned to the house for the final hour of the proceedings. To those gazing at the stage from the plush seats of the house throughout the event, the audience onstage formed the mass of Roman citizenry, dynamic scenery installing itself within the proscenium. Astute observers may have sensed their machinations, but the onstage micro-events were of little import alongside the macrocosmic views the house afforded. A projection above the stage space, and equal to it in size, gave the house-bound audience the same view available on each of the television screens onstage, and between the two an LED ticker, like those delivering news snippets to Times Square, offered context, history, and commentary for each of the plays (in between the contemporary news updates noted above). Key historical events not captured by Shakespeare (or cut by Toneelgroep) tracked quickly across the ticker whenever war engulfed Rome. Data and statistics took prime of place here: each character's death was marked, dated, and recorded in the ticker's zooming historical record. The ticker also made tweeting spectators into participants in the construction of the historical narrative: select tweets were displayed regularly among the historical and contemporary updates. The Twitter activities of those onstage filled out the comprehensive view for those watching from the house. As certain observations passed across the ticker (such as my own jotting, "From the audience/house politics is history . . . #romantragedies," the house view allowed for a moment of critical distance to actively construct the play's meanings as it proceeded. This, too, modeled a form of spectatorship that increasingly characterizes contemporary politics: the expert observer offering varying degrees of punditry, from professional analysts in peer-reviewed publications, to televised talking heads of dubious pedigree, to citizen bloggers interpreting for smaller constituencies. Such efforts also gestured toward the play's integration with contemporary politics, an effect made more explicit when the LED ticker would turn again to headlines from the news of November 2012, allowing Operation Pillar of Defense to make its way onto the stage at BAM. Toneelgroep has been performing *Roman Tragedies* since 2007. The production is thus nearly as old as Twitter itself, though email was used in place of Twitter prior to May 2010 (there are still internet stations onstage where spectators can send emails but I did not see much activity at these). As a spectator in November 2012, I have trouble imagining a performance as loaded with specific resonances as those available that weekend. Certain world historical events immediately come to mind as corollaries to the intrigues represented: Coriolanus's wrangling with populism reiterated many themes of the US presidential election recently past, while Antony and Cleopatra's private decadence conjured up the sex scandal that had toppled CIA Director David Petraeus the same month. And, of course, there was also Gaza. My research into the United Nations Security Council had led me to spend that week glued to my Twitter feed, to news reports, to live video of Council media events, and the like. I had engaged precisely the form of contemporary political and historical spectatorship that Toneelgroep would model onstage at BAM. Having my own life reflected so immediately in art forced me to take stock of the ways in which my acts of everyday spectatorship form a constituent part of the contemporary political sphere. Finding myself staged as audience member shed new light on the ethics and efficacies of being an observer to global political violence. *Roman Tragedies* was largely bloodless: deaths were marked by an actor falling onto a rolling platform ("Excellent use of Ekkyklema," one observer tweeted and hastily photographed from above, like documentary evidence of a war crime. Between this blood-lessness and the gray, institutional space the set evoked, *Roman Tragedies* proved to be primarily interested in the antiseptic spaces where war is fought beyond the battlefield in 2012, these are as much the Security Council chamber as the twitterverse. Far from "dramatiz[ing] the dangers of (and desire for) distraction in a hypermediated world" (Corbett and Zaiontz 2011:117), as some critical takes on the production suggest, *Roman Tragedies* in fact demonstrates the centrality of mediated spaces (old and new) in the increasingly theatricalized milieu of global politics. Neither dangerous nor safe, desirable nor undesirable, media like Twitter extend the space in which war is fought while amplifying the theatrical strategies of those who wage it. The actions of the IDF, as Operation Pillar of Defense spilled out onto Twitter's servers, demonstrated that such digital technologies are not distractions but fronts in their own right. Twitter has become one place where words and images can first be contested, a particular battle that extends beyond the official cessation of hostilities. That the IDF indicated and recorded some of the bloody effects of the war in tweets also demonstrates that this front is not divorced from, or an era sure of, the physical battlefield. *Roman Tragedies* deftly incorporates social media, specifically Twitter, to reflect back on its audience their place in a digital theatre of war. The audience of *Roman Tragedies* was neither invited nor authorized to intervene in the history it watched. This audience was not empowered to participate in the events as they unfolded. Rather, digital, photographic, and spectatorial engagements rendered material the usually invisible forms of participation that attend all theatre, be it on a stage in Elizabethan England or on a news broadcast from twenty-first-century Gaza. Spectatorship requires the active production of meaning by the spectator; in all theatre, the audience must make sense of the narrative from the material immediately available to it. The integration of Twitter in the *Roman Tragedies* not only brought contemporary historical and political events onto the stage to be incorporated into the meanings made, but charged the audience with the work of writing that history in the moment. A Twitter history is exceedingly ephemeral . On 18 November 2012, at 6:00 pm when the show began again at BAM, I logged into my Twitter account at home to experience the production once more. Following live updates of the #romantragedies hashtag, I retraced the history I had lived a day earlier, as new spectators wrote the show for me from Coriolanus's rise, to Brutus's betrayal, to the fall of Antony and Cleopatra. On 19 November, I would be back at work on my research, following Twitter now to see what end to the Gaza conflict might be in sight. Agreement was reached on a cease-fire on 21 November, and my view became historical once more from the house composing a comprehensive view of the scene. As an active process of making meaning, spectatorship is much the same in theatre as in war, and the lessons from each realm apply to the other. *Roman Tragedies'* reflections on the forms of spectatorship available to twenty-first century global citizens suggest that how, where, and why we watch world historical events establishes our political relationship with those events and so our integration into the history they will become. Staging the Twitter war offers new ways to use theatre to do politics and write history.

Note

1   James R. Ball III, "Staging the Twitter War: Toneelgroep Amsterdam's Roman Tragedies," *The Drama Review*, Volume 57, Number 4, Winter 2013 (T220), pp. 163–170.

Bibliography

Alqassam Brigade. 2012a. Twitter post, 17 November, 6:22 am. http://twitter.com/alqassambrigade.
Alqassam Brigade. 2012b. Twitter post, 20 November, 7:28 pm. http://twitter.com/alqassambrigade.
Ball, James R, III. 2012. Twitter post, 17 November, 6:39 pm. http://twitter.com/jamesreedball.
Bishop-Stone, Sarah. 2012a. Twitter post, 17 November, 1:43 pm. http://twitter.com/sbishopstone.
Bishop-Stone, Sarah. 2012b. Twitter post, 17 November, 3:40 pm. http://twitter.com/sbishopstone.
Bishop-Stone, Sarah. 2012c. Twitter post, 17 November, 5:13 pm. http://twitter.com/sbishopstone.

Corbett, Natalie, and Keren Zaiontz. 2011. "The Politics of Distraction: Spectatorial Freedom and (dis) Enfranchisement in Toneelgroep's 'Roman Tragedies.'" *Canadian Theatre Review* (Summer): 117–20.

Frisbie, Claire. 2012. Twitter post, 17 November, 7:08 pm. http://twitter.com/planetaclaire.

IDFSpokesperson. 2012a. Twitter post, 14 November, 9:29 am. http://twitter.com/IDFSpokesperson.

IDFSpokesperson. 2012b. Twitter post, 14 November, 10:45 am. http://twitter.com/IDFSpokesperson.

IDFSpokesperson. 2012c. Twitter post, 14 November, 10:49 am. http://twitter.com/IDFSpokesperson.

IDFSpokesperson. 2012d. Twitter post, 14 November, 1:22 pm. http://twitter.com/IDFSpokesperson.

IDFSpokesperson. 2012e. Twitter post, 20 November, 5:34 pm. http://twitter.com/IDFSpokesperson.

Kanthou, Haritini. 2012. Twitter post, 17 November, 4:35 pm. http://twitter.com/hkanthou.

Lorenzetti, Nicole. 2012. Twitter post, 17 November, 5:04 pm. http://twitter.com/niccilor.

natty_ijs. 2012. Twitter post, 17 November, 7:09 pm. http://twitter.com/natty_ijs.

Schachter, Aaron. 2012. "The Gaza Twitter War." PRI's *The World,* 22 November. www.theworld.org/2012/11/the-gaza-twitter-war (23 March 2013).

Sutter, John D. 2012. "Will Twitter War Become the New Norm?" CNN.com, 19 November. www.cnn.com/2012/11/15/tech/social-media/twitter-war-gaza-israel (23 March 2013).

Verkerk, Mariana. 2012. Twitter post, 17 November, 8:12 pm. http://twitter.com/marianaverkerk.

Way, Geoffrey. 2011. "Social Shakespeare: Romeo and Juliet, Social Media, and Performance." *Journal of Narrative Theory* 41, 3: 401–420.

Yang, Cynthia. 2012. Twitter post, 17 November, 2:57 pm. http://twitter.com/cynthiayang.

APPENDIX 2: INTERVIEW WITH IVO VAN HOVE BY JOHAN REYNIERS

Ivo van Hove: "Theatre is the art form of the 20th century"

Interview by Johan Reyniers, translated by David Willinger and Pieter Vermeulen[1]

Where did the urge to produce theatre come from?
Where and how did it start?

Ivo van Hove: It started very early. When I was little, I used to spend a lot of time with my maternal grandparents. Right from the start, I was staging performances. My younger brother, perforce, had to collaborate. We used to hang a curtain and did our acting outside, with our grandparents as our sole audience. So the urge to make something that could be shown was already there.

Later on, I was at a boarding school in the town of Hoogstraten. There was no class on Wednesday afternoons, so we were allowed to do other things. I was part of a theatre group. I started when I was eleven. We were once featured on *Tienerklanken* [*Sounds of Teens*], a television program of the time.

Once a year we made a production that would get put on two or three times in April or May, something we all worked towards. I used to play a clown in white-face. I don't remember the title. I didn't have a deep need to act, or else I'd have kept it up.

After high school, I studied law for three years. I wasn't an outstanding student, but I never got left back either, and always passed with honors. I excelled at divorce law, even though it was the hardest course of study. But in the middle of the third year I decided to quit. I thought: if I keep going ahead with this, I'm going to become a lawyer. And I didn't want that.

Even though it's also a kind of theatre

Indeed. It's all about text interpretation. You start looking for certain elements in libraries so as to find a way to read a text in a way nobody else has thought of, and win a lawsuit. I never regretted having done that for a couple of years. It still proves quite useful. That's how I learned to process large amounts of information in a short period of time.

After that I went to the RITCS, which I didn't find very interesting. Some teachers even said: you don't need to come to class, you know enough already. That's where I met Peter van Kraaij [later a TGA dramaturg, Ed.], who was studying in the film department as of the second year. And there was the one and only Alex Van Royen, who explained that theatre was serious business. André Van den Bunder taught semiotics of film. That's how my passion for film came about and how I got introduced to Antonioni's work. I didn't understand it, but it fascinated me.

Jan Versweyveld showed up at a party. He'd been studying and living in Brussels up until the previous year. It all happened in that one night, in a manner of speaking. [Jan Versweyveld has been the life partner and in-house scenographer of Ivo van Hove ever since. JR] On account of Jan I used to spend a lot of time with the visual arts students from the Fine Arts Academy in Antwerp. Guy Cassiers was in his class, which is why, during my school years, I wound up putting on my first performances working largely with visual artists. *Rumors* was created in the spring of 1981. *Disease Germs* and *Like in the War* (*Als in de oorlog*) followed, independent of any school context.

For our final exam, we had to put on a comedy, *Same Time Next Year* by Bernard Slade. There were eight of us, and everybody had to direct one scene. I found the play dull and told myself, I'm not going to do this. I want to make my own choice. So I did *Marokko*, which consisted of the first monologue from *Big and Small* by Botho Strauss. Alex Van Royen came to see it, but didn't say a word. The following day he said, 'Yesterday night I saw *no* theatre seven times, and bad theatre one time.' I was happy to be doing bad theatre. At least it was theatre.

You did your first plays outside of the official structures. Did you have to or was it by conscious choice?

Rumors was performed in a former launderette. A friend of Jan's had decided to live there. It still needed to be refurbished before we could make use of the space. We were consciously working site-specifically as we didn't like real theatres.

Annie De Clerck from the BRT [former hostess of a well-known cultural show. BRT is the state-owned Flemish television station. Ed.] came to film us. I sat there in my leather jacket, fulminating against the official theatre. In our view, it was stone-cold dead, horrible, a joke. We didn't want to be associated with it in any way.

During those early years we never applied for any subsidies [unheard of in Belgium at the time. Ed.] We preferred to do it on our own. No one got paid. For a period of time, we ran a *grand café* just across from the Academy in Antwerp. Our only intention was to generate enough money to put on more plays, and to buy our freedom. We used the 20,000 francs we made to pay the actors for *Agatha*.

In a side room off the bar, we had a candle factory, Aktine. The idea came from Jan's family, very Catholic they were. They'd used it [to raise money for church-sponsored charities] for 'the Congo.' One of our co-workers put on a nice suit and went around to all the priests with a car full of Easter candles. That's how we received support from the church for the sole purpose of making subversive theatre. We were real entrepreneurs!

Military service was still obligatory in Belgium back then. I opted for the civilian branch of military service so I wouldn't have to stop making theatre. But first we needed to think of a structure. So we founded a not-for-profit: AKT. Jan was named artistic director. That allowed me to do my military service. One time they came to do an audit on us, and I think they saw what we were up to. But they also saw that we weren't just twiddling our thumbs, so they didn't charge us with any infractions.

AKT stood for Antwerps Kollektief voor Teaterprodukties. That's a joke, as there never was an actual collective.

Guy Cassiers studied graphic arts, he wasn't an actor. How did you come to the decision to let him perform in Rumors? Did you cast him?

We used to hang out together. Guy might have said: 'I'll do it.' We had thirty people on stage for that performance, and not one actor in the whole bunch. The audience also consisted of thirty people, forming a mirror image.

Our audience was, at least as I remember it, not the usual theatre audience. It was an avant-garde public, more interested in visual arts. The idea of attending site-specific theatre was still very new. *Disease Germs* was performed in Montevideo for two or three weeks, a hangar where large-scale art exhibitions were organized. Very hip, but not chic. We were allowed to use the space for free, as a form of in-kind support.

Your theatre of that time has been characterized as physical and visual, not verbal. Was it a kind of performance art?

It certainly was influenced by performance art. We were somewhere in between. *Wild Lords* and *Wonders of Mankind* would be called montage performances these days. We used to hand out individual assignments to the actors for them to develop. After a while we'd culled some fragments from what they brought in. Then I'd go off and edit the performance. The theatre wasn't language-based.

The press didn't publish a word about what we did. However, David Willinger, an American professor, had been researching theatre in Belgium for a year and wrote an article that appeared in *De Standaard*. He said he'd seen only one magnificent show in all that time, and it was entitled *Rumors*. Not a single journalist knew what he was talking about! So I suddenly got famous for a play that no one had seen! Only with the next performance, *Disease Germs*, did the press start showing up.

The beginning of the 1980s is the time of the 'no future' generation: high youth unemployment rate, Reagan and Thatcher conducting their right-wing policies, the recrudescence of the Cold War, fear of the atom bomb. . .

We weren't that political. We weren't interested in Reagan and Thatcher. We didn't make any political statements, unless perhaps indirectly. Nuclear weapons, now that was something. I lay awake for three nights running after our teacher explained to us how the atom bomb worked and the damage it could do. The awareness of evil. The 1982 anti-nuclear demonstration is the only one I ever participated in.

Indeed there was a lot of unemployment, but we didn't give a damn about money. My great idol was Fassbinder. He had a theatre in Munich. With the subsidies he received, he'd stage a theatre play and make a movie with the same cast. That was our inspiration.

We were deliberately *outside* of the social context. Not opposed, but outside.

Did you have any contact with other theatre makers of your generation, such as Jan Fabre or Jan Lauwers?

We'd shoot each other hostile looks in the same bars. We saw each other's work and naturally decided it was terrible. I saw *Asch*, the first performance by Anne Teresa De Keersmaeker. It was different from her later work. I really liked her *Fase*. Liking it felt safe too because it was dance.

The director Jan Decorte was our *godfather*. He wasn't actually all that much older than me, only eight years. But when you're that young the difference seems enormous. He was the first to stage a new repertoire in a far-out way. It wasn't entirely comprehensible, but the new way of performing was fascinating.

The Beursschouwburg [theatre space in the heart of Brussels] was really like a temple. If you put stuff on there, you'd made it. It was *the* place of Decorte and De Keersmaeker. Also around at the time were such initiatives and individuals as De Mannen van den Dam, Pol Dehert and Herman Gillis with Arca Theatre, Sam Bogaerts. They were all working toward a new kind of repertoire. That's what I went to see.

In 1984, AKT merged with Vertikaal making it into AKT/Vertikaal. What were the implications for the further development of your work?

Ronnie Commissaris, the director of Vertikaal, had seen our show *Agatha* and couldn't believe that we could produce such a thing without any money. We had nice-looking posters and were attracting large crowds. Due to the merger with Vertikaal, which did get subsidies, we suddenly had three million francs per year. All praise to Ronnie Commissaris, for taking us in. After a year, however, it hit me that I was doing all the work. So I let it be known that I wanted to become the leader of the group. Ronnie wasn't in favor of that happening, so he put up a second contender: Arne Sierens. I can still remember us both waiting our turn for an interview with the board. Ronnie tried to convince me to drop out of the running, which isn't the right way to handle me. That's when I start fighting. I had the actors on my side, such as Luk de Koninck, Peter Van Asbroeck, and Goele Derick. But also Jan and Peter van Kraaij, the dramaturg. One of my strong points is that I've always managed to surround myself with a good team. For a director to go it on their own is a pretty useless state of affairs in theatre. So I won the battle, but it was painful.

AKT/Vertikaal lasted for three years. After that, contacts formed there with Sam Bogaerts's De Witte Kraai. Lucas Vandervorst was also there, as well as Warre Borgmans, *the* super actor. We were still in negotiation with Sam when he was asked to go to Eindhoven to work at Zuidelijk Toneel. Lucas then assumed leadership of De Witte Kraai, and that's how the merger with AKT/Vertikaal into De Tijd came about, in 1987. Why the merger? I wanted things to start happening on a larger scale. Story of my life. The arrangement didn't last more than a couple of years though. Why? Because there wasn't enough room for two of us. Lucas wasn't seeking a large audience, but I was. Luckily, I was able to go to Het Zuidelijk Toneel, where I was offered the possibility of a new platform from which to operate.

That's how it's always been with me. There wasn't any conscious ambition or strategy. I've never gone looking for it. Anytime I wanted something bigger to happen, it just came to pass. The only thing driving us was an artistic inclination. We wanted to be able to make the work we wanted to make.

How did you end up at Het Zuidelijk Toneel in 1990?

At that time, it was still a 'toneelvoorziening,' a large presenting house that invited various directors to come do shows with them. Eric Antonis was the artistic director. He knew us from De Warande [cultural center] in Turnhout. When they were looking for a successor [Antonis was about to become head of Antwerpen 1993, JR], I was asked to come on as artistic director and I immediately said I would.

By the time I started at Het Zuidelijk Toneel, I'd already planned out my program for the first season. I intended to direct two productions, *South* by Julien Green and *Ajax/Antigone*. Two tragedies in one night was more than they could wrap their minds around. They said, 'We've still got costumes left over from *Pinocchio*, why don't you put on a show that could use them?' I said I'd think about it. I didn't do it of course. I called them one week later to say that I couldn't figure out how to do it, and went ahead with my original plan. We immediately got selected for the [annual prestigious Dutch-Flemish] Theaterfestival.

I also reconceived the place into a real theatre company, which I didn't tell the board before I did it. I'd always say: thank you very much for the suggestion, and then go right ahead and do what I'd planned to begin with.

In Het Zuidelijk Toneel's brochure for 1993–94 you write: 'Making theatre is always a form of wandering, asking questions until there are no more answers to give.' What did this mean to you? To whom are you asking these questions? To yourself, the public?

Yes, but not that consciously. For me that too is something that's basically the same, really. After watching *The Roman Tragedies*, hundreds of questions will remain unanswered, if all goes well. These questions are also literally projected onto monitors and screens after the applause. I'm more interested in question marks than in exclamation points. And by the same token, I'm not very interested in judging whether a given thing is good or if it's bad. It's obvious that Macbeth isn't a good person, but we knew that ahead of time, so our attention needs to be focused on other issues.

Isn't that a typical avant-garde standpoint? But today, artists are also expected to give answers, to take positions, to come up with solutions

I'm deeply convinced that it's a mistake to expect answers from art. Good art is always timeless in a way. The need to make explicit connections to social issues is by definition inartistic. What's wrong with one's having a relationship to beauty? Value isn't only to be found in practicality. Most of today's theatre falls short in that respect. What does a Rothko painting tell us, or a Van Gogh flower? You remember them from magazines and it hits you: I think I know that. But then I see such a flower in a museum and I can stand there staring at it for a whole hour, that's how much it shocks me. Why is that? It's something irrational. You can try to find the right words for it but a nerve has been touched, that's the most important thing.

I still remember seeing a play by Castellucci, *Giulio Cesare*. I came home and was pinned to the ground. Jan said: you're so pale, what's wrong? I said: I've seen something, I don't know what, but it was phenomenal.

In the book Ten Years Zuidelijk Toneel, actor Steven Van Watermeulen called the company 'an over-professionalized organization'

I consider professionalism a necessity. I've always been very much into figuring out how to create the best possible conditions for topnotch productions.

Steven also mentions 'the ardent yet detached power of Het Zuidelijk Toneel, they still don't know how to deal with our remotely heated passion'

That's still the case. Last season I put on *After the Rehearsal/Persona*. The one part is passion, the other is cool and detached. Both are contained in me, like yin and yang.

Of course I'm both my mother and my father. My father was a sociable man, a pharmacist in the center of town. On Sunday he would go to church. Not so much for Mass, but so he could go to the pub afterwards, talking to people and buying rounds. My mother, on the contrary, is a homemaker. She likes to be around people but also likes to close the curtains. I embody both personalities.

It's actually alright that our productions haven't only received kudos. That's what has enabled us to stick to our own path. I never measured my professional development against what Wim Van Gansbeke, Pol Arias [Flemish critics. Ed.], or whoever thought I should do. The tension that comes from not being celebrated all the time can only be good for us, that's what I feel. It helps the work to go against the grain at times.

After ten years at Zuidelijk Toneel, you moved over to Toneelgroep Amsterdam, the largest theatre company in the Netherlands. Your first plays there were The Massacre at Paris by Marlowe in an adaptation of Hafid Bouazza, and Con Amore, a stage version of the libretto of Monteverdi's opera Poppea. Quite radical choices

Too radical, indeed.

Do you want to elaborate on that? How do you see it in retrospect?

If I were to do it again, I'd do it differently. But things went the way they went, and something beautiful came out of it. I was in my early forties when I got there. I was up to something new and my thinking was: Toneelgroep Amsterdam, this is *the* place for experimenting on a large scale. I asked Walter Van Beirendonck to do costumes for *The Massacre*, Harry de Wit to do the music, and Jeroen Kooimans as video artist. Jan did the set design. It was pretty crowded on the stage, and I had put myself in last place. As a director I had nowhere to go, and it started going against my own nature. Wigs, out-sized scenery. But it was by my own choice, and that's the way I'd truly wanted it.

I realized that, as artistic director, I needed to clarify which hat I was wearing at any given moment, to any employee, actor, or whomever. In the rehearsal room these days I tell them: Guys, I'm not in my role of artistic director, so this isn't the right moment to bring up this topic, not right now. I've been way too sloppy in those areas. But there also were some people back then who did their best to make life miserable for me.

At Toneelgroep Amsterdam, your work suddenly became much warmer, brighter, and more colorful, despite the dark themes. Why was that? Was it due to having a different ensemble? Was it the influence of the international repertoire you programmed at Holland Festival? Or was it more on a personal level?

None of the above, even though they're certainly related to it. First and foremost it's due to a number of changes going on in the Netherlands as well as in the world, such as the assassinations of Pim Fortuyn and Theo van Gogh.

Colleagues attacked me because I was working on my marriage cycle plays around that time. They found it scandalous that I was doing that while two people in the Netherlands were lying dead on the streets, so to speak. 'In Berlin they're organizing an evening around Theo van Gogh, and what are you doing?' I told them: At this particular moment I think Amsterdam needs something different, more warmth. I find those current events incredibly important, but I don't know what to do with the subject on stage *right now*.

Sometimes you just need some distance. Sometimes it's better to hold it in reserve for a while. Theatre isn't set up for rapid fire response. And I was proven right: *A Perfect Wedding* seems to have been a great success. In my opinion, I hit a nerve by *not* relating to the times in a direct way.

I subscribe to Richard Sennett's theory that says that great changes in society have emotional consequences on peoples' lives. I believe that's what was going on for me and my theatre back at that point in time.

How do you make your selection of plays? Do you do it all on your own or is it more of a joint decision? Do you look for a play using a certain theme as jumping off point? I can't really imagine you sitting on your sofa, reading the collected works of Shakespeare

No, but I studied them so they're still somewhere on my hard drive. It's really tough to get to a decision. Ultimately, the choice is mine since I've got to believe in it 180 percent. I can't work with themes, it's not my way. I get further from just addressing the plays themselves. Then at a certain point you leave the text behind, and it gets to: now I'm just going to do *Persona*, period. But why, I still don't know. It's like falling in love.

I don't have a list of plays, which is a terrible calamity. I'm not easily led by others, even though I'd like to be. So I talk a lot with my dramaturgs, as well as other people. For *The Antonioni Project,* for example. I hadn't seen the whole trilogy, but I had seen *La notte* and *L'eclisse*. In a book on his films, I noticed that one kept referring to the other, and that's how the project came about in just one weekend. The text in those films is very thin, but nonetheless has a lot to say about what goes on in relationships during a time of great changes: the atom bomb, the stock market crash. He translates all that turmoil into the emotional lives of individuals.

At the end of this season, you'll be staging **The Fountainhead.** *You referred to this book by Ayn Rand as early as seven years ago*

When I read it, I instantly thought: here's a theatre play written in the O'Neill style. But I couldn't get the rights. So I told my dramaturg: keep on trying every three months. I think they must have thought that somebody was sure to adapt it for the screen and were unwilling to release the rights. But now we finally managed.

I was talking to Benjamin Barber one morning [American political scientist, JR]. I've known him for quite some time now, and he was here presenting his new book in Amsterdam. We spoke about Syria, and of course about Ayn Rand. He'd suggested I consider Ibsen's *Brand*, and I say: 'yes, but . . . we've already had an adaptation of it made by a dramaturg, but it doesn't speak to me.' Barber says a few things, I take a couple of notes. And it suddenly hits me: 'Hey!' and then it clicks.

Since you did Rumors you haven't written any more scripts

I discovered that other people are better at it. There are two things that I would have liked to do. Become a writer, but I'm unable to imagine anything from scratch, which is exactly what a writer does. And I would have liked to become a rock singer, but I can't sing.

Peter Verhelst, Hafid Bouazza, and Tom Lanoye all made adaptations of extant plays for you to direct. It's striking that the only new, original work TGA is doing is being written by foreigners: Charles Mee and Richard Maxwell. The largest national theatre company doesn't produce any new plays by Dutch-language authors. Don't you think that continuing on the same track will be problematic?

That list is seriously incomplete actually. We produced *Mind the Gap* by Stefan Hertmans. Oscar van den Boogaard wrote *Nacht van de bonobo's* for us, and Gerardjan Rijnders wrote *Snaren*. Agreed, I'm not the person directing those plays, but they were put on by Toneelgroep Amsterdam.

In Flanders, theatre companies and producing houses are forced by decree to commission new texts to be written by local playwrights. But if you look at the results, what's the point of imposing such a stipulation?

Wouldn't a culture of playwriting naturally emerge if a whole lot of plays get written, as from the mass a certain number of really great ones would have to be among them? Out of nothing, comes nothing?

I admit that this is my weak point. It's not my natural habitat. And it does have something to do with control. I'm really afraid the day will come when the script I commissioned arrives and I'm forced to say that it's worthless. In that case you're just stuck with it.

In my view, there is simply no difference between new work whether it be by Dutch people, or Flemish, or whatever nationality. Charles Mee tends to come closest to what I consider original and good. I wish I had someone like Patrice Chéreau had his Koltès, but unfortunately I haven't found such a person around here. The English playwright Simon Stephens is going to write a short play for me now. There's good chemistry between us. And I'm sure the same will happen with Tom Lanoye. *The Russians! [De Russen!]* was more than just a translation of two plays by Chekhov; it was full of new scenes.

Are there any extant pieces by authors from here that you would like to stage?

Hugo Claus [important Flemish playwright, novelist and poet, now deceased]. But everyone's continually doing him these days. So I feel that it wouldn't be suitable for me to.

It's mostly his novels that are being adapted. His plays are barely ever done

I promise you that the minute I get a chance to be in charge of a Flemish theatre, the first play I put on with them will be one by Hugo Claus. *A Bride in the Morning [Een bruid in de morgen].*

You've put a lot of film scripts on stage: Faces, Opening Night, Teorema, The Antonioni Project, Rocco and His Brothers, Cries and Whispers, Scenes From a Marriage, After the Rehearsal/Persona. *Does it all have to do with the content for you? Or is it the form that appeals to you, as a different sort of text, other than theatre plays offer? You often dig deep into the past for texts for your repertoire, from Shakespeare up until—most recently—O'Neill. The scenarios are often much more recent; the oldest date back to the 1960s*

Those scenarios are all about certain themes that you aren't going to be able to find so easily in a play. *Cries and Whispers* is about dying and its connotations. I hadn't found that subject adequately dealt with in any theatre play. I wanted to depict death on the stage. *Rocco and His Brothers* is about emigration. What is it really about? There's this mother and her four sons, which opens up a variety of attitudes regarding emigration: The youngest son wants to go back to his roots, the middle son is trying to adapt, and another comes into his own outside the family unit. It isn't just a family drama, but a social drama too. Theatrically speaking my work with film scenarios represents a great challenge.

To get back to your previous question: By bringing film scripts into the theatre I've made a contribution to building a new repertoire. We've been pioneers in that domain, and that has had great influence both locally and abroad.

A mega-production like The Roman Tragedies *has the quality of eventfulness. People are allowed to eat and drink during the show, they sit alongside us onstage and can change places in the middle. Don't you run the risk that the event itself might come to dominate? That the audience will go away retaining only the memory of having been able to sit wherever they wanted onstage and that they were allowed to eat and drink?*

You're still going to have to sit a real long time, just to experience it at that level. It finally starts petering out. By the last hour it starts to run down, with people wandering around, and the play grinding to a halt. You watch Cleopatra slowly dying. And still, as a spectator, you manage to take something away with you, something that really gets under your skin.

I'm deeply convinced that each spectator comes to a show for an independent personal reason. Some because they like to watch certain actors onstage. Others for the intellectual aspect.

Still others because they finally want to see *Coriolanus* put on stage. Well, if I intend to be a good director of a large-scale production, then I have to cater to all of them. Each spectator has to be able to find something in it for themselves.

How far do you go in early planning for a play? Is there still a lot that remains open once the rehearsals begin?

Processes for me work very slowly, no matter how efficient I may seem to be. I'm not a director who knows exactly where things will land before the rehearsals start. Yes, there are certain things I do know. Before *Long Day's Journey* rehearsal I'd already decided that the whole thing would be performed in bare feet. The actors stared at me, as it's not something they're crazy about doing, but they also know that it's not negotiable. In other ways I'm much easier. There's always a lot of room left for flexibility.

In my pre-planning phase I've looked into every sense, every thought, every scene from all sides, and gone over them with the dramaturg.

To accumulate a lot of baggage, and then to make sure you leave a lot of that baggage back at home, that's the art. Therein lies the art of directing.

That's why it's also the art of waiting. Someone once asked Jan: what do you think Ivo's greatest strength is as a director, and he answered: 'Patience.' I'm very well known as an extremely impatient person, but in the rehearsal room it's a whole different matter. Jan often says, 'If only you had as much patience elsewhere as you have there!' I can push, but if it's really necessary, I can really hang back as well.

How do you conduct a rehearsal? Do you have certain definite methods? Are there ways of drawing actors out, depending on the type of play you're doing?

It's evolved over time. I'll tell you how I do it now. The first day I read the text with the actors. After that I introduce the entire company, all those who want to attend in any case. I say, we're going to do this play. What I find particularly exciting about it is thus and so. We do a visual presentation of everything we've got in mind. The idea for the set is exhibited. Then the following days the actual rehearsing begins. Starting with Scene One. In the past we'd spend two weeks sitting around a table. I unlearned that in New York. You've only got four weeks in all to put a show on there, so you need to jump right in, and I experienced that as an emancipation.

I find it a lot better not to annoy the actors beforehand with all the baggage you've already got. You realize then that some things are better left unsaid because they're so obvious once you get to them, without you having to ask about it. The rehearsal process has to have something organic built in to it because they're eventually going to have to perform in an organic manner.

I rehearse over less time than I used to. I now work six weeks before opening night. *Roman Tragedies* took eleven weeks to put together. But six weeks is perfect in order for the company to maintain the right attention span. You manage to avoid the irritation that comes with repetition. There's also a tension that comes along with the approach of opening night. It's a process that continues to develop.

In the 2007–2008 brochure you wrote that Toneelgroep Amsterdam wanted to make big theatre for a big audience. Isn't that big audience relative in these times of television and the internet? How many spectators do you actually have?

Theatre, of course, is never large when juxtaposed with other media. But what we do is large in the context of theatre itself. The word 'large' is already implied. For me, it's also a matter of a *wide* audience. That isn't the masses. The budget we're given to enable our work also implies responsibility for making sure we attract a sizable number of people.

I've always got my eye on the accounting side, and it occupies quite a bit of my attention.

To which audience does Toneelgroep Amsterdam appeal?

It's quite varied. But it's a most natural fit for educated people, we have to be honest about that. Sixty percent of our audience members are one-time visitors, the rest returning ones. And right across from us, Joop van den Ende [the commercial producer, Ed.], whose Delamar Theater is located on the other side of the Leidseplein, has put up a building to house commercial theatre.

Has the relevance of the medium of theatre over the last thirty years come up? Does theatre play a role in a societal discussion?

Too little. *The Roman Tragedies* definitely has that kind of element in it, but it's not a point of reference in a social debate. That, of course, is an unfortunate situation.

I believe that the theatre very definitely has a social function. I went into it in the Machiavelli Lecture I recently gave. But as politicians never tire of saying in the Dutch media: the arts are a left-wing hobby, which is a contention it becomes difficult to go up against.

What has gone wrong? You've got advisory boards, commissions, and funding organizations throughout the cultural world that increasingly come between the arts organizations and politics. If the politicians fall over themselves to see which of them can make the most negative comments, then things start to get difficult. A baker will say to himself, 'Hmph, I don't get any subsidies. Why should they?' For that reason, we undoubtedly should stop using the word subsidies. We'd do better to talk about making investments. In the world of real estate, you invest. But in the arts it's called subsidies.

I think the current model is obsolete, and we've simply got to make a break with it. What the new model should look like, I'm not yet sure, but I do know we should be looking for one. The gulf between art and the political class has to go.

Germany's a good example of how things can be different: the artistic director (*intendant*) of any large company is there by direct political intervention. And that means that there's a commitment on the part of the authorities.

In his new book If Mayors Ruled the World *Benjamin Barber says that the cities of the world ought to take the lead. De facto, he says, they're already doing it. What role in this is reserved for the theatre?*

(*smiles*) He tells me that I'm mentioned in that book. The arts play an essential role in the city because they are concerned with creation. Creation brings inspiration, and thereby brings life to a city.

Barber has identified me as a prime example of an artist who can lay down links between cities. I naturally bow before that. I wouldn't give myself that attribution, but *he* certainly did cite our work as an example of it.

What you're referring to now is the East Village or Williamsburg, where all the artists are piled one on top of the other. I don't believe that that's what he's talking about. He's talking about the slum neighborhoods

I know he is. It's about that dreadful division in society. The light blazes for the people who can permit themselves an evening at Lincoln Center.

It's something I really give a lot of thought to. I also calculate all that it costs for two people to go out to the theatre. You have to pay for a baby-sitter, the cost of driving the car, paying for a glass to drink. I'm extremely conscious of all that. For that reason I always try to make sure that there are really cheap seats available. Rush tickets can also make a big difference. Students pay only 10 euros and any member of the Food Bank gets in for free.

I had a real scare in New York one time. At New York Theatre Workshop where I work you can accommodate 250 people. To see one of my shows there it costs $70. Seventy fucking dollars! Except on Sundays. By the time the actors have performed eight shows a week they're practically lying panting on the ground, and that's when the students are allowed in for $20.

By how much has Toneelgroep Amsterdam been set back by the government in the recent wave of subsidy reductions? Can you keep up the work you'd intended?

We were cut twelve percent. It's not insignificant. The way it went down is no secret. At a certain moment it became obvious that it would be unavoidable. I could have gone whining and complaining, but that'll get you nowhere. So then I said, twelve percent equals 650,000 Euros, that's the reality. What are we going to do about it?

First: We went off actively in search of interest within the business community. We found two sponsors—Accenture and Rabobank. Besides we set up a patronage fund: fifty or so individuals who give a certain sum each year, and they'll keep it up for a period of five years. *Long Day's Journey* was also co-produced for a certain amount from one individual. Over the course of one year we've already raised 350,000 for each of the coming four years.

Second: We went to our international partners. Told them there'd been cuts. That we'd dearly love to maintain the high level of quality. You want that too because we perform for you at the highest level. Our next big Shakespeare project is going to be co-produced with the Barbican in London and with the Théâtre de Chaillot in Paris. If you have a good story that jibes with their mission, then organizations may very well come up with a bit extra for you.

From co-productions we've already brought in 120,000 Euros, again for each of the coming four years. It means that I won't have to let anyone from my organization go. I definitely will have to eliminate a number of productions over the same four-year period— two regular ones, and two from the second company. And we'll also do one mega-production less, putting on only one instead of two. And I'm creating a show—as far as transport's concerned—for which the whole production can be squeezed into a single trailer—whereas they've always needed two in the past.

So I've had to do some trimming, but at the same time I've been careful to create circumstances that will allow me to avoid impinging on quality.

I'm always impressed with the optimism that comes along with all you say and do

That's the way I am. It's an attitude toward life. Or else I should just maybe pack up and die? What have I got to complain about? Look, this morning I woke up and had a terrific talk with Benjamin Barber out in the sun. After that I had a meeting about getting sponsors. With the actors I had a talk about the opening night of *The Seagull*. Then there was a rehearsal for *Long Day's Journey*. Somebody from London who's writing a book about theatre came to interview me. And now you've been sitting here for hours chatting with me about thirty years of putting on theatre. Our problems are luxurious ones.

I'm a Sunday's child. I've been here for twelve years now but it doesn't feel that way. I'm not bored yet. Everybody knows Toneelgroep Amsterdam, and they'd all like to come work here. I enjoy the fact that Ostermeier* wants to do a show with my actors. Isn't that phenomenal? I can make things possible that otherwise wouldn't be. This isn't my job, it's my life.

June 2017 Annex to *Etcetera* interview (2013) with Ivo van Hove

For several years now, your work has taken on a much more international allure. Toneelgroep Amsterdam is traveling the world over, from Seoul to Buenos Aires, from Avignon to Sydney. You've been active as a guest director in New York, London, Avignon, Paris. . . . This international dimension isn't that new actually; it was present from your earliest start

That's true. In the early eighties in Belgium you had the Kaaitheater Festival [experimental performance festival in Brussels] and De Singel [large presenting theatre in Antwerp]. Those were the first venues where international productions and performance art were on offer to see. You could see Bob Wilson's early work and The Wooster Group. With our first production, *Rumors* (1981), we got our first invitation to the Kaaitheater Festival. So, apparently, our work had sufficient validity to place in an international context. But at that point back then we had no organization. We did everything ourselves, and couldn't live up to that level of logistics. In hindsight that was naturally a big mistake. If I had to do it over again, I'd handle it in a whole other way. We'd also gotten an invitation to the Festival d'Automne in Paris. I had an appointment but on the day of it I canceled. I was too timid, didn't even know what I was supposed to do. What they call networking these days, that was beyond me. We actually did, however, make it to the Venice Biënnale with *The Wonders of Mankind*.

A few years later, the first guest directing gigs started getting booked. First in the Netherlands; that's where I did *Lulu* at Toneelgroep Amsterdam. That was a very big co-production. There were nineteen actors onstage. For Theater van het Oosten, I directed *Richard II*. In Hamburg, I did *The Bacchae*, and in Stuttgart, *Desire Under the Elms*. Owing to that, for the last five years, I've been working with stars like David Bowie, Juliette Binoche, and Jude Law. There's been an enormous amount of publicity. But that international dimension was there right from the start, and it's never let up. I've always envisioned our work through an international lens.

Back then it was surely harder to take text theatre abroad than physical theatre, because the language barrier didn't get in the way. How important is that in connection with the introduction of super-titles?

Today, such a thing would be unimaginable. But we were the first to make structural use of super-titling.

Still, it's exceptional that in this day and age an English-language audience is prepared to watch a many hour-long Shakespeare play without understanding anything that's being said on stage. Is that a consequence of globalization or has it come about through the power of your theatrical language?

Both, I think, but especially the latter. In England we really made a breakthrough with Shakespeare, and that, after all, really is an art. We approach it in a freer way than they can. We're not attached to Shakespearean English. And therefore our way of acting is more relaxed. They have a whole slew of do's and don'ts. We have no such tradition. We do it differently, but absolutely retain a respect for the original. We present the story of *Julius Caesar* in such a way that it makes them say: we've never seen the like before. With *A View From the Bridge*, it didn't go like that. I may have cut five lines of dialogue, no more. And yet it hits them a whole other way. They say: now we've finally come to discover this play. That's because we always strive as much for content as for the level of visual dramaturgical transparency. The questions we ask ourselves are: what's really going on here? And how ought we present it onstage?

It is striking that it took the British watching Shakespeare in another language for it to be opened up for them

And now they want me to go direct Shakespeare for them in English. But that I've refused to do. It's buried so deep in their genes that the text can only be spoken in a certain way. I call that "singing the text." But I want it to be spoken, both out of their thoughts and feelings. Not to make an aria out of it.

On account of an important producer, there's been game-changer for them. On account of *A View From the Bridge*. After the run at The Young Vic we transferred the show to the West End. That means that you're working in a commercial environment and have to pull in a thousand people each evening, and that eight times a week! And we pulled it off! Now nobody can say it's impossible to reach an audience interested in extreme work.

Do they regard your work abroad differently than in the Netherlands? Here you've worked many years in the nation's largest institution. You're establishment. In New York you always do one-offs Off-Broadway. You had an avant-garde image. Has that changed? Ben Brantley from* The New York Times *has called you the maximalist minimalist. That means that you achieve the maximal effect with the most minimal means.

That's what I did with *A View From the Bridge*. You can also reverse it. Which is what we did with *Kings of War*. With a maximal infusion of means we went straight to the gist of the work and we arrive at the absolute minimal. I find Brantley's the best definition of our work anyone has come up with so far.

You work in disparate environments. Isn't it extremely different working on Broadway than at Toneelgroep Amsterdam?

The only really great difference is keeping a company of actors together. In that case team-building is the greatest aim. In casting calls I go out looking for people who if put together I believe will be able to form an ensemble. It isn't necessarily by throwing the eleven best players in the world together that you'll get the best football club. In the first week of rehearsal I try to meld freelancers into a real ensemble. And I'm not alone in this effort. There is Jan (Versweyveld). I always work with Tal (Yarden) if there's video involved. An D'Huys or Wojciech Dziedzic do the costumes. They're involved in the process throughout. The set designer doesn't walk in late in the process or the guy for the lights only show up in the last week. I also always have a dramaturg. In England and America they don't use them, there's only an assistant director. So, it's not just me and the actors, I've got a fixed team that also engages them in discussion. So, first and foremost it has always been team-building. That has always been the case when I've worked with Toneelgroep Amsterdam or the Comédie Française with their permanent ensemble or with a group of freelancers like on Broadway or at the National Theatre in London. It automatically makes a space for our way of thinking.

A View From the Bridge *has always been considered a naturalistic play that took place in a specific milieu in a specific place: Italian immigrants in Red Hook, Brooklyn. You made a timeless Greek tragedy out of it*

It's funny, but I myself never thought about that. I discovered that Miller had written two versions of the play. The first he described as a contemporary Greek tragedy. At Peter Brook's instigation he wrote a second version for London. In that one he injected a lot of Italian local color. That's particularly in evidence in the stage directions and a couple of extra secondary characters: As a result the play developed a naturalistic tradition: Italian immigrants who eat spaghetti and so forth. I used the text from the second version and the conceptual content of the first. When joined together they accrue added value: one plus one equals three.

Does your work in the Netherlands and your international work exercise an influence on each other?

When international directors come to work at Toneelgroep Amsterdam, that represents an influence on Dutch theatre in general. There are a large number of fine directors in the Netherlands, but they each have their own shop already. We can give a boost to the Dutch theatre scene by letting them see other approaches. A show plays for a couple of days and then takes off again. When foreign directors put on shows more times, often with a Dutch company, the result is more far-reaching.

Do you also intend to internationalize the Toneelgroep Amsterdam acting ensemble?

We've directed two English language productions: *Antigone* and *Obsession*. That generated new energy and new ideas, which we'll be exploring further as time goes by. In a period where people are to a greater and greater extent turning inward to their own countries and their own roots, this is one of the ways in which art, by way of contrast, can be an antidote to nationalism.

Four years ago you were pessimistic about the relevance of theatre. Roman Tragedies *hadn't become a point of reference in the larger social discussion. That seems to have changed. Your work now tends to be read as more political than was formerly the case*

I'm aware that my shows are being categorized differently on that level. Take the title, *Kings of War*. There has been discussion about it. With the result that it's been used in newspaper columns regarding debates in the Upper House (in the Dutch parliament). It's turned into a flashpoint for questions of leadership in the media.

We've stuck our neck out pretty far with *The Fountainhead*. It's about a society that is going more and more in a liberal [neo-liberal, free market. Ed.] direction, in which the individual is ever more focused on themselves. The show has put everyone in conflict because Rand's politics are oriented to the right and because she's so decisive about the choices life forces you to make, whatever the dilemmas one faces. *The Damned* not only drew the French president as audience, but later the whole French government, on an individual basis. There must, it seems, have been talk of it even at high-level ministerial meetings. About a Belgian who's finger's firmly on the pulse of a nation that's being torn asunder by extreme nationalism and the glance at the outside. That dilemma is implanted in the production.

My work has always been politically tinted. But in the old days, nobody noticed it. With *Roman Tragedies* in the Netherlands, the talk centered mostly on the form. About how the audience was allowed onstage and so forth. But that's only a means to an end. In other countries, the political aspects were much more rapidly recognized. Here, if an actor fails to wear a toupee like Geert Wilders then it doesn't qualify as political theatre. There's got to be a one-for-one equivalency. That's not my thing. I have a closer feeling towards the Greeks' relationship with theatre work that has to be concerned with the polis, that's focused on social concerns. Politics is merely a sub-unit of it. I'm not directly focused on current affairs, but am with all the slow-motion landslides, the gradual changes. They inspire me to go deeper, to zoom out to the big picture.

That's how the two-years' old Kings of War *could be seen by Rebecca Mead in* The New Yorker *during the week of the American election, as 'the first great theatrical work of the Trump era'*

Take 'Guernica.' Picasso painted it after an unprepossessing Basque town had gotten leveled to the ground by a bombing. The painting isn't a realist depiction of the place. Picasso has sublimated the victim and turned it into something universal. And exactly in that way has he grasped the grisly horror of it all. That act of aggression would have remained merely anecdotic if it had been realistically treated.

You've now been working for 37 years. Very few artists can say that they've worked with a hero from their youth. But that's exactly what happened with you and David Bowie. But not long after the opening of Lazarus, on his 69th birthday, he passed away. What meaning does this hold for you?

The death of Bowie was my first wake-up call, and a loud one too. I'm now 58, so I still have 11 years to go. It really gives me pause. I saw how driven he was working on his new album, the accompanying videos, and also a bit with *Lazarus*. And all the while he was fatally ill. Why did he do it? That's artistry. It was existentially necessary for him. It made me realize more than ever that Bowie wasn't just a rock icon. He was a great artist. I've got a heavy year behind me, but people tell me how great I look. That's also true. I've got my eye on next season. I've never had the slightest feeling of burn-out. I'm enormously motivated and also find great satisfaction in my work. Same when it doesn't always work out, because that of course does happen. I can live with it with no problem. I live and die by the theatre.

I've done things that I wouldn't do that way again. I always had a good reason for everything I did in my shows, but didn't always manage to pull it off right. I always make things the way I want to. If you never take a risk to avoid failing, than you'll never find anything. So I sometimes take enormous risks. When I wanted to do *The Fountainhead*, everyone told me not to do it. Especially for political reasons. But I went ahead and did it anyway.

How would the young van Hove seem in relation to the van Hove from today?

When I look back and see filmed versions of interview segments from before, then I see someone remarkably at ease and wise. But back then I thought it was completely different. I can easily understand how people back then wanted to work with me. You saw someone who radiated confidence, who knew what he was talking about. Who wasn't middle-of-the-road. He may want things that other people didn't, but he doesn't care. Not in an aggressive way, but purposeful without being too vain. I think that the young van Hove isn't so very different from who I am now.

Notes

*   Thomas Ostermeier, major German director
1   Excerpted from: Johan Reyniers, "Toneel is de kunstvorm van de eenentwintigste eeuw: toesprak met Ivo van Hove," *Etcetera*, 30th Anniversary edition, 18 September 2013, 5–9, 17–19.

INDEX